Case Studies
in
Business Ethics

Fifth Edition

Edited by
Al Gini
Loyola University Chicago

Upper Saddle River, NJ 07458

Library of Congress Cataloging-in-Publication Data

Case studies in business ethics / [edited by] Al Gini.—5th ed.
    p. cm.
  Includes bibliographical references.
  ISBN 0-13-112746-2
   1. Business ethics—Case studies. I. Gini, Al, 1944-

HF5387.C36 2003
174'.4—dc22

2003064769

VP, Editorial Director: Charlyce Jones Owen
Senior Acquisitions Editor: Ross Miller
Assistant Editor: Wendy Yurash
Editorial Assistant: Carla Worner
Marketing Manager: Kara Kindstrom
Marketing Assistant: Jennifer Lang
Managing Editor: Joanne Riker
Production Editor: Randy Pettit
Manufacturing Manager: Nick Sklitsis
Manufacturing Buyer: Christina Helder
Cover Design: Bruce Kenselaar
Composition: Laserwords, Inc.
Printer/Binder: Phoenix Book Tech

Credits and acknowledgments borrowed from other sources and reproduced, with permission, in this textbook appear on appropriate page within text.

Pearson Prentice Hall™ is a trademark of Pearson Education, Inc.
Pearson® is a registered trademark of Pearson plc
Prentice Hall® is a registered trademark of Pearson Education, Inc.

Pearson Education LTD.
Pearson Education Australia PTY, Limited
Pearson Education Singapore, Pte. Ltd
Pearson Education North Asia Ltd
Pearson Education, Canada, Ltd
Pearson Educación de Mexico, S.A. de C.V.
Pearson Education—Japan
Pearson Education Malaysia, Pte. Ltd

10 9 8 7 6 5 4 3 2 1
ISBN 0-13-112746-2

Contents

————●————

Preface *ix*

Introduction to Ethical Reasoning • THOMAS DONALDSON, PATRICIA H. WERHANE *1*

The Case Method • THOMAS DONALDSON *13*

ONE • Business or Ethics 23

CASE STUDY
The Parable of the Sadhu • BOWEN H. MCCOY *24*

CASE STUDY
Into the Mouths of Babes • JAMES TRAUB *29*

CASE STUDY
Tylenol's Rebound • CARL CANNON *36*

TWO • Communication in Business: Internal and External 40

ESSAY
Sex, Lies, and Advertising • GLORIA STEINEM *41*

CASE STUDY
Uptown, Dakota, and PowerMaster • N. CRAIG SMITH *54*

CASE STUDY
Volvo's Crushing Blow • RONALD M. GREEN *59*

iv   Contents

CASE STUDY

Toy Wars • MANUEL G. VELASQUEZ   *62*

CASE STUDY

The Case of the Contested Firearms • GEORGE BRENKERT   *65*

CASE STUDY

Italian Tax Mores • ARTHUR L. KELLY   *70*

CASE STUDY

Whistleblowing and Employee Loyalty • RONALD DUSKA   *72*

CASE STUDY

Some Paradoxes of Whistleblowing • MICHAEL DAVIS   *76*

ESSAY

A Hero—And a Smoking-Gun Letter • WENDY ZELLER, STEPHANIE FOREST ANDERSON, LAURA COHN   *86*

THREE • Pollution and Environment   *88*

ESSAY

Shades of Green: Business, Ethics, and the Environment • R. EDWARD FREEMAN, JESSICA PIERCE, RICHARD DODD   *89*

CASE STUDY

Save the Turtles • ROGENE A. BUCHHOLZ   *99*

CASE STUDY

Edible Carpets, Anyone!? Interface Corporation a Sustainable Business • JOE DESJARDINS, JANALLE AARON   *105*

CASE STUDY

The Hazards of Enterprise • JOHN HASNAS   *111*

CASE STUDY

Texaco in the Ecuadorean Amazon • DENIS G. ARNOLD   *113*

FOUR • Diversity in the Workplace *116*

ESSAY

A Defense of Programs of Preferential Treatment • RICHARD WASSERSTROM *118*

ESSAY

Reverse Discrimination as Unjustified • LISA H. NEWTON *122*

ESSAY

Racism in the Workplace • AARON BERNSTEIN *126*

CASE STUDY

Texaco: The Jelly Bean Diversity Fiasco • MARIANNE M. JENNINGS *130*

CASE STUDY

Denny's • RONALD M. GREEN *137*

CASE STUDY

Global United: Melba Moore • JOHN R. HUNDLEY III *140*

CASE STUDY

Management Dilemma • FRED E. SCHUSTER *142*

FIVE • Work Life Balance and Gender Issues *144*

ESSAY

Management Women and the New Facts of Life • FELICE N. SCHWARTZ *146*

ESSAY

Women in the Workplace • AL GINI *156*

ESSAY

Child Care Comes to Work • BONNIE HARRIS *169*

CASE STUDY

Gender Issues at Your House   •   JOHN HASNAS   *172*

CASE STUDY

Worth the Effort   •   RAYMOND S. PFEIFFER, RALPH P. FORSBERG   *175*

CASE STUDY

Foreign Assignment   •   THOMAS DUNFEE, DIANA ROBINSON   *177*

CASE STUDY

Sexual Discrimination at Eastern Airlines   •   AL GINI   *179*

SIX • Corporate Obligations and Responsibilities: Everything Old is New Again   *183*

CASE STUDY

The Fall of Michael Milken   •   O.C. FREELL, JOHN FRAEDICH   *184*

CASE STUDY

Enron: From Paragon to Pariah   •   LISA H. NEWTON   *190*

CASE STUDY

"The Good Old Boys at WorldCom"   •   DENNIS MOBERG, EDWARD ROMAR   *205*

ESSAY

The Adelphia Story   •   DEVIN LEONARD   *213*

CASE STUDY

The Ford Pinto   •   W. MICHAEL HOFFMAN   *222*

CASE STUDY

Radials, Rollovers, and Responsibility: An Examination of the Ford Firestone Case   •   ROBERT NOGGLE, DANIEL PALMER   *229*

CASE STUDY
A.H. Robins: The Dalkon Shield   •   AL GINI, T. SULLIVAN   *249*

SEVEN • Multinationals   *257*

ESSAY
The Ethical Wealth of Nations   •   THOMAS DONALDSON   *258*

CASE STUDY
AIDS and Life-Saving Medicine: Responsibilities   •   OLIVER F. WILLIAMS   *268*

CASE STUDY
Chrylser and Gao Feng: Corporate Responsibility for Religious
and Political Freedom in China   •   MICHAEL A. SANTORO   *277*

ESSAY
The Great Non-Debate over International Sweatshops   •   IAN MAITLAND   *279*

CASE STUDY
Shell Oil in Nigeria   •   JOHN BOATRIGHT   *291*

CASE STUDY
Levi Strauss & Co. and China   •   EDWIN M. EPSTEIN, TIMOTHY PERKINS, COLLEEN O'CONNELL,
CARIN OROSCO, MARK RICKEY, MATTHHEW SCOBLE   *294*

EIGHT • Privacy, Ethics, and Technology   *299*

ESSAY
Technology and Ethics: Privacy in the Workplace   •   LAURA P. HARTMAN   *300*

ESSAY
Virtual Morality: A New Workplace Quandary   •   MICHAEL J. MCCARTHY   *316*

ESSAY

Rippers, Portal Users, and Profilers: Three Web-Based Issues
for Business Ethicists   •   MARTIN CALKINS   *318*

CASE STUDY

Cyberethics: Seven Short Cases   •   RICHARD A. SPINELLO, HERMAN T. TAUANI   *328*

CASE STUDY

E-Mail Policy at Johnson & Presser   •   RICHARD A. SPINELLO   *333*

NINE • Leadership   *336*

ESSAY

Leadership: An Overview   •   AL GINI   *337*

ESSAY

The Call of Leaders   •   GARY WILLS   *345*

ESSAY

Ethics: Take It From the Top   •   MAYNARD M. DOLECHECK, CAROLYN C. DOLECHECK   *352*

ESSAY

Ways Women Lead   •   JUDY L. RUSENA   *360*

ESSAY

Moral Mazes: Bureaucracy and Managerial Work   •   ROBERT JACKALL   *367*

ESSAY

Not a Fool, Not a Saint   •   THOMAS TEAL   *382*

ESSAY

Visionary's Dream Led to Risky Business   •   PETER BEHR, APRIL WITT   *385*

ESSAY

Former Tyco Executives are Charged   •   MARK MAREMONT, JERRY MARKON   *394*

Preface

---•---

If doing business were simple and ethical decisionmaking always obvious, there would be no need for this book or any textbook on the topic of business ethics. But clearly such is not the case. Like most things in life, business is complex and the pursuit of ethics is often convoluted. Sadly, because it is hard to combine these two enterprises, we too often simply dismiss business ethics, accuse it of being an oxymoron, or proclaim that it is impossible to achieve because of the technical complexity and intellectual nuances involved.

The reality is that, whether in our professional or private lives, doing the right thing for the right reason is never easy. But just because it is difficult does not mean that we need not bother to try, or that it cannot be done. We are, to paraphrase Jean-Paul Sartre, moral mammals required by our status and situation to decide, make choices, seek meaning. None of us are absolved, says Sartre; we all must choose our way through life. We all must decide on what is right, what is wrong, what is acceptable and unacceptable conduct in regard to ourselves and others.

Some critics, of course, will say that, while this all may be true, in business ethics the situation is much more complex, the choices are much more difficult, and the dilemmas are much more confusing because of what is at stake: success, status, stuff, wealth, position, property. These critics claim that there is a long history (e.g., Niccoló Machiavelli, *The Prince*) of maintaining separate standards for personal and business (and/or political) conduct. According to Otto von Bismarck, it is the way of the world. Success in the public realm requires a certain amount of ethical schizophrenia, what he would call *real politik.*

As a discipline, business ethics wants to deny this dichotomy. Business is not disconnected from the people it serves. Business is part of life. Life, labor, and business are all of a piece. They should not be separate "games" played by separate "rules." Like all other activities in life, business is required to ask, "What ought to be done in regard to others?" and "What rights and obligations do we have and share with others?"

What business ethics is advocating is that people apply in the workplace those commonsensical rules and standards learned at home, from the lectern, and from the pulpit. The moral issues facing a person are age-old, and they are essentially the same issues facing a business—only written large. According to R. Edward Freeman, of the Darden School of Business, ethics is "how we treat each other, every day, person to person. If you want to know about a company's ethics, look at how it treats people—customers, suppliers, and employees. Business is about people. And business ethics is about how customers and employees are treated."

What is being asked of the business community is neither extraordinary nor excessive: a decent product at a fair price; honesty in advertisements; fair treatment of employees, customers, suppliers, and competitors; a strong sense of responsibility to the communities it inhabits and serves; and the production of a reasonable profit for the financial risk-taking of its stockholders and owners. In the words of General Robert Wood Johnson, founder of Johnson & Johnson:

> The day has passed when business was a private matter—if it ever really was. In a business society, every act of business has social consequences and may arouse public interest. Every time business hires, builds, sells or buys, it is acting for the . . . people as well as for itself, and it must be prepared to accept full responsibility.

Case Studies in Business Ethics is an attempt to bring together in a single package an overview of ethical reasoning, an explanation of the case method, essays to read, ideas and issues to ponder, and cases to debate. It is my hope that these readings will be both interesting and informative to teachers and students alike.

The first edition of this text (1984) was the brainchild solely of Thomas Donaldson. Editions two (1990), three (1993), and four (1996) were the products of the efforts of both of us. For good or ill, the responsibility for this fifth edition fell entirely on my shoulders. Tom's pressing professional schedule and expanded family responsibilities prohibited him from coediting this project with me. Nevertheless, I want to publicly thank Tom for all of his efforts over the years on this project, for his accomplishments and contributions to the field of business ethics, and for his friendship and collegiality.

A few other thanks also need to be noted. I owe a great deal of gratitude to my longtime associate Mark D. Schneider for his diligence in preparing this manuscript. I also want to thank April White, my graduate assistant, for her day-to-day production efforts. And I want especially to thank Ross Miller and Wendy Yurash of Prentice Hall for making this book possible yet again.

AL GINI

Loyola University Chicago

Introduction to Ethical Reasoning

Thomas Donaldson

Patricia H. Werhane

What is the basis for making ethical decisions? Should Joan challenge Fred the next time he cracks a chauvinist joke? Should John refrain from lying on his job application despite his temptation to do so? What, if anything, should make Hillary decide that eating meat is corrupting, whereas vegetarianism is uplifting? It is obvious that the kind of evidence required for an ethical decision is different from that needed to make a nonethical one; but what is the nature of the difference? These questions give rise to a search for a *method* of ethical justification and decision making, a method that will specify the conditions that any good ethical decision should meet.

To see how such questions arise concretely, consider the following case.[1]

Some years ago, a large German chemical firm, BASF, decided to follow the lead of many other European firms and build a factory in the United States. BASF needed land, lots of it (1,800 acres), an inexpensive labor pool, almost 5 million gallons of fresh water every day, a surrounding area free of import taxes, and a nearby railroad and ocean port. Obviously, only a handful of locations could meet all these requirements. The spot the company finally picked seemed perfect, an area near the coast of South Carolina called Beaufort County. It purchased 1,800 acres.

South Carolina and Beaufort County were pleased with BASF's decision. The surrounding area, from which the company would pick its workers, was economically depressed and per capita income stood well below the national average. Jobs of any kind were desperately needed. Even the Governor of South Carolina and his staff were eager for BASF to build in South Carolina, and although BASF had not yet finalized its exact production plans, the State Pollution Central Authority saw no problems with meeting the State pollution laws. BASF itself said that although it would dump chemical byproducts into the local Colleton River, it planned not to lower the river's quality.

But troubled started immediately. To see why, one needs to know that Beaufort County is the home of the internationally famous resort area called "Hilton Head." Hilton Head attracts thousands of vacationers every year—most of them with plenty of money—and its developers worried that the scenic splendor of the area might be marred by the air and water pollution. Especially concerned about water pollution, resort developers charged that the proposed chemical plant would pollute the Colleton River. They argued that BASF plants in Germany had polluted the Rhine and, in Belgium, the Schelde River. Further, they noted that on BASF's list of proposed expenditures, pollution control was allocated only one million dollars.

The citizens of Beaufort County, in contrast to the Hilton Head Developers, welcomed BASF. They presented the company with a petition bearing over 7,000 signatures

This article is a revised version of one appearing in Thomas Donaldson and Patricia H. Werhane, eds., *Ethical Issues in Business*, 2nd, 4th, 5th, 6th, and 7th ed. (Englewood Cliffs, N.J.: Prentice Hall, 1983).

endorsing the new plant. As one local businessman commented, "I would say 80 percent of the people in Beaufort County are in favor of BASF. Those who aren't rich." (William D. McDonald, "Youth Corps Looking for Jobs," *The State*, February 23, 1970.)

The manager of BASF's U.S. operations was clearly confronted by an economic and moral dilemma. He knew that preventing massive pollution was virtually impossible and, in any case, outrageously expensive. The eagerness of South Carolina officials for new industry suggested that pollution standards might be "relaxed" for BASF. If it decided to go ahead and build, was the company to push for minimum pollution control it could get away with under the law? Such a policy might maximize corporate profits and the financial interests of the shareholders, while at the same time it would lower the aesthetic quality of the environment. It might make jobs available to Beaufort County while ignoring the resort industry and the enjoyment of vacationers. Moreover, the long-term effects of dumping chemicals were hard to predict, but past experience did not give the manager a feeling of optimism. Pollution seemed to be not only a business issue, but a *moral* one. But how should the manager sort out, and eventually decide upon, such a moral issue?

To solve his moral problem, BASF's manager might try a variety of strategies. He might, for example, begin by assuming that he has three basic options: (1) Build with minimal pollution control; (2) build with maximal pollution control; or (3) do not build.

Then, he might reason:

The consequences of option 1 will be significant but tolerable water pollution, hostility from the Hilton Head Developers, high short-term corporate profits, and satisfied shareholders.

The consequences of option 2 will be unnoticeable pollution, no complaints from the Hilton Head Developers, high pollution-control costs, low profits, and unsatisfied stockholders.

The consequences of 3 will be approval from the Hilton Head Developers, low short-term profits (while a search for a new location is underway), strong disapproval from the local townspeople.

My job from a *moral* perspective is to weigh these consequences and consider which of the alternatives constitutes a maximization of good. Who will benefit from each decision? How many people will be adversely affected and in what ways?

Or the manager might reason:

Both BASF Corporation and I are confronted with a variety of *duties, rights,* and *obligations.* First there is the company's obligation to its stockholders, and my duty as manager is to protect the economic interests and rights of our stockholders. Next there are the rights of those Beaufort residents and visitors in the area to clean air and water. Finally there are the rights of other property owners in the area, including the Hilton Head Developers, not to be harmed unreasonably by other industries. There is an implied obligation to future generations to protect the river. And finally, there are broader considerations: Is this an act I would want others to do? What kind of moral example will I be setting?

My job from a *moral* perspective is to balance and assess these duties, rights, and obligations, and determine which have priority.

Finally, the manager might reason:

> I cannot confront a moral problem from either the abstract perspective of "consequences," or of "duties, rights, and obligations." Instead, I must use a concrete concept of *human nature* to guide my deliberations. Acts that aid persons to develop their potential human nature are morally good; ones that do the opposite are bad.
>
> I believe that the crucial potentialities of human nature include such things as health, knowledge, moral maturity, meaningful employment, political freedom, and self-respect.
>
> My job from a *moral* perspective is to assess the situation in terms of its harmony or disharmony with these basic concepts of human potential.

Notice how different each of these approaches is. The first focuses on the concept of *consequences*; the second on *duties, rights, and obligations*; and the third on *human nature*. Of course, the three methods may overlap; for example, applying the concept of "human nature" in the third approach may necessitate referring to concepts drawn from the first and second, such as "consequences" and "rights," and vice versa. Even so, the approaches reflect three classical types of ethical theory in the history of philosophy. Each has been championed by a well-known traditional philosopher, and most ethical theories can be categorized under one of the three headings. The first may be called *consequentialism*, the second, *deontology*, and the third, *human nature ethics*.

CONSEQUENTIALISM

As its name implies, a consequentialist theory of ethical reasoning concentrates on the consequences of human actions, and all actions are evaluated in terms of the extent to which they achieve desirable results. Such theories are also frequently labeled *teleological*, a term derived from the Greek word *telos*, which means "end" or "purpose." According to consequentialist theories, the concepts of right, wrong, and duty are subordinated to the concept of the end or purpose of an action.

There are at least two types of consequentialist theory. The first—advocated by only a few consequentialists—is a version of what philosophers call *ethical egoism*. It construes right action as action whose consequences, considered among all the alternatives, maximizes *my* good—that is, action that benefits *me* the most or harms *me* the least. The second type—advocated by most consequentialists—denies that right action concerns only *me*. Rather, right action must maximize *overall* good; that is, it must maximize good (or minimize bad) from the standpoint of the entire human community. The best-accepted label for this type of consequentialism is *utilitarianism*. This term was coined by the eighteenth-century philosopher Jeremy Bentham, although its best-known proponent was the nineteenth-century English philosopher John Stuart Mill. As Bentham formulated it, the principle of utility states that an action is right if it produces the greatest balance of pleasure or happiness and unhappiness in light of alternative actions. Mill supported a similar principle, using what he called the "proof" of the principle of utility—namely, the recognition that the only proof for something's being desirable is that someone actually desires it. Since everybody desires pleasure or happiness, it follows, according to Mill, that happiness is the most desirable thing. The purpose of moral action is to achieve greatest overall happiness, and actions are evaluated in terms of the extent to which they contribute to this end. The most desirable state of affairs, the greatest good and the goal of morality, said Mill, is the "greatest happiness for the greatest number.

While later utilitarians accept the general framework of Mill's argument, not all utilitarians are hedonists. That is, not all utilitarians equate "the good" with pleasure or happiness. Some utilitarians have argued that in maximizing the "good," one must be concerned not only with maximizing pleasure, but with maximizing other things, such as knowledge, moral maturity, and friendship. Although it could be claimed that such goods also bring pleasure and happiness to their possessor, it is arguable whether their goodness is ultimately *reducible* to whatever pleasure they bring. These philosophers are sometimes called *pluralistic utilitarians*. Still other philosophers have adapted utilitarianism to modern methods of economic theory by championing what is known as *preference utilitarianism*. Instead of referring to the maximization of specific goods, such as pleasure or knowledge, preference utilitarians understand the ultimate foundation of goodness to be the set of preferences people actually possess. One person prefers oysters to strawberries; another prefers rock music to Mozart. Each person has a set of preferences, and so long as the set is internally consistent, it makes no sense to label one set morally superior to another. Preference utilitarianism thus interprets right action as that which is optimal among alternatives in terms of everyone's preferences. Disputes, however, rage among preference utilitarians and their critics over how to specify the meaning of *optimal.*

Bentham and Mill thought that utilitarianism was a revolutionary theory, both because it accurately reflected human motivation and because it had clear application to the political and social problems of their day. If one could measure the benefit or harm of any action, rule, or law, they believed, one could sort out good and bad social and political legislation as well as good and bad individual actions.

But how, specifically, does one apply the traditional principle of utility? To being with, one's race, religion, intelligence, or condition of birth is acknowledged to be irrelevant in calculating one's ultimate worth. Each person counts for "one," and no more than "one." Second, in evaluating happiness, one must take into account not only present generations, but ones in the future. In calculating the effects of pollution, for instance, one must measure the possible effects pollution might have on health, genetics, and the supply of natural resources for future generations. Third, pleasure or happiness is measured *in toto* so that the thesis does not reduce to the idea that "one ought to do what makes the most persons happy." Utilitarianism does not reduce to a dictatorship of majority interests. One person's considerable unhappiness might outweigh the minor pleasures of many other persons added together. Utilitarians also consider the long-term consequences for single individuals. For instance, it might be pleasurable to drink a full bottle of wine every evening, but the long-term drawbacks of such a habit might well outweigh its temporary pleasures.

Finally, according to many utilitarians (such as Mill), some pleasures are *qualitatively* better than others. Intellectual pleasure, for example, is said to be higher than physical pleasure. "Better to be Socrates unsatisfied," writes Mill, "than a pig satisfied." The reasons that drove Mill to formulate this qualitative distinction among pleasures are worth noting. Since Mill believed that the optimal situation was one of "greatest happiness for the greatest number," than what was he to say about a world of people living at the zenith of merely *physical* happiness? If science could invent a wonder drug, like the "soma" in Aldous Huxley's *Brave New World*, which provided a permanent state of drugged happiness (without even a hangover), would the consequence be a perfect world? Mill believed not, and to remedy this difficulty in his theory, he introduced *qualitative levels* of happiness. For example, he said that the happiness of understanding Plato is "higher" than that of drinking three martinis. But how was Mill to say *which* pleasures were higher? Here he retreated to an ingenious proposal: When deciding which of two pleasures is higher, one should poll the group of persons who are experienced—that is, who know *both* pleasures. Their decision will indicate which is the higher pleasure. Ah, but might the majority decision not be wrong? Here Mill provides no clear answer.

Modern-day utilitarians divide themselves roughly into two groups: *act utilitarians* and *rule utilitarians*. An *act* utilitarian believes that the principle of utility should be applied to individual acts. Thus one measures the consequences of each *individual action* according to whether it maximizes good. For example, suppose a certain community were offered the opportunity to receive a great deal of wealth in the form of a gift. The only stipulation was that the community force some of its citizens with ugly, deteriorated homes to repair and beautify them. Next, suppose the community held an election to decide whether to accept the gift. An act utilitarian would analyze the problem of whether to vote for or against the proposal from the standpoint of the *individual voter*. Would an individual's vote to accept the gift be more likely to maximize the community's overall good than would a vote to the contrary?

A *rule* utilitarian, on the other hand, believes that instead of considering the results of specific actions, one must weight the consequences of adopting a *general rule* exemplified by that action. According to the rule utilitarian, one should act according to a general rule which, if adopted, would maximize good. For example, in the hypothetical case of the community deciding whether to accept a gift, a rule utilitarian might adopt the rule "Never vote in a way that lowers the self-respect of a given class of citizens." She might accept this rule because of the general unhappiness that would ensue if society systematically treated some persons as second-class citizens. Here the focus is on the general rule and not on the individual act.

Critics raise objections to utilitarianism. Perhaps the most serious objection is that it is unable to account for justice. Because the utilitarian concentrates on the consequences of an action for a majority, the employment of the principle of utility can be argued to allow injustice for a small minority. For example, if overall goodness were maximized in the long run by making slaves of 2 percent of the population, utilitarianism seemingly is forced to condone slavery. But clearly this is unjust.

Utilitarianism's obvious response is that such slavery will not, as a matter of empirical fact, maximize goodness. Rule utilitarians, as we have seen, can argue that society should embrace the rule "Never enslave others," because following such a principle will, in the long run, maximize goodness. Even so, the battle continues between utilitarians and their critics. Can utilitarianism account for the widely held moral conviction that injustice to a minority is wrong *regardless* of the consequences? The answer is hotly contested.

Another criticism concerns the determination of the good to be maximized. Any consequentialist has the problem of identifying and ranking whatever is to be maximized. For a utilitarian such as Mill, as we have seen, the problem involves distinguishing between higher and lower pleasures. But for pluralistic utilitarians, a similar problem exists: What is the basis for selecting, for example, friendship and happiness as goods to be maximized and not, say, aesthetic sensitivity? And even granted that this problem can be solved, there is the future problem of arbitrating trade-offs between goods such as happiness and friendship when they *conflict.* When one is forced to choose between enhancing happiness and enhancing friendship, which gets priority? And under what conditions?

An interesting fact about consequentialist reasoning is that most of us employ it to some degree in ordinary decisions. We weigh the consequences of alternatives in choosing colleges, in deciding on a career, in hiring and promoting others, and in many other judgments. We frequently weigh good consequences over bad ones and predict the long- and short-term effects of our choices. We often even cite consequentialist-style principles—for example, "No one should choose a college where he or she will be unhappy," or, "No one should pollute the environment when his or her action harms others."

However, for a variety of reasons including the objections to utilitarianism mentioned earlier, some philosophers refuse to acknowledge consequentialism as an adequate theory of ethics. They argue that the proper focus for ethical judgments should not be consequences, but moral *precepts*—that is, the rules, norms, and principles we use to guide our actions. Such philosophers are known as *deontologists*, and the next section will examine their views.

DEONTOLOGY

The term *deontological* comes from the Greek word for "duty," and what is crucial according to the deontologist are the rules and principles that guide actions. We shall discuss here two approaches to deontological ethical reasoning that have profoundly influenced ethics. The first is that of the eighteenth-century philosopher Immanuel Kant and his followers. This approach focuses on duty and universal rules to determine right actions. The second—actually a subspecies of deontological reasoning—is known as the "social contract" approach. It focuses not on individual decision making, but on the general social principles that rational persons in certain ideal situations would agree upon and adopt.

Kantian Deontology

Kant believed that ethical reasoning should concern activities that are rationally motivated and should utilize precepts that apply universally to all human actions. To this end, he opens his treatise on ethics by declaring

> It is impossible to conceive anything at all in the world, . . . which can be taken as good without qualification except a *good* will.[2]

This statement sums up much of what Kant wants to say about ethics and is worth unraveling. What Kant means is that the only thing that can be good or worthwhile without any provisos or stipulations is an action of the will freely motivated for the right reasons. Other goods such as wealth, beauty, and intelligence are certainly valuable, but they are not good *without gratification* because they have the potential to create both good and bad effects. Wealth, beauty, and intelligence can be bad when they are used for purely selfish ends. Even human happiness—which Mill held as the highest good—can, according to Kant, create complacency, disinterest, and excessive self-assurance under certain conditions.

According to Kant, reason is the faculty that can aid in the discovery of correct moral principles; thus it is *reason*, not *inclination*, that should guide the will. When reason guides the will, Kant calls the resulting actions ones done from "duty." Kant's use of the term *duty* turns out to be less formidable than it first appears. Kant is simply saying that a purely good and free act of the will is one done not merely because you have an *inclination* to do it, but because you have the right reasons for doing it. For example, suppose you discover a wallet belonging to a stranger. Kant would say that despite one's inclination to keep the money (which the stranger may not even need), one should return it. This is an act you know is right despite your inclinations. Kant also believes you should return the wallet even when you believe the *consequences* of not returning it are better. Here his views are at sharp odds with consequentialism. Suppose that the stranger is known for her stinginess, and you plan to donate the money to a children's hospital. No matter. For Kant, you must return the wallet. Thus the moral worth lies in the act itself and not in either your happiness or the consequences brought about by the act. Acts are good because they are done for the sake of what is right and not because of the consequences they might produce.

But how do I know what my duty is? While it may be clear that one should return a wallet, there are other circumstances in which one's duty is less evident. Suppose you are in a six-person lifeboat at sea with five others and a seventh person swims up? What is one's duty here? And how does one even know that what one *thinks* is right *is* right? To settle such problems, Kant claims that duty is more than doing merely what you "feel" is right. Duty is acting with *respect for other rational beings*. It almost goes without saying, then, that "acting from duty" is not to be interpreted as action done in obedience to local, state, or national laws, since these can be good or bad. Instead, "duty" is linked to the idea of universal principles that should govern all our actions.

But is there any principle that can govern *all* human beings? Kant believes the answer is yes, and he calls the highest such principle the "categorical imperative." He formulates the categorical imperative in three ways (although we shall only consider two formulations here). The first formulation, roughly translated, is

> One ought only to act such that the principle of one's act could become a universal law of human action in a world in which one would hope to live.

For example, one would want to live in a world where people followed the principle "Return property that belongs to others." Therefore, one should return the stranger's wallet. We do not, however, want to live in a world where everyone lies. Therefore, one should not adopt the principle "Lie whenever it seems helpful."

The second formulation of the categorical imperative is

> One ought to treat others as having intrinsic value in themselves, and *not* merely as means to achieve one's ends.

In other words, one should respect every person as a rational and free being. Hitler treated one group of persons as nonpersons in order to achieve his own ends, and thus he acted contrary to the categorical imperative. Another instance of treating persons as means would occur if a teacher looked up the grade records of new students to determine how to assign grades in her own class. She would be treating students as if they had no control over their destinies. Such actions are immoral according to Kant because they fail to respect the inherent dignity of rational beings.

Ethical reasoning for Kant implies adopting principles of action and evaluating one's actions in terms of those principles. Even Kant grants that the evaluation is sometimes difficult. For example, there is the problem of striking the proper level of generality in choosing a principle. A principle that read, "If one is named John Doe and attends Big State University and has two sisters, then he should borrow fifty dollars without intending to repay it," is far too specific. On the other hand, the principle "You should always pay your debts" might be too general, since it would require that a starving man repay the only money he possesses to buy a loaf of bread. Because of the problem of striking the proper degree of generality, many modern deontologists have reformulated Kant's basic question to read, "Could I wish that everyone in the world would follow this principle *under relevantly similar conditions?*"

As with utilitarianism, critics challenge deontological reasoning. Some assert that fanatics such as Hitler could at least *believe* that the rule "Persecute Jews whenever possible" is one that the world should live by. Similarly, a thief might universalize the principle "Steal whenever you have a good opportunity." Moreover, a strict interpretation of deontological ethical reasoning is said to allow no exceptions to a universal principle. Such strict adherence to universal principles might encourage moral rigidity and might fail to reflect the diversity of responses required by complex moral situations. Finally, critics argue that, in a given case, two principles may conflict without there being a clear way to decide which principle or rule should take precedence. Jean-Paul Sartre tells of his dilemma during World War II when he was forced to choose between staying to comfort his ill and aging mother and fighting for the freedom of France. Two principles seemed valid: "Give aid to your father and mother," and "Contribute to the cause of freedom." But with conflicting principles, how is one to choose? Nevertheless, deontological ethical reasoning represents a well-respected and fundamentally distinctive mode of ethical reasoning, one which, like consequentialism, appears in the deliberations of ordinary persons as well as philosophers. We have all heard actions condemned by the comment "What would it be like if everyone did that?"

The Contractarian Alternative

Kant assumes that the categorial imperative is something all rational individuals can discover and agree upon. A different version of deontology is offered by many philosophers who focus less on the actions of individuals and more on the principles that govern society at large. These include two philosophers whose writings appear in our book: the seventeenth-century political philosopher John Locke and the twentieth-century American philosopher John Rawls. They and others try to establish universal principles of a just society through what might be called "social contract thought experiments." They ask us to imagine what it would be like to live in a situation where there are no laws, no social conventions, and no political state. In this so-called state of nature, we imagine that rational persons gather to formulate principles or rules to govern political and social communities. Such rules would resemble principles derived through the categorical imperative in that they are presumable principles to which every rational person would agree and which would hold universally.

Locke and Rawls differ in their approach to establishing rules or principles of justice, and the difference illustrates two distinct forms of contractarian reasoning. Locke argues from a "natural rights" position, while Rawls argues from a "reasonable person" position. Locke claims that every person is born with, and possesses, certain basic rights that are "natural." These rights are inherent to a person's nature, and they are possessed by everyone equally. Like other inherent traits, they cannot be taken away. They are, in the words of the Declaration of Independence, "inalienable." When rational persons meet to formulate principles to govern the formation of social and political communities, they construct a social contract that is the basis for an agreement between themselves and their government and whose rules protect natural rights. Rights, then, become deontological precepts by which one forms and evaluates rules, constitutions, government, and socioeconomic systems. While many philosophers disagree with Locke's view that each of us has inherent or *natural* rights, many do utilize a theory of human rights as the basis for justifying and evaluating political institutions.

Rawls adopts a different perspective. He does not begin from a natural rights position. Instead, he asks which principles of justice rational persons would formulate if they were behind a "veil of ignorance"—that is, if each person knew nothing about who he or she was. That is, one would not know whether one were old or young, male or female, rich or poor, highly motivated or lazy, or anything about one's personal status in society. Unable to predict which principles, if picked, will favor them personally, Rawls argues, persons will be forced to choose principles that are fair to all.

Rawls and Locke are not in perfect agreement about which principles would be adopted in such hypothetical situations, and more will be said about their views later in this book. For now it is important to remember that the social contract approach maintains a deontological character. It is used to formulate principles of justice that apply universally. Some philosophers note, however, that from an original position in a "state of nature" or behind a "veil of ignorance," rational persons *could* adopt consequentialist principles as rules for a just society. Thus, while the social contract approach is deontological in style, the principles it generates are not necessarily ones that are incompatible with consequentialism.

In the moral evaluations of business, all deontologists—contractarians included—would ask questions such as the following:

1. Are the rules fair to everyone?
2. Do the rules hold universally even with the passage of time?
3. Is every person treated with equal respect?

What may be missing from a deontological approach to ethical reasoning is a satisfactory means of coping with valid exceptions to general rules. Under what circumstances, if any, are exceptions allowed? Deontologists believe that they can answer this question, but their solutions vary. Suffice it to say that deontologists, just as utilitarians, have not convinced everyone.

HUMAN NATURE ETHICS

According to some contemporary philosophers, the preceding two modes of ethical reasoning exhaust all possible modes. That is to say, all theories can be classified as either teleological or deontological. Whether this is true cannot be settled here, but it will be helpful to introduce briefly what some philosophers consider to be a third category, namely, the *human nature* approach.

A *human nature* approach assumes that all humans have inherent capacities that constitute the ultimate basis for all ethical claims. Actions are evaluated in terms of whether they promote or hinder, coincide with or conflict with these capacities. One of the most famous proponents of this theory was the Greek philosopher Aristotle. In Aristotle's opinion, human beings have inherent *potentialities*, and thus human development turns out to be the struggle for self-actualization or, in other words, the perfection of inherent human nature. Consider the acorn. It has the natural potential to become a sturdy oak tree. Its natural drive is not to become an elm or a cedar or even a stunted oak, but to become the most robust oak tree possible. Diseased or stunted oak trees are simply deficient; they are instances of things in nature whose potential has not been fully developed. Similarly, according to Aristotle, persons are born with inherent potentialities. Persons, like acorns, naturally are oriented to actualize their potentialities, and for them this means more than merely developing their physical potential. It also means developing their mental, moral, and social potential. Thus, human beings in this view are seen as basically good; evil is understood as a deficiency that occurs when one is unable to fulfill one's natural capacities.

It is important to understand that the concept of human nature need not be an individualistic one. According to Aristotle, persons are "social" by nature and cannot be understood apart from the larger community in which they participate. "Man," Aristotle wrote, is a "social animal." For Aristotle, then, fulfilling one's natural constitution implies developing wisdom, generosity, and self-restraint, all of which help to make one a good member of the community.

The criterion for judging the goodness of any action is whether or not the action is compatible with one's inherent human capacities. Actions that enhance human capacities are good; those that deter them are bad unless they are the best among generally negative alternatives. For example, eating nothing but starches is unhealthy, but it is clearly preferable to starving.

This theory puts great emphasis on the nature of persons, and obviously how one understands that "nature" will be the key to determining both what counts as a right action and how one defines the proper end of human action in general. Aristotle argued that intelligence and wisdom are uniquely human potentialities and consequently that intellectual virtue is the highest virtue. The life of contemplation, he believed, is the best sort of life, in part because it represents the highest fulfillment of human nature. Moral virtue, also crucial in Aristotle's theory, involves the rational control of one's desires. In action where a choice is possible, one exercises moral virtue by restraining harmful desires and cultivating beneficial ones. The development of virtue requires the cultivation of good habits, and this in turn leads Aristotle to emphasize the importance of good upbringing and education.

One problem said to affect human nature theories is that they have difficulty justifying the supposition that human beings *do* have specific inherent capacities and that these capacities are the same for all humans. Further, critics claim that it is difficult to warrant the assumption that humans are basically good. Perhaps the famous psychoanalyst Sigmund Freud is correct in his assertion that at bottom we are all naturally aggressive and selfish. Third, critics complain that it is difficult to employ this theory in ethical reasoning, since it appears to lack clear-cut rules and principles for use in moral decision making. Obviously, any well-argued human nature ethic will take pains to spell out the aspects of human nature which, when actualized, constitute the ultimate ground for moral judgments.

CONCLUSION

The three approaches to ethical reasoning we have discussed—consequentialism, deontology, and human nature ethics—all present theories of ethical reasoning distinguished in terms of their basic methodological elements. Each represents a type or model of moral reasoning that is applicable to practical decisions in concrete situations. Consider, for example, the case study with which we began our discussion, involving BASF and its proposed new plant. As it happened, BASF chose option 3 and decided to build elsewhere. In making his decision, did the BASF manager actually use any or all of the methods described earlier? Although we cannot know the answer to this question, it is clear, as we saw earlier, that each method was applicable to his problem. Indeed, the three methods of moral reasoning are sufficiently broad that each is applicable to the full range of problems confronting human moral experience. The question of which method, if any, is superior to the others must be left for another time. The intention of this essay is not to substitute for a thorough study of traditional ethical theories—something for which there is no substitute—but to introduce the reader to basic modes of ethical reasoning that will help to analyze the ethical problems in business that arise in the remainder of this book.

NOTES

1. "BASF Corporation vs. The Hilton Head Island Developers," in *Business and Society*, Robert D. Hay et al., eds. (Cincinnati: South-Western Publishing Co., 1984), pp. 100–12.
2. Immanuel Kant, *Groundwork of the Metaphysic of Morals*, trans. H.J. Paton (New York: Harper & Row, 1948, 1956), p. 61.

The Case Method

Thomas Donaldson

Professor Charles Gragg of the Harvard Business School, himself a master of the case method, once said the belief that knowledge can simply be "told" and passed on is "the great delusion of the ages."[1] Gragg's remark concurs with the view of Socrates, the Greek philosopher, whose well-known style of teaching was never a one-way street, with the instructor talking and the student listening, but rather a two-way exchange in which the student actively participated by questioning, searching, and answering. Thus the fundamental basis of the case method, the belief that knowledge cannot simply be "told," is in step with an age-old norm of good teaching. And it is a norm that for centuries has been recognized as valid by philosophers. One should not be surprised, then, to learn that the case method is gaining wide acceptance even outside schools of business. Philosophers, theologians, and social scientists are using it to confront issues of public policy, distributive justice, and ethics.

The purpose of this essay is to describe the case method, its strategies and aims, and to apply it to the teaching of ethics.

THE CASE METHOD: A DIFFERENT STYLE OF LEARNING

"You can lead a person to the university," someone once quipped, "but you can't make him think." What too often passes for learning is the repetition of facts by students during standardized exams. The case method, however, does not allow a student the luxury of memorizing a body of accepted wisdom. Rather, it forces the student to confront a set of facts that demands analysis; and these facts, the student soon discovers, are not understood by the application of memorized truths.

Thus, a philosophy of education undergirds the case method—namely, that people must be taught to think well in the presence of new situations and to arrive at reasoned courses of action. In this way the method emphasizes *judgment* as much as *understanding*. Moreover, it attempts to develop skills of judgment that can be applied to situations in the real world. Although it varies from practitioner to practitioner, the case method may be defined as a method of instruction that confronts students with descriptions of realistic human events, and then requires the students to analyze, evaluate, and make recommendations about those events.

What is known today as the case method began at Harvard University in 1908 with the opening of the new business school. The business school's first catalog stated that the "problem method" would be utilized "as far as practicable." After years of struggle and experimentation, the case method reached maturity at Harvard

---

from 1919 to 1942 under the encouragement of the dean of the business school, Wallace Donham. It was during these years that the method became the trademark of the Harvard Business School, a position it retains to this day.

THE ROLE OF THE INSTRUCTOR

Just as there is no such thing as a "typical" case, there is no such thing as a "typical" case-method teaching style. Each instructor develops his or her own questions, responses, and style. Certain pedagogical virtues, however, are obvious, such as approachability, enthusiasm, and articulateness.[2]

The responsibilities of the instructor using a case-method approach have been summed up as follows:

1. Assign cases for discussion
2. Act as a responsible member of the group delegated to provoke argumentative thinking
3. Guide discussions through remarks and questions toward points of major importance
4. Take a final position on the viewpoints at the end of the discussion *if* the instructor chooses[3]

Sometimes an instructor has a remarkable teaching experience in which it is necessary only to ask an opening question—"Mr. Y., would you begin our discussion?"—and the class is off and running. More frequently, the instructor must help the discussion through contributions of his or her own. To accomplish this, the instructor may

1. Ask further questions
2. Restate and reconstruct what has been said
3. Voice his or her own opinions and draw upon his or her knowledge of fact[4]

To open a discussion, an instructor may ask such questions as

Do you see a problem in this case? If so, what is it?
Would someone volunteer to give us a brief sketch of the facts in the case?
(Or simply) What's happening in this case?

Once the discussion is underway, the instructor may invite a student to play the part of one of the managers who has a central role in the case. Thus, the instructor might ask, "What would you do if you were Mr. Jones?" Indeed, unless an instructor pushes a student to speak in terms of decisions, the advantage of the case method may be undercut as the discussion regresses into a fragmented series of general observations.

Discussion leaders frequently summarize or attempt to interpret a student's remark. Doing so has a double advantage: It helps to confirm what the student actually meant, and it helps to ensure that other students interpreted the remark correctly. In a surprisingly large number of cases, the student will want to qualify a remark once it has been interpreted by the instructor. This has the welcome consequence of encouraging the student to reflect upon both the nature of the view being expressed and the reasons for it.

Professor Andrews has summarized the role of the instructor as follows:

> The instructor provides the impromptu services which any group discussion requires. He keeps the proceedings orderly. He should be able to ask questions which . . . advance . . . group thinking and at the same time reveal the relevance of talk that has gone before. . . . He needs the sense of timing which tells him that a discussion is not moving fast enough to make good use of available time or is racing away from the comprehension of half the class. . . . He exercises control over an essentially "undirected" activity, but at the same time he keeps out of the way. . . . Since unpredictable developments always distinguish real learning, he examines his class rather than his subject. His workshop is not the study but the classroom. . . . He must himself be a student.[5]

An instructor may block a direct question from a student. When a student asks a specific question about the material, the instructor may decide that to answer the question would stifle the thinking of other students. Hence the instructor may reply by saying "Well, what does the class think?" or "My opinion is X, but is that really the right opinion?" Here the attempt is to turn the question into a catalyst rather than a retardant of the ongoing discussion.

The following are sample questions asked by case-method instructors:

Where does this idea lead?

You said X. May I add Y?

Do others disagree?

Do you mean X?

Do you have more to say about Y?

Do you think that is true in all cases?

How does that apply to the situation in the case?

Is your point related to Ms. Y's?

What does that have to do with the bigger question?[6]

An instructor can do more than ask questions. He or she can identify unstated assumptions that one of the participants is making and hold them up to the class for inspection. Or if a discussion is really dragging, the instructor may frankly ask the class what's wrong and attempt to generate discussion about the *process* of the discussion itself. (Sometimes this will have surprising results.) Blackboards can be used to list options, relevant facts, pros and cons, and assumptions.

When a discussion is well under way, it is not unusual for an instructor to retire to an inconspicuous place and simply observe.

THE ROLE OF THE STUDENT

In the case method, the active cooperation of the student is essential. Previous schooling habituates a student to the role of receiver. In the case method, this previous schooling must be undone; the student must learn the habit of being active, of being a force in the teaching process. Hence the student must master a number of skills. First he or she must learn to synthesize material on his or her own. Although infrequently an instructor's summary of the main lines of the preceding discussion will help the student to integrate important aspects of the discussion, ordinarily the act of synthesis must be undertaken by the student. Equally important, the student must learn to separate irrelevant from relevant information. (Cases are frequently constructed intentionally to contain both kinds.) Finally, the student must invest sufficient time in preparing a case to make the discussion productive. With other methods, a failure to prepare is problematic; with the case method, it is disastrous.

Sometimes students benefit from discussing a case in a small, preclass group. In such a group they often discover crucial items around which ordinary group discussions will turn; moreover they gain experience in the presentation of ideas.

Discouragement is routine when students begin the case method. They jump to the conclusion that they are making no progress because they are accustomed to defining "progress" differently. After discussing the first case or two, they recognize that not all issues have been resolved, and may be left with a sense of incompleteness, like hearing a piece of music with no resolving chord. Gradually, however, they will experience a growing confidence in their ability to analyze complex case materials and, in turn, a growing conviction of the value of the case method. At this stage it is not uncommon for the original skepticism to turn to an uncritical endorsement of the method.

THE CASE METHOD APPLIED TO ETHICS

Any given method is related to the function and object of the method's activity. Thus, we should begin by noting—as Aristotle and others have before us—that the end or aim of ethical enquiry is different from that of empirical enquiry. Whereas the goal of empirical enquiry is factual or empirical knowledge, the goal of ethical enquiry is ethical insight. By "ethical insight" I mean insight about good and bad, right and wrong, and permissible and impermissible behavior. We want to be able to distinguish false or irrational convictions (e.g., that of first-century Romans that when a slave owner was killed by one of his slaves, *all* of his slaves should be executed) from correct ones (e.g., the more modern conviction that this Roman custom was unfair). Although ethics intersects frequently with matters of taste, and hence involves a certain amount of relativity, the very possibility of ethical insight recognizes a difference in the truth status of the belief that torturing children for sport is permissible, and the belief that it is not.

Ethical and empirical knowledge must be distinguished because although they both may be kinds of knowledge, they not only have different subjects but different epistemological foundations. The belief that salt is soluble in water is a piece of empirical knowledge because it is known through experience. It depicts a "fact," and if one were to doubt it, the proper response would be to take a pinch of salt and throw it into water. But the belief that patricide is wrong is an *ethical* belief, not an empirical one, and doubters may well not be persuaded by undertaking the "experiment" of killing their fathers. Indeed, it is difficult to see just what killing one's father could possibly "prove" about the rightness or wrongness of patricide.

The reasoning necessary to make sense of ethical issues has a different logic from that of empirical reasoning. Consider the traditional distinction offered by philosophers such as Aristotle and Aquinas between practical and theoretical reasoning. The end of theoretical reasoning is a general concept, while that of practical reasoning is an action. Thus, using theoretical reasoning I might conclude from the fact that all ravens I have seen are black to the general proposition that all ravens are black. Or I might reason from the premises that all healthy corporations have a strong corporate culture, and that the XYZ Corporation is a healthy corporation, to the deductive conclusion that the XYZ Corporation has a strong corporate culture. Both would be pieces of theoretical reasoning.

However, in practical reasoning, the tables are turned. I reason from the acknowledgment of a general value or desire to a practical action, and I do so typically through a process of means-ends reasoning. Thus, given that I hold the value of "honoring valid contracts," and that I believe that giving you a check in the amount of $10,000 is a means of "honoring a valid contract," my reasoning may lead me to write you a check in the amount of $10,000.

Notice that I have employed means-ends reasoning; that is, I reason that writing the check is a *means* of honoring the contract, but that my process of reasoning is not deductive in nature. The necessary conclusion that is characteristic of deductive reasoning is absent in practical reasoning. For although writing a check for $10,000 is one means of achieving my value, it may not be the only means. I might similarly honor the contract by giving you $10,000 in cash, or by arranging to release you from a prior debt. So whereas the conclusion that "XYZ Corporation has a strong corporate culture" is necessarily true if the premises, "All healthy corporations have a strong corporate culture" and "XYZ Corporation is a healthy corporation" are true, it does not follow necessarily that *if* I hold the value of honoring valid contracts and *if* I believe that writing you a check is a means of honoring a valid contract, I *will* write you a check. It does not even necessarily follow that I *should* write you a check.

Practical reasoning occurs in a variety of contexts, not only those dealing with ethics. It occurs whenever one employs means-ends reasoning as a guide for action. Yet ethical reasoning, in contrast to nonethical reasoning, has another identifying feature: It necessarily involves evaluation of ends and principles as well as means. If I assume that I want to sell a given piece of property and reason about the best means of selling it, I am using a practical, though not necessarily ethical, mode of reasoning. Ethical reasoning also requires that I deliberate about the act of selling itself, and that I evaluate whether the end of selling the piece of property is morally justified. This feature adds to the complexity of business decisions enormously. For insofar as we can assume that the end or guiding principle of a corporation is the maximization of profit, our reasoning about corporate behavior is simplified. Moral analysis, however, requires that at least from time to time the corporate goal of profit maximization itself come under scrutiny.

Let us now apply our conclusion about ethical reasoning to the matter of teaching business ethics through cases.

The first thing to notice is that adapting the case method to ethics is relatively easy because this method emphasizes practical reasoning, which is a crucial component of ethical reasoning. Cases traditionally have been used to hone a student's judgment in concrete business situations. They emphasize means-ends reasoning and can be used to do the same when the ends are not only market share and profits, but fairness and corporate integrity. A major pedagogical difference between traditional business subjects and that of ethics, however, stems from ethics' concern with ends and principles. Because ethics requires investigation of values to be achieved as well as the means used to achieve them, cases must be adapted to evaluate broader issues. As we shall see, this implies a difference in the structure of cases and the style of pedagogy.

To begin with, teaching ethics requires a different selection of cases. Cases must be structured to raise issues about ends and principles, and this implies a backing away from the traditional insistence, associated with the Harvard case method, that every case must pose a decision-making problem confronted by an individual manager. A case dealing with the FDA's decision to ban the manufacture of Laetrile may not yield to the traditional format of "What should manager A do now?" Yet it may be a good case nonetheless if it confronts students with some of the difficult trade-offs between the liberties of individual actors in a market, and the (supposed) well-being of consumers.

Nor is the enormous detail championed by some case-method practitioners always necessary. Whereas practical reasoning always occurs in the context of a maze of facts, reasoning about ends sometimes thrives in rarefied atmospheres. Consider, for example, the following "case," which is only two sentences long:

> Two equally qualified candidates, one of whom is a black female and the other a white male, have applied for a job. Should the prospective employer hire the black female?

Admirably brief, these two sentences could serve as the focus of a highly profitable, hour-long discussion.

Cases alone are not sufficient when teaching business ethics and should be augmented by theoretical material. The examination of ends and principles is enhanced by reference to the inquiries of others. Whereas it may be possible to gain a reasonable sense of good marketing practice merely through an analysis of cases (although I have my doubts even here), it is nearly impossible to do so in the case of ethics. Again, unlike empirical disciplines, basic ethical knowledge owes little to experience per se. Like mathematics, ethics requires sustained reflection on specific concepts. Thus, just as teaching mathematics would be impossible through an approach involving nothing but cases, so too would ethics. One benefits greatly by examining the theoretical investigations of specialists in the field of ethics, and it follows that any casebook should be supplemented by theoretical materials.

Even as the structure of cases must be adapted to the teaching of ethics, so too must the instructor's teaching style. The "neutrality" of the instructor is a well-respected fixture of the case method in its ordinary setting. Should instructors be similarly neutral when teaching ethics? Although the answer is somewhat a matter of opinion, there seems little reason for sacrificing openness in ethical contexts. We are reminded of the long-standing Socratic irony: Socrates believed that virtue could not be taught, yet he spent his life teaching virtue. The solution to the seeming paradox, of course, is that Socrates believed that one teaches ethics in a quite different manner than one teaches other disciplines. One does not convey facts to the student; instead one plays the role of midwife, attempting to engage the student in a process of reflection that will yield ethical understanding. The truths of ethics cannot be drummed into one's head; rather they must instead be discovered and respected by oneself. Otherwise, they cannot be "known" in a meaningful sense.

Because of this, the instructor must struggle to preserve his or her own openness in the face of the student's own investigations. But openness should not be confused with moral relativism. As the philosopher Ralph Barton Perry notes, it "is easy to raise doubts, to point out the ignorance and conflicting evidence that beset the mind on every side. It is well to do this and an honest and trained mind will do it . . . (but) if beliefs are demolished, they should be built again, or others built in their place."[7]

Openness does not imply that there are no givens in ethics. As in any practical sphere, some things can be assumed: We can assume that murder, torture, and the intentional harming of innocents is bad, and that fairness and happiness are good. Documents such as the United Nation's *Universal Declaration of Human Rights* are good examples of how much we have in common even with peoples of distant lands and different tastes. Signed by virtually every country in the world, the *Declaration* lays down a basic floor of values that deserve the name "universal": rights to freedom, adequate medical care, safe working conditions, participation in government, and the ownership of property. So too, an instructor teaching ethics can make certain basic assumptions about values without compromising his pedagogical openness.

In empirical science, success implies that we have discovered the structure of the subject—and finally of the world itself—by perception and experiment. In ethical theory, success implies that we in some sense create the structure of the world, and that we do so in the image of a design that is beautiful and not ugly. As the German philosopher Immanuel Kant once remarked, "Things in nature act according to laws; only people act in accordance with the *concept* of laws." In business, people should be guided by concepts not only related to profitability and efficiency, but of professional integrity, responsibility, and fairness. The latter concepts demand an attention to ends and principles that is uncharacteristic of traditional case-method technique. Thus case-method instructors must make a concession to the unique demands of the discipline of ethics.

SHORTCOMINGS OF THE CASE METHOD

The case method is not foolproof. Like any other method, it is susceptible to the foibles and failings of those who use it and, badly handled, produces classroom disasters. At its worst, the method becomes a boring exposure to the prejudices of others.

Cases necessarily oversimplify business situations. Whereas cases can imitate reality by demanding decisions on the basis of incomplete facts (no real-world decision maker has *all* the facts), cases are at odds with reality in presenting a "static" rather than a dynamic decision-making context. A case presents a situation in which the action has already occurred, but everyday situations unfold gradually, and every hour brings fresh information to the decision maker. Hence the skills of knowing when to seek new information, and of knowing when the proper moment has arrived to make a decision, are not developed by the case method.

Essential to a good case discussion is adequate discussion time. A case done hurriedly is an unrewarding experience in which most of the analysis is either superficial or wrong. At first, students may find the discussion of many problems in a short time stimulating. But soon the frustration of approaching case after case without in-depth analysis will bring discouragement with the entire method.

Finally, although the case method is an excellent method for most students, one or two students may benefit little if at all. However, this is not a characteristic drawback of the case method per se, since every approach to teaching misses some students. Indeed, a special advantage of the case method is that it can bring to life a joy in learning for students who have been turned off by traditional methods.

STRUCTURING THE LEARNING EXPERIENCE

The following are suggestions for designing a case discussion process.

Lecturing in Conjunction with Cases

Depending on the style and preference of a given instructor, a lecture may precede or follow a case discussion. Most instructors in business ethics courses use cases only as one part of their course, with lectures and discussions of theoretical material constituting the remaining parts.

Time

A case may occupy a full class period or, in the instance of exceedingly long and complicated cases, two or more periods. Two or three short cases can sometimes be discussed in an hour. Even the shortest of cases (perhaps a paragraph or two in length) will usually require twenty minutes of discussion times.

Call Lists

Some instructors work entirely with volunteers, but others call on specific students, especially in the beginning, to get things moving. Calling on students increases pressure on them to be prepared, although some instructors and students find such pressure uncomfortable and distracting. Of those who do call on students, many use "call lists" containing the names of participants and their frequency of participation. Near the end of a discussion, an instructor may stop recognizing volunteers and move to call on those who haven't yet participated.

Assigning Additional Work

The usual assignment for students is to read and study the case carefully. With complicated cases, instructors sometimes ask for a brief written analysis to be submitted on the day of the discussion.

Role Playing

Role playing is a device sometimes used to simulate a living situation. Choosing an opportune moment, the instructor invites a student (or students) to assume the role of a participant in the case. In a case dealing with government regulation, for example, one student may remark that the corporation's best option is to stall the regulatory agency. The teacher, knowing that other students do not agree with this strategy, may ask, "Does anyone want to play the role of the regulator?" When someone accepts the invitation and responds directly to the student who advocates stalling, the former student has a chance to respond directly to the regulator. Such exchanges can enliven a discussion and reveal difficulties that otherwise might be glossed over.

Concluding Evaluation

At the end of a discussion, some instructors will ask for a vote among various options that have been explored in the discussion. This is not to affirm that correct answers are simple products of democratic vote, but to indicate how others have interpreted the points made in the discussion.

Grading

The method of grading, of course, is the prerogative of the instructor. Most instructors, however, try to form a general impression of a student's performance and then record it either after each class discussion or at one or two points during the semester.

Students may also be given exams that ask them to analyze cases in a written essay. In ethics courses where theoretical material is being covered in addition to cases, it is common to ask students to analyze a case by using concepts drawn from the theoretical readings.

The case method, though not foolproof, offers clear rewards. Socrates' insight that moral truth cannot simply "be told" is reflected in the case method's emphasis on analysis, discussion, and decision making. Like any method, it is subject to the failings of its practitioners. Like any method, it must be carefully adapted to the special territory it covers. But handled properly it can spark the search for skills and values of utmost human import. It can, perhaps more effectively than any other method, demonstrate the need for intellectual solutions to practical problems.

NOTES

1. Charles I. Gragg, "Because Wisdom Can't Be Told," in *The Case Method at the Harvard Business School,* ed. Malcolm P. McNair (New York: McGraw-Hill, Inc., 1954), p, 10.
2. Kenneth R. Andrews, "The Role of the Instructor in the Case Method," in *The Case Method at the Harvard Business School,* ed. Malcolm P. McNair (New York: McGraw-Hill, Inc., 1954), p. 99.
3. Gragg, "Wisdom Can't Be Told," p. 12.
4. Andrews, "Role of the Instructor," p. 105.
5. Ibid., 98–99.
6. Ibid., 105–6.
7. Ralph Barton Perry, *The Citizen Decides: A Guide to Responsible Thinking in Time of Crisis* (Bloomington: Indiana University Press, 1951), Chapter VII.

SUGGESTED SUPPLEMENTARY READINGS

ANDREWS, KENNETH R., ed. *The Case Method of Teaching Human Relations and Administration.* Cambridge, Mass.: Harvard University Press, 1953.

ANDREWS, KENNETH R. "The Role of the Instructor in the Case Method," in *The Case Method at the Harvard Business School,* ed. Malcolm P. McNair. New York: McGraw-Hill, Inc., 1954, pp. 98–109.

CANTOR, NATHANIAL B. "Learning Which Makes a Difference," in *To Study Administration by Cases,* ed. Andrew Towl. Cambridge, Mass.: Harvard University Press, 1969, pp. 153–58.

COPELAND, MELVIN P. "The Genius of the Case Method in Business Instruction," in *The Case Method at the Harvard Business School,* ed. Malcolm P. McNair. New York: McGraw-Hill, Inc., 1954, pp. 25–33.

GLOVER, JOHN D., and RALPH M. HOWER. "Some Comments on Teaching by the Case Method," in *The Case of Teaching Human Relations and Administration,* ed. Kenneth R. Andrews. Cambridge, Mass.: Harvard University Press, 1953, pp. 13–24.

MCNAIR, MALCOLM P., ed. *The Case Method at the Harvard Business School.* New York: McGraw-Hill, Inc., 1954.

STENZEL, ANNE, and HELEN FEENEY. *Learning by the Case Method.* New York: The Seabury Press, Inc, 1970.

Chapter One

———•———

Business or Ethics

THE WORD *PARABLE* means "comparison" or "judgment". "The Parable of the Sadhu" asks us to compare, to judge, to make a moral choice. What was an Indian holy man (a sadhu) doing unconscious and unclothed at 15,500 feet on a Himalayan mountain slope? Were the people who found him now responsible for him? Should the group or any single individual have taken responsibility for his safety? Does this parable parallel the distinction often made between individual ethical decision making (personal ethics) and collective decision making (professional or business ethics)? Is there an absolute right or wrong to be found here?

As "The Parable of the Sadhu" demonstrates, relatively few issues in life are ever clear-cut, especially when they involve a complex series of facts and decisions. However, there are times when the issues, though complex, are clear and demand our attention. Such is the case with two classic examples of what's right and wrong in business ethics: the Beech-Nut apple juice incident and the Tylenol tampering episode.

The Beech-Nut incident asks the question "Why would one of America's most venerable food companies knowingly produce apple juice that completely omitted apples from its recipe and contained nothing but sugar water and vitamin C?" After all, Beech-Nut is not a "mom-and-pop" outfit, but a firm that annually earned 17 to 20 percent of the $760 million produced by the annual U.S. baby food market. This was a firm that was managed (at the top) by a president and vice-president who were pillars of the community. So how did it happen that Beech-Nut broke its sacred trust with the public—"Safe Food for Healthy Kids"?

The Tylenol tampering episode and the position that top management at Johnson & Johnson took begs the question "In doing the right thing, can a corporation and business also do well?" Is the lesson of this case that honesty works and that the truth can be effective both ethically and economically? Or is the real lesson a cynical self-serving one vis-à-vis Mark Twain: "When in doubt tell the truth. It will disarm your friends and befuddle your enemies."

Case Study

The Parable of the Sadhu

Bowen H. McCoy

It was early in the morning before the sun rose, which gave them time to climb the treacherous slope to the pass at 18,000 feet before the ice steps melted. They were also concerned about their stamina and altitude sickness, and felt the need to press on. Into the chance collection of climbers on that Himalayan slope an ethical dilemma arose in the guise of an unconscious, almost naked sadhu, an Indian holy man. Each climber gave the sadhu help but none made sure he would be safe. Should somebody have stopped to help the sadhu to safety? Would it have done any good? Was the group responsible? Since leaving the sadhu on the mountain slope, the author, who was one of the climbers, has pondered these issues. He sees many parallels for business people as they face ethical decisions at work.

Last year, as the first participant in the new six-month sabbatical program that Morgan Stanley has adopted, I enjoyed a rare opportunity to collect my thoughts as well as do some travelling. I spent the first three months in Nepal, walking 600 miles through 200 villages in the Himalayas and climbing some 120,000 vertical feet. On the trip my sole Western companion was an anthropologist who shed light on the cultural patterns of the villages we passed through.

During the Nepal hike, something occurred that has had a powerful impact on my thinking about corporate ethics. Although some might argue that the experience has no relevance to business, it was a situation in which a basic ethical dilemma suddenly intruded into the lives of a group of individuals. How the group responded I think holds a lesson for all organizations no matter how defined.

THE SADHU

The Nepal experience was more rugged and adventuresome than I had anticipated. Most commercial treks last two or three weeks and cover a quarter of the distance we traveled.

My friend Stephen, the anthropologist, and I were halfway through the 60-day Himalayan part of the trip when we reached the high point, an 18,000-foot pass over a crest that we'd have to traverse to reach the village of Muklinath, an ancient holy place for pilgrims.

Six years earlier I had suffered pulmonary edema, an acute form of altitude sickness, at 16,500 feet in the vicinity of Everest base camp, so we were understandably concerned about what would happen at 18,000 feet. Moreover, the Himalayas were having their wettest spring in 20 years, hip-deep powder and ice had already driven us off one ridge. If we failed to cross the pass, I feared that the last half of our "once in a lifetime" trip would be ruined.

The night before we would try the pass, we camped at a hut at 14,500 feet. In the photos taken at that camp, my face appears wan. The last village we'd passed through was a sturdy two-day walk below us, and I was tired.

During the late afternoon, four backpackers from New Zealand joined us, and we spent most of the night awake, anticipating the climb. Below we could see the fires of two other parties, which turned out to be two Swiss couples and a Japanese hiking club.

To get over the steep part of the climb before the sun melted the steps cut in the ice, we departed at 3:30 A.M. The New Zealanders left first, followed by Stephen and myself, our porters and Sherpas, and then the Swiss. The Japanese lingered in their camp. The sky was clear, and we were confident that no spring storm would erupt that day to close the pass.

At 15,500 feet, it looked to me as if Stephen were shuffling and staggering a bit, which are symptoms of altitude sickness. (The initial stage of altitude sickness brings a headache and nausea. As the condition worsens, a climber may encounter difficult breathing, disorientation, aphasia, and paralysis.) I felt strong, my adrenaline was flowing, but I was very concerned about my ultimate ability to get across. A couple of our porters were also suffering from the height, and Pasang, our Sherpa sirdar (leader), was worried.

Just after daybreak, while we rested at 15,500 feet, one of the New Zealanders, who had gone ahead, came staggering down toward us with a body slung across his shoulders. He dumped the almost naked, barefoot body of an Indian holy man—a sadhu—at my feet. He had found the pilgrim lying on the ice, shivering and suffering from hypothermia. I cradled the sadhu's head and laid him out on the rocks. The New Zealander was angry. He wanted to get across the pass before the bright sun melted the snow. He said, "Look, I've done what I can. You have porters and Sherpa guides. You care for him. We're going on!" He turned and went back up the mountain to join his friends.

I took a carotid pulse and found that the sadhu was still alive. We figured he had probably visited the holy shrines at Muklinath and was on his way home. It was fruitless to question why he had chosen this desperately high route

instead of the safe, heavily traveled caravan route through the Kali Gandaki gorge. Or why he was almost naked and with no shoes, or how long he had been lying in the pass. The answers weren't going to solve our problem.

Stephen and the four Swiss began stripping off outer clothing and opening their packs. The sadhu was soon clothed from head to foot. He was not able to walk, but he was very much alive. I looked down the mountain and spotted below the Japanese climbers marching up with a horse.

Without a great deal of thought, I told Stephen and Pasang that I was concerned about withstanding the heights to come and wanted to get over the pass. I took off after several of our porters who had gone ahead.

On the steep part of the ascent where, if the ice steps had given way, I would have slid down about 3,000 feet, I felt vertigo. I stopped for a breather, allowing the Swiss to catch up with me. I inquired about the sadhu and Stephen. They said that the sadhu was fine and that Stephen was just behind. I set off again for the summit.

Stephen arrived at the summit an hour after I did. Still exhilarated by victory, I ran down the snow slope to congratulate him. He was suffering from altitude sickness, walking 15 steps, then stopping, walking 15 steps, then stopping, Pasang accompanied him all the way up. When I reached them, Stephen glared at me and said: "How do you feel about contributing to the death of a fellow man?"

I did not fully comprehend what he meant.

"Is the sadhu dead?" I inquired.

"No," replied Stephen, "but he surely will be!"

After I had gone, and the Swiss had departed not long after, Stephen had remained with the sadhu. When the Japanese had arrived. Stephen had asked to use their horse to transport the sadhu down to the hut. They had refused. He had then asked Pasang to have a group of our porters carry the sadhu. Pasang had resisted the idea, saying that the porters would have to exert all their energy to get themselves over the pass. He had thought they could not carry a man down 1,000 feet to the hut, reclimb the slope, and get across safely before the snow melted. Pasang had pressed Stephen not to delay any longer.

The Sherpas had carried the sadhu down to a rock in the sun at about 15,000 feet and had pointed out the hut another 500 feet below. The Japanese had given him food and drink. When they had last seen him he was listlessly throwing rocks at the Japanese party's dog, which had frightened him.

We do not know if the sadhu lived or died.

For many of the following days and evenings Stephen and I discussed and debated our behavior toward the sadhu. Stephen is a committed Quaker with deep moral vision. He said, "I feel that what happened with the sadhu is a good example of the breakdown between the individual ethic and the corporate ethic. No one person was willing to assume ultimate responsibility for the sadhu. Each was willing to do his bit just so long as it was not too inconvenient. When it got to be a bother, everyone just passed the buck to someone else and took off. Jesus was relevant to a more individualistic stage of society, but how do we interpret his teaching today in a world filled with large, impersonal organizations and groups?"

I defended the larger group, saying, "Look, we all cared. We all stopped and gave aid and comfort. Everyone did his bit. The New Zealander carried him down below the snow line. I took his pulse and suggested we treat him for hypothermia. You and the Swiss gave him clothing and got him warmed up. The Japanese gave him food and water. The Sherpas carried him down to the sun and pointed out the easy trail toward the hut. He was well enough to throw rocks at a dog. What more could we do?"

"You have just described the typical affluent Westerner's response to a problem. Throwing money—in this case food and sweaters—at it,

but not solving the fundamentals!" Stephen retorted.

"What would satisfy you?" I said. "Here we are, a group of New Zealanders, Swiss, Americans, and Japanese who have never met before and who are at the apex of one of the most powerful experiences of our lives. Some years the pass is so bad no one gets over it. What right does an almost naked pilgrim who chooses the wrong trail have to disrupt our lives? Even the Sherpas had no interest in risking the trip to help him beyond a certain point."

Stephen calmly rebutted, "I wonder what the Sherpas would have done if the sadhu had been a well-dressed Nepali, or what the Japanese would have done if the sadhu had been a well-dressed Asian, or what you would have done, Buzz, if the sadhu had been a well-dressed Western woman?"

"Where, in your opinion," I asked instead, "is the limit of our responsibility in a situation like this? We had our own well-being to worry about. Our Sherpa guides were unwilling to jeopardize us or the porters for the sadhu. No one else on the mountain was willing to commit himself beyond certain self-imposed limits."

Stephen said, "As individual Christians or people with a Western ethical tradition, we can fulfill our obligations in such a situation only if (1) the sadhu dies in our care, (2) the sadhu demonstrates to us that he could undertake the two-day walk down to the village, or (3) we carry the sadhu for two days down to the village and convince someone there to care for him."

"Leaving the sadhu in the sun with food and clothing, while he demonstrated hand-eye coordination by throwing a rock at a dog, comes close to fulfilling items one and two," I answered. "And it wouldn't have made sense to take him to the village where the people appeared to be far less caring than the Sherpas, so the third condition is impractical. Are you really saying that, no matter what the implications, we should, at the drop of a hat, have changed our entire plan?"

THE INDIVIDUAL VS. THE GROUP ETHIC

Despite my arguments, I felt and continue to feel guilt about the sadhu. I had literally walked through a classic moral dilemma without fully thinking through the consequences. My excuses for my actions include a high adrenaline flow, a superordinate goal, and a once-in-a-lifetime opportunity—factors in the usual corporate situation, especially when one is under stress.

Real moral dilemmas are ambiguous, and many of us hike right through them, unaware that they exist. When, usually after the fact, someone makes an issue of them, we tend to resent his or her bringing it up. Often, when the full import of what we have done (or not done) falls on us, we dig into a defensive position from which it is very difficult to emerge. In rare circumstances we may contemplate what we have done from inside a prison.

Had we mountaineers been free of physical and mental stress caused by the effort and the high altitude, we might have treated the sadhu differently. Yet isn't stress the real test of personal and corporate values? The instant decisions executives make under pressure reveal the most about personal and corporate character.

Among the many questions that occur to me when pondering my experience are: What are the practical limits of moral imagination and vision? Is there a collective or institutional ethic beyond the ethics of the individual? At what level of effort or commitment can one discharge one's ethical responsibilities? Not every ethical dilemma has a right solution. Reasonable people often disagree; otherwise there would be no dilemma. In a business context, however, it is essential that managers agree on a process for dealing with dilemmas.

The sadhu experience offers an interesting parallel to business situations. An immediate response was mandatory. Failure to act was a decision in itself. Up on the mountain we could not resign and submit our résumés to a headhunter. In contrast to philosophy, business involves action and implementation—getting things done. Managers must come up with answers to problems based on what they see and what they allow to influence their decision-making processes. On the mountain, none of us but Stephen realized the true dimensions of the situation we were facing.

One of our problems was that as a group we had no process for developing a consensus. We had no sense of purpose or plan. The difficulties of dealing with the sadhu were so complex that no one person could handle it. Because it did not have a set of preconditions that could guide its action to an acceptable resolution, the group reacted instinctively as individuals. The cross-cultural nature of the group added a further layer of complexity. We had no leader with whom we could all identify and in whose purpose we believed. Only Stephen was willing to take charge, but he could not gain adequate support to care for the sadhu.

Some organizations do have a value system that transcends the personal values of the managers. Such values, which go beyond profitability, are usually revealed when the organization is under stress. People throughout the organization generally accept its values, which, because they are not presented as a rigid list of commandments, may be somewhat ambiguous. The stories people tell, rather than printed materials, transmit these conceptions of what is proper behavior.

For 20 years I have been exposed at senior levels to a variety of corporations and organizations. It is amazing how quickly an outsider can sense the tone and style of an organization and the degree of tolerated openness and freedom to challenge management.

Organizations that do not have a heritage of mutually accepted, shared values tend to become unhinged during stress, with each individual bailing out for himself. In the great takeover battles we have witnessed during past years, companies that had strong cultures drew the wagons around them and fought it out, while other companies saw executives, supported by their golden parachutes, bail out of the struggles.

Because corporations and their members are interdependent, for the corporation to be strong the members need to share a preconceived notion of what is correct behavior, a "business ethic," and think of it as a positive force, not a constraint.

As an investment banker I am continually warned by well-meaning lawyers, clients, and associates to be wary of conflicts of interest. Yet if I were to run away from every difficult situation, I wouldn't be an effective investment banker. I have to feel my way through conflicts. An effective manager can't run from risk either; he or she has to confront and deal with risk. To feel "safe" in doing this, managers need the guidelines of an agreed-on process and set of values within the organization.

After my three months in Nepal, I spent three months as an executive-in-residence at both Stanford Business School and the Center for Ethics and Social Policy at the Graduate Theological Union at Berkeley. These six months away from my job gave me time to assimilate 20 years of business experience. My thoughts turned often to the meaning of the leadership role in any large organization. Students at the seminary thought of themselves as antibusiness. But when I questioned them they agreed that they distrusted all large organizations, including the church. They perceived all large organizations as impersonal and opposed to individual values and needs. Yet we all know of organizations where people's values and beliefs are respected and their expressions encouraged. What makes the difference? Can we identify

the difference and, as a result, manage more effectively?

The word "ethics" turns off many and confuses more. Yet the notions of shared values and an agreed-on process for dealing with adversity and change—what many people mean when they talk about corporate culture—seem to be at the heart of the ethical issue. People who are in touch with their own core beliefs and the beliefs of others and are sustained by them can be more comfortable living on the cutting edge. At times, taking a tough line or a decisive stand in a muddle of ambiguity is the only ethical thing to do. If a manager is indecisive and spends time trying to figure out the "good" thing to do, the enterprise may be lost.

Business ethics, then, has to do with the authenticity and integrity of the enterprise. To be ethical is to follow the business as well as the cultural goals of the corporation, its owners, its employees, and its customers. Those who cannot serve the corporate vision are not authentic business people and, therefore, are not ethical in the business sense.

At this stage of my own business experience. I have a strong interest in organizational behavior. Sociologists are keenly studying what they call corporate stories, legends, and heroes as a way organizations have of transmitting the value system. Corporations such as Arco have even hired consultants to perform an audit of their corporate culture. In a company, the leader is the person who understands, interprets, and manages the corporate value system. Effective managers are then action-oriented people who resolve conflict, are tolerant of ambiguity, stress, and change, and have a strong sense of purpose for themselves and their organizations.

If all this is true, I wonder about the role of the professional manager who moves from company to company. How can he or she quickly absorb the values and culture of different organizations? Or is there, indeed, an art of management that is totally transportable? Assuming such fungible managers do exist, is it proper for them to manipulate the values of others?

What would have happened had Stephen and I carried the sadhu for two days back to the village and become involved with the villagers in his care? In four trips to Nepal my most interesting experiences occurred in 1975 when I lived in a Sherpa home in the Khumbu for five days recovering from altitude sickness. The high point of Stephen's trip was an invitation to participate in a family funeral ceremony in Manang. Neither experience had to do with climbing the high passes of the Himalayas. Why were we so reluctant to try the lower path, the ambiguous trail? Perhaps because we did not have a leader who could reveal the greater purpose of the trip to us.

Why didn't Stephen with his moral vision opt to take the sadhu under his personal care? The answer is because, in part, Stephen was hard-stressed physically himself, and because, in part, without some support system that involved our involuntary and episodic community on the mountain, it was beyond his individual capacity to do so.

I see the current interest in corporate culture and corporate value systems as a positive response to Stephen's pessimism about the decline of the role of the individual in large organizations. Individuals who operate from a thoughtful set of personal values provide the foundation for a corporate culture. A corporate tradition that encourages freedom of inquiry, supports personal values, and reinforces a focused sense of direction can fulfill the need for individuality along with the prosperity and success of the group. Without such corporate support, the individual is lost.

That is the lesson of the sadhu. In a complex corporate situation, the individual requires and deserves the support of the group. If people cannot find such support from their organization, they don't know how to act. If such support is forthcoming, a person has a stake in the success of the group, and can add much to the process of establishing and maintaining a corporate culture. It is management's challenge to be sensitive to individual needs, to shape them, and to direct and focus them for the benefit of the group as a whole.

For each of us the sadhu lives. Should we stop what we are doing and comfort him; or should we keep trudging up toward the high pass? Should I pause to help the derelict I pass on the street each night as I walk by the Yale Club en route to Grand Central Station? Am I his brother? What is the nature of our responsibility if we consider ourselves to be ethical persons? Perhaps it is to change the values of the group so that it can, with all its resources, take the other road.

Case Study

Into the Mouth of Babes

James Traub

It is well within the reach of most white-collar criminals to assume an air of irreproachable virtue, especially when they're about to be sentenced. But there was something unusually compelling about the hearing of Niels L. Hoyvald and John F. Lavery as they stood before Judge Thomas C. Platt of the United States District Court in Brooklyn last month—especially in light of what they were being sentenced for. As president and vice president of the Beech-Nut Nutrition Corporation, Hoyvald and Lavery had sold millions of bottles of "apple juice" that they knew to contain little or no apple juice at all—only sugars, water, flavoring and coloring. The consumers of this bogus product were babies.

One prosecutor of the case, Thomas H. Roche, had summed up Beech-Nut's behavior as "a classic picture of corporate greed and irresponsibility." The company itself had pleaded guilty the previous fall to 215 counts of violating Federal food and drug laws, and had agreed to pay a $2 million fine, by far the largest ever imposed in the 50-year history of the Food, Drug and Cosmetic Act. Beech-Nut had confessed in a press release that it had broken a "sacred trust."

Yet there was Niels Hoyvald, 54 years old, tall, silver-haired, immaculately dressed, standing before Judge Platt with head bowed, as his attorney. Brendan V. Sullivan Jr., described him as "a person we would be proud to have in our family." When it was Hoyvald's turn to address the judge, he spoke firmly, but then his voice cracked as he spoke of his wife and mother: "I can hardly bear to look at them or speak to them." he said. "I ask for them and myself, please don't send me to jail."

Judge Platt was clearly troubled. He spoke in a semiaudible mutter that had the crowd in the courtroom craning forward. Though it was "unusual for a corporate executive to do time for consumer fraud," he said, he had "no alternative" but to sentence Hoyvald to a prison term of a year and a day, plus fines totaling $100,000. He then meted out the same punishment to the 56-year old Lavery, who declined to speak on his own behalf. He received his sentence with no show of emotion.

The combination of babies, apple juice and a well-known name like Beech-Nut makes for a potent symbol. In fact, apple juice is not especially nutritious (bottlers often fortify it with extra Vitamin C), but babies love it and find it easy to digest. Parents are pleased to buy a product that says "no sugar added"—as Beech-Nut advertised—and seem to regard is as almost as pure and natural as mother's milk. That, of course, was the sacred trust Beech-Nut broke, and is now struggling to repair. The company's share of the $760 million United States baby-food market has dropped from a high of 20 percent in 1986, when Beech-Nut and the two executives were indicted, to 17 percent this year. Its losses in the fruit-juice market have been even more dramatic. Richard C. Theuer, the company's president since 1986, still gets a stream of letters from outraged parents "who don't realize that it was a long time ago." Some of them, he says are "almost obscene."

If parents are outraged by Beech-Nut's actions, many people are also baffled. Even after the trial and verdict, the question of motive lingers: why would two men with impeccable records carry out so cynical and reckless a fraud? Except for Theuer, no current Beech-Nut employee who was involved in the events of the trial agreed to be interviewed for this article, nor did Hoyvald or Lavery. But a vivid picture of the economic and psychological concerns that impelled the company along its ruinous course emerges from court documents and a wide range of interviews. The Beech-Nut baby food scandal is a case study in the warping effects of blind corporate loyalty.

For three-quarters of century after its founding in 1891 as a meatpacking company, Beech-Nut expanded steadily into a large, diversified food concern, eventually including Life Savers, Table Talk pies, Tetley tea, Martinson's coffee, chewing gum and, of course, baby food. The company had an image straight from Norman Rockwell—pure, simple, healthful. In 1969, Beech-Nut was taken over by the Squibb Corporation. Only four years later, a remnant of the old company was spun off and taken private by a group led by a lawyer, Frank C. Nicholas. The company that emerged from the Squibb umbrella sold only baby food, and, as in earlier years, regularly divided with Heinz the third or so of the market not controlled by Gerber. It was a completely new world for Beech-Nut's newly independent owners, and an extremely precarious one. Beech-Nut was in a continuous financial bind.

After an expensive and unsuccessful effort in the mid-1970's to market Beech-Nut as the "natural" baby food, the imperative to reduce costs became overwhelming. In 1977, when a Bronx-based supplier, who would later take the name Universal Juice, offered Beech-Nut a less-expensive apple-juice concentrate, the company abandoned its longtime supplier for the new source. The savings would never amount to much more than $250,000 a year, out of a $50 million-plus manufacturing budget, but Beech-Nut was under the gun.

At the time, the decision may have seemed insignificant. Ira Knickerbocker, head of agricultural purchasing at the main Beech-Nut plant in Canajoharie, N.Y., who has since retired, says that in 1977 the new concentrate was only slightly less expensive than the competition's. "There was never a question about the quality or anything else," he insists. Yet no other baby-food company, and no large apple-juice manufacturer, ever bought significant quantities of concentrate from Universal. In early 1981, Heinz would return the product to Universal after samples had failed to pass conventional laboratory tests and the supplier refused to let company officials visit the plant.

Another Federal prosecutor, John R. Fleder, contends that the low price of the Universal concentrate, which eventually reached 25 percent below the market, "should have been enough in itself to tip off anybody" that the concentrate was diluted or adulterated.

Jack B. Hartog, a supplier who had sold Beech-Nut much of its apple concentrate until 1977, agrees with Fleder: "There was no question about it in the trade."

John Lavery, Beech-Nut's vice president of operations and manager of the plant in Canajoharie, did not question the authenticity of the concentrate. After spending his entire career at Beech-Nut, Lavery had risen to a position in which he managed almost 1,000 employees. In the small hamlets around Canajoharie, a company town in rural Montgomery County, northwest of Albany, Lavery was known-as a figure of propriety and rectitude. "He was as straight and narrow as anything you could come up with," says Ed Gros, an engineer who worked with Lavery at Beech-Nut. Lavery was a fixture in the Methodist church, on the school board and in community organizations.

In 1978, after initial testing indicated the presence of impurities in the new concentrate, Lavery agreed to send two employees to inspect the "blending facility" that Universal's owner, Zeev Kaplansky, claimed to operate in New Jersey. The two reported that all they could find was a warehouse containing a few 55-gallon drums. The bizarre field trip aroused further suspicions among executives at the Canajoharie plant, but only one, Jerome J. LiCari, head of research and development, chose to act on them.

LiCari sent samples of the concentrate to an outside laboratory. The tests, he reported to Lavery, indicated that the juice was adulterated, probably with corn syrup. Rather than return the concentrate, or demand proof of its authenticity, as Heinz would do three years later, Lavery sent down the order that Kaplansky sign a "hold-harmless agreement," indemnifying Beech-Nut against damages arising from consumer and other complaints (Ironically, in May 1987 Beech-Nut settled a class-action suit against it totalling $7.5 million.)

LiCari, however, was scarcely satisfied by Lavery's legalistic approach. Like Lavery, LiCari was also every bit the local boy. Born and raised in neighboring Herkimer County, he had worked in the Beech-Nut plant during summers home from college, and, after 14 years with Beech-Nut, he had achieved his greatest ambitions. Yet it was LiCari who accepted the solitary role of institutional conscience. In April 1979, and again in July, he sent samples of the concentrate to a second laboratory, in California. The April test again found signs of adulteration, but the July test did not. LiCari concluded that Kaplansky had switched from corn syrup to beet sugar, an adulterant that current technology could not detect. Once again he approached Lavery, suggesting that Beech-Nut require Kaplansky to repurchase the concentrate. This time, Lavery instructed that the concentrate be blended into mixed juices, where adulteration is far harder to detect. Lavery's attorney, Steven Kimelman, says that his client does not recall his rationale for the decision, but argues that on this matter, as on others, he acted in concert with other executives, including LiCari.

Lavery and LiCari were locked in a hopeless conflict of roles, values, and personality. Steven Kimelman characterizes Lavery as "more like a general. He's the kind of guy who gives orders, and he has no trouble making up his mind; LiCari was too much of a scientist type to him, and not practical enough." LiCari had become consumed by the issues of the concentrate. By spring of 1981 he was working almost full time on tests to determine its purity. Finally, on Aug. 5, LiCari circulated a memo to executives, including Lavery. "A tremendous amount of circumstantial evidence," he wrote, makes for "a grave case against the current supplier" of apple concentrate. No matter what the cost, LiCari concluded, a new supplier should be found.

Several days later, LiCari was summoned to Lavery's office, where, as he told the jury, "I was threatened that I wasn't a team player, I wasn't working for the company, threatened to be fired." The choice could not have been more stark: capitulate, or leave.

Many of those who know Lavery find this picture of him simply unbelievable. The Canajoharie view is that Lavery was victimized. Ed Gros, Lavery's former colleague, speculates that LiCari "had a personal vendetta" against Lavery. Ira Knickerbocker blames the Government. Yet even Lavery's friends admit to a kind of moral bafflement. "I've lost a lot of sleep over this," says a former company vice president, Bill Johnsey.

Steven Kimelman denies that Lavery threatened LiCari, but concedes that his client made a "mistake in judgment." The mistake was in not kicking the matter up to Hoyvald when he received the Aug. 5 memo, Kimelman insists that Lavery "thought that LiCari tended to overreact," and in any case felt that there was no other concentrate whose purity he could entirely trust. In fact, LiCari's tests showed no signs of adulteration in several other, more expensive, concentrates. A harsher view is that Lavery acted quite consciously. "He just didn't care," says Thomas Roche, one of the prosecutors. "He showed an extraordinary amount of arrogance. I think his sole objective was to show Beech-Nut and Nestlé's (since 1979, the corporate parent) that he could do well."

Or perhaps Lavery had simply blinded himself to the consequences of his acts. The apple juice had become merely a commodity and the babies merely customers. One exchange between another prosecutor, Kenneth L. Jost, and an executive at the Canajoharie plant, Robert J. Belvin, seemed to sum up Lavery's state of mind:

> "Mr. Belvin, what did you do when you found that Beech-Nut had been using a product in what is called apple juice that was not in fact apple juice?"
>
> "I—I became very upset."

Business or Ethics**33**

"Why were you very upset?"

"Because we feed babies . . ."

"Did you ever hear Mr. Lavery express a sentiment similar to that you have just described to the jury?"

"No."

By 1979, Beech-Nut's financial condition had become so parlous that Frank Nicholas admitted failure and sold the company to Nestlé S.A., the Swiss food giant. Nestlé arrived with $60 million in working capital and a commitment to restore a hallowed brand name to health. The view in the food industry was that Beech-Nut had been rescued from the brink. Yet evidence presented at the trial gives the exact opposite impression—of a Procrustean bed being prepared for nervous managers. Hoyvald, who chose to testify on his own behalf, admitted that in 1981, his first year as chief executive, he had grandiosely promised Nestlé that Beech-Nut would earn $700,000 the following year, though there would be a negative cash flow of $1.7 million. Hoyvald had arrived at Nestlé only a year before, but he was a seasoned executive in the food business. The answer nevertheless shot back from Switzerland: the cash flow for Beech-Nut, as for all other Nestlé subsidiaries, would have to be zero or better. "The pressure," as he conceded, "was on."

Hoyvald testified that he knew nothing about adulterated concentrate until the summer of 1982. In January 1981, however, LiCari had sent to both Lavery and Hoyvald a copy of an article in a trade magazine discussing signs of adulteration in apple juice, and had written and attached a memo noting, among other things, that "Beech-Nut has been concerned over the authenticity of fruit juice products." LiCari also told the jury that in August of that same year, several weeks after his disastrous confrontation with Lavery, he went to Beech-Nut's corporate headquarters in Fort Washington, Pa., to appeal to Hoyvald—an uncharacteristic suspension of his faith in the chain of command. Hoyvald had been appointed president only four months earlier, and LiCari testified that he liked and trusted his new boss, whom he felt had a mandate from Nestlé to restore Beech-Nut's prestige. The meeting in Fort Washington persuaded LiCari that he had finally found an ally. Hoyvald, LiCari testified, "appeared shocked and surprised" at LiCari's report, and left him feeling "that something was going to be done and they would stop using it."

Then, month after month, nothing happened. Finally, at a late-fall company retreat at a ski resort in Vermont, LiCari raised the issue with Hoyvald one last time. Hoyvald told him, he testified, that he was unwilling to fire Lavery. (In his own testimony, Hoyvald denied that either meeting had taken place.)

LiCari was now convinced that the company was bent on lawbreaking, as he later testified, and rather than acquiesce, he quit, in January 1982. His allies concerned with quality control remained behind, but evidently none was stubborn or reckless enough to press his point.

Hoyvald, like Lavery, was a man with an exemplary background, though one that was a good deal more varied and sophisticated than his subordinate's. Born and raised in a provincial town in Denmark, he had relocated to the United States and received his Master of Business Administration degree from the University of Wisconsin in 1960. An ambitious man, Hoyvald had hopscotched across five companies before joining Beech-Nut as head of marketing in 1980, with the promise that he would be promoted to president within a year. Throughout his career, Hoyvald's watchword had been "aggressively marketing top quality products," as he wrote in a three-page "Career Path" addendum to a 1979 resumé. He had turned around the faltering Plumrose Inc., a large food company, by emphasizing quality, and he viewed the job at Beech-Nut as a chance to do just that.

In June 1982, Hoyvald's principles were abruptly tested when the quality of his own product was decisively challenged. A trade association, the Processed Apples Institute, had initiated an investigation into long-standing charges of adulteration throughout the apple-concentrate business. By April 1982, an investigator working of the institute, a former New York City narcotics detective named Andrew Rosenzweig (who is now chief investigator for the Manhattan District Attorney's office), was prowling around the Woodside, Queens, warehouse of a company called Food Complex, which was Universal's manufacturing arm. By diligent questioning, and searching by flashlight through a dumpster in the middle of many nights, Rosenzweig discovered that Food Complex omitted apples from its recipe altogether, and that its biggest customer was Beech-Nut. On June 25, Rosenzweig tracked a tanker full of sugar water out of the Food Complex loading dock and up the New York State Thruway to Canajoharie, where he planned to confront management with his findings. He was hoping to persuade the company to join a civil suit being prepared against Universal and Food Complex; but, expecting the worst, he secretly tape-recorded the ensuing conversation.

At the trial, the tape proved to be a damning piece of evidence. In the course of the discussion, Lavery and two other executives, instead of disputing Rosenzweig's claim that Beech-Nut was making juice from suspect concentrate, unleashed a cascade of tortuous rationalizations. When Rosenzweig explained that the trade association had made new strides in lab testing, Lavery, obviously panicking, suddenly announced: "At this point, we've made our last order from" Universal. But despite considerable pressure, Lavery refused to give Rosenzweig samples of the concentrate, and declined to join the suit. The one anxiety he expressed was the possibility of bad publicity.

On June 28, Paul E. Hillabush, the head of quality assurance at Canajoharie, called Hoyvald to tell him of Rosenzweig's visit. Hillabush testified that he suggested Beech-Nut recall the product. But Beech-Nut would not only have had to switch to a new and more expensive concentrate, it would have had to admit publicly that the product it had been selling since 1978 was bogus. The cover-up, which Lavery had begun three years earlier with the order to blend the concentrate in mixed juices, was attaining an irresistible momentum.

Hoyvald made the fateful decision to reject Hillabush's advice, and to devote the next eight weeks to moving the tainted products as fast as possible. It would be aggressive marketing, though not of a quality product.

The Apple Institute's suit, as it turned out, was only the first wave to hit the beach. Federal and state authorities had been investigating suppliers of adulterated concentrate since the spring, and the trail led them, too, to Canajoharie. On July 29, an inspector from the United States Food and Drug Administration arrived at the plant, announced that samples taken from supermarket shelves had proved to be adulterated, and took away cases of apple juice ready to be shipped. On Aug. 11, Paul Hillabush received a call from an old friend, Maurice Guerrette, an assistant director with the New York State Department of Agriculture and Markets, who reported much the same conclusion. Guerrette recalls receiving one of the great shocks of his life when Hillabush tried to laugh the whole thing off. It was only then that he realized—as would each investigator in his turn—that Beech-Nut was not the victim of a crime, but its conscious perpetrator.

Guerrette's phone call persuaded Lavery and others—incorrectly, as it turned out—that a seizure action was imminent. After consulting with Hoyvald, executives in Canajoharie decided to move the entire inventory of tainted juice out of the state's jurisdiction. And so, on the night of Aug. 12, nine tractor-trailers from Beech-Nut's trucking company were loaded with 26,000 cases of juice and taken in a ghostly caravan to a warehouse in Secaucus, N.J. One of America's most venerable food companies was fleeing the law like a bootlegger.

By the late summer of 1982, Beech-Nut was racing to unload its stock before regulators initiated a seizure action. On Sept. 1, Hoyvald managed to unload thousands of cases of juice from the Secaucus warehouse to Puerto Rico, despite the fact that the Puerto Rican distributor was already overstocked. Two weeks later, Hoyvald overruled his own lawyers and colleagues, who again suggested a recall, and ordered a feverish "foreign promotion"; under certain circumstances, American law does not prohibit the selling abroad of products banned at home. Within days, 23,000 cases were trucked at great expense from the company's San Jose, Calif., plant to Galveston, Tex., where they were off-loaded for the Dominican Republic, where they were sold at a 50 percent discount.

While Beech-Nut's sales staff shipped the evidence out to sea, its lawyers were holding the Federal and state agencies at bay. On Sept. 24, lawyers scheduled a meeting with F.D.A. officials that was designed to placate their adversaries. It worked. Three more weeks passed before the F.D.A. Administrator, Taylor M. Quinn, threatened to seize the juice, and thus finally wrung from the company a pledge to begin a nationwide recall. New York State authorities, less patient, threatened a seizure before Beech-Nut hurriedly agreed to a state recall. But the delay allowed Niels Hoyvald to virtually complete his master plan.

By the middle of November Hoyvald could boast, in a report to his superior at Nestlé: "The recall has now been completed, and due to our many delays, we were only faced with having to destroy approximately 20,000 cases. We received adverse publicity in only one magazine." As it turned out, of course, Hoyvald's self-congratulation was premature.

Further Federal and state investigations exposed details of the cover-up, as well as the fact that Beech-Nut had continued to sell the juice in its mixed-juice product for six months after the recall. New York State sued Beech-Nut for selling an adulterated and misbranded product, and imposed a $250,000 fine, by far the largest such penalty ever assessed in the state for consumer violations. In November 1986, the United States Attorney obtained indictments of Hoyvald, Lavery, Beech-Nut, Zeev Kaplansky and Kaplansky's colleague Raymond H. Wells, the owner of Food Complex. Beech-Nut eventually settled by agreeing to pay a $2 million fine. Kaplansky and Wells, who had earlier settled the apple-institute with a financial agreement and by ceasing production of their concentrate, also pleaded guilty, and await sentencing. The F.D.A. referred the case to the Justice Department for criminal prosecution.

The case against Hoyvald and Lavery seemed overwhelming—so overwhelming that Lavery's first attorney suggested he plead guilty. Why did Lavery and Hoyvald insist on standing trial? Because both men, by most reports are still convinced that they committed nothing graver than a mistake in judgment.

Hoyvald and Lavery seem to think of themselves as corporate patriots. Asked by one of the prosecutors why the entire inventory of concentrate was not destroyed once it came under suspicion, Hoyvald shot back testily: "And I could have called up Switzerland and told them I had just closed the company down. Because that is what would have been the result of it."

The questions of what Nestlé would have said, or did say, was not resolved by the trial. Jerome LiCari testified that in 1980 and 1981 he had expressed his concerns to six different

Nestlé officials, including Richard Theuer, who was then a vice president of Nestlé and would become Beech-Nut's president in 1986. In an extraordinary effort to clear its reputation, Nestlé brought all six officials to court, mostly from Switzerland, and each one either contradicted LiCari's account or stated he had no memory of the alleged conversation. Nestlé acutely sensitive to its public image, which was tarnished in the 1970's and early 80's when it aggressively promoted infant formula in third-world countries despite public health concerns, sparking international controversy and boycott campaigns.

Nestlé has defended its subsidiary's acts as vigorously as it defended its own in the past. The company has spent what sources close to the case estimate as several million dollars in defending the two executives, and has agreed to keep both men on the payroll—at annual salaries of $120,000 and $70,000—until their current appeals are exhausted.

In a memo sent to Canajoharie employees after the verdict, James M. Biggar, president of Nestlé's American operations, claimed that LiCari had confused "what he wished he had said" with "what he actually said or did," and faulted management only for failing to keep an "open door."

Richard Theuer, the man Nestlé chose to replace Hoyvald, promises to keep that door open. He hopes to convince the public that at "the new Beech-Nut" decisions will be taken, as he says, "on behalf of the babies."

Case Study

Tylenol's Rebound

Carl Cannon

It's "easier to turn water into wine than to bring back Tylenol. It is dead."

That obituary by the head of a large advertising agency came at the height of the Tylenol crisis, which began a year ago this coming Friday. In the bitter wake of seven deaths in the Chicago area from cyanide-laced Extra-Strength Tylenol capsules, millions of bottles were yanked off the shelves by panicky retailers, unsure of their own liability, and by a confounded manufacturer, Johnson & Johnson. A product that had become almost a household word virtually disappeared in the first weeks after the tragedy.

From 35.4% of the over-the-counter analgesic market before the killings, Tylenol sank to a shaky 18.3% at the end of last year, when the red-and-white capsules began to reappear on the shelves. Johnson & Johnson, an international health-products giant based in New Brunswick, N.J., saw its stock price plunge.

"TEXTBOOK" RECOVERY PLAN

But that ad executive has since profusely apologized. Today, through a recovery plan that some say will be studied in textbooks on marketing, advertising and public relations, the product that only 12 months ago was "buried" by doomsayers has more than a 28.6% share of the $1.2-billion non-prescription pain reliever market, or more than 80% of its total before the crisis.

Johnson & Johnson's management, its agency, Compton Advertising, the unique confidence the public had in the product itself and even the news media share credit for the resurgence of Tylenol. It came against difficult odds, against a backdrop of national fear and a host of copycat crimes that not only threatened Tylenol but for a time case a pall over the entire non-prescription analgesic industry as well. It was expensive—Johnson & Johnson's massive product recall, media messages and tests of the capsules cost it in the tens of millions of dollars. And it has permanently affected the way non-prescription drugs are packaged as makers of everything from aspirin to eye drops followed Johnson & Johnson's lead in tamper-proofing.

Within the first few hours after the poisonings were traced to Tylenol capsules, Johnson & Johnson set up a task force of its top executives to first assess the damage to the company and then determine how to overcome it.

Over the next two weeks, during which this task force and a Compton Advertising team struggled to come up with a plan for recovery, outside marketing experts were advising that the only course was to change the name and come out with a "new" product. But there was legitimate concern that if such a tactic as merely reissuing Tylenol under a different name were tried, the press would quickly learn of it and the situation for the company would be worse.

There was no feeling within the company or within the agency that the name Tylenol should be dropped, according to Richard Earle, Compton's senior vice president and creative director, and Thomas Lom, senior vice president and managing supervisor for the advertising agency, both of whom worked on the recovery plan.

Tylenol was introduced in the late 1950's to the medical profession and built its reputation in those first years on being medically endorsed as a substitute for aspirin. The company contends its research shows that 70% of the users of the product first tried it on the recommendation of a physician. "With that kind of a profile as a foundation, advertising for the product began in 1976," Earle said. "We did some research and found that it was pretty well known among consumers then as a substitute for aspirin. Over the years our commercials used ordinary people with hidden cameras and showed the relief of actual headaches. The whole emphasis of our campaigns was how well the product worked."

ADVERTISING CRITICIZED

It was a type of advertising that had been criticized by other Madison Avenue agencies as both boring and insulting to viewers. Critics say consumers were not naive enough to believe that people featured in the commercials were unaware they were on camera. But sales results had proved these critics wrong. Viewers obviously not only believed the advertising, but had faith in the product as well. This was later to stand the company in good stead in the midst of the crisis when competing products saw an opportunity to increase their market share at Tylenol's expense.

The first major decision by Johnson & Johnson, even before the crisis task force was set up, according to a company spokesman who took part, was to pull two lots of Tylenol capsules of the shelves in Chicago. The second was to halt all advertising. In the next few days capsules were taken off shelves across the country.

Johnson & Johnson's next step was to launch consumer research, to judge how the public perceived the company. "Then it was deemed necessary to make sure consumers got rid of Tylenol capsules," a Johnson & Johnson spokesman said. To accomplish this, Compton ran newspaper ads 10 days after the tragedy offering to swap Tylenol tablets for

Tylenol capsules. "The press had informed the public so well that the whole country realized the danger was not in tablets, so the response was good" Lom said.

At the same time, decisions were being made to investigate tamper-resistant packaging, to develop marketing strategies to rebuild the brand—coupons for consumers and discounts for retailers—and to figure out the type of advertising to employ once the crisis was over.

During this period the company also obtained a letter from the Food and Drug Administration stating that the agency was satisfied that there had been no criminal tampering with the product at the plant in which it was manufactured. "We were encountering people in our research who still expressed some lingering doubt, who thought perhaps the damage had been done on our premises," a company spokesman said. Johnson & Johnson widely exhibited the FDA letter to the press to try to erase the doubts.

Then the counterattack—a low-key one—began. "We wrote some ad copy which was essentially a corporate statement," Earle said. "We felt the public should be told that Tylenol would be back. We wrote a commercial early but it was held up and not aired for about four weeks.

The reluctance was born of uncertainty, according to the Compton team. "The company had worries of stirring everything up. So we did some research. Starting a week after the tragedy, we began to conduct man-on-the-street interviews to get a good reading of the general mood of the country. Over the next four weeks, we interviewed more than 800 people in 12 or 15 cities and found little negative feeling against the company itself. Many said they would buy Tylenol again if it were packaged in tamper-proof containers.

"But Mr. Burke (James E. Burke, chairman and chief executive of Johnson & Johnson) wanted to go slowly. He decided not to rush in.

There were some concern over the timing. It was very close to Halloween and we were afraid it might spark a 'copycat' crime," Earle said.

AIRED "ROADBLOCK" AD

It was finally concluded that, since the Tylenol killings had been so extensively covered in the press and since Compton's research showed that the public wanted to hear from the company, the commercial should be run. "Our statement was rewritten many times," Lom said.

The first Tylenol commercial after the killings was what ad agencies and networks call a "roadblock": A viewer would see the same commercial no matter which of the three television networks was being watched at, say, 9 p.m. The ad featured Dr. Thomas N. Gates, medical director of McNeil Consumer Products, the Johnson & Johnson subsidiary that produces the analgesic. Gates, obviously used as a symbol of reliability, urged trust in the product and promised tamper-resistant containers.

"We thought about that spot hard and long," acknowledged a Johnson & Johnson spokesman. "There was some risk that it would be interpreted as being too commercial. After all, there were no capsules on the shelves for people to even buy. But, fortunately, it did what the country was expecting from the company and told them Tylenol would be back and it would be safe."

Long thought was given, too, to the press conference by Burke in which he announced—five weeks after McNeil Consumers Products withdrew 22 million bottles from the market—that Tylenol would start to reappear on store shelves in triple-sealed, tamper-resistant packages.

"We had more than 200 inquiries from the media and there simply was no other way" to answer them all, a company spokesman said. Burke appeared in New York and was linked by television to 29 other cities across the country. He said it was a "moral imperative" not to be destroyed by a "terrorist" act. And Johnson & Johnson emerged with the perception of being a responsible company and a champion of consumers.

GRANTED ACCESS TO MEDIA

Both Earle and Lom acknowledge that "a lot that might have been handled by advertising at this time was handled in a public relations sense." They mean that over these weeks Johnson & Johnson executives made themselves extremely available to the press. Burke and aides accepted virtually any and all appearances on talk shows, for instance, in an attempt to get across the company's viewpoint.

Still, according to one of those involved, the Johnson & Johnson task force agonized over a request for an appearance on "60 Minutes" because of the combative and sometimes abrasive style of questioning often used on the show. Among the seven key members of the Burke task force, two voted against the appearance. "We discussed it at length, and decided we had nothing to hide and the rest of the press had done a very complete job, and we thought '60 Minutes' would, too."

Burke not only appeared, but CBS reporter Mike Wallace and a camera crew were also allowed to attend and film a strategy session of the task force. In the telecast, as it had publicly and editorially most other places, the company won empathy from its plight.

It was a plight that would have sunk a smaller and less diverse company than Johnson & Johnson. If Tylenol had been its lone product, the story probably would have been different. As it was, Johnson & Johnson took a $100-million pretax write-off on the Tylenol losses for 1982. Tylenol contributed an estimated 7% of Johnson & Johnson's worldwide sales of $5.4 billion and between 15% and 20% of its profits of $467.6 million in 1981.

Still, despite Tylenol's vulnerability, competitors made surprisingly small headway in grabbing off chunks of its market share. For one thing, some of their products, too, were adulterated in a wave of copycat incidents at the height of the scare. Consumers were frightened by then of most analgesic capsules.

There was apparently an amazing level of brand loyalty. Anacin, the next-biggest seller, picked up only an estimated 1% to give it a 13.5% market share, and Datril's share remained at less than 1%.

A Johnson & Johnson official said the company is currently in litigation with some of its insurance firms over whether or not the company was covered for such product-tampering resulting in deaths.

Finally, the company was confident enough to return to pretty much the same type of advertising it had done before the crisis— non-actors with headaches. On Jan. 3, a San Diego woman appeared in an ad, expressing her trust in the brand. An announcer pointed out the new tamper-resistant packaging, but the crisis was never mentioned.

"We reviewed our advertising campaign just the other day," a company spokeswoman said last week. "We decided to go with the same thing with about the same level of spending."

Chapter Two

———————•———————

Communication in Business:
Internal and External

ETHICS IS PRINCIPALLY about how we interact with each other and treat each other, person to person, face to face, day in and day out. Business ethics, by extension, concerns how businesses treat other businesses as well as how businesses and individuals interact with each other. One of our primary modes of interaction is communication; thus the ethical issues surrounding both internal and external business communication are of vital interest to business people and business ethicists. Central to the concept of communication is information: how it is managed, gathered, and disseminated, as well as by whom and to whom.

Advertising and marketing are at the core of any discussion regarding the ethics of business communication, especially regarding truthfulness and disclosure. What are the ethical boundaries that should constrain a sales pitch? A marketing campaign? An internal memo? A report to the stockholders? Especially when it comes to advertising, the cry of business is often *caveat emptor*—"let the buyer beware." It is often argued that the job of business is to sell its products, while the job of consumers is to spend their money wisely. Short of outright falsehood or flagrant deception, business should do whatever it can to attract consumers' dollars, especially in a competitive marketplace. Many critics of the ethics of advertising have suggested that advertising is nothing more than thinly veiled psychological warfare waged against the buying public. That is, the public are manipulated, cajoled, coerced, and otherwise bamboozled into buying goods and services that they would not buy were the portrayal accurate and informative, especially without the emotional and psychological ploys so often used in advertising. A proper ethical evaluation of advertising requires caution, subtlety, and a highly nuanced analysis. This is true with respect not only to what is being presented, but also to what is omitted.

In addition, ethics concerns itself with the intended target of advertising—to whom are these ads intended to appeal? Ethicists often argue that we need to take into account the intended audience of the advertisement, as well as the nature of the product being advertised. Selling designer jeans to an adult audience is ethically different, for example, from selling toys to children, or extrapotent alcoholic beverages to the working poor. These are complicated issues, and guidance from business and law texts is not sufficient to define how business should talk about its products to the buying public. We require coherent ethical guidelines to determine what's right and wrong in marketing/advertising.

The cases and essays in this chapter subject marketing and advertising to close ethical scrutiny. "Sex, Lies, and Advertising" begins by considering the portrayal of women in advertising, the use of sex appeal, and the overall impact of advertising on women (as well as the nature of the products being targeted toward women). "Uptown, Dakota, and PowerMaster" considers the ethical implications of marketing specific tobacco and alcoholic beverages to the minority community, particularly the low-income sector of that market. "Volvo's Crushing Blow" allows us to examine how advertisements can mislead without lying and invites us to consider what ethical guidelines should govern how products are portrayed in ads. "Toy Wars" considers the nature of toy marketing and raises interesting considerations about the ethical responsibilities of both advertisers and consumers. "The Case of the Contested Firearms" analyzes some interesting issues regarding the sale, marketing, and distribution of firearms. "Italian Tax Mores" contributes an interesting new twist to considerations regarding tax-form filing.

As we shall see in chapter eight, information has great value to business, and privileged access to that information is granted to individuals within the business/corporation. What are the ethical guidelines that govern the keeping of trade secrets? The protection of internal business communications? What should an employee do when confronted by an ethical issue arising from a specific business practice, or how should an employee act, specifically because she or he has special access to the goings-on within a particular company? This is usually called whistleblowing, and there are a number of thorny, interrelated, moral issues surrounding whistleblowing that require careful attention. We begin our examination of whistleblowing with the article "Whistleblowing and Employee Loyalty" and "Some Paradoxes of Whistleblowing." "A Hero—And A Smoking-Gun Letter" presents some insights in the effects of whistleblowing in the now infamous Enron debacle.

Essay

Sex, Lies, and Advertising

Gloria Steinem

About three years ago, as *glasnost* was beginning and *Ms.* seemed to be ending, I was invited to a press lunch for a Soviet official. He entertained us with anecdotes about new problems of democracy in his country. Local Communist leaders were being criticized in their media for the first time, he explained, and they were angry.

From "Sex, Lies, and Advertising" by Gloria Steinem. *Ms. Magazine,* July/August 1990. Reprinted by permission.

"So I'll have to ask my American friends," he finished pointedly, "how more *subtly* to control the press." In the silence that followed, I said, "Advertising."

The reporters laughed, but later, one of them took me aside: How *dare* I suggest that freedom of the press was limited? How dare I imply that his newsweekly could be influenced by ads?

I explained that I was thinking of advertising's media-wide influence on most of what we read. Even newsmagazines use "soft" cover stories to sell ads, confuse readers with "advertorials," and occasionally self-censor on subjects known to be a problem with big advertisers.

But, I also explained, I was thinking especially of women's magazines. There, it isn't just a little content that's devoted to attracting ads, it's almost all of it. That's why advertisers—not readers—have always been the problem for *Ms.* As the only women's magazine that didn't supply what the ad world euphemistically describes as "supportive editorial atmosphere" or "complementary copy" (for instance, articles that praise food/fashion/beauty subjects to "support" and "complement" food/fashion/beauty ads), *Ms.* could never attract enough advertising to break even.

"Oh, *women's* magazines," the journalist said with contempt. "Everybody knows they're catalogs—but who cares? They have nothing to do with journalism."

I can't tell you how many times I've had this argument in twenty-five years of working for many kinds of publications. Except as moneymaking machines—"cash cows" as they are so elegantly called in the trade—women's magazines are rarely taken seriously. Though changes being made by women have been called more far-reaching than the industrial revolution—and though many editors try hard to reflect some of them in the few pages left to them after all the ad-related subjects have been

covered—the magazines serving the female half of this country are still far below the journalistic and ethical standards of news and general interest publications. Most depressing of all, this doesn't even rate an exposé.

If *Time* and *Newsweek* had to lavish praise on cars in general and credit General Motors in particular to get GM ads, there would be a scandal—maybe a criminal investigation. When women's magazines from *Seventeen* to *Lear's* praise beauty products in general and credit Revlon in particular to get ads, it's just business as usual.

I

When *Ms.* began, we didn't consider *not* taking ads. The most important reason was keeping the price of a feminist magazine low enough for most women to afford. But the second and almost equal reason was providing a forum where women and advertisers could talk to each other and improve advertising itself. After all, it was (and still is) as potent a source of information in this country as news or TV and movie dramas.

We decided to proceed in two stages. First, we would convince makers of "people products" used by both men and women but advertised mostly to men—cars, credit cards, insurance, sound equipment, financial services, and the like—that their ads should be placed in a women's magazine. Since they were accustomed to the division between editorial and advertising in news and general interest magazines, this would allow our editorial content to be free and diverse. Second, we would add the best ads for whatever traditional "women's products" (clothes, shampoo, fragrance, food, and so on) that surveys showed *Ms.* readers used. But we would ask them to come in *without* the usual quid pro quo of "complementary copy."

We knew the second step might be harder. Food advertisers have always demanded that women's magazines publish recipes and articles on entertaining (preferably ones that name their products) in return for their ads; clothing advertisers expect to be surrounded by fashion spreads (especially ones that credit their designers); and shampoo, fragrance, and beauty products in general usually insist on positive editorial coverage of beauty subjects, plus photo credits besides. That's why women's magazines look the way they do. But if we could break this link between ads and editorial content, then we wanted good ads for "women's products," too.

By playing their part in this unprecedented mix of *all* the things our readers need and use, advertisers also would be rewarded: ads for products like cars and mutual funds would find a new growth market; the best ads for women's products would no longer be lost in oceans of ads for the same category; and both would have access to a laboratory of smart and caring readers whose response would help create effective ads for other media as well.

I thought then that our main problem would be the imagery in ads themselves. Carmakers were still draping blondes in evening gowns over the hoods like ornaments. Authority figures were almost always male, even in ads for products that only women used. Sadistic, he-man campaigns even won industry praise. (For instance, *Advertising Age* had hailed the infamous Silva Thin cigarette theme, "How to Get a Woman's Attention: Ignore Her," as "brilliant.") Even in medical journals, tranquilizer ads showed depressed housewives standing beside piles of dirty dishes and promised to get them back to work.

Obviously, *Ms.* would have to avoid such ads and seek out the best ones—but this didn't seem impossible. The *New Yorker* had been selecting ads for aesthetic reasons for years, a practice that only seemed to make advertisers more eager to be in its pages. *Ebony* and *Essence* were asking for ads with positive black images, and though their struggle was hard, they weren't being called unreasonable.

Clearly, what *Ms.* needed was a very special publisher and ad sales staff. I could think of only one woman with experience on the business side of magazines—Patricia Carbine, who recently had become a vice president of *McCall's* as well as its editor in chief—and the reason I knew her name was a good omen. She had been managing editor at *Look* (really *the* editor, but its owner refused to put a female name at the top of his masthead) when I was writing a column there. After I did an early interview with Cesar Chavez, then just emerging as a leader of migrant labor, and the publisher turned it down because he was worried about ads from Sunkist, Pat was the one who intervened. As I learned later, she had told the publisher she would resign if the interview wasn't published. Mainly because *Look* couldn't afford to lose Pat, it *was* published (and the ads from Sunkist never arrived).

Though I barely knew this woman, she had done two things I always remembered: put her job on the line in a way that editors often talk about but rarely do, and been so loyal to her colleagues that she never told me or anyone outside *Look* that she had done so.

Fortunately, Pat did agree to leave *McCall's* and take a huge cut in salary to become publisher of *Ms.* She became responsible for training and inspiring generations of young women who joined the *Ms.* ad sales force, many of whom went on to become "firsts" at the top of publishing. When *Ms.* first started, however, there were so few women with experience selling space that Pat and I made the rounds of ad agencies ourselves. Later, the fact that *Ms.* was asking companies to do business in a different way meant our saleswomen had to make many times the usual number of calls—first to convince agencies and then client companies besides—and to present endless amounts of research. I was often asked to do a final ad presentation, or see some higher decision maker, or speak to women employees so executives could see the interest of women they worked with. That's why I spent more time persuading advertisers than editing or writing for *Ms.* and why I ended up with an unsentimental education in the seamy underside of publishing that few writers see (and even fewer magazines can publish).

Let me take you with us through some experiences, just as they happened:

Cheered on by early support from Volkswagen and one or two other car companies, we scrape together time and money to put on a major reception in Detroit. We know U.S. carmakers firmly believe that women choose the upholstery, not the car, but we are armed with statistics and reader mail to prove the contrary: a car is an important purchase for women, one that symbolizes mobility and freedom.

But almost nobody comes. We are left with many pounds of shrimp on the table, and quite a lot of egg on our face. We blame ourselves for not guessing that there would be a baseball pennant play-off on the same day, but executives go out of their way to explain they wouldn't have come anyway. Thus begins ten years of knocking on hostile doors, presenting endless documentation, and hiring a full-time saleswoman in Detroit; all necessary before *Ms.* gets any real results.

This long saga has a semihappy ending: foreign and, later, domestic carmakers eventually provided *Ms.* with enough advertising to make cars one of our top sources of ad revenue. Slowly, Detroit began to take the women's market seriously enough to put car ads in other women's magazines, too, thus freeing a few pages from the hothouse of fashion-beauty-food ads.

But long after figures showed a third, even a half, of many car models being bought by women, U.S. makers continued to be uncomfortable addressing women. Unlike foreign carmakers, Detroit never quite learned the secret of creating intelligent ads that exclude no one, and then placing them in women's magazines to overcome past exclusion. (*Ms.* readers were so grateful for a routine Honda ad featuring rack and pinion steering, for instance, that they sent fan mail.) Even now, Detroit continues to ask, "Should we make special ads for women?" Perhaps that's why some foreign cars still have a disproportionate share of the U.S. women's market.

In the *Ms.* Gazette, we do a brief report on a congressional hearing into chemicals used in hair dyes that are absorbed through the skin and may be carcinogenic. Newspapers report this too, but Clairol, a Bristol-Myers subsidiary that makes dozens of products—a few of which have just begun to advertise in *Ms.*—is outraged. Not at newspapers or newsmagazines, just at us. It's bad enough that *Ms.* is the only women's magazine refusing to provide the usual "complementary" articles and beauty photos, but to criticize one of their categories—*that* is going too far.

We offer to publish a letter from Clairol telling its side of the story. In an excess of solicitousness, we even put this letter in the Gazette, not in Letters to the Editors where it belongs. Nonetheless—and in spite of surveys that show *Ms.* readers are active women who use more of almost everything Clairol makes than do the readers of any other women's magazine—*Ms.* gets almost none of these ads for the rest of its natural life.

Meanwhile, Clairol changes its hair coloring formula, apparently in response to the hearings we reported.

Our saleswomen set out early to attract ads for consumer electronics: sound equipment, calculators, computers, VCRs, and the like. We know that our readers are determined to be included in the technological revolution. We know from reader surveys that *Ms.* readers are buying this stuff in numbers as high as those of magazines like *Playboy*; or "men 18 to 34," the prime targets of the consumer electronics industry. Moreover, unlike traditional women's products that our readers buy but don't need to read articles about, these are subjects they want covered in our pages. There actually *is* a supportive editorial atmosphere.

"But women don't understand technology," say executives at the end of ad presentations. "Maybe not," we respond, "but neither do men—and we all buy it."

"If women *do* buy it," say the decision makers, "they're asking their husbands and boyfriends what to buy first." We produce letters from *Ms.* readers saying how turned off they are when salesmen say things like "Let me know when your husband can come in."

After several years of this, we get a few ads for compact sound systems. Some of them come from JVC, whose vice president, Harry Elias, is trying to convince his Japanese bosses that there is something called a women's market. At his invitation, I find myself speaking at huge trade shows in Chicago and Las Vegas, trying to persuade JVC dealers that showrooms don't have to be locker rooms where women are made to feel unwelcome. But as it turns out, the shows themselves are part of the problem. In Las Vegas, the only women around the technology displays are seminude models serving champagne. In Chicago, the big attraction is Marilyn Chambers, who followed Linda Lovelace of *Deep Throat* fame as Chuck Traynor's captive and/or employee. VCRs are being demonstrated with her porn videos.

In the end, we get ads for a car stereo now and then, but no VCRs; some IBM personal computers, but no Apple or Japanese ones. We notice that office magazines like *Working Woman* and *Savvy* don't benefit as much as they should from office equipment ads either. In the electronics world, women and technology seem mutually exclusive. It remains a decade behind even Detroit.

Because we get letters from little girls who love toy trains, and who ask our help in changing ads and box-top photos that feature little boys only, we try to get toy-train ads from Lionel. It turns out that Lionel executives *have* been concerned about little girls. They made a pink train, and were surprised when it didn't sell.

Lionel bows to consumer pressure with a photograph of a boy *and* a girl—but only on some of their boxes. They fear that, if trains are associated with girls, they will be devalued in the minds of boys. Needless to say, *Ms.* gets no train ads, and little girls remain a mostly unexplored market. By 1986, Lionel is put up for sale.

But for different reasons, we haven't had much luck with other kinds of toys either. In spite of many articles on child-rearing; an annual listing of nonsexist, multiracial toys by Letty Cottin Pogrebin; Stories for Free Children, a regular feature also edited by Letty; and other prizewinning features for or about children, we get virtually no toy ads. Generations of *Ms.* saleswomen explain to toy manufacturers that a larger proportion of *Ms.* readers have preschool children than do the readers of other women's magazines, but this industry can't believe feminists have or care about children.

When *Ms.* begins, the staff decides not to accept ads for feminine hygiene sprays or cigarettes: they are damaging and carry no appropriate health warnings. Though we don't think we should tell our readers what to do, we do think we should provide facts so they can decide for themselves. Since the antismoking lobby has been pressing for health warnings on cigarette ads, we decide to take them only as they comply.

Philip Morris is among the first to do so. One of its brands, Virginia Slims, is also sponsoring women's tennis and the first national polls of women's opinions. On the other hand, the Virginia Slims theme, "You've come a long way, baby," has more than a "baby" problem. It makes smoking a symbol of progress for women.

We explain to Philip Morris that this slogan won't do well in our pages, but they are convinced its success with some women means it will work with *all* women. Finally, we agree to publish an ad for a Virginia Slims calendar as a test. The letters from readers are critical—and smart. For instance: Would you show a black man picking cotton, the same man in a Cardin suit, and symbolize the antislavery and civil rights movements by smoking? Of course not. But instead of honoring the test results, the Philip Morris people seem angry to be proven wrong. They take away ads for *all* their many brands.

This costs *Ms.* about $250,000 the first year. After five years, we can no longer keep track. Occasionally, a new set of executives listens to *Ms.* saleswomen, but because we won't take Virginia Slims, not one Philip Morris product returns to our pages for the next sixteen years.

Gradually, we also realize our naiveté in thinking we *could* decide against taking cigarette ads. They became a disporportionate support of magazines the moment they were banned on television, and few magazines could compete and survive without them; certainly not *Ms.*, which lacks so many other categories. By the time statistics in the 1980s showed that women's rate of lung cancer was approaching men's, the necessity of taking cigarette ads has become a kind of prison.

General Mills, Pillsbury, Carnation, DelMonte, Dole, Kraft, Stouffer, Hormel, Nabisco: you name the food giant, we try it. But no matter how desirable the *Ms.* readership, our lack of recipes is lethal.

We explain to them that placing food ads *only* next to recipes associates food with work. For many women, it is a negative that works *against* the ads. Why not place food ads in diverse media without recipes (thus reaching more men, who are now a third of the shoppers in supermarkets anyway), and leave the recipes to specialty magazines like *Gourmet* (a third of whose readers are also men)?

These arguments elicit interest, but except for an occasional ad for a convenience food, instant coffee, diet drinks, yogurt, or such extras as avocados and almonds, this mainstay of the publishing industry stays closed to us. Period.

Traditionally, wines and liquors didn't advertise to women: men were thought to make the brand decisions, even if women did the buying. But after endless presentations, we begin to make a dent in this category. Thanks to the unconventional Michel Roux of Carillon Importers (distributors of Grand Marnier, Absolut Vodka, and others), who assumes that food and drink have no gender, some ads are leaving their men's club.

Beermakers are still selling masculinity. It takes *Ms.* fully eight years to get its first beer ad (Michelob). In general, however, liquor ads are less stereotyped in their imagery—and far less controlling of the editorial content around them—than are women's products. But given the underrepresentation of other categories, these very facts tend to create a disproportionate number of alcohol ads in the pages of *Ms.* This in turn dismays readers worried about women and alcoholism.

We hear in 1980 that women in the Soviet Union have been producing feminist *samizdat* (underground, self-published books) and circulating them throughout the country. As punishment, four of the leaders have been exiled. Though we are operating on our usual shoestring, we solicit individual contributions to send Robin Morgan to interview these women in Vienna.

The result is an exclusive cover story that includes the first news of a populist peace movement against the Afghanistan occupation, a prediction of *glasnost* to come, and a grass-roots, intimate view of Soviet women's lives. From the popular press to women's studies courses, the response is great. The story wins a Front Page award.

Nonetheless, this journalistic coup undoes years of efforts to get an ad schedule from Revlon. Why? Because the Soviet women on our cover *are not wearing makeup.*

Four years of research and presentations go into convincing airlines that women now make travel choices and business trips. United, the first airline to advertise in *Ms.*, is so impressed with the response from our readers that one of its executives appears in a film for our ad presentations. As usual, good ads get great results.

But we have problems unrelated to such results. For instance: because American Airlines flight attendants include among their labor demands the stipulation that they could choose to have their last names preceded by "Ms." on their name tags—in a long-delayed revolt against the standard. "I am your pilot, Captain Rothgart, and this is your flight attendant, Cindy Sue"—American officials seem to hold the magazine responsible. We get no ads.

There is still a different problem at Eastern. A vice-president cancels subscriptions for thousands of copies on Eastern flights. Why? Because he is offended by ads for lesbian poetry journals in the *Ms.* Classified. A "family airline," as he explains to me coldly on the phone, has to "draw the line somewhere."

It's obvious that *Ms.* can't exclude lesbians and serve women. We've been trying to make that point ever since our first issue included an article by and about lesbians, and both Suzanne Levine, our managing editor, and I were lectured by such heavy hitters as Ed Kosner, then editor of *Newsweek* (and now of *New York Magazine*), who insisted that *Ms.* should "position" itself *against* lesbians. But our advertisers have paid to reach a guaranteed number of readers, and soliciting new subscriptions to compensate for Eastern would cost $150,000, plus rebating money in the meantime.

Like almost everything ad-related, this presents an elaborate organizing problem. After days of searching for sympathetic members of the Eastern board, Frank Thomas, president of the Ford Foundation, kindly offers to call Roswell Gilpatrick, a director of Eastern. I talk with Mr. Gilpatrick, who calls Frank Borman, then the president of Eastern. Frank Borman calls me to say that his airline is not in the business of censoring magazines: *Ms.* will be returned to Eastern flights.

Women's access to insurance and credit is vital, but with the exception of Equitable and a few other ad pioneers, such financial services address men. For almost a decade after the Equal Credit Opportunity Act passes in 1974, we try to convince American Express that women are a growth market—but nothing works.

Finally, a former professor of Russian named Jerry Welsh becomes head of marketing. He assumes that women should be cardholders, and persuades his colleagues to feature women in a campaign. Thanks to this 1980s series, the growth rate for female cardholders surpasses that for men.

For this article, I asked Jerry Welsh if he would explain why American Express waited so long. "Sure," he said, "they were afraid of having a 'pink' card."

Women of color read *Ms.* in disproportionate numbers. This is a source of pride to *Ms.* staffers, who are also more racially representative than the editors of other women's magazines. But this reality is obscured by ads filled with enough white women to make a reader snowblind.

Pat Carbine remembers mostly "astonishment" when she requested African American, Hispanic, Asian, and other diverse images. Marcia Ann Gillespie, a *Ms.* editor who was previously the editor in chief of *Essence*, witnesses ad bias a second time: having tried for *Essence* to get white advertisers to use black images (Revlon did so eventually, but L'Oréal, Lauder, Chanel, and other companies never did), she sees similar problems getting integrated ads for an integrated magazine. Indeed, the ad world often creates black and Hispanic ads only for black and Hispanic media. In an exact parallel of the fear that marketing a product to women will endanger its appeal to men, the response is usually, "But your [white] readers won't identify."

In fact, those we are able to get—for instance, a Max Factor ad made for *Essence* that Linda Wachner gives us after she becomes president—are praised by white readers, too. But there are pathetically few such images.

> By the end of 1986, production and mailing costs have risen astronomically, ad income is flat, and competition for ads is stiffer than ever. The 60/40 preponderance of edit over ads that we promised to readers becomes 50/50; children's stories, most poetry, and some fiction are casualties of less space; in order to get variety into limited pages, the length (and sometimes the depth) of articles suffers; and, though we do refuse most of the ads that would look like a parody in our pages, we get so worn down that some slip through. Still, readers perform miracles. Though we haven't been able to afford a subscription mailing in two years, they maintain our guaranteed circulation of 450,000.

Nonetheless, media reports on *Ms.* often insist that our unprofitability must be due to reader disinterest. The myth that advertisers simply follow readers is very strong. Not one reporter notes that other comparable magazines our size (say, *Vanity Fair* or the *Atlantic*) have been losing more money in one year than *Ms.* has lost in sixteen years. No matter how much never-to-be-recovered cash is poured into starting a magazine or keeping one going, appearances seem to be all that matter. (Which is why we haven't been able to explain our fragile state in public. Nothing causes ad-flight like the smell of nonsuccess.)

My healthy response is anger. My not-so-healthy response is constant worry. Also an obsession with finding one more rescue. There is hardly a night when I don't wake up with sweaty palms and pounding heart, scared that we won't be able to pay the printer or the post office; scared most of all that closing our doors will hurt the women's movement.

Out of chutzpah and desperation, I arrange a lunch with Leonard Lauder, president of Estée Lauder. With the exception of Clinique (the brainchild of Carol Phillips), none of Lauder's hundreds of products has been advertised in *Ms.* A year's schedule of ads for just three or four of them could save us. Indeed, as

the scion of a family-owned company whose ad practices are followed by the beauty industry, he is one of the few men who could liberate many pages in all women's magazines just by changing his mind about "complementary copy."

Over a lunch that costs more than we can pay for some articles, I explain the need for his leadership. I also lay out the record of *Ms.*: more literary and journalistic prizes won, more new issues introduced into the mainstream, new writers discovered, and impact on society than any other magazine; more articles that became books, stories that became movies, ideas that became television series, and newly advertised products that became profitable; and, most important for him, a place for his ads to reach women who aren't reachable through any other women's magazine. Indeed, if there is one constant characteristic of the ever-changing *Ms.* readership, it is its impact as leaders. Whether it's waiting until later to have first babies, or pioneering PABA as sun protection in cosmetics, *whatever Ms.* readers are doing today, a third to a half of American women will be doing three to five years from now. It's never failed.

But, he says, *Ms.* readers are not *our* women. They're not interested in things like fragrance and blush-on. If they were, *Ms.* would write articles about them.

On the contrary, I explain, surveys show they are more likely to buy such things than the readers of, say, *Cosmopolitan* or *Vogue*. They're good customers because they're out in the world enough to need several sets of everything: home, work, purse, travel, gym, and so on. They just don't need to read articles about these things. Would he ask a men's magazine to publish monthly columns on how to shave before he advertised Aramis products (his line for men)?

He concedes that beauty features are often concocted more for advertisers than readers. But *Ms.* isn't appropriate for his ads anyway, he explains. Why? Because Estée Lauder is selling "a kept-woman mentality."

I can't quite believe this. Sixty percent of the users of his products are salaried, and generally resemble *Ms.* readers. Besides, his company has the appeal of having been started by a creative and hardworking woman, his mother, Estée Lauder.

That doesn't matter, he says. He knows his customers, and they would *like* to be kept women. That's why he will never advertise in *Ms.*

In November 1987, by vote of the Ms. Foundation for Education and Communication (*Ms.*'s owner and publisher, the media subsidiary of the Ms. Foundation for Women), *Ms.* was sold to a company whose officers, Australian feminists Sandra Yates and Anne Summers, raised the investment money in their country that *Ms.* couldn't find in its own. They also started *Sassy* for teenage women.

In their two-year tenure, circulation was raised to 550,000 by investment in circulation mailings, and, to the dismay of some readers, editorial features on clothes and new products made a more traditional bid for ads. Nonetheless, ad pages fell below previous levels. In addition, *Sassy*, whose fresh voice and sexual frankness were an unprecedented success with young readers, was targeted by two mothers from Indiana who began, as one of them put it, "calling every Christian organization I could think of." In response to this controversy, several crucial advertisers pulled out.

Such links between ads and editorial content were a problem in Australia, too, but to a lesser degree. "Our readers pay two times more for their magazines," Anne explained, "so advertisers have less power to threaten a magazine's viability."

"I was shocked," said Sandra Yates with characteristic directness. "In Australia, we think you have freedom of the press—but you don't."

Since Anne and Sandra had not met their budget's projections for ad revenue, their investors forced a sale. In October 1989, *Ms.* and *Sassy* were bought by Dale Lang, owner of *Working Mother, Working Woman,* and one of the few independent publishing companies left among the conglomerates. In response to a request from the original *Ms.* staff—as well as to reader letters urging that *Ms.* continue, plus his own belief that *Ms.* would benefit his other magazines by blazing a trail—he agreed to try the ad-free, reader-supported *Ms.* you hold now and to give us complete editorial control.

II

Do you think, as I once did, that advertisers make decisions based on solid research? Well, think again. "Broadly speaking," says Joseph Smith of Oxtoby-Smith, Inc., a consumer research firm, "there is no persuasive evidence that the editorial context of an ad matters."

Advertisers who demand such "complementary copy," even in the absence of respectable studies, clearly are operating under a double standard. The same food companies place ads in *People* with no recipes. Cosmetics companies support the *New Yorker* with no regular beauty columns. So where does this habit of controlling the content of women's magazines come from?

Tradition. Ever since *Ladies Magazine* debuted in Boston in 1828, editorial copy directed to women has been informed by something other than its readers' wishes. There were no ads then, but in an age when married women were legal minors with no right to their own money, there was another revenue source to be kept in mind: husbands. "Husbands may rest assured," wrote editor Sarah Josepha Hale, "that nothing found in these pages shall cause her [his wife] to be less assiduous in preparing for his reception or encourage her to 'usurp station' or encroach upon prerogatives of men."

Hale went on to become the editor of *Godey's Lady's Book*, a magazine featuring "fashion plates": engravings of dresses for readers to take to their seamstresses or copy themselves. Hale added "how to" articles, which set the tone for women's service magazines for years to come: how to write politely, avoid sunburn, and—in no fewer than 1,200 words—how to maintain a goose quill pen. She advocated education for women but avoided controversy. Just as most women's magazines now avoid politics, poll their readers on issues like abortion but rarely take a stand, and praise socially approved life-styles, Hale saw to it that *Godey's* avoided the hot topics of its day: slavery, abolition, and women's suffrage.

What definitively turned women's magazines into catalogs, however, were two events: Ellen Butterick's invention of the clothing pattern in 1863 and the mass manufacture of patent medicines containing everything from colored water to cocaine. For the first time, readers could purchase what magazines encouraged them to want. As such magazines became more profitable, they also began to attract men as editors. (Most women's magazines continued to have men as top editors until the feminist 1970s.) Edward Bok, who became editor of the *Ladies' Home Journal* in 1889, discovered the power of advertisers when he rejected ads for patent medicines and found that other advertisers canceled in retribution. In the early twentieth century, *Good Housekeeping* started its institute to "test and approve" products. Its Seal of Approval became the grandfather of current "value-added" programs that offer advertisers such bonuses as product sampling and department store promotions.

By the time suffragists finally won the vote in 1920, women's magazines had become too entrenched as catalogs to help women learn how to use it. The main function was to create a desire for products, teach how to use products, and make products a crucial part of gaining social approval, pleasing a husband, and performing as a homemaker. Some unrelated articles and short stories were included to persuade women to pay for these catalogs. But articles were neither consumerist nor rebellious. Even fiction was usually subject to formula: if a woman had any sexual life outside marriage, she was supposed to come to a bad end.

In 1965, Helen Gurley Brown began to change part of that formula by bringing "the sexual revolution" to women's magazines—but in an ad-oriented way. Attracting multiple men required even more consumerism, as the Cosmo Girl made clear, than finding one husband.

In response to the workplace revolution of the 1970s, traditional women's magazines—that is, "trade books" for women working at home—were joined by *Savvy, Working Woman*, and other trade books for women working in offices. But by keeping the fashion/beauty/entertaining articles necessary to get traditional ads and then adding career articles besides, they inadvertently produced the antifeminist stereotype of Super Woman. The male-imitative, dress-for-success woman carrying a briefcase became the media image of a woman worker, even though a blue-collar woman's salary was often higher than her glorified secretarial sister's, and though women at a real briefcase level are statistically rare. Needless to say, these dress-for-success women were also thin, white, and beautiful.

In recent years, advertisers' control over the editorial content of women's magazines has become so institutionalized that it is written into "insertion orders" or dictated to ad salespeople as official policy. The following are recent typical orders to women's magazines:

- Dow's Cleaning Products stipulates that ads for its Vivid and Spray 'n Wash products should be adjacent to "children or fashion editorial"; ads for Bathroom Cleaner should be next to "home furnishing/family" features; and so on for other brands. "If a magazine fails for 1/2 the brands or more," the Dow order warns, "it will be omitted from further consideration."

- Bristol-Myers, the parent of Clairol, Windex, Drano, Bufferin, and much more, stipulates that ads be placed next to "a full page of compatible editorial."

- S. C. Johnson & Son, makers of Johnson Wax, lawn and laundry products, insect sprays, hair sprays, and so on, orders that its ads "*should not be opposite extremely controversial features or material antithetical to the nature/copy of the advertised product*" (italics theirs).

- Maidenform, manufacturer of bras and other apparel, leaves a blank for the particular product and states: "The creative concept of the——— campaign, and the very nature of the product itself appeal to the positive emotions of the reader/consumer. Therefore, it is imperative that all editorial adjacencies reflect that same positive tone. The editorial must not be negative in content or lend itself contrary to the——— product imagery/message (e.g., *editorial relating to illness, disillusionment, large size fashion, etc.*)" (italics mine).

- The De Beers diamond company, a big seller of engagement rings, prohibits magazines from placing its ads with "adjacencies to hard news or anti-love/romance themed editorial."

- Procter & Gamble, one of this country's most powerful and diversified advertisers, stands out in the memory of Anne Summers and Sandra Yates (no mean feat in this context): its products were not to be placed in *any* issue that included *any* material on gun control, abortion, the occult, cults, or the disparagement of religion. Caution was also demanded in any issue covering sex or drugs, even for educational purposes.

Those are the most obvious chains around women's magazines. There are also rules so clear they needn't be written down: for instance, an overall "look" compatible with beauty and fashion ads. Even "real" nonmodel women photographed for a woman's magazine are usually made up, dressed in credited clothes, and retouched out of all reality. When editors do include articles on less-than-cheerful subjects (for instance, domestic violence), they tend to keep them short and unillustrated. The point is to be "upbeat." Just as women in the street are asked, "Why don't you smile, honey?" women's magazines acquire an institutional smile.

Within the text itself, praise for advertisers' products has become so ritualized that fields like "beauty writing" have been invented. One of its frequent practitioners explained seriously that "It's a difficult art. How many new adjectives can you find? How much greater can you make a lipstick sound? The FDA restricts what companies can say on labels, but we create illusion. And ad agencies are on the phone all the time pushing you to get their product in. A lot of them keep the business based on how many editorial clippings they produce every month. The worst are products," like Lauder's as the writer confirmed, "with their own name involved. It's all ego."

Often, editorial becomes one giant ad. Last November, for instance, *Lear's* featured an elegant woman executive on the cover. On the contents page, we learned she was wearing Guerlain makeup and Samsara, a new fragrance by Guerlain. Inside were full-page ads for Samsara and Guerlain antiwrinkle cream. In the cover profile, we learned that this executive was responsible for launching Samsara and is Guerlain's director of public relations. When the *Columbia Journalism Review* did one of the few articles to include women's magazines in coverage of the influence of ads, editor Frances Lear was quoted as defending her magazine because "this kind of thing is done all the time."

Often, advertisers also plunge odd-shaped ads into the text, no matter what the cost to the readers. At *Woman's Day*, a magazine originally founded by a supermarket chain, editor in chief Ellen Levine said, "The day the copy had to rag around a chicken leg was not a happy one."

Advertisers are also adamant about where in a magazine their ads appear. When Revlon was not placed as the first beauty ad in one Hearst magazine, for instance, Revlon pulled its ads from all Hearst magazines. Ruth Whitney, editor in chief of *Glamour*, attributes some of these demands to "ad agencies wanting to prove to a client that they've squeezed the last drop of blood out of a magazine." She also is, she says, "sick and tired of hearing that women's magazines are controlled by cigarette ads." Relatively speaking, she's right. To be as censoring as are many advertisers for women's products, tobacco companies would have to demand articles in praise of smoking and expect glamorous photos of beautiful women smoking their brands.

I don't mean to imply that the editors I quote here share my objections to ads: most assume that women's magazines have to be the way they are. But it's also true that only former editors can be completely honest. "Most of the pressure came in the form of direct product mentions," explains Sey Chassler, who was editor in chief of *Redbook* from the sixties to the eighties.

We got threats from the big guys, the Revlons, blackmail threats. They wouldn't run ads unless we credited them.

But it's not fair to single out the beauty advertisers because these pressures came from everybody. Advertisers want to know two things: What are you going to charge me? What *else* are you going to do for me? It's a holdup. For instance, management felt that fiction took up too much space. They couldn't put any advertising in that. For the last ten years, the number of fiction entries into the National Magazine Awards has declined.

And pressures are getting worse. More magazines are more bottom-line oriented because they have been taken over by companies with no interest in publishing.

I also think advertisers do this to women's magazines especially because of the general disrespect they have for women.

Even media experts who don't give a damn about women's magazines are alarmed by the spread of this ad-edit linkage. In a climate the *Wall Street Journal* describes as an unacknowledged depression for media, women's products are increasingly able to take their low standards wherever they go. For instance: newsweeklies publish uncritical stories on fashion and fitness. The *New York Times Magazine* recently ran an article on "firming creams," complete with mentions of advertisers. *Vanity Fair* published a profile of one major advertiser, Ralph Lauren, illustrated by the same photographer who does his ads, and turned the life-style of another, Calvin Klein, into a cover story. Even the outrageous *Spy* has toned down since it began to go after fashion ads.

And just to make us really worry, films and books, the last media that go directly to the public without having to attract ads first, are in danger, too. Producers are beginning to depend on payments for displaying products in movies, and books are now being commissioned by companies like Federal Express.

But the truth is that women's products—like women's magazines—have never been the subjects of much serious reporting anyway. News and general interest publications, including the "style" or "living" sections of newspapers, write about food and clothing as cooking and fashion, and almost never evaluate such products by brand name. Though chemical additives, pesticides, and animal fats are major health risks in the United States, and clothes, shoddy or not, absorb more consumer dollars than cars, this lack of information in serious. So is ignoring the contents of beauty products that are absorbed into our bodies through our skins, and that have profit margins so big they would make a loan shark blush.

III

What could women's magazines be like if they were as free as books? as realistic as newspapers? as creative as films? as diverse as women's lives? We don't know. But we'll only find out if we take women's magazines seriously. If readers were to act in a concerted way to change traditional practices of *all* women's magazines and the marketing of *all* women's products, we could do it. After all, they are operating on our consumer dollars; money that we now control. You and I could:

- write to editors and publishers (with copies to advertisers) that we're willing to pay *more* for magazines with editorial independence, but will *not* continue to pay for those that are just editorial extensions of ads;
- write to advertisers (with copies to editors and publishers) that we want fiction, political reporting, consumer reporting—whatever is, or is not, supported by their ads;
- put as much energy into breaking advertising's control over content as into changing the images in ads, or protesting ads for harmful products like cigarettes;
- support only those women's magazines and products that take *us* seriously as readers and consumers.

Those of us in the magazine world can also use the carrot-and-stick technique. For instance: pointing out that, if magazines were a regulated medium like television, the demands of advertisers would be against FCC rules. Payola and extortion could be punished. As it is, there are probably illegalities. A magazine's postal rates are determined by the ratio of ad to edit pages, and the former costs more than the latter. So much for the stick.

The carrot means appealing to enlightened self-interest. For instance: there are many studies showing that the greatest factor in determining an ad's effectiveness is the credibility of its surroundings. The "higher the rating of editorial believability," concluded a 1987 survey by the *Journal of Advertising Research*, "the higher the rating of the advertising." Thus, an impenetrable wall between edit and ads would also be in the best interest of advertisers.

Unfortunately, few agencies or clients hear such arguments. Editors often maintain the false purity of refusing to talk to them at all. Instead, they see ad salespeople who know little about editorial, are trained in business as usual, and are usually paid by commission. Editors might also band together to take on controversy. That happened once when all the major women's magazines did articles in the same month on the Equal Rights Amendment. It could happen again.

It's almost three years away from life between the grindstones of advertising pressures and readers' needs. I'm just beginning to realize how edges got smoothed down—in spite of all our resistance.

I remember feeling put upon when I changed "Porsche" to "car" in a piece about Nazi imagery in German pornography by Andrea Dworkin—feeling sure Andrea would understand that Volkswagen, the distributor of Porsche and one of our few supportive advertisers, asked only to be far away from Nazi subjects. It's taken me all this time to realize that Andrea was the one with a right to feel put upon.

Even as I write this, I get a call from a writer for *Elle*, who is doing a whole article on where women part their hair. Why, she wants to know, do I part mine in the middle?

It's all so familiar. A writer trying to make something of a nothing assignment; an editor laboring to think of new ways to attract ads; readers assuming that other women must want this ridiculous stuff; more women suffering for lack of information, insight, creativity, and laughter that could be on these same pages.

I ask you: Can't we do better than this?

Case Study

Uptown, Dakota, and PowerMaster

N. Craig Smith

UPTOWN

In December 1989, the R.J. Reynolds Tobacco Co. (RJR) announced plans to introduce Uptown, a menthol cigarette designed to appeal strongly to black smokers. Cigarette sales had declined 6% in 1989 alone and tobacco companies were aggressively seeking new customers. While 29% of the adult U.S. population smoked at that time, the figure was 34% for blacks. Market research showed 69% of black smokers preferred menthol as against 27% for all smokers. RJR's Salem already was the top-selling menthol cigarette with a 6.8% market share (a 1% share was around $250 million in sales), but research suggested many blacks would favor the lighter menthol planned for Uptown. The company's marketing plan for the Philadelphia test market included advertising suggesting glamour, high fashion and nightlife, with the slogan "Uptown. The place. The taste." It would run in black newspapers and in black-oriented magazines such as *Jet* and *Ebony*. Research on the Uptown name suggested it was "classy sounding" and, accordingly, the product packaging was black and gold, in contrast to the usual green for menthol cigarettes. Moreover, the cigarettes were to be packed with the filters down, a response to a research finding showing that many blacks opened cigarette packs from the bottom. In short, RJR had studied carefully the market and customer needs and responded with a sharply focused marketing program targeting black smokers.

For a number of years, public health officials had attacked cigarette advertising directed at specific groups, especially minorities. Statistics showed that during the 1980s the gap between the number of black and white smokers was widening, as whites were more likely to quit. However, the attack on RJR's marketing plans for Uptown by the black Health and Human Services Secretary, Louis W. Sullivan, was unprecedented. In a January 18, 1990, speech to medical students at the University of Pennsylvania (in the city where RJR planned to test market Uptown) he said: "This brand is cynically and deliberately targeted toward black Americans. At a time when our people desperately need the message of health promotion, Uptown's message is more disease, more suffering and more death for a group already bearing more than its share of smoking-related illness and mortality. At a time when we must cultivate greater personal responsibility among our citizens, Uptown's slick and sinister advertising proposes instead a greater degree of personal irresponsibility." In a letter to RJR's CEO, Sullivan wrote, "I strongly urge you to cancel your plans to market a brand of cigarettes that is specifically targeted to black smokers."

Sullivan's speech received extensive media coverage. Among those commenting on his remarks, Reed Tuckson, the D.C. health commissioner, noted: "The prevalence of smoking is by far the single most important issue that accounts for the poor quality of health for people of color in this country. The predatory behavior and the degree of intensity to which these companies market their products of death and disease for the sake of profit is just immoral." An RJR spokeswoman initially commented: "We believe that black smokers have the right to buy products that fit their preference. The introduction of a new brand will not affect the decision to smoke." However, on January 19, RJR announced that it had cancelled plans for Uptown. Peter Hoult, executive vice president for marketing commented: "We regret that a small coalition of antismoking zealots apparently believes that black smokers are somehow different from others who choose to smoke. This represents a loss of choice for black smokers and a further erosion of the free enterprise system."

RJR's conflict with Sullivan did not end with Uptown. Confidential RJR documents leaked to the Advocacy Institute were released to the press to coincide with a Senate hearing on cigarette advertising targeting specific groups. This time, the marketing plans were for a new brand that targeted women.

DAKOTA

RJR had planned to test market Dakota in April, 1990. It was positioned against Philip Morris Co.'s Marlboro, the leading cigarette brand with a 26% overall market share and the leading brand among women. Marlboro was the most popular entry-level brand for teenage women and was smoked by almost half of young female smokers aged 18 to 24. RJR saw an opportunity in addressing a weakness in Marlboro's appeal to women:

the difficulty for a woman to completely identify with the "Marlboro man" image. Women were "one of the few bright spots" in the shrinking cigarette market, with a rate of smoking declining, but not as fast as for males. Moreover, while there were still more adult male smokers (32%) than females (27%), among teens, girls smoked at higher rates than boys. Philip Morris had pioneered female cigarettes in the late 1960s with Virginia Slims, the dominant brand with a 3% share. While around a dozen other brands only held in total a 3% market share, there had been much activity in the late 1980s; for example, BAT Industries' Capri, a much thinner cigarette, had gained a 0.5% market share in 16 months, prompting Philip Morris to launch Superslims and other innovations. As a marketing VP for Liggett commented, "if the female segment keeps growing, more companies will come into it." RJR was no exception.

Dakota was not positioned as a conventional female cigarette with a "soft, feminine sell." Its image was rugged. The target customer was a white, 18–24 year-old, "virile" female, with only a high school degree and for whom work was a job, not a career. Her free time was spent with her boyfriend, doing whatever he was doing, including tractor pulls and hot rod shows. Proposed promotions included "hunk-oriented" premiums, such as calendars, that would tie in with Dakota-sponsored male strip shows. The Dakota cigarette would be similar in taste and number of puffs to a Marlboro. Again, RJR had developed a marketing program clearly aimed at a well-defined target market.

Women's groups already had been strongly critical of the increased efforts by tobacco companies to target women. Twisting the Virginia Slims ad slogan, they were telling women smokers: "You've come the *wrong* way, baby." The Women's Tennis Association had been pressured to end its ties with Philip Morris, the sponsor of the Virginia Slims tennis tour. The marketing VP of Philip Morris commented that it was "reprehensible at best and sexist at worst to assume that adult women are not capable of making their own decisions about whether or not to smoke." Another industry spokesperson noted that it's "prudent marketing to go after your market." The demise of Uptown prompted increased attention to the targeting of women and the suggestion that they too could "resist exploitation by the tobacco industry." Having noted that slim cigarettes appealed to women with a "freedom from fat" message, one commentator suggested Sullivan should "blast cigarette companies for targeting women." With the announcement of RJR's plans for Dakota, Sullivan was able to oblige. He was also critical of the Virginia Slims tennis tour for fostering "a misleading impression that smoking is compatible with good health."

Primed by the Uptown story, commentators offered more insightful analysis on the controversy over target marketing, going beyond charges of "exploitation" and "manipulation." Consumer vulnerability was suggested in explanation: "Dakota is an unscrupulous attempt to exploit a vulnerable group" (Kornheiser 1990); "the company is under heavy fire for a plan to market the new brand to one of the industry's most vulnerable segments: young, poorly-educated, blue-collar women" (Freedman and McCarthy 1990). Target marketing was acknowledged as a standard marketing tool and a tactic of choice among tobacco companies because in a declining market the best opportunities were with specific groups the poor, the young, blacks and Hispanics. These perceived vulnerable groups were left because "The well-to-do and well-educated . . . have quit smoking. Those who remain are the disadvantaged. It's logical to target them, except you are sending a message society can't accept." Targeting had become hazardous for tobacco companies because "targeting specific consumer groups suggests they're creating victims" (Freedman and McCarthy 1990).

However, the hazards of targeting were not restricted to tobacco. The alcohol industry soon realized that it too faced the prospect of similar pressures and going "down Tobacco Road" (Abramson 1991). With driving after drinking the leading cause of death among teenagers, the industry had already faced criticism over targeting youth from groups and public health officials, such as Surgeon General Koop.

POWERMASTER

Like the tobacco industry, alcohol producers, also faced with declining consumption, were increasingly targeting their marketing programs, especially at heavy users. These targets included "the most vulnerable elements of society," according to Michael Jacobson of the Center for Science in the Public Interest (CSPI), a consumer advocacy group coordinating a coalition of 22 public interest groups critical of the emphasis on black and Hispanic consumers in advertisements for malt liquor. A CSPI video, "Marketing Booze to Blacks," suggested alcohol was connected to many social problems, from spousal and child abuse to homicide. The Beer Institute charged the Center with elitism: "The elitists at CSPI believe that only middle- to upper-class white males have the capacity to view ads without endangering themselves" (Folt 1991). In San Francisco, the city's health commissioner commented: "It is the height of irresponsibility for the beer industry to target poor ethnic communities with these genocidal beer promotions." Community leaders charged that heavy promotion of "high octane" malt liquor in black and Latino neighborhoods resulted in social problems similar to those created by crack cocaine. The following year, another new product introduction was to go the way of Uptown and Dakota.

In 1990, G. Heileman Brewing Co., the fifth largest brewer in the U.S., had seen its volumes decline for the seventh year in a row. Market share was also down. It was in bankruptcy proceedings and desperately in need of successful new product introductions. It had developed 40% of the 87 new beer products introduced in the 1980s. While beer consumption was on the decline (along with most other alcoholic beverages), the $500m. malt liquor market was growing. It experienced a 7% volume increase to 79.7 m. 2.5-gallon cases in 1990, about 3% of the total beer market. Some malts had even seen annual increases of 25–30%. Malt liquor, brewed from a base that contains a higher degree of fermentable sugars than regular beer, has a higher alcohol content, is paler in color and has a more aromatic and malty taste. It was disproportionately consumed in low income neighborhoods, where its appeal was attributed to its "quicker high." Heileman dominated the malt liquor market with a volume market share of around one-third. In July, 1991, it planned to introduce Power-Master, which at 5.9% alcohol was 31% stronger than Heileman's Colt 45, the market leader, and had 65% more alcohol than regular beer. Heileman had spent more than $2m on research and marketing for the brand.

The announcement of PowerMaster had anti-alcohol groups and black leaders up in arms. CSPI and other groups asked the brewer to stop distribution of the product because "higher octane alcoholic beverages have no place on the market, especially in communities where residents already suffer disproportionately from alcohol and other drug problems." Boycotts were planned. Surgeon General Antonia Novello described the promotion of PowerMaster as "socially irresponsible." PowerMaster's target marketing to minorities also was criticized by Congressional representatives. On June 20, 1991, the Bureau of Alcohol, Tobacco and Firearms (BATF) announced that its approval of the PowerMaster label was a mistake and required Heileman to drop the word *power* because it was a veiled reference to alcohol strength. (The Federal Alcohol Administration Act banned the mention of alcohol content on beer labels to discourage competition on that basis.) On July 3, Heileman announced that it would discontinue PowerMaster following BATF's withdrawal of approval for its label, because "the brand name was the product," commented the Heileman director of marketing. BATF gave the brewer four months to sell existing stocks.

Anti-alcohol groups criticized the agency because it made its move only after public outrage over PowerMaster's potency and the targeting of low-income blacks, who suffer disproportionately from alcohol-related diseases (CSPI found that black men had a 40% higher death rate from cirrhosis of the liver than whites). Industry commentators, anticipating further action by BATF against power claims widely used by malt liquor brands, suggested this would "strip away the whole basis for business" in the category. Also under scrutiny was advertising that associated malt liquors with aphrodisiacs, drug use, and street gangs. The director of the National Coalition to Prevent Impaired Driving commented: "Alcohol producers will think twice before targeting vulnerable, inner-city groups again." While a *New York Times* editorial had lambasted Heileman for "deliberately zeroing in on a section of society that already has problems enough," the president of the Beer Institute accused critics of PowerMaster of "patronizing" blacks and Hispanics. The trade journal *Beverage World* in its obituary to PowerMaster said it became "a magnet of controversy from the moment it reared its alcohol-enhanced head. Federal officials, industry leaders, black activists, and media types weighed in with protests that PowerMaster . . . was an example of bad product, bad marketing, and, essentially, a bad idea."

Later in 1991, BATF cracked down on other malt liquors, such as Black Sunday, Crazy Horse, and St. Ides, while cans of PowerMaster fast became collectors' items. Some observers noted the failure of some black organizations and media to criticize alcohol and tobacco and educate on health effects, suggesting they were "bought off" by these industries. *Fortune* described PowerMaster as one of the biggest business goofs of 1991, noting that "targeting black consumers with anything less wholesome than farina has become politically risky." A line extension of Colt 45, Colt 45 Premium, was introduced by Heileman in May 1992 and described by BATF as being identical in content to PowerMaster.

SOURCES

ABRAMSON, JILL (1991). "Selling Moderation, Alcohol Industry Is at Forefront of Efforts to Curb Drunkenness," *Wall Street Journal*, May 21, p. A1.

ALTERS, DIANE (1989). "As Youths Are Urged to Stay Sober, Beer Ad Blitz Tries to Lure Them," *Boston Sunday Globe*, June 25, p. 1.

BUREAU OF NATIONAL AFFAIRS (1991). "Brewer Decides to Withdraw New High Alcohol Malt Liquor," *Antitrust and Trade Regulation Report*, Vol. 61, No. 1524 (July 11), p. 41.

CHICAGO TRIBUNE (1991). "U.S. Seeking to Dilute New Malt Liquor's Name," *Chicago Tribune*, June 21, p. 10.

COHEN, RICHARD (1990). "More Work for Dr. Sullivan," *Washington Post*, January 30, p. A19.

CORNWELL, RUPERT (1991). "Out of the West: Trouble Brews for a Powerful Beer," *The Independent*, July 3, p. 10.

FARNHAM, ALAN (1992). "Biggest Business Goofs of 1991," *Fortune*, January 13, p. 81.

FOLTZ, KIM (1991). "Alcohol Ads Aimed at Blacks Criticized," *New York Times*, January 16, p. D6.

FREEDMAN, ALIX M. (1991). "Potent New Heileman Malt Is Brewing Fierce Industry and Social Criticism," *Wall Street Journal*, June 17, p. B1.

FREEDMAN, ALIX M. (1991). "Malt Advertising That Touts Firepower Comes Under Attack by U.S. Officials," *Wall Street Journal*, July 1, p. B1.

FREEDMAN, ALIX M. (1991). "Heileman, Under Pressure, Scuttles PowerMaster Malt," *Wall Street Journal*, July 5, p. B1.

FREEDMAN, ALIX M. and MICHAEL J. MCCARTHY (1990). "New Smoke from RJR Under Fire," *Wall Street Journal*, February 20, p. B1.

GARDNER, MARILYN (1990). "Women and Cigarettes: Smoking out the Truth," *Christian Science Monitor*, January 30, p. 14.

GLADWELL, MALCOLM (1990). "HHS Chief Assails Tie Between Tobacco Firms, Sporting Events," *St. Petersburg Times*, February 24, p. 6A.

GLATER, JONATHAN (1992). "Federal Crackdown Alcohol, Regulators Target Ads Over Claims of Potency," *San Francisco Chronicle*, July 24, p. B1.

HARDIE, CHRIS (1994). "Heileman Shipments Cut in Half Since '83," *La Crosse Tribune*, January 13.

HILTS, PHILIP J. (1990). "Health Chief Assails a Tobacco Producer for Aiming at Blacks," *New York Times*, January 19, p. A1.

INMAN, DAVID (1990). "Blacks Strike Back at Ad Campaigns; Amidst Uproar, Will Marketing Change?" *Sunday Tennessean*, April 8, p. ID.

JACKSON, DERRICK Z. (1991). "Miller's Mockery," *Boston Globe*, December 29, p. 63.

KORNHEISER, TONY (1990). "Cigarettes and Virile Chicks," *Washington Post*, February 23, p. B1.

LACEY, MARC (1992). "Marketing of Malt Liquor Fuels Debate," *Los Angeles Times*, December 15, p. A32.

LANG, PERRY (1990). "Hard Sell to Blacks of Potent Malt Brew Called 'Irresponsible,'" *San Francisco Chronicle*, November 3, p. A2.

ROTHENBERG, RONDALL (1989). "Groups Plan to Protest Malt Liquor Campaigns," *New York Times*, August 23, p. D17.

SPECTER, MICHAEL (1990). "Sullivan Denounces Reynolds Tobacco; New Brand Said Aimed at Blacks," *Washington Post*, January 19, p. A1.

SPECTER, MICHAEL (1990). "Reynolds Cancels Plans to Market New Cigarette; Uptown Brand Attacked as Aimed at Blacks," *Washington Post*, January 20, p. A3.

WALDMAN, PETER (1989). "Tobacco Firms Try Soft, Feminine Sell; But in Targeting Women, They Spark Backlash," *Wall Street Journal*, December 19, p. B1.

Case Study

Volvo's Crushing Blow

Ronald M. Green

The title card reads "June 12, 1990 Austin, Texas," Visuals move between crowd shots and views of a giant pickup truck with 6-foot-high tires identified as "Bear Foot." The truck drives over a line of cars, leaving only Volvo station wagon intact. "There's one car still standing out there" says an announcer over the public address system. A voice-over adds "Apparently, not everyone appreciates the strength of a Volvo."

In October 1990, executives at Volvo and their advertising agency Scali, McCabe, Sloves were pleased. Their "Bear Foot" spots were adding a sly touch of humor to Volvo's tradition of promoting the safety and reliability of its cars. The ads, first broadcast early in the month on several cable channels, and appearing in print versions in *Forbes* and *Car & Driver*, were also drawing critical praise. In a review of car advertising. *USA Today* described the "Bear Foot" spots as one of the most effective television promotions of the 1991 model year.

But by the end of the month "Bear Foot" had turned into a nightmare for Volvo and Scali. Late in October, James Mattox, attorney general of Texas, announced that he was pressing charges against Volvo North America Corporation, the car maker's American arm. In a lawsuit, Mattox charged that the ads had been shot after production people had reinforced the Volvos and sawed through the pillars on the competing cars. The ads, he told the press, were "a hoax and a sham."

Volvo reacted quickly. Within a week of Mattox's public announcement, the firm withdrew the spots and began running corrective ads explaining its decision in 19 Texas newspapers, *USA Today*, and the *Wall Street Journal*. Volvo also agreed to reimburse the

attorney general's office $316,250 for investigative costs and legal fees.

Volvo's corrective ads took the form of a letter "to all interested consumers" from Joseph L. Nicolato, company president-CEO. The letter stated that the advertising "inaccurately characterized the event as a car-crushing exhibition when in fact it was a dramatization of the actual event in Vermont."

The letter continued:

> On Oct. 30 Volvo management learned for the first time that the film production team had apparently made modifications to two of the vehicles. There were two reasons for the modifications, first, to enable the filming to be done without threatening the safety of the production crew, and second, to allow the demonstration Volvo to withstand the number of runs by the "monster truck" required for filming.

As Volvo issued its statement it was still unclear who had authorized the modifications. Perretti Productions, New York, had handled production of the commercial for Scali but Jim Perretti, the spot's director, was unavailable for comment.

In a separate statement to the press, 'Volvo's manager of public relations, Bob Austin, said that an investigation was under way to deter-

---

mine what caused the mistake. He explained that Milt Gravatt, the importer's marketing services manager, had been in Austin during the shoot but had not been on site at every moment during the 15 to 18 hours over two days it took to film the commercial.

"[Mr. Gravatt] assured us he did not see anything improper," said Austin. "We normally go down to a shoot to be nearby in case we can do anything to facilitate the production, but our basic attitude is to let the professionals do it. At this point, it is unclear what happened when, and who authorized it."

Executives at Scali expressed confusion and dismay. Agency chairman-CEO Marvin Sloves told reporters, "The agency never authorized any alterations of any vehicles at the shoot. We knew of no alterations made to create any misleading impression. I am just overwhelmed and shocked by the whole thing."

Sloves insisted that the agency creative team on site had not seen the alterations being made. "They say, and I believe them, that we had no idea they were doing anything to alter the cars to create a misleading impression." Although the spot itself was a dramatization, Sloves added. "This was a real live thing we had documentation for."

Stephanie Frawley, a development specialist at the Arthritis Foundation of Vermont supported the claim that the ads were based on fact. The Foundation, she said, had sponsored a "monster truck" event at the fairgrounds in Essex, Vermont, two years earlier and of the four cars that participated, a Volvo was the only one that was not crushed. From other people who were there, and from photos we have it was obvious, she said "Volvo is telling the truth".

Specialists in advertising law disagreed over the legal norms relevant to the "Bear Foot" spots. Felix Kent, an advertising lawyer with Hall, Dickler, Lawler, Kent & Friednan, said that a U.S. Supreme Court decision in the 1970s clearly established that demonstration ads could not use any form of mock-ups

or deception. But Rick Kunit, a partner at Frankfurt, Garbus, Klein & Selz, said that "for the past 10 years or so we've been able to be fairly free about not putting the dramatization and recreation and similar supers basically because a lot of the time you get enough in the context of the commercial that people know it's a dramatization."

As November wore on, Volvo weighed the course of its future advertising. Speaking for the company, Bob Austin insisted that Volvo had no intention of backing off from its emphasis on safety which has been featured in advertising virtually since the company entered the U.S. market in 1956. "Volvo was built around a solid set of basic values safety, reliability, and longevity," Austin said, "We will have to allow the public to decide whether they believe in Volvo."

As for Scali's future on the $40 million account, "We will establish what happened and take appropriate corrective action," said Austin, who acknowledged that some outsiders had suggested Volvo fire the agency.

"Any conversation of that type would be premature," Austin added. "We have resisted the temptation to throw a body out there for the media."

Some advertising industry professionals saw major damage to the industry in the "Bear Foot" incident. DeWitt Helm, president of the Association of National Advertisers, said the episode "feeds the fuel of activists and overly zealous regulators. It's giving all advertising and business a tarnish and black eye we don't deserve."

But not every consumer agreed. Donna Gates, a Chicago public relations executive, said the flap over the ads would not have changed her mind about the car. "As a Volvo owner, I think it's a wonderful car," she said. "It feels like a little tank. I feel very safe in it."

On November 18, 1990, in the wake of a highly publicized scandal involving its "Bear Foot" commercial, Scali, McCabe, Sloves ended a twenty-three-year relationship by resigning the Volvo account. Loss of its oldest, largest flagship account was estimated to cost the agency $40 million in revenues and to require the layoff of thirty-five to fifty staffers.

"I'm devastated by it," said Marvin Sloves, the chairman and chief executive of the agency he had founded twenty-three years earlier with Sam Scali and Ed McCabe. Resigning the account, he said, "was the right thing to do. The executives at Volvo deserve a chance to put this thing behind them."

According to William Hoover, the senior vice-president of marketing for Volvo Cars of North America, an investigation showed that the production company hired by Scali apparently knew the demonstration was a fake. "The agency had to accept responsibility and the only thing to do was to resign," said Hoover.

Despite the resignation, questions remained over who had authorized and who knew of the product rigging that took place at the production shoot June 12 in Austin.

In an interview in October, before Volvo had been contacted by the Texas attorney general's office, Dean Stefanides, Scali executive vice-president and group creative director, explained that the idea for the spot initially came from an account executive at the agency who learned from a friend that a real monster truck exhibition in Vermont had used a Volvo in a lineup of other cars. In that event, the Volvo was the only car uncrushed. Engineering personnel at Volvo confirmed that Volvo's roof supports were theoretically strong enough to sustain the 11,000 pound weight of a monster truck.

"We looked into it and substantiated it. We thought the Volvo audience would find it funny or campy, even though they might not go to those events," Stefanides said. He added that it was simply a fresh and creative way to continue Volvo's long-running safety demonstration spots. Scali subsequently hired Perretti Productions to oversee production of the commercial.

Perretti, in turn handed the re-creation of the Vermont event to International Productions, a company based in Phoenix, Arizona, that specializes in the promotion and production of motor sport events.

Lesse Spindler, promotion director of International Productions, said that his company did not have any advertising responsibility during the shoot. Our understanding was that we were to recreate that event. The issue of bracing the Volvos came up during the contract negotiation stage with Perretti said Spindler, but "they elected not to because of the cost factor."

According to Spindler, the first of the three Volvos used in the shoot was not reinforced and was crushed early in the day by the monster truck. Once that car was crushed work to brace the remaining two Volvos immediately got under way. Wooden supports were added to the second Volvo and the third was reinforced with steel. "The decision was also made to weaken the structures of competing cars by cutting their roof supports.

Those at the scene had included Jim Perretti; John Slaven; Scali executive vice-president and management representative; Dean Stefanides; and Larry Hempel, another Scali executive vice-president and group creative director. An initial Volvo inquiry revealed that a Volvo management representative, Milt Gravait, had been at the site from early morning until about 6:30 P.M. At that point, the shooting was declared a wrap and Volvo and top Scali management left the scene. Apparently some filming continued after that using one or more modified Volvos.

Sources reported that before the airing of the spots, Scali submitted to the TV networks a producer's report vouching for the accuracy of the commercial and stating that no special effects or techniques had been used.

Whatever its causes, the episode marked a serious setback for an agency whose creativity had long been the envy of others in the industry.

Over the years, Scali had put Perdue and its foul-faced chairman on the map and had held kosher Hebrew National franks accountable to "a higher authority."

Mark Messing, a Scali senior vice-president, noted that the agency could have avoided the fiasco by labeling the ad a "reenactment."

"Rookie error," he said.

Case Study

Toy Wars

Manuel G. Velasquez

Early in 1986, Tom Daner, president of the advertising company of Daner Associates, was contacted by the sales manager of Crako Industries, Mike Teal.[1] Crako Industries is a family-owned company that manufactures children's toys and had long been a favorite and important client of Daner Associates. The sales manager of Crako Industries explained that the company had just developed a new toy helicopter. The toy was modeled on the military helicopters that had been used in Vietnam and that had appeared in the "Rambo" movies. Mike Teal explained that the toy was developed in response to the craze for military toys that had been sweeping the nation in the wake of the Rambo movies. The family-owned toy company had initially resisted moving into military toys, since members of the family objected to the violence associated with such toys. But as segments of the toy market were increasingly taken over by military toys, the family came to feel that entry into the military toy market was crucial for their business. Consequently, they approved development of a line of military toys, hoping that they were not entering the market too late. Mike Teal now wanted Daner Associates to develop a television advertising campaign for the toy.

The toy helicopter Crako designers had developed was about one and one-half feet long, battery-operated, and made of plastic and steel. Mounted to the sides were detachable replicas of machine guns and a detachable stretcher modeled on the stretchers used to lift wounded soldiers from a battlefield. Mike Teal of Crako explained that they were trying to develop a toy that had to be perceived as "more macho" than the top-selling "G.I. Joe" line of toys. If the company was to compete successfully in today's toy market, according to the sales manager, it would have to adopt an advertising approach that was even "meaner and tougher" than what other companies were doing. Consequently, he continued, the advertising clips developed by Daner Associates would have to be "mean and macho." Television advertisements for the toy, he suggested, might show the helicopter swooping over buildings and blowing them up. The more violence and mayhem the ads suggested, the better. Crako Industries was relying heavily on sales from the new toy, and some Crako managers felt that the company's future might depend on the success of this toy.

Tom Daner was unwilling to have his company develop television advertisements that would increase what he already felt was too much violence in television aimed at children. In particular, he recalled a television ad for a tricycle with a replica machine gun mounted on the handlebars. The commercial showed the tricycle being pedaled through the woods by a small boy as he chased several other boys fleeing before him prospect of letting their imaginations loose on the project, several feeling that they could easily produce an attention-grabbing ad by "out-violencing" current television programming. The Creative Department, in fact, quickly produced a copy-script that called for videos showing the helicopter "flying out of the sky with machine guns blazing" at a jungle village below. This kind of ad, they felt, was exactly what they were being asked to produce by their client, Crako Industries.

But after viewing the copy, Tom Daner refused to use it. They should produce an ad, he insisted, that would meet their client's needs but that would also meet the guidelines of the national networks. The ad should not glorify violence and war but should somewhat support cooperation and family values. Disappointed and somewhat frustrated, the Creative Department went back to work. A few days later they presented a second proposal: An ad that would show the toy helicopter flying through the family room of a home as a little boy plays with it; then the scene shifts to show the boy on a rock rising from the floor of the family room: the helicopter swoops down and picks up the boy as though rescuing him from the rock where he had been stranded. Although the Creative Department was mildly pleased with their attempt, they felt it was too "tame." Tom liked it, however, and a version of the ad was filmed.

A few weeks later Tom Daner met with Mike Teal and his team and showed them the film. The viewing was not a success. Teal turned down the ad. Referring to the network regulations, which other toy advertisements were breaking as frequently as motorists broke the 55 mile per hour speed law, he said, "That commercial is going only 55 miles an hour when I want one that goes 75." If the

next version was not "tougher and meaner." Crako Industries would be forced to look elsewhere.

Disappointed, Tom Daner returned to the people in his Creative Department and told them to go ahead with designing the kind of ad they had originally wanted: "I don't have any idea what else to do." In a short time the Creative Department had an ad proposal on his desk that called for scenes showing the helicopter blowing up villages. Shortly afterwards a small set was constructed depicting a jungle village sitting next to a bridge stretching over a river. The ad was filmed using the jungle set as a background.

When Tom saw the result he was not happy. He decided to meet with his Creative Department and air his feelings. "The issue here," he said, "is basically the issue of violence. Do we really want to present toys as instruments for beating up people? This ad is going to promote aggression and violence. It will glorify dominance and do it with kids who are terrifically impressionable. Do we really want to do this?" The members of the Creative Department, however, responded that they were merely giving their client what the client wanted. That client, moreover, was an important account. The client wanted an aggressive "macho" ad, and that was what they were providing. The ad might violate the regulations of the television networks, but there were ways to get around the networks. Moreover, they said, every other advertising firm in the business was breaking the limits against violence set by the networks. Tom made one last try: why not over a dirt path. At one point the camera closed in over the shoulder of the boy, focused through the gun sight, and showed the gun sight apparently trying to aim at the backs of the boys as they fled before the tricycle's machine gun. Ads of that sort had disturbed Tom Daner and had led him to think that advertisers should find other ways of promoting these toys. He suggested, therefore, that instead of promoting the Crako helicopter through violence, it should be presented in some other manner. When Teal asked what he had in mind, Tom was forced to reply that he didn't know. But at any rate, Tom pointed out, the three television networks would not accept a violent commercial aimed at children. All three networks adhered to an advertising code that prohibited violent, intense, or unrealistic advertisements aimed at children.

This seemed no real obstacle to Teal, however. Although the networks might turn down children's ads when they were too violent, local television stations were not as squeamish. Local television stations around the country regularly accepted ads aimed at children that the networks had rejected as too violent. The local stations inserted the ads as spots on their non-network programming, thereby circumventing the Advertising Codes of the three national networks. Daner Associates would simply have to place the ads they developed for the Crako helicopter through local television stations around the country. Mike Teal was firm: if Daner Associates would not or could not develop a "mean and tough" ad campaign, the toy company would move their account to an advertiser who would. Reluctantly. Tom Daner agreed to develop the advertising campaign. Crako Industries accounted for $1 million of Daner's total revenues.

Like Crako Industries, Daner Associates is also a family-owned business. Started by his father almost fifty years ago, the advertising firm that Tom Daner now ran had grown dramatically under his leadership. In 1975 the business had grossed $3 million; ten years later it had revenues of $25 million and provide a full line of advertising services. The company was divided into three departments (Creative, Media, and Account Executive), each of which had about 12 employees. Tom Daner credited much of the company's success to the many new people he had hired, especially a group with M.B.A.s who had developed new marketing

strategies based on more thorough market and consumer analyses. Most decisions, however, were made by a five-person executive committee consisting of Tom Daner, the Senior Account Manager, and the three-department heads. As owner president, Tom's views tended to color most decisions, producing what one of the members called a "benevolent dictatorship." Tom himself was an enthusiastic, congenial, intelligent, and widely read person. During college he had considered becoming a missionary priest but had changed his mind and was now married and the father of three daughters. His personal heros included Thomas Merton, Albert Schweitzer, and Tom Dooley.

When Tom Daner presented the Crako deal to his Executive Committee, he found they did not share his misgivings. The other Committee members felt that Daner Associates should give Crako exactly the kind of ad Crako wanted: one with a heavy content of violence. Moreover, the writers and artists in the Creative Department were enthused with the market the toy as an adventure and fantasy toy? Film the ad again, he suggested, using the same jungle backdrop. But instead of showing the helicopter shooting at a burning village, show it flying in to rescue people from the burning village. Create an ad that shows excitement, adventure, and fantasy, but no aggression. "I was trying," he said later, "to figure out a new way of approaching this kind of advertising. We have to follow the market or we can go out of business trying to moralize to the market. But why not try a new approach? Why not promote toys as instruments that expand the child's imagination in a way that is positive and that promotes cooperative values instead of violence and aggression?"

A new film version of the ad was made, now showing the helicopter flying over the jungle set. Quick shots and heightened background music give the impression of excitement and danger. The helicopter flies dramatically through the jungle and over a river and bridge to rescue a boy from a flaming village. As lights flash and shoot haphazardly through the scene the helicopter rises and escapes into the sky. The final ad was clearly exciting and intense. And it promoted saving of life instead of violence against life.

It was clear when the final version was shot, however, that it would not clear the network censors. Network guidelines require that sets in children's ads must depict things that are within the reach of most children so that they do not create unrealistic expectations. Clearly the elaborate jungle set (which cost $25,000 to construct) was not within the reach of most children, and consequently most children would not be able to recreate the scene of the ad by buying the toy. Moreover, network regulations stipulate that in children's ads scenes must be filmed with normal lighting that does not create undue intensity. Again clearly the helicopter ad, which created excitement by using quick changes of light and fast cuts, did not fall within these guidelines.

After reviewing the film Tom Daner reflected on some last-minute instructions Crako's sales manager had given him when he had been shown the first version of the ad: The television ad should show things being blown up by the guns of the little helicopter and perhaps even some blood on the fuselage of the toy; the

ad had to be violent. Now Tom had to make a decision. Should he risk the account by submitting only the rescue mission ad? Or should he let Teal also see the ad that showed the helicopter shooting up the village, knowing that he would probably prefer that version if he saw it? And was the rescue mission ad really that much different from the ad that showed the shooting of the village? Did it matter that the rescue mission ad still violated some of the network regulations? What if he offered Teal only the rescue mission ad and Teal accepted the "rescue approach" but demanded he make it more violent; should he give in? And should Tom risk launching an ad campaign that was based on this new untested approach? What if the ad failed to sell the Crako toy? Was it right to experiment with a client's product, especially a product that was so important to the future of the client's business? Tom was unsure what he should do. He wanted to show Teal only the rescue mission commercial, but he felt he first had to resolve these questions in his own mind.

NOTE

1. Although the events described in this case are real, all names of the individuals and the companies involved are fictitious; in addition, several details have been altered to disguise the identity of participants.

Case Study

The Case of the Contested Firearms

George Brenkert

"Our lawyers are handling the current case," said Bob Graham, CEO of Magnum Industries, a major gun manufacturer doing business across the United States. "I want you to come up with some overall plan as to where we should be going. Start with a clean slate. What should we be doing with regard to manufacturing and marketing in our handgun division?

Should we try to defend our current practices? What about altering them? In what ways? What are our responsibilities and to whom?" Those were the marching orders given to John Diller, Senior VP for Marketing. Diller had been recently been hired by Graham in the hope that he could help the beleaguered firm find a way out of its current difficulties. These difficulties had been brought upon them by increasing numbers of lawsuits filed against them and public charges which accused them of everything from crass indifference to moral culpability in the deaths and injuries of those caused by handguns.

Magnum had been very successful in recent years in the development and marketing of new firearms. Though Magnum offered a full range of firearms, including hunting rifles and target pistols, this market had leveled off. In response, several years ago, it had introduced two other models that had attracted special attention. One was a small, semi-automatic pistol, the Defender, which had a barrel length of only 2.75 inches and an overall length of 5 inches. It was easily concealable, lightweight, and powerful. The other was a special model, the Wildfire, which they advertised as "the gritty answer to tough problems." With a 40 round detachable magazine, a combat-style trigger guard, and surfaces specially treated to resist fingerprints, it had captured the imagination of movie makers, gun magazines and chat rooms on the Internet. There was no doubt that these two models had helped shore up their sales in recent years. But it was these two models that were under attack by the anti-gun lobby and their lawyers. These attacks had not been numerous and had been dismissed by most gun makers as unlikely to succeed until lately. Now the situation seemed to be changing.

THE LEGAL AND MORAL COMPLAINTS

What had particularly caught the attention of Magnum (and that of all other gun manufacturers) was the verdict of a federal jury in New York City that had found nine gun makers collectively liable for several shootings, even though plaintiff lawyers could not prove what brand of gun had been used in any of the cases. The jury had determined that the manufacturers were liable because of their negligent marketing and distribution of handguns. Even though the manufacturers were ordered to pay only 13% of the full amount, one of the plaintiffs was awarded an eye-popping $3.95 million.[1]

The jury found that manufacturers had oversupplied their products in states with weak gun laws, leading to illegal sales in those with strict regulations, like New York.[2] Elisa Barnes, the plaintiff's chief lawyer in this case, claimed that "the gun makers made no attempts to keep their products from falling into criminal hands, like requiring wholesalers not to supply dealers suspected of selling the weapons to questionable buyers." "They don't care" asserted Michael Feldberg, attorney for one of the plaintiffs.[3] In describing the overall situation, Ms. Barnes said: "This huge pool (of handguns) is like toxic waste. It's been sent down the river by different companies."[4]

Now Chicago, New Orleans, Miami, Atlanta, Newark (N.J.), Cleveland (Ohio), and Bridgeport (Connecticut) had filed similar suits; Philadelphia, Baltimore, and Los Angeles also had lawsuits under consideration. Chicago's action sought $433 million in damages, claiming that gun manufacturers have created a public nuisance and burdened the city with extra costs for public hospitals as well as extra police and fire protection.[5]

No one was denying that most large cities continue to be faced with high levels of violent crime. Many of these crimes are committed with firearms that are possessed and used illegally. Firearms were used to commit 69% of all homicides in 1995 and 68% in 1996. In 1995, there were 35,957 deaths attributable to firearms.[6] The high level of gun violence has had a particularly drastic impact on young persons; homicide is the second leading cause of death for youths aged 15–19.

In 1997, in Chicago alone, there were 8,866 robberies, 4,390 aggravated batteries and 3,963 aggravated assaults in which handguns were used. That same year, only 147 robberies were committed in the city with a firearm other than a handgun. Overall, approximately 87% of firearms used in all crimes in Chicago are handguns. A recent survey showed that 45% of persons arrested in the city obtained their guns in the illegal firearms market. Although most major cities faced the same general set of problems, they approached the legal issues in different ways.

The New Orleans suit, for example, raised a number of relatively straightforward but disturbing issues. It claimed that gun manufacturers, by failing to incorporate appropriate safety devices to prevent use by children and other unauthorized persons, had failed to "personalize" handguns. The suit claimed that at least 30 patents for personalized guns have been granted since 1976. Designs such as combination locks, magnetic locks, radio frequency locks, and encoded chip locks are among the devices patented in attempts to limit the unauthorized use of handguns. Under the Louisiana product liability statute, a manufacturer can be held liable for damage caused by a product that is unreasonably dangerous in design. Under this doctrine, just as car manufacturers have been held liable for failing to install seat belts and air bags, gun makers should be liable for failing to install feasible safety systems.[7] The New Orleans suit alleges that guns that fail to incorporate safety systems to prevent their use by children and other unauthorized users are unreasonably dangerous in design. As a result, the United States leads the world in the number of children who are killed or injured by handguns, with "an average of more than four accidental shootings of children under 15 occur[ring] each day, one of whom dies every other day."[8]

Other cities, such as Chicago (and New York), have taken a more aggressive and less traditional approach to litigation, arguing that gun manufacturers oversupply guns in nearby suburban communities. These guns then end up in Chicago, a city with one of the strictest gun control laws in the nation. This is a result, the City of Chicago contends, of the sales practices of dealers in surrounding communities as well as the manufacturing and marketing practices of the gun manufacturers.

Many of the firearms illegally possessed in Chicago were purchased in a way that should have put the defendant dealers on reasonable notice that the buyer was not obtaining firearms for his own lawful use. For example, Stanley Malone, a resident of Bellwood, Illinois, purchased fourteen pistols from **Bell's Gun & Sport Shop** and from **Suburban Sporting Goods** between August, 1994 and June, 1996. He purchased the majority of these firearms to resell to gang members, making a profit of about $60 per firearm ("a straw purchase").[9] Other individuals made similar multiple purchases of handguns over similar periods of time. Sales clerks often made recommendations to undercover police officers regarding means of purchasing the guns to avoid investigation by the Bureau of Alcohol, Tobacco, and Firearms and other authorities. Clerks frequently disregarded comments about how these "buyers" wanted to settle scores with someone. In short, the City of Chicago claims that the practices of dealers in the surrounding communities have caused a large underground market for illegal firearms to flourish within its city limits, making it easy for Chicago residents to obtain firearms in clear violation of the "spirit" of the law.

The role of manufacturers and distributors in this process, the City of Chicago claims, is to knowingly oversupply or "saturate" the market with handguns in areas where gun control laws are less restrictive, knowing that they will be resold in jurisdictions where they cannot be sold legally. By shipping large numbers of firearms to these jurisdictions, the gun manufacturers enhance their profits while disclaiming any knowledge of or responsibility for where their products end up or how they are used. They also distribute substantial quantities of firearms through low-end retailers such as pawn shops and gun stores known to be frequented by criminals and gang members. They choose not to supervise, regulate, or standardize their network of distributors and dealers because such practices would limit sales in one of their most lucrative markets.

In addition, gun manufacturers are alleged to design and advertise their products to appeal to illicit buyers (both directly and indirectly), including those who wish to use them for criminal purposes. Among the design features of these handguns are: 1) surfaces that offer "resistance to fingerprints"; 2) short barrel lengths and overall lengths; 3) lightweight, detachable magazines; and 4) semi-automatics that can be easily modified to fully automatic. Some models tout the fact that they do not have a hammer, meaning that they are easier to withdraw from a pocket (for quick firing) without snagging on clothing. Advertisements include descriptions of guns as "assault-type pistols" that "deliver more gutsy performance and reliability than any other gun on the market." Another is advertised as being "[c]onsidered the ultimate hideaway, undercover, backup gun available anywhere." The manufacturer, the S. W. Daniels Corporation, marketed this 9-millimeter semiautomatic pistol as the "weapon of choice of the drug lords of the 80s."[10] Another manufacturer called one of its products the "Streetsweeper."[11]

THE GUN INDUSTRY AND THE NATIONAL RIFLE ASSOCIATION

Although they rarely dispute the magnitude of crime problems in major cities, the "pro-gun" sector takes issue with the legal and moral claims made against gun makers. To most gun manufacturers the legal reasoning and arguments above have seemed sophistical and dangerous. The National Rifle Association has held that "this is the beginning [of an attempt] to accomplish . . . through the back door . . . what could not be accomplished through the legislative front door—the elimination of private gun ownership in America."[12]

The attempt to control the misuse of guns in this manner is fraught with other problems as well, according to the pro-gun group. "What's next," Wayne Lapierre, spokesman and CEO of the NRA asked, "blaming car manufacturers instead of drunk drivers. . . . Under this theory of law you could eliminate virtually every manufactured product in America."[13] Ralph Boyd, a lawyer who advises gun industries, agreed. "The auto industry makes vehicles that exceed . . . the lawful speed limit in any jurisdiction. What would stop someone from using this type of legal theory from saying, 'Hey, you know those commercials that show cars speeding across the countryside, making tight turns on mountains, zipping around pylons on race courses? Why isn't that negligent marketing? Why isn't the auto industry responsible for all the accidents resulting from excessive speed?'"[14]

Of course the gun industry has sought innovation in style, weight, size, capacity, and speed so as to boost its sales.[15] It is merely responding to the increased competition it faces and the softening of its markets. In general, it feels that its responsibility ends once its product are sold to licensed distributors. "The job of policing gun runners should be left to the Bureau of Alcohol, Tobacco and Firearms, which has never required manufacturers to track their products to the street."[16] Since it considers these lawsuits to pose significant dangers to legitimate rights, the NRA has introduced legislation in at least 20 states that would preclude local governments from suing gun manufacturers and distributors. The latest bill, proposed in Florida, is the toughest, making it a felony for any local official to file a lawsuit of this type.[17]

Besides, gun makers argue, someone ought to raise some questions about the ethics of the lawyers and cities who have brought legal suits against them. Outside of the case in New York, they have little reason, based on the present and past record, to believe that these suits will succeed. Indeed, they have with remarkable consistency been rejected. Instead, they are using these suits to apply financial pressure, or coercion, against the gun makers to pay the cities what amounts to extortion. And yet there have been few complaints raised against such moral tactics. Defenders of the gun makers see this as simply another example of individuals failing to take responsibility for their own behavior and seeking Big Brother, or rather some big law firm, to do for them what people will not do for themselves. It is the morals and lawful behavior of individuals which needs to be addressed in our society, not that of the gun makers.

DILLER'S DILEMMA

In light of all these charges and counter-charges and with significant legal threats in clear view, Magnum needed a coherent plan regarding both its response to the suits and the operation of its business in this new environment. John wondered what he should recommend. The theories of public nuisance, of product liability, and of collective liability advanced in the lawsuits seemed to extend well beyond their past applications. Besides, this was not simply a legal challenge to gun makers. Strong moral charges against the gun manufacturers were also part of the situation they faced. Magnum had to be prepared for all these charges. John wondered whether society and the gun manufacturers

had responsibilities for the actions of other adults. How far back up the commercial path should responsibility be pushed and under what conditions? Should Magnum alter its design or marketing of the Defender or the Wildfire? John worried that he would have to have some idea how to answer these questions when he made his recommendation to Graham regarding both their immediate response to this legal situation and their long run approach to producing and marketing firearms.[18]

NOTES

1. Chris Hawke, "Jury Finds Gun Maker Negligence Responsible for Shooting." *Agence France Press*, Feb. 12, 1999. The case was that of Hamilton v. Accu-Tek. No. 95-0049.
2. Joseph P. Fried, "9 Gun Makers Called Liable for Shootings," *New York Times*, Feb. 12, 1999.
3. Ibid.
4. Tom Hays, "AP-Gens-on-Trail," *AP Online*. Feb. 12, 1999.
5. Resa King, "Firepower for the Antigun Lobby," *Business Week*, Feb. 1, 1999.
6. David Kairys, "Legal Claims of Cities Against the Manufacturers of Handguns," *Temple Law Review* 71 (Spring 1998), 2.
7. "Background Information on New Orleans Lawsuit Against Gun Industry," http://www.handguncontrol.org/legalaction/noqa.htm, Hand Gun Control, Feb. 19, 1999.
8. Kairys, 2.
9. Cf. City of Chicago and Country of Cook v. Beretta et al.
10. Daniel Wise. *New York Law Journal*, January 7, 1999.
11. Kairys. 4.
12. Chris Hawke, "NRA Concerned About Gun Suit Verdict," United Press International, February 12, 1999.
13. Ibid.
14. Laura Mansnerus, "Cities' Suits Against Gun Makers Raise Complicated Legal Issues," *Star Tribune* (Minneapolis, MN), Februaryz 14, 1999.
15. Cf. King.
16. Cf. Hays.
17. Sharon Walsh, "NRA Pushing to Block Gun Suits." *Washington Post*. Feb. 26, 1999.
18. Thomas M. Jones gave me insightful help in preparing this case.

Case Study

Italian Tax Mores

Arthur L. Kelly

The Italian federal corporate tax system has an official, legal tax structure and tax rates just as the U.S. system does. However, all similarity between the two systems ends there.

The Italian tax authorities assume that no Italian corporation would ever submit a tax return which shows its true profits but rather would submit a return which understates actual profits by anywhere between 30 percent and 70 percent; their assumption is essentially correct. Therefore, about six months after the annual deadline for filing corporate tax returns, the tax authorities issue to each corporation an "invitation to discuss" its tax return. The purpose of this notice is to arrange a personal meeting between them and representatives of the corporation. At this meeting, the Italian revenue service states the amount of corporate income tax which it believes is due. Its position is developed from both prior years' taxes actually paid and the current year's return; the amount which the tax authorities claim is due is generally several times that shown on the corporation's return for the current year. In short, the corporation's tax return and the revenue service's stated position are the opening offers for the several rounds of bargaining which will follow.

The Italian corporation is typically represented in such negotiations by its *commercialista*, a function which exists in Italian society for the primary purpose of negotiating corporate (and individual) tax payments with the Italian tax authorities; thus, the management of an Italian corporation seldom, if ever, has to meet directly with the Italian revenue service and probably has a minimum awareness of the details of the negotiation other than the final settlement.

Both the final settlement and the negotiations are extremely important to the corporation, the tax authorities, and the *commercialista*. Since the tax authorities assume that a corporation *always* earned more money this year than last year and *never* has a loss, the amount of the final settlement, i.e., corporate taxes which will actually be paid, becomes, for all practical purposes, the floor for the start of next year's negotiations. The final settlement also represents the amount of revenue the Italian government will collect in taxes to help finance the cost of running the country. However, since large amounts of money are involved and two individuals having vested personal interests are conducting the negotiations, the amount of *bustarella*—typically a substantial cash payment "requested" by the Italian revenue agent from the *commercialista*—usually determines whether the final settlement is closer to the corporation's original tax return or to the fiscal authority's original negotiating position.

Whatever *bustarella* is paid during the negotiation is usually included by the *commercialista* in his lump-sum fee "for services rendered" to his corporate client. If the final settlement is favorable to the corporation, and it is the *commercialista's* job to see that it is, then the corporation is not likely to complain about the amount of its *commercialista's* fee, nor will it ever know how much of that fee was represented by *bustarella* and how much remained for the *commercialista* as payment for his negotiating services. In any case, the tax authorities will recognize the full amount of the fee as a tax deductible expense on the corporation's tax return for the following year.

About ten years ago, a leading American bank opened a bank subsidiary in a major Italian city. At the end of its first year of operation, the bank was advised by its local lawyers and tax accountants, both from branches of U.S. companies, to file its tax return "Italian-style," i.e., to understate its actual profits by a significant amount. The American general manager of the bank, who was on his first overseas assignment, refused to do so both because he considered it dishonest and because it was inconsistent with the practices of his parent company in the United States.

About six months after filing its "American-style" tax return, the bank received an "invitation to discuss" notice from the Italian tax authorities. The bank's general manager consulted with his lawyers and tax accountants who suggested he hire a *commercialista*. He rejected this advice and instead wrote a letter to the Italian revenue service not only stating that his firm's corporate return was correct as filed but also requesting that they inform him of any specific items about which they had questions. His letter was never answered.

About sixty days after receiving the initial "invitation to discuss" notice, the bank received a formal tax assessment notice calling for a tax of approximately three times that shown on the bank's corporate tax return; the tax authorities simply assumed the bank's original return had been based on generally accepted Italian practices, and they reacted accordingly. The bank's general manager again consulted with his lawyers and tax accountants who again suggested he hire a *commercialista* who knew how to handle these matters. Upon learning that the *commercialista* would probably have to pay *bustarella* to his revenue service counterpart in order to reach a settlement, the general manager again chose to ignore this advisors. Instead, he responded by sending the Italian revenue service a check for the full amount of taxes due according to the bank's American-style tax return even though the due date for the payment was almost six months hence; he made no reference to the amount to corporate taxes shown on the formal tax assessment notice.

Ninety days after paying its taxes, the bank received a third notice from the fiscal authorities. This one contained the statement, "We have reviewed your corporate tax return for 19— and have determined that [the lira equivalent of] $6,000,000 of interest paid on deposits is not an allowable expense for federal tax purposes. Accordingly, the total tax due for 19— is lira 3." Since interest paid on deposits is any bank's largest single expense item, the new tax assessment was for an amount many times larger than that shown in the initial tax assessment notice and almost fifteen times larger than the taxes which the bank had actually paid.

The bank's general manager was understandably very upset. He immediately arranged an appointment to meet personally with the manager of the Italian revenue service's local office. Shortly after the start of their meeting, the conversation went something like this:

GENERAL MANAGER: "You can't really be serious about disallowing interest paid on deposits as a tax deductible expense.

ITALIAN REVENUE SERVICE: "Perhaps. However, we thought it would get your attention. Now that you're here, shall we begin our negotiations?"[1]

NOTE

1. For readers interested in what happened subsequently, the bank was forced to pay the taxes shown on the original tax assessment, and the American manager was recalled to the United States and replaced.

Case Study

Whistleblowing and Employee Loyalty

Ronald Duska

There are proponents on both sides of the issue—those who praise whistleblowers as civic heroes and those who condemn them as "finks." Maxwell Glen and Cody Shearer, who wrote about the whistleblowers at Three Mile Island say, "Without the *courageous* breed of assorted company insiders known as whistleblowers—workers who often risk their livelihoods to disclose information about construction and design flaws—the Nuclear Regulatory Commission itself would be nearly as idle as Three Mile Island. . . . That whistleblowers deserve both gratitude and protection is beyond disagreement."[1]

Still, while Glen and Shearer praise whistleblowers, others vociferously condemn them. For example, in a now infamous quote, James Roche, the former president of General Motors said:

> Some critics are now busy eroding another support of free enterprise—the loyalty of a management team, with its unifying values and cooperative work. Some of the enemies of business now encourage an employee to be *disloyal* to the enterprise. They want to create suspicion and disharmony, and pry into the proprietary interests of the business. However this is labeled—industrial espionage, whistleblowing, or professional responsibility—it is another tactic for spreading distinty and creating conflict.[2]

From Roche's point of view, not only is whistleblowing not "courageous" and not deserving of "gratitude and protection" as Glen and Shearer would have it, it is corrosive and impermissible.

Discussions of whistleblowing generally revolve around three topics: (1) attempts to define whistleblowing more precisely, (2) debates about whether and when whistleblowing is permissible, and (3) debates about whether and when one has an obligation to blow the whistle.

In this paper I want to focus on the second problem, because I find it somewhat disconcerting that there is a problem at all. When I first looked into the ethics of whistleblowing it seemed to me that whistleblowing was a good thing, and yet I found in the literature claim after claim that it was in need of defense, that there was something wrong with it, namely that it was an act of disloyalty.

If whistleblowing is a disloyal act, it deserves disapproval, and ultimately any action of whistleblowing needs justification. This disturbs me. It is as if the act of a good Samaritan is being condemned as an act of interference, as if the prevention of a suicide needs to be justified.

In his book *Business Ethics*, Norman Bowie claims that "whistleblowing . . . violate(s) a *prima facie* duty of loyalty to one's employer." According to Bowie, there is a duty of loyalty that prohibits one from reporting his employer or company. Bowie, of course, recognizes that this is only a *prima facie* duty, that is, one that can be overridden by a higher duty to the public good. Nevertheless, the axiom that whistleblowing is disloyal is Bowie's starting point.[3]

Bowie is not alone. Sissela Bok sees "whistleblowing" as an instance of disloyalty:

The whistleblower hopes to stop the game; but since he is neither referee nor coach, and since he blows the whistle on his own team, his act is seen as a *violation of loyalty*. In holding his position, he has assumed certain obligations to his colleagues and clients. He may even have subscribed to a loyalty oath or a promise of confidentiality. . . . Loyalty to colleagues and to clients comes to be pitted against loyalty to the public interest, to those who may be injured unless the revelation is made.[4]

Bowie and Bok end up defending whistleblowing in certain contexts, so I don't necessarily disagree with their conclusions. However, I fail to see how one has an obligation of loyalty to one's company, so I disagree with their perception of the problem and their starting point. I want to argue that one does not have an obligation of loyalty to a company, even a *prima facie* one, because companies are not the kind of things that are properly objects of loyalty. To make them objects of loyalty gives them a moral status they do not deserve and in raising their status, one lowers the status of the individuals who work for the companies. Thus, the difference in perception is important because those who think employees have an obligation of loyalty to a company fail to take into account a relevant moral difference between persons and corporations.

But why aren't companies the kind of things that can be objects of loyalty? To answer that we have to ask what are proper objects of loyalty. John Ladd states the problem this way, "Granted that loyalty is the wholehearted devotion to an object of some kind, what kind of thing is the object? Is it an abstract entity, such as an idea or a collective being? Or is it a person or group of persons?"[5] Philosophers fall into three camps on the question. On one side are the idealists who hold that loyalty is devotion to something more than persons, to some cause or abstract entity. On the other side are what Ladd calls "social atomists," and these include empiricists and utilitarians, who think that at most one can only be loyal to individuals and that loyalty can ultimately be explained away as some other obligation that holds between two people. Finally, there is a moderate position that holds that although idealists go too far in postulating some super-personal entity as an object of loyalty, loyalty is still an important and real relation that holds between people, one that cannot be dismissed by reducing it to some other relation.

There does seem to be a view of loyalty that is not extreme. According to Ladd, " 'loyalty' is taken to refer to a relationship between persons—for instance, between a lord and his vassal, between a parent and his children, or between friends. Thus the object of loyalty is ordinarily taken to be a person or a group of persons."[6]

But this raises a problem that Ladd glosses over. There is a difference between a person or a group of persons, and aside from instances of loyalty that relate two people such as lord/vassal, parent/child, or friend/friend, there are instances of loyalty relating a person to a group, such as a person to his family, a person to this team, and a person to his country. Families, countries, and teams are presumably groups of persons. They are certainly ordinarily construed as objects of loyalty.

But to what am I loyal in such a group? In being loyal to the group am I being loyal to the whole group or to its members? It is easy to see the object of loyalty in the case of an individual person. It is simply the individual. But to whom am I loyal in a group? To whom am I loyal in a family? Am I loyal to each and every individual or to something larger, and if to something larger, what is it? We are tempted to think of a group as an entity of its own, an individual in its own right, having an identity of its own.

To avoid the problem of individuals existing for the sake of the group, the atomists insist that a group is nothing more than the individuals who comprise it, nothing other than a mental fiction by which we refer to a group of individuals. It is certainly not a reality or entity over and above the sum of its parts, and consequently is not a proper object of loyalty. Under such a position, of course, no loyalty would be owed to a company because a company is a mere mental fiction, since it is a group. One would have obligations to the individual members of the company, but one could never be justified in overriding those obligations for the sake of the "group" taken collectively. A company has no moral status except in terms of the individual members who comprise it. It is not a proper object of loyalty. But the atomists go too far. Some groups, such as a family, do have a reality of their own, whereas groups of people walking down the street do not. From Ladd's point of view the social atomist is wrong because he fails to recognize the kinds of groups that are held together by "the ties that bind." The atomist tries to reduce these groups to simple sets of individuals bound together by some externally imposed criteria. This seems wrong.

There do seem to be groups in which the relationships and interactions create a new force or entity. A group takes on an identity and a reality of its own that is determined by its purpose, and this purpose defines the various relationships and roles set up within the group. There is a division of labor into roles necessary for the fulfillment of the purposes of the group. The membership, then, is not of individuals who are the same but of individuals who have specific relationships to one another determined by the aim of the group. Thus we get specific relationships like parent/child, coach/player, and so on, that don't occur in other groups. It seems then that an atomist account of loyalty that restricts loyalty merely to individuals and does not include loyalty to groups might be inadequate.

But once I have admitted that we can have loyalty to a group, do I not open myself up to criticism from the proponent of loyalty to the company? Might not the proponent of loyalty to business say: "Very well. I agree with you. The

atomists are short-sighted. Groups have some sort of reality and they can be proper objects of loyalty. But companies are groups. Therefore companies are proper objects of loyalty."

The point seems well taken, except for the fact that the kinds of relationships that loyalty requires are just the kind that one does not find in business. As Ladd says, "The ties that bind the persons together provide the basis of loyalty." But all sorts of ties bind people together. I am a member of a group of fans if I go to a ball game. I am a member of a group if I merely walk down the street. What binds people together in a business is not sufficient to require loyalty.

A business or corporation does two things in the free enterprise system: It produces a good or service and it makes a profit. The making of a profit, however, is the primary function of a business as a business, for if the production of the good or service is not profitable, the business would be out of business. Thus nonprofitable goods or services are a means to an end. People bound together in a business are bound together not for mutual fulfillment and support, but to divide labor or make a profit. Thus, while we can jokingly refer to a family as a place where "they have to take you in no matter what," we cannot refer to a company in that way. If a worker does not produce in a company or if cheaper laborers are available, the company—in order to fulfill its purpose—should get rid of the worker. A company feels no obligation of loyalty. The saying "You can't buy loyalty" is true. Loyalty depends on ties that demand self-sacrifice with no expectation of reward. Business functions on the basis of enlightened self-interest. I am devoted to a company not because it is like a parent to me; it is not. Attempts of some companies to create "one big happy family" ought to be looked on with suspicion. I am not devoted to it at all, nor should I be. I work for it because it pays me. I am not in a family to get paid, I am in a company to get paid.

The cold hard truth is that the goal of profit is what gives birth to a company and forms that particular group. Money is what ties the group together. But in such a commercialized venture, with such a goal, there is no loyalty, or at least none need be expected. An employer will release an employee and an employee will walk away from an employer when it is profitable for either one to do so.

Not only is loyalty to a corporation not required, it more than likely is misguided. There is nothing as pathetic as the story of the loyal employee who, having given above and beyond the call of duty, is let go in the restructuring of the company. He feels betrayed because he mistakenly viewed the company as an object of his loyalty. Getting rid of such foolish romanticism and coming to grips with this hard but accurate assessment should ultimately benefit everyone.

To think we owe a company or corporation loyalty requires us to think of that company as a person or as a group with a goal of human fulfillment. If we think of it in this way we can be loyal. But this is the wrong way to think. A company is not a person. A company is an instrument, and an instrument with a specific purpose, the making of profit. To treat an instrument as an end in itself, like a person, may not be as bad as treating an end as an instrument, but it does give the instrument a moral status it does not deserve; and by elevating the instrument we lower the end. All things, instruments and ends, become alike.

Remember that Roche refers to the "management team" and Bok sees the name "whistleblowing" coming from the instance of a referee blowing a whistle in the presence of a foul. What is perceived as bad about whistleblowing in business from this perspective is that one blows the whistle on one's own team, thereby violating team loyalty. If the company can get its employees to view it as a team they belong to, it is easier to demand loyalty. Then the rules governing teamwork and team loyalty will apply. One reason the appeal to a team

and team loyalty works so well in business is that businesses are in competition with one another. Effective motivation turns business practices into a game and instills teamwork.

But businesses differ from teams in very important respects, which makes the analogy between business and a team dangerous. Loyalty to a team is loyalty within the context of sport or a competition. Teamwork and team loyalty require that in the circumscribed activity of the game I cooperate with my fellow players, so that pulling all together, we may win. The object of (most) sports is victory. But winning in sports is a social convention, divorced from the usual goings on of society. Such a winning is most times a harmless, morally neutral diversion.

But the fact that this victory in sports, within the rules enforced by a referee (whistleblower), is a socially developed convention taking place within a larger social context makes it quite different from competition in business, which, rather than being defined by a context, permeates the whole of society in its influence. Competition leads not only to victory but to losers. One can lose at sport with precious few consequences. The consequences of losing at business are much larger. Further, the losers in business can be those who are not in the game voluntarily (we are all forced to participate) but who are still affected by business decisions. People cannot choose to participate in business. It permeates everyone's lives.

The team model, then, fits very well with the model of the free market system, because there competition is said to be the name of the game. Rival companies compete and their object is to win. To call a foul on one's own teammate is to jeopardize one's chances of winning and is viewed as disloyalty.

But isn't it time to stop viewing corporate machinations as games? These games are not controlled and are not ended after a specific time. The activities of business affect the lives of everyone, not just the game players. The analogy of the corporation to a team and the consequent appeal to team loyalty, although understandable, is seriously misleading, at least in the moral sphere where competition is not the prevailing virtue.

If my analysis is correct, the issue of the permissibility of whistleblowing is not a real issue since there is no obligation of loyalty to a company. Whistleblowing is not only permissible but expected when a company is harming society. The issue is not one of disloyalty to the company, but of whether the whistleblower has an obligation to society if blowing the whistle will bring him retaliation.

NOTES

1. Maxwell Glen and Cody Shearer, "Going After the Whistle-blowers," *Philadelphia Inquirer*, Tuesday, August 2, 1983, Op-ed page, p. 11A.
2. James M. Roche, "The Competitive System, to Work, to Preserve, and to Protect," *Vital Speeches of the Day* (May 1971): 445.
3. Norman Bowie, *Business Ethics* (Englewood Cliffs, N.J.: Prentice Hall, 1982), pp. 140–143.
4. Sissela Bok, "Whistleblowing and Professional Responsibilities," *New York University Education Quarterly* 2 (1980): 3.
5. John Ladd, "Loyalty," *The Encyclopedia of Philosophy* 5:97.
6. Ibid.

Case Study

Some Paradoxes of Whistleblowing

Michael Davis

By "paradox," I mean an apparent—and, in this case, real—inconsistency between theory (our systematic understanding of whistleblowing) and the facts (what we actually know, or think we know, about whistleblowing). What concerns me is not a few anomalies, the exceptions that test a rule, but a flood of exceptions that seems to swamp the rule.

This paper has four parts. The first states the standard theory of whistleblowing. The second argues that the standard theory is paradoxical, that it is inconsistent with what we know about whistleblowers. The third part sketches what seems to me a less paradoxical theory of whistleblowing. The fourth tests the new theory against one classic case of whistleblowing, Roger Boisjoly's testimony before the presidential commission investigating the *Challenger* disaster ("the Rogers Commission").

I use that case because the chief facts are both uncontroversial enough and well known enough to make detailed exposition unnecessary. For the same reason, I also use that case to illustrate various claims about whistleblowing throughout the paper.

JUSTIFICATION AND WHISTLEBLOWING

The standard theory is not about whistleblowing as such but about justified whistleblowing—and rightly so. Whether this or that is, or is not, whistleblowing is a question for lexicographers. For the rest of us, mere moral agents, the question is: when, if ever, is whistleblowing justified?

We may distinguish three (related) senses in which an act may be "justified." First, an act may be something morality permits. Many acts, for example, eating fruit at lunch, are morally justified in this weak sense. They are (all things considered) morally all right, though some of the alternatives are morally all right too. Second, acts may be morally justified in a stronger sense. Not only is doing them morally all right, but doing anything else instead is morally wrong. These acts are *morally required*. Third, some acts, though only morally justified in the weaker sense, are still required all things considered. They are mandatory because of some non-moral consideration. They are rationally (but not morally) required.

I shall be concerned here only with moral justification, that is, with what morality permits or requires. I shall have nothing to say about when other considerations, for example, individual prudence or social policy, make (morally permissible) whistleblowing something reason requires.

Generally, we do not *need* to justify an act unless we have reason to think it wrong (whether morally wrong or wrong in some other way). So, for example, I do not need to justify eating fruit for lunch today, though I would if I were allergic to fruit or had been keeping a fast. We also do not need a justification if we believe the act in question wrong. We do not need a justification because, insofar as an act is wrong, justification is impossible. The point of justification is to show to be right an act the rightness of which has been put in (reasonable) doubt.

Insofar as we believe the act wrong, we can only condemn or excuse it. To condemn it is simply to declare it wrong. To excuse it is to show that, while the act was wrong, the doer had good reason to do it, could not help doing it, or for some other reason should not suffer the response otherwise reserved for such a wrongdoer.

Most acts, though what morality permits or requires, need no justification. There is no reason to think them wrong. Their justification is too plain for words. Why then is whistleblowing so problematic that we need *theories* of its justification? What reason do we have to think whistleblowing might be morally wrong?

Whistleblowing always involves revealing information that would not ordinarily be revealed. But there is nothing morally problematic about that: after all, revealing information not ordinarily revealed is one function of science. Whistleblowing always involves, in addition, an actual (or at least declared) intention to prevent something bad that would otherwise occur. Nothing morally problematic in that either. That may well be the chief use of information.

What seems to make whistleblowing morally problematic is its organizational context. A mere individual cannot blow the whistle (in any interesting sense); only a member of an organization, whether a current or a former member, can. Indeed, he can only blow the whistle on his own organization (or some part of it). So, for example, a police officer who makes public information about a burglary ring, though a member of an organization, does not blow the whistle on the burglary ring (in any interesting sense). She simply alerts the public. Even if she came by the information working undercover in the ring, her revelation could not be whistleblowing. While secret agents, spies, and other infiltrators need a moral justification for what they do, the justification they need differs from that whistleblowers need. Infiltrators gain their information under false pretenses. They need a justification for that deception.[1]

Whistleblowers generally do not gain their information under false pretenses.

What if, instead of being a police officer, the revealer of information about the burglary ring were an ordinary member of the ring? Would such an informer be a (justified) whistleblower?

I think not. The burglary ring is a criminal organization. The whistleblower's organization never is, though it may occasionally engage in crime (knowingly or by inadvertence). So, even a burglar who, having a change of heart, volunteers information about his ring to the police or the newspaper, does not need to justify his act in the way the whistleblower does. Helping to destroy a criminal organization by revealing its secrets is morally much less problematic than whistleblowing.

What then is morally problematic about the whistleblower's organizational context? The whistleblower *cannot* blow the whistle using just any information obtained in virtue of membership in the organization. A clerk in Accounts who, happening upon evidence of serious wrongdoing while visiting a friend in Quality Control, is not a whistleblower just because she passes the information to a friend at the *Tribune*. She is more like a self-appointed spy. She seems to differ from the whistleblower, or at least from clear cases of the whistleblower, precisely in her relation to the information in question. To be a whistleblower is to reveal information with which one is *entrusted*.

But it is more than that. The whistleblower does not reveal the information to save his own skin (for example, to avoid perjury under oath).[2] He has no excuse for revealing what his organization does not want revealed. Instead, he claims to be doing what he should. If he cannot honestly make that claim—if, that is, he does not have that intention—his revelation is not whistleblowing (and so, not justified as whistleblowing), but something analogous, much as pulling a child from the water is not a rescue, even if it saves the child's life, when the "rescuer" merely believes herself to be salvaging old clothes.

What makes whistleblowing morally problematic, if anything does, is this high-minded but unexcused misuse of one's position in a generally law-abiding, morally decent organization, an organization that prima facie deserves the whistleblower's loyalty (as a burglary ring does not).[3]

The whistleblower must reveal information the organization does not want revealed.

But, in any actual organization, "what the organization wants" will be contested, with various individuals or groups asking to be taken as speaking for the organization. Who, for example, did what Thiokol wanted the night before the *Challenger* exploded? In retrospect, it is obvious that the three vice presidents, Lund, Kilminster, and Mason, did not do what Thiokol wanted—or, at least, what it would have wanted. At the time, however, they had authority to speak for the company—the conglomerate Morton-Thiokol headquartered in Chicago—while the protesting engineers, including Boisjoly, did not. Yet, even before the explosion, was it obvious that the three were doing what the company wanted? To be a whistleblower, one must, I think, at least temporarily lose an argument about what the organization wants. The whistleblower is disloyal only in a sense, the sense the winners of the internal argument get to dictate. What can justify such disloyalty?

THE STANDARD THEORY

According to the theory now more or less standard,[4] such disloyalty is morally permissible when:

S1. The organization to which the would-be whistleblower belongs will, through its product or policy, do serious and considerable harm to the public (whether to users of its product, to innocent bystanders, or to the public at large);

S2. The would-be whistleblower has identified that threat of harm, reported it to her immediate superior, making clear both the threat itself and the objection to it, and concluded that the superior will do nothing effective; and

S3. The would-be whistleblower has exhausted other internal procedures within the organization (for example, by going up the organizational ladder as far as allowed)—or at least made use of as many internal procedures as the danger to others and her own safety make reasonable.

Whistleblowing is morally required (according to the standard theory) when, in addition:

S4. The would-be whistleblower has (or has accessible) evidence that would convince a reasonable, impartial observer that her view of the threat is correct; and

S5. The would-be whistleblower has good reason to believe that revealing the threat will (probably) prevent the harm at reasonable cost (all things considered).

Why is whistleblowing morally required when these five conditions are met? According to the standard theory, whistleblowing is morally required, when it is, because "people have a moral obligation to prevent serious harm to others if they can do so with little cost to themselves."[5] In other words, whistleblowing meeting all five conditions is a form of "minimally decent samaritanism" (a doing of what morality requires) rather than "good samaritanism" (going well beyond the moral minimum).[6]

A number of writers have pointed out that the relation between the first three conditions and the full five does not seem to be that between the morally permissible and the morally required.[7] If, for example, the whistleblower lacks evidence that would convince a reasonable, impartial observer of the threat in question (S4), her whistleblowing could not prevent harm. Since it could not prevent harm, her whistleblowing would not be even morally permissible: what could make morally permissible an attempt to help a stranger when the attempt will probably fail and the cost be high both to the would-be samaritan and to those to whom she owes a competing obligation? The most that can be said for blowing the whistle where only conditions S1–S3 are met seems to be that the whistleblower has an excuse when (without negligence) she acts on inadequate evidence. So, for many writers, the standard view is that S1–S5 state sufficient conditions for morally

required whistleblowing even though S1–S3 do not state sufficient conditions for morally permissible whistleblowing but (at best) for morally excusable whistleblowing.

The standard theory is not a definition of whistleblowing or even of justified whistleblowing. The theory purports to state sufficient conditions, not necessary conditions (a "when" but *not* an "only when"). But these sufficient conditions are supposed to identify the central cases of morally justified whistleblowing. Since a theory that did only that would be quite useful, we cannot object to the theory merely because it is incomplete in this way. Incomplete only in this way, the theory would be about as useful as theories of practical ethics ever are.

THREE PARADOXES

That's the standard theory: where are the paradoxes? The first paradox I want to call attention to concerns a commonplace of the whistleblowing literature. Whistleblowers are not minimally decent samaritans. If they are samaritans at all, they are good samaritans. They always act at considerable risk to career and generally at considerable risk to their financial security and personal relations.[8]

In this respect, as in many others, Roger Boisjoly is typical. Boisjoly blew the whistle on his employer, Thiokol: he volunteered information, in public testimony before the Rogers Commission, that Thiokol did not want him to volunteer. As often happens, both his employer and many who relied on it for employment reacted hostilely. Boisjoly had to say goodbye to the company town, to old friends and neighbors, and to building rockets; he had to start a new career at an age when most people are preparing for retirement.

Since whistleblowing is generally costly to the whistleblower in some such large way as this, the standard theory's minimally decent samaritanism provides *no* justification for the central cases of whistleblowing.[9] That is the first paradox, what me might call "the paradox of burden."

The second paradox concerns the prevention of "harm." On the standard theory, the would-be whistleblower must seek to prevent "serious and considerable harm" in order for the whistleblowing to be even morally permissible. There seems to be a good deal of play in the term "harm." The harm in question can be physical (such as death or disease), financial (such as loss of or damage to property), and perhaps even psychological (such as fear or mental illness). But there is a limit to how much the standard theory can stretch "harm." Beyond that limit are "harms" like injustice, deception, and waste. As morally important as injustice, deception, and waste can be, they do not seem to constitute the "serious and considerable harm" that can require someone to become even a minimally decent samaritan.

Yet, many cases of whistleblowing, perhaps most, are not about preventing serious and considerable physical, financial, or psychological harm. For example, when Boisjoly spoke up the evening before the *Challenger* exploded, the lives of seven astronauts sat in the balance. Speaking up then was about preventing serious and considerable physical, financial, and psychological harm—but it was not whistleblowing. Boisjoly was then serving his employer, not betraying a trust (even on the employer's understanding of that trust); he was calling his superiors' attention to what he thought they should take into account in their decision, not publicly revealing confidential information. The whistleblowing came after the explosion, in testimony before the Rogers Commission. By then, the seven astronauts were beyond help, the shuttle program was suspended, and any further threat of physical, financial, or psychological harm to the "public" was—after discounting for time—negligible.

Boisjoly had little reason to believe his testimony would make a significant difference in the booster's redesign, in safety procedures in the shuttle program, or even in re-awakening concern for safety among NASA employees and contractors. The *Challenger*'s explosion was much more likely to do that than anything Boisjoly could do. What Boisjoly could do in his testimony, what I think he tried to do, was prevent falsification of the record.[10]

Falsification of the record is, of course, harm in a sense, especially a record as historically important as that the Rogers Commission was to produce. But falsification is harm only in a sense that almost empties "harm" of its distinctive meaning, leaving it more or less equivalent to "moral wrong." The proponents of the standard theory mean more by "harm" than that.

De George, for example, explicitly says that a threat justifying whistleblowing must be to "life or health."[11] The standard theory is strikingly narrower in its grounds of justification than many examples of justified whistleblowing suggest it should be. That is the second paradox, the "paradox of missing harm."

The third paradox is related to the second. Insofar as whistleblowers are understood as people out to prevent harm, not just to prevent moral wrong, their chances of success are not good. Whistleblowers generally do not prevent much harm. In this too, Boisjoly is typical. As he has said many times, things at Thiokol are now much as they were before the disaster. Insofar as we can identify cause and effect, even now we have little reason to believe that—whatever his actual intention—Boisjoly's testimony actually prevented any harm. So, if whistleblowers must have, as the standard theory says (S5), "good reason to believe that revealing the threat will (probably) prevent the harm," then the history of whistleblowing virtually rules out the moral justification of whistleblowing. That is certainly paradoxical in a theory purporting to state sufficient conditions for the central cases of justified whistleblowing. Let us call this "the paradox of failure."

A COMPLICITY THEORY

As I look down the roll of whistleblowers, I do not see anyone who, like the clerk from Accounts, just happened upon key documents in a cover-up.[12] Few, if any, whistleblowers are mere third-parties like the good samaritan. They are generally deeply involved in the activity they reveal. This involvement suggests that we might better understand what justifies (most) whistleblowing if we understand the whistleblower's obligation to derive from *complicity* in wrongdoing rather than from the ability to prevent harm.

Any complicity theory of justified whistleblowing has two obvious advantages over the standard theory. One is that (moral) complicity itself presupposes (moral) wrongdoing, not harm. So, a complicity justification automatically avoids the paradox of missing harm, fitting the facts of whistleblowing better than a theory which, like the standard one, emphasizes prevention of harm.

That is one obvious advantage of a complicity theory. The other is that complicity invokes a more demanding obligation than the ability to prevent harm does. We are morally obliged to avoid doing moral wrongs. When, despite our best efforts, we nonetheless find ourselves engaged in some wrong, we have an obligation to do what we reasonably can to set things right. If, for example, I cause a traffic accident, I have a moral (and legal) obligation to call help, stay at the scene till help arrives, and render first aid (if I know how), even at substantial cost to myself and those to whom I owe my time, and even with little likelihood that anything I do will help much. Just as a complicity theory avoids the paradox of missing harm, it also avoids the paradox of burden.

What about the third paradox, the paradox of failure? I shall come to that, but only after remedying one disadvantage of the complicity theory. That disadvantage is obvious: we do not yet have such a theory, not even a sketch. Here, then, is the place to offer a sketch:

Complicity Theory. You are morally required to reveal what you know to the public (or to a suitable agent or representative of it)[13] when:

C1. what you will reveal derives from your work for an organization;

C2. you are a voluntary member of that organization;

C3. you believe that the organization, though legitimate, is engaged in serious moral wrongdoing;

C4. you believe that your work for that organization will contribute (more or less directly) to the wrong if (but *not* only if) you do not publicly reveal what you know;

C5. you are justified in beliefs C3 and C4; and

C6. beliefs C3 and C4 are true.

The complicity theory differs from the standard theory in several ways worth pointing out here. The first is that, according to C1, what the whistleblower reveals must derive from his work for the organization. This condition distinguishes the whistleblower from the spy (and the clerk in Accounts). The spy seeks out information in order to reveal it; the whistleblower learns it as a proper part of doing the job the organization has assigned him. The standard theory, in contrast, has nothing to say about how the whistleblower comes to know of the threat she reveals (S2). For the standard theory, spies are just another kind of whistleblower.

A second way in which the complicity theory differs from the standard theory is that the complicity theory (C2) explicitly requires the whistleblower to be a *voluntary* participant in the organization in question. Whistleblowing is not—according to the complicity theory— an activity in which slaves, prisoners, or other involuntary participants in an organization engage. In this way, the complicity theory makes explicit something implicit in the standard theory. The whistleblowers of the standard theory are generally "employees." Employees are voluntary participants in the organization employing them.

What explains this difference in explicitness? For the samaritanism of the standard theory, the voluntariness of employment is extrinsic. What is crucial is the ability to prevent harm. For the complicity theory, however, the voluntariness is crucial. The obligations deriving from complicity seem to vary with the voluntariness of our participation in the wrongdoing. Consider, for example, a teller who helps a gang rob her bank because they have threatened to kill her if she does not: she does not have the same obligation to break off her association with the gang as someone who has freely joined it. The voluntariness of employment means that the would-be whistleblower's complicity will be more like that of one of the gang than like that of the conscripted teller.[14]

A third way in which the complicity theory differs from the standard theory is that the complicity theory (C3) requires moral wrong, not harm, for justification. The wrong need not be a new event (as a harm must be if it is to be *prevented*). It might, for example, consist in no more than silence about facts necessary to correct a serious injustice.

The complicity theory (C3) does, however, follow the standard theory in requiring that the predicate of whistleblowing be "serious." Under the complicity theory, minor wrongdoing can no more justify whistleblowing than can minor harm under the standard theory.[15] While organizational loyalty cannot forbid whistleblowing, it does forbid "tattling," that is, revealing minor wrongdoing.

A fourth way in which the complicity theory differs from the standard theory, the most important, is that the complicity theory (C4)

requires that the whistleblower believe her work will have contributed to the wrong in question if she does nothing but does *not* require that she believe that her revelation will prevent (or undo) the wrong. The complicity theory does not require any belief about what the whistleblowing can accomplish (beyond ending complicity in the wrong in question). The whistleblower reveals what she knows to prevent complicity in the wrong, not to prevent the wrong as such. She can prevent complicity (if there is any to prevent) simply by publicly revealing what she knows. The revelation itself breaks the bond of complicity, the secret partnership in wrongdoing, that makes her an accomplice in her organization's wrongdoing.[16] The complicity theory thus avoids the third paradox, the paradox of failure, just as it avoided the other two.

The fifth difference between the complicity theory and the standard theory is closely related to the fourth. Because publicly revealing what one knows breaks the bond of complicity, the complicity theory does not require the whistleblower to have enough evidence to convince others of the wrong in question. Convincing others, or just being able to convince them, is not, as such, an element in the justification of whistleblowing.

The complicity theory does, however, require (C5) that the whistleblower be (epistemically) justified in believing both that his organization is engaged in wrongdoing and that he will contribute to that wrong unless he blows the whistle. Such (epistemic) justification may require substantial physical evidence (as the standard theory says) or just a good sense of how things work. The complicity theory does not share the standard theory's substantial evidential demand (S4).

In one respect, however, the complicity theory clearly requires more of the whistleblower than the standard theory does. The complicity theory's C6—combined with C5—requires not only that the whistleblower be *justified* in her beliefs about the organization's wrongdoing and her part in it, but also that she be *right* about them. If she is wrong about either the wrongdoing or her complicity, her revelation will not be justified whistleblowing. This consequence of C6 is, I think, not as surprising as it may seem. If the would-be whistleblower is wrong only about her own complicity, her revelation of actual wrongdoing will, being otherwise justified, merely fail to be justified *as whistleblowing* (much as a failed rescue, though justified as an attempt, cannot be justified as a rescue). If, however, she is wrong about the wrongdoing itself, her situation is more serious. Her belief that wrong is being done, though fully justified on the evidence available to her, cannot justify her disloyalty. All her justified belief can do is *excuse* her disloyalty. Insofar as she acted with good intentions and while exercising reasonable care, she is a victim of bad luck. Such bad luck will leave her with an obligation to apologize, to correct the record (for example, by publicly recanting the charges she publicly made), and otherwise to set things right.

The complicity theory says nothing on at least one matter about which the standard theory says much, going through channels before publicly revealing what one knows. But the two theories do not differ as much as this difference in emphasis suggests. If going through channels would suffice to prevent (or undo) the wrong, then it cannot be true (as C4 and C6 together require) that the would-be whistleblower's work will contribute to the wrong if she does not publicly reveal what she knows. Where, however, going through channels would *not* prevent (or undo) the wrong, there is no need to go through channels. Condition C4's if-clause will be satisfied. For the complicity theory, going through channels is a way of finding out what the organization will do, not an independent requirement of justification. That, I think, is also how the standard theory understands it.[17]

A last difference between the two theories worth mention here is that the complicity theory is only a theory of morally required whistleblowing while the standard theory claims as well to define circumstances when whistleblowing is morally permissible but not morally required. This difference is another advantage the complicity theory has over the standard theory. The standard theory, as we saw, has trouble making good on its claim to explain how whistleblowing can be morally permissible without being morally required.

TESTING THE THEORY

Let us now test the theory against Boisjoly's testimony before the Rogers Commission. Recall that under the standard theory any justification of that testimony seemed to fail for at least three reasons: First, Boisjoly could not testify without substantial cost to himself and Thiokol (to whom he owed loyalty). Second, there was no serious and substantial harm his testimony could prevent. And, third, he had little reason to believe that, even if he could identify a serious and considerable harm to prevent, his testimony had much chance of preventing it.

Since few doubt that Boisjoly's testimony before the Rogers Commission constitutes justified whistleblowing, if anything does, we should welcome a theory that—unlike the standard one—justifies that testimony as whistleblowing. The complicity theory sketched above does that:

C1. Boisjoly's testimony consisted almost entirely of information derived from his work on booster rockets at Thiokol.

C2. Boisjoly was a voluntary member of Thiokol.

C3. Boisjoly believed Thiokol, a legitimate organization, was attempting to mislead its client, the government, about the causes of a deadly accident. Attempting to do that certainly seems a serious moral wrong.

C4. On the evening before the *Challenger* exploded, Boisjoly gave up objecting to the launch once his superiors, including the three Thiokol vice presidents, had made it clear that they were no longer willing to listen to him. He also had a part in preparing those superiors to testify intelligently before the Rogers Commission concerning the booster's fatal field joint. Boisjoly believed that Thiokol would use his failure to offer his own interpretation of his retreat into silence the night before the launch, and the knowledge that he had imparted to his superiors, to contribute to the attempt to mislead Thiokol's client.

C5. The evidence justifying beliefs C3 and C4 consisted of comments of various officers of Thiokol, what Boisjoly had seen at Thiokol over the years, and what he learned about the rocket business over a long career. I find this evidence sufficient to justify his belief both that his organization was engaged in wrongdoing and that his work was implicated.

C6. Here we reach a paradox of *knowledge*. Since belief is knowledge if, but only if, it is *both* justified *and* true, we cannot *show* that we know anything. All we can show is that a belief is now justified and that we have no reason to expect anything to turn up later to prove it false. The evidence now available still justifies Boisjoly's belief both about what Thiokol was attempting and about what would have been his part in the attempt. Since new evidence is unlikely, his testimony seems to satisfy C6 just as it satisfied the complicity theory's other five conditions.

Since the complicity theory explains why Boisjoly's testimony before the Rogers Commission was morally required whistleblowing, it has passed its first test, a test the standard theory failed.

NOTES

I should thank Vivian Weil for several discussions provoking this paper, as well as for commenting on several drafts; members of the Program in Ethics, Science, and Environment, Oregon State University, for raising several hard questions after I read an early version of this paper to them, April 24, 1996; those who asked questions (including my co-panelist, Roger Boisjoly) at a session of the annual meeting of the Northwest Section of the American Society of Engineering Educators, Oregon Institute of Technology, Klamath Falls, Oregon, April 26, 1996; the editors of *Business and Professional Ethics Journal*; and, last, attendees at a symposium sponsored by the Centre for Professional Ethics, University of Central Lancashire, Preston, England, November 12, 1996.

1. This is, I think, one (but not the only) reason to reject the forgotten—but perceptive—definition of whistleblowing in Frederick Elliston, John Keenan, Paula Lockhart, and Jane van Schaick, *Whistleblowing Research: Methodological and Moral Issues* (New York: Praeger, 1984), p. 15: "An act of whistleblowing occurs when: 1) an individual performs an action or series of actions intended to make information public; 2) the information is made a matter of public record; 3) the information is about possible or actual, nontrivial wrongdoing in an organization; and 4) the individual who performs the action is a member or former member of the organization." While this definition confounds whistleblowers with spies, informers, and the like, and is designed for research on whistleblowing rather than for developing a justification, its wrong-based approach makes it closer to the complicity theory offered below than to the standard theory. (Though the book has four authors, they credit the whole of the first chapter, including this definition, to someone else, Deborah Johnson.)

2. I do not mean that, for some purpose, for example, a whistleblower protection act, it might not be convenient to include among whistleblowers those who reveal information unwillingly. What I mean is that, for purposes of developing a general theory of justified whistleblowing, such cases are uninteresting. Avoiding contempt of court or Congress generally provides sufficient justification for testifying about serious wrongdoing, and avoiding perjury, a sufficient justification for telling the truth, a stronger justification than can either the standard theory or the alternative I shall offer.

3. There is, of course, a problem about organizational loyalty, especially when the organization is a business and it understands its employees as instruments rather than members. While justifying whistleblowing is easier the less loyalty one owes the organization in question, we will learn more if we focus on the harder cases, those where we admit significant obligations of loyalty. So, that is what I do here.

4. Throughout this paper, I take the standard theory to be Richard T. De George's version in *Business Ethics, 3rd* (New York: Macmillan, 1990), pp. 200–214 (amended only insofar as necessary to include non-businesses as well as businesses). Why treat De George's theory as standard? There are two reasons: first, it seems the most commonly cited; and second, people offering alternatives generally treat it as the one to be replaced. The only obvious competitor, Norman Bowie's, is distinguishable from De George's

on no point relevant here. See his *Business Ethics* (Englewood Cliffs, NJ: Prentice-Hall, 1982), p. 143.

5. De George, 200. Later, 214, De George says something more daring: "It is not implausible to claim both that we are morally obliged to prevent harm to others at little expense to ourselves, and that we are morally obliged to prevent great harm to a great many others, even at considerable expense to ourselves." De George (quite rightly) considers the opportunity to prevent great harm (as distinct from serious harm) so rare that he can safely ignore it.

6. There is now a significant literature on the responsibilities of the minimally decent samaritan. See, for example: Peter Singer, "Famine, Affluence, and Morality," *Philosophy and Public Affairs* 7 (Spring 1972): 229–243; Alan Gewirth, *Reason and Morality* (Chicago: University of Chicago Press, 1978), 217–230; Patricia Smith, "The Duty to Rescue and the Slippery Slope Problem," *Social Theory and Practice* 16 (Spring 1990): 19–41; John M. Whelan, "Charity and the Duty to Rescue," *Social Theory and Practice* 17 (Fall 1991): 441–456; and David Copp, "Responsibility for Collective Inaction," *Journal of Social Philosophy* 22 (Fall 1991): 71–80.

7. See, for example, David Theo Goldberg, "Tuning In to Whistle Blowing," *Business and Professional Ethics Journal* 7 (Summer 1988): 85–94.

8. For an explanation of why whistleblowing is inevitably a high risk undertaking, see my "Avoiding the Tragedy of Whistleblowing," *Business and Professional Ethics Journal* 8 (Winter 1989): 3–19.

9. Indeed, I am tempted to go further and claim that, where an informant takes little or no risk, we are unlikely to describe her as a whistleblower at all. So, for example, I would say that using an internal or external "hot-line" is whistleblowing only when it is risky. We are, in other words, likely to consider using a hot-line as disloyalty (that is, as "going out of channels") only if the organization (or some part of it) is likely to respond with considerable hostility to its use.

10. After I presented this paper in Klamath Falls, Boisjoly told me that, though his motive for testifying as he did was (as I surmised) to prevent falsification of the record, part of his reason for wanting to prevent that was that he wanted to do what he could to prevent the managers responsible for the disaster from having any part in redesigning the boosters. This *secondary* motive is, of course, consistent with the complicity theory.

11. De George, 210: "The notion of *serious* harm might be expanded to include serious financial harm, and kinds of harm other than death and serious threats to health and body. But as we noted earlier, we shall restrict ourselves here to products and practices that produce or threaten serious harm or danger to life and health."

12. See Myron Peretz Glazer and Penina Migdal Glazer, *The Whistleblowers: Exposing Corruption in Government and Industry* (New York: Basic Books, 1989), for a good list of whistleblowers (with detailed description of each); for an older list (with descriptions), see Alan F. Westin, *Whistle-blowing! Loyalty and Dissent in the Corporation* (New York: McGraw-Hill, 1981).

13. The problems with "public" in any definition of "whistleblowing" are well known (perhaps even notorious). I simply ignore them here. For our purposes, the public to whom the whistleblower reveals information is that individual or group to whom she must reveal it in order to end her complicity. Who is the public will vary with circumstances.

14. Do I claim that slaves, prisoners, inmates in a mental hospital, or students in a school cannot blow the whistle—or, at least, cannot do so justifiably? Well, not exactly. That the usual lists of whistleblowers include no involuntary participants in wrongdoing is, I think, important evidence for the claim that involuntary participants cannot blow the whistle. But, since how we have used a word does not determine how we can use it (especially a word like "whistleblowing" where usage is still evolving), that evidence is hardly decisive. What I think is clear is that involuntary participants will not have the same obligation of loyalty as the typical whistleblower; hence, any theory justifying their "going public" will have a somewhat different structure than the theory developed here. What about *voluntary* participants who are not employees, such as unpaid volunteers in a political campaign? While the complicity theory clearly counts them as capable of justified whistleblowing, the standard theory must make some special provision.

15. If the revelation seems likely to prevent harm as well, or to undo some injustice as well, that will, of course, strengthen the justification, making better a justification already good enough. But, according to the complicity theory, such good consequences are not necessary for justification.

16. We are, of course, assuming the standard case of whistleblowing where complicity involves only information. We can imagine more complicated cases where, in addition to information, there are benefits from the wrongdoing (say, a bonus derived from past wrongdoing). In such complex cases, revealing information (including the bonus) may not be all that is morally required but, even so, it will, I think, end the complicity relevant to whistleblowing. That, however, is a matter about which I am still thinking.

17. Compare De George, 211: "By reporting one's concern to one's immediate superior or other appropriate persons, one preserves and observes the regular practices of firms, which on the whole promote their order and efficiency; this fulfills one's obligation of minimizing harm, and *it precludes precipitous whistle blowing.*" (Italics mine.)

Essay

A Hero—And A Smoking-Gun Letter

Wandy Zeller, Stephanie Forest Anderson, Laura Cohn

At last, someone in the sordid Enron Corp. scandal seems to have done the right thing. Thanks to whistle-blower Sherron S. Watkins, a no-nonsense Enron vice-president, the scope and audacity of the accounting mess is becoming all too clear. Her blunt Aug. 15 letter to Enron CEO Kenneth L. Lay warns that the company might "implode in a wave of accounting scandals." And now that her worst fears have been realized, it is also clear that Watkins' letter went far beyond highlighting a few accounting problems in a handful of off-balance-sheet partnerships. Watkins' letter lays bare for all to see the underbelly of Enron's get-rich-quick culture.

Watkins, 42, a former Arthur Andersen accountant who remains Enron's vice-president for corporate development, put her finger on the rot: top execs who, at best, appeared to close their eyes to questionable accounting maneuvers; a leadership that had lost sight of ordinary investors and the basic principles of accounting; and watchdogs—the outside auditors and lawyers whose own involvement may have left them too conflicted to query the nature of the deals. Perhaps the question shouldn't be how Enron collapsed so quickly—but why it didn't implode sooner.

Lay's response to Watkins' complaints is nearly as damning as her letter itself. Yes, he talked to her for an hour. And, yes, he ordered an outside investigation. But contrary to Watkins' advice, he appointed the company's longtime Houston law firm, Vinson & Elkins, despite the obvious conflict: V & E had worked on some of the partnerships. And Enron and V & E agreed there would be no "second-guessing" of Andersen's accounting and no "detailed analysis" of each and every transaction, according to V & E's Oct. 15 report. The inquiry was to consider only if there was new factual information that warranted a broader investigation. V & E declined comment.

Surprise: V & E concluded that a widespread investigation wasn't warranted. It simply warned that there was a "serious risk of adverse publicity and litigation." And Watkins' letter reveals the inadequacy of Lay's response in the months following CEO Jeffrey K. Skilling's sudden Aug. 14 resignation for "personal reasons." His departure triggered the letter. Lay never fully disclosed the partnerships or explained their impact to investors, even as he vowed there were no accounting issues and "no other shoe to fall." Even after Enron revealed on Oct. 16 a $1.2 billion hit to shareholder equity related to the partnerships, Lay continued to express ignorance about details of these deals and support for Chief Financial Officer Andrew S. Fastow, who managed and had stakes in certain partnerships. But on Oct. 24, Fastow was removed from his job and promptly left the company.

Watkins, an eight-year Enron veteran, is not some disgruntled naysayer who is easy to dismiss. Her lawyer, Philip H. Hilder, says she became familiar with some of the partnership dealings when she worked in June and July in Fastow's finance group. Her position allowed her to review the valuation of certain assets being sold into the partnerships, and that's when she saw "computations that just didn't jibe," says Hilder.

Former executives say the Tomball (Tex.) native was tenacious and competent. "She wasn't really an alarmist," says one former Enron employee. Her mother, Shirley Klein Harrington, a former high school accounting teacher, calls her daughter "a very independent, outspoken, good Christian girl, who's going to stand up for principle whenever she can." Watkins had previously worked at Andersen in Houston and New York and then for Germany's Metallgesellschaft AG.

At those companies, she befriended Jeffrey McMahon, whom she helped recruit. Now the CFO at Enron, McMahon "complained mightily" about the Fastow partnerships to Skilling, Watkins told Lay in the letter. "Employees question our accounting propriety consistently and constantly," she claimed. McMahon didn't return calls. Skilling has denied getting any warnings about accounting.

Watkins didn't stop there. Five days after she wrote to Lay, Watkins took her concerns directly to an Andersen audit partner, according to congressional investigators. He in turn relayed her questions to senior Andersen management on the Enron account. It's not known what, if any, action they took.

Of course, Skilling and Andersen execs shouldn't have needed a letter and a phone call from Watkins to figure out something was seriously amiss. Red flags abounded. And Watkins, for one, had no trouble putting her finger on questionable accounting practices. She wondered if Enron was hiding losses in off-balance-sheet entities while booking large profits from the deals. At the same time, the outside partnerships were backed with Enron stock—a tactic sure to backfire when it was falling—and no outsiders seemed to have any capital at risk. Was Enron creating income essentially by doing deals with itself? "It sure looks to the layman on the street that we are hiding losses in a related company and will compensate that company with Enron stock in the future," she wrote.

In the end, Watkins grasped one thing that Enron's too-clever-by-half dealmakers didn't: Enron's maneuvering didn't pass the smell test. Even if Enron and its high-priced auditors and lawyers can ultimately show that they followed the letter of the law, it matters little. As Watkins herself wrote, if Enron collapses, "the business world will consider the past successes as nothing but an elaborate accounting hoax." And that seems destined to become Enron's epitaph.

Chapter Three

———•———

Pollution and Environment

THE ESKIMO AND some subcultures in India regard pollution as a philosophical concept. For such persons, to pollute is to injure the harmony that exists between people and nature. Hence, one should avoid polluting not only the physical environment but also one's social environment. In western Europe and the United States, we have tended to view pollution more narrowly. We have defined it largely in a physical manner, referring primarily to air pollution, water pollution, radiation pollution, waste-disposal pollution, and noise pollution. For our present purposes, we shall define *pollution* as "the presence in the environment of a substance produced by human beings that renders the environment less fit for life."

Concern about pollution mushroomed during the 1960s with the appearance of such books as Rachel Carson's *Silent Spring*, a chilling forecast of the destruction that pesticides such as DDT could bring to bird and animal populations. During the 1960s, not only were DDT and other pesticides restricted by congressional legislation, but broad regulatory mechanisms were also established under such acts as the Clean Air Act and the Clean Water Act. Unfortunately, for Congress to put legal teeth into its legislation sufficient to force business into compliance, these acts were forced to wait until the early 1970s and the passage of the Clean Air Amendments Act and the Clean Water Amendments Act.

An economic concept crucial to an understanding of pollution issues is that of *external cost*. Economists define external costs as "costs of production borne by someone other than the producer."

Under this definition, the production of steel would involve both external and internal costs. Producing steel requires iron ore, coal, and skilled labor. These are all internal costs, since they are borne directly by the producer. But steel production also typically involves the discharge of pollutants such as sulfur dioxide and sulfur trioxide into the atmosphere, and such pollutants are notorious for defacing and weakening steel and marble structures. And since the structures damaged are typically not owned by the steelmaking firms themselves, these costs must be counted as external ones. From an ethical point of view then, the push is to make external costs internal. In other words, the push is either to require the steel company to compensate those who are harmed by the pollution, or—as is usually done—to require the company to pay for pollution-control devices sufficient to deter pollution damage.

Becoming clearer about pollution issues requires a healthy sense of realism. The goal of *zero discharge*—in other words, no pollution at all—is probably a dream. Pollution experts note that the cost of eliminating pollutants from a given production process is inversely and exponentially related to the percentage of pollution remaining. That is, as the manufacturer spends money to control pollution, the first 50 percent of the pollution is relatively inexpensive to eliminate; but eliminating each remaining percentage point of pollution is dramatically more expensive. Indeed, for many production processes, eliminating 100 percent of the pollution is infinitely expensive or, practically speaking, impossible.

Although as a nation and a world we are more aware of the issue and dangers of pollution then we were when the first edition of this text was published (1984), the dire effects and consequences of pollution seem to be escalating rather than receding. Problems regarding endangered species of animals, the waste of precious resources, the growing accumulation of garbage and toxic waste, deforestation, the loss of plant life, and the growing pollution of fresh and salt water continue to proliferate at a pace and rate that could endanger all forms of life on earth. The essay "Shades of Green: Business, Ethics, and the Environment" lays out many of the problems and many of the tough questions posed by pollution. It also challenges us to think about business, ethics, and the environment as different parts of the same puzzle rather than as three separate problems that can and should be addressed separately. "Save the Turtles" is a case about the decimation and possible extinction of six species of sea turtles that have existed since the time of the dinosaurs. This case raises the questions: "Do these turtles, and by extension most if not all animals, have a right to exist for their own sake?" "Should we create and enforce laws that protect this value as well as provide specific animals a haven from extinction?"

Some of the cases in this section focus on the extent to which corporations must exercise internal moral responsibility in addition to simply following laws regarding environmental use. The "Texaco in the Ecuadorean Amazon" case also deals with the problem of trade-offs between pollution and economic survival. Ecuador possesses lush rain forests and rich oil reserves, but it can't have one without hurting the other. "The Hazards of the Enterprise" case is purely fictional. But sometimes fiction highlights the facts of an issue better than the actual facts. Finally, "Edible Carpets, Anyone!?" examines the short- and long-term consequences of chemically polluting our environment and our bodies in the pursuit of products that supposedly constitute the "good life."

Essay

Shades of Green: Business, Ethics, and the Environment

R. Edward Freeman, Jessica Pierce, Richard Dodd

THE CHALLENGE OF BUSINESS LEADERSHIP TODAY

It is possible for business leaders to make money, do the right thing, and participate in saving the earth. It is possible to fit these ideas together, but it is not easy. We have to warn you here and now that we don't have any quick solutions, magic bullets, or foolproof formulas for success. The issues are too difficult and messy for any such nonsense. Instead we are going to suggest how to begin to understand the concepts of business, ethics, and the environment so that they can work together.

This is an exercise about possibilities. Instead of showing the myriad ways that business, ethics, and the environment conflict and lead to impossible choices, we are going to ask the question. "How is it possible to put these ideas together?"[1] In today's world and the one we are creating for our children, all three are necessary. Our businesses must continue to create value for their financiers and other stakeholders. In an interconnected global economy, we can no longer afford the ethical excesses that many see as characteristic of the last several decades. And, if we are to leave a livable world for our children and their children, we simply must pay attention to environmental matters.

Most of the methods, concepts, ideas, theories, and techniques that we use in business do not put business, ethics, and the environment together. From discounted cash flow to human resources planning, neither ethics nor the environment are central to the way we think about business.

Everyone shares the joke about the very idea of "business ethics" as an oxymoron, two words whose definitions are contradictory. Much of business language is oriented toward seeing a conflict between business and ethics. We routinely juxtapose profits with ethics, as if making an ethical decision costs profits.[2] We sometimes qualify difficult choices that distribute harms and benefits to communities and employees as "business decisions," signaling that business and ethics are not compatible.[3]

The environment fares no better. It is seen as a necessary evil, a cost to be minimized or a regulation with which to comply. We almost never think about the environment as central to the main metaphors of business, its strategic and people management systems, unless, of course, there is some regulation that constrains business strategy, a mess to be cleaned up or a public issue that pits executives against environmentalists. Historically, business people have been neither encouraged nor discouraged to get involved with environmental concerns. Our models and theories of business have traditionally been simply *silent* on the subject of the environment. The world of the 1990s, however, is beginning to make a great deal of noise.

More and more citizens see themselves as environmentalists. Governments are increasing their cooperative actions to address global environmental concerns such as global warming and biodiversity. And interest groups are beginning to propose solutions to problems that involve business decision-making outside of and beyond government regulation.

So, what we desperately need are some new ideas, concepts, and theories that allow us to think about business, ethics, and the environment in one full breath. We need to see these issues as going together rather than in conflict. Today's challenge to business leadership is sustaining profitability, doing the right thing, and being green.

THE ENVIRONMENT: IT'S EVERYWHERE

Early on the morning of March 24, 1989, the super tanker Exxon *Valdez* ran aground on Bligh Reef in Prince William Sound off the coast of Alaska. In the days following the accident, every action or inaction by Exxon executives, government officials and environmentalists was subjected to an unprecedented public scrutiny.

In addition to the damage caused by the release of millions of gallons of oil into the ecosystem, the *Valdez* incident symbolizes an important milestone in business history. The environment is an issue that has come to stay. It is not a fad, passing fancy, or the issue of the day.

There is not a single aspect of our world today that can escape the scrutiny of environmental analysis. Pollution of air, water, and land; the production and disposal of hazardous wastes; solid waste disposal; chemical and nuclear spills and accidents; global warming and the greenhouse effect; ozone depletion; deforestation and desertification; biodiversity; and overpopulation are a few of the issues that today's executive needs to understand to be environmentally literate.

We are treated to daily doom and gloom press reports about the state of the earth. Scientists have "discovered" that global warming is or is not a problem, is or is not caused by solar storms, is or is not related to the emission of greenhouse gases, and so forth. We want to know the answer, the whole truth, "just the facts," about the environment, and we get disturbed by so many conflicting reports.

The truth is this: there is no one truth about the environment. The truth is also this: we have not lived in a way that respects the environment and preserves it for our children's children.

OUR CHILDREN'S FUTURE: A WAGER

Let's assume an optimistic scenario that implies that the gloomy forecasts are all wrong. Maybe there is enough land for landfills for generations to come. Global warming may be elusive. Many chemicals may well be harmless. The destruction of forests may be insignificant and worth the benefits of development. Clean and healthful water may someday be plentiful. And it may be that we can invent the technology we need to compensate for whatever damage we actually have done to the earth.

Are you willing to bet the future of your children on this optimistic scenario? If it is wrong, or even partially wrong, with respect to, say, global warming, then there will be no inhabitable world left for our children. Like Pascal's Wager,[4] we are going to assume that it is reasonable to bet that there is, in fact, an environmental crisis. The consequences of being wrong are too great to bet otherwise.

Yet the great majority of responses to the environmental crisis have been at best ineffective. The main response mode has been to marshal the public policy process to legislate that the air and water be cleaner, and to assign the costs of doing so to states, localities, and businesses. Twenty plus years of environmental regulation in the United States has led to "environmental gridlock." There is disagreement and contention at several important levels.

First of all, as we stated earlier, there isn't any one truth about the state of the environment. Many (but not all) individual scientific "facts" are disputable. There is widespread disagreement about the scientific answers to environmental questions, even about how the questions should be stated.

Second, among those who agree about the science around a particular issue, there is still disagreement about the appropriate public policy. Even if we agree that greenhouse gases lead to global warming, we may well disagree that limiting carbon dioxide emissions to 1990 levels will solve the problem.

Third, there is disagreement about the underlying values. How should we live? By exploiting the earth's resources? By conserving the earth's resources? By living with nature? Should we be vegetarians to improve the ability of advanced societies to feed the hungry and use land efficiently? Should we recycle or should we consume green products or should we build an ethic of "anti-consumption," of saving the earth rather than consuming it?

These three levels of disagreement lead to gridlock, especially in a public policy process that purports to base policy on facts rather than values. Overlay these three levels of disagreement on a litigious system of finding, blaming, and punishing polluters of the past and the result is a conversation about the environment that goes nowhere fast.

We believe that this public policy process needs to change, that we need to have a better conversation about the environment and the role of governments, but we are not willing to wait for these changes to take place. Instead we want to suggest another mode of response to the environmental crisis: business strategy. If we can come to see how business activity can take place, systematically, in environmentally friendly ways, then we can respond to the environmental crisis in lasting and effective ways.[5]

THE BASICS OF BUSINESS: WHAT DO YOU STAND FOR?

At the thousands of McDonald's franchises around the world one thing is the same: McDonald's values. "QVC" means Quality, Value, and Cleanliness, and the very idea of McDonald's is built around realizing these values. This is why at any McDonald's anywhere you get good quality, fast-food, a clean restaurant, and a good comparative price. The very meaning of McDonald's encompasses these values, and everyone, from CEO to fry cook, has to understand their job in terms of these values.

Strangely enough, a tiny company, only a fraction of the size of McDonald's works the same way. The company is called Johnsonville Sausage in Johnsonville and Sheboygan, Wisconsin. It is highly profitable, fast growing, and is based on different values from McDonald's. At Johnsonville Sausage the operating philosophy is self-improvement. The company exists in order for the individuals in it to realize their goals and to continue to improve themselves.

There is a revolution afoot in business today. And it is a revolution with values at its core. Sparked by Tom Peters and Bob Waterman's bestselling book, *In Search Of Excellence,* the rediscovery of Edward Demming's ideas on the productive workplace and the role of values and quality, and the countless programs for individual and organizational change that have been ignited by an increasingly competitive global marketplace, business today is turning to values.[6]

At one level, this emphasis on values cuts against the traditions of business. It has always been assumed that business promotes only one primary value—profits. Both the academic research and the how-to books on business are full of ideas on how to become more profitable. And profits are important as they are the lifeblood of business. But surely the purpose of life is not simply to breathe or to have our hearts go on beating. As important as these activities are, we humans are capable of more, of standing for some principles, or caring for others, or creating value for ourselves and others. Even those few people who care only for themselves still must be good enough citizens to avoid trampling on the rights and projects of others.

Organizations are no different. Profits are important, necessary—add any words you want—but there is more. Businesses can, and often do, stand for something more than profitability. Some, like IBM, stand for creating value for customers, employees, and shareholders. Others, like Merck, stand for the alleviation of human suffering. Still others, like Mesa Petroleum, may well stand for creating value for shareholders only, but even those companies must do so within the confines of the law and public expectations that could be turned into law.

This concern for values can be summarized in the idea of enterprise strategy, or asking the question, "What do you stand for?"

The typical strategy process in a company asks someone to think about these questions: (1) What businesses are we in? (2) What is our competitive advantage in these businesses? (3) How can we sustain competitive advantage? What product/market focus should we take? What needs to change in order to be successful?

Some set of these questions goes into every company architecture of its portfolio of businesses. Even small businesses have to have some business plan, perhaps in the mind of the entrepreneur, which articulates how that small business creates, captures, and sustains value.

But, if this values revolution in business is meaningful, there is a prior question, the question of enterprise strategy. "What do you stand for?" By articulating an answer to this question, thereby setting forth a statement of the core values of the organization, the strategy questions mentioned earlier will have some context in which they can be answered. For instance, if you stand for human dignity and some basic idea of human rights for all, then there are probably some markets that you will not serve, and some products and services that you will not provide. If you stand for quality, cleanliness, and value, then there are certain business opportunities that you will forego because you cannot produce the quality service, or do it in a clean environment, or provide it at a price that gives good value.

Now all of this may sound rather fanciful, but the basic point is that businesses have discovered that articulating some bedrock, some foundation, some basic values has enormous benefits. The business becomes focused around these values. People, from executives to mail clerks, begin to believe in them or are attracted to the firm because of these values. In short, business strategy just makes more sense in the context of values.

It is easy to see how thinking about the environment and about ethics are compatible with the values revolution. By clearly stating and understanding the core beliefs that an organization has or wants to adopt about ethical issues such as honesty, integrity, dignity of individuals, caring about others, and so on, policies that are straightforward and easily implementable can be designed. By clearly thinking through a position on the environment—whether it is just complying with the law or trying to leave the earth better than we found it—we can begin to marshal resources to realize these basic beliefs.

Executives can begin to meet the challenge of leadership we articulated earlier—being profitable, doing the right thing, and helping to save the earth—by understanding and articulating an enterprise strategy, an answer to the question, "What do we stand for?" From huge DuPont to little Ben and Jerry's, from oil and chemical companies to retail boutiques, articulating what you stand for on the environment is step one to a greener world, one that we can pass along to our children.

IT'S NOT EASY BEING GREEN

There are many ways that businesses can adopt strategies that are more friendly toward the environment. None of them are simple. In the words of that great philosopher, Kermit the Frog, "It's not easy being green."

We want to suggest that there are four primary "shades of green," and each has its own logic, and each has many interpretations. Let's call these shades: (1) light green; (2) market green; (3) stakeholder green; and (4) dark green. You can think of these shades as phases of development of a company's strategy, moving from light green to dark green, but keep in mind that each shade has its own logic. It isn't necessary to move from one shade to the next. And each shade offers its own way to create and sustain value, so that business, ethics, and the environment go together. Here's a brief thumbnail sketch of the logic of each shade of green.

Light Green, or Legal Green, is a shade with which most companies are familiar. Being Light Green involves complying with the following principle:

Light Green Principle

Create and sustain competitive advantage by ensuring that your company is in compliance with the law.

The logic of Light Green relies on the public policy process to drive its strategy. But, it is a mistake to think that no competitive advantage is possible for every company has to obey the law—a mistake on two counts.

First, as Michael Porter and his colleagues have argued, countries with strict environmental standards seem to gain an edge in global marketplaces—they become more efficient and have better technology. Secondly, within an industry, companies actively can pursue public policies that fit with their special competitive advantage. By innovating with technology and know-how, a company gains an advantage over a competitor who cannot comply as efficiently. Light Green thinking thus creates the possibility for competitive advantage.

Market Green logic is different. Rather than focus on the public policy process. Market Green logic focuses on customers. The following principle is at work:

Market Green Principle

Create and sustain competitive advantage by paying attention to the environmental preferences of customers.

Market Green strategies are based on the greening of the customer, a fast-growing yet controversial phenomenon. Today's customer-focused, market-driven company cannot afford to miss the fact that customers prefer environmentally friendly products—and without added costs. Again it is easy to see that creating and sustaining competitive ad-

vantage is a matter of "better, cheaper, faster." Companies that can meet these environmental needs will be the winners. Customer perceptions about the shade of green of the company will be crucial, but most importantly the products and services have to perform.

McDonald's decision to ban Styrofoam cartons was driven in part by customers' perceptions that polystyrene was bad for the environment. But if the new containers made from treated paper cannot be recycled or biodegraded, customer needs will not have been met, and someone else will produce a more environmentally friendly burger.

Market Green logic just applies good old-fashioned "smell the customer" thinking to the environment. Note that this may or may not be in conjunction with Legal Green. Market Green logic roots competitive advantage in customer needs and the ability of the customer-driven company to deliver on these needs. There is nothing unusual except giving up the costly belief that environmentally friendly products always entail higher costs and competitive disadvantages. Notice that Market Green logic can apply to the industrial sector as well as the consumer sector and to services as well as products.

Stakeholder Green is a shade darker than Market Green. It applies Market Green logic to key stakeholder groups such as customers, suppliers, employees, communities, shareholders, and other financiers. There are many different ways to slice the stakeholder pie. Companies can seek to maximize the benefits of one group, or they can seek to harmonize the interests of all groups. The point is that Stakeholder Green gets its color from responding to the needs of some or all stakeholder groups. It obeys the following principle:

Stakeholder Green Principle

Create and sustain competitive advantage by responding to the environmental preferences of stakeholders.

Stakeholder Green strategies are based on a more thoroughgoing adoption of environmental principles among all aspects of a company's operations. Many companies have adopted a version of Stakeholder Green by requiring suppliers to meet environmental requirements and by setting strict standards for the manufacturing process. Paying attention to recyclable material in consumer packaging, educating employees on environmental issues, participating in community efforts to clean up the environment, and appealing to investors who want to invest in green companies are all a part of Stakeholder Green. This shade is different because it does not require one action or a focused set of actions; rather, it requires anticipating and responding to a whole set of issues regarding the environment. As such it is more complicated than the earlier shades. The logic of Stakeholder Green is similar to the logic of quality processes. Unless quality processes permeate a company at all levels, they are doomed to fail. There are different levels of commitment to Stakeholder Green, just as there are different levels of commitment to quality, but any effective commitment must be pervasive.

Dark Green is a shade for which few companies strive. Being Dark Green commits a company to being a leader in making environmental principles a fundamental basis for doing business. Dark Green suggests the following principle:

Dark Green Principle

Create and sustain value in a way that sustains and cares for the earth.

To most business people this principle will sound pretty idealistic or fanciful. Their skepticism only points out how much we have ignored the environment in our ways of thinking about business. Indigenous people know that this principle must be obeyed. We teach our children to care for their things and the things—such as our homes and land—that we

share. It is not a large stretch of the imagination to expect that the same values are possible in business.

Dark Green logic is not antibusiness, though many people will believe it is. Humans create value for each other, and *business* is the name we have given that process. Dark Green logic just says that we must respect and care for the earth in this process of value creation.

There are more than four shades of green. Look at these four as anchors that can define what is possible for your company. Dark Green is not for everyone, while Light Green may be more universal. Indeed Dark Green raises more questions than it answers. It reminds us that the very idea of "living with the earth" or "treating the earth with respect" are difficult issues that bring forth deep philosophical questions.

Our argument is not that we should find the optimal shade for everyone, but that variation is good. That is, imagine a world in which there are thousands of enterprises each trying to realize competitive advantage through environmental means. Undoubtedly, many of these innovations will fail, but some will succeed, and many will lead to other, more important innovations. It is only through a large-scale process of many small innovations that real, lasting change can occur. Perhaps while such innovation is emerging, someone, somewhere, will invent a revolutionary "pollution machine" that will cure all of our environmental ills, or some official will "discover" the perfect set of regulations. All well and good if that happens, but we are suggesting a more modest and, we believe, more workable approach.

TOUGH QUESTIONS

Ultimately how we run our companies reflects our commitment to how we want to live. Our values are lived through our behavior. Someone who espouses green values but who does nothing to realize those values lives in bad faith or self-deception. Bad faith means that we say one thing and do another, and self-deception means we are not honest with ourselves about what we truly believe and how we really want to live. Ethics, in life and in business, starts with an assumption of good faith and self-awareness, or at least an acknowledgment of the difficulties involved in being authentic to our true beliefs.

Nowhere do we see these issues more plainly than in environmental values. Talk is cheap, and its price is related to a shared history and culture of not living in a way that guarantees our children a future. We believe there are many ways to live—indeed many ways to live in an environmentally sustainable way—but we also know that our values have not always led us in any sustainable direction.

The point is that we do depend on the natural world and, especially today, the natural world depends on us for its survival. Humans have the capability to destroy life on earth, and such a capability implies a responsibility to live ethically. We argue that any shade of green that you adopt raises important questions about our responsibility to live ethically. We explore three of these philosophical challenges here. Briefly they are conservation, social justice, and ecology.

The conservation challenge tells us to conserve the earth's resources for the future and is a minimal response to Our Children's Future Wager.

The social justice challenge tells us that there are many ways to improve the institutions that we have created. It focuses on those who have been mistreated by those institutions—women, minorities, indigenous people—and traces a connection between their mistreatment and the way we view the environment.

The ecological challenge comes in many forms, but it asks us to view the Earth as a living organism and to find a way to talk about the Earth and its creatures in our human-centered moral discourse. We should live in a way that is sustainable and self-renewing, rather than destructive of current resources.

Each of these three philosophies challenges our ways of doing business. It is easiest to integrate conservation with the normal ways we think about business, but we argue that what is necessary to meet. Our Children's Future is a conversation that takes all three philosophies into account. We need to understand how we redefine business and make it consistent with each of these three views.

BARRIERS TO A GREEN CONVERSATION

If we are going to explore how we can rethink business along an environmental dimension, and if the outcome of this conversation is to be not one but many different ways of creating and sustaining value, then we must be on the lookout for barriers that will prevent us from engaging the tough issues. We believe that most of these barriers are our own inabilities to entertain new ideas: our mind-sets. We have identified five mind-sets that all say that our project, the integration of business, ethics, and the environment into new modes of thinking, is impossible.

The Regulatory Mind-set

This mind-set sees the environment as a part of the business-government relationship to be spelled out in terms of regulation or public policy. The Regulatory Mind-set says that the best way to take care of the environment is through the public policy process that produces laws and rules with which business must comply. It discounts the possibility and the wisdom of voluntary initiatives that stem from deeply held environmental values, or even the desire to respond to environmental preferences. While the recent history of concern with the environment has usually meant the passage of laws and their attendant regulations, the debate today goes far beyond a regulatory mind-set. Regulation lags the real world, and regulation inevitably entails unforeseen consequences. Our question for the Regulatory Mind-set is: Are you confident that government, as it currently works, will create a sustainable future for your children?

The Cost/Benefit Mind-set

The Cost/Benefit Mind-set is sometimes closely related to the Regulatory Mind-set simply because many regulatory regimes use cost/benefit methods to determine "proper" regulations. The Cost/Benefit Mind-set says that cleaning up the environment or making products and services more environmentally friendly has costs and benefits. And we should go only so far as the benefits outweighing the costs.

There are several problems with this view. The first is that if you focus on costs and benefits, you will fail to use "innovation." The argument is similar to the quality approach. By focusing on the cost of quality, managers make wrong decisions. Instead by focusing on quality processes that involve extraordinary customer service or stretch goals such as zero defects, human innovation takes over and drives quality up and costs down. The Cost/Benefit Mind-set says that there is a contradiction between "environmentally friendly" and costs. Many companies are discovering that by adopting one or more of the shades of green that we recommend here, they are making money and becoming more environmentally friendly. By focusing on costs and benefits, managers inevitably are led to ask the wrong questions.

The second problem with the Cost/Benefit Mind-set is that it assumes one particular set of underlying values: economic ones. Many environmentalists, executives, and other thinkers have questioned the priority of our current ways of thinking about economics. All value is not economic value, and anyone who believes that it is, is trying to get us to live in a certain way. Does the last gorilla have just an economic value? What about the beauty of the Grand Tetons? What about the futures of our children? Human life is rich and complex and is not reducible solely to an economic calculation. It is degrading to all of us to think that we only value people and things in economic terms.

The Constraint Mind-set

Still, many will argue that the main purpose of business is to create and sustain economic value, and everything else from ethics to the environment to meaningful work is best viewed as a side constraint. The business of business is business. Anything else should be viewed as not the main objective of business.

There is a nugget of truth here, like there is in all of these prevalent mind-sets. Economic value has been the main focus of business, and other kinds of value have been seen as constraining a kind of unfettered capitalism, driven by the urge to win, succeed, and compete. A more thoughtful analysis of economic value creation, however, shows that it is impossible to separate out economic, political, social, and personal aspects of value. When the employees of Delta buy a jet for the company, when Johnson & Johnson recalls Tylenol, when Body Shop employees volunteer to help the homeless, when Mattel donates money to the part of Los Angeles destroyed by riots, all of these actions imply it is possible for a company to be driven by economics and by ethics. No one is arguing that economics is unimportant, but we are insisting that the reduction of all human value creation and value sustaining activity to economic measures misses the mark. Business does more, as Adam Smith realized, and to reduce capitalism to economics endangers our free society.[7]

The Sustainable Development Mind-set

It may seem strange to lump what is supposed to be a way to save the earth with mind-sets that prevent environmental progress. Obviously not all discussions of sustainable development act as barriers, but one recent discussion simply misses the mark. The Brundtland Report, the basis of the Rio Earth Summit in 1992, called on governments to redefine economic activity to become sustainable. The problem with this view is that it calls on governments to have an intrusive role in the process of value creation, and if we have learned anything from the collapse of state socialism, it is that governments and centralized approaches do not work very well. Ultimately, a worldwide regime of environmental cooperation could become a worldwide hegemony of democratic freedom, especially if combined with the other mind-sets. Decisions on the future of whole industries and companies could become a matter just of government's beliefs about what is sustainable.

Recall our view, that there is no one truth about the environment. We believe that it is necessary to adopt a radically decentralized approach, which focuses on shared values, and a conversation about those shared values. If such an approach is not viable, then we should see the heavy hand of the state as part and parcel of our failure to integrate business, ethics, and the environment.

The Greenwashing Mind-set

The Greenwashing Mind-set pervades many discussions of the environment. Characteristic of it is the view that business could never act on values other than profit maximization. And whenever we see a company engaged in something that looks like it might be good for the environment, we should be deeply skeptical. Really, if truth be told, the company is probably trying to make money, or avoid some future cost, or engage in other narrowly self-interested schemes. Many environmental programs at companies are, on this view, cleverly disguised attempts to be seen as green, while really continuing in an environmentally destructive mode.

Many times when we have presented these ideas to groups that contained people who were deeply committed to environmental values but had little real contact with the inner workings of business, there has been an assumption that "business is bad."[8]

Surely, there are attempts to greenwash—portray trivial changes to products, services, and processes in grand and glorious environmental terms. And we should look carefully at such claims. However, the assumption that therefore all business attempts at environmental action are suspect simply does not follow.

We want to suggest that we be skeptical of all grand environmental claims, whether they be from business, government, environmental groups, or scientists. The arena is very uncertain and complex, and the Greenwashing Mind-set makes our task impossible, so we shall set this mind-set aside. Of course, businesses want to make money, but it doesn't follow that the environment must be left out of the equation, or that profit is the only value that counts.

SUMMARY

We have chosen a difficult project—we want to engage you in a conversation about how to think about business, ethics, and the environment together rather than separately. We are optimistic that the fruits of such a conversation can make a difference, to us and to our children. If you are confident that your children have a safe and secure future then you don't need to wrestle with the questions that this conversation raises, and you don't need to examine your values and behavior to see if there needs to be change, but we do not share your confidence.

We do not have confidence that the future is secure, nor do we have confidence that our current institutions, as well meaning as they may be, are doing all that is necessary. We are confident that if we can begin to think about business in environmentally sound ways, we can make real progress.

NOTES

1. We have no doubt that there can be and indeed are multiple conflicts. These conflicts are a result of the conceptual schemes we've brought to bear on these issues. Our argument is that we need a new conceptual scheme, one that considers the possibility that these ideas can fit together.
2. That many see "ethics" and "profits" as contradictory is evident from the reading of a great deal of the literature on business theory and business ethics.
3. Of course, these "business decisions" are moral in nature. They distribute harms and benefits to other stakeholders, usually shareholders.
4. Philosopher Blaise Pascal proposed the following wager in the seventeenth century: Suppose Christianity is correct. If you are not a believer you are in for a seriously hot eternity in Hell. So, it is rational to believe in Christianity or to act as if it is correct. Now, Pascal's Wager doesn't work in its original form because it is a tenet of both Christianity and liberalism that individuals can decide for themselves whether to mortgage their own future in eternity for a few temporal moments of pleasure during life on earth. Our Children's Wager doesn't suffer from the same logical defect because the point is that our children will not get to make those choices if we do not begin to live differently. We have used *children* in the sense of future generations, which include, but are not limited to, existing children.
5. Our approach is radical—at least for business theorists and environmentalists. Most writing about the environment acts as if business is evil, and most writing on business acts as if business is separate from the environment. We want to stake out some new territory.
6. Note that this shift to values is not always in moral terms, even though Freeman and Gilbert argue that it should be. Many executives see these values as instrumental, leading to profits.
7. Adam Smith was primarily concerned about justice.
8. For a more careful analysis of this idea, see R. Edward Freeman, "The Business Sucks Story," The Darden School Working Papers (Charlottesville, VA: University of Virginia, 1996).

Case Study

Save the Turtles

Rogene A. Buchholz

The Endangered Species Act was originally passed in 1973 to protect animal species threatened with extinction. It marked the first time a law had been passed in the United States that recognized that animals have a right to exist for their own sake, and that animals must be protected both from human beings and from projects that threaten their existence. The law was based in part on the notion that animals have an intrinsic value apart from their value for human welfare. As such, a law was needed to protect this value as well as give animals a haven from extinction. Since the law's passage, various animals have been placed on the endangered list when their species have become threatened for one reason or another.[1]

Since 1978 all six species of sea turtles found in U.S. waters have been labeled threatened and have been placed on the endangered list to protect them from further decimation. Sea turtles are powerful and imposing creatures that evolved about the time of the dinosaurs. They are fascinating in their own right, and some people are loath to see them disappear. Turtle populations in North America have declined in recent years due to the development of beaches where they breed; butchery of nesting females and theft of eggs from their nests; oil slicks; eating plastic garbage; and nets used to catch fish and shellfish.[2]

The Kemp Ridley sea turtle nests only on one beach—near Rancho Nuevo, Mexico— and is one of the world's most threatened species of sea turtles. The Kemp Ridley's population has declined from 40,000 nesting females a day in the late 1940s to 10,000 in 1960 to little more than 500 in the 1980s. The decline continues at an annual rate of about 3 percent. Their nesting beach is now protected by a detachment of Mexican marines who guard the site against poachers. Shrimp nets are the major suspect in their continuing decline. According to some estimates, approximately 48,000 sea turtles are caught each year on shrimp trawlers in the southeast, and about 11,000 of these turtles die because of drowning, since they must come to the surface every hour or so to breathe. About 10,000 of the turtles that die are Loggerheads, and 750 are Kemp Ridleys.[3]

The Kemp Ridley has a diameter of about 32 inches and may weigh as much as 85 pounds. The breeding season starts in early April and lasts through the first week of September. During this period biologists from the United States and Mexico, together with a contingent of volunteers from both countries, work at the Rancho Nuevo site to improve the turtles' reproduction rate. After a female turtle digs her nest in the sand and lays her 100 or so eggs, she leaves the scene and heads out to sea the moment her clutch has been buried. When left unguarded, the nest may be victimized by predators. To protect the eggs, volunteers transfer them to nests in a nearby corral guarded by the marines.[4]

The shrimping industry disputes government figures showing a close correlation between the number of dead turtles found on beaches and the number of trawlers working in the vicinity. While any one boat may not catch many turtles, the cumulative impact of approximately 7,000 offshore commercial vessels towing 4 to 5 million hours per year can be serious. Shrimpers claim dead turtles are mostly victims of pollution or disease rather than shrimpers' nets. There is evidence supporting both points of view, but there is no doubt that shrimpers are killing a number of turtles along with other nonshrimp organisms. For every pound of shrimp caught, 9 pounds of fish, such as juvenile trout, redfish, whiting, and flounder, are dumped dead over the side of the boat in what is called the by-catch.[5] The by-catch has become more of a problem as shrimping has increased.

Americans eat an average of 2.4 pounds of shrimp a year, making it the most popular seafood in the country. In 1988, 331 million pounds of shrimp, worth $506 million, were caught. The shrimping industry provides jobs for many people in the southeastern part of the United States. More than 30,000 commercial fishermen and their families rely on shrimp for their livelihood, and many more work in shoreside processing plants.[6] Many shrimpers are second and third generation, following in the paths of their fathers and grandfathers. As such, the industry has great social as well as economic value, and any threat to the industry is likely to be met with great resistance.[7]

THE SOLUTION

Such a threat appeared in the form of turtle excluder devices (TEDs), which act as trapdoors in the nets of the shrimpers. The TED is a panel of large-mesh webbing or a metal grid inserted into the funnel-shaped nets of the shrimpers. When these nets are dragged along the bottom of the ocean, shrimp and other small animals pass through the TED and into the narrow bag at the end of the funnel where the catch is collected. Sea turtles, sharks, and other marine species too large to get through the panel are deflected out the trapdoor. The problem is that some of the shrimp escape as well, as much as 20 percent or more of the catch, according to some estimates.[8]

Some fishermen call the TEDs a trawler elimination device. They claim the TEDs, which are about 3 feet in diameter, are dangerous, wasteful, expensive, and unnecessary, often lead to wholesale losses of catch. "Would you all like to go to work with a big hole in the back of your pants?" asked the wife of a Louisiana fisherman. "That's what they're asking us to do. We can't pull a TED." Many shrimpers simply refuse to use TEDs in spite of laws requiring their installation.[9]

Ironically, TEDs were developed to save the shrimp industry. Since the law requires that endangered species in the public domain be protected regardless of the cost, the industry was in danger of being totally shut down if environmental groups were to sue the industry or the federal government. To prevent a total shutdown, the National Marine Fisheries Service (NMFS) sought a technological solution. Between 1978 and 1981 the NMFS spent $3.4 million developing and testing the TED device. By 1981, the agency was promoting voluntary usage of the device and in 1983 began distributing free TEDs to further encourage shrimpers to use them. However, shrimpers rejected the TEDs, claiming they were difficult to use and lost a significant percentage of the shrimp catch.[10]

As more dead turtles washed ashore, environmental groups like Greenpeace and the Center for Marine Conservation demanded an end to the killing. Since the voluntary approach to TEDs had failed, the U.S. Fish and Wildlife Service mandated the use of TEDs, and the Center for Marine Conservation threatened to sue the NMFS and close down the industry completely. Industry representatives agreed to phase in use of TEDs, but rank-and-file fishermen rose up in rebellion. They vowed civil disobedience against what they saw as a threat to their survival, and filed lawsuit after lawsuit, which were all eventually lost in court.[11]

The fight then moved to Congress where the Endangered Species Act was up for renewal. It was hoped that Congress would not require the devices until a study was done to determine (1) whether the turtles to be protected were really endangered; (2) if so, whether the TEDs would protect them; and (3) whether there were better ways, such as increased use of hatcheries, to protect the sea turtle population.[12] After prolonged debate, amendments were passed in early fall 1988 that made the use of TEDs mandatory by May 1, 1989, but only in offshore waters, with the exception that regulations already in effect in the Canaveral, Florida, area remain in effect. Regulations for inshore areas were to go into effect by May 1, 1990, unless the secretary of commerce determined that other conservation measures were proving equally effective in reducing sea turtle mortality by shrimp trawling. Further testing was to be done on TEDs under inshore conditions, but until 1990, inshore turtles had virtually no protection.[13]

FURTHER CONTROVERSY

Disaster struck almost immediately after the amendments were passed. Record numbers of dead turtles began washing up on beaches from Georgia to New Smyrna Beach, Florida. From October to December 1980–1986, 32 Kemp Ridleys had washed ashore, but during these same months in 1988, 70 dead Kemp Ridleys washed ashore along with several other species of sea turtles. Altogether, 201 dead turtles were counted, and since there were 150 to 200 boats working in the area, shrimpers were again blamed.[14] In December 1988 environmentalists pressured the state of Florida into requiring emergency use of TEDs in state waters off Florida's northeast coasts. Florida's mandated use of TEDs was now set for an earlier date than required by the federal government.[15]

As the May 1 federal deadline for implementing TEDs drew closer, fishermen in Louisiana rallied to oppose installation of the device. Officials from across the South pledged to help stop TED legislation from being implemented. Governor Roemer of Louisiana said that state wildlife agents should boycott TED laws until studies showed conclusively that the device worked. Roemer said he would take his concerns to Washington, D.C., and tell George Bush to "read my lips."[16]

Louisiana congressional representatives persuaded the secretary of commerce, who was responsible for implementing TED regulations, to further delay their implementation. This would allow shrimpers additional time to buy and install the devices. Only warnings would be issued through the end of June while a National Academy of Sciences committee studied the issue.[17] However, shrimpers who were caught many times not pulling a TED would be branded flagrant abusers of the new law and could be held liable for civil penalties of up to $12,000 per violation.[18] When the warning period ended, penalties as high as $10,000 would go into effect and the catch confiscated. Criminal violators—those who repeatedly thumbed their noses at the law—could be convicted of a felony and fined $20,000 in addition to losing their catch. Emotions ran high in some Louisiana communities, and many shrimpers vowed to break the law by not pulling TEDs, and dared officials to haul them off to jail. Some vowed to shoot the man who tried to take away their living.[19]

In order to comply with the regulations, many shrimpers installed and tried to use the device. Then nature struck with the largest bloom of seaweed in several years, which clogged the excluder panels and prevented much of a shrimp catch from being taken. Shrimpers who had installed TEDs cut them out of their nets, and the Coast Guard temporarily suspended the regulations for Louisiana coastal waters. Representatives from the state hoped that the secretary of commerce would make the suspension permanent.[20]

Then the secretary of commerce, after initially telling the Coast Guard not to enforce the law, reversed himself. When the shrimpers heard this, they streamed into port to protest, blocking shipping channels in Galveston and Corpus Christi, Texas, as well as several Louisiana locations. The blockade in Galveston halted all ship and ferry traffic, although by midafternoon the shrimpers agreed to let ferries pass through the blockade. The blockade threatened to shut down Houston's oil refineries. There was some violence. An Alabama man was arrested after firing a semiautomatic rifle from his boat in Galveston, and two men were arrested in Corpus Christi for throwing an object through a window of a 41-foot Coast Guard patrol boat. Angry fishermen set fire to a huge pile of TEDs on shore.[21]

The secretary of commerce then announced that he was suspending the use of TEDs until the National Academy of Sciences completed its study. Environmental groups filed suit, claiming that the secretary had caved in to terrorism and had put the Bush administration on a collision course with the Endangered Species Act. Robert E. McManus, president of the Center for Marine Conservation, said the secretary of commerce's decision "is a capitulation to organized violence, assaults against government and private property and individuals, and legitimizes organized efforts by a minority of shrimpers to promote illegal activity."[22]

Meanwhile, researchers for the National Marine Fisheries Service released the results of their research, which showed that nets equipped with TEDs resulted in only a 2 to 5 percent reduction in the shrimp catch. These results were at considerable variance with the 20 to 50 percent loss claimed by shrimpers. The results were based on 1,555 hours of trawling off the coast of Louisiana, which produced 12,185 pounds of shrimp in nets equipped with TEDs and 12,391 pounds of shrimp in nonequipped nets. Shrimpers accused the researchers of fudging their data to keep sea turtle research money flowing into their organization.[23]

Experts on the use of TEDs defended their results and accused the shrimpers of refusing to learn how to use the devices correctly. They argued that if TEDs were installed properly the shrimp catch could even be increased. But shrimpers, as victims of a depressed economy that resulted in an increase in the number of competing boats thus contributing to stagnant prices, believed they were fighting for their lives. TEDs were seen as the deathblow to a dying industry, and research data regarding the use of TEDs were rejected. With such a hardened position, nothing short of a court-ordered settlement seemed likely to resolve the issue.[24]

With respect to the lawsuit filed by environmental groups, a federal judge refused to immediately force offshore shrimpers to use TEDs, but directed the secretary of commerce to enforce some immediate turtle protection until he ruled on the TEDs issue. The judge stated that the secretary of commerce's decision to suspend the use of TEDs left sea turtles totally unprotected, but it was not the court's responsibility to determine what protection was appropriate. The secretary then published regulations that required shrimpers to limit their tows to 105 minutes so that any sea turtles caught would not drown. Environmental groups were unhappy with these results, and said they would appeal the judge's decision, arguing that restricting tow times is not nearly as effective in protecting the turtles as TEDs.

They claimed that turtles could not survive even 90 minutes underwater.[25]

In order to enforce the trawl limits, the secretary of commerce planned to embargo shrimping altogether for 30 minutes after each 105-minute period. The normal trawl times for shrimpers ranged between 2 and 6 hours. Shrimping would be banned for 11 half-hour periods during a 24-hour day. This fixed routine would allow Coast Guard officials to spot violators. Fishermen who pulled TEDs, however, would not have to adhere to this schedule.[26]

After the Coast Guard reported that 88 percent of the shrimp fleet was not complying with the shorter tow times, the secretary withdrew the limited tow times and required TEDs to be installed once again.[27] The new regulations were to go into effect Friday, September 8, 1989, but until September 22 violators would not be fined if they immediately installed a TED upon being caught. Violators caught between September 22 and October 15 would be eligible for reduced fines if they purchased and installed TEDs; otherwise, the fines ranged between $8,000 and $20,000 depending on the circumstances. Agents of the federal government could also confiscate both the boats and their catch.[28]

When President Bush visited New Orleans in September 1989 to address the U.S. Hispanic Chamber of Commerce and the National Baptist Convention, shrimpers and their families lined his motorcade route protesting the use of TEDs, and more than 50 shrimpers blocked nearby waterways. Instead of confronting the shrimpers, the Coast Guard issued citations that could have amounted to $55,000 per vessel. Shrimpers, who sealed off Belle Pass in Lafourche Parish and the Intracoastal Waterway near Intercoastal City, were cited under two little-used maritime laws. Many shrimpers were cited for one count of anchoring in and blocking a narrow channel and two counts of violating a safety zone as designated by a port captain.[29]

Shrimpers then protested an editorial that appeared in the *Times-Picayune* under the headline "Shrimpers as Scofflaws." The protest took place outside the newspaper's main offices in downtown New Orleans. The shrimpers resented being compared to outlaws and wanted the newspaper to listen to their side.[30] The president of Concerned Shrimpers of America then said his group might sue the federal government for cash compensation for losses caused by being forced to use TEDs. Comparisons were made with ranchers who are subsidized by the federal government if endangered animals feed on their cattle. These payments are designed to stop ranchers from killing the endangered species.[31]

To protect shrimpers from an unfair competitive advantage given to countries that did not require the use of TEDs or other actions to protect endangered sea turtles, Congress considered a law barring these cheaper imports. Even though imports constitute 80 percent of shrimp consumption in this country, the law was not expected to have much of an impact. Most of the shrimp imported into the United States are produced by an aquaculture industry that relies on shrimp farming. China and Ecuador, for example, each of which accounts for about 104 million pounds of shrimp imports, run aquaculture industries. The import provision was inserted into a spending bill by U.S. Senators J. Bennett Johnston and John Breaux, both from Louisiana. The measure ordered the state department to negotiate agreements with countries that do not protect sea turtles to institute similar turtle protection measures to those found in the United States.[32]

In February 1990 shrimpers sued the federal government again, saying TED laws placed an unconstitutional burden on their businesses. The suit was filed in federal court in Corpus Christi, Texas, and sought immediate suspension of the regulations requiring the use of TEDs for offshore shrimpers. Attorney Robert Ketchand, who filed the suit on behalf of the Concerned Shrimpers of America,

called the TED laws "regulatory taking" of shrimpers' profits.[33]

The controversy had now come full circle, with the shrimpers pursuing the cause through the courts as they did before the amendments to the Endangered Species Act were passed. Nothing yet has been resolved, and a solution to the problem seems nowhere in sight.

1. Is there a technological solution to this problem, or is the nature of the controversy so political at this point that the parties to the controversy have ceased to believe a technological solution exists? If so, what kind of a political solution will work to resolve the controversy?

2. Should the fishermen be paid compensation for the losses they claim because of using TEDs? How should these losses be determined? Who should pay for the protection of endangered species? What is a fair resolution of this issue?

3. Is the on-again nature of the regulations a serious problem? Was the secretary of commerce right in suspending TED regulations when shrimpers blockaded ports along the Gulf Coast? What else could have been done at this point?

4. What should be done now? Is our system structured in such a way that it can resolve conflicts of this nature? What makes this conflict different from others that seem to get resolved without resort to violence or stonewalling tactics that drag on forever?

NOTES

1. Roderick Frazier Nash, *The Rights of Nature: A History of Environmental Ethics* (Madison: University of Wisconsin Press, 1989), pp. 175–179.

2. Jack and Anne Rudlow, "Shrimpers and Lawmakers Collide over a Move to Save the Sea Turtles," *Smithsonian*, December 1989. p. 47.

3. Ibid.

4. "TEDs Couldn't Keep Gilbert from Attacking Turtle's Beach," *Times-Picayune* (New Orleans), September 20, 1988, p. A-4.

5. Rudlow, "Shrimpers and Lawmakers Collide," p. 49.

6. Ibid., p. 47.

7. Ibid., p. 49.

8. Ibid., p. 45.

9. Christopher Cooper, "La. Shrimpers Get Break on TEDs," *Times-Picayune* (New Orleans), July 11, 1989, p. B-1.

10. Rudlow, "Shrimpers and Lawmakers Collide," p. 50.

11. Ibid.

12. Susan Finch, "Congress May Delay TEDs Date," *Times-Picayune* (New Orleans), July 16, 1988, p. A-13.

13. Endangered Species Act Amendments of 1988, Conference Report 100-928 to Accompany H.R. 1467, House of Representatives, 100th Congress, 2d Session, p. 5.

14. Rudlow, "Shrimpers and Lawmakers Collide," pp. 50–51.

15. Ibid., pp. 52–53.

16. Christopher Cooper, "Shrimpers Vow to Defy Law on TEDs," *Times-Picayune* (New Orleans), April 9, 1989, p. B-1.

17. Rudlow, "Shrimpers and Lawmakers Collide," pp. 52–53.

18. Christopher Cooper, "TED Honeymoon May Be a Short One," *Times-Picayune* (New Orleans), May 6, 1989, p. B-2.

19. Christopher Cooper, "Furious Shrimpers Flouting TEDs Law," *Times-Picayune* (New Orleans), July 9, 1989, p. B-1.

20. Cooper, "La. Shrimpers Get Break on TEDs." p. B-1.

21. Christopher Cooper, "Shrimpers' TEDs Protest Turns Violent," *Times-Picayune* (New Orleans), July 23, 1989, p. A-1.

22. Christopher Cooper, "Environmentalists Plan Legal Challenge of TEDs Suspension," *Times-Picayune* (New Orleans), July 26, 1989, p. B-1.

23. James O'Byrne, "Research Disputes Shrimpers' Claims," *Times-Picayune* (New Orleans), July 27, 1989, p. A-1.

24. Ibid.

25. Rick Raber and Christopher Cooper, "Judge Refuses to Force Shrimpers to Use TEDs," *Times-Picayune* (New Orleans), August 4, 1989, p. A-1.

26. Christopher Cooper, "Trawling Schedules Start for Shrimpers," *Times-Picayune* (New Orleans), August 8, 1989, p. A-1.

27. Rudlow, "Shrimpers and Lawmakers Collide," p. 55.

28. Christopher Cooper, "Commerce Department Reinstates TED Regulation," *Times-Picayune* (New Orleans), September 6, 1989, p. A-1.

29. Christopher Cooper, "555,000 Fines Are Urged for TEDs Blockage," *Times-Picayune* (New Orleans), September 13, 1989, p. B-1.

30. Christopher Cooper, "Shrimpers Picket Newspaper to Protest Blockade Editorial." *Times-Picayune* (New Orleans), September 22, 1989, p. B-5.

31. "Shrimpers May Sue U.S. for Losses," *Times-Picayune* (New Orleans), October 4, 1989, p. B-5.

32. Rick Raber, 'TED Provision OK'd for Shrimp Imports," *Times-Picayune* (New Orleans), October 21, 1989, p. A-4.

33. Christopher Cooper, "Shrimpers File Federal Suit against TEDs," *Times-Picayune* (New Orleans), February 22, 1990, p. B-1.

Case Study

Edible Carpets, Anyone!?
Interface Corporation, a Sustainable Business

Joe DesJardins
Janalle Aaron

The old cliché suggests that business ethics is, like jumbo shrimp and working vacations, an oxymoron. To that list, one might wish to add "industrial ecology." Yet if Interface Corporation, a Georgia-based carpeting manufacturer, has its way, industrial ecology will become the standard for twenty-first century manufacturing and the model for sustainable business.

The concept of industrial ecology requires manufacturing processes be designed to mimic biological processes. Since 1994, Interface has worked to transform its business operations to become a leader in industrial ecology. In the words of their Mission Statement:

Interface will become the first name in commercial and institutional interiors worldwide through its commitment to people, process, product, place and profits. We will strive to create an organization wherein all people are accorded unconditional respect and dignity: one that allows each person to continuously learn and develop. We will focus on product (which includes service) through constant emphasis on process quality and engineering, which we will combine with careful attention to our customers' needs so as always to deliver superior value to our customers, thereby maximizing all stakeholders' satisfaction. We will honor the places where we do business by endeavoring to become the first name in industrial ecology, a corporation that cherishes nature and restores the environment. Interface will lead by example and validate by results, including profits, leaving the world a better place than when we began, and we will be restorative through the power of our influence in the world."

But it was not always this way.

Interface was founded in 1973 when Ray Anderson, current chairman of the board, recognized a growing market for flexible floor coverings for office environments. Interface soon began manufacturing and distributing modular carpet tiles, essentially carpeting that can easily be installed and replaced in modular sections. Over the years the company has grown to its current status as the world's leading producer of soft-surfaced modular floor coverings. Through the years Interface has grown by over 50 acquisitions. Today, Interface is a global company with sales offices in over 100 countries, 26 factories, more than 7,000 employees, and annual sales in excess of $1.3 billion.

For more than two decades, Interface could rightly be described as a typical and responsible business. They were a good corporate citizen, treated their employees, customers, and suppliers well, and produced a quality product. Like most business, Interface believed that it was fulfilling its social responsibility simply by responding to consumer demand as reflected in the market and by obeying the law. It was, in short, doing all that society asked of it.

Carpet manufacturing, however, is not normally thought of as an environmentally commendable industry. Most carpeting is derived from petroleum, a non-renewable resource. Petroleum-based products are synthesized with fiberglass and PVC, two known carcinogens, to create the fibers used to manufacture carpeting. The carpeting is dyed, and the waste produced from this process can contain various toxins and heavy metals. Carpet manufacturing factories are heavy industrial producers of CO_2 emissions. Used carpeting, especially nylon-based products, is not recycled and therefore usually ends up in landfills. One estimate holds that carpeting products add nearly 10 million pounds to American landfills each day.[1] Interface estimates that over 5 billion pounds of its own carpeting now exists in landfills. This carpet waste is toxic and nonbiodegradable. Thus, for twenty-five years Interface was living up to normal standards of corporate social responsibility in a way that was environmentally dreadful.

The company's transformation from one that merely sold floor coverings while complying with social expectations to a leader in environmental responsibility was dramatic. Anderson states that

> For the first twenty-one years of Interface's existence. I never gave one thought to what we took from or did to the Earth, except to be sure we obeyed all laws and regulations. Frankly, I didn't have a vision, except "comply, comply, comply." I had heard statesmen advocate "sustainable development," but I had no idea what it meant.

The traditional standard of corporate social responsibility, a standard which asks business only to respond to consumer demand and obey the law, no longer seemed sufficient. Reflecting on this friction between ecological responsibility and compliance with the demands of the law and the marketplace. Anderson now believes that "In the future, people like me will go to jail."[2]

By all accounts Interface's dramatic transformation has been spearheaded by the personal commitment of Ray Anderson. As Anderson recounts the story, his own conversion began with a book on sustainable business. In 1994 he was invited to deliver a keynote address at a conference of Interface managers. The conference was called to review Interface's environmental activities and Anderson realized that he had little to offer on this topic. In preparation for the address. Anderson read Paul Hawken's *Ecology of Commerce*, a book that provided a vision and rationale for sustainable business practices.[3] The resulting speech challenged Interface's employees to turn the company into a model of sustainable business.

FRAMEWORKS FOR SUSTAINABLE BUSINESS

"Sustainability" and "sustainable development" have perhaps become overused phrases in recent years. To some, sustainability is little more than environmental window-dressing to rationalize the status quo. From this perspective, a sustainable business simply is one that can continue business as usual for the long-term. But this superficial understanding is not what Hawken, or Anderson, had in mind. Their concept of sustainable business can be traced to a U.N. report authored by then-Prime Minister Gro Bruntland of Norway in which sustainability was defined as the ability "to meet the needs of the present without compromising the ability of future generations to meet their own needs."

True sustainability requires radical changes in the status quo and a recognition that compliance is not enough. To meet the needs (and not simply the desires) of the present without jeopardizing the morally equal needs of future generations requires action along three dimensions: economic, ecological, and social. These "three pillars of sustainability" require that business activities be economically,

ecologically, and socially sustainable. As reflected in the Mission Statement quoted previously. Interface has committed itself to becoming sustainable on all three grounds.

The three pillars of sustainability suggest that no business can be truly sustainable unless it satisfies three related and mutually dependent criteria. A sustainable business must be *economically* sustainable, which means not just that it be profitable but that it be capable of maintaining profitability over the long-term. A business that maintains revenues by liquidating its capital is not sustainable in this sense, nor is one that does not reinvest in capital, that takes on expenses greater than revenues, or that relies exclusively on nonrenewable resources. A sustainable business must also be *ecologically* sustainable, which means that it must recognize the biophysical limits to its activities. The worldwide fishing industry is an example of an unsustainable industry because it has harvested fish at a rate that the ocean's ecosystems cannot sustain. The automotive industry is learning that the internal combustion engine, with its reliance on nonrenewable fossil fuels and resultant CO_2 pollution, is not ecologically sustainable, but fuel-cell-driven cars may well be. Finally, a business must be *socially* or *ethically* sustainable. A company, such as Enron, that relies on a strategy of "pushing the envelope" on fraud, or a global business that ignores or disrespects local culture, is unsustainable. So, too, is a company the exploits child labor, mistreats its employees, or makes profits by defrauding its investors, deceiving its customers, or squeezing its suppliers.

More generally, three global facts show why these criteria of sustainable business are ultimately connected. First, worldwide poverty and inequality, judged according to any reasonable measure of quality of life, show that tremendous economic growth in the near term would be required to meet even the basic needs of hundreds of millions of people. Quite literally, billions of people lack basic minimal levels of clean water, adequate nutrition, health care, or education. The amount of economic growth required to meet the very real present needs of billions of people is staggering. Second, even conservative estimates hold that worldwide population will increase significantly in the coming decades, with most of the increase coming in the already poor urban areas in the undeveloped world. The problems of poverty and inequality will increase exponentially in the face of this population growth. Third, the only source for the resources needed to address these problems is the productive capacity of the earth and there are already clear signs that the biosphere is under stress from present economic activity.

In light of these factors, it seem unduly optimistic to assume that economic growth and business as usual can meet the basic needs of the billions of people already lacking, plus the hundreds of millions of children who will join them in the very near future, without causing the already fragile biosphere to collapse. It is also morally repugnant to think that business as usual can continue without attention to these real and fundamental needs of the world's poor. Yet, attempting to meet these needs by continuously growing the economy threatens the earth's capacity to sustain the very lives we seek to protect.

The three general sustainability criteria can be applied more specifically to business. Some refer to similar criteria as the "triple bottom line" of sustainable business.[4] This "triple bottom line" holds that business must be judged by its performance on three bottom lines: financial, ecological, and ethical. In fact, this was the type of strategy being pursued by Paul Hawken in the book that so inspired Anderson. To be sustainable, business ought to be arranged in such a way that it adequately meets the economic expectations of society (i.e., jobs, income, goods and services) in an efficient and sustainable manner. But in meeting these responsibilities, business must also be arranged in a way that supports, rather than degrades, the ability of the biosphere to sustain life, especially but not exclusively human life, over the long term. Business also ought to be arranged in ways that address minimum demands of social justice.

Some models exist for what such sustainable economic and business institutions might look like. *Natural Capitalism,* a more recent book co-authored by Hawken, provides both a framework for and numerous examples of sustainable business practice.[5] Interface is prominently featured in this book as a model for sustainable business. *Natural Capitalism* offers four strategies for creating sustainable business: radical resource productivity (or eco-efficiency); biomimicry; service and flow economy; and investment in natural capital. These strategies can be thought of as reasonable means for attaining the three pillars/triple-bottom-line sustainability goals. *Natural Capitalism* argues that business can and must be made more efficient in use of natural resources and energy, suggesting that even a ten-fold increase in resource and energy efficiency is already attainable with present technologies. Biomimicry involves redesigning industrial systems to mimic biological processes, essentially enabling the constant reuse of materials and the elimination of waste. The service and flow economy would have business create value by providing services rather than by selling products. Instead of purchasing light bulbs, carpeting, copying machines, and air conditioners, the service economy has business renting or leasing illumination, floor-covering, copying, or climate control services. By investing in natural capital business comes to recognize and value the significant benefits provided by living systems and natural resources. The ultimate capital on which all business relies is natural capital, not financial capital. Just as it would be a mistake to spend one's financial capital without reinvestment, so it is a mistake to spend one's natural capital without reinvesting.

SUSTAINABLE PRACTICE AT INTERFACE

This sustainability model permeates all aspects of Interface's business. Their corporate vision statement commits itself

> To be the first company that, by its deeds, shows the entire industrial world what sustainability is in all its dimensions: People, process, product, place and profits—by 2020—and in doing so we will become restorative through the power of influence.

In its annual reports and on the company's website Interface explains why this goal is so important:

> Here's the problem in a nutshell. Industrialism developed in a different world from the one we live in today: fewer people, less material well-being, plentiful natural resources. What emerged was a highly productive, take-make-waste system that assumed infinite resources and infinite sinks for industrial wastes. Industry moves, mines, extracts, shovels, burns, wastes, pumps and disposes of four million pounds of material in order to provide one average, middle-class American family their needs for a year. Today, the rate of material throughput is endangering our prosperity, not enhancing it. At Interface, we recognize that we are part of the problem. We are analyzing all of our material flows to begin to address the task at hand.
>
> What's the solution? We're not sure, but we have some ideas. We believe that there's a cure for resource waste that is profitable, creative and practical. We must create a company that addresses the needs of society and the environment by developing a system of industrial production that decreases our costs and dramatically reduces the burdens placed upon living systems. This also makes precious resources available for the billions of people who need more. What we call the next industrial revolution is a momentous shift in how we see the world, how we operate within it, what systems will prevail and which will not. At Interface, we are completely reimagining and redesigning everything we do, including the way we define our business. Our vision is to lead the way to the next industrial revolution by becoming the first sustainable corporation, and eventually a restorative enterprise. It's an

extraordinarily ambitious endeavor; a mountain to climb that is higher than Everest.

To attain this goal, Interface has articulated seven steps along the way. Again from the company's own literature, these steps are:

1. **Eliminate Waste**—The first step to sustainability, QUEST is Interface's campaign to eliminate the concept of waste, not just incrementally reduce it.

2. **Benign Emissions**—We're focusing on the elimination of molecular waste emitted with negative or toxic impact into our natural systems.

3. **Renewable Energy**—We're reducing the energy used by our processes while replacing non-renewable sources with sustainable ones.

4. **Closing the Loop**—Our aim is to redesign our processes and products to create cyclical material flows.

5. **Resource Efficient Transportation**—We're exploring methods to reduce the transportation of molecules (products and people) in favor of moving information. This includes plant location, logistics, information technology, video-conferencing, e-mail, and telecommuting.

6. **Sensitivity Hookup**—The goal here is to create a community within and around Interface that understands the functioning of natural systems and our impact on them.

7. **Redesign Commerce**—We're redefining commerce to focus on the delivery of service and value instead of the delivery of material. We're also engaging external organizations to create policies and market incentives that encourage sustainable practices.

The relationships among these steps and the synergies created by them can be seen in what is perhaps the most significant transformation at Interface. Interface is making a transition from a company that manufactures and sells carpeting to become a company that provides floor-covering services. This is very much the shift to the service and flow economy described in *Natural Capitalism.*

On a traditional business model, carpet is sold to consumers who, once they become dissatisfied with the color or style or once the carpeting becomes worn, are responsible for disposal of the carpet, typically sending the old carpeting to landfills. There is little incentive here for the manufacturer to produce long-lasting or easily recyclable carpeting. The old-time manufacturing strategy of planned obsolescence seems the rational corporate strategy in this situation. But once Interface shifted to leasing floor-covering services, incentives are created to produce long-lasting, easily replaceable and recyclable carpets. By selling carpeting services rather than the carpeting itself, Interface thereby accepts responsibility for the entire life-cycle of the product it markets. Because they retain ownership and are responsible for maintenance, Interface strives to produce carpeting that can be easily replaced in sections rather than in its entirety, that is more durable, and that can eventually be remanufactured. Redesigning their carpets and shifting to a service lease have also improved production efficiencies and reduced material and energy costs significantly. Consumers benefit by getting what they truly desire at lower costs and fewer burdens.

Thus, the shift to becoming a service provider addresses several of the seven goals outlined above. By providing carpeting in modules and by being responsible to replace worn sections, Interface has made great strides to eliminate waste. Strong incentives exist to create a fully closed loop process; carpeting that will be taken back is designed to be recycled and remanufactured. What was formely waste now becomes resource, and any material that is destined for the landfill represents lost potential revenues. Because Interface's own employees will be recycling and remanufacturing its waste products, there is also a strong incentive to produce non-toxic and benign products. This shift truly does pioneer a new business model of delivering service and value rather than simply delivering the material of a planned obsolescence product model. Finally, a service lease creates

an on-going and stable relationship with customers, something that should benefit both the business and its customer.

A second area in which Interface has made great strides towards sustainability is in the design of their manufacturing plants. In the late 1990s, Interface was building a new manufacturing plant in Shanghai, China. Consciously looking for design changes that would radically increase energy efficiency, its engineers redesigned the piping and pumping process throughout the plant. The original and standard design included 14 large pumps with 95 horsepower and an intricate system of small pipes arranged throughout the factory. With normal plant design, the factory is set up first and the pipes are then arranged to flow throughout the pre-existing design. Such an approach results in many secondary pipes coming off of the major trunk, and many bends and turns throughout the system. In this case, Interface's engineers laid out the pipes first, emphasizing a more efficient and straighter design. The new design and larger pipes reduced friction and allowed smaller and fewer pumps. Ultimately the redesign required pumping capacity of only 7 horsepower, a 92 percent savings on energy efficiency, and resulted in a simplified and therefore more reliable production process, and an overall reduction in capital expenditures.[6]

In the decade that Interface has been moving towards a sustainable model its economic outlook has been mixed. In the first four years, Interface's revenues doubled, its employment almost doubled, and its profits increased almost three-fold. The recession of the early 2000s resulted in a noticeable downturn in Interface's business. Nevertheless, the company is committed to a sustainable future. Ray Anderson's vision continues to inspire the company:

We look forward to the day when our factories have no smokestacks and no effluents. If successful, we'll spend the rest of our days harvesting yesteryear's carpets, recycling old petro-chemicals into new materials, and converting sunlight into energy. There will be zero scrap going into landfills and zero emissions into the ecosystem. Literally, it is a company that will grow by cleaning up the world, not by polluting or degrading it.[7]

NOTES

1. See P. Warshall. "The Tensile and the Tantric," *Whole Earth* 90: 4–7, summer 1997, as quoted in *Natural Capitalism* by Paul Hawken, Amory Lovins, and Hunter Lovins (Boston: Little Brown, 1999), p. 77.
2. *"In the Future, People Like Me Will Go to Jail,"* in *Fortune.* May 24, 1999, pp. 190–200. Other quotes from the Interface Mission Statement are from the company website: www.interface.com. Further information for this case was taken from *Mid-Course Correction: Toward a Sustainable Enterprise: the Interface Model* by Ray Anderson (White River Junction, VT.: Chelsea Green Publishers, 1999), a public lecture and interview with Anderson at St. John's University, and *Natural Capitalism.*
3. *Ecology of Commerce*, by Paul Hawken (New York: Harper Business Books, 1994).
4. The "triple bottom line" was most notably introduced in John Elkington. *Cannibals with Forks: The Triple Bottom Line of 21st Century Business* (Gabriola Island, British Columbia: New Society Publishers, 1998).
5. *Natural Capitalism.*
6. As described in *Natural Capitalism*, pp. 116–117.
7. *Interface Sustainability Report*, 1997, as quoted in *Natural Capitalism*, pp. 168–169.

Case Study

The Hazards of the Enterprise

John Hasnas

Upon graduating from Middle State University's MBA program last year, you were pleased to be offered a position with Kirk Enterprise, an American based multinational conglomerate. Originally started in the 1950's, the company grew rapidly due to its ability to supply NASA with several of the synthetic materials required by the space program for the development of space suits and heat shields. As the company grew, its product line diversified with one of its major successes being the development of long-lasting batteries for use in both automated probes and manned spacecraft. As the technology developed for the space program was found to have widespread commercial uses, Kirk Enterprises was able to exploit its competitive advantages to grow into a conglomerate supplying the international demand for this technology.

For many years, the company has been one of the world's largest suppliers of long-lived, large-scale batteries. However, it has become increasingly difficult to retain this position. The requirements of the Clean Air Act and especially California's state legislation mandating zero emission automobiles by the turn of the century has stimulated demand for powerful, long-lasting batteries for use in electric cars. This has greatly increased the number of competitors vying with Kirk for this market. In addition, American environmental regulations have reduced Kirk's ability to compete with producers of low cost batteries located in other countries. This is because the process of manufacturing the batteries produces measurable quantities of both lead and mercury, substances whose discharge into the environment is strictly controlled in the United States. The cost of separating these materials from the other byproducts and disposing of them in accordance with Environmental

Protection Agency regulations has put Kirk at a competitive disadvantage relative to manufacturers located in countries without such controls and regulations.

Last year, Kirk made a major commitment to winning the competition in the market for the new electric car batteries. Accordingly, Kirk organized a new subdivision known as Impulse Power, Inc. devoted exclusively to the manufacture of these batteries. In deciding where to locate the new plant it proposed to build for Impulse, Kirk considered several sites both within the United States and abroad. The most favorable location appeared to be in the South American country of Parador. This had three main advantages over the other candidates. The first was the low cost of labor. The second was the site's location on the Miramonie river which empties into the Pacific Ocean and would facilitate shipment of the finished batteries to California. The third was the likelihood of being able to negotiate favorable business conditions with the Paradorian government.

One reason Kirk Enterprises had been interested in hiring you was the reputation of Middle State's graduates as being prepared to deal with matters of international business. Accordingly, after spending your initial year at the main headquarters in Orgainia, Florida, it was decided that you could be of value in Parador. As a result, you became the assistant to Jordy LaForge, Impulse's chief negotiator with the Paradorian government. You have spent the last month working with LaForge amassing information concerning Parador's tax, labor, and environmental law and preparing your negotiating strategy. You have learned that there are practically no labor or environmental regulations in Parador beyond a minimum wage requirement of $.57 per hour. Accordingly, LaForge decided to devote his attention in the negotiations to the tax issue.

Over the same period of time, you have been studying the operation of the proposed plant according to the documents submitted to the Paradorian government. The industrial waste generated by the manufacturing process is to be dumped into the Miramonie river which will carry it into the Pacific. Apparently, the company has no plans to separate the mercury and lead out of this effluvium. The reason the discharge of these elements into waterways is banned in the United States is that fish ingest these elements which are then absorbed into their tissues. When the fish are caught and eaten by human beings, the mercury and lead are ingested as well. Both these elements are neurotoxins which attack the human central nervous system and lead, which is easily absorbed, is especially dangerous to children even at relatively low levels. You are concerned by this because you know that most of the native Paradorians who live along the coast make their living by fishing and that fish is a staple of the native diet.

The negotiating sessions began last week. LaForge has been extremely skillful at keeping the discussion focused on the issue of tax concessions. In the first session the only time environmental concerns came close to being addressed was when the Paradorian negotiator asked, "Is the plant safe?" to which LaForge replied, "Of course, perfectly safe."

This response bothered you and you discussed it with LaForge after the meeting adjourned. When you inquired whether he thought he had made a false representation concerning the plant's safety, he responded, "All I said was that the plant was safe. That statement can be interpreted in many ways. And besides, the plant is safe. We're not making explosives or nuclear weapons." Still unsatisfied, you pressed him by asking, "But what about the mercury and lead that will be dumped into the river?" At this point, LaForge became impatient with you and stated, "Look, this is not Sunday school. These negotiations concern big money. We're not hiding anything. Our proposed manufacturing processes and methods of waste disposal are a matter of public record. It's the Paradorians' job to protect their country's environment. If they are not concerned enough to do their homework, I'm certainly not going to do it for them. Besides, it's the EPA regulations back home that are undermining our position in the global market. Why do you think we're locating this plant in Parador, anyway?"

LaForge's last comment greatly disturbed you and you decided to speak to Diana Troy, the head of Impulse's development team and LaForge's immediate superior. You explained the situation to her and asked whether it was company policy to mislead the Paradorian negotiators and whether the reason Impulse was locating in Parador was to avoid American environmental regulations. Troy assured you that such was not the case and that company policy had always been to be forthright and above board in all negotiations. She thanked you for bringing the matter to her attention and assured you that she would talk to LaForge about it.

Although this set your mind at ease at first, as the negotiations continued, LaForge made no attempt to correct his statement about the plant's safety and seemed to you to be skillfully preventing the subject of the proposed plant's environmental impact from being discussed.

After two weeks, you went to see Troy again. She seemed considerably less hospitable than at your last meeting, claiming that she was very busy and could only give you five minutes. Upon inquiring whether anything had been done concerning Impulse's negotiating posture with regard to environmental issues, she told you that she had raised the matter with William Riker, the Vice President of Kirk's battery subdivision who is to be the first CEO of Impulse. Troy claims that he instructed her that if the negotiations were going well, she should not "rock the boat," and that the matter was now out of her hands.

The negotiations have been going well and LaForge has been successful in obtaining several favorable tax concessions for the company. He has told you that he expects to wrap things up within two weeks and has scheduled the last negotiating session for October 29. When you asked him whether he intended to raise the issue of the plant's environmental impact before then, he responded, "Get serious," and then added jokingly, "You're not going to hand me any 'Save the Whales' literature are you?"

You realize that you have a limited amount of time to decide what action, if any, you should take with regard to this situation. What should you do?

Case Study

Texaco in the Ecuadorean Amazon

Denis G. Arnold

Ecuador is a small nation on the northwest coast of South America. During its 173-year history, Ecuador has been one of the least politically stable South American nations. In 1830

Ecuador achieved its independence from Spain. Ecuadorean history since that time has been characterized by cycles of republican government and military intervention and rule.

The period from 1960–1972 was marked by instability and military dominance of political institutions. From 1972–1979 Ecuador was governed by military regimes. In 1979 a popularly elected president took office, but the military demanded and was granted important governing powers. The democratic institutional framework of Ecuador remains weak. Decreases in public sector spending, increasing unemployment, and rising inflation have hit the Ecuadorean poor especially hard. World Bank estimates indicate that in 1994 thirty-five percent of the Ecuadorean population lived in poverty, and an additional seventeen percent were vulnerable to poverty.

The Ecuadorean Amazon is one of the most biologically diverse forests in the world and is home to an estimated five percent of the Earth's species. It is home to cicadas, scarlet macaws, squirrel monkeys, freshwater pink dolphins, and thousands of other species. Many of these species have small populations, making them extremely sensitive to disturbance. Indigenous Indian populations have lived in harmony with these species for centuries. They have fished and hunted in and around the rivers and lakes. And they have raised crops of cacao, coffee, fruits, nuts, and tropical woods in *chakras*, models of sustainable agroforestry.

Ten thousand feet beneath the Amazon floor lies one of Ecuador's most important resources: rich deposits of crude oil. Historically, the Ecuadorean government regarded the oil as the best way to keep up with the country's payments on its $12 billion foreign debt obligations. For twenty years American oil companies, led by Texaco, extracted oil from beneath the Ecuadorean Amazon in partnership with the government of Ecuador. (The U.S. is the primary importer of Ecuadorean oil.) They constructed four hundred drill sites and hundreds of miles of roads and pipelines, including a primary pipeline that extends for 280 miles across the Andes. Large tracts of forest were clear-cut to make way for these facilities. Indian lands, including *chakras*, were taken and bulldozed, often without compensation. In the village of Pacayacu the central square is occupied by a drilling platform.

Officials estimate that the primary pipeline alone has spilled more than 16.8 million gallons of oil into the Amazon over an eighteen-year period. Spills from secondary pipelines have never been estimated or recorded; however, smaller tertiary pipelines dump ten thousand gallons of petroleum per week into the Amazon, and production pits dump approximately 4.3 million gallons of toxic production wastes and treatment chemicals into the forest's rivers, streams, and groundwater each day. (By comparison, the *Exxon Valdez* spilled 10.8 million gallons of oil into Alaska's Prince William Sound.) Significant portions of these spills have been carried downriver into neighboring Peru.

Critics charge that Texaco ignored prevailing oil industry standards that call for the reinjection of waste deep into the ground. Rivers and lakes were contaminated by oil and petroleum; heavy metals such as arsenic, cadmium, cyanide, lead, and mercury; poisonous industrial solvents: and lethal concentrations of chloride salt, and other highly toxic chemicals. The only treatment these chemicals received occurred when the oil company burned waste pits to reduce petroleum content. Villagers report that the chemicals return as black rain, polluting what little fresh water remains. What is not burned off seeps through the unlined walls of the pits into the groundwater. Cattle are found with their stomachs rotted out, crops are destroyed, animals are gone from the forest, and fish disappear from the lakes and rivers. Health officials and community leaders report adults and children with deformities, skin rashes, abscesses, headaches, dysentery, infections, respiratory ailments, and disproportionately high rates of cancer. In 1972 Texaco signed a contract requiring it to turn over all of its operations to Ecuador's national oil company, Petroecuador, by 1992. Petroecuador inherited antiquated equipment, rusting pipelines, and uncounted toxic waste sites. Independent estimates place the cost of cleaning up the production pits alone at 600 million dollars. From 1995–1998 Texaco spent 40 million dollars on cleanup operations in Ecuador. In exchange for these efforts the government of Ecuador relinquished future claims against the company.

Numerous international accords—including the 1972 Stockholm Declaration on the Human Environment signed by over one hundred countries, including the United States and Ecuador—identify the right to a clean and healthy environment as a fundamental human right and prohibit both state and private actors from endangering the needs of present and future generations. Ecuadorean and Peruvian plaintiffs, including several indigenous tribes, have filed billion-dollar class-action lawsuits against Texaco in U.S. courts under the Alien Tort Claims Act (ATCA). Enacted in 1789, the law was designed to provide noncitizens access to U.S. courts in cases involving a breach of international law, including accords. Texaco maintains that the case should be tried in Ecuador. However, Ecuador's judicial system does not recognize the concept of a class action suit and has no history of environmental litigation. Furthermore, Ecuador's judicial system is notoriously corrupt (a poll by George Washington University found that only sixteen percent of Ecuadoreans have confidence in their judicial system) and lacks the infrastructure necessary to handle the case (e.g., the city in which the case would be tried lacks a courthouse). Texaco defended its actions by arguing that it is in full compliance with Ecuadorean law and that it had full approval of the Ecuadorean government.

In May 2001 U.S. District Judge Jed Rakoff rejected the applicability of the ATCA and dismissed the case on grounds of forum non conveniens. Judge Rakoff argued that since "no act taken by Texaco in the United States bore materially on the pollution-creating activities," the case should be tried in Ecuador and Peru. In October 2001 Texaco completed a merger with Chevron Corporation. Chevron and Texaco are now known as Chevron Texaco Corporation. In August 2002 the U.S. Court of Appeals for the Second Circuit upheld Judge Rakoff's decision.

NOTE

This case was prepared by Denis G. Arnold and is based on James Brooke, "New Effort Would Test Possible Coexistence of Oil and Rain Forest," *The New York Times*, February 26, 1991; Dennis M. Hanratty, ed., *Ecuador: A Country Study*, 3rd ed. (Washington D.C.: Library of Congress, 1991); Anita Isaacs, *Military Rule and Transition in Ecuador, 1972–92* (Pittsburgh: University of Pittsburgh Press, 1993); *Ecuador Poverty Report* (Washington D.C.: The World Bank, 1996); Joe Kane, *Savages* (New York: Vintage Books, 1996); Eyal Press, "Texaco on Trial," *The Nation*, May 31, 1999; "Texaco and Ecuador," *Texaco: Health, Safety and the Environment*, 27 September 1999. <www.texaco.com/she/index.html> (16 December 1999); and *Aguinda v. Texaco, Inc.*, 142 F. Supp. 2d 534 (S.D.N.Y. 2001).

Chapter Four

———————————•———————————

Diversity in the Workplace

FORMER NEW JERSEY Senator and Presidential candidate Bill Bradley has argued that "slavery was America's original sin, and race remains our unresolved dilemma." Derrick Bell, internationally recognized African-American legal scholar, couldn't agree more. The U.S. Constitution, the Bill of Rights, and the Declaration of Independence, says Bell, suggest, specify, and argue that all human beings have an equal right to life, liberty, the pursuit of happiness, equal protection under the law, and an equal opportunity for, if not an absolute guarantee of, an equal outcome. These documents claim that all human beings are equal and, therefore, everyone must be treated equally or similarly unless there are compelling reasons why they should be treated differently. In 1964 Title VII of the Civil Rights Act attempted to update, encapsulate, and bring into the workplace the spirit of our "founding documents":

> It shall be unlawful employment practice for an employer to fail or refuse to hire or discharge any individual or otherwise to discriminate against any individual with respect to his compensation, terms, conditions, or privileges of employment because of such individual's race, color, religion, sex, or national origin.

This is our creed, our faith commitment, our mantra, says Bell, but it is not our lived reality.

We are not, says Bell, a society based on equal opportunity and merit. Rather, we are a society based on race and racism. In this society, says Bell, pigmentation and, to a real extent, gender radically influence our opportunities, options, and outcomes. Emancipation, argues Bell, did not abolish slavery; it only changed it. We have always treated persons unequally for such characteristics as race, sex, or ethnic background. Sadly, he concludes, we are a society that discriminates by disposition, habit, and institutional tradition. Bell believes that only continued education and legislation can eradicate racism, and that one of the best and most common places for this to occur is in the workplace. He agrees with former President Clinton that affirmative action needs to be augmented and mended, but certainly not ended!

Regardless of ethnicity, gender, or class, work is perhaps our most common cultural link. As adults there is nothing we do more in our lives than work. We do not eat as much, recreate as much, or play as much as we do work. Sociologist Frank Tannenbaum argues that we are a nation of workers/employees. We are dependent upon each other for our means of livelihood and our lifestyles. In work we acquire salaries, stuff, and success. Work is one of the major ways by which we come to know ourselves and be known by others. Work is a means by which we achieve status and identity. Work offers us meaning, molds us, and offers us models by which to evaluate reality. The lessons we learn in our work and in the workplace become the metaphors we apply to life and the means by which we digest the world. The meter and measure of work serve as our mapping device to explain and order the geography of life. Our work circumscribes what we know, how we know it, and how we select and categorize the things we choose to see, react to, or respond to. Work influences our use of language; our values and priority structures; our political, cultural, and class awareness; and our repertoire of personal and professionally learned skills and behaviors. As Samuel Butler wrote, "Every [person's] work, whether it be literature or music or pictures or architecture or anything else, is always a personal portrait of [who they are]."

Jobs affect our lives. The rules and regulations of our jobs influence how individual workers think and behave both on and off the job. Given all of this, should we not use the workplace as a living laboratory for social reform and impose certain rules and regulations in an attempt to achieve the spirit of equality amid the physical reality of our diversity? Although our historical past may have seemed, at least, to be a monoculture (WASP, that is, white), in fact, our recent past and near future depict a portrait of diversity and heterogeneity. (According to the U.S. Department of Labor population statistics: 1996—74 percent Anglo, 12 percent black, 10.27 percent Latin, 3.3 percent Pacific Rim, Projections for 2050—53 percent Anglo, 13.6 percent black, 24.47 percent Latin, 8.2 percent Pacific Rim.) In order to accommodate the needs of this "new melting pot" and in order to overcome Derrick Bell's fear of habitual and institutional prejudice, we must continue the struggle to achieve equality. And in pursuing this goal we must remain ever mindful of the words of John F. Kennedy: "All of us do not have equal talents, but all of us should have an equal opportunity to develop our talents."

"A Defense of Programs of Preferential Treatment" is a qualified defense of affirmative action programs. The article recognizes that reverse discrimination is unjust. But the article argues that it is acceptable if it is not as unjust as the practices of discrimination it is designed to eliminate. "Reverse Discrimination as Unjustified" claims that reverse discrimination is always wrong because—even in the pursuit of the highest goals—it is internally illogical and continues the patterns of injustice done to others because of their race, sex, or ethnic background. "Racism in the Workplace" is an article that concludes that no matter what the legal prohibitions in place, workplace prejudice and the harassment of minorities have not entirely ceased. The "Texaco" and the "Denny's" cases show us how prejudice and harassment keep occurring in both complicated and secretive, as well as blatant and obvious, ways in corporations and places of business. "Global United: Melba Moore" is a very interesting case. Is she a victim of racial prejudice or gender bias, or do her co-workers not like her for purely personal and private reasons? The last case in this section,

"Management Dilemma" isn't about race. Rather it deals with other forms of prejudice that are experienced in the workplace, such as ageism, sexism, and stereotypes regarding being single versus being married, or being financially well off versus being financially in need.

Essay

A Defense of Programs of Preferential Treatment

Richard Wasserstrom

Many justifications of programs of preferential treatment depend upon the claim that in one respect or another such programs have good consequences or that they are effective means by which to bring about some desirable end, e.g., an integrated, equalitarian society. I mean by "programs of preferential treatment" to refer to programs such as those at issue in the *Bakke* case—programs which set aside a certain number of places (for example, in a law school) as to which members of minority groups (for example, persons who are non-white or female) who possess certain minimum qualifications (in terms of grades and test scores) may be preferred for admission to those places over some members of the majority group who possess higher qualifications (in terms of grades and test scores).

Many criticisms of programs of preferential treatment claim that such programs, even if effective, are unjustifiable because they are in some important sense unfair or unjust. In this paper I present a limited defense of such programs by showing that two of the chief arguments offered for the unfairness or injustice of these programs do not work in the way or to the degree supposed by critics of these programs.

The first argument is this. Opponents of preferential treatment programs sometimes assert that proponents of these programs are guilty of intellectual inconsistency, if not racism or sexism. For, as is now readily acknowledged, at times past employers, universities, and many other social institutions did have racial or sexual quotas (when they did not practice overt racial or sexual exclusion), and many of those who were most concerned to bring about the eradication of those racial quotas are now untroubled by the new programs which reinstitute them. And this, it is claimed, is inconsistent. If it was wrong to take race or sex into account when blacks and women were the objects of racial and sexual policies and practices of exclusion, then it is wrong to take race or sex into account when the objects of the policies have their race or sex reversed. Simple considerations of intellectual consistency—of what it means to give racism or sexism as a reason for condemning these social policies and practices—require that what was a good reason then is still a good reason now.

The problem with this argument is that despite appearances, there is no inconsistency involved in holding both views. Even if contemporary preferential treatment programs which contain quotas are wrong, they are not wrong for the reasons that made quotas against

Richard Wasserstrom, "A Defense of Programs of Preferential Treatment," originally published in 24 *UCLA Law Review,* 581, Copyright 1977, The Regents of the University of California. All rights reserved.

blacks and women pernicious. The reason why is that the social realities do make an enormous difference. The fundamental evil of programs that discriminated against blacks or women was that these programs were a part of a larger social universe which systematically maintained a network of institutions which unjustifiably concentrated power, authority, and goods in the hands of white male individuals, and which systematically consigned blacks and women to subordinate positions in the society.

Whatever may be wrong with today's affirmative action programs and quota systems, it should be clear that the evil, if any, is just not the same. Racial and sexual minorities do not constitute the dominant social group. Nor is the conception of who is a fully developed member of the moral and social community one of an individual who is either female or black. Quotas which prefer women or blacks do not add to an already relatively overabundant supply of resources and opportunities at the disposal of members of these groups in the way in which the quotas of the past did maintain and augment the overabundant supply of resources and opportunities already available to white males.

The same point can be made in a somewhat different way. Sometimes people say that what was wrong, for example, with the system of racial discrimination in the South was that it took an irrelevant characteristic, namely race, and used it systematically to allocate social benefits and burdens of various sorts. The defect was the irrelevance of the characteristic used—race—for that meant that individuals ended up being treated in a manner that was arbitrary and capricious.

I do not think that was the central flaw at all. Take, for instance, the most hideous of the practices, human slavery. The primary thing that was wrong with the institution was not that the particular individuals who were assigned the place of slaves were assigned there arbitrarily because the assignment was made in virtue of an irrelevant characteristic, their race. Rather, it seems to me that the primary thing that was and is wrong with slavery is the practice itself—the fact of some individuals being able to own other individuals and all that goes with that practice. It would not matter by what criterion individuals were assigned; human slavery would still be wrong. And the same can be said for most if not all of the other discrete practices and institutions which comprised the system of racial discrimination even after human slavery was abolished. The practices were unjustifiable—they were oppressive—and they would have been so no matter how the assignment of victims had been made. What made it worse, still, was that the institutions and the supporting ideology all interlocked to create a system of human oppression whose effects on those living under it were as devastating as they were unjustifiable.

Again, if there is anything wrong with the programs of preferential treatment that have begun to flourish within the past ten years, it should be evident that the social realities in respect to the distribution of resources and opportunities make the difference. Apart from everything else, there is simply no way in which all of these programs taken together could plausibly be viewed as capable of relegating white males to the kind of genuinely oppressive status characteristically bestowed upon women and blacks by the dominant social institutions and ideology.

The second objection is that preferential treatment programs are wrong because they take race or sex into account rather than the only thing that does matter—that is, an individual's qualifications. What all such programs have in common and what makes them all objectionable so this argument goes, is that they ignore the persons who are more qualified by bestowing preference on those who are less qualified in virtue of their being either black or female.

There are, I think, a number of things wrong with this objection based on qualifications, and not the least of them is that we do not live in a society in which there is even the serious pretense of a qualification requirement for many jobs of substantial power and authority. Would anyone claim, for example, that the persons who comprise the judiciary are there because they are the most qualified lawyers or the most qualified persons to be judges? Would anyone claim that Henry Ford II is the head of the Ford Motor Company because he is the most qualified person for the job? Part of what is wrong with even talking about qualifications and merit is that the argument derives some of its force from the erroneous notion that we would have a meritocracy were it not for programs of preferential treatment. In fact, the higher one goes in terms of prestige, power and the like, the less qualifications seem ever to be decisive. It is only for certain jobs and certain places that qualifications are used to do more than establish the possession of certain minimum competencies.

But difficulties such as these to one side, there are theoretical difficulties as well which cut much more deeply into the argument about qualifications. To begin with, it is important to see that there is a serious inconsistency present if the person who favors "pure qualifications" does so on the ground that the most qualified ought to be selected because this promotes maximum efficiency. Let us suppose that the argument is that if we have the most qualified performing the relevant tasks we will get those tasks done in the most economical and efficient manner. There is nothing wrong in principle with arguments based upon the good consequences that will flow from maintaining a social practice in a certain way. But it is inconsistent for the opponent of preferential treatment to attach much weight to qualifications on this ground, because it was an analogous appeal to the good consequences that the opponent of preferential treatment thought was wrong in the first place. That is to say, if the chief thing to be said in favor of strict qualifications and preferring the most qualified is that it is the most efficient way of getting things done, then we are right back to an assessment of the different consequences that will flow from different programs, and we are far removed from the considerations of justice or fairness that were thought to weigh so heavily against these programs.

It is important to note, too, that qualifications—at least in the educational context—are often not connected at all closely with any plausible conception of social effectiveness. To admit the most qualified students to law school, for example—given the way qualifications are now determined—is primarily to admit those who have the greatest chance of scoring the highest grades at law school. This says little about efficiency except perhaps that these students are the easiest for the faculty to teach. However, since we know so little about what constitutes being a good, or even successful lawyer, and even less about the correlation between being a very good law student and being a very good lawyer, we can hardly claim very confidently that the legal system will operate most effectively if we admit only the most qualified students to law school.

To be at all decisive, the argument for qualifications must be that those who are the most qualified deserve to receive the benefits (the job, the place in law school, etc.) because they are the most qualified. The introduction of the concept of desert now makes it an objection as to justice or fairness of the sort promised by the original criticism of the programs. But now the problem is that there is no reason to think that there is any strong sense of "desert" in which it is correct that the most qualified deserve anything.

Let us consider more closely one case, that of preferential treatment in respect to admission to college or graduate school. There is a logical gap in the inference from the claim that a person is most qualified to perform a task, e.g., to be a good student, to the conclusion that he or she deserves to be admitted as a student. Of course, those who deserve to be admitted should be admitted. But why do the most qualified deserve anything? There is simply no necessary connection between academic merit (in the sense of being the most qualified) and deserving to be a member of a student body. Suppose, for instance, that there is only one tennis court in the community. Is it clear that the two best tennis players ought to be the ones permitted to use it? Why not those who were there first? Or those who will enjoy playing the most? Or those who are the worst and, therefore, need the greatest opportunity to practice? Or those who have the chance to play least frequently?

We might, of course, have a rule that says that the best tennis players get to use the court before the others. Under such a rule the best players would deserve the court more than the poorer ones. But that is just to push the inquiry back one stage. Is there any reason to think that we ought to have a rule giving good tennis players such a preference? Indeed, the arguments that might be given for or against such a rule are many and varied. And few if any of the arguments that might support the rule would depend upon a connection between ability and desert.

Someone might reply, however, that the most able students deserve to be admitted to the university because all of their earlier schooling was a kind of competition, with university admission being the prize awarded to the winners. They deserve to be admitted because that is what the role of the competition provides. In addition, it might be argued, it would be unfair now to exclude them in favor of others, given the reasonable expectations they developed about the way in which their industry and performance would

be rewarded. Minority-admission programs, which inevitably prefer some who are less qualified over some who are more qualified, all possess this flaw.

There are several problems with this argument. The most substantial of them is that it is an empirically implausible picture of our social world. Most of what are regarded as the decisive characteristics for higher education have a great deal to do with things over which the individual has neither control nor responsibility: such things as home environment, socioeconomic class of parents, and, of course, the quality of the primary and secondary schools attended. Since individuals do not deserve having had any of these things vis-à-vis other individuals, they do not, for the most part, deserve their qualifications. And since they do not deserve their abilities they do not in any strong sense deserve to be admitted because of their abilities.

To be sure, if there has been a rule which connects, say, performance at high school with admission to college, then there is a weak sense in which those who do well at high school deserve, for that reason alone, to be admitted to college. In addition, if persons have built up or relied upon their reasonable expectations concerning performance and admission, they have a claim to be admitted on this ground as well. But it is certainly not obvious that these claims of desert are any stronger or more compelling than the competing claims based upon the needs of or advantages to women or blacks from programs of preferential treatment. And as I have indicated, all rule-based claims of desert are very weak unless and until the rule which creates the claim is itself shown to be a justified one. Unless one has a strong preference for the status quo, and unless one can defend that preference, the practice within a system of allocating places in a certain way does not go very far at all in showing that is the right or the just way to allocate those places in the future.

A proponent of programs of preferential treatment is not at all committed to the view that qualifications ought to be wholly irrelevant. He or she can agree that, given the existing structure of any institution, there is probably some minimal set of qualifications without which one cannot participate meaningfully within the institution. In addition, it can be granted that the qualifications of those involved will affect the way the institution works and the way it affects others in the society. And the consequences will vary depending upon the particular institution. But all of this only establishes that qualifications, in this sense, are relevant, not that they are decisive. This is wholly consistent with the claim that race or sex should today also be relevant when it comes to matters such as admission to college or law school. And that is all that any preferential treatment program—even one with the kind of quota used in the *Bakke* case—has ever tried to do.

I have not attempted to establish that programs of preferential treatment are right and desirable. There are empirical issues concerning the consequences of these programs that I have not discussed, and certainly not settled. Nor, for that matter, have I considered the argument that justice may permit, if not require, these programs as a way to provide compensation or reparation for injuries suffered in the recent as well as distant past, or as a way to remove benefits that are undeservedly enjoyed by those of the dominant group. What I have tried to do is show that it is wrong to think that programs of preferential treatment are objectionable in the centrally important sense in which many past and present discriminatory features of our society have been and are racist and sexist. The social realities as to power and opportunity do make a fundamental difference. It is also wrong to think that programs of preferential treatment are in any strong sense either unjust or unprincipled. The case for programs of preferential treatment could, therefore, plausibly rest both on the view that such programs are not unfair to white males (except in the weak, rule-dependent sense described above) and on the view that it is unfair to continue the present set of unjust—often racist and sexist—institutions that comprise the social reality. And the case for these programs could rest as well on the proposition that, given the distribution of power and influence in the United States today, such programs may reasonably be viewed as potentially valuable, effective means by which to achieve admirable and significant social ideals of equality and integration.

Essay

Reverse Discrimination as Unjustified

Lisa H. Newton

I have heard it argued that "simple justice" requires that we favor women and blacks in employment and educational opportunities, since women and blacks were "unjustly" excluded from such opportunities for so many years in the not so distant past. It is a strange argument, an example of a possible implication of a true proposition advanced to dispute the

Lisa H. Newton, "Reverse Discrimination as Unjustified," *Ethics* 83 (1973). Reprinted by permission of The University of Chicago Press.

proposition itself, like an octopus absent-mindedly slicing off his head with a stray tentacle. A fatal confusion underlies this argument, a confusion fundamentally relevant to our understanding of the notion of the rule of law.

Two senses of justice and equality are involved in this confusion. The root notion of justice, progenitor of the other, is the one that Aristotle (*Nichomachean Ethics* 5. 6; *Politics* 1, 2; 3. 1) assumes to be the foundation and proper virtue of the political association. It is the condition which free men establish among themselves when they "share a common life in order that their association bring them self-sufficiency"—the regulation of their relationship by law, and the establishment, by law, of equality before the law. Rule of law is the name and pattern of this justice; its equality stands against the inequalities—of wealth, talent, etc—otherwise obtaining among its participants, who by virtue of that equality are called "citizens." It is an achievement—complete, or, more frequently, partial—of certain people in certain concrete situations. It is fragile and easily disrupted by powerful individuals who discover that the blind equality of rule of law is inconvenient for their interests. Despite its obvious instability, Aristotle assumed that the establishment of justice in this sense, the creation of citizenship, was a permanent possibility for men and that the resultant association of citizens was the natural home of the species. At levels below the political association, this rule-governed equality is easily found; it is exemplified by any group of children agreeing together to play a game. At the level of the political association, the attainment of this justice is more difficult, simply because the stakes are so much higher for each participant. The equality of citizenship is not something that happens of its own accord, and without the expenditure of a fair amount of effort it will collapse into the rule of a powerful few over an apathetic many. But at least it has been achieved, at some times in some places; it is always worth trying to achieve, and

eminently worth trying to maintain, wherever and to whatever degree it has been brought into being.

Aristotle's parochialism is notorious; he really did not imagine that persons other than Greeks could associate freely in justice, and the only form of association he had in mind was the Greek *polis*. With the decline of the *polis* and the shift in the center of political thought, his notion of justice underwent a sea change. To be exact, it ceased to represent a political type and became a moral ideal: the ideal of equality as we know it. This ideal demands that all men be included in citizenship—that one Law govern all equally, that all men regard all other men as fellow citizens, with the same guarantees, rights, and protections. Briefly, it demands that the circle of citizenship achieved by any group be extended to include the entire human race. Properly understood, its effect on our associations can be excellent: it congratulates us on our achievement of rule of law as a process of government but refuses to let us remain complacent until we have expanded the associations to include others within the ambit of the rules, as often and as far as possible. While one man is a slave, none of us may feel truly free. We are constantly prodded by this ideal to look for possible unjustifiable discrimination, for inequalities not absolutely required for the functioning of the society and advantageous to all. And after twenty centuries of pressure, not at all constant, from this ideal, it might be said that some progress has been made. To take the cases in point for this problem, we are now prepared to assert, as Aristotle would never have been, the equality of sexes and of persons of different colors. The ambit of American citizenship, once restricted to white males of property, has been extended to include all adult free men, then all adult males including ex-slaves, then all women. The process of acquisition of full citizenship was for these groups a sporadic trail of half-measures, even now not complete; the steps on the road to full equality are marked by leg-islation and judicial decisions which are only recently concluded and still often not en-forced. But the fact that we can now discuss the possibility of favoring such groups in hir-ing shows that over the area that concerns us, at least, full equality is presupposed as a basis for discussion. To that extent, they are full cit-izens, fully protected by the law of the land.

It is important for my argument that the moral idea of equality be recognized as logical-ly distinct from the condition (or virtue) of jus-tice in the political sense. Justice in this sense exists *among* a citizenry, irrespective of the num-ber of the populace included in that citizenry. Further, the moral ideal is parasitic upon the political virtue, for "equality" is unspecified—it means nothing until we are told in what respect that equality is to be realized. In a political con-text, "equality" is specified as "equal rights"—equal access to the public realm, public goods and offices, equal treatment under the law—in brief, the equality of citizenship. If citizenship is not a possibility, political equality is unintelligi-ble. The ideal emerges as a generalization of the real condition and refers back to that con-dition for its content.

Now, if justice (Aristotle's justice in the po-litical sense) is equal treatment under law for all citizens, what is injustice? Clearly, injustice is the violation of that equality, discriminating for or against a group of citizens, favoring them with special immunities and privileges or depriving them of those guaranteed to the others. When the southern employer refuses to hire blacks in white-collar jobs, when Wall Street will only hire women as secretaries with new titles, when Mississippi high schools rou-tinely flunk all black boys above ninth grade, we have examples of injustice, and we work to restore the equality of the public realm by en-suring that equal opportunity will be provid-ed in such cases in the future. But of course, when the employers and the schools *favor* women and blacks, the same injustice is done.

Just as the previous discrimination did, this re-verse discrimination violates the public equali-ty which defines citizenship and destroys the rule of law for the areas in which these favors are granted. To the extent that we adopt a program of discrimination, reverse or other-wise, justice in the political sense is de-stroyed, and none of us, specifically affected or not, is a citizen, a bearer of rights—we are all petitioners for favors. And to the same ex-tent, the ideal of equality is undermined, for it has content only where justice obtains, and by destroying justice we render the ideal meaningless. It is, then, an ironic paradox, if not a contradiction in terms, to assert that the ideal of equality justifies the violation of jus-tice, it is as if one should argue, with William Buckley, that an ideal of humanity can justify the destruction of the human race.

Logically, the conclusion is simple enough: all discrimination is wrong *prima facie* because it violates justice, and that goes for reverse dis-crimination too. No violation of justice among the citizens may be justified (may overcome the *prima facie* objection) by appeal to the ideal of equality, for that ideal is logically dependent upon the notion of justice. Reverse discrimina-tion, then, which attempts no other justifica-tion than an appeal to equality, is wrong. But let us try to make the conclusion more plausi-ble by suggesting some of the implications of the suggested practice of reverse discrimina-tion in employment and education. My argu-ment will be that the problems raised there are insoluble, not only in practice but in principle.

We may argue, if we like, about what "dis-crimination" consists of. Do I discriminate against blacks if I admit none to my school when none of the black applicants are quali-fied by the tests I always give? How far must I go to root out cultural bias from my applica-tion forms and tests before I can say that I have not discriminated against those of differ-ent cultures? Can I assume that women are not strong enough to be roughnecks on my oil rigs, or must I test them individually? But this controversy, the most popular and well-argued aspect of the issue, is not as fatal as two others which cannot be avoided: if we are regarding the blacks as a "minority" victimized by discrimination, what is a "minority"? And for any group—blacks, women, whatever—that has been discriminated against, what amount of reverse discrimination wipes out the initial discrimination? Let us grant as true that women and blacks were discriminated against, even where laws forbade such discrimination, and grant for the sake of argument that a history of discrimination must be wiped out by reverse discrimination. What follows?

First, are there other groups which have been discriminated against? For they should have the same right of restitution. What about American Indians, Chicanos, Appalachian Mountain whites, Puerto Ricans, Jews, Cajuns, and Orientals? And if these are to be included, the principle according to which we specify a "minority" is simply the criterion of "ethnic (sub) group," and we're stuck with every hyphenated American in the lower-middle class clamoring for special privileges for *his* group—and with equal justification. For be it noted, when we run down the Harvard roster, we find not only a scarcity of blacks (in comparison with the proportion in the population) but an even more striking scarcity of those second-, third-, and fourth-generation ethnics who make up the loudest voice of Middle America. Shouldn't they demand *their* share? And eventually, the WASPs will have to form their own lobby, for they too are a minority. The point is simply this: there is no "majority" in America who will not mind giving up just a bit of their rights to make room for a favored minority. There are only other minorities, each of which is discriminated against by the favoring. The initial injustice is then repeated dozens of times, and if each minority is granted the same right of restitution as the others, an entire area of rule

governance is dissolved into a pushing and shoving match between self-interested groups. Each works to catch the public eye and political popularity by whatever means of advertising and power politics lend themselves to the effort, to capitalize as much as possible on temporary popularity until the restless mob picks another group to feel sorry for. Hardly an edifying spectacle, and in the long run no one can benefit: the pie is no larger—it's just that instead of setting up and enforcing rules for getting a piece, we've turned the contest into a free-for-all, requiring much more effort for no larger a reward. It would be in the interests of all the participants to re-establish an objective rule to govern the process, carefully enforced and the same for all.

Second, supposing that we do manage to agree in general that women and blacks (and all the others) have some right of restitution, some right to a privileged place in the structure of opportunities for a while, how will we know when that while is up? How much privilege is enough? When will the guilt be gone, the price paid, the balance restored? What recompense is right for centuries of exclusion? What criterion tells us when we are done? Out experience with the Civil Rights movement shows us that agreement on the terms cannot be presupposed: a process that appears to some to be going at a mad gallop into a black takeover appears to the rest of us to be at a standstill. Should a practice of reverse discrimination be adopted, we may safely predict that just as some of us begin to see "a satisfactory start toward righting the balance," others of us will see that we "have already gone too far in the other direction" and will suggest that the discrimination ought to be reversed again. And such disagreement is inevitable, for the point is that we could not *possibly* have any criteria for evaluating the kind of recompense we have in mind. The context presumed by any discussion of restitution is the context of rule of law: law sets the rights of men and simultaneously sets the method for remedying the violation of those rights. You may expect suffering from others and/or damage payments for yourself if and only if the others have violated your rights; the suffering you have endured is not sufficient reason for them to suffer. And remedial rights exist only where there is law: primary human rights are useful guides to legislation but cannot stand as reasons for awarding remedies for injuries sustained. But then, the context presupposed by any discussion of restitution is the context of preexistent full citizenship. No remedial rights could exist for the excluded; neither in law nor in logic does there exist a right to *sue* for a standing to sue.

From these two considerations, then, the difficulties with reverse discrimination become evident. Restitution for a disadvantaged group whose rights under the law have been violated is possible by legal means, but restitution for a disadvantaged group whose grievance is that there was no law to protect them simply is not.

First, outside of the area of justice defined by the law, no sense can be made of "the group's rights," for no law recognizes that group or the individuals in it, *qua* members, as bearers of rights (hence *any* group can constitute itself as a disadvantage minority in some sense and demand similar restitution). Second, outside of the area of protection of law, no sense can be made of the violation of rights (hence the amount of the recompense cannot be decided by any objective criterion). For both reasons, the practice of reverse discrimination undermines the foundation of the very ideal in whose name it is advocated; it destroys justice, law, equality, and citizenship itself, and replaces them with power struggles and popularity contests.

NOTE

A version of this paper was read at a meeting of the Society for Women in Philosophy in Amherst, Massachusetts, 5 November 1972.

Essay

Racism in the Workplace

Aaron Bernstein

When Wayne A. Elliott was transferred in 1996 from a factory job to a warehouse at Lockheed Martin Corp.'s sprawling military-aircraft production facilities in Marietta, Ga., he says he found himself face to face with naked racism. Anti-black graffiti was scrawled on the restroom walls. His new white colleagues harassed him, Elliott recalls, as did his manager, who would yell at him, call him "boy," and tell him to "kiss my butt." He complained, but Elliot says the supervisor was no

help. Instead, he assigned Elliott, now 46, to collecting parts to be boxed, which involves walking about 10 miles a day. Meanwhile, the eight whites in his job category sat at computer terminals and told him to get a move on—even though Elliott outranked them on the union seniority list.

The atmosphere got even uglier when Elliott and a few other blacks formed a small group in 1997 called Workers Against Discrimination, which led to the filing of two

---

class actions. One day, he and the other two black men among the 30 warehouse workers found "back-to-Africa tickets" on their desks, he says, which said things like "Just sprinkle this dingy black dust on any sidewalk and piss on it, and, presto! hundreds of n—s spring up!" They reported this, but the Lockheed security officials who responded took the three victims away in their security cars as if they were the wrongdoers, he says, and interrogated them separately.

Then, one day in 1999, according to Elliott, a hangman's noose appeared near his desk. "You're going to end up with your head in here," Elliott recalls a white co-worker threatening. Another noose appeared last November, he says. He and the other whites "hassle me all the time now, unplugging my computer so I lose work, hiding my bike or chair; it's constant," says Elliott, who gets counseling from a psychologist for the stress and says he has trouble being attentive to his two children, ages 7 and 8, when he's at home.

Lockheed spokesman Sam Grizzle says the company won't comment on any specific employee. But regarding the suits, which Lockheed is fighting, he says, "we do not tolerate, nor have we ever tolerated, harassment or discrimination of any form. We take such complaints very seriously, and we always have investigated them and taken appropriate action when needed."

The alleged incidents at Lockheed are part of an extensive pattern of charges of racial hatred in U.S. workplaces that *BusinessWeek* investigated over a two-month period. Nearly four decades after the Civil Rights Act of 1964 gave legal equality to minorities, charges of harassment at work based on race or national origin have more than doubled, to nearly 9,000 a year, since 1990, according to the Equal Employment Opportunity Commission.

The problem is not confined to small Southern cities such as Marietta. In addition to high-profile suits at Lockheed, Boeing, and Texaco, dozens of other household names face complaints of racism in their workforce. Noose cases have been prosecuted in cosmopolitan San Francisco and in Detroit, with a black population among the largest in the nation.

It's true that minorities' share of the workforce grew over the decade, which could have led to a corresponding rise in clashes. Yet racial harassment charges have jumped by 100% since 1990, while minority employment grew by 36%. What's more, most charges involve multiple victims, so each year the cases add up to tens of thousands of workers—mostly blacks, but also Hispanics and Asians.

It's hard to reconcile such ugly episodes with an American culture that is more accepting of its increasing diversity than ever before. Today, immigrants from every ethnic and racial background flock to the U.S. There is a solid black middle class, and minorities are active in most walks of life, from academia to the nightly news. When we do think about race, it's usually to grapple with more subtle and complex issues, such as whether affirmative action is still necessary to help minorities overcome past discrimination, or whether it sometimes constitutes reverse discrimination against whites.

To some extent, the rise in harassment cases may actually reflect America's improved race relations. Because more minorities believe that society won't tolerate blatant bigotry anymore, they file EEOC charges rather than keep quiet out of despair that their complaints won't be heard, says Susan Sturm, a Columbia University law professor who studies workplace discrimination. Many cases involve allegations of harassment that endured for years.

Multimillion-dollar settlements of racial discrimination or harassment claims at such companies as Coca-Cola Co. and Boeing Co. also give victims greater hope that a remedy is available. Such suits became easier in 1991, after Congress passed a law that allowed jury trials and compensatory and punitive damages in race cases. "It's like rape, which everyone kept silent about before," says Boeing human resources chief James B. Dagnon. "Now, prominent individuals are willing to talk publicly about what happened, so there's a safer environment to speak up in."

But many experts say they are seeing a disturbing increase in incidents of harassment. Minority workers endure the oldest racial slurs in the book. They're asked if they eat "monkey meat," denigrated as inferior to whites, or find "KKK" and other intimidating graffiti on the walls at work.

Even office workers are not exempt. In May, 10 current and former black employees at Xerox Corp. offices in Houston filed harassment charges with the EEOC. One, Linda Johnson, says she has suffered racial slurs from a co-worker since 1999, when glaucoma forced her to quit the sales department and become a receptionist. Last year, a white colleague doctored a computer photo of her to make her look like a prostitute, she says. After she complained, her boss printed out the picture and hung it in his office, her charge says. "I tried to do what company procedures suggested and complain to my supervisor, then on up to human resources at headquarters," says Johnson, 47. "But they just sweep it under the rug." Xerox declined to comment on her case.

Worse yet are hangman's nooses, a potent symbol of mob lynchings in America's racial history. The EEOC has handled 25 noose cases in the past 18 months, "something that only came along every two or three years before." says Ida L. Castro, outgoing EEOC chairwoman. Management lawyers concur that racial harassment has jumped sharply. "I've seen more of these cases in the last few years than in the previous 10, and it's bad stuff," says Steve Poor, a partner at Seyfarth, Shaw, Fairweather & Geraldson, a law firm that helps companies defend harassment and discrimination suits.

Some lay the blame on blue-collar white men who think affirmative action has given minorities an unfair advantage. Their feelings may be fueled by the long-term slide in the wages of less-skilled men, which have lagged inflation since 1973. Since many whites see little evidence of discrimination anymore, the small number who harbor racist views feel more justified in lashing out at minorities, whom they perceive as getting ahead solely due to their race, says Carol M. Swain, a Vanderbilt University law professor who is writing a book about white nationalism.

SILENCE

Incidents of open racism at work occur below the national radar because all the parties have powerful incentives to keep it quiet. Plaintiffs' lawyers don't want employees to go public before a trial for fear of prejudicing their case in court *BusinessWeek* spoke for more than a month with some lawyers before they agreed to let their clients talk. Even then, most workers refused to give their names, fearful of retaliation. Management and plaintiffs' lawyers alike say it takes tremendous nerve to file a suit or EEOC charges, given the likelihood that co-workers or bosses will strike back. Since 1990, the number of minorities filing charges of retaliation with the EEOC after they complained about racial mistreatment has doubled, to 20,000 a year.

Companies have an even greater desire to avoid bad publicity. Many suits end when employers settle. They routinely buy employees' silence with extra damage award money.

Because racial harassment allegations can be so embarrassing, they pose a difficult challenge for companies. Some quickly go on the offensive and take steps to change. Other employers hunker down for a fight, arguing that allegations are inaccurate or exaggerated. Northwest

Airlines Corp., for example, is fighting charges made by black construction workers who found a noose last July at the airline's new terminal under construction at Detroit Metro Airport. Northwest also recently settled two noose-related suits, although it denied liability. Northwest spokeswoman Kathleen M. Peach says none of the noose incidents "rise to the level of harassment. You have to ask was it a joke at a construction site? Or was it in a cargo area where a lot of ropes are used? It's not as cut-and-dried as it seems."

Some employers dismiss nooses and slurs as harmless joking. This seems to be the view taken by Lakeside Imports Inc., New Orleans' largest Toyota Motor Corp. dealer. Last August, it signed a consent decree with the EEOC to settle charges brought by six black salesmen in its 50-person used car department. The men said that their manager. Chris Mohrman, hit and poked them with two 3 1/2-foot-long sticks with derogatory words on them that he called his "n—sticks."

Lakeside brushed aside the incident; according to case depositions. Mohrman's manager at the time, a white man named David Oseng, had hired the black salesmen. When he heard what was going on. Oseng said in his deposition, he told the dealership's top brass. Oseng said the top two managers "told me they were tired of all the problems with the n—s. And if we hired another n—,[I] would be terminated."

Lakeside lawyer Ralph Zatzkis says the dealer didn't admit any guilt and denies that anything serious happened. He says the sticks, which the EEOC obtained by subpoena, did have writing on them, but "those weren't racial remarks." Zatzkis dismissed the episode as "horseplay." Mohrman and the black salesmen left Lakeside and couldn't be reached. Zatzkis says Lakeside's top managers declined to comment.

Frivolous harassment charges do occur, say experts, but they're rare. "It takes a lot of energy to raise a complaint, and you can make major mistakes assuming what the employees' motives are," warns Haven E. Cockerham, head of human resources at R.R. Donnelley & Sons Co., which is fighting a class action for alleged racial discrimination and harassment that included claims of whites donning KKK robes.

Consider Adelphia Communications Corp., a $2.9 billion cable-TV company based in Coudersport, Pa. In February, the EEOC filed suit on behalf of Glenford S. James, a 12-year veteran, and other black employees in the company's Miami office. A manager there racially harassed minorities "on a daily basis" after he took over in August, 1999, the suit says. The manager twice put a noose over James's door, it says. Once, says the complaint, the manager told an employee to "order monkey meat or whatever they eat" for James.

In a suit filed in June, James says that Adelphia didn't stop the problem until he complained to the EEOC in May, 2000. Then, the manager was terminated or resigned. Adelphia declined to comment. However, its brief in the EEOC suit admits that the manager displayed a noose and "made inappropriate statements of a racial nature." The brief says Adelphia "promptly and severely disciplined" the manager "as a result of his actions." The manager couldn't be reached.

REVENGE

Whites who stand up for co-workers also can run into trouble. Ted W. Gignilliat, a worker at the Marietta facility of Lockheed since 1965, says he was harassed so badly for speaking up about two nooses that he had to take a leave of absence. He says he was threatened, his truck was broken into, and he got anonymous phone calls at work and at home—one telling him he would "wind up on a slab, dead." In March, 2000, a psychologist told Gignilliat to stop work: he went on disability leave until May of this year. He now works as an alarm-room operator in the plant's fire station. "It's in the middle of the security office, with guards, but I feel they will retaliate against me again for stepping forward," says Gignilliat.

Usually, of course, minorities bear the brunt of revenge. Roosevelt Lewis, who delivers Wonder bread for an Interstate Bakeries Corp. bakery in San Francisco, says his white superiors have been making his life miserable ever since he and other blacks filed a race suit in 1998. A jury awarded them $132 million last year (late reduced by a judge to $32 million). Lewis says this only exacerbated the behavior. "They're trying to make you insubordinate, to create an excuse to fire you," charges Lewis. He says he has complained to higher-ups, but the hassling continues.

Jack N. Wiltrakis, Interstate's head of human resources, says the company has a hotline to headquarters in Kansas City but has received no complaints. "If they have a problem, it's incumbent on them to tell us," he says. Interstate, which has 34,000 workers in 64 bakeries around the U.S., has been sued for race problems in New York, Orlando, Indianapolis, and Richmond, Va. It has settled the two cases, denying liability, and is still fighting the others, including Lewis'. Wiltrakis says the suits haven't prompted Interstate to launch new policies.

In the end, racist behavior by employees lands at the door of corporate executives. They face a dilemma: If they admit there's a problem, the company is exposed to lawsuits and negative publicity. But denial only makes matters worse. Until more employers confront the rise of ugly racism head on, Americans will continue to see behavior they thought belonged to a more ignominious age.

Case Study

Texaco: The Jelly Bean Diversity Fiasco

Marianne M. Jennings

In November, 1996, Texaco, Inc., was rocked by the disclosure of tape-recorded conversations among three executives about a racial discrimination suit pending against the company. The suit, seeking $71 million, had been brought by 6 employees, on behalf of 1500 other employees, who alleged the following forms of discrimination:

> I have had KKK printed on my car. I have had my tires slashed and racial slurs written about

me on bathroom walls. One co-worker blatantly called me a racial epithet to my face.

Throughout my employment, three supervisors in my department openly discussed their view that African-Americans are ignorant and incompetent, and, specifically, that Thurgood Marshall was the most incompetent person they had ever seen.

Sheryl Joseph, formerly a Texaco secretary in Harvey, Louisiana was given a cake for her birthday which occurred shortly after she announced that she was pregnant. The cake depicted a black

---

pregnant woman and read. "Happy Birthday, Sheryl. It must have been those watermelon seeds."

The suit also included data on Texaco's workforce:

| 1989 | Minorities as a percentage of Texaco's workforce | 15.2% |
| 1994 | Minorities as a percentage of Texaco's workforce | 19.4% |

# of Years to Promotion by Job Classification

Minority Employees	Job	Other Employees
6.1	Accountant	4.6
6.4	Senior Accountant	5.4
12.5	Analyst	6.3
14.2	Financial Analyst	13.9
15.0	Assistant Accounting Supervisor	9.8

Senior Managers

	White	Black
1991	1,887	19
1992	2,001	21
1993	2,000	23
1994	2,029	23

Racial Composition (% of Blacks) by Pay Range

Salary	Texaco	Other Oil Companies
$ 51,100	5.9%	7.2%
$ 56,900	4.7%	6.5%
$ 63,000	4.1%	4.7%
$ 69,900	2.3%	5.1%
$ 77,600	1.8%	3.2%
$ 88,100	1.9%	2.3%
$ 95,600	1.4%	2.6%
$106,100	1.2%	2.3%
$117,600	0.8%	2.3%
$128,800	0.4%	1.8%

(African-Americans make up 12% of the U.S. population)

The acting head of the EEOC wrote in 1995, "Deficiencies in the affirmative-action programs suggest that Texaco is not committed to insuring comprehensive, facility by facility, compliance with the company's affirmative-action responsibilities."

Faced with the lawsuit, Texaco's former treasurer, Robert Ulrich, senior assistant treasurer, J. David Keough, and senior coordinator for personnel services, Richard A. Lundwall, met and discussed the suit. A tape transcript follows:

They look through evidence, deciding what to turn over to the plaintiffs.

LUNDWALL: Here, look at this chart. You know, I'm not really quite sure what it means. This chart is not mentioned in the agency, so it's not important that we even have it in there. . . . They would never know it was here.

KEOUGH: They'll find it when they look through it.

LUNDWALL: Not if I take it out they won't.

The executives decide to leave out certain pages of a document; they worry that another version will turn up.

ULRICH: We're gonna purge the [expletive deleted] out of these books, though. We're not going to have any damn thing that we don't need to be in them—

LUNDWALL: As a matter of fact, I just want to be reminded of what we discussed. You take your data and . . .

KEOUGH: You look and make sure it's consistent to what we've given them already for minutes. Two versions with the restricted and that's marked clearly on top—

ULRICH: But I don't want to be caught up in a cover-up. I don't want to be my own Watergate.

LUNDWALL: We've been doing pretty much two versions, too. This one here, this is strictly my book, your book . . .

ULRICH: Boy, I'll tell you, that one, you would put that and you would have the only copy. Nobody else ought to have copies of that.

LUNDWALL: O.K.?

ULRICH: You have that someplace and it doesn't exist.

LUNDWALL: Yeah, O.K.

ULRICH: I just don't want anybody to have a copy of that.

LUNDWALL: Good, No problem.

ULRICH: You know, there is no point in even keeping the restricted version anymore. All it could do is get us in trouble. That's the way I feel. I would not keep anything.

LUNDWALL: Let me shred this thing and any other restricted version like it.

ULRICH: Why do we have to keep the minutes of the meeting anymore?

LUNDWALL: You don't, you don't.

ULRICH: We don't?

LUNDWALL: Because we don't, no, we don't because it comes back to haunt us like right now—

ULRICH: I mean, the pendulum is swinging the other way, guys.

The executives discuss the minority employees who brought the suit.

LUNDWALL: They are perpetuating an us/them atmosphere. Last week or last Friday I told . . .

ULRICH: [Inaudible.]

LUNDWALL: Yeah, that's what I said to you, you want to frag grenade? You know, duck, I'm going to throw one. Well, that's what I was alluding to. But the point is not, that's not bad in itself but it does perpetuate us/them. And if you're trying to get away and get to the we . . . you can't do that kind of stuff.

ULRICH: [Inaudible.] I agree. This diversity thing. You know how black jelly beans agree. . . .

LUNDWALL: That's funny. All the black jelly beans seem to be glued to the bottom of the bag.

ULRICH: You can't have just we and them. You can't just have black jelly beans and other jelly beans. It doesn't work.

LUNDWALL: Yeah. But they're perpetuating the black jelly beans.

ULRICH: I'm still having trouble with Hanukkah. Now, we have Kwanza (laughter).

The release of the tape prompted the Reverend Jesse Jackson to call for a nationwide boycott of Texaco. Sales fell 8%, Texaco's stock fell 2%, and several institutional investors were preparing to sell their stock.

Texaco did have a minority recruiting effort in place and the "jelly bean" remark was tied to a diversity trainer the company had hired. The following are excerpts from Texaco's statement of vison and values:

Respect for the Individual

Our employees are our most important resource. Each person deserves to be treated with respect and dignity in appropriate work environments, without regard to race, religion, sex, age, national origin, disability or position in the company. Each employee has the responsibility to demonstrate respect for others.

The company believes that a work environment that reflects a diverse workforce, values diversity, and is free of all forms of discrimination, intimidation, and harassment is essential for a productive and efficient workforce. Accordingly, conduct directed toward any employee that is unwelcome, hostile, offensive, degrading, or abusive is unacceptable and will not be tolerated.

A federal grand jury began an investigation at Texaco to determine whether there had been obstruction of justice in the withholding of documents.

Within days of the release of the tape, Texaco settled its bias suit for $176.1 million, the largest sum ever allowed in a discrimination case. The money will allow a 11% pay raise for blacks and other minorities who joined in the law suit.

Texaco's chairman and CEO, Peter I. Bijur, issued the following statement after agreeing to a settlement:

Texaco is facing a difficult but vital challenge. It's broader than any specific words and larger than any lawsuit. It is one we must and are attacking head-on.

We are a company of 27,000 people worldwide. In any organization of that size, unfortunately, there are bound to be people with unacceptable, biased attitudes toward race, gender and religion.

Our goal, and our responsibility, is to eradicate this kind of thinking wherever and however it is found in our company. And our challenge is to make Texaco a company of limitless opportunity for all men and women.

We are committed to begin meeting this challenge immediately through programs with concrete goals and measurable timetables.

I've already announced certain specific steps, including a redoubling of efforts within Texaco to focus on the paramount value of respect for the individual and a comprehensive review of our diversity programs at every level of our company.

We also want to broaden economic access to Texaco for minority firms and increase the positive impact our investments can have in the minority community. This includes areas such as hiring and promotion; professional services such as advertising, banking, investment management and legal services; and wholesale and retail station ownership.

To assist us, we are reaching out to leaders of minority and religious organizations and others for ideas and perspectives that will help Texaco succeed in our mission of becoming a model of diversity and workplace equality.

It is essential to this urgent mission that Texaco and African-Americans and other minority community leaders work together to help solve the programs we face as a company—which, after all, echo the problems faced in society as a whole.

Discrimination will be extinguished only if we tackle it together, only if we join in a unified, common effort.

Working together, I believe we can take Texaco into the 21st century as a model of diversity. We can make Texaco a company of limitless opportunity. We can make Texaco a leader in according respect to every man and woman.

Even after the announcement, Texaco stock was down $3 per share, a loss of $800 million total, and the boycott was continued. Texaco's proposed merger with Shell Oil began to unravel as Shell's CEO expressed concern about Texaco's integrity. However, after the settlement, additional information about the case began to emerge.

Holman W. Jenkins, Jr. wrote the following piece for the *Wall Street Journal:*

Quietly, corporate America is debating whether Texaco's Peter Bijur did the right thing.

Mr. Bijur gets paid to make the hard calls, and with the airwaves aflame over "nigger" and "black jelly beans," Texaco took a battering in the stock and political markets. He had every reason for wanting to put a stop-loss on the media frenzy. "Once the taped conversations were revealed," he says, settling was "reasonable and honorable." So now Texaco is betting $176 million that paying off minority employees and their lawyers is the quickest way out of the news.

But as the company's own investigation showed, the truly inflammatory comments reported in the media never took place. They were purely a fabrication by opposing lawyers, and trumpeted by a credulous *New York Times*. And some digging would have shown this problem cropping up before in the career of Mike Hausfeld, lead attorney for the plaintiffs.

In an antitrust case years ago, he presented a secret recording that he claimed showed oil executives conspiring to threaten gasoline dealers. But a check by the same expert who handled the Nixon Watergate tapes showed no such thing. Says Larry Sharp, the Washington antitrust lawyer who opposed Mr. Hausfeld: "To put it generously, he gave himself the benefit of the doubt in making the transcript."

But this time the lie has been rewarded, and the broader public, unschooled in legal cynicism, heads home believing Texaco an admitted racist.

The catechism of corporate crisis management says you can't fight the media. Mr. Bijur had to consider that Jesse Jackson was threatening a boycott if Texaco failed to "regret, repent and seek renewal." Mr. Jackson pointedly added that "any attempt to shift to denial would add insult to injury"—a warning against trying to spread some egg to the faces of those who were fooled by the fake transcript.

There may have been wisdom, if not valor, in Mr. Bijur's decision to run up the white flag. But he also evinced symptoms of Stockholm Syndrome, telling CNN that Texaco was just the "tip of the iceberg" of corporate racism. Ducking this fight so ignominiously may yet prove a penny-wise, pound-foolish strategy. The City of Philadelphia has decided to dump its Texaco holdings anyway, partly out of fear of more litigation.

What else could Texaco have done? It could have apologized for any offense, but stuck up for its former treasurer Bob Ulrich, who was wronged by the phony transcript and stripped of his medical benefits by Texaco. And the company could have vowed to fight the lawsuit like the dickens, arguing that Texaco is not the cause of society's racial troubles but has tried to be part of the solution.

Start with the tapes: A fair listening does not necessarily reveal a "racist" conversation by executives at Texaco, but certainly a candid conversation about the problems of race at Texaco. They spoke of "jelly beans" dividing into camps of "us" and "them," an honest representation of life at many companies, not just in the oil patch.

Mr. Bijur could have made this point, starting with the *New York Times*, which has been embroiled in its own discrimination lawsuit with Angela Dodson, once its top-ranking black female. In a complaint filed with New York City's Human Rights Commission, she claims the paper was "engaged in gender-based harassment and disability-based discrimination . . . because *The Times* no longer wanted me, as a black person, to occupy a position as Senior editor."

Her deepest ire is reserved for *Times* veteran Carolyn Lee, who is white and more accustomed to being lauded as a champion of women and minorities. Ms. Dodson told the *Village Voice*: "It got to the point that whenever I was in her presence or earshot she made remarks [about other black people] that could only be taken as negative."

This sounds remarkably like the anecdotes filed in the Texaco complaint. All an outsider can safely conclude is that race makes everything more complicated, as sensitivity begets sensitivity. Mr. Bijur would have done more for racial understanding had he used his platform to open up this subject.

Yes, the cartoonist racists are out there, he might have said, but the *Times* coverage of Texaco only found cartoonist racists. The paper could have looked to its own experience for another story—a story about how garden-variety interpersonal conflict can land even decent people in the snares of racial mistrust.

This is what affirmative action, by throwing people together, was supposed to get us past. And it may be no accident that our most quota-ridden newspaper, *USA Today*, jumped off the bandwagon on the Texaco tapes, noting the ambiguity of whether the "jelly bean" remarks were meant to be hostile or friendly to blacks.

And McPaper kept on asking intelligent questions, like whether the *New York Times* had been "used by plaintiffs in the case to promote a faulty but more inflammatory transcript?" ("Not unless the court was used," answered *Times* Business Editor John Geddes, sounding like a lawyer himself.)

So Mr. Bijur was not facing a uniformly hopeless media torrent. The truth, even a complicated truth, catches up with the headlines eventually.

In time, he might have found surprising allies drifting to his side. The *New Republic* and the *New Yorker* have run thoughtful articles arguing that businesses should be allowed to use quotas but shouldn't be subject to harassment litigation if they don't. Right now, we do the opposite: Forbid companies to promote by quota, then sue them under federal "adverse impact" rules when they don't.

In effect, liberal voices are arguing that business could do more for minorities with less conflict if freedom of contract were restored. The world is changing, and companies have their own reasons nowadays for wanting minorities around. They need input from different kinds of people on how to deal with different kinds of people. No doubt this is why McPaper feels free to thumb its nose at the conformity crowd on stories like Texaco and church-burnings. (See September's *Harvard Business Review* for what business is thinking about diversity now.)

If companies were set free to assemble the work forces most useful to them, they could sweep away a heap of excuses for recrimination. Whites couldn't feel cheated out of jobs. Blacks wouldn't end up at companies that want them only for window-dressing. And the world could go back to feeling OK about being an interesting place. We might even allow that cultural patterns other than racism may explain why so many rednecks, and so few blacks, become petroleum engineers.

Mr. Bijur may have made the best of a bad deal for his shareholders. Whether it was best for America is a different judgment.[1]

Richard Lundwall, the executive who taped the sessions with the other executives was charged with one count of obstruction of justice. Lundwall had turned over the tapes of the conversations to lawyers for the plaintiffs in the discrimination suit on October 25, 1996. Lundwall had been terminated.

Texaco hired attorney Michael Armstrong to investigate the underlying allegations. Mr. Armstrong found the tapes had not been transcribed correctly.

As part of its settlement, Texaco agreed to, at a cost of $55 million, assign a task force to police hiring and promotion as well as requiring mentors for black employees and sensitivity training for white employees.

The following interview with CEO Bijur appeared in *Business Week:*

Q: How did your legal strategy change once the news of the tapes was printed?

A: When I saw [the story], I knew that this lawsuit was pending and moving forward. I made the judgment that we needed to accelerate the settlement process. And those discussions on settlement commenced almost immediately.

Q: It has been reported that you didn't get the board of directors involved with the settlement talks and other issues. Why not?

A: You're drawing conclusions that are erroneous. The board was fully involved throughout the entire process. I talked to numerous directors personally. We had several board and executive committee meetings. The board was fully supportive of our actions.

Q: Have you met with shareholders?

A: Yes, of course. I went down to [New York] and met with the Interfaith Center on Corporate Responsibility, which is a group of religious shareholders. I expressed our position on this and listened carefully to their position and got some good counsel and guidance. But I wanted to provide our side of the issue as well. I have met with [New York State Comptroller] Carl McCall and [New York City Comptroller] Alan Hevesi about concerns that they had, and I will continue to meet with other shareholders as I normally do.

Q: Why do you think the oil industry has such a poor reputation on issues of racial diversity and gender equality? How does Texaco stack up against the others?

A: The percentage of minorities within Texaco is just about average for the petroleum industry. We have made really significant progress in the last several years in improving the percentage. But there are some very interesting points that need to be examined to place in context what may be going on in this industry. I just read a study that showed that in 1995, there were only nine petroleum engineering minority graduates that came out of all engineering schools in the United States—only nine. That's not an excuse. But it is indicative of why it is difficult for this industry to have a lot of people in the pipeline. Now, of course, that does not apply to accountants, finance people, and anybody else. But we are a very technically oriented industry.

Q: Have you personally witnessed discrimination at Texaco?

A: In the nearly 31 years I have been with Texaco, I have never witnessed an incident of racial bias or prejudice. And had I seen it, I would have taken disciplinary action. I've never seen it.

Q: Is there a widespread culture of insensitivity at Texaco?

A: I do not think there is a culture of institutional bias within Texaco. I think we've got a great many very good and decent human beings, but that unfortunately we mirror society. There is bigotry in society. There is prejudice and injustice in society. I am sorry to say that, and I am sorry to say that

probably does exist within Texaco. I can't do much about society, but I certainly can do something about Texaco.

Q: What are your views on affirmative action?

A: Texaco's views on affirmative action have not changed a bit. We have supported affirmative action, and we will continue to support affirmative action.

Q: This is your first big trial since taking over. What have you learned?

A: I've learned that as good as our programs are in the company—and they really are quite good, even in this area—there's always more we can do. We've got to really drill down into the programs. We've got to make certain that they're meeting the objectives and goals we've set for them.

Q: Are there other lessons in terms of your style of management?

A: I don't think I would do anything different the next time than what I did this time.

Q: How will you make sure the spirit as well as the letter of the policy is followed at Texaco?

A: We're going to put more and more and more emphasis on it until we get it through everybody's head: Bigotry is not going to be tolerated here.[2]

Robert W. Ulrich was indicted in 1997. Mr. Lundwall entered a "not guilty" plea on July 8, 1997, and J. David Keough has sued Texaco for libel. Texaco named Mary Bush, a financial consultant, as its first black female board member.

As Lundwall's prosecution has proceeded, new discoveries have been made. For example, "purposeful erasures" have been found on the tapes.

In an interim report on its progress toward the settlement goals, Texaco revealed the following:

Polishing the Star

As part of its settlement of a discrimination lawsuit brought by black employees, Texaco has moved on a half-dozen fronts to alter its business practices.

Hiring Asked search firms to identify wider arrays of candidates. Expanded recruiting at historically minority colleges. Gave 50 scholarships and paid internships to minority students seeking engineering or technical degrees.

Career Advancement Wrote objective standards for promotions. Developing training program for new managers. Developing a mentoring program.

Diversity Initiatives Conducted two-day diversity training for more than 8,000 of 20,000 U.S. employees. Tied management bonuses to diversity goals. Developing alternative dispute resolution and ombudsman programs.

Purchasing Nearly doubled purchases from minority- or women-owned businesses. Asking suppliers to report their purchases from such companies.

Financial Services Substantially increased banking, investment management and insurance business with minority- and women-owned firms. A group of such firms underwrote a $150 million public financing.

Retailing Added three black independent retailers, 18 black managers of company-owned service stations, 12 minority or female wholesalers, 13 minority- or women-owned Xpress Lube outlets and 6 minority- or women-owned lubricant distributors.

In May 1998, the Texaco executives were acquitted of all criminal charges.

NOTES

1. Reprinted with permission of *The Wall Street Journal* © 1996 Dow Jones & Company, Inc. All rights reserved.
2. Smart, Tim. "Texaco: Lessons From A Crisis-in-Progress." Reprinted from December 2, 1996, issue of *Business Week* by special permission, © 1997 by McGraw Hill, Inc.

Case Study

Denny's

Ronald M. Green

On the morning of April 1, 1993, 21 agents of the Secret Service Uniformed Division entered the West Street, Annapolis Denny's restaurant for breakfast. The agents were part of a detail assigned to protect President Clinton while he addressed the American Society of Newspaper Editors at the U.S. Naval Academy in Annapolis. The unit hoped to grab a quick bite before returning to the Naval Academy to set up metal-detecting equipment.

Six black Secret Service Agents, including Alfonso Dyson, Leroy Snyder, and Robin Thomson, sat together. Their white colleagues sat at neighboring tables. The entire detail was dressed in full uniform—badges, black shoes, black pants with wide gold stripes, white shirts, black ties, and guns strapped on. All 21 agents, who had less than an hour to eat, ordered quickly, one after another, but the six black agents, who sat together, waited

50 minutes after ordering without being served. Watching as their white colleagues finished second and third helpings, agent Robin Thompson complained to their waitress. She replied that their meals were on the way. Thompson then asked to see the manager, but the waitress said he was on the phone. White agents report that the waitress rolled her eyes after turning to leave the black agents' table. The agents saw several dishes sitting for several minutes under heat lamps next to the kitchen. Meanwhile, a small group of white customers who had entered the uncrowded restaurant after the black agents, were promptly served.

When the other agents had finished their meals, and after numerous complaints, the black agents stood to leave. Only then was food offered to them. The agents refused it because there was no time to eat. The food arrived so late and after so many complaints that the agents believed they were effectively denied service. "We had to go to Roy Rogers and eat in the van," said agent Dyson.

Ironically, the incident occurred the same day that Flagstar, Denny's parent corporation, settled a federal lawsuit in California by a consent decree in which Denny's agreed to stop allegedly discriminatory treatment of black customers. Now Denny's faced another suit, soon filed by the six Secret Service agents, who claimed that the chain violated their civil rights during the April 1 incident. Agent Thompson said he "felt humiliated" by the events of that April morning. "I was somewhat invisible that day. I felt we (black and white agents) were coequals. But after I left the restaurant, I felt belittled, less than a person. This should not happen to anyone." Agent Alfonso Dyson said that he concluded that poor service was not the reason for the delay. "You would never think it would happen to you, especially not in full uniform. I was definitely unprepared. I had let my guard down."

This incident was part of a larger pattern of discrimination of which the Denny's chain was being accused. (See Exhibit 1.) The lawsuit filed by the Secret Service agents brought Denny's under renewed fire. At a press conference, the agents said that the Secret Service had been supportive of their effort, adding that the decision to break from the agency's traditional stoicism and file the lawsuit had been difficult.

As the agents' suit grabbed headlines, the NAACP demanded negotiations with Flagstar Corporation to amend their alleged discriminatory hiring and serving practices. Rupert Richardson, an NAACP member, pointing to the California consent decree and the Annapolis incident, said, "There has got to be something radically wrong with Denny's, because the moment you take care of a problem here, it pops up somewhere else." Around the country, editorial writers blasted the chain and held it up as an example of how far the United States was from eliminating racism.

Denny's top management was caught unprepared by the intensity and extent of the criticisms. The company thought of itself as a family-oriented business, serving reasonably priced food 24-hours a day in a sit-down, friendly atmosphere. Over the years, Denny's had tried to distinguish itself from many other fast food chains by its emphasis on sit-down service and by the creation of a welcoming atmosphere with practices like complimentary meals on customers' birthdays. Flagstar Corporation, the parent company, owns some of the nation's largest restaurant chains. In addition to Denny's, its franchises include Hardee's, Quincy's Family Steakhouse, and El Pollo Loco. Flagstar also owns Canteen Company, a food services and concessions business. With 3.7 billion dollars in sales in 1992, and nearly 2,000 restaurants nationwide, Flagstar is one of the nation's largest corporations, employing 120,000 people. There are 1,460 Denny's Restaurants nationwide alone, employing 46,000 people. Seventy percent of these restaurants are owned by Flagstar, while the others are owned and operated by individual franchisers. After the Annapolis incident, sales were down in restaurants across the nation, and Flagstar's stock was trading near the lowest price since the company went public in 1989.

Flagstar executives, realizing that their company was in trouble and insisting that these incidents were not examples of company policy, struggled to understand and explain the cause of the widespread allegations. Thirty-six percent of Flagstar's employees are minorities, twenty percent of whom are black (twice the proportion of the U.S. population). But Flagstar has no senior black managers, and no minority officers or directors. Only one of its franchises is minority owned. Although Flagstar obviously had a lack of minority leadership, Marilyn Loven, a San Francisco management and diversity consultant offered a sympathetic view of the company's problems. In most cases, she claimed, discrimination results from employees acting individually without the approval of management. A company can have enlightened, well-intentioned leaders, only to be undercut by low-level front line employees. She argued that no company can eliminate racism, "but any company that doesn't spend a lot of time educating employees is going to run into problems."

Jerome Richardson, head of Flagstar, readily accepted some of the blame. The company has recently come through a long period of financial turbulence. Richardson sold Flagstar in 1979, bought it out again in 1989, and took it public. In 1992, Kohlberg Kravis Roberts invested $300 million to acquire 47% of the company. Richardson acknowledges that constantly dealing with finances blinded him to other aspects of running a corporation. "I should have invested the time earlier, and I regret it."

Whatever the causes, Denny's, with numerous charges of discrimination facing it and a tarnished reputation, had run into serious problems. Flagstar executives now confronted an urgent responsibility—convincing the public and their employees that they truly believed that discrimination is bad business. Richardson, with a company $2 billion in debt, summed up the challenge. "We need all the customers we can get."

EXHIBIT 1

1990: Marcus Daniels accuses Denny's manager of harassing him for his skin color. Tyrone Jackson, a Denny's employee, alleges that he was ordered not to allow blacks to receive separate checks.

October, 1992: U.S. Justice Department informs Denny's that it plans to file lawsuit alleging discriminatory practices against black customers in Northern California. Government offers Denny's opportunity to settle complaint.

March 24, 1993: Black customers file class-action lawsuit in San Francisco, accusing Denny's of discrimination. Complaint is also filed with the Equal Opportunity Commission alleging job discrimination and asking the company to hire a civil rights monitor.

March 25: Denny's reaches settlement with Justice Department, promising to train employees against racial discrimination and to hire a civil rights monitor.

April 1: A waitress at a Denny's restaurant in Annapolis, Maryland, allegedly refuses to serve breakfast to six black Secret Service agents. The Justice Department demands an explanation. Federal judge approves consent decree between Denny's and U.S. Justice Department. Denny's agrees to reinforce policies of equitable treatment and to communicate guidelines to all employees.

Other: Individual charges of discrimination on April 1, April 18, April 24, May 7, May 8, May 9, May 10, May 20, and May 26, 1993.

Case Study

Global United: Melba Moore

John R. Hundley III

The Global United Manufacturing Company employs over 1500 people in its headquarters in Cleveland, Ohio. The company has several government contracts and thus is subjected annually to an equal employment opportunity compliance review conducted by a federal agency. The company has an affirmative action program to implement its policy of equal employment opportunity. The government's compliance staff has found the company's affirmative action program to be comprehensive and the company to be serious in its attempts to correct any deficiencies uncovered by the review.

The purchasing department of Global United is responsible for ordering all manufacturing materials, office supplies, and services. The department is headed by the chief purchasing agent, Pete Wilson. Reporting to Pete are five supervisors, each having responsibility for purchasing different types of goods and services. Each supervisor has a staff of several buyers, a stenographer, and a typist.

Most of the buyers are college graduates or have a college background with equivalent experience. The buyers are considered semi-professional employees and are given considerable leeway in their purchasing decisions. The buyers must exercise considerable tact in dealing with the many salesmen who call on Global.

Under the various provisions of the company's affirmative action program (and as required by various governmental orders), all major suppliers and subcontractors must certify that they are equal employment opportunity employers and that they have an affirmative action program. The purchasing department is responsible for seeing that the necessary certifications are received from each supplier and subcontractor.

However, over the years the purchasing department itself had employed only a few black employees. During an annual compliance review in February, the EEOC (Equal Employment Opportunity Commission) compliance staff pointed out that Global was deficient in employing blacks in its purchasing department. Pete Wilson and the five supervisors reporting to him agreed that they would make a special effort to employ black buyers.

In August Melba Moore, a young black woman, began her employment with Global as a clerk-typist in the purchasing department. She had attended a junior college in Cleveland and had studied several courses in business administration. After a year and a half of college. Melba left school due to marriage. Upon leaving college, Melba went to work as a clerk-typist in the accounting department of a chemical company headquartered in Cleveland. Melba worked for the chemical company for three years before leaving due to pregnancy.

When her son, Jeff, reached age one, Melba decided to re-enter the labor market and again, assist in earning the family income. Melba's husband, Bob, was employed as a marketing representative by a major oil

This case was prepared by John R. Hundley III of the University College Division, Washington University. Used by permission. All names are disguised.

company and was assigned to a territory in the Ohio area. Although Bob earned a fairly good income, both Bob and Melba wanted to save enough money to purchase a home.

During her first several months on the job, Melba performed in an outstanding manner. She learned her job quickly and reached a high output level as a typist. Melba formed cordial relationships with the other employees in the purchasing department, and she was very pleasant with the salesmen who called on Global.

In January one of the buyers under supervisor Tom Schmitt left Global to accept a position with another company. After discussion of possible ways to fill the vacant buyer's position. Pete Wilson and Tom Schmitt decided to offer the promotion to Melba. Melba accepted the promotion and was moved under Tom Schmitt's supervision. The company was pleased that it had been able to upgrade a black female employee to fill this semiprofessional position. Melba thus became one of the few black people to occupy a comparable position in the company, although the company did employ many blacks in lower occupational jobs.

However, after several months as a buyer. Melba began to complain to Tom Schmitt about discriminatory actions on the part of other members of the department. Melba cited examples of not receiving phone messages or copies of departmental memoranda on several occasions. She also mentioned an incident where one of the typists refused to do her work because another buyer had already given her some work. Melba further stated that she felt certain supervisors in other departments were biased.

Tom talked with Melba for several hours, advising her that these incidents should "be taken for what they are and no more—irritations that cannot be avoided in the business world." Tom advised Melba that even Pete Wilson didn't receive all of his phone messages and that this was not necessarily a subtle form of discrimination on the part of her coworkers. Melba told Tom that these incidents were attempts "to remind me that I'm the least important person in the department." Melba further stated, "I'm not important here, so if I'm out a day or so, my work won't suffer—someone else will do it or it'll wait."

After Melba became a buyer, her attendance began to slip. During a six-month period, Melba missed fifteen days. On each occasion Melba had seemingly good reasons for being absent, but this amount of absence was far more than customary in the purchasing department.

Melba was shaken by the following incident. She invited several of her co-workers to a "home decorating" party over a weekend. A representative of a home decorating firm planned to display his merchandise and provide Melba with a commission on any merchandise sold as a result of the party. None of the men or women working for Tom Schmitt whom Melba invited attended the party. One of the buyers said he planned a trip on that date. Another buyer became ill several days prior to the party and was unable to attend. A stenographer in the unit decided not to attend since she did not know anyone else attending the party. Even though several employees of the company attended the party. Melba was disturbed that no one from the purchasing department attended. She made it a point to tell Tom Schmitt about this experience on Monday morning and she commented. "This shows again that the whites in this department are against me and don't care about my feelings."

In previous discussions of problems in relationships with co-workers. Melba usually had reacted negatively to Tom's advice. No amount of reassurance or personal counseling had convinced Melba that her beliefs were without foundation. Tom wondered what action, if any, he should take regarding the latest incident.

Case Study

Management Dilemma

Fred E. Schuster

Stan Fritzhill, Manager of the Data Analysis Department of Aerostar, Inc., a small research firm; pondered how he should utilize a salary increase budget of $32,900 (10% of total payroll) to reward the five semi-professional employees in his unit. He knew that he did not have to spend the full budget, but under no circumstances could he exceed it. In his opinion, all of these individuals were properly paid in relation to their relative performance and seniority one year (12 months) ago, when he last adjusted their compensation. The rate of inflation last year was 7%.

Fritzhill had assembled a summary of his performance appraisals (see Appendix I) and other pertinent data to assist in determining his recommendations, which he knew were needed immediately.

QUESTIONS FOR DISCUSSION

1. Is the information provided in the column titled "personal circumstances" relevant to Mr. Fritzhill's decision? Why or why not?
2. Is the information provided in the column titled "years in department" relevant to Mr. Fritzhill's decision? Why or why not?
3. If it appears that an employee has been unfairly denied raises in the past, should special "make-up" raises be given? Are there any employees in this case who appear to have been unfairly treated?
4. How should Fritzhill distribute the money? What role, if any, should inflation play in his deliberations?

APPENDIX A

Name	Present Salary	Title	Salary Grade	Years in Dept.	Performance	Personal Circumstances
John Mason	$72,000	Analyst	6	5	Acceptable quality, several important deadlines have been missed but may not be his fault.	Married. Large family dependent on him as sole support.
G. W. Jones	$66,000	Analyst	6	2	Outstanding. Sometimes a bit "pushy" in making requests and suggestions about the department.	Single. No dependents. Has no pressing need for money. Reported to lead a rather "wild" life outside the office
Jane Boston	$56,000	Junior Analyst	5	8	Consistently an excellent performer, though not assigned to the full range of duties of an analyst. Dependable. Often initiates improvements in work methods.	Married. Husband is a successful architect. Children in high school.
Ralph Schmidt	$73,000	Senior Analyst	7	15	Acceptable, but not outstanding. Few original contributions recently. Seems to be a "plodder." Content to get by with minimum performance and participation.	Married. Financially pressed because he has 2 children in college (one plans to go on to Med. School).
Hillary Johnson	$58,000	Junior Analyst	5	6	Acceptable volume of performance, but continues to make costly mistakes. Has repeatedly been warned about this over last years.	Single. Has a dependent mother who is chronically ill.

Chapter Five

———•———

Work Life Balance and Gender Issues

THE POPULAR TV show of the late 1950s and early 1960s *Leave It to Beaver* was a sitcom and not a documentary. And yet a lot of people then (and perhaps even now) thought it represented the perfect portrait of the American family—Dad at work and Mom at home with the kids. Sociologist Stephanie Coontz maintains that the model of Dad earning a living and Mom in the kitchen resonates with a deep-seated bias regarding what we then thought to be natural and proper: Men were providers, women were nurturers. In her book *The Way We Never Were: American Families and the Nostalgia Trap*, she argues that this model existed for only a short-lived moment in the cultural history of this country.

Perhaps the single most important event in the American labor market in the second half of the twentieth century was the unprecedented entry of large numbers of women into the workforce seeking full-time employment and careers. Depending on how you crunch the numbers and whose numbers you accept, there are in excess of 66 million women working in full-time jobs in America; that is, women represent between 49 and 51 percent of the entire workforce. An equally important statistic is that working couples (either DINKS, "Double Income No Kids," or DISKS, "Double Income Some Kids") now make up 39 percent of the workforce.

Fueling this trend of women in the workforce were the impact of the feminist movement, changes in social custom, the evolving needs of business, more educational opportunities, the need to seek individual identity, and perhaps most immediately, the rising cost of a middle-class lifestyle. But whatever the reason or reasons, in less than forty years the structure of the workforce, the workplace, and the American family radically altered. In contrast to the 1950s and 1960s when 43 percent of all families (with or without children) made do on a single income, only 14 percent of today's families have just one income earner. So-called traditional families, in which the father is the sole breadwinner and the mother is a full-time homemaker caring for children, are now a minority of two-parent households with children. In the 1980s this type of family composed 15 percent of all households. As of this publication some experts now suggest that this figure has risen to about 25 percent. Bradley K. Googins, a professor in the Graduate School of Social Work at Boston University, has put together a handy chart, which graphically captures the magnitude of change that occurred in the prototypical U.S. family between 1950 and 1990:

1950	1990
Three children	One child
Mother at home	Mother at work
Parents age twenty-two when first child born	Parents age thirty-five when first child is born
Mother and father married fifteen years	Parents divorced; father remarried
Grandmother lives in house	Grandmother in extended-care facility
Family eats out a few times per year	Family eats out three times per week
Children and mother part of scout troops	Children alone participate in after-school activities and lessons

According to Googins, it is almost incomprehensible that these radically different families were only a generation apart. Today's families are diverse, defy stereotypes, and operate under a constantly changing series of rules, demands, and expectations. Today's families are more mobile, less stable as units, and much more dependent on institutions, such as day-care centers, schools, restaurants, and elder service agencies to carry out what were once strictly family roles and functions. No matter how much we wistfully romanticize the 1950s model of the traditional family, said Googins, in reality, it is now nothing more than a statistical anomaly. Nowadays, Dad's at work, Mom's at work, and we're not always altogether sure who's taking care of the children!

With women in the workplace, "the great American time crunch" has become collective, communal, and familial. With both Mom and Dad on the job and working an ever-expanding day, our lives have become hectic attempts to balance work, home, family, and a rapidly diminishing social and leisure calendar. Although there is no more time in the day than there was when wives didn't work and were in charge of the home front, there is now twice as much to do and less and less time to do it. When the hours devoted to home and family responsibilities are added to paid work hours, most working adults today are responsible for the equivalent of one and one-half to two full-time jobs. According to economist Juliet Schor, the 5 P.M. dads of the 1950s and 1960s are becoming an "endangered species," and more and more of them are being transmogrified into 8 or 9 P.M. dads. As one hardworking dad put it, "Either I can spend time with my family or support them. Not both. If I didn't work the overtime, my wife would have to work much longer hours to make up the difference" And working women, said Schor, find themselves in much the same bind. According to her calculations, the total working time of employed mothers now averages in excess of sixty-five hours per week, and this figure can jump to seventy to eighty hours per week depending on the number and age of her children, her marital status, the type of job, and her wage scale.

Clearly we are facing a challenge. Clearly the entrance of women into the workforce has necessitated a fundamental reevaluation of our ideas about sexual equality, sexual role modeling, the purpose and function of marriage, the responsibilities of parenthood, and the logistics of child rearing. In effect, a major revolution has been taking place in American society, one that affects virtually all of our domestic, social, and economic arrangements. How we work and the problems of finding a balance between our work and our private lives say a great deal about us as a nation and a culture, and about the quality of our individual lives.

The essays and cases in this section try to address some of the issues of women entering the workplace and the problem of trying to achieve a balance in work and the rest of life for both men and women. "Women in the Workplace" offers us an overview of the entire phenomenon and its general impact on our lives. "Management Women and the New Facts of Life" is the article that sparked the still ongoing debate about creating a "mommy track" for women who want careers and kids. The article "Child Care Comes to Work" speak to the various pieces of the work/life puzzle. That is, how does one go about finding a balance between kids, home, career, commuting, and chores? The last few cases in this section speak to specific problems women experience on the job. "Gender Issues at Your House" and "Worth the Effort?" provide the reader with realistic workplace scenarios of what can happen when a sexual harassment charge is made. "Foreign Assignment" focuses on how women are perceived on the job by colleagues and customers. "Sexual Discrimination at Eastern Airlines?" is a curious and complicated case about gender identity, gender bias, public perception, and corporate identity.

Essay

Management Women and the New Facts of Life

Felice N. Schwartz

The cost of employing women in management is greater than the cost of employing men. This is a jarring statement, partly because it is true, but mostly because it is something people are reluctant to talk about. A new study by one multinational corporation shows that the rate of turnover in management positions is 2 1/2 times higher among top-performing women than it is among men. A large producer of consumer goods reports that one half of the women who take maternity leave return to their jobs late or not at all.

And we know that women also have a greater tendency to plateau or to interrupt their careers in ways that limit their growth and development. But we have become so sensitive to charges of sexism and so afraid of confrontation, even litigation, that we rarely say what we know to be true. Unfortunately, our bottled-up awareness leaks out in misleading metaphors ("glass ceiling" is one notable example), veiled hostility, lowered expectations, distrust, and reluctant adherence to Equal Employment Opportunity requirements.

Career interruptions, plateauing, and turnover are expensive. The money corporations invest in recruitment, training, and development is less likely to produce top executives among women than among men, and the invaluable company experience that developing executives acquire at every level as they move up through management ranks is more often lost.

The studies just mentioned are only the first of many, I'm quite sure. Demographic realities are going to force corporations all across the country to analyze the cost of employing women in managerial positions, and what they will discover is that women cost more.

But here is another startling truth: The greater cost of employing women is not a function of inescapable gender differences. Women *are* different from men, but what increases their cost to the corporation is principally the clash of their perceptions, attitudes, and behavior with those of men, which is to say, with the policies and practices of male-led corporations.

It is terribly important that employers draw the right conclusions from the studies now being done. The studies will be useless—or worse, harmful—if all they teach us is that women are expensive to employ. What we need to learn is how to reduce that expense, how to stop throwing away the investments we make in talented women, how to become more responsive to the needs of the women that corporations *must* employ if they are to have the best and the brightest of all those now entering the work force.

The gender differences relevant to business fall into two categories: those related to maternity and those related to the differing traditions and expectations of the sexes. Maternity is biological rather than cultural. We can't alter it, but we can dramatically reduce its impact on the workplace and in many cases eliminate its negative effect on employee development. We can accomplish this by addressing the second set of differences, those between male and female socialization. Today, these differences exaggerate the real costs of maternity and can turn a relatively slight disruption in work schedule into a serious business problem and a career derailment for individual women. If we are to overcome the cost differential between male and female employees, we need to address the issues that arise when female socialization meets the male corporate culture and masculine rules of career development—issues of behavior and style, of expectation, of stereotypes and preconceptions, of sexual tension and harassment, of female mentoring, lateral mobility, relocation, compensation, and early identification of top performers.

The one immutable, enduring difference between men and women is maternity. Maternity is not simply childbirth but a continuum that begins with an awareness of the ticking of the biological clock, proceeds to the anticipation of motherhood, includes pregnancy, childbirth, physical recuperation, psychological adjustment, and continues on to nursing, bonding, and child rearing. Not all women choose to become mothers, of course, and among those who do, the process varies from case to case depending on the health of the mother and baby, the values of the parents, and the availability, cost, and quality of child care.

In past centuries, the biological fact of maternity shaped the traditional roles of the sexes. Women performed the home-centered functions that related to the bearing and nurturing of children. Men did the work that required great physical strength. Over time, however, family size contracted, the community assumed greater responsibility for the care and education of children, packaged foods and household technology reduced the work load in the home, and technology eliminated much of the need for muscle power at the workplace. Today, in the developed world, the only role still uniquely gender related is childbearing. Yet men and women are still socialized to perform their traditional roles.

Men and women may or may not have some innate psychological disposition toward these traditional roles—men to be aggressive, competitive, self-reliant, risk taking; women to be supportive, nurturing, intuitive, sensitive, communicative—but certainly both men and women are capable of the full range of behavior. Indeed, the male and female roles have already begun to expand and merge. In the decades ahead, as the socialization of boys and girls and the experience and expectations of young men and women grow steadily more androgynous, the differences in workplace behavior will continue to fade. At the moment, however, we are still plagued by disparities in perception and behavior that make the integration of men and women in the workplace unnecessarily difficult and expensive.

Let me illustrate with a few broadbrush generalizations. Of course, these are only stereotypes, but I think they help to exemplify the kinds of preconceptions that can muddy the corporate waters.

Men continue to perceive women as the rearers of their children, so they find it understandable, indeed appropriate, that women should renounce their careers to raise families. Edmund Pratt, CEO of Pfizer, once asked me in all sincerity, "Why would any woman choose to be a chief financial officer rather than a full-time mother?" By condoning and taking pleasure in women's traditional behavior, men reinforce it. Not only do they see parenting as fundamentally female, they see a career as fundamentally male—either an unbroken series of promotions and advancements toward CEOdom or stagnation and disappointment. This attitude serves to legitimize a woman's choice to extend maternity leave and even, for those who can afford it, to leave employment altogether for several years. By the same token, men who might want to take a leave after the birth of a child know that management will see such behavior as a lack of career commitment, even when company policy permits parental leave for men.

Women also bring counterproductive expectations and perceptions to the workplace. Ironically, although the feminist movement was an expression of women's quest for freedom from their home-based lives, most women were remarkably free already. They had many responsibilities, but they were autonomous and could be entrepreneurial in how and when they carried them out. And once their children grew up and left home, they were essentially free to do what they wanted with their lives. Women's traditional role also included freedom from responsibility for the financial support of their families. Many of us were socialized from girlhood to expect our husbands to take care of us, while our brothers were socialized from an equally early age to complete their educations, pursue careers, climb the ladder of success, and provide dependable financial support for their families. To the extent that this tradition of freedom lingers subliminally, women tend to bring to their employment a sense that they can choose to change jobs or careers at will, take time off, or reduce their hours.

Finally, women's traditional role encouraged particular attention to the quality and substance of what they did, specifically to the physical, psychological, and intellectual development of their children. This traditional focus may explain women's continuing tendency to search for more than monetary reward—intrinsic significance, social importance, meaning—in what they do. This too makes them more likely than men to leave the corporation in search of other values.

The misleading metaphor of the glass ceiling suggests an invisible barrier constructed by corporate leaders to impede the upward mobility of women beyond the middle levels. A more appropriate metaphor, I believe, is the kind of cross-sectional diagram used in geology. The barriers to women's leadership occur when potentially counterproductive layers of influence on women—maternity, tradition, socialization—meet management strata pervaded by the largely unconscious preconceptions, stereotypes, and expectations of men. Such interfaces do not exist for men and tend to be impermeable for women.

One result of these gender differences has been to convince some executives that women are simply not suited to top management. Other executives feel helpless. If they see even a few of their valued female employees fail to return to work from maternity leave on schedule or see one of their most promising women plateau in her career after the birth of a child, they begin to fear there is nothing they can do to infuse women with new energy and enthusiasm and persuade them to stay. At the same time, they know there is nothing they can do to stem the tide of women into management ranks.

Another result is to place every working woman on a continuum that runs from total dedication to career at one end to a balance between career and family at the other. What women discover is that the male corporate culture sees both extremes as unacceptable. Women who want the flexibility to balance their families and their careers are not adequately committed to the organization. Women who perform as aggressively and competitively as men are abrasive and unfeminine. But the fact is, business needs all the talented women it can get. Moreover, as I will explain, the women I call career-primary and those I call career-and-family each have particular value to the corporation.

Women in the corporation are about to move from a buyer's to a seller's market. The sudden, startling recognition that 80% of new entrants in the work force over the next decade will be women, minorities, and immigrants has stimulated a mushrooming incentive to "value diversity."

Women are no longer simply an enticing pool of occasional creative talent, a thorn in the side of the EEO officer, or a source of frustration to corporate leaders truly puzzled by the slowness of their upward trickle into executive positions. A real demographic change is taking place. The era of sudden population growth of the 1950s and 1960s is over. The birth rate has dropped about 40%, from a high of 25.3 live births per 1,000 population in 1957, at the peak of the baby boom, to a stable low of a little more than 15 per 1,000 over the last 16 years, and there is no indication of a return to a higher rate. The tidal wave of baby boomers that swelled the recruitment pool to overflowing seems to have been a one-time phenomenon. For 20 years, employers had the pick of a very large crop and were able to choose males almost exclusively for the executive track. But if future population remains fairly stable while the economy continues to expand, and if the new information society simultaneously creates a greater need for creative, educated managers, then the gap between supply and demand will grow dramatically and, with it, the competition for managerial talent.

The decrease in numbers has even greater implications if we look at the traditional source of corporate recruitment for leadership positions—white males from the top 10% of the country's best universities. Over the past decade, the increase in the number of women graduating from leading universities has been much greater than the increase in the total number of graduates, and these women are well represented in the top 10% of their classes.

The trend extends into business and professional programs as well. In the old days, virtually all MBAs were male. I remember addressing a meeting at the Harvard Business School as recently as the mid-1970s and looking out at a sea of exclusively male faces. Today, about 25% of that audience would be women. The pool of male MBAs from which corporations have traditionally drawn their leaders has shrunk significantly.

Of course, this reduction does not have to mean a shortage of talent. The top 10% is at least as smart as it always was—smarter, probably, since it's now drawn from a broader segment of the population. But it now consists increasingly of women. Companies that are determined to recruit the same number of men as before will have to dig much deeper into the male pool, while their competitors will have the opportunity to pick the best people from both the male and female graduates.

Under these circumstances, there is no question that the management ranks of business will include increasing numbers of women. There remains, however, the question of how these women will succeed—how long they will stay, how high they will climb, how completely they will fulfill their promise and potential, and what kind of return the corporation will realize on its investment in their training and development.

There is ample business reason for finding ways to make sure that as many of these women as possible will succeed. The first step in this process is to recognize that women are not all alike. Like men, they are individuals with differing talents, priorities, and motivations. For the sake of simplicity, let me focus on the two women I referred to earlier, on what I call the career-primary woman and the career-and-family woman.

Like many men, some women put their careers first. They are ready to make the same trade-offs traditionally made by the men who seek leadership positions. They make a career decision to put in extra hours, to make sacrifices in their personal lives, to make the most of every opportunity for professional development. For women, of course, this decision also requires that they remain single or at least childless or, if they do have children, that they be satisfied to have others raise them.

Some 90% of executive men but only 35% of executive women have children by the age of 40. The *automatic* association of all women with babies is clearly unjustified.

The secret to dealing with such women is to recognize them early, accept them, and clear artificial barriers from their path to the top. After all, the best of these women are among the best managerial talent you will ever see. And career-primary women have another important value to the company that men and other women lack. They can act as role models and mentors to younger women who put their careers first. Since upwardly mobile career-primary women still have few role models to motivate and inspire them, a company with women in its top echelon has a significant advantage in the competition for executive talent.

Men at the top of the organization—most of them over 55, with wives who tend to be traditional—often find career women "masculine" and difficult to accept as colleagues. Such men miss the point, which is not that these women are just like men but that they are just like the *best* men in the organization. And there is such a shortage of the best people that gender cannot be allowed to matter. It is clearly counterproductive to disparage in a woman with executive talent the very qualities that are most critical to the business and that might carry a man to the CEO's office.

Clearing a path to the top for career-primary women has four requirements:

1. Identify them early.
2. Give them the same opportunity you give to talented men to grow and develop and contribute to company profitability. Give them client and customer responsibility. Expect them to travel and relocate, to make the same commitment to the company as men aspiring to leadership positions.
3. Accept them as valued members of your management team. Include them in every kind of communication. Listen to them.

4. Recognize that the business environment is more difficult and stressful for them than for their male peers. They are always a minority, often the only woman. The male perception of talented, ambitious women is at best ambivalent, a mixture of admiration, resentment, confusion, competitiveness, attraction, skepticism, anxiety, pride, and animosity. Women can never feel secure about how they should dress and act, whether they should speak out or grin and bear it when they encounter discrimination, stereotyping, sexual harassment, and paternalism. Social interaction and travel with male colleagues and with male clients can be charged. As they move up, the normal increase in pressure and responsibility is compounded for women because they are women.

Stereotypical language and sexist day-to-day behavior do take their toll on women's career development. Few male executives realize how common it is to call women by their first names while men in the same group are greeted with surnames, how frequently female executives are assumed by men to be secretaries, how often women are excluded from all-male social events where business is being transacted. With notable exceptions, men are still generally more comfortable with other men, and as a result women miss many of the career and business opportunities that arise over lunch, on the golf course, or in the locker room.

The majority of women, however, are what I call career-and-family women, women who want to pursue serious careers while participating actively in the rearing of children. These women are a precious resource that has yet to be mined. Many of them are talented and creative. Most of them are willing to trade some career growth and compensation for freedom from the constant pressure to work long hours and weekends.

Most companies today are ambivalent at best about the career-and-family women in their management ranks. They would prefer that all employees were willing to give their all to the company. They believe it is in their best interests for all managers to compete for the top positions so the company will have the largest possible pool from which to draw its leaders.

"If you have both talent and motivation," many employers seem to say, "we want to move you up. If you haven't got that motivation, if you want less pressure and greater flexibility, then you can leave and make room for a new generation." These companies lose on two counts. First, they fail to amortize the investment they made in the early training and experience of management women who find themselves committed to family as well as to career. Second, they fail to recognize what these women could do for their middle management.

The ranks of middle managers are filled with people on their way up and people who have stalled. Many of them have simply reached their limits, achieved career growth commensurate with or exceeding their capabilities, and they cause problems because their performance is mediocre but they still want to move ahead. The career-and-family woman is willing to trade off the pressures and demands that go with promotion for the freedom to spend more time with her children. She's very smart, she's talented, she's committed to her career, and she's satisfied to stay at the middle level, at least during the early child-rearing years. Compare her with some of the people you have there now.

Consider a typical example, a woman who decides in college on a business career and enters management at age 22. For nine years, the company invests in her career as she gains experience and skills and steadily improves her performance. But at 31, just as the investment begins to pay off in earnest, she decides to have a baby. Can the company afford to let her go home, take another job, or go into business for herself? The common perception now is yes, the corporation can afford to lose her unless, after six or eight weeks or even three months of disability and maternity leave, she returns to work on a full-time schedule with the same vigor, commitment, and ambition that she showed before.

But what if she doesn't? What if she wants or needs to go on leave for six months or a year or, heaven forbid, five years? In this worst-case scenario, she works full-time from age 22 to 31 and from 36 to 65—a total of 38 years as opposed to the typical male's 43 years. That's not a huge difference. Moreover, my typical example is willing to work part-time while her children are young, if only her employer will give her the opportunity. There are two rewards for companies responsive to this need: higher retention of their best people and greatly improved performance and satisfaction in their middle management.

The high-performing career-and-family woman can be a major player in your company. She can give you a significant business advantage as the competition for able people escalates. Sometimes too, if you can hold on to her, she will switch gears in mid-life and re-enter the competition for the top. The price you must pay to retain these women is three-fold: you must plan for and manage maternity, you must provide the flexibility that will allow them to be maximally productive, and you must take an active role in helping to make family supports and high-quality, affordable child care available to all women.

The key to managing maternity is to recognize the value of high-performing women and the urgent need to retain them and keep them productive. The first step must be a genuine partnership between the woman and her boss. I know this partnership can seem difficult to forge. One of my own senior executives came to me recently to discuss plans for her maternity leave and subsequent return to work. She knew she wanted to come back. I wanted to make certain that she would. Still, we had a somewhat awkward conversation, because I knew that no woman can predict with

certainty when she will be able to return to work or under what conditions. Physical problems can lengthen her leave. So can a demanding infant, a difficult family or personal adjustment, or problems with child care.

I still don't know when this valuable executive will be back on the job full-time, and her absence creates some genuine problems for our organization. But I do know that I can't simply replace her years of experience with a new recruit. Since our conversation, I also know that she wants to come back, and that she *will* come back—part-time at first—unless I make it impossible for her by, for example, setting an arbitrary date for her full-time return or resignation. In turn, she knows that the organization wants and needs her and, more to the point, that it will be responsive to her needs of working hours and child-care arrangements.

In having this kind of conversation it's important to ask concrete questions that will help to move the discussion from uncertainty and anxiety to some level of predictability. Questions can touch on everything from family income and energy level to child care arrangements and career commitment. Of course you want your star manager to return to work as soon as possible, but you want her to return permanently and productively. Her downtime on the job is a drain on her energies and a waste of your money.

For all the women who want to combine career and family—the women who want to participate actively in the rearing of their children and who also want to pursue their careers seriously—the key to retention is to provide the flexibility and family supports they need in order to function effectively.

Time spent in the office increases productivity if it is time well spent, but the fact that most women continue to take the primary responsibility for child care is a cause of distraction, diversion, anxiety, and absenteeism—to say nothing of the persistent guilt experienced by all working mothers. A great many women, perhaps most of all women who have always performed at the highest levels, are also frustrated by a sense that while their children are babies they cannot function at their best either at home or at work.

In its simplest form, flexibility is the freedom to take time off—a couple of hours, a day, a week—or to do some work at home and some at the office, an arrangement that communication technology makes increasingly feasible. At the complex end of the spectrum are alternative work schedules that permit the woman to work less than full-time and her employer to reap the benefits of her experience and, with careful planning, the top level of her abilities.

Part-time employment is the single greatest inducement to getting women back on the job expeditiously and the provision women themselves most desire. A part-time return to work enables them to maintain responsibility for critical aspects of their jobs, keeps them in touch with the changes constantly occurring at the workplace and in the job itself, reduces stress and fatigue, often eliminates the need for paid maternity leave by permitting a return to the office as soon as disability leave is over, and, not least, can greatly enhance company loyalty. The part-time solution works particularly well when a work load can be reduced for one individual in a department or when a full-time job can be broken down by skill levels and apportioned to two individuals at different levels of skill and pay.

I believe, however, that shared employment is the most promising and will be the most widespread form of flexible scheduling in the future. It is feasible at every level of the corporation except at the pinnacle, for both the sort and the long term. It involves two people taking responsibility for one job.

Two red lights flash on as soon as most executives hear the words "job sharing": continuity and client-customer contact. The answer to

the continuity question is to place responsibility entirely on the two individuals sharing the job to discuss everything that transpires—thoroughly, daily, and on their own time. The answer to the problem of client-customer contact is yes, job sharing requires reeducation and a period of adjustment. But as both client and supervisor will quickly come to appreciate, two contacts means that the customer has continuous access to the company's representative, without interruption for vacation, travel, or sick leave. The two people holding the job can simply cover for each other, and the uninterrupted, full-time coverage they provide together can be a stipulation of their arrangement.

Flexibility is costly in numerous ways. It requires more supervisory time to coordinate and manage, more office space, and somewhat greater benefits costs (though these can be contained with flexible benefits plans, prorated benefits, and, in two-paycheck families, elimination of duplicate benefits). But the advantages of reduced turnover and the greater productivity that results from higher energy levels and greater focus can outweigh the costs.

A few hints:

Provide flexibility selectively. I'm not suggesting private arrangements subject to the suspicion of favoritism but rather a policy that makes flexible work schedules available only to high performers.

Make it clear that in most instances (but not all) the rates of advancement and pay will be appropriately lower for those who take time off or who work part-time than for those who work full-time. Most career-and-family women are entirely willing to make that trade-off.

Discuss costs as well as benefits. Be willing to risk accusations of bias. Insist, for example, that half time is half of whatever time it takes to do the job, not merely half of 35 or 40 hours.

The woman who is eager to get home to her child has a powerful incentive to use her time effectively at the office and to carry with her reading and other work that can be done at home. The talented professional who wants to have it all can be a high performer by carefully ordering her priorities and by focusing on objectives rather than on the legendary 15-hour day. By the time professional women have their first babies—at an average age of 31—they have already had nine years to work long hours at a desk, to travel, and to relocate. In the case of high performers, the need for flexibility coincides with what has gradually become the goal-oriented nature of responsibility.

Family supports—in addition to maternity leave and flexibility—include the provision of parental leave for men, support for two-career and single-parent families during relocation, and flexible benefits. But the primary ingredient is child care. The capacity of working mothers to function effectively and without interruption depends on the availability of good, affordable child care. Now that women make up almost half the work force and the growing percentage of managers, the decision to become involved in the personal lives of employees is no longer a philosophical question but a practical one. To make matters worse, the quality of child care has almost no relation to technology, inventiveness, or profitability but is more or less a pure function of the quality of child care personnel and the ratio of adults to children. These costs are irreducible. Only by joining hands with government and the public sector can corporations hope to create the vast quantity and variety of child care that their employees need.

Until quite recently, the response of corporations to women has been largely symbolic and cosmetic, motivated in large part by the will to avoid litigation and legal penalties. In some cases, companies were also moved by a genuine sense of fairness and a vague discomfort and frustration at the absence of women above the middle of the corporate pyramid.

The actions they took were mostly quick, easy, and highly visible—child care information services, a three-month parental leave available to men as well as women, a woman appointed to the board of directors.

When I first began to discuss these issues 26 years ago, I was sometimes able to get an appointment with the assistant to the assistant in personnel, but it was only a courtesy. Over the past decade, I have met with the CEOs of many large corporations, and I've watched them become involved with ideas they had never previously thought much about. Until recently, however, the shelf life of that enhanced awareness was always short. Given pressing, short-term concerns, women were not a front-burner issue. In the past few months, I have seen yet another change. Some CEOs and top management groups now take the initiative. They call and ask us to show them how to shift gears from a responsive to a proactive approach to recruiting, developing, and retaining women.

I think this change is more probably a response to business needs—to concern for the quality of future profits and managerial talent—than to uneasiness about legal requirements, sympathy with the demands of women and minorities, or the desire to do what is right and fair. The nature of such business motivation varies. Some companies want to move women to higher positions as role models for those below them and as beacons for talented young recruits. Some want to achieve a favorable image with employees, customers, clients, and stockholders. These are all legitimate motives. But I think the companies that stand to gain most are motivated as well by a desire to capture competitive advantage in an era when talent and competence will be in increasingly short supply. These companies are now ready to stop being defensive about their experience with women and to ask incisive questions without preconceptions.

Even so, incredibly, I don't know of more than one or two companies that have looked into their own records to study the absolutely critical issue of maternity leave—how many women took it, when and whether they returned, and how this behavior correlated with their rank, tenure, age, and performance. The unique drawback to the employment of women is the physical reality of maternity and the particular socializing influence maternity has had. Yet to make women equal to men in the workplace we have chosen on the whole not to discuss this single most significant difference between them. Unless we do, we cannot evaluate the cost of recruiting, developing, and moving women up.

Now that interest is replacing indifference, there are four steps every company can take to examine its own experience with women:

1. Gather quantitative data on the company's experience with management-level women regarding turnover rates, occurrence of and return from maternity leave, and organizational level attained in relation to tenure and performance.

2. Correlate this data with factors such as age, marital status, and presence and age of children, and attempt to identify and analyze why women respond the way they do.

3. Gather qualitative data on the experience of women in your company and on how women are perceived by both sexes.

4. Conduct a cost-benefit analysis of the return on your investment in high-performing women. Factor in the cost to the company of women's negative reactions to negative experience, as well as the probable cost of corrective measures and policies. If women's value to your company is greater than the cost to recruit, train, and develop them—and of course I believe it will be— then you will want to do everything you can to retain them.

We have come a tremendous distance since the days when the prevailing male wisdom saw women as lacking the kind of intelligence that would allow them to succeed in business. For decades, even women themselves have harbored an unspoken belief that they couldn't make it because they couldn't be just like men, and nothing else would do. But now that women have shown themselves the equal of men in every area of organizational activity, now that they have demonstrated that they can be stars in every field of endeavor, now we can all venture to examine the fact that women and men are different.

On balance, employing women is more costly than employing men. Women can acknowledge this fact today because they know that their value to employers exceeds the additional cost and because they know that changing attitudes can reduce the additional cost dramatically. Women in management are no longer an idiosyncrasy of the arts and education. They have always matched men in natural ability. Within a very few years, they will equal men in numbers as well in every area of economic activity.

The demographic motivation to recruit and develop women is compelling. But an older question remains: Is society better for the change? Women's exit from the home and entry into the work force has certainly created problem—an urgent need for good, affordable child care; troubling questions about the kind of parenting children need; the costs and difficulties of diversity in the workplace; the stress and fatigue of combining work and family responsibilities. Wouldn't we all be happier if we could turn back the clock to an age when men were in the workplace and women in the home, when male and female roles were clearly differentiated and complementary?

Nostalgia, anxiety, and discouragement will urge many to say yes, but my answer is emphatically no. Two fundamental benefits that were unattainable in the past are now within our reach. For the individual, freedom of choice—in this case the freedom to choose career, family, or a combination of the two. For the corporation, access to the most gifted individuals in the country. These benefits are neither self-indulgent nor insubstantial. Freedom of choice and self-realization are too deeply American to be cast aside for some wistful vision of the past. And access to

our most talented human resources is not a luxury in this age of explosive international competition but rather the barest minimum that prudence and national self-preservation require.

Essay

Women in the Workplace

Al Gini

Perhaps the single most important event in the American labor market in the twentieth century has been the unprecedented entry of large numbers of women into the workforce.

> When the history of the last quarter of the 20th century is written scholars may well conclude that the nation's most important social development has been the rise to positions of power and influence of its most vigorous majority: American women. So many women have flocked to the labor force . . . that more Americans are now employed than ever before. This is no less than a revolutionary change, one that has created profound shifts not only in the family and the workplace but also in basic U.S. economic policy making.[1]

When Freud cited work and love as the foundations of human behavior, he might as well have used the words work and family. These are the two major institutions on which any society is based. Work and family are the two primary pillars of human existence, and every society in every age must grapple with the delicate mechanisms and relationships that influence and support these two fundamental phenomena.[2] As we step onto Bill Clinton's proverbial "bridge to the twenty-first century," the sheer numbers of women who have entered the workforce threaten to

irreparably alter both the quality and quantity of our work and family lives. And, like it or not, we must be prepared to adapt or modify some of our most sacred social ideals and stereotypes about work and the family.

Cultural critic Barbara Ehrenreich once commented that in the 1960s the stereotypical liberated women was a braless radical, hoarse from denouncing the twin evils of capitalism and patriarchy.[3] Today's stereotype is more often a blue-suited executive carrying an attaché case and engaging in leveraged buyouts—before transmogrifying into a perfect mother, gourmet cook, and seductive lover in the evenings. Neither stereotype is or ever was perfectly true, but they can tell us a great deal about what many women and men would like to believe. What is true, according to newspaper columnist Carol Kleiman, is that the official organizational policy of most workplaces continues to operate as if white men constituted the majority of the workforce and most women are still at home managing the multiple roles of homemaking and child-rearing. As a result, both male and female employees must cope with the mounting stress of balancing work and family demands.[4] Workplaces need to accept and accommodate the inescapable demographic fact that since the mid-1980s, women and minority males make up the majority of the workforce.[5]

Women have always been part of the workforce and working mothers are not simply a "new demographic phenomenon of the later-half of the 20th century."[6] Stephanie Coontz has documented that women's active participation in the workforce has always been dependent on need, circumstance, and, to a very large extent, "cultural permission," which has varied over the years. A classic example is "Rosie the Riveter" the icon of American women during World War II. When the GI Joe husbands, brothers, and sons of "Rosie" marched off to war, "Rosie" marched into factories across America and took on complicated new jobs, gained new skills, and produced both the necessary domestic goods and the military hardware needed to win the war, doing her bit to once again "make the world safe for democracy." When the war was won and our GIs came home, many of the women were happy to leave the workplace to the men. Others were reluctant to give up their newly won responsibilities, independence, and income, and expressed a desire to continue working. Management, however, went to extraordinary lengths to purge women from high-paying and nontraditional jobs. The women who wanted or needed to work were not expelled from the labor force, but were downgraded to lower-paid, "female" jobs. Nevertheless, according to Coontz:

> Even at the end of the purge, there were more women working than before the war, and by 1952 there were two million more wives at work than at the peak of wartime production. The jobs available to these women, however, lacked the pay and the challenges that had made war time work so satisfying, encouraging women to define themselves in terms of home and family even when they were working.[7]

During the war, working as "Rosie the Riveter" was a badge of honor, a mark of distinction,

a woman's patriotic duty. After the war, however, "cultural permission" once again shifted. *Esquire* magazine called working wives a "menace," and *Life* termed married women's employment a "disease." Being a full-time wife and mother was lauded as a woman's true vocation, the only job that could provide a woman with a "sense of fulfillment, of happiness, of complete pervading contentment."[8]

Sixty years ago, the notion of an unfulfilled homemaker was for most—but certainly not all—women unheard of. Prior to World War II, the maintenance of a house and, often, a large family was a full-time occupation and acknowledged as such. Those women who did venture outside the home in search of full- or part-time employment did so either out of dire financial need or in an attempt to earn a little "pin money" to subsidize a few household extras. Only in recent years have the everyday tasks of meal-making and home maintenance become less than full-time jobs. When combined with the decrease in family size, large numbers of women became, in the view of many, underemployed and underestimated.

It wasn't until the late 1950s and early 1960s, however, that women once again received "cultural permission" to enter the workforce in search of jobs or careers and a new sense of identity. Contributing to this cultural shift were the feminist movement and its impact on social consciousness, technological advances in the information and communications industries, the conversion from a manufacturing to a service economy, increased access to education, fair employment and affirmative action legislation, and the ever-increasing costs of a higher standard of living. Women now find full-time work outside the home not only possible and desirable, but, in many cases, financially necessary.

At the beginning of the twentieth century, only 5 million of the 28 million working Americans were women. One-quarter of these were teenagers and only a very few were married. As recently as 1947, women accounted for fewer than 17 million of the 59 million employed. Since that time, however, six of every ten additions to the workforce have been women. Between 1969 and 1979 women took on two-thirds of the 20 million newly created jobs;[9] between 1980 and 1992 women accounted for 60 percent of the increase in the American workforce.[10]

In 1984 the Census Bureau reported that for the first time in our history the prototype of American worker—the adult white male—no longer made up the majority of the labor force.[11] Women and minority men now hold approximately 57 percent of all jobs. In 1995, 57.5 million women were in the labor force of 125 million. In 1960, 35.5 percent of all women and 78.8 percent of all men worked full-time; by 1995, those numbers had risen to 55.6 percent of all women and 70.8 percent of all men.[12]

Depending on how you crunch the numbers, women now make up 46 to 49 percent of the entire workforce. Between 1947 and 1995 women's participation in the workforce increased 17 percent. Some demographers predict that women may represent a simple majority of the workforce early in the twenty-first century.[13] The Bureau of Labor Statistics more conservatively estimates that women will maintain but not necessarily exceed their present percentage in the workforce. They project that in 2005 the total labor force will be 150.5 million workers, and that 71.8 million of them will be women.[14]

While single and divorced women have long had relatively high labor force participation rates, fewer than 25 percent of married women were working full-time in 1960. That number today is 33.3 million, or 61 percent of married women. Of these working married women 70.2 percent have children under seventeen years of age.[15] It is estimated that two-thirds of all mothers are now in the labor force. Two-job families now make up 58 percent of married couples with children.[16] One

set of statistics indicates that 20 percent of women in double-income families earn more than their husbands.[17] More recent research conducted by the Women's Voice Project, an ongoing study by the Center for Policy Alternatives in Washington, suggests that as many as 55 percent of all married women earn at least half of their family's income.[18]

According to social commentator John W. Wright, an unmistakable sign of the social change going on in the workplace is the significant increase in the number of women who return to work after having a baby. In 1976, about 31 percent of the women who gave birth returned to or entered the labor force, by 1985 it had climbed to 48 percent.[19] In a series of interviews I conducted with human resources specialists, most estimated that at their places of employment 75 percent of new mothers returned to work within twelve weeks of giving birth.

Fueling these rising statistics are the ever-widening professions now open to women. While traditional "women's" jobs such as nurses, teachers, librarians, and clerical workers are still predominantly women, the proportion of female engineers, architects, and public officials—while still small—has more than doubled since 1960.[20] Classes in law and medical schools are now typically composed of 40 to 50 percent women.

According to the Department of Labor special report "Working Women Count," 30 percent of working women are engaged in service and sales jobs, 13.1 percent have factory, craft, construction, or technical jobs or jobs in the transportation industry, 27.6 percent of working women have professional or executive jobs, and 40 percent of all corporate middle-management positions are held by women.[21] In general, although women are grossly overrepresented at the entry and low levels of all kinds of work, it is clear that the historical distinctions between "women's" work and "men's" work have begun to blur.

Obviously, the entrance of women into the labor market has changed the composition of the workforce, the workplace, and the structure of family life. According to "Working Women Count," it is now expected that 99 percent of all American women will work for pay sometime during their lives.[22] The 1950s traditional family—dad at work and mom at home with the kids—is no longer the predominant pattern; nontraditional families are now the majority.[23] Again, depending on whose figures you are willing to accept, it is estimated that fewer than 15 percent of all households fit the traditional family model.[24] As recently as 1960, 43 percent of all families conformed to the single-earner model,[25] but in less than thirty-six years we have become a nation of DINKS (Double-Income-No-Kids) and DISKS (Double-Income-Some-Kids) families. According to sociologist Uma Sekaran, "The number of two-career families, single-parent families, and unmarried working couples living together is steadily increasing. This population constitutes more than 90 percent of today's labor force. Organizations are . . . beginning to feel the impact of this new breed of employee."[26]

In addition, women are now demanding the right to define themselves in the way that men always have—through their jobs. Being a wife, a mother, a homemaker has over the course of the past two or three generations simply changed until it no longer meets the definition of work to which most people now subscribe. It has been suggested that when the first wave of female baby boomers arrived at college in the early 1960s, many expected to marry shortly thereafter and raise children.[27]Not anymore! According to a survey cited by Arlie Russell Hochschild, less than 1 percent of 200,000 female college freshmen wanted to be a "full-time homemaker." In a 1986 survey of female college seniors, 80 percent thought it was "very important" to have a career.[28] Nine years later, 86 percent of recent female college graduates defined themselves as "careerist."[29]

Women now want to be known by their accomplishments and occupations and not merely as "Mrs. John Smith" or "Johnny's mommy." When First Lady Barbara Bush gave the commencement speech at Wellesley College in 1991, many members of the all-female student body protested her appearance because her most significant accomplishment was being somebody's wife.[30] Gloria Emerson has pointed out that every twelve-year-old boy in America knows what must be done to achieve identity and "make it" as a man: Money must be made. Nothing else is as defining or as masculine as this.[31] Women now want to forge their own identity by means of paid employment—the principal definition of work. In the words of demographer Daniel Yankelovich, women now view a paid job as "a badge of membership in the larger society and an almost indispensable symbol of self-worth."[32]

In a very real sense women's desire to define themselves through work was spurred by Betty Friedan, Gloria Steinem, and the feminist movement. The "new breed" of women sought to be autonomous agents, able to guide and direct themselves, determining their purpose and role in life by their own choices and actions. They no longer wanted to be viewed as "second-class citizens," relegated to hearth and home, and totally dependent on men. In addition to the ideological motivations, however, practical reasons played an important role. Many women sought jobs or careers to keep up with the ever-increasing costs of middle-class existence: suburban homes, safe cars, good schools, kids' music lessons, and prestigious colleges.

As recently as 1980, only 19 percent of working women said that their incomes were necessary to support their family, while 43 percent said they worked to bring in extra money.[33] In 1995, however, 44 percent of employed women said that they worked out of necessity, and only 23 percent to earn extra cash. The survey concluded that most married working women now view their incomes as essential to their family's well-being.[34] The new piece of cynical conventional wisdom currently circulating around college campuses today reads something like this: "Guys, look around. Don't just marry the pretty one. Marry the smart one. The one who's got the best chance of landing a good job. Why? Because you're going to need each other to acquire the things and lifestyle that your parents managed to achieve on one salary!" For example, in 1989, 79 percent of homes bought were purchased by two-income households.[35] Some realtors estimate that in the mid-1990s, that number rose to 85 percent.[36]

The bottom line is that women may once have entered the workforce out of desire, but, today, they stay because of need. Not only have they been granted "cultural permission" to seek work, they have now acquired a financial imperative to do so. In the most recent past, most women had three choices about employment: Don't work at all, work part-time, or work full-time. Now, like men, their options have been reduced to one.

As a final note on the many ways in which women's increased presence in the workforce has changed family life, one must mention divorce. Ninety percent of men and women marry, but 50 percent of all first marriages end in divorce, and an alarming 60 percent of second marriages also end in divorce.[37] The traumatic effect of divorce is felt by all members of a family, especially the children. Because of America's rising divorce rates in the last fifty years, 60 percent of all children will live in a single-parent household for a significant period of time before they are eighteen.[38] Although 70 percent of divorced adults will remarry, 25 percent of all children grow up primarily in a one-parent household.[39]

Whatever the causes of a divorce, the practical and financial fallout of the separation is much harder on the woman. According to psychologist Lenore Weitzman, in the first year after divorce women experience a 73 percent loss in their standard of living, whereas men experience a 42 percent gain.[40] Even when divorced fathers dutifully comply with child-support payments and remain emotionally involved with their children, the primary responsibility for children's day-to-day and long-term well-being falls to the mother.

Divorce is now an accepted part of our social tapestry. Another trend gaining acceptance is single motherhood, from unmarried teenage mothers to adult women who choose to have children out of wedlock (à la TV's *Murphy Brown*). One of the major lessons now learned by women and girls alike is self-sufficiency. According to Karen Nussbaum, former head of the U.S. Department of Labor's Women's Bureau, "There should be no girl out there [anymore] who thinks someone else is going to take care of [her]." Life has changed and the expectations of women must also change. For women work is now less of an option and more of a necessity. "If girls [today] aren't working when they get out of high school," Nussbaum has stated, "they will be at some point."[41] While, for many women, work can be a badge of honor and a symbol of self-worth, it has also become a fundamental element of survival.

JUSTICE ON THE JOB

Women are now being recruited more than men for entry positions in various industries. In this way, corporations can claim, at least prima facie, that they are complying with the rules of affirmative action and open employment. The issue for most women is not getting a job, but, what happens to them once they have it. Although not all women encounter prejudicial behavior, too many are forced to endure personal and institutional resistance to their careers and professional advancement.

According to management scholar Judy Rosener, few women encounter a level playing field on the job. Most are forced to cope with a problem she calls "sexual static." Rosener argues that most male managers and workers—especially those over the age of forty—see females in the workplace, first and foremost, as females, not as colleagues. Too many men are unable to see female coworkers outside their traditional sex roles—as mothers, sisters, daughters, and potential mates. Sexual static interferes with communication and hampers normal business conduct between men and women, resulting in mixed signals, misunderstanding, embarrassment, anger, confusion, and fear.[42] Sexual static, suggests business ethicist Patricia Werhane, may make a work environment hostile or just uncomfortable. It may be "sexually charged" or create an atmosphere in which "men and women feel uneasy about their professional interrelationships and how these might be misinterpreted as sexual ones."[43]

Sexual static is not the same thing as sexual harassment. Sexual static is more insidious. Sexual harassment is about inappropriate sexual comments, unwelcome sexual advances, or requests for sexual favors as a condition of an individual's employment, advancement, or success. Sexual static is an attempt to avoid and defuse even the suggestion of sexual harassment. It is the tension that occurs when men and women are not sure how to comport themselves in a business or social environment. The personal sexual insecurity of male managers often leads to dysfunctional corporate decision-making. A senior male attorney at a major firm admitted, "We have a real bright woman who has what it takes to be a partner, but I can't bring myself to vote to promote her because she turns me on, and it

gets in my way." Fear of gossip motivates other men. "Every time I promote a woman," reported a fifty-year-old male advertising executive, "I worry about people suspecting I have a romantic interest in her."[44]

Rosener and Werhane agree that although everyone involved loses both personally and professionally in an atmosphere of sexual static, women are the primary victims. Sexual static perpetuates stereotypical female roles, denies women the opportunity to acquire new skills and experiences, too often denies women the support of a senior male mentor who can act as a role model, and, finally, precludes professional objectivity.[45] Professional objectivity maintains that management practices should be unbiased and impersonal. It requires that the most skilled and effective persons be hired and promoted to leadership positions. Unfortunately, concludes Werhane, "we live in a society in which business is conducted in an atmosphere where merit or worthiness is the ideal but not the practice."[46] Not only do we not live in a sex-gender-color-ethnic-age–neutral environment, sexual static reinforces the divisive notion that men and women are two separate and competitive species loosely connected by sex, children, and financial arrangements.

The major organizational problem facing working women is the proverbial glass ceiling—an invisible barrier that keeps women from ascending to the highest levels of management. The glass ceiling does not just apply to elite workers aspiring to corporate management; it also refers to the institutional and personal prejudices that women encounter in every kind of job at every level in the workplace. A majority of American women in the workplace, regardless of race, class, type of job, or job location, feel that the glass ceiling is keeping them in their place. According to the nationally based report "Working Women Count," more than 60 percent of women believe that they have little or no opportunity for advancement.[47]

Even though women now represent 46 to 49 percent of the workforce, more than 97 percent of all senior management is still male. Where women are starting to achieve representation equal with their numbers is in the lower and middle ranks of management. Even those women who manage to pass through this transparent barrier often find themselves in jobs that have a "glass floor," that is, where their every move can be seen and scrutinized, and where their first big mistake has them figuratively crashing down.

Business Week has reported that half the lowest management levels are staffed with female workers and that soon the middle ranks will be, too. Overall, women now occupy an unprecedented 41 to 43 percent of lower- and middle-management positions.[48] However, a report by Catalyst, Inc., released in October 1996 found that only 10 percent of the top jobs at the nation's 500 largest companies are held by women. Alarmingly, 105 of these 500 companies have no female corporate officers at all, and only 2.4 percent of all the women employed in these 500 companies have achieved the rank of chairperson, president, CEO, or executive vice president. Only four of the twenty-four "Best Companies for Women to Work For," featured in a *Business Week* cover story, had women in more than 25 percent of their corporate officer posts in 1996.[49]

In a related report, Catalyst announced that women's representation on boards of directors of Fortune 500 companies had finally exceeded 10 percent. Of the 6,123 Fortune 500 board seats, women now hold 626, or 10.2 percent. Altogether, 83 percent of Fortune 500 companies have at least one woman on their boards. According to Sheila Wellington, president of Catalyst, while these numbers are important, they're "absolutely minuscule. What this shows is that people who say the

gains have been made, so let's move on, are dead wrong. It shows that the number of women who have made it to the apex are still so few. . . . Clearly, there's a lot more work to be done."[50]

The absence of women from positions of power in business is also reflected in our political system. In 1995, the seventy-fifth anniversary of women's suffrage in America. The Center for Policy Alternatives reported that across the nation, women represented only 20 percent of state legislators, 25 percent of statewide elective executive officers, 10 percent of U.S. representatives, 8 percent of U.S. senators, and 2 percent of governors.[51] As Katherine Spillar, national coordinator for the Fund for the Feminist Majority, so wryly put it, "At the current rates of increase it will be four hundred and seventy-five years before women reach equality in executive suites."[52]

Some critics suggest that those few women who have broken through the glass ceiling have done so not by embracing feminism but by outperforming men on their own terms. These are classic careerists, who happen to be women. Like any dedicated careerist, they did their jobs, made their numbers, and, when necessary, did battle. In fact, according to Chicago-based consultants Megan Buffington and Jane Neff, some of these successful women are more combative and ruthless than their male counterparts because they feel they have to prove they can be rough, tough, and resilient. Buffington and Neff call this the "only bra in the room syndrome" and cite Chicago's first female mayor, Jane Byrne, as its icon.

By all accounts Byrne may have been "lady" when the situation required but in her heart she was one of the boys. A longtime operative in Richard J. Daley's political machine, Byrne earned her spurs because she did her job, could keep a secret, and over the years built up alliances. After Daley died, she rose to his post. In a tough campaign that "reeked of testosterone," as one pundit put it, she convinced the electorate that she had more of the "right stuff" than her rival. After she was out of office, she said in an interview that she really hated losing the mayor's job because she had worked so hard at it; she had wanted to be an effective mayor, and she feared that people attributed her mistakes not just to miscalculation or shortcomings of character, but to being "just a woman."

According to Buffington and Neff, a characteristic of these types of achievers is their lack of empathy for and support of other working women, especially their subordinates. Having achieved success by playing hardball and working hard, they expect the same from others. Having made it despite being a woman, their focus is on success and not sensitivity. They tend to be intolerant of office schmoozing or signs of friendship in the office, such as birthday celebrations. They leave their private lives at home, and they expect others to do so as well. But, worst of all, out of either a twisted sense of elitism or simple selfishness, too many of these successful women do not reach back to mentor other women. Some of them seem to think "I made it without any help, and if you're any good so will you" or "since I'm already here, there's no more room at the table." Buffington and Neff suggest that consequently, many women do not like to work for female bosses. In a recent Gallop poll conducted in twenty-two countries, women overwhelmingly preferred male to female bosses in all but three countries surveyed (India, where they preferred to work for women, and El Salvador and Honduras, where they were evenly split in their preferences). In the United States 45 percent of men and women surveyed prefer a man as a boss while only 20 percent prefer a woman (the rest did not indicate a preference).[53]

Although the term *glass ceiling* is metaphorical, the effect it describes is very real. Not only does it prohibit some women from advancing to senior corporate management, it also denies women on the shop floor and in the lower offices equal opportunities for training, advancement, and promotion. Worse still, it has a limiting effect on salaries. According to the Department of Labor, the second most common complaint voiced by the 250,000 women surveyed as part of its study "Working Women Count," was "unequal and unfair pay."[54] Even though the Equal Pay Act passed Congress in 1963 and the discrepancy between men's and women's pay has narrowed, the gap remains significant. In 1993 in annual earnings of full-time, full-year workers, women earned 71 cents for every dollar earned by a man in the same job, and in 1996 the International Labor Organization reported that a majority of women in America earn 75 cents for every dollar earned by men doing the same job.[55]

Nationwide it is estimated that, on average, women with college degrees earn slightly more than men with high-school degrees and $10,000 a year less than men with comparable educations. Of the women who took part in the "Working Women Count" survey, 23 percent had part-time jobs (less than 35 hours per week) and 77 percent had full-time jobs (40 hours or more per week). Their income reporting was as follows: 16.3 percent earned less than $10,000 per year; 39 percent earned $10,000 to $25,000; 15.8 percent earned $25,000 to $35,000; 10.4 percent earned $35,000 to $50,000; and 4.8 percent earned $50,000 to $75,000. It is worth noting that 71.1 percent of these women earned less than $35,000 per year, and 58 percent earned less than $25,000. At the same time, 35 percent of the sample reported being the sole support of themselves and their families.[56] While women may nearly constitute the simple majority of the workforce, it was clear that they are a long way from matching men in pay.

Another factor that impedes women's advancement at work is babies. According to the Women's Bureau of the Department of Labor the greatest concern of working women is finding a way to balance work, family, and child care. Never has the number of women with young children in the workplace been higher. Sixty-seven percent of women with children under eighteen are working or actively seeking employment. This includes 54 percent of mothers with children under three, 58 percent of mothers with children under six, and 75 percent of mothers with school-age children. These mothers report that juggling kids and work results in a constant state of anxiety, fatigue, frustration, and guilt, both on and off the job. As one working woman told me, "I don't even know what I should feel bad about first! The job? Because I always feel I should be working harder? The kids? Because I miss them so much, and I know I'm missing so much. The house? Because it doesn't feel like a home anymore, it's just a place where we live. Or, my husband? Good old—what the hell is his name?!"

In the "Working Women Count" survey, 56 percent of mothers complained about not being able to find adequate, affordable childcare services, 49 percent wanted paid leaves "to care for a newborn and sick relatives," and 35 percent wanted more "flexible working schedules" in an attempt to balance the day-to-day necessities of work and private life.[57] In some sense, these demands and desires reflect a piece of "occupational wisdom" that all working women have been forced to absorb: "You can take time to baby a client, but you can't take time to baby your own baby."[58]

In 1989, in an attempt to address the needs of babies, women, and men, Felice Schwartz published an article in which she proposed that corporations establish two parallel working tracks for female employees: the "career primary" track and the "career and family" track. Those who chose the career primary track would be considered for any and all tasks, and the career and family track women would be given more limited responsibilities

than their career primary colleagues. Schwartz also proposed that at different points in a woman's career she could change career tracks. In this way, corporations would be able to retain experienced employees, and women could pursue their careers without being forced to totally abdicate their responsibilities as mothers.[59] Critics immediately attacked Schwartz's ideas and relabeled her categories the "breeders" versus the "achievers." Although Schwartz offered her track system as a means of balancing the needs of women, children, and families, many commentators saw her proposal as a passport to permanent second class status and a one-way ticket to a mediocre career. The "mommy track," as her proposal was commonly called, was seen as singling out women for complete parental responsibility or sacrifice. The mommy track became not a new alternative, but a dead end.

In a 1997 article in *Fortune* magazine Betsy Morris argued that the issues raised by Schwartz—balancing careers, babies, and long-term family responsibilities—have neither been resolved nor gone away. In fact, Morris claims things have gotten much worse. For all their politically correct talk, most companies don't much care about or like kids.

> Today, in the corridors of business as elsewhere, families are getting more lip service than ever. Being on the right side of work and family issues—having the proper programs, letting Mom and Dad slip out to watch a T-ball game—is very PC. But corporate America harbors a dirty secret. People in human resources know it. So do a lot of CEOs, although they don't dare discuss it. Families are no longer a big plus for a corporation; they are a big problem. An albatross. More and more, the business world seems to regard children not as the future generation of workers but as luxuries you're entitled to after you've won your stripes. Its fine to have kid's pictures on your desk—just don't let them cut into your billable hours.[60]

Companies want all their employees to clock as much time as possible. They are interested in results, productivity, and success, not child-care commitments and kindergarten recitals. In the spirit of full disclosure, Morris suggested, all corporate manuals should carry a warning: "Ambitious workers beware. If you want to have children, proceed at your own risk. You must be very talented, or on very solid ground, to overcome the damage a family can do to your career."[61]

JUSTICE AT HOME

The problems, prejudices, and injustices that women face in the workplace are, unfortunately, mirrored and often intensified on the home front. As Arlie Hochschild put it, "Women can have fame and fortune, office affairs, silicon injections, and dazzling designer clothes. But the one thing they can't have, apparently, is a man who shares the work at home."[62] There is a price to pay for having "made it," and, by all accounts, women are picking up most of the tab. In her important book *The Second Shift*, Hochschild claims that even though women have won certain rights in the workplace, they have not won many rights at home—in fact, many women are losing ground. According to Hochschild, women in dual-income families not only carry the burdens and responsibilities of their profession, but 80 percent of working women also carry the burden of a second job—caring for the home, the kids, and the husband.

On average, Hochschild claims, in the 1960s and 1970s American women worked around the house 15 hours more per week than men did. Over a year, this adds up to women putting in "an extra month of twenty-four-hour days" on household chores. One study showed that "women averaged three hours a day on housework while men averaged 17 minutes; women spent fifty minutes a day of time exclusively with their children; men spent 12 minutes." According to Hochschild's

computations, 61 percent of men do little or no housework, 21 percent attempt, on an irregular basis, to do their share of household chores, and only 18 percent of men share housework equally.[63] In effect, the second shift means that women put in a double day: They're on duty at work, they're on duty at home. As one angry woman put it, "I do my half. I do half of his half. And the rest doesn't get done!"[64]

Some of Hochschild's findings are unexpected (for example, working-class husbands did more around the house than ostensibly more liberal, middle-class professional husbands), but the cultural causes of the second shift phenomenon are painfully predictable. Most men feel that their work is more important than their wives' jobs. Although their wives' salaries may be necessary, most men, because they earn more and because they have been traditionally seen as the head of the family, view their work as the primary ingredient defining household status. Although domestic chores may be aesthetically and hygienically necessary, they are neither creative nor important and therefore are not the concern of the progenitor and main provider of the family. Most men believe that women are natural nurturers and are better suited for child care.

Hochschild argues that the sudden surge of women into the workplace has not been accompanied by a new cultural understanding of both marriage and work that would have made this transition smoother. Families have changed, women have changed, work has changed, but most workplaces have remained inflexible in the face of their workers' family demands. At home, most men have yet to fundamentally adapt their lifestyles to accommodate the changes in women's lives. Because of this absence of change, said Hochschild, and because of the burdens of the second shift, the movement of women into the workforce in search of identity, independence, and financial security remains at best a "stalled revolution."[65]

In her most recent book, *The Time Bind*, Hochschild suggests that the revolution not only is still "stalled" but that the burdens and fallout of the second shift have gotten more complex. Even with men actively contributing to child care and household chores, men and women still find themselves desperately trying to juggle their commitments to family and work. The demands of a workaholic corporate system and the needs of families and children have us rushing from one responsibility to another and have us trapped in a "time bind" of guilt. Unfortunately, Hochschild says, "many working families are both prisoners and architects of the time bind in which they find themselves."[66] They want it all: great jobs, great families, and all the goodies that go along with it. But the increased energy and time they pump into work is taken from the home, and their lives become more emotionally stressful. Surprisingly, Hochschild discovered, in her three-year study of a "family friendly" Fortune 500 firm, that for a growing number of two-career couples, when work and family compete, work wins. Many workers choose to escape into work because life at home has become a "frantic exercise in beat-the-clock, while work, by comparison, seems a haven of grown-up sociability, competence and relative freedom."[67]

According to Hochschild, the roles of home and work have begun to reverse. Work has become a form of "home" (a village of associates, peers, coworkers) and home has become "hardwork" (a locus of duty, chores, and demanding personalities). Work is the new "neighborhood," where we spend most of our time, where we talk to friends and develop relationships and expertise. Meanwhile, home is now where we are least secure and most harried. "At home the divorce rate has risen, and the emotional demands have become more baffling and complex. In addition to teething, tantrums and the normal develop-

ment of growing children, the needs of elderly parents are creating more tasks for the modern family—as are the blending, unblending, reblending of new step parents, step children, exes, and former in-laws,"[68] By comparison work is less chaotic, cleaner, more enriching, and much less personal. As one female worker admitted to Hochschild, "I put in for [overtime]. . . . I get home, and the minute I turn the key, my daughter is right there . . . the baby is still up . . . the dishes are still in the sink. . . . My husband is in the other room hollering at my daughter, 'I don't ever get any time to talk to your mother. You're always monopolizing her time!' They all come at me at once."[69]

Is it any wonder that work becomes home and home becomes work? Work is less demanding, a surrogate, a refuge from our troubled private lives. It is also a place where conflicts that originate in the home can be discussed, debated, and subjected to sympathetic scrutiny. In the sanctuary of work, says Hochschild, increasing numbers of women are discovering the "great male secret"—work can be an escape from the pressures of home. In the words of a James Thurber character as he leaves for work after a long weekend of kit and kin, "Ah, thank God it's Monday!" Somewhat reluctantly, Hochschild concludes that for more and more women "the world of 'male' work seems more honorable and valuable than the 'female' world of home and children."[70] The paradoxical result of such a shift, suggests Hochschild, is altogether clear: That for which we work—families—is that which is most hurt by our work!

Hochschild implies that every dual-career family needs a full-time wife. In my review of *The Time Bind* I argued that given Hochschild's findings and insights, perhaps the only way to save the family is to change it.

In the future, individuals who want to "have it all"—children and a career—without shortchanging one or the other, or both, will be required to enter into a communal marriage involving six precertified adults. Two of them will work full-time in order to support the family; two will be in charge of the house and kids; and two of them will be held in ready reserve, to fill in wherever they are needed. Divorce will be forbidden; all property will be owned in joint tenancy; sleeping arrangements are negotiable; and sex will be strictly optional. Hey, why not give it a try? Nothing else seems to be working.[71]

Women have changed. The economy has changed. The workplace has changed. Families have changed. Unfortunately, most men have not changed, either privately or professionally. The rules of work also have not changed sufficiently to accommodate the new reality. Are women in the workplace to stay? Absolutely! Women report that they both need and want to work. Current research also suggests that no matter how taxing and hectic their lives, women who do paid work feel less depressed, have a higher sense of personal worth, and are happier and more satisfied than women who do not have jobs. Do men need women in the workplace? Yes! Demographic trends regarding birthrates, urban population patterns, and college graduation rates necessitate women's active participation in the workplace. Do men want women in the workplace? Yes and no. For a lot of men, women simply represent another group of individuals to compete with for jobs, salaries, promotions; and for some men there yet remains a sense of social awkwardness about women's roles and men's appropriate response.

For too many men, women's commitment to work and their general dependability remains suspect because of "the one immutable, enduring difference between men and women . . . maternity."[72] On the job, families and babies are seen as a vulnerability, an impediment rather than a normal and necessary part of life that should be accommodated. According to Betsy Morris, in an interesting shift in values,

the new ultimate male status symbol "is not a fancy car or a fancy second home, or a wife with a fancy career. You've really made it, buddy, if you can afford a wife that doesn't work. She may be a drag on earnings, but she provides a rare modern luxury: peace on the home front."[73]

Finally, will women rise in the ranks and assume power proportional to their numbers in the workplace? I fear not. But the reasons are much more straightforward and much less gender-specific and sexually biased than some social commentators would have us think. To begin with, the rules of work are, by and large, still being written by men, and these rules communicate an indifference to any concerns beyond the job at hand. As both Robert Bly and Gloria Emerson have argued, the primary masculine imperative is to fulfill their role as worker-provider. Consequently, most workplace rules reflect primarily professional, and not personal, issues. Second, although it is true that the predominantly male corporate structure has been unwilling to share the power base, this reluctance is not necessarily misogynistic in its origins. The term *power* comes from the Latin *posse*: to do, to be able, to change, to influence, to affect. Power is about control or the ability to produce intended results. To have power is to possess the capacity to control or direct change. The first maxim of power is self-perpetuation; nobody gladly gives up power. This principle is not testosterone-based or predominantly masculine in its origins. It is purely Machiavellian, that is, those who have power (in this case, men) will give it up only reluctantly. The goal of power, said Machiavelli, is not to allow change, because change always leads to the alienation of power and of the status quo, and an alteration of the status quo is never in the best interest of those who possess power. Although the issue at hand is the power of the "good-old-boy network," we are not talking about a cabal of evil men conspiring to keep women in their place. In effect, the motivating principle involved in this and every power struggle is much more visceral than simple machismo.

Things are not going to radically change anytime soon, but gradual change is occurring. As singer-actress-director. Barbra Streisand said upon her 1992 induction into the Women in Film Hall of Fame, "Not so long ago we were referred to as dolls, tomatoes, chicks, babes, broads. We've graduated to being called tough cookies, foxes, bitches and witches. I guess that's progress."[74]

NOTES

1. "Changing Profile of the U.S. Labor Force." *U.S. News & World Report*, September 2, 1985, 46–47.

2. Bradley K. Googins, *Work/Family Conflicts* (New York: Auburn House, 1991), 1, 286.

3. Barbara Ehrenreich, "Strategies of Corporate Women." *New Republic*, January 27, 1987, 28.

4. Carol Kleiman, "On the Job," *Chicago Tribune*, November 1, 1998, Jobs section, 1.

5. Kathryn M. Borman, "Fathers, Mothers, and Child Care in the 1980s," in K. M. Borman et al., eds., *Women in the Workplace: Effects on Families* (Trenton, N.J.: Ablex Publishing, 1984), 73.

6. Stephanie Coontz, *The Way We Never Were: American Families and the Nostalgia Trap* (New York: Basic Books, 1992), 31–41.

7. Ibid., 31.

8. Ibid., 32.

9. Ralph E. Smith, ed., *The Subtle Revolution: Women at Work* (Washington, D.C.: Urban Institute, 1979), 1.

10. "Are Men Becoming the Second Sex?" *Chicago Tribune*, February 9, 1997, Women's News secton, 6.

11. "Sixth Annual Salary Survey," *Working Woman*, January 5, 1985, 65.

12. *Statistical Abstract of the United States*, 116th ed., no. 626, "Employment Status of Women" (Latham, Md.: Bernan Press, 1996), 400.

13. Borman, "Fathers, Mothers, and Child Care in the 1980s," 73.

14. John Schmeltzer, "Daughters Will Face Many of Mom's Barriers at Work," *Chicago Tribune*, April 28, 1994, Business section, 1.

15. *Statistical Abstract of the United States*, 116th ed., no. 626.

16. Arlie Russell Hochschild, *The Second Shift* (New York: Viking, 1989), 2.

17. Ibid., 93–94; Daniel Evan Weiss, *The Great Divide: How Females and Males Really Differ* (Crofton, Md.: Poseidon Press, 1991), 32.

18. Carol Kleiman, "Women's Voices Poll Speaks of Solutions as Well as Questions," *Chicago Tribune*, November 12, 1996, Business section, 3.

19. John W. Wright, *The American Almanac of Jobs and Salaries* (New York: Avon, 1997), 650–51.

20. *Working Woman*, January 1985, 65.

21. *Working Women Count! A Report to the Nation*, U.S. Department of Labor Women's Bureau, 1994, 13; Lisa Anderson, "Women Escape Affirmative Action Feud," *Chicago Tribune*, May 16, 1995, 1.

22. *Working Women Count*, 10.

23. Coontz, *The Way We Never Were*, 23.

24. Googins, *Work/Family Conflicts*, 95.

25. Ibid., 4.

26. Ibid., 5.

27. Sara Ann Friedman, *Work Matters* (New York: Viking, 1996), xii.

28. Hochschild, *The Second Shift*, 263.

29. Maureen Brendan, Director, Career Center and Placement, Loyola University, Chicago, 1996.

30. Friedman, *Work Matters*, xii.

31. Gloria Emerson, *Some American Men* (New York: Simon and Schuster, 1985), 32.

32. Daniel Yankelovich, "The New Psychological Contracts at Work." *Psychology Today*, May 1978.

33. Roper Starch Worldwide survey, quoted in *Working Woman*, October 1995, 22.

34. Ibid.

35. Coontz, *The Way We Never Were*, 266.

36. David R. Koller, president, Cornerstone Realty Advisors, Inc., Chicago, 1996.

37. Coontz, *The Way We Never Were*, 22.

38. Googins, *Work/Family Conflict*, 22.

39. Coontz, *The Way We Never Were*, 3, 15.

40. Hochschild, *The Second Shift*, 249.

41. Schmeltzer, "Daughters Will Face Many of Mom's Barriers at Work," 2.

42. Judith Rosener, "Coping with Sexual Static," *New York Times Magazine*. December 7, 1986, 89ff.

43. Patricia H. Werhane, "Sexual Static and the Ideal of Professional Objectivity," in A. R. Gini and T.J. Sullivan, eds., *It Comes with the Territory* (New York: Random House, 1989), 170.

44. Rosener, "Coping with Sexual Static."

45. Werhane, "Sexual Static and the Ideal of Professional Objectivity," 173.
46 Ibid., 171.
47. *Working Women Count,* 36.
48. Amanda T. Segal and Wendy Zeller, "Corporate Women," *Business Week,* June 8, 1992, 76.
49. "Breaking Through," *Business Week,* February 17, 1997, 64. Survey by Catalyst, Inc., a New York research firm that focuses on women in business.
50. Barbara Sullivan, "Women Cross 10% Barrier in Presence on Boards," *Chicago Tribune,* Dec. 12, 1996, Business section, 1–2.
51. "The State of the States for Women and Politics" (Washington, D.C.: Center for Policy Alternatives, n.d.), 2–3.
52. Segal and Zeller, "Corporate Women," 74.
53. Mike Dorning, "Poll Details Global Role of Gender Bias," *Chicago Tribune,* March 27, 1996, 1.
54. *Working Women Count,* 20.
55. Carol Kleiman, "Equal Pay for Work of Equal Value: A Gender-Free Gain," *Chicago Tribune,* September 17, 1996, Business section, 3.
56. *Working Women Count,* 13.
57. Ibid., 31–32.
58. Hochschild, *The Second Shift,* 96.

59. Felice N. Schwartz, "Management Women and the New Facts of Life," *Harvard Business Review,* January–February 1989, 65–76.
60. Betsy Morris, "Is Your Family Wrecking Your Career?" *Fortune,* March 17, 1998, 71–72.
61. Ibid., 72.
62. Ibid., 26.
63. Ibid., 3–4, 260.
64. Ibid., 259.
65. Ibid., 12.
66. Arlie Russell Hochschild, *The Time Bind* (New York: Metropolitan Books, 1997), 249.
67. Laura Shapiro, "The Myth of Quality Time," *Newsweek,* May 12, 1997, 64.
68. Arlie Russell Hochschild, "There's No Place Like Work," *New York Times Magazine,* April 20, 1997, 53.
69. Ibid., 53.
70. Ibid., 84.
71. Al Gini, "Work, Time, and Hochschild," *Metropolis,* WBEZ, Chicago, May 21, 1997.
72. Schwartz, "Management Women and the New Facts of Life," 66.
73. Morris, "Is Your Family Wrecking Your Career?" 72.
74. Friedman, *Work Matters,* 231.

Essay

Child Care Comes to Work

Bonnie Harris

On a recent workday at her Irvine office, Traci Renner held a staff meeting, e-mailed clients, met with her boss and prepared a public relations proposal—all between diaper changes, feedings and play time with her 9-month-old son, Lucas, who rolled around the floor by her desk.

"It's nice to know I don't have to panic when my child care falls through at the last minute, like today," said Renner, stuffing a teething ring into her son's waiting mouth.

"Besides, I just like having him here with me sometimes."

At a time more families are seeing both parents hold full-time jobs, the 40-employee Benjamin Group public relations agency where Renner works is addressing child care in a way that many companies wouldn't dare—and its efforts have drawn national attention. Sick child? Work the day from home. Nanny canceled? Bring the kids on in.

Even though a tight job market and booming economy have prompted scores of employers to expand worker benefits and strike better work-life balances, officials say such workplace improvements haven't applied as much to child-care support.

It's taken nearly 20 years, for example, for the number of on-site corporate day-care centers to reach 8,000 nationally; in 1982 there were 204, according to a dependent-care consulting group in Michigan.

Operating costs, liability concerns and reams of licensing applications and inspections have deterred companies from making the on-site child-care leap.

But at Benjamin Group's Irvine offices, it's not uncommon to see Renner and other parents toting their children around the office, plopping them in a beanbag chair during meetings or putting them down for a nap in one of several office cribs.

Not everyone sees such an arrangement as practical or beneficial to the workplace. But as a result of this casual kid-friendly attitude and other programs for employees, the Silicon Valley–based agency has been repeatedly recognized by *Working Mother* magazine as one of the country's best companies to work for.

And by the end of this month, the company's employees in Irvine will be able to enroll their children in an on-site day-care center called Executive Sweet, making it the first on-site, corporate child-care center in Orange County, according to state officials. Los Angeles County has just a few such centers. The Bay Area has 11.

"I'm surprised there aren't more," said John Gordon, a spokesman for the state Department of Social Services, which oversees day-care licensing. "I would have expected at least to see some of the larger companies heading in that direction."

But Sheri Benjamin, chief executive of Benjamin Group, said she has an idea why such child-care efforts are so unusual.

It's been a two-year process to open her company's on-site center, even requiring the entire Orange County office to move from Santa Ana to a larger site in Irvine with enough square footage to accommodate 20 children and enough room for an enclosed, grassy outdoor play area.

"Do you know how difficult it is?" asked Benjamin, who also set up an on-site center at the agency's headquarters in the Silicon Valley. "It's exhausting. But we've seen the payoffs. We were committed to this."

After two years of code inspections, building changes and licensing approvals, Benjamin said, she is now waiting on final approval from fire officials so she can officially open the center at the Irvine offices.

The trend in corporate child-care centers began in the 1980s in the health-care industry, with hospitals—and their large numbers of shift workers—leading the way, officials said. Employees at Hoag Hospital in Newport Beach have access to a day-care center that operates on its campus, but the center is not considered a corporate, on-site center because it is also open to the public.

Law firms and financial companies later began adding child care to their list of benefits, and now officials said they are seeing it splash into the technology industry, Motorola Inc., for one, boasts 12 on-site child-care centers in the U.S. and two abroad.

Cisco Systems Inc. runs an on-site center for roughly 100 children in San Jose and Amgen Inc., a biotechnology company in Thousand Oaks, recently expanded its 8-year-old center to accommodate 300, ranging in age from 6 weeks to 5 years.

"Child-care benefits, especially on-site child-care centers, are worth more than any amount of money," said Ilene Hoffer, a spokeswoman for Bright Horizons, which provides employer-sponsored on-site child care for more than 325 clients worldwide. "It's a competitive recruitment and retention tool for companies. If one company in an industry does it, many others tend to follow suit. They'd be crazy not to in this market."

Sharman Stein, a senior editor for *Working Mother* magazine, said employers are often put off by the cost of providing on-site child care, which can exceed $ 100.000 a year. But with the number of working mothers now topping 26 million, Stein said, she expects to see more companies begin "testing the waters," perhaps by providing emergency backup child care first.

At least 30 companies in California (a dozen in Orange County) offer such off-site services, designed to give working parents a safety net should their regular day-care arrangements fall through.

Typically, officials say, a working family will experience six to eight child-care breakdowns every year.

"It's just a no-brainer for companies to do everything they can to keep their working parents happy," Stein said. "We've seen time and time again that in order for employees to be productive, they have to feel like home base is covered."

At Benjamin Group, the office sometimes turns *into* home base, with 5-year-olds raiding the staff refrigerator or cozying up with a video in the company lounge.

What some bosses may frown on as a distraction, though, has evolved into what employees said is an unusual perk. With a staff of more than 30 women and a handful of dads, there is never a shortage of hands to pitch in if a child needs tending when the parent needs to concentrate on work. There is a lounge with sofas and a VCR, and plenty of toys, they said.

"Half the time I bring her in here, I don't know where she is," said account manager Morag Rich, referring to her 6-month-old daughter, Brenna.

"I'll get busy on something and then I have to walk through the office going. 'Who has the baby?' "

Added associate Christine Eastman, who joined the firm six months ago: "I don't even have kids, and I'm telling you, coming into the office after lunch and seeing the receptionist bouncing a baby on her knee is just plain fun."

The arrangement has been practiced in the agency's Orange County office for years while the company searched for a location that would meet the host of building restrictions required to operate a day-care center, said Benjamin, the chief executive, whose own children "grew up" in the center she opened nine years ago at the company's headquarters.

"When we started this back then, people thought we were bonkers, especially being the small company that we were. But we strongly believed it was the right thing to do," she said. "Now it's an enviable benefit in the workplace. And the returns have far outweighed any investment we've made."

In Orange County, there is already a list of employees who plan to enroll their children on the first day, Benjamin said. The company offers day-care subsidies that vary depending on salaries, but average about $266 per child per month.

The agency's general manager, Lisa Zwick, who is expecting her first child next month, said the new day-care center "made a huge difference" in her decision to return to work after the baby is born.

"It is such a relief to know I can come back here and have the baby in day care, but still so close by, while I work," she said. "All my friends are jealous."

Case Study

Gender Issues at Your House

John Hasnas

DOMINIQUE FRANCON

You are Dominique Francon, a senior account representative in the advertising department of the successful architecture magazine, *Your House*. In this position, you supervise the junior account reps who directly contact potential advertisers to sell advertising space. You and Peter Keating, the other senior account representative, are each responsible for half the staff, although your half consistently out-performs Keating's. Both of you report directly to Henry Cameron, the manager of the advertising department. Recently, you were excited to learn that Cameron will soon be promoted to the magazine's editorial board. Since by any performance standard your results are greatly superior to Keating's, you feel sure that you are slated to replace Cameron.

You think of yourself as a self-assured and assertive woman and have a strong desire to succeed in what you view as the male-dominated publishing industry. Accordingly, you behave in what you consider a professional manner at all times. Although somewhat demanding, you are never unfair to your subordinates; a combination that you believe helps account for your staff's superior bottom-line performance. You feel some regret that this posture prevents you from developing the kind of work-place friendships that others do, but you see this as part of the price you have to pay to make it as a woman manager. You keep a strict separation between your social and professional lives and would never

consider pursuing a personal relationship with any of your co-workers. In addition, you are a hard worker, typically putting in many hours beyond the 40 per week required by your position.

You get along fairly well with everyone at the magazine except Ellsworth Toohey, one of the senior editors. Even before the run-in you had with him last year, you considered Toohey to be a typical "male chauvinist pig." Toohey, a man in his mid-fifties from Lubbock. Texas, habitually engages in behavior that you find offensive and demeaning to the women who work at the magazine. Regardless of their position, he typically addresses the women on the staff as "Honey" or "Dear" and refers to them collectively as the magazine's "fillies." In addition, he will invariably greet them with some comment on their appearance such as "Looking good today, Dear" or "Nice dress. I don't know how I'll keep my mind on my work while you're around, Honey."

Last year, after a private meeting in his office concerning the advertising budget, Toohey asked you to go out with him. You told him that since he was a superior of yours whose judgment could have an effect on your future career, you thought it would be inappropriate and that you had a personal policy of never dating co-workers. Rather than accept your refusal, Toohey responded to this by saying. "Oh, loosen up. People go out with co-workers all the time. Let your hair down. I guarantee you won't be disappointed." Although you found

---

this to be both condescending and offensive, you retained your calm and said. "Mr. Toohey, you are putting me in a very awkward situation. I don't think it would be a good idea and I'd appreciate it if you would drop the subject."

A few days following this, you overheard two of the female secretaries discussing Toohey at lunch. Upon inquiring, you learned that he had propositioned many of the single women at the magazine, something that upset several of them. The final straw, however, came the following week when you were leaning over to take a drink from the water fountain. Toohey, who was passing by at the time, said, "Whoa, nice view!" and when you stood up. "Have you reconsidered my proposal of last week? You should get to know me better. I can really be of help to you in this business."

Following this incident, you went immediately to the manager of personnel, Howard Roark, to complain. Roark listened to your description of both incidents and your claim that other female employees had had similar experiences and told you he would look into it. Less than a week later, he came by your office to say that the problem had been taken care of and if you had any further trouble with Toohey to inform him immediately. Although you have no idea what action Roark took, it was clear something had been done. From that point on, Toohey never said a word to you that was not strictly business related. His manner toward you had become completely cold and formal, and he seemed to try to avoid you whenever possible.

This state of affairs suited you fine until today. Yesterday afternoon, you were shocked to learn that the editorial board had voted to promote Peter Keating to manager of the advertising department. The editorial board is made up of the senior managers and editors and is empowered to fill any opening at the managerial level by majority vote. The board presently has nine members, none of whom are women.

Upset, you had gone to Roark's office to ask why you had been passed over. He informed you that although the vote was as close as it possibly could be, the board elected to go with Keating because it was impressed with his "people skills." However, when you came in this morning, one of your account reps asked you what you had ever done to Toohey. When you asked her what she meant, she said that she had been talking to the secretary who had kept the minutes of yesterday's Board meeting, and she had said that Toohey really had it in for you. Before you could stop yourself, you heard yourself saying. "Why, that son of a bitch. I'll sue him for sexual harassment and the entire board for sex discrimination."

When you calmed down, you found yourself wondering whether this was, in fact, a case of sexual harassment or sex discrimination. You also found yourself wondering what would be the best steps for you to take in this situation. What should you do? (You may ask to meet with either Roark or Toohey or both in addition to any other action you deem appropriate.)

ELLSWORTH TOOHEY

You are Ellsworth Toohey, a senior editor of the successful architecture magazine, *Your House.* This position has both editorial and managerial responsibilities. As an editor, you both decide which articles will be printed in the magazine and make editorial recommendations regarding them. However, as a senior editor, you are also a member of the editorial board, which makes the important managerial decisions for the magazine. The board is comprised of the nine men who are senior managers or editors. It has responsibility for planning the magazine's budget, establishing editorial policy, and selecting those who are to be hired or promoted to managerial positions.

You were born in 1937 in Lubbock, Texas. Your family was extremely poor and you always had to work as a boy, but you managed to put yourself through college, getting a B.A. in English. Following graduation, you married your college sweetheart, got a position as a reporter for the *Dallas Morning News*, and began your career. By 1982, you had worked your way up to editor of the *Morning News*. At that time, you left Dallas to join the staff of *Your House*, then a new magazine just starting out. You were quite happy with your new position and things were going very well for you until your wife died 18 months ago. After a very rough 6 or 7 months, you began to put your life back together and have rededicated yourself to your work, perhaps in order to compensate for some of the emptiness in your personal life.

You think of yourself as a skilled professional, but one who has never forgotten the importance of a friendly demeanor that your Southern upbringing impressed upon you. Accordingly, you try to maintain an informal and friendly manner with your co-workers and subordinates. You will often chat with the male employees about sports or politics. You also try to make small talk with the female employees, although you find this more difficult since your upbringing and life experience seems to have left you ignorant of what subjects are of interest to women. You have a personal policy of attempting to greet all co-workers with a complementary comment in an effort to overcome the intimidating effect your high-level position can have on lower-level employees. Even when you don't know their names, you might greet an employee with a comment such as, "Nice suit, Son." or "Looking good today, Dear."

You believe you get along fairly well with everyone at the magazine except Dominique Francon, one of the two senior account representatives in the advertising department. A senior account representative supervises the junior account reps who directly contact potential advertisers to sell advertising space. Even before the run-in you had with her last year, you considered Francon to be an example of an "uptight, feminist bitch"; cold, aloof, and demanding. She had the reputation for driving the accounts reps under her unmercifully hard while hardly ever dispensing a "Nice job" or "Well done." Although her section usually sold the most advertising, in your opinion these results came at the expense of a happy workforce.

Last year, about six months after your wife's death, you made what you now consider some terrible errors in judgment. Seeking escape from your loneliness, you asked several of the single women at the magazine to go out with you. Since you had not asked a woman out in over 35 years, you were not particularly good at it and felt foolish and inept trying to do so.

One day last year, you were having a private meeting with Francon in your office concerning the advertising budget. It was one of those days when you were feeling particularly lonely and couldn't stand the thought of going home to an empty house again. As a result, you asked Francon to go out with you despite the negative impression you had of her personality. To your surprise, she did not turn you down directly, but simply stated that she had a policy against dating people from the office. At the time, you interpreted this to mean that she would like to go out with you, but was concerned with the appearance of impropriety. Rather than let the matter drop, you said something to the effect that she should not be so concerned with appearances and that people on the magazine's staff go out with each other all the time. However, Francon responded by saying that she thought it would create an awkward situation and that she would rather not.

A week later, Francon was getting a drink at the water fountain when you passed by. After saying hello, you said "Have you reconsidered my proposal of last week? I would really like to get to know you better. I know you're trying to make a career in publishing.

I have a lot of experience in the field. Maybe I can be of some help to you." To your surprise, she just stormed off.

The next thing you knew, Howard Roark, the manager of personnel, was in your office telling you that Francon had complained to him that you were sexually harassing her as well as other women on the magazine's staff. Angry and extremely embarrassed, you admitted to Roark that you had been lonely since your wife's death and had asked several women out. You assured him that since these actions had apparently been misinterpreted, you would not do so again. Since then, although you still have endeavored to remain on friendly terms with most of the women at the magazine, you have never been familiar with Francon again. You have kept all your dealings with her on a formal and professional level.

Yesterday, the editorial board met to vote on who should be named manager of the advertising department now that the former manager, Henry Cameron, had been promoted to senior manager and member of the editorial board. Although four members of the board wanted to promote Francon because of her section's superior sales performance, Cameron, now a board member, recommended Peter Keating, the other senior account representative. Cameron stated that he thought Keating had more "people skills" than did Francon and would make a better manager. You certainly agreed with this and said so. In the end, the board voted 5–4 to promote Keating.

Today, you learned that upon hearing that Keating had been promoted rather than her, Francon had told one of her account reps that she was going to sue you and the magazine for sexual harassment and sex discrimination. Your initial reaction to this was to exclaim. "Isn't that just like the bitch." However, after you calmed down, you realized that this could present a damaging situation both for you and the magazine. What should you do? (You may ask to meet with either Roark or Francon or both in addition to any other action you deem appropriate.)

Case Study

Worth the Effort?

Raymond S. Pfeiffer
Ralph P. Forsberg

HANDLING SEXUAL HARASSMENT

Violet Spear had done her homework. But then, she felt she had to in order to know whether or not she should file a grievance against her colleague, Theo Lucasey. Violet did not want to jeopardize her job as a junior marketing executive by appearing to be a "bad sport," "overly sensitive woman," or any "hysterical female." Theo had called her all of these in the last few months when she complained to him about his conduct toward her.

Violet was trying to find out whether the way Theo had been treating her constituted sexual harassment. What she found out was interesting. First, she looked for the legal guidelines for sexual harassment. Under Title VII of the 1964 Civil Rights Act, sexual harassment is defined as

> Unwelcome sexual advances, requests for sexual favors, and other verbal or physical conduct of a sexual nature constitute sexual harassment when (1) submission to such conduct is made either explicitly or implicitly a term or condition of an individual's employment, (2) submission to or rejection of such conduct by an individual is used as the basis for employment decisions affecting such individual, or (3) such conduct has the purpose or effect of unreasonably interfering with an individual's work performance or creating an intimidating, hostile, or offensive working environment.[1]

This seemed pretty clear to Violet and seemed to definitely apply to the way Theo had been treating her.

Violet is very successful in her marketing position. She attributes part of her success to the fact that her clients trust her professionalism as well as her knowledge of her job. Part of what Violet sees as important to her professional image is her wardrobe: she dresses in very conservative business suits that are feminine yet reassuring to her conservative male clients. Before Theo's remarks, no one had ever referred to her wardrobe as anything but tasteful or stylish.

Theo was transferred from a regional branch about six months earlier and almost immediately began to make comments to Violet whenever they worked together. At first it had just been things like "Very nice suit," but soon he began to add a growl or a low barking noise to his comments. She had called him on this right away, but he accused her of being overly sensitive. The comments continued and gradually became more suggestive. Again Violet told him to keep his comments to himself. He responded by accusing her of being a bad sport.

The situation reached its peak about a week ago when once again Theo made a comment about her clothes: "That suit is so sexy I can't stand it. Why don't we go into my office where you can take it off so I can get some work done? You know what kind of work I mean, right?"

Violet replied angrily, "Why don't you just knock it off. Act like a grown man instead of a 14-year-old with a hormone problem. I simply will not tolerate these remarks any more. One more and I'm going to have to file a complaint."

"Don't be a hysterical female, dear. Those business suits of yours really turn me on. I've always had a thing for women who dress in those 'power suits.' I like power. Why not just stop wearing those clothes? Maybe then I'll be able to control myself," was Theo's response.

Violet had walked away in disgust. In the next week she looked up the harassment guidelines and talked to a number of women at her office about what had happened. When she asked what to do, the replies were not encouraging. One woman said it couldn't be harassment, because Theo wasn't her boss and had no power over her employment. Another said that she had no confidence that any of the male executives would take her complaints seriously. A third said that unless one of the male executives actually witnessed the harassment, nothing would be done. In all, five different women expressed the sentiment that no male executive would take her seriously, and probably they'd believe Theo's comment about her being overly sensitive or hysterical.

"It's the way men are. Must be genetic. No government guidelines are going to reverse 41,000 years of habit," one had said.

Violet was confused. The terms of the guidelines seemed to cover Theo's action—work was becoming oppressive. Yet she had gotten no encouragement from other women at the company. She had also come across some statistics that stated that 67 percent of the women who complained of harassment lost their jobs within one year, either by being fired or by voluntarily leaving. The same source stated that only 9 percent of the complaints ever resulted in the harassment ceasing. There was a procedure for sexual harassment claims at Violet's firm, but each step of the process involved some male executive who might react just as the other women predicted.

Violet is afraid of being labeled a complainer or a troublemaker. She began to think Theo's comments might be correct, maybe if she just stopped wearing those suits he'd leave her alone. She didn't want to compromise her career; she had worked too hard and been too professional to give it up for a jerk like Theo. But her clients responded well to her professional style of dressing and had never insulted her like Theo. Would they be bothered by a switch in her wardrobe? Yet if she didn't complain, work would continue to be oppressive, and there was no telling how many other women Theo would insult. Violet has to make a decision about how she's going to get this problem Resolved. Put yourself in her position to complete the analysis and reach a decision.

NOTE

1. "Guidelines on Discrimination on the Basis of Sex" (Washington, DC: Equal Employment Opportunity Commission, November 10, 1980).

Case Study

Foreign Assignment

Thomas Dunfee, Diana Robertson

Sara Strong graduated with an MBA from UCLA four years ago. She immediately took a job in the correspondent bank section of the Security Bank of the American Continent. Sara was assigned to work on issues pertaining to relationships with correspondent banks in Latin America. She rose rapidly in the section and received three good promotions in three years. She consistently got high ratings from her superiors, and she received particularly high marks for her professional demeanor.

In her initial position with the bank, Sara was required to travel to Mexico on several occasions. She was always accompanied by a male colleague even though she generally handled similar business by herself on trips within the United States. During her trips to Mexico she observed that Mexican bankers seemed more aware of her being a woman and were personally solicitous to her, but she didn't discern any major problems. The final decisions on the work that she did were handled by male representatives of the bank stationed in Mexico.

A successful foreign assignment was an important step for those on the "fast track" at the bank. Sara applied for a position in Central or South America and was delighted when she was assigned to the bank's office in Mexico City. The office had about twenty bank employees and was headed by William Vitam. The Mexico City office was seen as a preferred assignment by young executives at the bank.

After a month, Sara began to encounter problems. She found it difficult to be effective in dealing with Mexican bankers—the clients. They appeared reluctant to accept her authority and they would often bypass her in important matters. The problem was exacerbated by Vitam's compliance in her being bypassed. When she asked that the clients be referred back to her, Vitam replied, "Of course that isn't really practical." Vitam made matters worse by patronizing her in front of clients and by referring to her as "my cute assistant" and "our lady banker." Vitam never did this when only Americans were present, and in fact treated her professionally and with respect in internal situations.

Sara finally complained to Vitam that he was undermining her authority and effectiveness; she asked him in as positive a manner as possible to help her. Vitam listened carefully to Sara's complaints, then replied: "I'm glad that you brought this up, because I've been meaning to sit down and talk to you about my little game-playing in front of the clients. Let me be frank with you. Our clients think you're great, but they just don't understand a woman in authority, and you and I aren't going to be able to change their attitudes overnight. As long as the clients see you as my assistant and deferring to me, they can do business with you. I'm willing to give you as much responsibility as they can handle your having. I *know* you can handle it. But we just have to tread carefully. You and I know that my remarks in front of clients don't mean anything. They're just a way of playing the game Latin style. I know it's frustrating for you, but I really need you to support me on this. It's not going to affect your promotions, and for the most part you really will have responsibility for these client's accounts. You just have to act like it's my responsibility." Sara replied that she would try to cooperate, but that basically she found her role demeaning.

As time went on, Sara found that the patronizing actions in front of clients bothered her more and more. She spoke to Vitam again, but he was firm in his position, and urged her to try to be a little more flexible, even a little more "feminine."

Sara also had a problem with Vitam over policy. The Mexico City office had five younger women who worked as receptionists and secretaries. They were all situated at work stations at the entrance to the office. They were required to wear standard uniforms that were colorful and slightly sexy. Sara protested the requirement that uniforms be worn because (1) they were inconsistent to the image of the banking business and (2) they were demeaning to the women who had to wear them. Vitam just curtly replied that he had received a lot of favorable comments about the uniforms from clients of the bank.

Several months later, Sara had what she thought would be a good opportunity to deal with the problem. Tom Fried, an executive vice president who had been a mentor for her since she arrived at the bank, was coming to Mexico City; she arranged a private conference with him. She described her problems and explained that she was not able to be effective in this environment and that she worried that it would have a negative effect on her chance of promotion within the bank, Fried was very careful in his response. He spoke of certain "realities" that the bank had to respect and he urged her to "see it through" even though he could understand how she would feel that things weren't fair.

Sara found herself becoming more aggressive and defensive in her meetings with Vitam and her clients. Several clients asked that other bank personnel handle their transactions. Sara has just received an Average rating, which noted "the beginnings of a negative attitude about the bank and its policies."

Case Study

Sexual Discrimination at Eastern Airlines?

Al Gini

On December 28, 1983, a federal judge ordered Eastern Airlines to reinstate a pilot who had been fired following a sex-change operation in 1980. The pilot, who flew for the airline for 12 years as Kenneth Ulane, is now known as Karen Ulane. Before joining Eastern in 1968, Ulane had previously been an Army pilot and was decorated for valor in connection with missions flown in Vietnam.[1]

In 1979, following years of psychiatric consultation, Ulane took a leave of absence and underwent a sex-change operation in April 1980. When she returned to work, the airline would not reinstate her as a pilot. After refusing to accept other administrative positions, Eastern fired her on April 24, 1981. Ulane charged that her dismissal was a direct result of her sex-change operation and filed a sex-discrimination suit. "In terms of sexual discrimination," said one of her lawyers, "Karen Ulane was kind of a perfect control group. As a male pilot, Eastern's own witnesses acknowledge that she was one of their better pilots. When she changed her sex, she was all of a sudden not acceptable. Eastern was willing to retain one sex in their employ, but not willing to retain the other."[2] At the time, only two of Eastern's 4,200 pilots were women.

In an emotionally charged two-hour oral opinion, Judge John Grady found in favor of Ulane and berated Eastern for their "ostrich-like and contemptuous attitude toward transsexuals."[3] Grady based his decision on Title VII of the Civil Rights Act of 1964. This statute provides that

> It shall be an unlawful employment practice for an employer to fail or refuse to hire or to discharge any individual or otherwise to discriminate against any individual with respect to his compensation, terms, conditions or privileges of employment because of such individual's race, color, religion, sex, or national origin.

The specific question before the court, Judge Grady suggested, is whether the phrase "because of the individual's sex" encompasses a person such as the plaintiff who alleges that she is a transsexual or, alternatively, that having gone through sex-reassignment surgery, she is now no longer a man but a woman. In other words, is a person's sexual identity a protected category under the Civil Rights Act?[4]

Judge Grady pointed out that this section of the Civil Rights Act had originally prohibited discrimination on the basis of race but not sex. An amendment introducing sex into the statute was offered by a southern senator who hoped that by this gambit he would prevent the bill's passage. His ploy obviously did not work, but neither was there much discussion at that time concerning the scope of the term *sex*. Grady therefore set himself the task of defining *sex* in the context of Title VII. He first distinguished between our understanding of the terms *homosexual* and *transvestite* on the one hand, and *transsexual* on the other. The later group, he argued, have problems relative to their sexual identities as men or women, while the former do not. He indicated that, while the statute in question cannot reasonably be extended to matters of sexual preference it is an altogether different matter as to whether the matter of sexual identity is included in our general understanding of the term *sex*.[5]

In his ruling, Grady interpreted the word *sex* to reasonably include the question of sexual identity. He said that, prior to his participation in this case, he would have had no doubt that the question of gender was straightforward. But after hearing the testimony, he realized that there is no settled definition in the medical community as to what we mean by *sex*. He argued that sex is defined by something more than the biological. It is also defined by society, because the way an individual is perceived by society plays a crucial role in a person's sense of sexual identity.[6]

Having concluded that the term *sex* in Title VII reasonably includes the question of sexual identity, Grady then considered whether Ulane was indeed a transsexual. The defendants argued that Ulane is really a transvestite and hence is not protected by the statute. Grady contended that both the Gender Identity Board of the University of Chicago Medical School and her own doctor had found Ulane to be a transsexual. The defense countered that the plaintiff had only managed to persuade these medical practitioners—through some retrospective distortion—that she is transsexual. Grady dismissed this claim, saying that Ulane knew as much as most psychiatrists about her condition and the possible risks of her operation, and that she could hardly have any ulterior motive in undergoing such a radical procedures. He contended that the fact of Ulane's operation argues for her being a true transsexual, since she must have been aware that transvestites have very poor prognosis after sex-reassignment surgery.[7]

Grady then considered the question of whether Ulane had been discharged because of her sex. The evidence presented at the trial indicated that Eastern began to develop their brief leading to Ulane's discharge just after her surgery. Prior to that time, Eastern had no complaints about her performance as a pilot.[8] Eastern's legal department drafted two separate discharge letters which contained seven essential arguments, each of which they felt represented independent "nondiscriminatory" reasons for dismissal.[9]

1. Eastern alleged that because of Ulane's "underlying psychological problem" her presence in the cockpit represented an unjustifiable safety hazard to passengers and crew. Grady argued that Eastern was prejudiced from the start and had invented all sorts of dangers that inhered in the so-called "underlying psychological problem." Furthermore, Eastern never gave Ulane a fair hearing on this issue or the opportunity to show that they were wrong or at least had no reason for concern in her particular situation.[10]

2. Eastern charged that Ulane's medical certification was not unconditional after her surgery. Here, Grady compared her case to that of alcoholic pilots, whose certificates are also conditional. The FAA had, in fact, indicated that Ulane was fit to fly, and had ordered her to undergo periodic counseling only in order to help her deal with any problems created by unfriendly co-workers.[11]

3. Eastern complained that sex-reassignment surgery does not solve the underlying psychological problem. Grady indicated that there was no evidence of change in the plaintiff's psychological adjustment profile. Ulane, therefore, would be no more dangerous in the cockpit than before her surgery. Moreover, the judge cited evidence that such surgery actually decreases the patient's anxieties and makes them more stable in regard to their own sense of self-esteem. Grady concluded that the fact of transsexuality does not in itself constitute a safety problem, any more than does, say, left-handedness.[12]

4. Eastern claimed that Ulane's presence in the cockpit would counteract its efforts to assure the public that airline travel is safe. Grady drew a parallel here between Eastern and those who at one time believed that black salesclerks or waiters

would drive customers away. The American public, said Grady, is a lot smarter than Eastern gives them credit for, and rejected their contention as prejudicial.[13]

5. Eastern alleged that, by virtue of her operation, Ulane was no longer the same person they had hired, and that, knowing what they do now, they would not have hired her in the first place. According to Grady, Eastern reacted to the situation as a public-relations problem: "A transsexual in the cockpit? The public wouldn't accept it! We will be the laughing stock of the airline industry! We have got to do something about it!" Grady ruled that this line of argumentation was a virtual admission of discrimination based on sex.[14]

6. Eastern alleged that Ulane had failed to disclose to the company the medication and medical and psychiatric treatments she had received over the years for her condition. Grady pointed out that the drugs Ulane had taken were approved by the FAA as not being dangerous. Therefore, he concluded that her flying ability was not impaired by the medication she was taking. He again drew a parallel between Ulane and male pilots who were alcoholics. Alcoholic pilots rarely, if ever, disclose their problems to the company, but they are not fired for that, even though the dangers of alcohol are well known. Female hormones, on the other hand, have no known effects on flying ability. Grady contended that Eastern had not followed its normal procedure in this case as a result of its initial prejudice against Ulane. If one employee is fired for failure to disclose, all should be treated alike.[15]

7. Eastern alleged that Ulane had instigated publicity damaging to Eastern Airlines. Grady countered that the company must have known that this case would inevitably draw publicity even as it drew up its letters of discharge. Besides, Eastern had raised no similar fuss when some of its female employees were featured nude in *Playboy* magazine.[16]

Grady dismissed all of Eastern's justifications for firing Ulane as mere pretexts. He concluded that, but for her being a transsexual, Ulane would not have been discharged.

I am satisfied from this evidence that while some transsexuals, just as some tall people and some left-handers, some fat people, and some Irishmen would not be safe airline pilots, it is true that some transsexuals would not be safe airline pilots. But it cannot be said with any rationality that all transsexuals are unsafe airline pilots. Neither can it be said with any rationality that it is impossible to make this determination of whether or not a safety hazard is really involved on an individualized basis.[17]

Grady ordered Ulane reinstated with back pay and seniority. The amount of the award was not set during the hearing, but was estimated at about $142,000. Ulane had been receiving an annual salary of $50,000 at the time of her dismissal in 1981.[18]

Eastern said it would appeal what it calls Judge Grady's "novel view of the law" and stated that "Eastern remains confident that its position in this case is correct under the law."[19] Grady indicated that if the U.S. Courts of Appeals rules that transsexuals are not protected under Title VII, he will reconsider the question of whether Ulane could claim discrimination because she is a woman. Ulane had originally contended that she was fired because she is a transsexual and a woman. Grady said he was unsure if he could rule that Ulane is a woman. "I don't think I can find the plaintiff is both a transsexual and a woman," he said. "She's either one or the other. . . ."[20]

In the end, Judge Grady saw Eastern's dismissal of Ulane as an attempt by the company to maintain its image at the expense of a good employee's career. But, according to labor-relations attorney Gerald Skoning, the basic premise behind Grady's decision—that sexual identity is defined by something more than the number of X and Y chromosomes present at birth—could have far more extensive implications.[21] Until now the courts have generally refused to grant employment protection for homosexuals under Title VII, saying that although it prohibits discrimination based on sex, it was not intended to prohibit discrimination based on "sexual preference." Many legal scholars believe, however, that if Grady's ruling is upheld on appeal, the decision may be used to try to win protection for homosexuals. Although other scholars are not sure Grady's decision can be extended that far, the ruling, if upheld, not only protects reassigned transsexuals, but all men who feel like a woman but have not undergone surgery.[22]

UPDATE

"Transsexual Pilot Loses Job Appeal"
Adrienne Drell
Chicago Sun Times
August 3, 1984

A federal appeals court ruled yesterday that Karen Ulane, a former Eastern Airlines pilot fired after undergoing a sex-change operation, is not entitled to regain her job.

The 7th Circuit Court of Appeals reversed a Dec, 28 decision by U.S. District Judge John F. Grady that Eastern had violated federal sex discrimination laws.

The 12-page opinion by a three-judge panel, written by Harlington Woods Jr., said *the law does not cover transsexuals or anyone with a "sexual identity disorder. . . ."*

The appellate court said federal law "implies that it is unlawful to discriminate against women because they are women and against men because they are men. . . . A prohibition against discrimination based on an individual's sex is not synonymous with a prohibition against discrimination based on an individuals's sexual identity disorder or discontent with the sex into which they were born."

Ulane is entitled to any "personal belief about her sexual identity she desires," the opinion notes. "But even if one believes that a woman can be so easily created from what remains of a man, that does not decide this case."

NOTES

1. *New York Times*, December 29, 1983, p. 18.
2. Ibid.
3. *Chicago Tribune*, January 1, 1984.
4. *Karen Frances Ulane v. Eastern Airlines, Inc., et al.*, No. 81 C 4411, U.S. District Court, Northeastern Illinois.
5. Ibid., p. 5.
6. Ibid., p. 6.
7. Ibid., pp. 15, 16, 17.
8. Ibid., p. 19.
9. Ibid., p. 33.
10. Ibid., p. 22.
11. Ibid., p. 27.
12. Ibid., p. 30.
13. Ibid., p. 32.
14. Ibid., p. 14.
15. Ibid., p. 15.
16. Ibid., p. 16.
17. *Chicago Tribune*, January 11, 1984, sect. 2, p. 8.
18. *Ulane v. Eastern Airlines*, p. 47.
19. *New York Times*, December 29, 1983, p. 18.
20. *Chicago Tribune*, January 11, 1984, sect. 2, p. 8.
21. *Chicago Tribune*, January 8, 1984, p. 1.
22. Ibid., p. 10.

Chapter Six

•

Corporate Obligations and Responsibilities: Everything Old Is New Again

CONVENTIONAL WISDOM PARADOXICALLY tells us that even though change is constant, certain things never really change, and even when things appear to change, they wind up coming back again. This insight is clearly true in regard to certain aspects of men's fashion. For example, the width and pattern of ties are in a constant state of flux, but sooner or later, they all come around again. All the men I know over the age of forty-five possess at least three different widths of their very favorite paisley or striped tie. This general principle, I think, also applies to literature and fiction. What's that old rule of thumb about there being only twelve possible story lines? But even if this figure is wrong and should be doubled or even tripled, the fact is there are just so many plots, so many story lines, and so many possible dramatic options out there. When you think about it, isn't *West Side Story* a modernized version of *Romeo and Juliet*? Isn't *Star Wars* a futuristic reiteration of American Westerns, such as *How the West Was Won*? And aren't the various adventures of Indiana Jones a kitsch portrayal of the constant, age-old struggle between good and evil?

On a more serious note, the poet and philosopher George Santayana did suggest that conventional wisdom, far from being just a casual cliché, is often true. He warned us that things can and will repeat themselves again and again. And he reminded us, "Those who cannot remember the past are condemned to repeat it," again and again. It does not require an encyclopedic knowledge or a huge leap of imagination to come up with examples to substantiate Santayana's thesis. In the 1920s there was Charles Ponzi's "postal coupon scam," which in the 1970s reappeared as Robert Vesco's "mutual funds scam," which reappeared yet again in the 1980s with Charles Keating and the "multiple-book accounting scam" in the savings-and-loan industry. Then there was Ivan Boesky and Michael Milken (see, "The Fall of Michael Milken") in the 1980s and the charges of "insider trading," which have also been recently leveled at America's favorite "doyenne of domesticity," Martha

Stewart. Obviously and painfully, this theme of mistakes of the past reiterated in the present is dramatically portrayed in "Enron: From Paragon to Pariah," "The Good Old Boys at WorldCom," "The Adelphia Story," and "Radials, Rollovers, and Responsibility: An Examination of the Ford-Firestone Case." All of these cases are proof positive that, in the lines of the old popular song, "Everything old is new again".

In the literature of business ethics in the last twenty years, perhaps the single most discussed topic in the field has been the debate over the legal versus the moral status of the corporation. Legally, corporations are "fictitious persons" created by the law and empowered with certain rights and abilities that allow them to be recognized as financial entities, capable of carrying on commercial transactions, and as institutional citizens that can be be held accountable to regulation and taxation. In general outline, the legalities are relatively easy to state. However, the moral issues involved are much less clear and exact. Is a corporation responsible only to its stockholders? Is fiduciary success the only measure of corporate success? Are corporations moral agents in the same sense as individuals? Can corporations be held morally accountable for their decisions and behavior? Beyond the strict requirements of the law, what rules, rights, and obligations do corporations share with other stakeholders, that is, employees, customers, vendors, and the general community?

Even "good corporations" sometimes do "bad things". Included in this section is an example of a corporation and with a solid track record that temporarily lost its way and almost permanently lost its good name. A. H. Robins, ("A. H. Robins: The Dalkon Shield") naively and perhaps unintentionally produced a product that caused injury and harm to many women. But when Robins found out, it didn't come forward and tell the truth. Rather, it conspired to misinform its customers about the health factors involved in the Dalkon Shield. Why?

Case Study

The Fall of Michael Milken

O. C. Ferrell, John Fraedrich

Drexel Burnham Lambert, Inc. was an investment banking firm that rose to prominence during the 1980s, only to be toppled by one of the biggest scandals ever to hit Wall Street. Michael Milken, senior vice-president and head of Drexel's high-yield and convertible bond department, based in Beverly Hills, California, also succumbed to the scandal. Milken's and Drexel's rapid rise to the top came about as a result of their virtual creation and subsequent domination of the billion-dollar "junk bond" market that helped finance the 1980s takeover boom and change the face of corporate America. Their downfall was the result of a Securities and Exchange Commission (SEC) investigation that eventually led to Milken's incarceration and Drexel's bankruptcy.

THE "JUNK BOND KING"

Before Milken's ascent to the top of financial circles, junk bonds were a relatively obscure financial investment shunned by most investors. Junk bonds are debt securities that offer high rates of return at high risk. Often, they are securities that previously had been graded as "investment quality" but later were downgraded to low-grade, high-risk, high-yield status because of doubts about the issuer's financial strength. Drexel preferred to call these securities "high-yield bonds."

Michael Milken was the driving force behind Drexel's domination of the high-yield bond market. People familiar with the firm say Milken's office was responsible for 80 to 90 percent of Drexel's profits. In addition to bringing in huge profits for the company, Milken also amassed for himself a huge fortune. In the four-year period ending in 1987, he is believed to have made over $1.1 billion. In 1987 alone he earned $550 million in salary and bonuses—more than the firm he worked for—making him easily the highest-paid employee in history.

During the early 1980s, Milken recognized a tremendous opportunity in borrowing needs of relatively small companies. At that time, only about eight hundred companies issued bonds labeled investment grade, but there were thousands of firms with annual revenues of $25 million or more. Drexel's success was built on meeting those financing needs. The company's ability to raise capital through the high-yield bond market allowed many firms to borrow much-needed funds although they had not previously been considered creditworthy. In this sense, Drexel's activities

supported growth. Nevertheless, Milken and Drexel have been sharply criticized, particularly in recent years, because their financial activities helped fuel the bitter takeover battles of the 1980s. Investment analysts generally view junk bonds and the companies that issue them as risky and unsafe. Milken continues to defend the use of high-yield bonds; he argues that at the time, "We were matching capital to entrepreneurs who could use it effectively. We were creating investments that money managers needed in volatile markets."

THE CASE AGAINST MILKEN

In addition to criticism by some Wall Streeters, Drexel Burnham Lambert and Michael Milken also attracted the attention of the Securities and Exchange Commission, which between 1980 and 1985 launched four separate investigations into Drexel's activities. None of the investigations turned up enough evidence of wrongdoing to justify action. Only in 1986, when Ivan Boesky agreed to cooperate with prosecutors, was the government able to put together a case strong enough to warrant bringing charges against Drexel Burnham Lambert. During government investigations into a Wall Street insider-trader ring, Dennis Levine, a former Drexel investment banker, blew the whistle on Boesky. As a part of his deal with prosecutors, Boesky agreed to name people who had participated in insider trading and other illegal activities. Boesky's testimony led prosecutors to Drexel and to Milken, their number-one target.

In September 1988, after an investigation spanning two and a half years, the SEC filed a 194-page civil lawsuit against Drexel Burnham Lambert, Inc. The SEC also named Michael Milken, his brother Lowell, and other Milken aides in the suit. In its most sweeping enforcement action since the securities laws were written, the SEC charged Drexel with insider trading, stock manipulation, "parking" of securities to conceal their true ownership, false disclosures in SEC filings, maintaining false books and records, aiding and abetting capital rules violations, fraud in securities offerings materials, and various other charges. (Parking involves hiding ownership of securities by selling them to another with the understanding that they will be sold back to the original owner, usually at a prearranged time and price.)

The SEC suit also raised questions about Drexel's supervision of Milken's Beverly Hills' operations. Milken reported to Edwin Kantor, head of trading in New York. The two reportedly spoke several times a day over the phone, but otherwise Milken ran the office with little intervention. In an interview held after the investigation and ensuing criminal case were completed, Drexel Burnham Lambert's chief executive officer Fred Joseph stated that he was "appalled and surprised by the organized nature of the crime wave." In retrospect, he admitted to "surprising naiveté." With leadership so loose, it is not clear who, if anyone, was overseeing Milken's activities.

While the SEC was putting together its case, the U.S. Department of Justice was building a criminal case against Drexel and its employees. This effort was led by Rudolph Giuliani, the U.S. attorney for the Manhattan district. At the same time the SEC filed its civil suit against Drexel, Giuliani's office notified Michael Milken, his brother Lowell (who managed many of Michael's accounts), and two other key traders that they would probably soon be indicted on securities laws violations. Drexel Burnham Lambert was notified of its impending indictment a few weeks later. Notification of an impending indictment usually means the prosecution has completed its investigation and is prepared to go to court.

The SEC and the U.S. attorney's office had worked together, sharing resources, information, and investigators, and both had good cases. Their adversary was also well prepared. Drexel had 115 lawyers to the SEC's 15, and

the firm made it clear it could outspend the SEC. In fact, Drexel's legal defense budget was bigger than the entire SEC budget. Drexel had $2.3 billion in capital, and for two years it had been setting aside huge reserves to cover any litigation. Despite the bad publicity Drexel experienced, it continued to gain market share and became more profitable throughout the investigation. Even competitors were impressed by the loyalty of Drexel's clients, many of whom at the time of the SEC announcement vowed to remain loyal to Drexel and especially to Milken, who had helped many of them make millions of dollars.

Drexel Burnham Lambert faced charges from the U.S. attorney's office on securities, wire, and mail fraud as well as charges of racketeering under the Racketeering Influenced and Corrupt Organizations Act (RICO). RICO was enacted in 1970 to give the government a powerful weapon to go after organized crime; under the act, a person or business that commits two or more felonies as part of a pattern can be charged with racketeering. RICO allows prosecutors to charge entire organizations with crimes and to seize assets before trial to ensure payment of any subsequent penalties. In addition, RICO requires firms to forfeit any profits made or any property used during the period of wrongdoing. RICO laws carry heavy fines and long prison sentences, and they award triple damages to successful plaintiffs in civil suits.

RICO was first used against a securities firm in August 1988, when Giuliani's office indicated the five general partners of Princeton/Newport Partners, a small New Jersey-based investment firm, on racketeering charges. A former Drexel trader was involved in the transactions on which the partners were indicted. The firm folded within five months of the indictment. Princeton/Newport officials blamed the firm's demise on the fact that clients were scared off from doing business with a racketeer. At the time of the charges against

Drexel, some observers expressed surprise that Drexel itself was named rather than the senior executives as individual persons, as in the Princeton/Newport Partners case.

Giuliani's office set out to prove that Drexel used Boesky as a front for secretly trading some stocks. By so doing, Drexel could increase the price of takeover stocks so that it could get higher fees and trigger unwanted takeovers. The profits were then funneled back into the firm using dubious payments, with false paperwork covering the trail. In many cases Drexel's goal appeared to be power as much as profit—the ability to control the outcome of the deals it financed. Giuliani's case against the firm centered around a $5.3 million payment Boesky made in March 1987 to Drexel for "consulting services." The prosecution alleged this amount was actually part of the profits on stock that Drexel had parked with Boesky's firm. There were also allegations that Drexel and Boesky deliberately destroyed documents to cover up their activities. Of the six charges initially brought against Drexel, all involved transactions allegedly initiated by Michael Milken, and five of the six transactions allegedly involved Boesky. Drexel set out to discredit Boesky as Giuliani's office supported his claims against Drexel with written documentation and other informants—Charles Thurnher, James Dahl, Cary Maultesch, and Terrence Peizer—all of whom had worked for Michael Milken.

As the possibility of a court trial increased, defense lawyers began negotiations with prosecutors to drop the racketeering charges. They argued that RICO was intended to be used against the Mafia and that such charges would be unfair to business, disruptive to the equity and debt markets, and harmful to the economy. Giuliani initially wanted Drexel and its employees to waive their client-attorney privileges so that he could get access to Drexel's records on its own internal investigation of employees in the matter. After several rounds of negotiations, it was clear that Giuliani wanted a settlement. It was also clear that he would not hesitate to invoke the full force of the RICO statutes if he did not get one.

In December 1988, after spending more than $100 million on its legal defense and denying any misconduct or wrongdoing for more than two years, Drexel pleaded guilty to a six-count felony indictment on charges of securities, wire, and mail fraud and agreed to pay a record $650 million in fines and restitution. Drexel also gave in to the government demand that it had most vehemently opposed: It agreed to cooperate in all continuing investigations, including investigations of some of its own clients and employees—including Michael Milken. In return, the prosecutor dropped the racketeering charges against the company. CEO Fred Joseph said Drexel's decision was the only alternative that gave the company a chance to survive.

The settlement with the Justice Department was contingent on Drexel's settling with the SEC, which it did in the spring of 1989. Under that agreement, Drexel submitted to unprecedented federal supervision, agreed to a three-year probation, and had to appoint board members approved by the SEC. In addition, Drexel was required to move its Beverly Hills operation back to New York and to sever ties with Michael Milken. In the agreement, Drexel neither admitted nor denied guilt. By agreeing to plead guilty to the felony charges in which Michael Milken was also implicated and by cooperating with the prosecution in all continuing investigations, Drexel in effect withdrew all support from its most productive employee. The firm was also asked to withhold Milken's 1988 salary and bonus. Some saw the guilty plea as a bargaining chip that Drexel used to gain other concessions from the prosecutor and said Drexel was passing sentence on Milken before he got a trial. Milken's attorney later protested that this denied his client due process.

MILKEN IS INDICTED

Michael Milken was handed his own ninety-eight count felony indictment, including charges of racketeering, in March 1989. In June he resigned from Drexel to form his own company—just before the federal court approved the terms of the SEC settlement that would have forced his termination anyway. This, along with the fact that Milken continued to proclaim his innocence, widened a rift that had existed in the firm since 1978, when Milken had set up the junk bond operations on the West Coast. Milken's office had become a company within a company, employing about 600 of the elite among Drexel's 9,100 people. Those in "Drexel East," as they came to be called by those in the Beverly Hills office, were often jealous of the high commissions and big bonuses paid to the employees in the junk-bond department. Those in the West saw the men on the board as nonproducers who got rich off Milken and then sold him out to preserve their positions and capital.

Drexel Burnham Lambert CEO Joseph had been a principal negotiator in working out the settlement. He was caught between trying to wring as many concessions from Giuliani as he could and trying to keep an increasingly bitter work force of traders, analysts, and brokers from quitting. However, Joseph made matters worse for himself when, at the board meeting held to accept or reject the settlement, he and five of the other twenty-two members of the board voted against the agreement Joseph had just negotiated.

This token support fooled no one and, in the view of some, made him appear hypocritical, Joseph later admitted privately that what he had done had been a mistake. In talking with a client who happened to be a Milken supporter, Joseph mentioned that he viewed Giuliani as a worthy adversary and that the prosecutor could have come down harder on the firm if he had chosen to do so. The client

saw the prosecutor as having "taken Joseph, turned him, and made him his own." Many Milken loyalists within the firm regarded Joseph as a "traitorous wimp."

Some observers say that RICO is a tool that allows prosecutors to scare defendants into submission before getting close to court. Certainly, Joseph initially had no intention of settling, for he believed that firms that had recently settled with the government in other types of cases had not fared well. Other observers, however, are less sympathetic. The $650 million fine, they point out, is not due all at once and is partially (20 percent) tax deductible. Moreover, $650 million may not be a very significant penalty for a firm that made as much as $200 million on a single deal. In fact, for a while the most popular joke on Wall Street was that the "latest buyout" referred to the way Drexel handled the U.S. attorney's office.

Drexel Burnham Lambert did manage to avoid a lengthy court trial and its accompanying expense and publicity. It avoided the severe penalties of RICO, including jail sentences for top management and the stigma of a racketeering-conviction label. In addition, Drexel was not prohibited from doing business in the junk-bond market. It was, however, a convicted felon and without the services of Michael Milken and other key employees. And, although many clients remained loyal to the firm, others followed Milken or broke ties altogether. Drexel lost its dominance in the junk-bond market.

THINGS GET WORSE

To maintain some degree of profitability, Drexel sold its retail brokerage and mutual fund businesses and trimmed about 40 percent of its work force from the payroll. Despite Drexel Burnham Lambert's efforts to remain a player in financial markets, the collapse of the junk-bond market in late 1989 was the final blow to the company. Unable to maintain the liquidity needed to buy and sell huge quantities of securities, the company declared bankruptcy in February 1990.

In a plea-bargain arrangement, Michael Milken pleaded guilty on April 24, 1990, to six felony charges, ranging from mail and wire fraud to conspiracy and net-capital violations. He was sentenced to ten years in prison and three years of community service on his release. He must pay $200 million in fines and penalties as well as $400 million in restitution to victims of his crimes. Additionally, he was barred forever from the securities industry. In return, prosecutors dropped all charges against Lowell Milken (although he, too, was forever barred from the securities industry) and the remaining charges filed against Michael Milken in 1989.

Michael Milken was released to a halfway house in Los Angeles on January 3, 1993. After Milken served twenty-two months in federal prison, his original ten-year sentence was reduced to two years. He spent two months in the halfway house work-release program, but he is still barred by the Securities and Exchange Commission from the investment brokerage industry. His halfway house employment was through his lawyer's firm, Victor and Sandler, researching civil legal cases. In early 1993, it was estimated that Michael Milken had paid $1.1 billion in fines and settlements connected with his work in the securities business at Drexel Burnham Lambert.

After spending 22 months in a federal prison, Michael Milken at the age of 46 indicated that he had inoperable prostate cancer. Milken said he was the victim of a Wall Street witch hunt that had him as a prize trophy. Milken pointed out thousands of emerging businesses he helped to grow, including MCI, Turner Broadcasting, and the largest black-owned business, TLC Beatrice. In June of 1993, he was worth $500 million after paying

$1 billion in fines and settlements. He continues to work on 1,800 hours of court-ordered community service with a drug prevention program in inner-city Los Angeles. In a June 5, 1993 interview with Barbara Walters, on the television program *20/20*, he presented himself as a humanitarian, philanthropist, and builder of business. He told Walters in the interview that, "I was involved with over 3 million transactions in my career. Did we have an oversight in bookeeping in one or two transactions? Yes. No one thought it was criminal. I am not perfect, and I've never met a person who was."

NOTE

These facts are from Stephen J. Adler and Laurie P. Cohen, "Using Tough Tactics, Drexel's Lawyers May Advance While Appearing to Lose," *The Wall Street Journal*, October 12, 1988, p. 138; Laurie P. Cohen, "Drexel Lawyers, Justice Agency to Meet, Discuss RICO Status in Possible Charges," *The Wall Street Journal*, October 20, 1988, p. A3; Laurie P. Cohen, "Drexel Learns U.S. May Soon Ask an Indictment from Grand Jurors," *The Wall Street Journal*, October 19, 1988, p. A3; Laurie P. Cohen, "Drexel Pact Contains Concessions by U.S.," *The Wall Street Journal*, December 27, 1988, p. A3; Laurie P. Cohen, "Milken's Stiff 10-Year Sentence Is Filled with Incentives to Cooperate with the U.S.," *The Wall Street Journal*, November 23, 1990, p. A3; Laurie P. Cohen, "SEC, Drexel Expected to Request Approval of Proposed Settlement," *The Wall Street Journal*, June 15, 1989, p. B4; Laurie P. Cohen and Stephen J. Adler, "Indicting Milken, U.S. Demands $1.2 Billion of Financier's Assets," *The Wall Street Journal*, March 30, 1989, p. A1; John R. Ernshwiller, "Milken's Pursuit of Business Opportunity Built a Personal Fortune, Brought Drexel to the Fore," *The Wall Street Journal*, September 8, 1988, p. 7A; Michael Galen, with Dean Foust and Eric Schine," 'Guilty, Your Honor'; Now, Will Milken Help the Feds Nab Other Wall Street Criminals?" *Business Week*, May 7, 1990, pp. 33–34; Colin Lernster and Alicia Hills Moore, "I Woke Up with My Stomach Churning," *Fortune*, July 3, 1989, p. 120; Michael Milken, interviewed by Barbara Walters, *20/20*, June 5, 1993; Michael Milken, as told to James W. Michaels and Phyllis Berman, "My Story—Michael Milken," *Forbes*, March 16, 1992, pp. 78–100; "Milken Move," *USA Today*, December 28, 1992, p. B1; "Mixed Feelings About Drexel's Decision; Some Call It Wise; Others, a Lack of Will,"

The Wall Street Journal, December 23, 1988, p. B1; Thomas E. Ricks, "SEC's Failed Probes of Milken in Past Show Difficulty of Its Mission," *The Wall Street Journal,* January 30, 1989, p. A1; Michael Siconolfi, William Power, Laurie P. Cohen, and Robert Guenther, "Rise and Fall: Wall Street Era Ends as Drexel Burnham Decides to Liquidate; Junk Bonds' Creator Becomes Their Victim as Securities It Holds Plunge in Value," *The Wall Street Journal,* February 14, 1990, pp. A1, A12; Randall Smith, "How Drexel Wields Its Power in Market for High Yield Bonds," *The Wall Street Journal,* May 26, 1988, pp. 1, 12; James B. Stewart, Steven J. Adler, and Laurie P. Cohen, "Out on a Limb, Drexel's Milken Finds Himself More Isolated as Indictment Nears," *The Wall Street Journal,* December 23, 1988, p. A1; James B. Stewart and Daniel Hartzberg, "SEC Accuses Drexel of a Sweeping Array of Securities Violations," *The Wall Street Journal,* September 8, 1988, pp. 1B, 7B; James B. Stewart and Daniel Hartzberg, "U.S. Reportedly to Seek Charges Tied to Transactions of Princeton/Newport," *The Wall Street Journal,* August 4, 1988, pp. 2, 4; James B. Stewart, Daniel Hartzberg, and Laurie P. Cohen, "Biting the Bullet, Drexel Agrees to Plead Guilty and Pay Out a Record $650 Million," *The Wall Street Journal,* December 22, 1988, p. A1; "Still Drawing a Crowd," *USA Today,* January 6, 1993, p. B3; Steve Swartz, "Why Mike Milken Stands to Qualify for Guinness Book," *The Wall Street Journal,* March 31, 1989, p. A1; Steve Swartz and Bryan Burrough, "Tough Choice, Drexel Faces Difficulty Whether It Settles Case or Gambles on a Trial," *The Wall Street Journal,* September 9, 1988, pp. 1, 7; Blair S. Walker, "Milken Rewrites His Life Story," *USA Today,* June 7, 1993, p. 3B; Monci Jo Williams, "Can Fred Joseph Save Drexel?" *Fortune,* May 8, 1989, p. 89; and Monci Jo Williams, "Drexel's Profit and Potential Loss," *Fortune,* February 27, 1989, p. 8.

Case Study

Enron: From Paragon to Parish

Lisa H. Newton

PIPES TO RICHES IN WONDERLAND

Beginnings: Enron had its humble beginnings as a natural gas company. When Kenneth L. Lay became chairman and COO of Houston Natural Gas in June, 1984, the company owned pipelines, and it transported natural gas to customers. Utilities of all sorts had always been highly regulated, and the industry wasn't very interesting. But Ken Lay's vision had its origin in the President Ronald Reagan's deregulation agenda, which Lay had helped to further, and drew its operating practices from the Mergers and Acquisitions habits of the 1980s business community. He set out to grow the company into the biggest and most profitable energy company in the world, which, eventually, he almost did, at least on paper. He snapped up a small pipeline company in Florida, then (July, 1985) merged with InterNorth, Inc., to give him 40,000 miles of pipeline. Such size required a catchier name, so in 1986 Enron was born. (He'd thought of "Enteron" first, but changed it to "Enron" when he found out that enteron is another word for the digestive tract.)

Largely due to the lobbying efforts of Lay and others of his mind, most of the regulations came off the production and sale of energy in the last years of the 1980s. By 1989 Enron was trading natural gas on the commodities market. The next year Lay hired Jeffrey K. Skilling, a Harvard MBA, away from his consulting job at McKinsey & Co., to head up the new energy-trading operations. It was Skilling who transformed the operation from a simple transportation service to an immense trading center, a "gas bank" purchasing large amounts of natural gas from the producers and reselling it to customers here and abroad on long-term contracts. After that, market innovation and company growth outpaced each other through the decade. The company began trading online, increasing by orders of magnitude the speed with which its deals could be completed.

Deals: And what deals they were! If you can name it, you can buy and sell it. It wasn't just that Enron had turned natural gas into a commodity, a move that rapidly expanded to energy futures contracts. By the end, they were selling broadband, water, and weather derivatives—hedges against bad weather that might affect business operations.

But the major innovations were financial. Federal regulators permitted Enron to use "mark-to-market" accounting, a way of evaluating future income that works reasonably well in securities trading. In Enron's case, it allowed the company to calculate projected income as present profit, a practice that can be taken to extremes; in 1999, for instance, the company claimed a $65 million profit "based on its projections of natural-gas sales from a South American pipeline project. The pipeline had yet to be built."[1]

The *Star Wars* arrangements were typical. In 1993 Enron had formed a partnership with the California Public Employees Retirement System (Calpers) to invest in energy trades; each partner put in $250 million. The partnership, a "special purpose entity" (SPE) was called the Joint Energy Development Investments (JEDI, to the company's delight), and prospered, so they started another one. But Calpers wanted to cash out its first investment (JEDI I), to the tune of $383 million at that point, before it started JEDI II. That posed a problem for Enron. JEDI was not on its balance sheets (since, as an SPE, it was an outside partnership), and simply buying out Calpers would have put it on Enron's books, cutting the company's reported profits and increasing its debt by over half a billion dollars. This it did not want, so it went looking for some other (outside) party to buy Calpers' share. It found, or more accurately founded, Chewco Investments (named after Chewbacca

the Wookiee), a partnership of Enron executives and unidentified others. Enron then lent Chewco $132 million and then guaranteed a $240 million loan, toward Chewco's purchase of Calpers' share in JEDI I. That left $11.5 million to complete the purchase. The amount was significant: three percent of Chewco's capital had to come from "outsiders" in order for Chewco to be an independent company that doesn't show up on the books, and $11.5 million was more than three percent. In the event, even that amount was largely underwritten by Enron in the form of loans and subsidies, leading to the conclusion that from 1997 on, both Chewco and JEDI should have showed up on Enron's books as one enormous debt. But they didn't. Why didn't Enron's auditors, Arthur Andersen, insist on putting them there? The CEO of Andersen later explained that Enron had concealed its subsidies to that last three percent. For the moment, this accounting irregularity raised Enron's 1997 profits by 75%; keeping it going for the next three years resulted in $396 million in inflated profits.[2]

LJM2, again in company with its parent Enron, created a new set of four investment vehicles called the Raptors (we're now in *Jurassic Park*). The Raptors were funded with Enron Stock, and with stock from New Power, a publicly traded company that had been founded and spun off by Enron. New Power's stock had risen astronomically, providing Enron (which had kept a major stake in it) with a $370 million profit. The purpose of the Raptors was to hedge, or lock in, that profit, and profit from other start-up ventures. But again, Enron was insuring itself, and if anything happened to the price of New Power stock, Enron would have to absorb the loss both as stockholder and as insurer. Until that happened, of course, the Raptors were perfect for Enron's purposes, for since LJM2 was an "outside investor," they didn't have to show up on Enron's books as debt, which they were.

All this time Enron wasn't paying taxes. Enron had paid no income taxes in four of the last five years, making good use of about 900 subsidiaries in tax-haven countries to cover their revenues: this according to an analysis of its financial reports to its shareholders. It even collected $382 million in tax refunds. The subsidiaries chose prime vacation spots for their services; there were 692 in the Cayman Islands, 119 in the Turks and Caicos Islands, 43 on Mauritius, 8 in Bermuda, 6 in Barbados, 4 in Puerto Rico, 2 in Hong Kong, 2 in Panama, and one each in Aruba, the British Virgin Islands, Guam, Guernsey, and Singapore. In the year 2000, the company got $278 million in refunds; since stock options, with which they were very generous, do not have to be reported to the shareholders as an expense, but are deducted from company income for tax purposes.[3] Even Robert Hermann, the company's general tax counsel, wondered about this; by his own account, he asked Skilling at a 2000 meeting why it was that the company seemed to be doing so well, but paid so little in taxes! The answer, of course, was in his own division; Enron's skill in locating its partnerships offshore and keeping cash flow small had made the tax division a significant "profit center" for the company, saving $1 billion over the previous five years.[4]

Strategy: The impression left by all of the above is that Enron is in constant motion, always innovating, always daring, always out in front of some field, but also doing rather little to earn a living. Shortly into its meteoric course into the hearts and purses of investors, Enron's financial activities well outstripped its pipelines and its natural gas trade in the amount of money generated. And the financial activities' profits were, as the world would soon find out, bogus. Why were they doing this? What, quite literally, were they thinking?

The New Culture: The Enron "culture" has received a good deal of attention—perhaps too much. There is broad agreement on its

nature: ambition, greed, and contempt for everyone who wasn't part of the cheering section. Nothing mattered except getting rich, very rich, and the company was led by people (see next point) who were completely convinced that rich was what they deserved to be. Convinced of their natural superiority, Enron's day-to-day managers sent clear signals to ignore the law, the rules, the accounting practices, and all other manifestations of the lesser breeds without the New Economy. Their highest virtue was that they could break the rules and get away with it—in the face of the incredulity of their own more experienced colleagues, they could pull off deals that would enrich the shareholders, enrich themselves, and keep the company strong. Questions were not permitted. Those who stood in the way of the top people were quickly silenced, transferred, fired. When banks hesitated to invest in the new funds, they were given to understand that their continued opportunity to do business with Enron required that they overcome their hesitations. When Arthur Andersen auditors objected to keeping those new funds off the books, they were warned that Enron might take its lucrative consulting business to another auditing firm. Even at the end, in August 2001, when Chung Wu, a broker at UBS Paine Webber from Houston, e-mailed his clients to consider selling their Enron shares, given the difficulties that the company was experiencing, his employer rapidly reversed his recommendation—and fired him. There is no indication, anywhere, that any other banks, or other auditors, would have put up more resistance to the glamorous and admired schemes of the mighty Enron, ranked in March 2000 as the 6th largest energy company in the world (7th in the *Fortune* 500) (That rank, of course, was part of the history of misrepresentation at Enron. It was never profitable—even its energy trading in California brought in only .5% on sales.)[5] What is less clear is the origin and support for this "culture." Cultures do not make themselves. Logically, a "culture," in the sense intended, is no more than the cumulative accustomed acts of all the people who claim it as their own. Yet while the key players in the Enron debacle surely embodied the culture, they came aboard too late to have created it. More likely, they were recruited because they already fit it—they were entirely prepared to engage in the single-minded effort to raise earnings and keep them high, only on condition that they too could become rich, and had the ability and imagination both to create the financial instruments that made Enron's earnings possible and to sell the ideas to the appropriate clients. It is significant that the "culture" claimed for Enron happens to be identical with the national culture where money is concerned: admiration for the rich, tolerance for innovative rule-breakers, and an unshakeable conviction that government has no right to stand in the way of any person's efforts to get fabulously wealthy.

The New Accounting: When the van crashes into the retaining wall at 120 mph, at least three causal factors are present: the driver who lost control (was he paying attention?) the engine that brought the van to that speed (was it operating properly?), and the brakes that failed. In this particular crash, the drivers were the managers of Enron, who were apparently zipping along without a roadmap with little regard to the safety of the passengers (let alone the pedestrians), the engine was the unrestrained culture of greed and confidence in the business community that permeated the nation as a whole, and the brakes were the bankers and auditors who were supposed to be making good business judgments about the soundness of Enron's decision-making. In this case, "market discipline"—that is, the need to satisfy customers or go out of business—had put a fatal wound in the brakes, all of whom needed, or felt they needed, Enron

as a customer. There were holes in the brakes already—"mark-to-market" accounting allowed Enron to record as profits assets that were very difficult to evaluate, contracts for future income, income projected from deals made but not implemented, income fantasized. The permission to use that accounting had come from the federal government itself. But the major problem facing the others responsible for monitoring American business, the banks, the investment analysts, the accountants—Enron's outside auditors. Arthur Andersen Inc., especially—was that they had a very lucrative consulting relationship with Enron, and they were given to understand that they would lose it if they asserted and maintained accounting standards for Enron's deals.

Endgame Begins: In 2001 it all fell apart. At the beginning of the year Enron's stock had been good, not its all-time high of $90, reached in late Fall 2000, but a healthy $83. It should have been; it was bringing in substantial profits from the California energy crisis, complete with price spikes, blackouts, and lots of money for energy companies. But it wasn't going in the right direction. Jeffrey Skilling may not have known how bad things were when he accepted the office of CEO of Enron in February 2001; at that time the price of the stock was $79, and he cheerfully proclaimed that it should be $126. Not all of the decline was Enron's fault; much of that was due to the decline of Internet and telecom companies generally, plus falling gas prices. But the price of the stock was vitally important to Skilling: most of the SPEs that he had helped put together depended for their creditworthiness on the value of the Enron stock that backed them up. If the Raptors and other SPEs started losing money. Enron had promised to repay the investors with Enron stock. If Enron stock fell below $20, there would not be enough. The Raptors would be bankrupt, and Enron would follow them down the same tubes. Any rapid decline in any of the SPE stocks would trigger a domino effect from which there would be no recovery.

By March, 2001, a second rescue operation had to be mounted for the failing Raptors; 12 million Enron shares, worth at that moment $700 million, was needed to bail them out. Had the deal not been approved—and as above, until reminded of their dependency on Enron. Arthur Andersen had been inclined not to approve it—Enron would have had to report a $500 million loss for the first quarter of 2001. That news would have tanked the stock, which would have wiped out all the rest of the partnerships. The stock was below $50 in June 2001 when Federal regulators finally responded to the California crisis by putting strict price controls on the Western electricity market; it had not yet sunk below $40 on August 14, 2001, when Jeff Skilling—for reasons that may never be entirely clear—resigned from Enron. He swore that when he left the company was in good financial shape. Lay returned from his own retirement to take on the post of CEO. The unraveling of Enron was inevitable at that point. At this point the now-famous "whistleblower" turned up.

That isn't a fair name for what happened; it wasn't exactly a whistle that Enron Vice President Sherron S. Watkins blew. Hers was not (initially) a principled stance. She wanted the career and the money as much as anyone, but confronted with reality, she decided to tell Ken Lay about it instead of pretending it wasn't there. That alone makes her exceptional. She had gotten a temporary assignment to look into the LJM partnerships, including the Raptors, and was horrified by what she saw. On August 15, the day after Skilling resigned. Watkins wrote a long anonymous letter to Lay suggesting that Skilling knew what he was running away from. The letter spoke of the danger that "we will implode in a wave of accounting scandals," when the problems with Condor and Raptor came out;

there would be "suspicions of accounting improprieties," because of Enron's "aggressive accounting." In this memo, she coolly estimates the appropriate course of action according to the "probability of discovery" of the improper accounting for these SPEs: she concludes that the probability of discovery is high; therefore the company should "quantify [the losses], develop damage containment plans and disclose."[6] She follows up with a memo suggesting damage containment activity. That sounds more like your cell-phone ringing than a whistle to stop play.

But the warning fell stillborn; Lehman Brothers went on to recommend buying Enron stock on August 17, when it had dropped to $36 per share. Three days later, seeing no action on her end, Watkins called an old friend at Andersen to share her concerns. Two days after that, she met with Lay. An internal investigation, led by Enron's law firm, Vinson & Elkins LLP, began. Andrew Fastow reassured the investigators that the deals, while apparently questionable, were really sound, and repeated pledges of confidence in Enron's golden future. The investigations went into September 2001, including an interview with David Duncan of Andersen (who did not mention that Andersen was seething with controversy over the Enron transactions), but ceased before interviewing the top executives that Watkins had suggested.

On September 26, when the stock fell to $25 per share. Lay had an Internet "chat" with Enron employees. They had watched their 401(k) plans, stuffed with Enron stock, plunge to that level from $90 a year ago. Lay assured the employees that he, personally, was buying more Enron stock, which he characterized as an "incredible bargain," and he urged them to do the same. As the end of the third quarter became imminent, the habits acquired in previous years reasserted themselves. Enron worked out one more "prepay" deal for $350 million on September 28;

Enron and Qwest arranged a purchase of networks for another $112 million, a deal that made very little business sense. With all that cash to pump up earnings, third-quarter losses still had to be admitted, and somehow spun to the Wall Street analysts on whose approval the company depended. On October 8. Lay addressed the company's outside board of directors with the same bad news. But how bad was it? When the meeting was over, in which the demise of the Raptors had been cheerfully described as a one-time setback, the directors left thinking the company was basically in good shape. There were claims of future profitability, even as the company was on the ropes.

Enron's October 16 news release on its third-quarter problems had much the same message; the losses were one-time, non-recurring, and the company's future was rosy. An accounting error, he told a reporter on the phone, resulted in a $1.2 billion loss in equity. Where had all that money gone? Seems Enron had counted a Raptors' acknowledgement of $1.2 billion transferred from Enron to the SPEs as "shareholder equity." On October 18, when the *Wall Street Journal* found out about that one, it wrote a sharp article calling for better explanations. When Lay addressed investment fund managers later that day, trying to get them to hold their stock, or even buy more, he responded to their concerns, and the questions triggered by the article, by attacking the press and promising, over and over, that the loss was a one-time thing, that there were no more write-offs hiding in the books.

Not quite satisfied with that explanation, on October 22 the SEC launched an investigation into Enron. By the end of the day the stock stood at $20.65. On October 28 Lay announced the formation of a special investigative committee, headed up by the Dean of the University of Texas Law School, William Powers, who hired William R. McLucas, former SEC enforcement chief and currently with

the law firm of Wilmer, Cutler & Pickering to do the actual investigating. McLucas hired some accountants from Deloitte & Touche to look into the books, and they found all those hidden debts and all those cover-ups and all those overstatements of profits, and there was no longer any chance of keeping them hidden. When McLucas issued his report, the company was essentially finished.

There was one more attempt to save the company by selling it, to its smaller rival Dynegy. Cash was draining rapidly, as creditors called in debts, banks refused to lend, and even EnronOnline, the computer energy trading company, that generated most of Enron's actual revenue, was losing money. Its European trading operations, for which it had claimed a $53 million operating profit in the July-September quarter, turned out to have actually lost $21 billion.[7] What finally queered the deal with Dynegy was the sudden surfacing of fine print in many of the huge debts that Enron had contracted, providing that should the quality of Enron's credit rating be downgraded, the debts or large portions of them were payable immediately, in cash. None of these debts showed up on the books, since they were all part of the secret partnerships. Were the banks that supplied the money—J.P. Morgan and Citigroup—co-conspirators in a broad effort to defraud? The answer to that question may come out in a court of law.

Meanwhile, this was too much for Dynegy. On November 26, the deal officially died. Six days later, on December 2, 2001. Enron filed for bankruptcy.

Just in summary, to keep the moral point in focus: who ended up with the money? On October 22, the day that the stock plunged to $20.65. Lay convened the Enron employees, several thousand strong, and commiserated with them about the loss of their investments. He promised, even as he knew that bankruptcy was inevitable, that Enron would get it all back for them. That day he took a $4 million cash advance from the company. Over the next three days he took $19 million more, repaying $6 million by transferring Enron stock, which by then he was very glad to unload.[8] In the end, Ken Lay sold $37,683.887 in stock just before the crash came; Jeff Skilling cashed out $14,480,755, Lou Pai, Unit CEO, received $62,936,552.[9] Andrew Fastow had made $45 million on his LJM entities, at least as far as anyone has been able to determine.[10] Employees were in "lockdown," not permitted to sell their stock, between October 29 (about the time the employees would have figured that it would never go up again) and November 12, when it stood at $9.98. Effectively they were barred from selling until the bankruptcy, when it was worth nothing. Employees in their 50s and 60s saw retirement funds go from millions of dollars to nothing, and there was nothing they could do about it. Many, many people, who had done nothing to deserve it and everything not to deserve it, were mortally hurt.

THE SHREDDING OF ARTHUR ANDERSEN

Accounting firm Arthur Andersen has to take some of the responsibility for that hurt. Andersen had signed off on all of the deals that Enron had made, sometimes under pressure, but it had signed off. Further, despite doubts and periodic whimpering about the risk of it all. Andersen had profited from its participation; Enron was one of its biggest clients. Now the firm stood to lose badly.

It wasn't just the money. When the accounting profession had assumed the role of corporate honesty guarantors, the company's founder, Arthur Andersen himself, had been one of the most powerful arguers, and arguments, for trusting the profession with the job of telling the truth to the public. A man of unquestionable integrity himself, he had argued that the moral integrity of accountants could be counted on to protect the investors from the (well known) tendencies of businesses to cut corners. Through its 88-year history. Arthur Andersen especially, among the large accounting firms, had stood for that integrity. Everything rested on that reputation, and once lost, it would not be recovered. Before going on, it might be worth noting that for 60 years at least, that integrity held and the system worked.

Extraordinary pressures had descended upon Arthur Andersen and its competitors during the 1980s and 1990s. Accounting firms discovered, in the rapid growth of technology based industry, that they could sell their technology consulting services to the very firms they had been auditing, for very attractive prices. Both stood to gain: the accounting firm suddenly had a new and major source of income, and the hiring firm had, beside the value of the consulting services, an interesting source of influence with the watchdog supposedly scrutinizing it. As we saw above, that influence could be very serious indeed. But there was a downside to the new mixture of revenues. Recall the section on "the New Culture," above. Accounting had always been a gray and lumpishly unattractive profession, guaranteeing a safe income and a good retirement, but nothing glamorous. Now suddenly the Big Five had moved from the wallflower auditing culture to the swinging consultant culture, and all their people began to demand big bucks, really big bucks, to enjoy the lifestyles practiced by the investment bankers, and by their clients. Andersen had done very well; its consulting arm brought in barrels of money, divided among all the partners and associates, and everyone was happy.

But not for long. Greed, as Plato pointed out so long ago, is essentially unlimited. If I am enjoying a comfortable existence now, I immediately see that with more money I could enjoy a luxurious existence, and I want it, also immediately. Andersen's consultants were not happy sharing their huge earnings with the old-fashioned   stick-in-the-mud-rain-on-your-parade auditors. In a brutal divorce, they separated themselves as a unit from the company, and formed a new company (Accenture) to earn their money far away from all the poor relations. But by now the auditors had gotten used to that larger income, and they put pressure on their new managing partner. Joseph F. Berardino, to get it back for them. So they started recruiting consulting clients all over again, built the business quickly, and secured Enron as their largest client, one they could not afford to lose. (According to *Forbes*, Enron was paying Andersen, by the end, $1 million a week in auditing and consulting fees.[11])

Arthur Andersen's auditors had protested the practices of Enron in the past. As far back as December 1999. Andersen auditor Carl Bass expressed serious discomfort with Enron's "aggressive hedging strategy for derivatives," that is, their strategy of backing up derivatives with more derivatives—propping bets up with other bets, and Enron was not very good at betting. After a series of complaints from Bass, Enron appealed to David B. Duncan, the lead audit partner on the Enron account, to get rid of him, and contrary to all accepted practice, Andersen had acquiesced in the request and removed Bass in 2000, leaving David Duncan in control. They lived to regret that, but not for long.

When Arthur Andersen began to get all the bad news, its senior partners realized that they had a major problem. For the better part of two years there had been internal conflict in the firm's Chicago headquarters over the wisdom of approving Enron's dubious deals and techniques for improving the looks of the books. Minutes of meetings characterized Enron earnings-boosting practices as "high risk," and acknowledged that some might find

those practices downright dishonest. But after Bass's protests, and after all their arguments, they kept the client and signed off on whatever they were asked to sign off on. In March 2001, matters came to a head when Fastow and Skilling rescued failing Raptors by "cross-collateralization," linking for 45 days the debts and assets of all four Raptors. Andersen's Professional Services Group, a unit of senior partners that is supposed to have the last say in such matters, decided to call the game then and there. But David Duncan, now Andersen's lead partner on the Enron account, overrode the PSG. Everyone at Andersen knew that was bad news.

Arthur Andersen emphatically did not want another run-in with the SEC. It was a huge company, with $9 billion in sales in 2001 and 85,000 employees in 84 countries, one of the Big Five that audit the financial statements of the publicly traded companies in the U.S. It had a lot to lose. But just four months before the current crisis Andersen had been fined $7 million by the S.E.C., the largest ever assessed against an accounting firm, for signing off on false and misleading financial statements issued by another client, Waste Management.[12] Since then it had operated under a "cease and desist" order, legally forbidding them from allowing clients such liberties (essentially, they had to promise not to violate the law any more). Now here they were doing it again. The Waste Management case had used as evidence the contents of Andersen's own files, seized by the SEC and used against them. Were there Enron documents in the file that could be used similarly? Maybe there were. In the first weeks of October, instructions came down in Houston and in Chicago, to "follow the firm's document-retention policy" of destroying "extraneous" or unneeded documents. Duncan's office got to work and started destroying. Over the weekend of October 13–14, 2001, bag after plastic bag was filled with the shredded remains of

Enron documents. Vast number of e-mails were also deleted. The destruction went on sporadically until November 2001, until—and maybe even after—orders came from the SEC to preserve all documents having anything to do with Enron.[13]

When Joe Berardino found out about the shredding, he was genuinely horrified. Trouble from the SEC was bad, but a criminal indictment for obstruction of justice—which the shredding clearly was, if there was anything at all in the documents material to the Enron case, then under investigation from several government agencies—was much, much, worse. He immediately fired Duncan. But firing Duncan, observers recognized at the time, and claiming that the shredding was done without the knowledge of higher management, would not save the firm from criminal investigation. "Joseph F. Berardino, Andersen's managing partner and chief executive, tried to put the best face on the situation as he announced the firing. 'Based on our actions today, it should be perfectly clear that Andersen will not tolerate unethical behavior, gross errors in judgment or willful violation of our policies,' he said."[14] The prosecutor was not impressed. The action was intended to restore confidence in Andersen's integrity. It was, unfortunately, too late for that.

Was anything in those documents of any relevance to the case that the government wanted to make against Enron and Andersen? We will never know, but that, of course is just the point. If there is, in the popular mind, a clearer indication of guilt than the rush to destroy documents when a Federal inquiry is threatening, we'd be hard put to say what it is. Andersen destroyed itself in that weekend, and may have destroyed what is left of the officers of Enron in the process.

The jury retired to begin its deliberations in the criminal trial of Arthur Andersen for obstruction of justice on June 6, 2002. It took until June 15 to reach the verdict, guilty of obstruction. The jury may have made legal history in the process; it discovered the obstruction in Nancy Temple's memo to David Duncan, before the shredding even began, urging the deletion of certain words from a draft memorandum on the Enron account. But the prosecution hadn't advanced that theory in the course of the trial. To judge from the reaction, the prosecution hadn't even *thought* of that theory. One reason for its absence from the prosecution arguments may be that it doesn't seem to be a crime to recommend a change in wording of a draft memo. Had Andersen been convicted of something that isn't even a crime? Andersen's lawyers considered going back to Federal district Judge Melinda Harmon and asking her to set aside the verdict on those grounds.[15] And the guilty verdict put an end to anything that mattered in the Andersen case any way— there was no time for an appeal, there was no interest in a rehash. Enron's late "firing" of Andersen as its auditor was inconsequential, the state-by-state decisions to suspend the firm's license to practice in that state made no difference, and the sentence for obstruction handed down on October 17, 2002—five years probation and a $500,000 fine—was beside the point. Andersen's reputation for integrity was gone, its clients left immediately for other accounting firms, its partners were quickly hired away to continue work elsewhere, and very soon after the verdict the firm closed its doors. By the time the sentence was handed down, there were about 2,000 employees left, closing out operations, of the 85,000 they had had at one time. The Big Five had become Big Four.

Slowly, the wheels of justice for individuals are beginning to turn. Andrew S. Fastow will probably go to jail; he is charged with using off-the-books partnerships to fraudulently disguise the company's financial performance while enriching himself with millions—fraud, money laundering, conspiracy. The charges do justice to the context, portraying Enron "as a company where fraud and deceit were the workaday mechanisms used to disguise the failings of a corporation secretly spinning out of control." It's worth pointing out that he cheated everyone: he cheated government and investors alike by lying about the company's real assets, and cheated the company, siphoning off millions into his own pocket.[16] Enron will surely be sued, what's left of it, and good lawyers may figure out ways to get at the individual executives.[17] State Attorneys are now searching Wall Street records for proof that tainted investment advice caused investors to lose big on high-flying stocks.[18] Reform is talked about, but recent surveys suggest that fewer firms now than in 2001 make any attempt to separate their consultants from their auditors, and that means that the accounting firms aren't trying to make those separations either.[19] But nobody thinks we're going to trust business again very soon.[20]

THE ULTIMATE FAILURE OF THE SYSTEM

The events narrated here meant the end of Enron and the end of Arthur Andersen. They might mean the end of business as we know it. There seems to be general, if muted, agreement, that the Enron case has shown us a terrible, possibly lethal, weakness in our business system. When wrongdoing is this extensive, long-lived, and shockingly serious, we know well that whether it be the Roman Catholic Diocese of Boston or the high-flying New Economy businesses, the problem goes beyond the "few bad apples." Unlike the Roman Catholic Diocese of Boston, the regulatory institutions of the U.S. government cannot cure souls, but they can change the institutions, the laws and the practices and the expectations governing the practice of business. Does

Enron demonstrate that the current practices of the business world lead straight to the impoverishment of the citizens and, most likely, the ultimate demise of capitalism itself? Quite possibly. Let me count the ways.

The Financialization of All Things: We might first call attention to the new forms of trading with special attention to the new entities for sale. Enron, like so many companies, seemed to be buying, selling, creating, trading and otherwise using "derivatives," financial products whose value is tied to something else (movements of currency, whatever) whose purpose is to "hedge" other investments—the derivative is structured so that if whatever you're "hedging" falls, the "hedge" goes up, and it's very useful, like an insurance policy. But it isn't real; it's a bet. And when you hedge derivatives with derivatives (the practice that drove Carl Bass up the wall), you are propping fictions up with poetry and the likelihood of failure is very great, as we found out. Then there is the creative accounting generally, the purpose of which is to get profits and losses (selectively) off the books, off the shore, off the tax rolls. So sophisticated have these practices become that Enron referred to its tax division as a "profit center." Since when is your tax division a "profit center"? Well, it was the only one it had. In truth, the company had never been profitable under any acceptable definition of "profitability."

We can have no better example than the operations of Andrew Fastow. In detailing the charges against Fastow, the prosecutor pointed out that when he was Enron's CFO, he directed an elaborate scheme to steal money from the company using special-purpose entities that that invested in Enron's assets. Enron's board, which approved the creation of the entities and allowed Mr. Fastow to run them, was told that they would allow the company to sell underperforming assets to improve its balance sheet. But according to the government. Mr. Fastow struck a secret agreement with Richard

A. Causey—who, as Enron's chief accounting officer, was charged with overseeing the deals—promising that the assets could be sold back to Enron at a profit. Wall Street firms took part in some of the transactions, providing cash where needed.

The projects, since we're talking about business and the profit motive, are an interesting lot of losers. They included Cuiabá (a power plant in Brazil that wasn't making money so in September 1999 Fastow created LJM to buy part of the plant to take it off the books), and the Nigerian Barges (three electricity-generating power barges anchored off the coast of Nigeria, which were making no money so no one wanted to buy them). Then in December 1999, Merrill Lynch bought a share of the barges for $7 million, enough to get them off the books (remember 3% from an outside entity was all you needed to get them off the books): Enron provided $21 million. Of course Enron had promised to buy them back. In the beginning, Enron chalked up a nice profit on the sale ($12 million in earnings for the quarter and $28 million in cash flow). On June 29, 2000, LJM2 bought Merrill's stake for $7.5 million, and Enron paid LJM2 a solid fee for the deal. Then there was AVICI, the profit on whose stock was locked in by a hedging agreement with the SPE Raptor I, specifying future sale of AVICI at a high price (the stock was falling at the time.) Raptor I was actually a subsidiary of Talon, which was financed by Enron and LJM2. Fastow lied about Talon's independence, backdated the hedge so that Enron could avoid loss. Essentially, he was parking assets. How much of this sounds like the conduct of business at all? But the point of it is this: that this is what counts as business in the New Economy.

Fastow got rich. But where, in all that, was any value created? Who could make money except executives and investment bankers in on the scheme? And how much of this sort of

nonsense can go on before we lose all track of what business is all about? Enron never owned anything that created real value and made real money. We have a record of nothing but years of bad business and mismanagement, kept hidden by cover-ups.[21] Yet people got rich, and others wish to emulate them. Business is supposed to be about the transformation of resources into goods and services. I defy you to find me a profitable good or service in those transactions. Most of its purchases were ill-considered; most of its trades were losers; most of its revenue was padded or downright fictional. Enron was essentially a Ponzi scheme. And its schemes are not its alone.

The Wall Street Fixation: From the above, it is very clear that we have lost "market discipline," whatever that was supposed to be. Firms are not in the new system disciplined by consumer choice in the open market, such that the firm creating the greatest value wins the market. As we see, Enron created no value at all for the consumer. But everyone knows that the Market has to be kept happy; not the real market where goods and services are exchanged, but the Stock Market, the Nasdaq, NYSE, the analysts who rate your stock. Essentially, what we have here is the redefinition of business. As Adam Smith would have understood business, Enron's Business was null; there were very few real transactions. Most of the "businesses," such as they were, ran in the red. By the end, even the basic assets of the energy—the pipelines, the only real things they had—were sold to raise quarterly earnings. This transformation of business by Wall Street has other effects, most of them undesirable. Some of the motivations for this change were outlined earlier in the case: the need of the huge funds to grow their assets, for instance. But that need coincides nicely with the opportunity of insiders to make a huge amount of money by manipulating stock and cashing in stock options. Who decided that this is the way that business should be conducted? What was the role of the Stock Exchange originally? And how did it get to this point?

The Use of Private Sector Auditors: Who was watching the store? Under present business practices, we rely on the integrity of the accountants to keep the whole system honest. Can that possibly work? Well, yes. For starters, it worked for 60 years. More than that, the arrangement is typical of our handling of technical fields in the U.S. Consider the way we have always managed, or rather not (collectively) managed, our national health care. For 200 years and more, the health of the nation has been in the hands of a profession operating in screaming conflict of interest. If I go to the doctor because of the pain in my stomach, his interests in the situation are clear: do a careful history and examination ($500), refer me down the street to the X-Ray facility owned by his practice ($150), diagnose something in Latin which is serious but not incurable, prescribe twice-daily pills ($60 each) from the pharmaceutical company on whose board he sits and whose stock he owns, and make sure that whatever it is doesn't get well for at least six months. I promise you I would follow his prescriptions faithfully, my insurance company would reimburse, and no one would be any the wiser. It is most assuredly *not* in his interest to decide—on the basis of a history, a quick exam ($40), and 38 years of experience with such ailments—that it's a minor touch of gastritis, eat bland foods, stay off the alcohol, go home. But that's what he'll do, if that's what it is, and that's what I and everyone else in the country expect him to do. Our businesses, according to Adam Smith, are supposed to operate according to a "market" ethic—each party pursues his own interest vigorously and intelligently, and that Invisible Hand makes sure that everyone does better in the long run. Problem with that is, when it comes to a field I don't understand, like medicine. I can be vigorous as I like, but

not ultimately intelligent. (Don't talk to me about going online and *Google*-ing my disease and being able to second-guess the doctor. I'll never be able to do that.) So we have always expected our professions to adhere to what we know as the "professional" ethic—to serve only the interests of the client, or patient, or student, setting aside the interests of the professional himself. (After all, if I conducted my academic practice in my own interests. I'd cancel half my classes, set no exams, give everyone an A or a B and go home for the summer. The students wouldn't complain.) It is in the nature of a profession that it must enjoy essential autonomy, and be worthy of essential trust, for no one but his peers has a clue whether a professional is operating honestly.

Of course there are oversight bodies. There are Deans, Medical Boards, the Office of the Inspector General, Utilization Review committees at the insurance companies and the like. Maybe a professional could get away with dishonest taking advantage for a short period of time, but he would get caught and punished eventually.

True, but how long is eventually? As the Enron executives proved, you can get very rich in a short time—and then get offshore. But that's not the point. The point is that for 200 years and more, our professions have not let us down in any wholesale way. There have indeed been the "bad apples," President Bush's favorite term for the Enron players, but the professions have remained honest. When the accountants, in the person of Arthur Andersen, claimed that their professional integrity would be proof against the clear conflict of interest between their clients and themselves insofar as they wanted to tell the truth, the claim was entirely believable and, as we saw, it held up until very recently.

And then it stopped holding up, which is the story of the shredding of Arthur Andersen. Given the kinds of pressures that wealthy clients can now bring to bear on accountants, again outlined above, are we going to have to find another way to get the auditing done? What would that be?

In the denouement of Enron, the answer to that question will be posed, debated, posed again—and then possibly forgotten, for what are the alternatives? No one likes the idea of a government bureaucracy appointed to second-guess every business decision we make. But if business clearly cannot be trusted, where do we go from here?

The Careful Dismantling of All the Checks and Balances: If the accountants were supposed to be watching the store, and weren't, who was watching the accountants? A few years ago the Federal Accounting Standards Board, which is supposed to set accounting standards and monitor accounting, had made one attempt to force companies to list their stock options as compensation, which they are. In the unexpected political firestorm that followed, the Senate, led by Senator Joseph I. Lieberman, almost dismantled the Board. Suddenly there was tremendous political pressure to leave the stock options alone. Why were the lawmakers so adamant on a subject that seems to be technical and not applicable to their constituents—except for the good? That was our first real indication that our Congress is totally dependent upon the big money to keep it going. We had watched the cost of political campaigns go up, and clucked with appropriate disapproval, but it had not occurred to us that all that money would permanently distort our political process—not until Joe Lieberman, our proudest example of moral probity, stood up and claimed, contrary to fact, that it was the small investors that really profited from stock options. Increasingly, the financially central members of Congress are bought and paid for, and we can no longer use Congress—the public sector—as a counterweight to business—the private sector. The same people who bribed Congress to go for deregulation,

and then invented the deals that were now possible, ran the companies and made the profits. This was no accident.

Can business operate in the new freewheeling "deregulation" atmosphere? Possibly not. As Paul Krugman pointed out in January 2002, as the full scope of the debacle opened itself to the public, the effects go well beyond this case.

> It's not just a matter of the utter unfairness of it all—employees lose their life savings while crooked executives walk away rich. It's also a matter of what it takes to make capitalism work. Investors must be reasonably sure that reported profits are real, that executives won't use their positions to enrich themselves at the expense of stockholders and employees, that when insiders do abuse their positions their actions will be discovered and punished. Now we have seen a graphic demonstration that the system that was supposed to provide those assurances doesn't work. And nobody I know in the financial community thinks Enron was an isolated case.[22]

There's no point in overstating the case, of course, but it was veteran business writer Kurt Eichenwald, writing in *The New York Times* six months later, who raised the question first raised by Robert Heilbroner in his 1984 *Limits of American Capitalism:* Could capitalism, in its greed, destroy itself? Could the motive that is supposed to make capitalism work—unlimited self-interest—finally bring it down? He points out that capitalism has survived hostile monarchs, intelligent socialists, even terrorists—noticed the start-up businesses at Ground Zero? But Enron suggests that it may not survive the capitalists.

> The scandals that have oozed out of corporate America with alarming regularity in recent months have repeatedly featured executives betraying the marketplace for their own short-term interest. From Enron to Global Crossing, Adelphia to WorldCom, the details differ but the stories boil down to the same theme: the companies lied about their performance, and investors paid the price.[23]

This isn't just more of the same, the latest outbreak of "white-collar malfeasance . . . greedy executives cutting corners to make a profit."

> . . . the corporate calamities of the new millennium are of a different ilk, one that challenges the credibility of the financial reporting system, and in turn the faith of investors in the capital markets—the very engine that has driven capitalism to its success.[24]

He traces, briefly, the scandals and large-scale thefts of the 1920s and the reforms of the 1930s—at no point was the goodness of the game questioned, "but the government put in referees." The Securities Exchange Act of 1933 and 1934, the S.E.C. to enforce it, the strict rules of disclosure, and independent accountants to make sure it all was accurate and transmitted accurately to the investors. That whole edifice of protection turned out, in a moment, to be smoke; ". . . from company to company, insular boards of directors, incompetent internal auditors and underfunded regulatory oversight have allowed the perception of stringent standards and protection to wither."[25]

It was never, he points out, the legal protections that preserved capitalism. It was trust, the trust that business was generally honest, that did that. Now the trust is gone. He concludes that capitalism will live to prosper another day, because it's so profitable. Eventually, when capital becomes unavailable for business investments because no one can trust the market, capitalists will stop their (present and ongoing!) lobbying to cut back on regulations, and will support efforts to rebuild the protections of the 1930s. Until next time, that is; for as soon as this generation passes from the scene (a Wall Street generation is between 10 and 15 years), more executives, egged on by the spirit of capitalism and by the example of Lay and Skilling enjoying their millions, will pull the same tricks again—with the same results.

The Failure of the Citizen: If American Capitalism operates on the Iron Law of Greed, with the same inevitability as Haitian devastation and the incoming tide, are we condemned to repeat the cycle over and over again, as Eichenwald foresees? Benjamin Barber, analyst of American (and world) culture, thinks otherwise; we will conclude with his note of encouragement, published as an Op-Ed in *The New York Times* about a month after Eichenwald's piece.

The problem, as Barber sees it, is not that capitalism is sinful—we always knew *that*—but that we have lost faith in the democratic institutions that were always supposed to limit, in the name of the public interest of which they were custodians, the damage that capitalism can do.

> Politicians on both sides of the aisle long insisted the scandals could be traced to a few rotten apples in an otherwise healthy barrel; a few radicals worry that the barrel itself (the capitalist system) is rotten. But business malfeasance is the consequence neither of systemic capitalist contradictions nor private sin, which are endemic to capitalism and, indeed, to humanity. It arises from a failure of the instruments of democracy, which have been weakened by three decades of market fundamentalism, privatization ideology and resentment of government.[26]

His thesis is simplicity itself—while we look about the catastrophe landscape, crying to know who is in charge here—we forget that *we* were in charge here. Business was never supposed to work without social controls.

> Capitalism is not too strong; democracy is too weak. We have not grown too hubristic as producers and consumers; we have grown too timid as citizens, acquiescing to deregulation and privatization (airlines, accounting firms, banks, media conglomerates, you name it) and a growing tyranny of money over politics.[27]

The parallels between Enron-Andersen and the current administration of President George W. Bush are only too clear: as Enron abandoned all notions of stewardship of investors' resources, so Bush has abandoned all stewardship of the natural environment; as the executives of Enron assumed that because they were so rich and powerful they were exempt from the law of the land, so Bush exempts himself and the U.S. from all adherence to international agreements, treaties, and consultations; unilateralism, the repudiation of partnerships, the destruction of trust, and the headlong charge into anarchy characterize both the Bush administration and the business community it has fostered.

> Market fundamentalism, which defined the era of Ronald Reagan and Margaret Thatcher, encourages a myth of omnipotent markets. But this is as foolish and wrong-headed as the myth of omnipotent states, which reigned from the New Deal to the Great Society. It tricks people into believing their own common power represents some bureaucrat's hegemony over them, and that buying power is the same as voting power. But consumers are not citizens, and markets cannot exercise democratic sovereignty. The ascendant market ideology claims to free us, but it actually robs us of the civic freedom by which we control the social consequences of our private choices.[28]

We have foolishly given up our power to control the forces of the "markets," legal and illegal, in return for an illusory "freedom" to play those markets, not recognizing the controlling hands that guide their strings—to their advantage and to our loss and disgrace. We have sat mesmerized, mystified, by the amazing wealth and power tied up in deals that no one can understand. It is time to wake up. It is our job as citizens to secure the common good in public matters, *res publica*, which alone can bring order to the inherently disordered realm of unfettered capitalism.

NOTES

1. Peter Behr and April Witt, "Visionary's Dream Led to Risky Business," *Washington Post*, July 28, 2002, p. A1.

2. Allan Sloan, "Who Killed Enron?" *Newsweek*, January 21, 2002, p. 22.

3. David Cay Johnston, "Enron Avoided Income Taxes In 4 of 5 Years," *The New York Times*, A1, C8.

4. Behr and Witt, "Dream Job Turns Into a Nightmare," *Washington Post*, July 29, 2002, A1.

5. Gretchen Mergenson, "How 287 Turned Into 7: Lessons in Fuzzy Math," *The New York Times*, January 20, 2002, Money & Business 1, 12. "Another half-truth concerned Enron's appearance last year at No. 7 on the *Fortune* 500 list of largest American companies. The company's $101 billion in revenue placed it between the powerhouses Citigroup and I.B.M. on the list. But rising to that level occurred only because energy trading companies can record as revenue the total amount of their transactions, rather than the profits made on each trade as is typical at brokerage firms. If viewed this way, Enron's revenue would have been $6.3 billion last year, pushing it to the bottom half of the list, at No. 287, wedged between Automatic Data Processing and Campbell Soup."

6. Peter C. Fusaro and Ross M. Miller, *What Went Wrong at Enron: Everyone's Guide to the Largest Bankruptcy in U.S. History*, Hoboken, N.J., John Wiley and Sons, 2002. The complete text of Sherron Watkins' memo is on pages 185–191.

7. Behr and Witt, "Hidden Debts, Deals Scuttle Last Chance," *Washington Post*, August 1, 2002, A1.

8. Behr and Pitt, "Losses, Conflicts Threaten Survival", *Washington Post*, July 31, 2002, p. A1.

9. Allan Sloan, "Who Killed Enron?" *Newsweek*, January 21, 2002, p. 23.

10. Behr and Witt, op. cit.

11. Dan Ackman, "The Scapegoating of Arthur Andersen," *Forbes*, January 18, 2002.

12. Alex Berenson with Jonathan D. Glater, "A Tattered Andersen Fights for Its Future," *The New York Times*, January 13, 2002. Money & Business 1, 3.

13. Kurt Eichenwald and Floyed Norris, "Enron's Auditor Says It Destroyed Documents: A 'Significant Number' of Papers," *The New York Times*, January 11, 2002. pp. C1, C5. Floyd Norris, "Did Enron's Auditors Think They Had Something to Hide?" *The New York Times*, January 11, 2002, p. C1.

14. Floyd Norris, "For Andersen and Enron, the Questions Just Keep Coming: Reasons Behind a Firing Leave Firm Open to Criminal Inquiry," *The New York Times*, January 16, 2002, pp. C1, C8.

15. Kurt Eichenwald, "Andersen Team Weighs Asking Judge to Undo Guilty Verdict," *The New York Times*, June 19, 2002, pp. C1, C9.

16. Kurt Eichenwald, "An Ex-Official Faces Charges In Enron Deals," *The New York Times*, October 3, 2002, pp. A1, C4. David Barboza, "From Enron Fast Track to Total Derailment," *The New York Times*, October 3, 2002, pp. C1, C5.

17. Jeffrey Toobin, "Annals of Law: The Man Chasing Enron," *The New Yorker*, September 9, 2002, pp. 86–94. The Man in the Class Action Suit.

18. Patrick McGeehan, "States Talk Tough: Wall Street Sweats." *The New York Times*, October 20, 2002, Section 3, p. 1.

19. Gretchen Morgenson, "On Reform, It's Time to Walk the Walk," *The New York Times*, October 6, 2002, Section 3, p. 1.

20. Kurt Eichenwald, "Even If Heads Roll, Mistrust Will Live On," *The New York Times*, October 6, 2002, Section 3, p. 1.

21. Kurt Eichenwald, "Flinging Billions to Acquire Assets That No One Else Would Touch," (Unveiling the secret deals that allowed Enron to hide bad business decisions), *The New York Times*, October 3, 2002, p. C4.

22. Paul Krugman, "A System Corrupted," *The New York Times*, January 18, 2002, Op-Ed.

23. Kurt Eichenwald, "Could Capitalists Actually Bring Down Capitalism?" *The New York Times*, June 30, 2002, Week In Review, pp. 1. 5.

24. Ibid.

25. Ibid. p. 5.

26. Benjamin Barber, "A Failure of Democracy, Not Capitalism," *The New York Times*, July 29, 2002, Op-Ed.

27. Ibid.

28. Ibid.

Case Study

"The Good Old Boys at WorldCom"

Dennis Moberg
Edward Romar

2002 saw an unprecedented number of corporate scandals: Enron, Tyco, Global Crossing. In many ways, WorldCom is just another case of failed corporate governance, accounting abuses, and outright greed. But none of these other companies had senior executives as colorful and likable as Bernie Ebbers. A Canadian by birth, the six foot three inch former basketball coach and Sunday School teacher emerged from the collapse of WorldCom not only broke but with a personal net worth as a negative nine-digit number.[1] No palace in a gated community, no stable of racehorses, or multi-million dollar yacht to show for the telecommunications giant he created. Only debts and red ink—results some consider inevitable given his unflagging enthusiasm and entrepreneurial flair. There is no question that he did some pretty bad stuff, but he really wasn't like the corporate villains of his day: Andy Fastow of Enron,

Dennis Koslowski of Tyco, or Gary Winnick of Global Crossing.[2]

Personally, Bernie is a hard guy not to like. In 1998 when Bernie was in the midst of acquiring the telecommunications firm MCI, Reverend Jesse Jackson, speaking at an all-black college near WorldCom's Mississippi headquarters, asked how Ebbers could afford $35 billion for MCI but hadn't donated funds to local black students. Businessman LeRoy Walker, Jr., was in the audience at Jackson's speech, and afterwards set him straight. Ebbers had given over $1 million plus loads of information technology to that black college. "Bernie Ebbers," Walker reportedly told Jackson, "is my mentor."[3] Rev. Jackson was won over, but who wouldn't be by this erstwhile milkman and bar bouncer who serves meals to the homeless at Frank's Famous Biscuits in downtown Jackson, Mississippi, and wears jeans, cowboy boots, and a funky turquoise watch to work.

It was 1983 in a coffee shop in Hattiesburg, Mississippi that Mr. Ebbers first help create the business concept that would become WorldCom. "Who could have thought that a small business in itty bitty Mississippi would one day rival AT&T?" asked an editorial in Jackson, Mississippi's *Clarion-Ledger* newspaper.[4] Bernie's fall and the company's was abrupt. In June, 1999 with WorldCom's shares trading at $64, he was a billionaire,[5] and WorldCom was the darling of The New Economy. By early May of 2002, Ebbers resigned his post as CEO, declaring that he was "1,000 percent convinced in my heart that this is a temporary thing."[6] Two months later, in spite of Bernie's unflagging optimism, WorldCom declared itself the largest bankruptcy in American history.[7]

This case describes three major issues in the fall of WorldCom, the corporate strategy of growth through acquisition, the use of loans to senior executives, and threats to corporate governance created by chumminess and lack of arm's length dealing. The case concludes with a brief description of the hero of the case—whistle blower Cynthia Cooper.

THE GROWTH THROUGH ACQUISITION MERRY-GO-ROUND

From its humble beginnings as an obscure long distance telephone company WorldCom, through the execution of an aggressive acquisition strategy, evolved into the second largest long distance telephone company in the United States and one of the largest companies handling worldwide Internet data traffic.[8] According to the WorldCom website, at its high point the company:

- Provided mission-critical communications services for tens of thousands of businesses around the world
- Carried more international voice traffic than any other company

- Carried a significant amount of the world's Internet traffic
- Owned and operated a global IP (Internet Protocol) backbone that provided connectivity in more than 2,600 cities, and in more than 100 countries
- Owned and operated 75 data centers . . . on five continents." [Data centers provide hosting and allocation services to businesses for their mission critical business computer applications.[9]

WorldCom achieved its position as a significant player in the telecommunications industry through the successful completion of 65 acquisitions.[10] Between 1991 and 1997, WorldCom spent almost $60 billion in the acquisition of many of these companies and accumulated $41 billion in debt.[11] Two of these acquisitions were particularly significant. The MFS Communications acquisition enabled WorldCom to obtain UUNet, a major supplier of Internet services to business, and MCI Communications gave WorldCom one of the largest providers of business and consumer telephone service. By 1997, WorldCom's stock had risen from pennies per share to over $60 a share.[12] Through what appeared to be a prescient and successful business strategy at the height of the Internet boom, WorldCom became a darling of Wall Street. In the heady days of the technology bubble Wall Street took notice of WorldCom and its then visionary CEO, Bernie Ebbers. This was a company "on the make," and Wall Street investment banks, analysts and brokers began to discover WorldCom's value and make "strong buy recommendations" to investors. As this process began to unfold, the analysts recommendations, coupled with the continued rise of the stock of the stock market, made WorldCom stock desirable and the market's view of the stock was that it could only go up. As the stock value went up, it was easier for WorldCom to use stock as the vehicle to continue to purchase additional companies. The acquisition of MFS Communications and MCI Communications were, perhaps, the most significant in the long list of WorldCom acquisitions. With the acquisition of MFS Communications and its UUNet unit, "WorldCom (s)uddenly had an investment story to offer about the value of combining long distance, local service and data communications."[13] In late 1997, British Telecommunications Corporation made a $19 billion bid for MCI. Very quickly, Ebbers made a counter offer of $30 billion in World-Com stock. In addition, Ebbers agreed to assume $5 billion in MCI debt, making the deal $35 billion or 1.8 times the value of the British Telecom offer. MCI took WorldCom's offer making WorldCom a truly significant global telecommunications company.[14]

All this would be just another story of a successful growth strategy if it wasn't for one significant business reality-mergers and acquisitions, especially large ones, present significant managerial challenges in at least two areas. First, management must deal with the challenge of integrating new and old organizations into a single smooth functioning business. This is a time-consuming process that involves thoughtful planning and a considerable amount of senior managerial attention if the acquisition process is to increase the value of the firm to both shareholders and stakeholders. With 65 acquisitions in six years and several of them large ones, WorldCom management had a great deal on their plate. The second challenge is the requirement to account for the financial aspects of the acquisition. The complete financial integration of the acquired company must be accomplished, including and accounting of asset, debts, good will and a host of other financially important factors. This must be accomplished through the application of generally accepted accounting practices (GAAP).

WorldCom's efforts to integrate MCI illustrate several areas senior management did not address well. In the first place, Ebbers appeared to be an indifferent executive who "paid scant attention to the details of operations."[15] For example, customer service deteriorated. One business customer's service was discontinued incorrectly, and when the customer contacted customer service, he was told he was not a customer. Ultimately, the WorldCom representative told him that if he was a customer, he had called the wrong office because the office he called only handled MCI accounts.[16] This poor customer stumbled "across a problem stemming from WorldCom's acquisition binge: For all its talent in buying competitors, the company was not up to the task of merging them. Dozens of conflicting computer systems remained, local systems were repetitive and failed to work together properly, and billing systems were not coordinated."[17]

Poor integration of acquired companies also resulted in numerous organizational problems. Among them were:

1. Senior management made little effort to develop a cooperative mindset among the various units of WorldCom.
2. Inter-unit struggles were allowed to undermine the development of a unified service delivery network.
3. WorldCom closed three important MCI technical service centers that contributed to network maintenance only to open twelve different centers that, in the words of one engineer, were duplicate and inefficient.
4. Competitive local exchange carriers (Clercs) were another managerial nightmare. World-Com purchased a large number of these to provide local service. According to one executive, "(t)he WorldCom model was a vast wasteland of Clercs, and all capacity was expensive and very underutilized . . . There was far too much redundancy, and we paid far too much to get it."[18]

Regarding financial reporting, WorldCom used a liberal interpretation of accounting rules when preparing financial statements. In an effort to make it appear that profits were increasing, WorldCom would write down in one quarter millions of dollars in assets it acquired while, at the same time, it "included in this charge against earnings the cost of company expenses expected in the future. The result was bigger losses in the current quarter but smaller ones in future quarters, so that its profit picture would seem to be improving."[19] The acquisition of MCI gave WorldCom another accounting opportunity. While reducing the book value of some MCI assets by several billion dollars, the company increased the value of "good will," that is, intangible assets, a brand name, for example, by the same amount. This enabled WorldCom each year to charge a smaller amount against earnings by spreading these large expenses over decades rather than years. The net result was WorldCom's ability to cut annual expenses, acknowledge all MCI revenue and boost profits from the acquisition.

WorldCom managers also tweaked their assumptions about accounts receivables, the amount of money customers owe the company. For a considerable time period, management chose to ignore credit department lists of customers who had not paid their bills and were unlikely to do so. In this area, managerial assumptions play two important roles in receivables accounting. In the first place, they contribute to the amount of funds reserved to cover bad debts. The lower the assumption of non-collectable bills, the smaller the reserve fund required. The result is higher earnings. Secondly, if a company sells receivables to a third party, which WorldCom did, then the assumptions contribute to the amount or receivables available for sale.[20]

So long as there were acquisition targets available, the merry-go-round kept turning, and WorldCom could continue these practices. The stock price was high and accounting practices allowed the company to maximize the financial advantages of the acquisitions while minimizing the negative aspects. WorldCom and Wall Street could ignore the consolidation issues because the new acquisitions allowed management to focus on the behavior so welcome by everyone, the continued rise in the share price. All this was put in jeopardy when, in 2000, the government refused to allow WorldCom's acquisition of Sprint. The denial stopped the carousel and put an end to their acquisition-without-consolidation strategy and left management a stark choice between focusing on creating value from the previous acquisitions with the possible loss of share value or trying to find other creative ways to sustain and increase the share price.

In July 2002, WorldCom filed for bankruptcy protection after several disclosures regarding accounting irregularities. Among them was the admission of improperly accounting for operating expenses as capital expenses in violation of generally accepted accounting practices (GAAP). WorldCom has admitted to a $9 billion adjustment for the period from 1999 thorough the first quarter of 2002.

SWEETHEART LOANS TO SENIOR EXECUTIVES

Bernie Ebbers' passion for his corporate creation loaded him up on common stock. Through generous stock options and purchases Ebbers' WorldCom holdings grew and grew, and he typically financed these purchases with his existing holdings as collateral. This was not a problem until the value of WorldCom stock declined, and Bernie faced margin calls (a demand to put up more collateral for outstanding loans) on some of his purchases. At that point he faced a difficult dilemma. Because his personal assets were insufficient to meet the substantial amount required to meet the call, he could either sell some of his common shares to finance the margin calls or request a loan from the company to cover the calls. Yet, when the board learned of his problem, it refused to let him sell his shares on the grounds that it would depress the stock price and signal a lack of confidence about WorldCom's future.[21]

Had he pressed the matter and sold his stock, he would have escaped the bankruptcy financially whole, but Ebbers honestly thought WorldCom would recover. Thus, it was enthusiasm and not greed that trapped Mr. Ebbers. The executives associated with other corporate scandals sold at the top. In fact, other WorldCom executives did much, much better than Ebbers.[22] Bernie borrowed against his stock. That course of action makes sense if you believe the stock will go up, but it's the road to ruin if the stock goes down. Unlike the others, he intended to make himself rich taking the rest of the shareholders with him. In his entire career, Mr. Ebbers sold company shares only half a dozen times. Detractors may find him irascible and arrogant, but defenders describe him as a principled man.[23]

The policy of boards of directors authorizing loans for senior executives raises eyebrows. The sheer magnitude of the loans to Ebbers was breathtaking. The $341 million loan the board granted Mr. Ebbers is the largest amount any publicly traded company has lent to one of its officers in recent memory.[24] Beyond that, some question whether such loans are ethical. "A large loan to a senior executive epitomizes concerns about conflict of interest and breach of fiduciary duty," said former SEC enforcement official Seth Taube.[25] Nevertheless, 27% of major publicly traded companies had loans outstanding for executive officers in 2000 up from 17% in 1998 (most commonly for stock purchase but also home buying and relocation). Moreover, there is the claim that executive loans are commonly sweetheart deals involving interest rates that constitute a poor rate of return on company assets. WorldCom charged Ebbers slightly more than 2% interest, a rate considerably below that available

to "average" borrowers and also below the company's marginal rate of return. Considering such factors, one compensation analyst claims that such lending "should not be part of the general pay scheme of perks for executives . . . I just think it's the wrong thing to do."[26]

WHAT'S A NOD OR WINK AMONG FRIENDS?

In the autumn of 1998, Securities and Exchange Commissioner Arthur Levitt, Jr. uttered the prescient criticism, "Auditors and analysts are participants in a game of nods and winks.[27] It should come as no surprise that it was Arthur Andersen that endorsed many of the accounting irregularities that contributed to WorldCom's demise.[28] Beyond that, however, were a host of incredibly chummy relationships between WorldCom's management and Wall Street analysts.

Since the Glass-Steagall Act was repealed in 1999, financial institutions have been free to offer an almost limitless range of financial services to its commercial and investment clients. Citigroup, the result of the merger of Citibank and Travelers Insurance Company, who owned the investment bank and brokerage firm Salomon Smith Barney, was an early beneficiary of investment deregulation. Citibank regularly dispensed cheap loans and lines of credit as a means of attracting and rewarding corporate clients for highly lucrative work in mergers and acquisitions. Since WorldCom was so active in that mode, their senior managers were the target of a great deal of influence peddling by their banker, Citibank. For example, Travelers Insurance, a Citigroup unit, lent $134 million to a timber company Bernie Ebbers was heavily invested in. Eight months later, WorldCom chose Salomon Smith Barney, Citigroup's brokerage unit, to be the lead underwriter of $5 billion of it's bond issue.[29]

But the entanglements went both ways. Since the loan to Ebbers was collateralized by his equity holdings, Citigroup had reason to prop up WorldCom stock. And no one was better at that than Jack Grubman, Salomon Smith Barney's telecommunication analyst. Grubman first met Bernie Ebbers in the early 1990's when he was heading up the precursor to WorldCom, LDDS Communications. The two hit it off socially, and Grubman started hyping the company. Investors were handsomely rewarded for following Grubman's buy recommendations until stock reached its high, and Grubman rose financially and by reputation. In fact, *Institutional Investing* magazine gave Jack a Number 1 ranking in 1999,[30] and *Business Week* labeled him "one of the most powerful players on Wall Street."[31]

The investor community has always been ambivalent about the relationship between analysts and the companies they analyze. As long as analyst recommendations are correct, close relations have a positive insider quality, but when their recommendations turn south, corruption is suspected. Certainly Grubman did everything he could to tout his personal relationship with Bernie Ebbers. He bragged about attending Bernie's wedding in 1999. He attended board meeting at WorldCom's headquarters. Analysts at competing firms were annoyed with this chumminess. While the other analysts strained to glimpse any tidbit of information from the company's conference call, Grubman would monopolize the conversation with comments about "dinner last night."[32]

It is not known who picked up the tab for such dinners, but Grubman certainly rewarded executives for their close relationship with him.[33] Both Ebbers and WorldCom CFO Scott Sullivan were granted privileged allocations in IPO (Initial Public Offering) auctions. While the Securities and Exchange Commission allows underwriters like Salomon Smith Barney to distribute its allotment of new securities as it sees fit among its customers, this sort of favoritism has angered many small investors. Banks defend this practice by contending that providing high net worth individuals with favored access to hot IPOs is just good business.[34] Alternatively, they allege that greasing the palms of distinguished investors creates a marketing "buzz" around an IPO, helping deserving small companies trying to go public get the market attention they deserve.[35] For the record, Mr. Ebbers personally made $11 million in trading profits over a four-year period on shares from initial public offerings he received from Salomon Smith Barney.[36] In contrast, Mr. Sullivan lost $13,000 from IPOs, indicating that they were apparently not "sure things."[37]

There is little question but that friendly relations between Grubman and WorldCom helped investors from 1995 to 1999. Many trusted Grubman's insider status and followed his rosy recommendations to financial success. In a 2000 profile in *Business Week,* he seemed to mock the ethical norm against conflict of interest: "what used to be a conflict is now a synergy," he said at the time. "Someone like me . . . would have been looked at disdainfully by the buy side 15 years ago. Now they know that I'm in the flow of what's going on."[38] Yet, when the stock started cratering later that year, Grubman's enthusiasm for WorldCom persisted. Indeed, he maintained the highest rating on WorldCom until March 18, 2002 when he finally raised its risk rating. At that time, the stock had fallen almost 90% from its high two years before. Grubman's mea culpa was to clients on April 22 read, "In retrospect the depth and length of the decline in enterprise spending has been stronger and more damaging to WorldCom than we even anticipated."[39] An official statement from Salomon Smith Barney two weeks later seemed to contradict the notion that Grubman's analysis was conflicted, "Mr. Grubman was not alone in his enthusiasm for the future prospects of the company. His coverage was based purely on information yielded during his analysis and was not based on personal relationships."[40] Right.

On August 15, 2002 Jack Grubman resigned from Salomon where he had made as much as $20 million per year. His resignation letter read in part, "I understand the disappointment and anger felt by investors as a result of [the company's] collapse, I am nevertheless proud of the work I and the analysts who work with me did."[41] On December 19, 2002, Jack Grubman was fined $15 million and was banned for securities transactions for life by the Securities and Exchange Commission for such conflicts of interest.

The media vilification that accompanies one's fall from power unearthed one interesting detail about Grubman's character—he repeatedly lied about his personal background. A graduate of Boston University, Mr. Grubman claimed a degree from MIT. Moreover, he claimed to have grown up in colorful South Boston, while his roots were actually in Boston's comparatively bland Oxford Circle neighborhood.[42] What makes a person fib about his personal history is an open question. As it turns out, this is probably the least of Jack Grubman's present worries. New York State Controller H. Carl McCall sued Citicorp, Arthur Andersen, Jack Grubman, and others for conflict of interest. According to Mr. McCall, "this is another case of corporate coziness costing investors billions of dollars and raising troubling questions about the integrity of the information investors receive."[43]

THE HERO OF THE CASE

No integrity questions can be raised about Cynthia Cooper whose careful detective work as an internal auditor at WorldCom exposed some of the accounting irregularities apparently intended to deceive investors. Originally charged with responsibilities in operational

audit, Cynthia and her colleagues grew suspicious of a number of peculiar financial transactions and went outside their assigned responsibilities to investigate. What they found was a series of clever manipulations intended to bury almost $4 billion in misallocated expenses and phony accounting entries.[44]

A native of Clinton, Mississippi where WorldCom's headquarters was located, Ms. Cooper's detective work was conducted in secret, often late at night to avoid suspicion. The thing that first aroused her curiosity came in March, 2002 when a senior line manager complained to her that her boss, CFO Scott Sullivan, had usurped a $400 million reserve account he had set aside as a hedge against anticipated revenue losses. That didn't seem kosher, so Cooper inquired of the firm's accounting firm, Arthur Andersen. They brushed her off, and Ms. Cooper decided to press the matter with the board's audit committee. That put her in direct conflict with her boss, Sullivan, who ultimately backed down. The next day, however, he warned her to stay out of such matters.

Undeterred and emboldened by the knowledge that Andersen had been discredited by the Enron case and that the SEC was investigating WorldCom, Cynthia decided to continue her investigation. Along the way, she learned of a WorldCom financial analyst who was fired a year earlier for failing to go along with accounting chicanery.[45] Ultimately, she and her team uncovered a $2 billion accounting entry for capital expenditures that had never been authorized. It appeared that the company was attempting to represent operating costs as capital expenditures in order to make the company look more profitable. To gather further evidence, Cynthia's team began an unauthorized search through WorldCom's computerized accounting information system. What they found was evidence that fraud was being committed. When Sullivan heard of the ongoing audit, he asked

Cooper to delay her work until the third quarter. She bravely declined. She went to the board's audit committee and in June, Scott Sullivan and two others were terminated. What Ms. Cooper had discovered was the largest accounting fraud in U.S. history.[46]

As single-minded as Cynthia Cooper appeared during this entire affair, it was incredibly trying ordeal. Her parents and friends noticed that she was under considerable stress and was losing weight. According to the *Wall Street Journal*, she and her colleagues worried "that their findings would be devastating to the company [and] whether their revelations would result in layoffs an obsessed about whether they were jumping to unwarranted conclusions that their colleagues at World-Com were committing fraud. Plus, they feared that they would somehow end up being blamed for the mess.[47]

It is unclear at this writing whether Bernie Ebbers will be brought to bear for the accounting irregularities that brought down his second in command. Jack Grubman's final legal fate is also unclear. While the ethical quality of enthusiasm and sociability are debatable, the virtue of courage is universally acclaimed, and Cynthia Cooper apparently has it. Thus, it was not surprising that on December 21, 2002, Cynthia Cooper was recognized as one of three "Persons of the Year" by *Time* magazine.

NOTES

1. This is only true if he is liable for the loans he was given by WorldCom. If he avoids those somehow, his net worth may be plus $8.4 million according to the *Wall Street Journal* (see S. Pulliam & J. Sandberg [2002]. Worldcom Seeks SEC Accord As Report Claims Wider Fraud [November 5], A-1).
2. Colvin, G. (2002). Bernie Ebbers' Foolish Faith. *Fortune. 146*, (11 [November 25]), 52.
3. Padgett, T., & Baughn, A. J. (2002). The Rise and Fall of Bernie Ebbers. *Time, 159*, (19 [May 12]), 56+.
4. Morse, D., & Harris, N. (2002). In Mississippi, Ebbers is a Man to be Proud Of. *Wall Street Journal*, May 2, 2002, B-1.
5. Young, S., & Solomon, D. (2002). WorldCom Backs Chief Executive For $340 Million. *Wall Street Journal* (February 8), B-1.
6. Ibid.
7. Romero, Simon, & Atlas, Rava D. (2002). WorldCom's Collapse: The Overview. *New York Times*, (July 22), A-1.
8. Ibid.
9. WorldCom website, (www.worldcom.com/global/about/facts/).
10. Eichenwald, Kurt (2002). For WorldCom, Acquisitions Were Behind its Rise and Fall, *New York Times* (August 8), A-1.
11. Romero & Atlas, op. cit.
12. Browning, E. S. (1997). Is the Praise for WorldCom Too Much? *Wall Street Journal* (October 8), p. C-24. All acquisition amounts are taken from this article.
13. Eichenwald, Op. cit., p. A-3.
14. Ibid.
15. Ibid.
16. Ibid., p. A-2.
17. Ibid., p. A-4.
18. Ibid., p. A-5.
19. Ibid., p. A-4.
20. Ibid., p. A-5; Sender, Henry (2002), Inside the WorldCom Numbers Factory, *Wall Street Journal* (August 21), C-1.
21. Solomon, D., & Blumenstein, R. (2002). Telecom: Mississippi blues: Loans Proved to be Ebber's Downfall. *Wall Street Journal* (May 1), A-8.
22. According to David Leonhardt of the *New York Tones* (8/25/02, p. 10), Director Francesco Galesi made $31 million, John Sidgmore, the senior manager who replaced Ebbers as CEO, made $25 million, and CFO Scott Sullivan, who many think was responsible for the accounting abuses at WorldCom, pocketed $23 million.
23. Sandberg, J. (2002). Bernie Ebbers Bet the Ranch—Really—on WorldCom Stock. *Wall Street Journal* (April 14), A-13.
24. Salomon, D., & Sandberg, J. (2002). Leading the News. *Wall Street Journal* (November 6), A-3, report that Bernie used 8% of this load for personal use, an uncharacteristically self-serving move for Mr. Ebbers.
25. Young, S. (2002). Big WorldCom Loan May Have Spurred Inquiry. *Wall Street Journal* (March 14), A-3.
26. Lublin, J. S., & Young, S. (2002). WorldCom Loan to CEO of $341 Million is the Most Generous in Recent Memory. *Wall Street Journal* (March 15), A-4.
27. Byrne, J. A. (2002). Fall from grace: Joe Berardino Presided over the Biggest Accounting Scandals Ever and the Demise of a Legendary Firm. *Business Week* (August 12), 50+.
28. These amounted to over $9 million in overstated income. For an explanation as to how some of this was

done, see Elstrom, P. (2002). How to Hide $3.8 Billion in Expenses. *Business Week* (July 8), 41+.

29. Morgenson, G. (2002). More Clouds over Citigroup in Its Dealings with Ebbers. *New York Times* (November 3), 1.

30. Smith, R., & Salomon, D. (2002). Heard on the Street Ebbers' Exit Hurts WorldCom's Biggest Fan. *Wall Street Journal* (May 3), C-1.

31. Rosenbush, S. (2002). Inside the Telecom Game. *Business Week* (August 5), p. 34+.

32. Ibid.

33. On December 20, 2002, Jack Grubman was fined $15 million and was banned for securities transactions for life by the Securities and Exchange Commission for such conflicts of interest.

34. Editors. (2002). Citi Defends IPO Allocations to Shamed Worldcom Execs. *Euroweek* (August 30), 18.

35. Murray, A. (2002). Political Capital: Let Capital Markets, Not Financial Firms, Govern Fate of IPOs. *Wall Street Journal* (September 10), A-4.

36. Craig, S. (2002). Offerings Were Easy Money for Ebbers. *Wall Street Journal* (September 3), C-1.

37. Ibid.

38. Rosenbush, op. cit., 34.

39. Smith, op. cit., C-1.

40. Ibid.

41. Editors (2002), Salomon's Jack Grubman Resigns. *United Press International* (August 15), 10082777w0186.

42. Rosenbush, op. cit., 34.

43. Weil, J. (2002). Leading the News: An Ebbers Firm Got Citigroup loans. *Wall Street Journal* (October 14), A-3.

44. Pelliam, S. (2002). Questioning the Books: WorldCom Memos Suggest Plan to Bury Financial Misstatements. *Wall Street Journal* (July 9), A-8.

45. Orey, M. (2002). Career Journal: WorldCom-Inspired "Whistle-Blower" Law Has Weaknesses. *Wall Street Journal* (October 1), B-1.

46. Colvin, G. (2002). Wonder Women of Whistleblowing. *Fortune* (August 12), 56+.

47. Pelliam, S., & Solomon, D. (2002). Uncooking the Books: How Three Unlikely Sleuths Discovered Fraud at WorldCom. *Wall Street Journal* (October 30), A-1.

Essay

The Adelphia Story

Devin Leonard

Dale Cowburn was allergic to bee stings. He carried medication at all times in case he encountered an angry swarm. Last summer, however, while he was working in his barn, Cowburn was stung twice on the head. He had a heart attack and died on the spot.

The news traveled quickly through Coudersport, Pa., the town of 2,600 near the New York border where Cowburn had lived. One of the locals moved by his death was John Rigas, chairman and CEO of Adelphia Communications, the nation's sixth-largest cable television provider, a company with $3.6 billion in annual revenues and headquarters in—of all places—this rural town. Rigas knows about bees. He owns a farm outside town that sells Christmas trees, maple syrup, and honey.

Soon after Cowburn's death, there was a knock on the door at his house. It was Rigas' beekeeper. He'd been sent to destroy the offending insects.

More than just the town's richest man, Rigas was a 76-year-old worth billions. He owned the Buffalo Sabres hockey team. He hobnobbed with Ted Turner. But the silver-haired cable mogul told people in a humble whisper that he was just a small-town guy who loved helping his neighbors. He sent busloads of children to Sabres games. He used Adelphia's corporate jet to fly ailing people to faith healers and cancer treatment centers.

Townspeople flocked to the Masonic temple every year for Adelphia's Christmas party. At last year's celebration there were two towering Christmas trees, each decorated with 16,000 lights at the direction of John's wife, Doris. The Buffalo Philharmonic Orchestra played the Nutcracker Suite and Vaughan Williams' "Fantasia on 'Greensleeves.'" That was really something for a town like Coudersport. "Each December the Rigas family brings their world to us, and I am grateful," wrote a columnist in the local paper. "How many would have the opportunity to hear a symphony orchestra, were it not for their generosity?"

John Rigas was also revered in the cable business. He was one of the pioneers who had started stringing wires and urging customers to throw away their rabbit ears in the early 1950s. He was inducted into the Cable Television Hall of Fame last year. Colleagues praised him not just for his business accomplishments but for his good works in Coudersport. In a celebratory video, Decker Anstrom, CEO of the Weather Channel, said, "If there's one person I'd like my son to grow up to be, it would be John Rigas."

Then, in the blink of an eye, John Rigas lost everything—his company, his reputation, even the affection of his beloved Coudersport. Last March, Adelphia disclosed it was on the hook for $2.3 billion in off-balance-sheet loans the Rigas family had used mostly to buy company stock. Rigas resigned, as did his three sons—Michael, Tim, and James—who held top executive positions and sat on the board with their father. The independent directors now running the company say they discovered that under the Rigases, nothing was as it seemed. They say Adelphia inflated subscriber numbers. Routine expenses like service calls had been booked as capital items, inflating Adelphia's reported cash flow. But what was perhaps most unsettling was the unabashed manner in which the Rigases had helped themselves to shareholder dollars.

Adelphia financed the family's $150 million purchase of the Sabres. It paid $12.8 million in 2001 for office furniture and design services provided by Doris Rigas. Even John Rigas' good works were tainted. Adelphia paid a Rigas family partnership that owns the Sabres $744,000 for "luxury-box rentals, hockey tickets, and other entertainment costs." That means shareholders probably picked up the tab for all those children who went to games. The same goes for the beekeeper's visit to Cowburn's house. It turns out the primary source of income at Rigas' farm wasn't honey sales; it was providing landscaping, snow removal, and other maintenance duties for Adelphia.

As Adelphia slid toward bankruptcy—it filed for Chapter 11 protection in June—the entire cable industry was affected. The stock of competitors like Comcast and Charter fell because Wall Street feared they might have similar secrets. Investors dumped shares of entertainment companies like Disney, afraid that Adelphia wouldn't pay its programming bills. Two federal grand juries are sorting through the wreckage, and indictments are expected soon. The Securities and Exchange Commission has set up an office in Coudersport and is preparing a civil suit.

The Rigases have spent the past several months sequestered in their family compound outside Coudersport. They refused to talk to *Fortune*, referring all questions to criminal attorney Paul Grand, who denies they did anything wrong.

Citizens of Coudersport no longer speak so worshipfully about John Rigas. But even now there are people who praise him as a principled man who refused, for instance, to allow porn channels on his cable systems. The John Rigas they describe believed in small-town values: strong families, hard work, church on Sunday. That's why, they say, he remained true to Coudersport all those years. But surely there was another reason. There were things John Rigas and his sons got away with in Coudersport that would never have been tolerated anywhere else.

John Rigas didn't impress anybody much when he first arrived in Coudersport in 1951. The son of a Greek immigrant who ran a hot dog restaurant in nearby Wellsville, N.Y., Rigas was a character. He was 5 feet 5 inches tall. He had a gap-toothed smile, a wandering left eye, and a lot of energy. His father had tried to entice him to work at the restaurant when he came home with an engineering degree from Rensselaer Polytechnic Institute in 1950. But after a few months at the grill, John thought better of it. He borrowed money from his dad and several other Greek businessmen and bought the Coudersport movie theater for $72,000. He sold tickets, made popcorn, and sometimes slept on a cot in the theater when he was too tired to drive home to Wellsville.

Back then Coudersport didn't seem like a place anybody would go to make a fortune. It was a one-stoplight town in the Allegheny Mountains, fat from any major highway. Main Street was four blocks of low-slung brick buildings dominated by the Potter County courthouse. It wasn't quaint; there was a hard edge, even a sense of desperation in the air Coudersport had missed nearly every economic boom in rural Pennsylvania. There was no coal to mine, no oil beneath the surface. The hills around town had been logged bare.

Family Assets, Sort Of: Some of the notable ways the Rigas family used shareholder dollars

On the receiving end . . .	Who's behind the entity	How much
Dobaire Designs	Adelphia paid this company, owned by Doris Rigas, for design services.	$371,000
Wending Creek Farms	Adelphia paid John Rigas' farm for lawn care and snowplowing.	$2 million
SongCatcher Films	Adelphia financed the production of a movie by Ellen Rigas.	$3 million
Eleni Interiors	The company made payments to a furniture store run by Doris Rigas and owned by John.	$12 million
The Golf Club at Wending Creek Farms	Adelphia began developing a ritzy golf club.	$13 million
Wending Creek 3656	The company bought timber rights that would eventually revert to a Rigas family partnership.	$26 million
Praxis Capital Ventures	Adelphia funded a venture capital firm run by Ellen Rigas' husband.	$65 million
Niagara Frontier Hockey LP	Adelphia underwrote the Rigases' purchase of the Buffalo Sabres hockey team.	$150 million
Highland 2000	Adelphia guaranteed loans to a Rigas family partnership, which used the funds to buy stock.	$1 billion
Total		$1,271,371,000

By the 1950s the joke was that the town hadn't felt the Great Depression because it hadn't known prosperity. Each spring when diplomas were passed out, the locals muttered. "Say good-bye to another graduating class at Coudersport High."

People who stayed behind weren't sure what to think about a man like John Rigas, who wore his ambition on his sleeve. "It's the same plague you see in other small communities," says Bruce Cahilly, a local attorney who befriended Rigas early on. "People who have more talent and expertise are perceived as threats." So John was snubbed when he moved to town with Doris, a former high school English teacher from a poor family in the Finger Lakes area. John was wounded. "I've never been accepted in this town," he complained to a friend later on. "I couldn't even get elected to the school board."

But he seemed determined to win everybody over. He stayed until midnight talking to moviegoers after the lights went up. He stopped people on Main Street to ask about their children. He began attending the Episcopal church preferred by the town's business leaders, even though he'd been raised in the Greek Orthodox faith.

With Doris' prodding, John also pursued other business opportunities. In 1952 he overdrew his bank account to buy the town cable franchise for $300 from a local hardware store owner who'd erected an antenna on Dutch Hill. A doctor and a state senator agreed to put up $40,000, and John was in the cable business. He wired up Coudersport. Four years later he and his brother Gus did the same in Wellsville.

By the mid-1960s Rigas could afford to build a house just outside town with a pool for his four children. He was invited to sit on the board of the local bank. For a man who wanted to be accepted, the offer meant a great deal. Besides, he could always use a loan.

John Rigas and his sons would become famous in the cable industry for taking huge risks and leveraging Adelphia to the hilt. That would not have surprised anybody in Coudersport. After wiring the town John acquired more rural cable systems in New York and Pennsylvania, and he bragged to friends about how much debt he was taking on to finance the deals. "Hey, I just borrowed $10 million," John blithely told Henry Lush, a local furniture store owner. His secretary was forever going to the bank and moving funds from account to account so that her boss could stay ahead of creditors. People who tried to collect debts discovered it was no simple matter. Bruce Cahilly once drove out to John's house to seek payment for some legal work. When all else failed, he grabbed two five-gallon cans of blue pool paint from the garage. "That's just as well," John shrugged. "Doris doesn't like blue. She wanted green."

John wasn't always so sanguine. There were times when he lay awake worrying. "Well, Angie," he told his secretary, "I'm either going to become a millionaire or I'm going to go bankrupt."

A lot of people in Coudersport would have been satisfied with a house, a pool, and a seat on the bank board. But John kept pushing himself. He and Doris drove their children just as hard. They raised Michael, Tim, James, and Ellen, their youngest, to be model students. No smoking, no drinking, no hitchhiking across the country like their cousins in Wellsville. Doris, locals say, seemed to feel that the family was too good for Coudersport and drove her children to outshine their classmates. John didn't cut them any slack either. Says Bob Currin, a retired social studies teacher who taught the Rigas children: "John always let them know they had it and they could do it—and they'd better do it." Michael, James, and Ellen were class valedictorians. Tim was on track for the same honor when a boy with a better academic record moved to town senior year and edged him out.

One by one the Rigas children went off to elite colleges. Michael, the oldest, went to

Harvard and then on to Harvard Law. Friends recall that he was smart and ambitious but monkish, usually spending Saturday nights studying.

Tim, the second child, was equally bright. He got a bachelor's degree in economics from Wharton, and he had a social life too. He played intramural volleyball and belonged to a singing group called the Penny Loafers.

James, the youngest of the boys, went to Harvard and then to Stanford Law School. He drank beer and played pinball, but he impressed everybody as a straight arrow. "He was the last person you would have thought would have gotten into trouble," says Steven Durlauf, a Harvard classmate.

For all their winning qualities, there was something odd about the Rigas boys. Unlike their father, they were awkward socially. When they attended their cousins' weddings in Wellsville, they stood in their tuxedos against the wall, arms crossed. "They didn't mingle," a Rigas family member says sadly. "They just stood there. Somebody said, 'They must be the bouncers.'"

The boys clearly preferred being with their immediate family in Coudersport. Not long after getting their degrees, Michael and Tim moved back in with their parents. Neither married, James spent a year and a half in San Francisco after Stanford, working at Bain & Co., but then he too returned to Coudersport, where he married and got a place of his own in town. "John just controlled everything with those boys," laments a relative. "He wouldn't give them any rope." (Ellen, the youngest child, went to Harvard and then pursued a career in music and film production in New York.)

All three sons went to work for their father. John couldn't have been happier. He now had three highly qualified young men to help run his cable company.

Adelphia was still a shoestring operation: John ran the company out of an office over a hardware store with three secretaries and a lineman. Once his sons joined the business, things changed rapidly. In 1981, Adelphia moved into an old church around the corner. People wondered what John was going to do with all that extra space. In 1985, Adelphia went from 53,538 subscribers to 122,500 after it acquired a cable system in Ocean County, N.J. When the Rigases took Adelphia public the next year, it had 370 full-time employees and deals on the table that would increase its subscribers to 253,767. By the mid-1990s Adelphia had moved into the old Coudersport High School building on Main Street, where the boys had gone to school. It was an odd place, perhaps, for what was now one of the nation's ten largest cable companies, managing 1.2 million subscribers. But the Rigas systems were the envy of their peers. They were clustered together in six areas—western New York Virginia, Pennsylvania, New England, Ohio, and coastal New Jersey—making it easier for Adelphia to control costs. That allowed Adelphia to enjoy 56% operating cash margins, the highest in the cable industry.

John and the boys came to be considered savvy businessmen. John was the resident wise man, but he was also obsessed with details. He knew every inch of his cable systems; he looked at every résumé that came in. Michael was responsible for the daily operations of the cable systems. Tim was CFO. James supervised Adelphia's push into new technologies, including telephone service.

Yet as the cable industry grew up, the Rigases operated as if they were a million miles away from prying investors. Says Tom Cady, a former Adelphia sales and marketing executive: "Decisions were made at the dinner table rather than in a boardroom or somebody's office." John and his sons showed up late for meetings so often that people joked that the family operated "on Rigas time." They were famous for not returning calls from analysts. Occasionally, when they spotted a cable acquisition they really liked, they simply kept it for themselves.

What's more, the Rigases structured Adelphia so that there were no checks and balances at the top. Adelphia issued class A shares with one vote each to the public, but the Rigases retained all the class B stock with ten votes per share. Therefore they got to pick the board of directors. John, the three boys, and Ellen's husband, Peter Venetis, held five of the nine board seats. They filled the other four with John's friends and business associates. Who else would want to travel to Coudersport for meetings anyway?

By all accounts Tim Rigas ran the financial side of the business like a Saudi prince. He was CFO, and he was also the chairman of the board's audit committee, which oversaw the CFO's work. So how effective was the audit committee? That's hard to say. Sources say attorneys for the company haven't been able to find minutes of any meeting that Tim ran. (A Rigas family spokesman says minutes do exist and were kept by an outside law firm.)

To anybody who'd followed John Rigas' career, what happened with Adelphia's financing was predictable. The small-town businessman who had boasted about his stomach for leverage now saddled Adelphia with outlandish amounts of debt. In 1996, Adelphia's debt was 11 times its market capitalization, an off-the-chart number. (By contrast, Comcast's ratio was 1.28; Cox Communication's was 0.45.) Bond-rating agencies constantly subjected Adelphia to credit reviews. Shareholders paid a price. A Salomon Smith Barney analyst noted that Adelphia's debt "has caused the stock to trade at the steepest discount to estimated net asset value of any cable operator."

Stranger still, Adelphia began commingling revenues from its own cable operations, family-owned systems, and loan proceeds in an account referred to internally, according to documents filed recently with the SEC, as the "cash-management system." It was a lot of money. After Adelphia made a series of acquisitions in 1999, its annual revenues reached $3 billion. From time to time the Rigas family dipped into the account for personal business. The company says the Rigases tapped the account earlier this year to pay $63 million in margin loans. They used $4 million from the account to buy Adelphia stock. Another $700,000 went to pay for Tim's membership at the Golf Club at Briar's Creek on John's Island, S.C.

The independent directors now running the company say neither the unusual account nor the family's withdrawals were approved by the board. The Rigas family spokesman insists that none of it was hidden from the directors.

The Rigases didn't particularly care if investors shied away from Adelphia's stock or if bond-rating agencies called their debt junk. They cared about Coudersport. As Adelphia prospered, John Rigas became the town's biggest benefactor. He hired many locals and paid them well. Employees built suburban-style houses. The newspaper store started selling fancy coffee. A gym opened on Main Street. The Adelphia Christmas party became the "fancy-dress event in Coudersport, a chance to hobnob with the Rigases and socialize in suits over catered canapés," says Donald Gilliland, managing editor of the *Potter Leader-Enterprise*.

John combed the local papers and sent checks to down-on-their-luck families. "I'd always know when he did that because I'd get calls saying, 'Thanks for the article, I just got a check from John Rigas,'" says John Anderson, managing editor of the *Wellsville Daily Reporter*. People seeking favors camped out in Rigas' favorite restaurants, waiting for the CEO to arrive for lunch. He rarely turned anybody down.

Coudersport treated the Rigases like royalty, and they behaved accordingly. John now traveled in a Gulfstream jet, which Adelphia purchased from King Hussein of Jordan. At the Adelphia Christmas party one year, the orchestra played selections from the musical *Camelot*. It was John's favorite music, the conductor told the audience.

Doris rarely ventured into town, sending servants to do her shopping. When she was seen, she was in one of her Toyota minivans, an employee behind the wheel. But everyone felt her presence. The Rigases accumulated a dozen or so houses in Coudersport and the surrounding area. Doris had most of them painted brown and surrounded by split-rail fences. She also helped design Adelphia's buildings, including its brick-and-marble headquarters on Main Street, which locals call the "mausoleum."

No expense seemed to be spared. One day John asked Jimmie Bruzzi, the town dry cleaner, what he thought of Doris' work. "John," Bruzzi replied, "that woman is costing you millions."

"Well, sometimes it's worth it," Rigas replied. "Because when she's bothering [the contractors], she's not bothering me."

The boys, for their part, seemed to owe their allegiance more to the family empire than to the town. Michael was the only one who showed interest in community service. He worked 16-hour days and still attended Coudersport Rotary Club meetings. Tim, too, worked hard, jetting around the country negotiating acquisitions. He dressed well, had lots of girlfriends, and belonged to nearly 20 golf clubs. But when he was home, Tim would take John to church and Doris to her favorite restaurant, the Beef 'N Barrel.

James seemed more interested in having his own fiefdom. He spent most of his time running Adelphia Business Solutions, a telephone service company spun off from the parent. He flew coach and stayed in midrange hotels. (Sources tell *Fortune* that of all the sons, James was the least involved in Adelphia's financial weirdness.) Yet even James behaved like royalty at times. He built a baronial house on a hill above town that made the neighbors feel like serfs, "I didn't realize until now I lived in the cottage down the lane," one of them is said to have complained.

Even Ellen lived in high style—on the company tab, no less. The company says she and her venture capitalist husband lived rent-free in a Manhattan apartment owned by Adelphia. The corporation also put up $3 million in production money for *Songcatcher*, her critically acclaimed film about a musicologist. John reportedly walked out of the Coudersport premiere when two women kissed onscreen. (Ellen Rigas and her husband have paid the back rent on the apartment to Adelphia.)

It struck some of the locals that the Rigases were rather free with shareholder money. Teresa Kisiel, Coudersport's tax collector, couldn't help noticing that Adelphia paid its real estate taxes and those of the Rigas family with a single check. It was no secret that shareholders were footing the bills for a planned golf course. Tim and John told people it would have specially bred sheepdogs to chase away Canada geese.

Sometimes people in Coudersport even wondered whether all the spending was legitimate. But the thought would pass. It seemed as though everyone in town had benefited from John's largesse. "He's our Greek god," Shirlee Lette, a local newspaper columnist, told a visiting reporter.

Oren Cohen thought there was something about the family's spending that didn't add up. Then a high-yield-bond analyst for Merrill Lynch (and now a principal at Trilogy Capital), Cohen had followed Adelphia for a decade. He'd noticed that the Rigases were buying their own stock aggressively, but he couldn't figure out how they were paying for it. They didn't appear to have the cash themselves. John Rigas made $1.4 million in 2000. Michael, Tim, and James each took home $237,000.

The Rigases didn't have any sources of income outside Adelphia. They never sold their stock, and it didn't pay a dividend. Cohen was pretty sure their private cable systems weren't throwing off cash. John couldn't be selling that much honey at his farm. But every time Cohen tried to get an explanation, Adelphia rebuffed him. "If everything was on the up and up, the answer would have been, 'Oh, we bought it with family funds,'" recalls the analyst. "But that was never the answer. It was always 'We're not telling you.'"

Last February, Cohen noticed that the Rigases had bought or were committed to buying $1.8 billion of Adelphia stock and convertible bonds. At the time of the purchases the stock had been trading at about $40 a share. Now it was at $20. If John and his sons were using borrowed money, the Rigases were in trouble. It was time to call Adelphia again. "It seems to me the Rigases are $900 million or $1 billion in the hole," Cohen said to the head of investor relations. "How's this stuff being funded?" He got the brush-off.

On March 27, Cohen nearly shouted for joy when he spied a footnote on the last page of Adelphia's quarterly earnings press release. It said Adelphia was liable for $2.3 billion in off-balance-sheet loans to the Rigas family. Near the end of a conference call that day, Cohen pressed Tim Rigas for details. Tim muttered something about family stock purchases and said he would provide details later.

That might have sufficed in the past, but it was just months after the disclosure of off-balance-sheet debt at Enron had led to the largest corporate bankruptcy in history. Adelphia's stock tumbled 35% in three days. The SEC began an investigation.

Things in Coudersport quickly spun out of control. John issued a statement acknowledging that "shareholders are looking for greater clarity and transparency." The stock continued to fall as Adelphia announced it would be restating earnings for 1999, 2000, and 2001.

The company delayed filing its 2001 annual report to sort out its books. On May 15, John resigned as chairman and CEO.

Rigas was succeeded by interim CEO Erland Kailbourne, a retired Fleet Bank executive and Adelphia "independent" director. Kailbourne was a consummate Rigas family insider, an old friend from Wellsville, and a lot of observers suspected that John might still pull strings.

But the truth is, the independent directors were livid. They'd signed off on the lending agreements, but they thought the Rigases were buying more cable systems, not taking out what were essentially margin loans to buy Adelphia stock. John had made them look like fools. Kailbourne and the three other independent directors hired David Boies, the attorney who led the case against Microsoft, to look into Adelphia's books.

John did not object. Neither did Michael, Tim, or James, who resigned soon after their father. Boies sent in forensic accountants, who discovered that a $167 million bond purchase by the family hadn't been paid for. They also unearthed what appeared to be evidence of fraud, "Certain employees of the company may have prepared documents, including wire transfer receipts and bank-paydown and draw-down notices. . . . to support accounting treatment of this transaction as a cash transaction." Adelphia later explained in an SEC filing. *Fortune* has learned that five members of the accounting department who worked under Tim Rigas are now cooperating with federal prosecutors.

The independent directors also discovered that even after the disastrous March 27 conference call, someone in the family withdrew $175 million from Adelphia's cash-management system to cover margin loans.

Adelphia's stock was soon worth pennies. The company was delisted by the Nasdaq because it didn't file its 2001 annual report. That triggered the default of $1.4 billion in

Adelphia convertible bonds. Bankruptcy was all but certain. The company desperately needed a loan to stay afloat. But Wall Street wasn't about to lend it any more money as long as the Rigases were around. The family still held 100% of the company's class B voting stock. Technically they still controlled Adelphia.

The problem was that John Rigas didn't think he'd done anything wrong. The day after he resigned as chairman and CEO, he startled the independent directors by showing up at a directors' meeting. Surely, he told them, this mess could be sorted out and things would get back to normal. No, John, said his old friends, you and the boys have to go. Lawyers from Boies' firm tried to negotiate a severance package with John but couldn't reach an agreement. Finally the independent directors gave the Rigas family an ultimatum: Turn over your voting shares to us, or we'll resign and go public with everything we've uncovered. After an all-night negotiating session on May 22 in Coudersport, the Rigases finally relinquished control at 5 A.M. Adelphia got a $1.5 billion bank loan. CEO Kailbourne says he hopes to take Adelphia through Chapter 11 and come out with a viable company.

The story, however, isn't over yet. There's a three-way wrestling match going on between the Rigases, the independent directors, and Deloitte & Touche, the company's auditor, over what people knew about Adelphia's finances and when they knew it. Predictably, the directors say Deloitte should have blown the whistle years ago, while Deloitte says the directors should have had better oversight. The Rigases, through their spokesman, say that both the directors and the outside auditors knew what was going on and didn't object.

John Rigas apparently still believes that he did nothing wrong. After weeks of silence, he told the *Buffalo News* that he'd been "de-pressed" lately and regretted disappointing "ordinary people." But his spirits were lifted by the hundreds of cards and letters he'd received from supporters. "It has been very inspirational to me and my family," Rigas told the paper. "I must say that most of the cards end with a message that is most meaningful and that is that 'You are in our prayers.' It does bring a tear to my eye."

If John Rigas showed up on Main Street in Coudersport tomorrow, some people would avoid him. Others might curse him. But the vast majority would pat him on the back and tell him to keep his chin up. They remember the checks, the Christmas parties, all the nice things he's done. Rigas knows that. But he hasn't been seen in town since everything fell apart at Adelphia. His friends say his health isn't good, and that must be part of it. But maybe there's another reason: He'd have to look everybody in the eye.

UPDATE

Soon after Leonard's story appeared in *Fortune,* John Rigas and his sons Timothy and Michael were arrested and charged with conspiracy to commit what a U.S. Attorney called "one of the largest and most egregious frauds ever perpetrated on investors and creditors." John Rigas was arrested on the morning of July 24 and led out in handcuffs, and television coverage of the event was widely credited with giving the stock market a boost that day. Prosecutors accused the Rigases of "systematically looting" Adelphia, and SEC officials said that the Rigases had overstated earnings and hidden $2.3 billion in debt from investors. The Rigases have pled not guilty to all the charges. Adelphia, meanwhile, sued the Rigases, and has apparently cut off all severance pay to John Rigas. Adelphia remains in business, but is still in Chapter 11.

Case Study

The Ford Pinto

W. Michael Hoffman

I

On August 10, 1978 a tragic automobile accident occurred on U.S. Highway 33 near Goshen, Indiana. Sisters Judy and Lynn Ulrich (ages 18 and 16, respectively) and their cousin Donna Ulrich (age 18) were struck from the rear in their 1973 Ford Pinto by a van. The gas tank of the Pinto ruptured, the car burst into flames and the three teen-agers were burned to death.

Subsequently an Elkhart County grand jury returned a criminal homicide charge against Ford, the first ever against an American corporation. During the following 20-week trial, Judge Harold R. Staffeldt advised the jury that Ford should be convicted of reckless homicide if it were shown that the company had engaged in "plain, conscious and unjustifiable disregard of harm that might result (from its actions) and the disregard involves a substantial deviation from acceptable standards of conduct."[1] The key phrase around which the trial hinged, of course, is "acceptable standards." Did Ford knowingly and recklessly choose profit over safety in the design and placement of the Pinto's gas tank? Elkhart County prosecutor Michael A. Cosentino and chief Ford attorney James F. Neal battled dramatically over this issue in a rural Indiana courthouse. Meanwhile, American business anxiously awaited the verdict which could send warning ripples through board rooms across the nation concerning corporate responsibility and product liability.

II

As a background to this trial some discussion of the Pinto controversy is necessary. In 1977 the magazine *Mother Jones* broke a story by Mark Dowie, general manager of *Mother Jones* business operations, accusing Ford of knowingly putting on the road an unsafe car—the Pinto—in which hundreds of people have needlessly suffered burn deaths and even more have been scarred and disfigured due to burns. In his article "Pinto Madness" Dowie charges that:

> Fighting strong competition from Volkswagen for the lucrative small-car market, the Ford Motor Company rushed the Pinto into production in much less than the usual time. Ford engineers discovered in pre-production crash tests that rear-end collisions would rupture the Pinto's fuel system extremely easily. Because assembly-line machinery was already tooled when engineers found this defect, top Ford officials decided to manufacture the car anyway—exploding gas tank and all—even though Ford owned the patent on a much safer gas tank. For more than eight years afterwards, Ford successfully lobbied, with extraordinary vigor and some blatant lies, against a key government safety standard that would have forced the company to change the Pinto's fire-prone gas tank. By conservative estimates Pinto crashes have caused 500 burn deaths to people who would not have been seriously injured if the car had not burst into flames. The figure could be as high as 900. Burning Pintos have become such an embarrassment to Ford that its advertising agency, J. Walter Thompson, dropped a line from the ending of a radio spot that read "Pinto leaves you with that warm feeling."

Ford knows that the Pinto is a firetrap, yet it has paid out millions to settle damage suits out of court, and it is prepared to spend millions more lobbying against safety standards. With a half million cars rolling off the assembly lines each year, Pinto is the biggest-selling subcompact in America, and the company's operating profit on the car is fantastic. Finally, in 1977, new Pinto models have incorporated a few minor alterations necessary to meet that federal standard Ford managed to hold off for eight years. Why did the company delay so long in making these minimal, inexpensive improvements?

Ford waited eight years because its internal "cost-benefit analysis," which places a dollar value on human life, said it wasn't profitable to make the change sooner.[2]

Several weeks after Dowie's press conference on the article, which had the support of Ralph Nader and auto safety expert Byron Bloch, Ford issued a news release attributed to Herbert T. Misch, vice president of Environmental and Safety Engineering at Ford, countering points made in the *Mother Jones* article. Their statistical studies significantly conflicted with each other. For example, Dowie states that more than 3,000 people were burning to death yearly in auto fires; he claims that, according to a National Highway Traffic Safety Administration (NHTSA) consultant, although Ford makes 24 percent of the cars on American roads, these cars account for 42 percent of the collision-ruptured fuel tanks.[3] Ford, on the other hand, uses statistics from the Fatality Analysis Reporting System (FARS) maintained by the government's NHTSA to defend itself, claiming that in 1975 there were 848 deaths related to fire-associated passenger-car accidents and only 13 of these involved Pintos; in 1976, Pintos accounted for only 22 out of 943. These statistics imply that Pintos were involved in only 1.9 percent of such accidents, and Pintos constitute about 1.9 percent of the total registered passenger cars. Furthermore, fewer than half of those Pintos cited in the FARS study were struck in the rear.[4] Ford

concludes from this and other studies that the Pinto was never an unsafe car and has not been involved in some 70 burn deaths annually as *Mother Jones* claims.

Ford admits that early model Pintos did not meet rear-impact tests at 20 mph but denies that this implies that they were unsafe compared to other cars of that type and era. In fact, its tests were conducted, according to Ford, some with experimental rubber "bladders" to protect the gas tank, in order to determine how best to have their future cars meet a 20 mph rear-collision standard which Ford itself set as an internal performance goal. The government at that time had no such standard. Ford also points out that in every model year the Pinto met or surpassed the government's own standards, and

> it simply is unreasonable and unfair to contend that a car is somehow unsafe if it does not meet standards proposed for future years or embody the technological improvements that are introduced in later model years.[5]

Mother Jones, on the other hand, presents a different view of the situation. If Ford was so concerned about rear-impact safety, why did it delay the federal government's attempts to impose standards? Dowie gives the following answer:

> The particular regulation involved here was Federal Motor Vehicle Safety Standard 301. Ford picked portions of Standard 201 for strong opposition way back in 1968 when the Pinto was still in the blueprint stage. The intent of 301, and the 300 series that followed it, was to protect drivers and passengers after a crash occurs. Without question the worst post-crash hazard is fire. Standard 301 originally proposed that all cars should be able to withstand a fixed barrier impact of 20 mph (that is, running into a wall at that speed) without losing fuel.
>
> When the standard was proposed, Ford engineers pulled their crash-test results out of their files. The front ends of most cars were no problem—with minor alterations they could stand

the impact without losing fuel. "We were already working on the front end," Ford engineer Dick Kimble admitted. "We knew we could meet the test on the front end." But with the Pinto particularly, a 20 mph rear-end standard meant redesigning the entire rear end of the car. With the Pinto scheduled for production in August of 1970, and with $200 million worth of tools in place, adoption of this standard would have created a minor financial disaster. So Standard 301 was targeted for delay, and with some assistance from its industry associates, Ford succeeded beyond its wildest expectations: the standard was not adopted until the 1977 model year.[6]

Ford's tactics were successful, according to Dowie, not only due to their extremely clever lobbying, which became the envy of lobbyists all over Washington, but also because of the pro-industry stance of NHTSA itself.

Furthermore, it is not at all clear that the Pinto was as safe as other comparable cars with regard to the positioning of its gas tank. Unlike the gas tank in the Capri which rode over the rear axle, a "saddle-type" fuel tank on which Ford owned the patent, the Pinto tank was placed just behind the rear bumper. According to Dowie,

> Dr. Leslie Ball, the retired safety chief for the NASA manned space program and a founder of the International Society of Reliability Engineers, recently made a careful study of the Pinto. "The release to production of the Pinto was the most reprehensible decision in the history of American engineering," he said. Ball can name more than 40 European and Japanese models in the Pinto price and weight range with safer gas-tank positioning.

> Los Angeles auto safety expert Byron Bloch has made an indepth study of the Pinto fuel system. "It's a catastrophic blunder," he says. "Ford made an extremely irresponsible decision when they placed such a weak tank in such a ridiculous location in such a soft rear end. It's almost designed to blow up—premeditated."[7]

Although other points could be brought out in the debate between *Mother Jones* and Ford, perhaps the most intriguing and controversial is the cost-benefit analysis study that Ford did entitled "Fatalities Associated with Crash-Induced Fuel Leakage and Fires" released by J. C. Echold, Director of Automotive Safety for Ford. This study apparently convinced Ford and was intended to convince the federal government that a technical improvement costing $11 per car which would have prevented gas tanks from rupturing so easily was not cost-effective for society. The costs and benefits are broken down in the following way:

Benefits

Savings:	180 burn deaths, 180 serious burn injuries, 2,100 burned vehicles
Unit Cost:	$200,000 per death, $67,000 per injury, $700 per vehicle
Total Benefit:	$180 \times (\$200,000) + 180 \times (\$67,000) + 2,100 \times (\$700) = \$49.5$ million.

Costs

Sales:	11 million cars, 1.5 million light trucks
Unit Cost:	$11 per car, $11 per truck
Total Cost:	$11,000,000 \times (\$11) + 1,500,000 \times (\$11) = \$137$ million

Component	1971 Costs
Future Productivity Losses	
Direct	$132,000
Indirect	41,300
Medical Costs	
Hospital	700
Other	425
Property Damage	1,500
Insurance Administration	4,700
Legal and Court	3,000
Employer Losses	1,000
Victim's Pain and Suffering	10,000
Funeral	900
Assets (Lost Consumption)	5,000
Miscellaneous	200
TOTAL PER FATALITY	$ 200,725

(Although this analysis was on all Ford vehicles, a breakout of just the Pinto could be done.) *Mother Jones* reports it could not find anybody who could explain how the $10,000 figure for "pain and suffering" had been arrived at.[8]

Although Ford does not mention this point in its News Release defense, it might have replied that it was the federal government, not Ford, that set the figure for a burn death. Ford simply carried out a cost-benefit analysis based on that figure. *Mother Jones*, however, in addition to insinuating that there was industry-agency (NHTSA) collusion, argues that the $200,000 figure was arrived at under intense pressure from the auto industry to use cost-benefit analysis in determining regulations. *Mother Jones* also questions Ford's estimate of burn injuries: "All independent experts estimate that for each person who dies by an auto fire, many more are left with charred hands, faces and limbs." Referring to the Northern California Burn Center which estimates the ratio of burn injuries to deaths at ten to one instead of one to one, Dowie states that "the true ratio obviously throws the company's calculations way off."[9] Finally, *Mother Jones* claims to have obtained "confidential" Ford documents which Ford did not send to Washington, showing that crash fires could be largely prevented by installing a rubber bladder inside the gas tank for only $5.08 per car, considerably less than the $11 per car Ford originally claimed was required to improve crash-worthiness.[10]

Instead of making the $11 improvement, installing the $5.08 bladder, or even giving the consumer the right to choose the additional cost for added safety, Ford continued, according to *Mother Jones*, to delay the federal government for eight years in establishing mandatory rear-impact standards. In the meantime, Dowie argues, thousands of people were burning to death and tens of thousands more were being badly burned and disfigured for life, tragedies many of which could have been prevented for only a slight cost per vehicle. Furthermore, the delay also meant that millions of new unsafe vehicles went on the road, "vehicles that will be crashing, leaking fuel and incinerating people well into the 1980s."[11]

In concluding this article Dowie broadens his attack beyond just Ford and the Pinto.

Unfortunately, the Pinto is not an isolated case of corporate malpractice in the auto industry. Neither is Ford a lone sinner. There probably isn't a car on the road without a safety hazard known to its manufacturer . . .

Furthermore, cost-valuing human life is not used by Ford alone. Ford was just the only company careless enough to let such an embarrassing calculation slip into public records. The process of willfully trading lives for profits is built into corporate capitalism. Commodore Vanderbilt publicly scorned George Washington and his "foolish" air brakes while people died by the hundreds in accidents on Vanderbilt's railroads.[12]

Ford has paid millions of dollars in Pinto jury trials and out-of-court settlements, especially the latter. *Mother Jones* quotes Al Slechter in Ford's Washington office as saying: "We'll never go to a jury again. Not in a fire case. Juries are just too sentimental. They see those charred remains and forget the evidence. No sir, we'll settle."[13] But apparently Ford thought such settlements would be less costly than the safety improvements. Dowie wonders if Ford would continue to make the same decisions "were Henry Ford II and Lee Iacocca serving 20-year terms in Leavenworth for consumer homicide."[14]

III

On March 13, 1980, the Elkhart County jury found Ford not guilty of criminal homicide in the Ulrich case. Ford attorney Neal summarized several points in his closing argument before the jury. Ford could have stayed out of the small car market which would have been the "easiest way," since Ford would have made more profit by sticking to bigger cars. Instead Ford built the Pinto "to take on the imports, to save jobs for Americans and to make a profit for its stockholders."[15] The Pinto met every fuel-system standard of any federal, state or local government, and was comparable to other 1973 subcompacts. The engineers who designed the car thought it was a good, safe car and bought it for themselves and their families. Ford did everything possible quickly to recall the Pinto after NHTSA ordered it to do so. Finally, and more specifically to the case

at hand, Highway 33 was a badly designed highway, and the girls were fully stopped when a 4,000-pound van rammed into the rear of their Pinto at at least 50 miles an hour. Given the same circumstances, Neal stated, any car would have suffered the same consequences as the Ulrichs' Pinto.[16] As reported in the *New York, Times* and *Time*, the verdict brought a "loud cheer" from Ford's Board of Directors and undoubtedly at least a sigh of relief from other corporations around the nation.

Many thought this case was a David against a Goliath because of the small amount of money and volunteer legal help Prosecutor Cosentino had in contrast to the huge resources Ford poured into the trial. In addition, it should be pointed out that Cosentino's case suffered from a ruling by Judge Staffeldt that Ford's own test results on pre-1973 Pinto's were inadmissible. These documents confirmed that Ford knew as early as 1971 that the gas tank of the Pinto ruptured at impacts of 20 mph and that the company was aware, because of tests with the Capri, that the over-the-axle position of the gas tank was much safer than mounting it behind the axle. Ford decided to mount it behind the axle in the Pinto to provide more trunk space and to save money. The restrictions of Cosentino's evidence to testimony relating specifically to the 1973 Pinto severely undercut the strength of the prosecutor's case.[17]

Whether this evidence would have changed the minds of the jury will never be known. Some, however, such as business ethicist Richard De George, feel that this evidence shows grounds for charges of recklessness against Ford. Although it is true that there were no federal safety standards in 1973 to which Ford legally had to conform and although Neal seems to have proved that all subcompacts were unsafe when hit at 50 mph by a 4,000-pound van, the fact that the NHTSA ordered a recall of the Pinto and not other subcompacts is, according to De George, "*prima facie* evidence that Ford's Pinto gas tank mounting was substandard."[18] De George argues that these grounds for recklessness are made even stronger by the fact that Ford did not give the consumer a choice to make the Pinto gas tank safer by installing a rubber bladder for a rather modest fee.[19] Giving the consumer such a choice, of course, would have made the Pinto gas tank problem known and therefore probably would have been bad for sales.

Richard A. Epstein, professor of law at the University of Chicago Law School, questions whether Ford should have been brought up on criminal charges of reckless homicide at all. He also points out an interesting historical fact. Before 1966 an injured party in Indiana could not even bring civil charges against an automobile manufacturer solely because of the alleged "uncrashworthiness" of a car; one would have to seek legal relief from the other party involved in the accident, not from the manufacturer. But after *Larson v. General Motors Corp.* in 1968, a new era of crashworthiness suits against automobile manufacturers began. "Reasonable" precautions must now be taken by manufacturers to minimize personal harm in crashes.[20] How to apply criteria of reasonableness in such cases marks the whole nebulous ethical and legal arena of product liability.

If such a civil suit had been brought against Ford, Epstein believes, the corporation might have argued, as they did to a large extent in the criminal suit, that the Pinto conformed to all current applicable safety standards and with common industry practice. (Epstein cites that well over 90% of U.S. standard production cars had their gas tanks in the same position as the Pinto.) But in a civil trial the adequacy of industry standards is ultimately up to the jury, and had civil charges been brought against Ford in this case the plaintiffs might have had a better chance of winning.[21] Epstein feels that a criminal suit, on the other hand, had no chance from the very outset, because the prosecutor would have had to establish criminal intent on the part of Ford. To use an analogy, if a hunter shoots at a deer and wounds an unseen person, he may be held civilly responsible but not criminally responsible because he did not intend to harm. And even though it may be more difficult to determine the mental state of a corporation (or its principal agents), it seems clear to Epstein that the facts of this case do not prove any such criminal intent even though Ford may have known that some burn deaths/injuries could have been avoided by a different placement of its Pinto gas tank and that Ford consciously decided not to spend more money to save lives.[22] Everyone recognizes that there are trade-offs between safety and costs. Ford could have built a "tank" instead of a Pinto, thereby considerably reducing risks, but it would have been relatively unaffordable for most and probably unattractive to all potential consumers.

To have established Ford's reckless homicide it would have been necessary to establish the same of Ford's agents since a corporation can only act through its agents. Undoubtedly, continues Epstein, the reason why the prosecutor did not try to subject Ford's officers and engineers to fines and imprisonment for their design choices is because of "the good faith character of their judgment, which was necessarily decisive in Ford's behalf as well."[23] For example, Harold C. MacDonald, Ford's chief engineer on the Pinto, testified that he felt it was important to keep the gas tank as far from the passenger compartment as possible, as it was in the Pinto. And other Ford engineers testified that they used the car for their own families. This is relevant information in a criminal case which must be concerned about the intent of the agents.

Furthermore, even if civil charges had been made in this case, it seems unfair and irrelevant to Epstein to accuse Ford of trading cost for safety. Ford's use of cost-benefit formulas, which must assign monetary values to human life and suffering, is precisely what the law demands in assessing civil liability suits.

The court may disagree with the decision, but to blame industry for using such a method would violate the very rules of civil liability. Federal automobile officials (NHTSA) had to make the same calculations in order to discharge their statutory duties. In allowing the Pinto design, are not they too (and in turn their employer, the United States) just as guilty as Ford's agents?[24]

IV

The case of the Ford Pinto raises many questions of ethical importance. Some people conclude that Ford was definitely wrong in designing and marketing the Pinto. The specific accident involving the Ulrich girls, because of the circumstances, was simply not the right one to have attacked Ford on. Other people believe that Ford was neither criminally nor civilly guilty of anything and acted completely responsibly in producing the Pinto. Many others find the case morally perplexing, too complex to make sweeping claims of guilt or innocence.

Was Ford irresponsible in rushing the production of the Pinto? Even though Ford violated no federal safety standards or laws, should it have made the Pinto safer in terms of rear-end collisions, especially regarding the placement of the gas tank? Should Ford have used cost-benefit analysis to make decisions relating to safety, specifically placing dollar values on human life and suffering? Knowing that the Pinto's gas tank could have been made safer by installing a protective bladder for a relatively small cost per consumer, perhaps Ford should have made that option available to the public. If Ford did use heavy lobbying efforts to delay and/or influence federal safety standards, was this ethically proper for a corporation to do? One might ask, if Ford was guilty, whether the engineers, the managers, or both are to blame. If Ford

had been found guilty of criminal homicide, was the proposed penalty stiff enough ($10,000 maximum fine for each of the three counts = $30,000 maximum), or should agents of the corporations such as MacDonald, Iacocca, and Henry Ford II be fined and possibly jailed?

A number of questions concerning safety standards are also relevant to the ethical issues at stake in the Ford trial. Is it just to blame a corporation for not abiding by "acceptable standards" when such standards are not yet determined by society? Should corporations like Ford play a role in setting such standards? Should individual juries be determining such standards state by state, incident by incident? If Ford should be setting safety standards, how does it decide how safe to make its product and still make it affordable and desirable to the public without using cost-benefit analysis? For that matter, how does anyone decide? Perhaps it is putting Ford, or any corporation, in a catch-22 position to ask it both to set safety standards and to competitively make a profit for its stockholders.

Regardless of how the reader answers these and other questions it is clear that the Pinto case raises fundamental issues concerning the responsibilities of corporations, how corporations should structure themselves in order to make ethical decisions, and how industry, government, and society in general ought to interrelate to form a framework within which such decisions can properly be made in the future.

NOTES

1. *Indianapolis Star*, March 9, 1980, sec. 3, p. 2.
2. Mark Dowie, "Pinto Madness," *Mother Jones*, Sept/Oct, 1977, pp. 18 and 20. Subsequently Mike Wallace for *60 Minutes* and Sylvia Chase for *20/20* came out with similar exposés.
3. Ibid., p. 30.
4. Ford News Release (Sept. 9, 1977), pp. 1–3.

5. Ibid., p. 5.

6. Dowie, "Pinto Madness," p. 29.

7. Ibid., pp. 22–23.

8. Ibid., pp. 24 and 28. Although this analysis was on all Ford vehicles a breakout of just the Pinto could be done.

9. Ibid., p. 28.

10. Ibid., pp. 28–29.

11. Ibid., p. 30.

12. Ibid., p. 32. Dowie might have cited another example which emerged in the private correspondence which transpired almost a half century ago between Lammot du Pont and Alfred P. Sloan, Jr., then president of GM, Du Pont was trying to convince Sloan to equip GM's lowest-priced cars, Chevrolets, with safety glass. Sloan replied by saying: "It is not my responsibility to sell safety glass. . . . You can say, perhaps, that I am selfish, but business is selfish. We are not a charitable institution—we are trying to make a profit for our stockholders." Quoted in Morton Mintz and Jerry S. Cohen, *Power, Inc.* (New York: The Viking Press, 1976), p. 110.

13. Ibid., p. 31.

14. Ibid., p. 32.

15. Transcript of report of proceedings in *State of Indiana v. Ford Motor Company*, Case No. 11-431, Monday, March 10, 1980, pp. 6202–3. How Neal reconciled his "easiest way" point with his "making more profit for stockholders" point is not clear to this writer.

16. Ibid., pp. 6207–9.

17. *Chicago Tribune*, October 13, 1979, p. 1, and sec. 2, p. 12; *New York Times*, October 14, 1979, p. 26; *Atlanta Constitution*, February 7, 1980.

18. Richard De George, "Ethical Responsibilities of Engineers in Large Organizations: The Pinto Case," *Business and Professional Ethics Journal*, vol. I, no. 1 (Fall 1981), p. 4. *New York, Times*, October 26, 1978, p. 103, also points out that during 1976 and 1977 there were 13 fiery fatal rear-end collisions involving Pintos, more than double that of other U.S. comparable cars, with VW Rabbits and Toyota Corollas having none.

19. Ibid., p. 5.

20. Richard A. Epstein, "Is Pinto a Criminal?" *Regulation*, March/April, 1980, pp. 16–17.

21. A California jury awarded damages of $127.8 million (reduced later to $6.3 million on appeal) in a Pinto crash where a youth was burned over 95% of his body. See *New York Times*, February 8, 1978, p. 8.

22. Epstein, p. 19.

23. Ibid., pp. 20–21.

24. Ibid., pp. 19–21.

Case Study

Radials, Rollovers, and Responsibility: An Examination of the Ford-Firestone Case

Robert Noggle, Daniel Palmer

I. THE ANATOMY OF A TIRE CRISIS

On August 9, 2000 executives of the Firestone Tire Corporation (a wholly owned subsidiary of the Japanese Bridgestone Corporation, hereafter referred to as Bridgestone/Firestone) announced the voluntary recall of an estimated 6.5 million tires, initiating the second largest tire recall in the United States to date.[1] The recall included the size P235/75R15 ATX, ATXII and Wilderness AT tires, many of which had been installed as original factory equipment on the popular Ford Explorer Sport Utility Vehicles (SUVs).[2] At the time of the announcement, the tires in question had been linked by the National Highway Traffic Safety Administration (NHTSA) and consumer advocacy groups to 270 complaints, 80 crashes and 46 deaths.[3] Most of these incidents involved Ford Explorers and occurred when tread separation caused blowouts that in turn led to vehicle rollovers. Later, NHSTA would raise its figures to include over 100 deaths and 500 injuries involving similar incidents, clearly linking this recall—the second largest in U.S. automotive history—with one the most infamous cases of product failure resulting in serious harms to consumers.[4] For months following the announcement, the Firestone recall and the injuries and deaths associated with Ford Explorers equipped with the tires were widely discussed in the media, bringing both the Firestone and Ford corporations to the center of public attention.

While the massive scope of the recall and the gravity of the accidents indicated by the numbers released by NHSTA brought the Ford/Firestone tire crisis to the center of public attention, the recall itself was simply the final attempt by Bridgestone/Firestone to respond to a problem that had plagued both Ford and Bridgestone/Firestone for years. Indeed, stability problems resulting from Ford Explorer prototypes equipped with Firestone tires had been discussed in company memos from as early as 1987.[5] Early tests on the Explorer prototype, code-named "UN46," indicated stability concerns. The Explorer was, in a word, tippy. The optimum way to deal with this problem would have been to widen the Explorer's wheel base and/or lower its center of gravity. However, such changes would have held up production more than what the top Ford executives were willing to tolerate. Ford engineers offered a back-up plan: they suggested that the Explorer's stability problems could be addressed in part simply by lowering the recommended tire pressure for use on the vehicles.[6] Throughout the pre-production tests on the Explorer, concerns continued to be raised concerning both the stability of the vehicle and tread separation problems on the vehicle's tires. Significantly, although Ford had approved the design of the Firestone ATX tires for use on the Explorer, tests conducted by both Ford and Bridgestone/Firestone

revealed problems with the tires when they were tested at the lower tire pressures that Ford had adopted in order to address the vehicle's stability problems.[7] Although these problems were noted, they were never fully addressed by either company. Thus, even before the Explorer went into production, a trend of ignoring red flags began that would eventually result in the infamous Bridgestone/Firestone tire recall of 2000.

Despite both companies' indications that there were concerns remaining about the vehicles and the tires, the Explorer was introduced into the American market in 1990. The first tread separation lawsuit against Ford and Firestone was filed shortly thereafter, in February of 1991, only one year after Ford began production of the Explorer.[8] By the mid-1990s both Ford and Firestone had already settled lawsuits for millions of dollars resulting from similar claims against the companies that would eventually issue in the 2000 recall.[9] Further, internal company documents indicate that both companies were tracking these problems and attempting to address them internally long before they came to public attention.[10] It was only after the Arizona State Game and Fish Department and State Farm Insurance Company had independently tracked tire problems and reported the data that NHSTA itself became aware of the abnormal rate of accidents resulting from Firestone-equipped Ford Explorers.[11] Even more telling to those familiar with the case was the fact that Ford had already begun a tire replacement program in Saudi Arabia and Venezuela stemming from similar patterns of accidents.[12]

At the time of this writing, definitive proof about what caused these accidents has yet to be put forward. However, a large body of evidence (some of which will be discussed briefly in this paper) suggests that several causal factors interacted to produce the deadly accidents. Tire experts have pointed to possible design flaws in the Firestone tires, to defects stemming from materials used in the production of the tires, and even to possible manufacturing irregularities resulting from labor problems at the plant where most of the tires that failed were produced.[13] In addition to whatever flaws may have existed in the tires, it is almost certain that the stability problems in the Explorers also played a crucial role in the accidents: the lower tire pressures which were Ford's own method for coping with these stability problems almost certainly exacerbated or contributed to the weaknesses in the tires themselves. In addition, the poor stability of the Explorers made them far more likely than other vehicles to roll over as a result of a tire blowout.[14] Whatever the exact causal story turns out to be, one thing that is certain is that the number and seriousness of the accidents associated with the Explorer and its Firestone tires are such that this case deserves the attention that has been lavished on it by the media. It turns out that the case presents a number of difficult normative questions that also deserve careful attention by business ethics.

II. RESPONDING TO THE CRISIS: FORD AND FIRESTONE REACT

As the media, public interest groups, and various governmental bodies continue to investigate the accidents, injuries, and deaths linked with Ford Explorers equipped with Firestone tires, those who work in applied ethics have also begun to sift through the ethical issues surrounding the case. Indeed, the case involves a bewildering tangle of ethical concerns, including, but certainly not limited to, questions of corporate responsibility, product safety and liability, corporate governance, government regulation, risk allocation, consumer access to product information, and even issues stemming from cross-cultural business practices. In this paper, however, we wish to concentrate on the questions it raises about the responsibilities that companies

have for the products they help to create. One theoretically interesting feature of this case is that the same set of defects and accidents have been linked to two corporations, each of which seems to be the maker of a different product. Indeed, much of the debate about this case is driven by conflicting statements, made by Ford and Firestone executives, about *which* product was defective and *which* company is responsible for the accidents and injuries that resulted. We will argue that the Ford/Firestone case is of particular importance for business ethics because it demonstrates that such questions are not as transparent as they might seem, and that answering them is not always as simple as one might think.

Our point of departure for addressing these issues will be the corporate responses that Bridgestone/Firestone and Ford offered in reaction to the increasing media and legal attention given to the safety of their products. Perhaps not surprisingly, as soon as word began to reach the public concerning the alleged problems that drivers were experiencing on Firestone equipped Explorers, both Ford and Firestone were quick to respond to the concerns, while at the same time attempting to divert any blame from themselves. Masatoshi Ono, the CEO of Firestone at the time, responded to the Houston television station KHOU's investigative report into the accidents by suggesting that they could be attributed to driver error and to poor tire maintenance by consumers.[15] Indeed, throughout the early stages of the mounting media coverage devoted to the Ford/Firestone tire crisis, Ono and other Bridgestone/Firestone representatives persisted in denying that their tires were defective or that the company was at fault for the accidents in any way. Even when Firestone's own internal investigation made it apparent that material and design irregularities appeared to exist in the tires under investigation, Firestone attempted to shift much of the blame onto Ford for recommending inappropriately low air pressure for the tires equipped on the Explorer.[16] Firestone officials also continued to stress the role of consumer maintenance. On Ford's part, Jacques Nasser, the CEO of Ford, maintained from the very beginning that the problem was wholly a Firestone tire issues. Nasser forcefully asserted that whatever the difficulties were that led to the accidents under consideration, they had nothing to do with the auto-maker, stating "this is about defective tires" and that "this is a Firestone tire issue, not a vehicle issue."[17]

In retrospect, the vigor with which both Ford and Firestone denied responsibility seems disingenuous. First, both companies were eager to absolve themselves of responsibility long before the scientific investigation into the precise technical factors that contributed to the accidents had been fully settled, a process, as noted, that is still to be finished. Second, as our overview of the case indicates, it is clear that whatever the nature of the technical problems involved, both Ford and Firestone were aware that the problems existed and were causing vehicle failures long before they released this information to either the public or to the appropriate regulatory agencies within the United States. In some sense then, both companies' responses to the crisis appear to be both a little too early and a little too late to be entirely convincing to those familiar with the details of the case.

There has, however, been an interesting difference in the public's reaction to Ford and Bridgestone/Firestone and their roles in and responsibility for the crisis. In the court of public opinion, Ford has fared much better than Bridgestone/Firestone. Bridgestone/Firestone's initial attempts to blame the victims, along with its failure to respond quickly to the problems in the first place, did not endear it to the general public. At the same time, Ford was relatively successful in deflecting public attention toward Bridge-

stone/Firestone. This is reflected in the fact that public surveys have consistently shown that consumer confidence in Firestone was much more deeply affected by the crisis than it was in Ford. For instance, polls have indicated that while 81% of those surveyed hold Firestone responsible for the accidents, only 8.5% hold Ford responsible. And while nearly 65% of consumers indicate that the incidents would influence their decision to buy Firestone products, only 35% indicated that it would influence their decision to purchase Ford products.[18] This suggests that the public accepted, at least to some significant degree, the reasoning by which Ford executives have attempted to absolve themselves from responsibility for the incidents in question.

In this paper, we will examine Ford's claim and the reasoning behind if. We will argue that Ford's position rests on untenable assumptions about how to assign moral responsibility for defects in complex products whose components are made by multiple companies. In particular, we will argue that simply noting that the tires were produced by Bridgestone/Firestone does not, in itself, show that Ford cannot be held responsible for accidents involving tire defects, even if those defects were the primary cause of the accidents. In doing so, we will develop an analysis that should be useful in better understanding of the factors that are morally relevant in determining corporate accountability in other complex cases of product liability.

III. WHOSE PRODUCT? WHICH COMPANY?

At one level, Nasser's sound bite, "It's a tire problem and not a vehicle problem," was obviously meant to assert that any defects that may exist in the Ford Explorer are located in the tires. However, as we suggested above, there is an important additional subtext to

Nasser's remarks. For Nasser's claim certainly suggests that the Firestone tires are an independent and distinct product from the Ford Explorers on which they were installed. After all, one would never say, for instance, that something is "an engine problem and not a vehicle problem" since an engine problem IS a vehicle problem. To say that something is a tire problem rather than a vehicle problem suggests that the tire is not a component of the vehicle in the way that an engine is. Moreover, it is to suggest that the *Explorer* itself is *Ford's* product, while the *ATX, ATXII, and Wilderness AT tires are Bridgestone/Firestone's* product.[19]

While it is obvious that a company must bear moral responsibility for defects in the products it creates, it would seem unfair to blame one company for defects in the products of an entirely separate company. The idea that it is unfair to hold one company responsible for defects in another company's products, combined with Ford's assertion that the Firestone tires are not Ford's product, together entail that it would be unfair to hold Ford responsible for failures in tires made by Bridgestone/Firestone. This line of thought certainly appeared to be an important part of Ford's initial public relations strategy. Because it appeals to common moral intuitions, it seems quite reasonable at first glance. As we shall see, however, it does not bear up well under more careful scrutiny.

Now of course Ford and Bridgestone/Firestone do have a business relationship—a rather long-lasting one, in fact. One result of that relationship is that Ford Explorers were equipped with Firestone tires. Thus, it is not simply happenstance that Firestone tires were on the Explorers; rather it was a result of deliberate actions taken by both companies. That much is clear enough. Things get somewhat murkier, however, when we try to characterize the relationship between Ford and Bridgestone/Firestone. And it turns out that the question of how to characterize this relationship is of paramount importance.

One way to characterize the relationship between the two companies would be to see Bridgestone/Firestone as a supplier to Ford. The tires supplied could then be seen as a component part in the finished product— namely the complete, ready-to-drive Ford Explorer. On this view, the tires are a part of the vehicle, and Bridgestone/Firestone acted as an outside supplier for this part on the Explorers.

On the other hand, we could see Ford as a mere conduit or middleman for Bridgestone/Firestone. From this perspective, Ford makes a product that requires another separate product before it can be used. This other product is a set of tires. From this perspective, Ford arranges to sell consumers a set of Firestone tires along with its own product, namely the Explorer. This way of seeing things would put Ford in the role of a mere retailer of tires, but a producer of vehicles. Support for this way of looking at the relationship between the vehicle and its tires might be derived from an analogy with gasoline: Gasoline is clearly a separate product from the vehicle, but for obvious practical reasons, Ford—or its dealers—sells vehicles with gasoline added. Additional support might be provided by the observation that Firestone put its own name on the tires, and even provided its own warranty for them— both of which are the kinds of things that a component part maker typically does not do.

So is Ford the manufacturer of a product which has Firestone tires as one of its components, or is it a mere retailer of tires to go with the product that it does make, namely the Explorer? This may seem like a merely verbal dispute on which nothing important could possibly turn. But it is not. It makes quite a lot of difference to some very common moral intuitions—and, perhaps more importantly, to our legal institutions—whether an item is a part of one's own product or merely a product that one is selling as a mere retailer. Common sense seems to favor holding retailers responsible for defects in products they sell only when they knew or should have known of the defects. After all, retailers are in the business of selling, not of manufacturing, and it seems unreasonable to require them to take responsibility for defects that they have no practical way to discover.

However, a manufacturer is generally held to a much higher standard of responsibility for defects—even when those defects are caused by defective components supplied by another company. For even if the defect arises because of a defective component supplied by another company, the defect still occurs in the product that is made by the manufacturing company. The manufacturing company, unlike the retailer, *is* in the business of creating products, and it seems reasonable to hold it responsible for defects in products that it makes. Of course the supplier of a defective component is also morally culpable, but this fact does not alleviate the manufacturer of its own responsibility to create safe products. Since the components are going into a product that the manufacturing company creates, the manufacturer's responsibility for the safety of the overall product creates a responsibility to make sure that all of the components of the product are safe—including any components made by outside companies. If such a component is defective, then both companies have violated their duty to produce safe products—the supplier has produced defective component, and the other company has produced a larger product which is also defective.

The foregoing analysis of what we take to be fairly standard initial intuitions shows why it makes a great deal of difference whether the Firestone tires are a product for which Ford is a mere retailer, or whether they are a component in a larger product of which Ford is the manufacturer. Boiled down, it is the difference between whether Ford's responsibility for the safety of the tires was the fairly minimal duty of non-negligence commonly assigned to retailers, or whether it was something approaching the strict liability of manufacturers. Obviously, it is much to Ford's advantage to portray itself as a mere retailer of the Firestone tires.

Legally, matters are somewhat more complex. Product liability law has evolved in roughly the direction suggested by the moral intuitions we have just discussed.[20] Like moral intuition, the rules of products liability law do tend to treat retailers somewhat differently from manufacturers. If the tires are in fact defective, in general, Ford might well be in a better legal position if it can portray the tires and the vehicles as separate products that were merely "bundled" together, and thus portray itself as a mere conduit—a retailer, in effect, for the tires. The legal specifies are extremely complex—partly because they are constantly evolving, and partly because they vary greatly from jurisdiction to jurisdiction.[21] Many jurisdictions have "shield laws" that prevent a plaintiff from suing a mere retailer for defects in a product that it did not produce when the manufacturer is available to be sued instead. And even in jurisdictions where it is possible to sue a mere retailer of a defective product, if such suit is successful, it is generally possible for the retailer to recover from the manufacturer whatever damages it had to pay to the plaintiff. The manufacturer, then, is in most jurisdictions the prime target for injured plaintiffs.[22] Mere retailers are generally able to escape ultimate legal liability for defects in products that they did not create. In fact, the case of a mere retailer is often even stronger when the actual manufacturer "is clearly and accurately identified on the label or other markings on the goods."[23] (Recall that Firestone did put its own name on the tires, and even provided its own warranty for them.)

On the other hand, manufacturers of a product with a defective component made by a separate company tend to be in a much less favorable legal position than mere retailers of defective products. In most cases, both the component part maker and the manufacturer of the larger product (often called the "assembler") are usually co-defendants. In some cases, the assembler might be sued separately and then have to sue the component part maker in a separate action. Either way, the court will at some point determine how to divide the burden of the damages awarded to the plaintiff between the assembler and the part maker. A number of different rules—which vary from jurisdiction to jurisdiction—govern how this is to occur. Most of them require that part maker and assembler share the burden, either equally or on the basis of comparative fault.[24]

So, keeping the caveats about legal complexity in mind, in general it appears to be better legally to be a mere retailer of a defective product than to be the manufacturer of a product with a defective component, even when that component is made by another company. So if Ford can successfully portray itself as a mere conduit or middleperson for the Firestone tires, it would stand some significant chance of making an early and favorable exit from what promises to be a mammoth legal battle.

In short, there are clearly potential advantages to Ford in portraying itself as a builder of cars and trucks, but a mere retailer of tires. The extent to which Nasser's comments were deliberately calculated to reap these benefits we cannot say, but it seems unlikely that these benefits would not have occurred to him or his advisers. In any event, Ford's strategy raises important questions about when something is a component of another product, and when it is a separate product "bundled" or packaged together and sold with some other product.

IV. THE METAPHYSICS OF PRODUCTS AND THE RESPONSIBILITY OF COMPANIES

It turns out that the question of whether something is a component or a product in its own right is more difficult than one would first imagine. And it turns out that tires present an especially difficult case—and thus an especially interesting one. It is worth emphasizing at the outset that even if we decide that tires should be viewed as a component of the Ford Explorer, this would not absolve Bridgestone/Firestone from responsibility for defects that might exist in those tires. Quite the contrary, of course: if the tires were defective as produced, then Bridgestone/Firestone produced a defective product and should bear the moral and legal consequences.[25] The more difficult and more interesting question is whether Ford should bear any similar moral or legal consequences in virtue of the fact that the Firestone tires were mounted as original equipment on the Explorers that it produced. Common intuitions as well as current legal rules suggest that the answer to that question depends on whether the tires are best seen as a separate product "bundled" with the Explorer, or as a component of the vehicle.

In earlier, days it was probably proper to view a tire as a separate product, "bundled" or sold along with the car, in much the same way that a battery might be packaged with a flashlight. The practice of having separate warranties for tires seems to reflect this understanding: since the tire was thought of as a separate product, it made perfect sense for its maker, the tire company, to provide a separate warranty for it to the ultimate consumer. Thus, while the tire came with the car and was indeed mounted onto the car, it was a product in its own right, and one that created a separate moral and legal relationship between the consumer and the tire maker—a relationship of a kind that did not exist between the consumer and the maker of, say, the car's head gasket. However, we will argue that the new realities of tire and vehicle manufacturing make this view no longer tenable.[26]

Our analysis of the relationship between tires and the vehicle will proceed by way of analogy. We will examine what we take to be two clear cases, one in which an item is clearly a component of another product, and the other in which it is not. Our goal will be to tease out those factors most salient in accounting for the difference between the "product metaphysics" of the two items. We will then use these factors to attempt to determine whether the Firestone ATX, ATXII, and Wilderness AT tires that were mounted on the Ford Explorer are best seen as a separate product, or whether they are best seen as components of the vehicle.

Our two clear cases will be the head gasket in the engine of a car, and the batteries in an ordinary, non-disposable flashlight. Notice that in both cases, we have one item that must be installed in a second item in order for that second item to function in the normal way. However, there is an important difference. The head gasket seems to be a clear case of a product that is so integrated into the "main" product—the car (or, perhaps, its engine)—that it seems to be an obvious case of a part or component of a product rather than a product in its own right. We take it that the flashlight battery is not a true component of the flashlight itself. Even if the batteries were sold with the flashlight, they seem to be a distinct product in a way that the head gasket is not. Intuitively, a defect in the head gasket would seem to be a defect in the engine itself, whereas a defect in a flashlight battery would not seem to be a defect in the flashlight itself. For example, we would generally not say, "The engine is fine; it's just got a bad head gasket," though

we often say, "The flashlight is fine; it's just got bad batteries."[27]

Of course, in one sense all products—including those that are components of other products—are products in the sense of being items that have been produced. The company that makes the head gasket—and let's assume that this is a separate company, that is a supplier to the car manufacturer—will rightly regard head gaskets as one of its products. So the notion of product we are using here is not the simple notion of "a thing produced." An item may be a product in the sense of being an "item produced," but it is a component part of another product if it is integrated into the larger product in such a way that from the consumer's point of view it no longer makes sense to regard it as a separate product. So while there is a sense in which the head gasket is a product, from the point of view of the final consumer, it is so fully integrated into the vehicle that it does not properly count as a separate product at all, but rather as a component of another product. In a sense, the consumer is not a consumer of the head gasket per se. Rather, she is a consumer of the larger product into which the head gasket is integrated.

So in the relevant sense, the head gasket is clearly a part of the car in a way that the flashlight battery is not part of the flashlight. But what does this difference amount to? We see three factors as being most salient in our commonsense judgment that the head gasket is so integrated into the vehicle as to be a component part of it, whereas the flashlight battery remains a separate and distinct product in its own right.

First, the flashlight battery is interchangeable in a way that a head gasket is not. Many different companies make flashlight batteries, and any one of them that is the right size can be used in the flashlight.[28] Indeed, the batteries that power the flashlight can be used interchangeably in a wide range of products having few features in common. Thus, I can easily take the batteries out of my flashlight and use them to power a radio, or a novelty talking fish, or a small personal electric fan, or any of a vast array of very different products that take the same size battery as my flashlight. By contrast, head gaskets are not interchangeable in this way; they are highly specialized. While replacement gaskets may be made by other companies besides the one that initially supplied the gasket to the auto-maker, each gasket is specifically engineered for a particular car. For instance, you cannot take the head gasket from a Honda Accord and put it into a Ford Taurus, even if the engines in the two cars are very similar in size. The criterion of interchangeability versus specialization seems relevant, then, to the question of whether an item is a separate product or a component of some other, more complex product.

Second, replacing the flashlight battery requires no specialized knowledge. The flashlight and its batteries are physically distinct enough that they can be separated easily and replaced by the consumer. The consumer is expected to change the batteries herself, in fact. By contrast, few consumers have the skills necessary to change their own head gaskets, and the acquisition of such skills is no trivial matter. In fact, the automobile manufacturer typically encourages consumers NOT to replace their own head gaskets. Instead, most car-makers have a certification system for identifying personnel with the proper aptitude for such jobs, and training programs to teach those skills. Ease of replaceability, then, seems to be a second factor that is relevant to the question of whether we have a component that is integrated into another product, or whether we have two separate products merely bundled together.

Third, a head gasket is engineered to fit the engine, but the flashlight is typically engi-neered to fit the battery. One would normally design a flashlight to take one of the several standard sizes of battery. Thus, one would decide whether one was designing a small, easily carried penlight, or a large, bright, durable flashlight suitable for security guards. This choice would dictate which SIZE of battery one's new flashlight would use, but by and large, one would typically design a flashlight to take SOME standard sized battery.[29] There is simply a standard, pre-existing, range of battery types available that the engineers of (non-disposable) flashlights can make use of when designing their product. On the other hand, with many automotive parts like the head gasket, the order of design runs the other direction, so to speak, with the component part being designed specifically for the product in which it will be used. One does not design an engine specifically to fit a certain, pre-existing head gasket. Rather, the engine is designed first, and its design dictates the design of the gasket. The fact that an engineer designs an item to fit into the larger product she is designing is a strong indication that the item is a part of the overall product, even if it is eventually supplied by an outside company. In other words, if item X's design is dictated by how it functions in the design of item Y, then item X is generally best seen as a component part of item Y.

So we have identified three main factors that distinguish the clear case of a head gasket, which is clearly a component of the vehicle, from the case of the battery, which is clearly a separate product that might nevertheless be "bundled" and sold with a flashlight. The first is a relative specialization. The second is ease of replacement. The third is what we might call the direction of the "engineering fit" between the item and the larger product—whether the item dictated the design of the product with which it is to be used, or whether the other product dictated its design. All of these factors seem to play a part in our impression that a flashlight battery is a separate product from the flashlight in which it is used, while a head gasket is a component of the engine in which it is used.

It is important to note that all three of these factors admit of degrees—none of them are all or nothing. First, an item may be more or less specialized, depending on how many other manufacturers make a suitable replacement. An item made only by one exclusive manufacturer is more specialized, and therefore less interchangeable than one which is made by a number of different manufacturers. Similarly, an item that can be installed on a larger number of different products is less specialized than an item that can only be installed on a smaller number of other products. Second, the ease of replacement is likewise a matter of degrees. At one extreme, it may require specialized equipment and proprietary information available only to persons licensed by the manufacturer of the larger product. A less extreme case would be an item that the average person cannot replace, but which can be replaced by someone who has above average mechanical skill and experience. Finally, the extent to which the design of the part is driven by the design of the larger product is a matter of degrees as well. The greater the number, extent, and importance of the constraints placed on the item by the design of the larger product, the more the item is integrated as a component of the larger product.

The fact that each of these factors admits of degrees implies that the property of being a component also admits of degrees. This is less counterintuitive than it may at first sound, if we think in terms of the notion of integration, which is a concept that does seem to admit of degrees. To be a component rather than a separate item is to be integrated into it in various ways, and integration does admit of degrees. Thus, an item is a component of another product to the degree that it

is integrated into that other product, where integration is defined in terms of the three factors we have discussed above—factors which admit of degrees. So while the ordinary uses of the term "component" does not make it apparent, it seems to us that the status of being a component is not, in fact, an all-or-nothing matter. This fact has an important implication, namely that there can be intermediate cases, in which an item is what we might call a "quasi-component." A quasi-component is not a separate product, although it is less fully integrated into the more complex product than a "full" component like a head gasket.

Interestingly, modern vehicle tires seem to be just such an intermediate case, a quasi-component, if you will. They are not separate products in the way that a battery is separate from a flashlight, but they are not as fully integrated into the vehicle as a head gasket is. In terms of interchangeability, modern vehicle tires seem to lie about midway between flashlight batteries and head gaskets. They are still interchangeable with tires of a specific type made by other companies (so that Ford could replace Firestone tires on its Explorers with similar tires made by Goodyear, for example). But they are rather more specialized than flashlight batteries. And they are significantly more specialized now than they were twenty or thirty years ago. For many vehicles, it is not enough simply to walk into a tire store and request a set of, say, 16-inch tires. In order to maintain the proper performance characteristics of the vehicle, it is often necessary to choose from a much more limited range of replacements.

Similarly, in terms of ease of replacement, tires lie somewhere between flashlight batteries and head gaskets. Like flashlight batteries, vehicle tires do require replacement. And unlike a head gasket, replacing tires does not require a major disassembly of the vehicle. But on the other hand, tires are rather unlike flashlight batteries in that very few consumers mount and balance their own tires. To be sure, the task does not require training or knowledge that is proprietary to the vehicle manufacturer or that is very much more demanding than changing spark plugs. The main barrier, it turns out, is equipment. But while the equipment needed to mount and balance tires is certainly out of reach of the average amateur mechanic, it is not out of the price range of vast numbers of small businesses and tire replacement franchises.

In terms of engineering direction of fit, tires again constitute an intermediate case. It is increasingly common for a vehicle manufacturer to contract with a tire maker to provide original equipment tires designed to fit the specifications of a particular vehicle. The case of the Ford Explorer, in fact, illustrates this development quite nicely. As we noted earlier, Ford provided specifications to Bridgestone/Firestone and approved the final design of the Firestone tires that were to be original equipment on the Explorer. Thus it is clear that the design of the Explorer exerted an important engineering influence over the design of the tires. Certainly the designer of an ordinary flashlight would not expect to exert that same level of influence over the design of the batteries to be supplied with it.

In fact, Ford's own engineers seem to have regarded the tires as a being a component of the complex vehicle they were designing. During the testing for the prototype for the Explorer. Ford engineers continually suggested ways to adapt the design of the tires to the vehicle as a whole in order to compensate for perceived vehicle performance weaknesses. And as we noted earlier, Ford's engineers used tire inflation pressure as a variable that was available for manipulation in their attempts to address the stability problems on the Explorer. The tires were not treated by Ford engineers as an independent product whose nature was already given, as batteries

are for the ordinary producers of flashlights, but as one element among others in the overall interaction of the vehicle that they were designing. This suggests that, wittingly or not, Ford was integrating the tires more fully into the vehicles they were producing. By these actions, Ford was helping to turn what may have once been a separate product into an item that is at least a quasi-component of the vehicle they were producing. By no means is Ford alone in this; Ford simply reflects what seems to be a trend in modern vehicle design toward seeing tires as an integral part of the ever more complex vehicles on which they are mounted. As vehicles become more complex, and as ever greater numbers of details come under engineering scrutiny, this trend is probably inevitable. Perhaps General Motors has already learned this lesson, for they recently became the first U.S. automaker to provide its own warranty for tires equipped on their vehicles.[30] Ironically, Ford is preparing to follow suit.[31]

V. MORAL RESPONSIBILITY FOR COMPONENT PARTS

It appears, then, that we should reject Nasser's claim that the Firestone tires are a completely separate product from the Ford Explorer. The reality is that they are at least a quasi-component of a very complex product of which Ford's engineers were the designers, and which was assembled by Ford Motor Company. In other words, the tires were, in very important respects, far more like a component than a separate product. If this conclusion is correct, then answering the question of what Ford's responsibility was for the defective tires requires an account of the responsibility of an assembler for defects in components supplied by another company.

We contend that an assembler retains an overarching moral responsibility for the product as a whole—what we shall call the "composite product"—a responsibility which is more than the sum of the responsibilities for each individual component. It is uncontroversial that the assembler bears responsibility for the actual assembly of the composite product from its various components and raw materials. This responsibility—call it "assembly responsibility"—is clearly something over and above the responsibility that the component makers have for making safe and non-defective components; it is the responsibility for assembling those components into a safe and non-defective composite product. The assembler also bears an unquestioned responsibility for the design of the composite product. Again, this responsibility—call it "design responsibility"—is a responsibility over and above the responsibility of the part makers for making safe and non-defective components; it is the responsibility for designing a safe and non-defective composite product into which those components will be integrated. Clearly, if things go wrong in the design or assembly of the composite product, the assembler is responsible. This is both common sense and, for the most part, the law as well.[32]

Both the design and assembly responsibilities of assemblers are widely recognized and explicitly stated in discussions of responsibility for product safety in the legal and business ethics literature. But what is less often noted, but equally implied by the assembler's overarching responsibility for the composite product, is a responsibility for the choice of components and suppliers thereof. The assembler has, as it were, ultimate responsibility for the composite product. This is because the composite product IS the assembler's product, and the assembler is just as fully responsible for it as any producer is for its product. And part of what the assembler does in producing the composite product is to choose appropriate components and to determine how they are to be integrated with

other components and raw materials to form the composite product. Call this third form of assembler responsibility "component selection responsibility." Notice that design responsibility implies (or perhaps derives from) a duty on the part of the assembler to design a composite product that is safe for consumers. Similarly, assembly responsibility implies (or derives from) a duty on the part of the assembler to assemble a composite product that is safe for consumers. By analogy then, we can conclude that component selection responsibility implies (or derives from) a duty on the part of the assembler to choose appropriate components to be integrated with other components and raw materials so as to produce a composite product that is safe for consumers.

To help support our claim that there is a duty of this third sort, let's consider a case in which an assembler clearly violates it. Suppose an assembler of airplanes has contracted to purchase fuel tanks from the lowest bidder. The lowest bidder, let us say, turns out to be a cut-rate metal fabrication company that has had well-documented and well-publicized quality-control problems in the recent past. Suppose that some of the fuel tanks supplied to the airplane assembler do in fact turn out to be defective, and that these defects lead to tragic accidents. Although it is unquestionable that the tank supplier acted wrongly in failing to correct known quality-control problems and consequently producing defective products, does that mean that the airplane assembler is in the clear, morally speaking? It seems quite obvious that the answer is no. The airplane assembler may be able to subcontract with another company to supply parts, but it cannot subcontract its ultimate moral responsibility for creating a safe product from whatever parts it chooses to use. Indeed, in the case before us, the assembler seems to have acted downright negligently, since it attempted to cut costs by using a cut-rate supplier that it knew (or should have known) produced low-quality components.

We assume that virtually everyone would agree that the aircraft assembler violated some duty. But what duty did the assembler violate? It did not violate any duty to design or assemble safe composite products. For, ex hypothesi, nothing went wrong in the design or assembly processes. What the assembler did was to act negligently in its choice of components. The fact that it seems clearly wrong for the assembler to have acted in this way supports the claim that there is a duty on the part of assemblers at least to exercise some degree of care in making decisions about what components to use in their composite products.

We conclude, then, that an assembler has a moral duty to its customers (at least) to take reasonable steps to ensure that it does not use defective components in its products, even when these are supplied by other companies. This seems to be the duty that the company using cut-rate fuel tanks has breached, and it seems to be the source of our intuitive judgment that such a company has acted immorally despite the fact that it produced no defective tanks. What it did produce was a defective airplane, and since the defect in the tanks became a defect in the airplanes in which the tanks were installed, the airplane assembler is at least partly guilty for producing defective airplanes. Because the components will become part of the larger product of the assembler, the assembler's duty to produce a safe product would appear, then, to imply a duty to guard against using defective components, even when they are supplied by other companies that have their own moral (and legal) obligations to guard against producing defective components.[33] Because this duty derives from the assembler's duty to ensure the safety of its own product, it cannot be simply shifted to the supplier.

The case of the airplane assembler represents the most straightforward way in which an assembler can violate its duty to choose appropriate components for assembly into a safe composite product: an assembler can be negligent in choosing components that it has reason to believe may be defective. There is, however, at least one other important way in which an assembler can violate this same duty.

Instead of choosing a component that the assembler has reason to believe is already defective, an assembler can negligently choose a component that may be reasonably expected to become defective under the use that the assembler proposes to make of it. For example, suppose that an assembler of space shuttle engines decides to cut costs by using O-rings that were made for the less harsh conditions of jet engines. The O-rings, let us say, are perfectly adequate for use in a jet engine. While there is, let us say, nothing inherently different about the function of an O-ring on a space shuttle engine, let us imagine that conditions in a space shuttle engine are such that they are likely to render anything less than very heavy duty O-rings brittle in a short time. Although there is, let us say, nothing technically wrong with either the design or assembly of the space shuttle engine or the O-rings, when the one is installed in the other, tragedy ensues. The non-defective O-rings become defective under the harsh conditions of the space shuttle engine, and consequently they fail. Now the assembler has not violated its design-related duty, nor its assembly-related duty, for, ex hypothesi, there has been no problem in either the design or the assembly of the engine. Nor has the assembler chosen a component that is defective in and of itself. Instead, the assembler has chosen a component that it should have known would be likely to become defective when used in the proposed way.[34]

Finally, we can imagine a more complicated kind of case that is a mixture of the two others.

In this kind of case, a dangerous situation arises because of a combination of morally dubious decisions by the assembler and a component that contains latent defects or relatively minor weaknesses. (We discuss this possibility not simply in order to make the discussion more complex, but because we believe that this mixed case bears important similarities to the Ford/Firestone case.) Suppose that Bill's Balloon Works is manufacturing a balloon with a suspended gondola for passengers. BBW anticipates that the balloon will be used to give short balloon rides to passengers, and that in most cases, the balloon's gondola will be filled to capacity. To secure the gondola to the balloon, BBW purchases lengths of rope from a rope-maker. Suppose that each length of rope will have to carry 490 pounds of weight when the balloon is loaded to capacity (which, as BBW anticipates, will be most of the time). Now, suppose that the rope supplier has two grades of heavy-duty rope. Grade A is rated up to 1,000 pounds, and grade B is rated up to 500 pounds. Suppose that grade A is much more expensive, and so, out of a desire to remain competitive and/or to increase its profit margin, BBW opts for grade B in order to cut costs.

Now as we have described the case, grade B is rated by the manufacturer to be appropriate for the use under consideration. However, the use BBW intends to make of it is at the outer edge of the rated capacity. Now suppose that the grade B rope that BBW purchased and used to secure the gondola turns out to have a very slight defect. Such a defect may never have been a problem if the rope had never been required to carry more than, say, 400 pounds, or if, on average, it had usually carried only 350 pounds, with only an occasional load of 490 pounds. However, at an almost constant load of 490 pounds, the undetected weakness causes the rope to break. Morally speaking, who is at fault?

Certainly the rope manufacturer must bear a sizable amount of moral (and, no doubt, legal) blame. After all, it supplied a rope that was defective even when used within its stated specifications. However, we think that it is clear that BBW's conduct has *also* been morally blameworthy. After all, BBW *knew* that it was not going to use the rope for loads in the midrange of the specifications, but rather at the very outer edge of what the rope-maker was willing to rate it. Now, it seems to us that, especially knowing what any responsible balloon maker must know about ropes, that BBW should know that IF there is any underlying weakness in the rope, using it at the edge of its rated capacity will exacerbate it.[35]

We contend that the assembler's duty to design a safe product includes a duty to take special care when using components in ways that could exacerbate any underlying weaknesses in its components—weaknesses that might exist undetected by the component part maker. The most straightforward way to discharge this duty would be to simply avoid such unexpectedly harsh uses of a component. Alternately, the assembler could undertake to have additional testing done to make sure that the component was free of defects which, though minor in some uses of the component, could lead to tragic component failure when the component is used in the way the assembler is considering. This is the duty that BBW has neglected when it made its conscious decision to use a component in a way that pushes up to the limits of what is rated as safe by the supplier when it could have used a much safer component instead. BBW has chosen to use the rope in a way that could be reasonably foreseen to exacerbate any latent undetected defects that may exist in it. Whether or not one would want to hold an assembler strictly liable for component defects that it had no practical way of knowing about, it certainly does seem reasonable to hold the assembler liable for actions that it knows or should know will exacerbate any latent, minor defects or weaknesses that might have gone unnoticed during testing predicated on a less harsh set of operating conditions. In short, while we certainly do not deny that the component maker has the obligation to ensure that its products are safe and free from defects, we contend that a manufacturer who makes use of component parts supplied by another company has a moral duty to guard against possible defects in component parts *especially when those parts are being used in ways that are out of the norm, and that can be reasonably expected to exacerbate any underlying weaknesses or defects that may not be apparent or dangerous when the component is used in a more standard way.*

At this point it is worth asking how quasi-components fit into this responsibility for component selection. Although it is tempting to think that the level of component choice responsibility should vary with the level of integration, there are reasons to reject this view. For what is important about the special responsibilities of assemblers is the question of choice. It is the assembler that has the choice about which components are to be used, and it is this choice that gives the assembler the responsibility to choose well. What separates an assembler from a mere retailer is that it makes choices about which components will be installed on the composite product it makes. This is a qualitatively different kind of decision from the decision that a mere retailer typically makes in deciding which product to sell, even if it is selling it bundled with its own product. Because the component is integrated into the composite product (and not merely sold along with it), the assembler's choices must address how the component will interact with the other components of the composite product. But these are just the choices that an assembler must also make about a quasi-component. What makes it a quasi-component instead of a separate product is the fact that it does interact with the other parts of the composite product in a way that a truly separate product does not. It is not a mere "black box" that delivers a specific output (like electric current) but whose other properties can be ignored.

To make matters a bit more concrete, return to the case of the Firestone tires and Ford Explorer. They were not merely a "black box" that could be counted upon simply to keep the wheel rims off the pavement but otherwise ignored. Instead, their performance characteristics were an important set of variables that had to be taken into account—and to some degree manipulated—by the engineers who were designing the composite product, namely the vehicle itself. Because it is integrated even to some extent into the composite product, questions about how the quasi-component will interact with the rest of the composite product arise and must be addressed. And they must be addressed by the assembler, who has a duty to be sure that they are addressed in the right way. In short, while a quasi-component is like a separate product in that it is somewhat more interchangeable and somewhat less specialized than a more paradigm case of a fully integrated component, it is like a true component in that its operational characteristics must be figured into the design and component choice decisions made by the assembler. Since the assembler must make the same kinds of choices about a quasi-component as about a more fully integrated component, and since the assembler's component choice responsibility derives from its duty to make such choices in a way that protects consumers, it appears that the assembler's duty with regard to quasi-components is not significantly different from its duty with regard to fully integrated components. In both cases, the duty is to make choices that will result in a safe and non-defective composite product.

VI. MEANWHILE, BACK AT FORD

There is a significant amount of evidence that Ford behaved in a manner similar to the balloon maker in our example. Its decision to lower the recommended inflation pressure of the Bridgestone/Firestone tires used on the Explorer from 35 to 26 p.s.i., while refusing to upgrade the construction of the tires to accommodate the greater stresses of use at these lower pressures, was similar to BBW's decision to use the lower grade of rope, even though it was going to be used at the edge of its zone of safe operation. In both cases, the assembler chose to make what might have been a safe use if only done occasionally in the typical operating condition of the component. In effect, the assembler in both cases decided to make what should have been a safety margin into the normal operational condition of the component.

It is well known to engineers, as well as to most of the driving public, that lower pressures in tires cause additional heat to build up and thus creates a greater potentiality for tire blowouts. In deciding to inflate the tires to a pressure that was at the very low end of the safe zone set by Bridgestone/Firestone, Ford assumed a much greater moral responsibility to make sure that the tires would remain safe under these new, harsher operating conditions. Ford seems clearly to have shirked this responsibility, especially since it knew that, according to its own specifications, the tires already had the lowest ratings for speed and temperature allowed by the Department of Transportation's Federal Motor Vehicle Safety Standard 109.[36] Even more damning is the fact that data available to Ford from the very initiation of its own tests using the Firestone tires indicated that the tires were not performing as expected. In fact, Goodyear, which had also been supplying Ford Explorers with tires that were made to specifications similar to those of the Firestone tires, refused to continue doing so in 1997, in large part because the company felt it could not meet the specifications and price demanded by Ford and still live up to their own quality standards.[37] This should have presented Ford executives with yet another red flag signaling both the potentiality for vehicle failures and their own responsibility to review their decision to continue using the low-rated Firestone tires while at the same time lowering the inflation pressure.

It turns out that these Goodyear tires provide an important clue about the cause of the failure of Firestone tires on Ford Explorers. The Goodyear tires, when equipped on Explorers and inflated to the same low pressures as the Firestones, performed somewhat better. This suggests that the Firestone tires were not as good as those made by Goodyear. On the other hand, there is evidence to suggest that when Firestone tires were installed on other vehicles, and inflated to more normal pressures, they did not experience a significantly higher failure rate than other tires. In fact, the Firestone tires apparently suffered a far greater failure rate from tread separation when mounted on Ford Explorers than on any other vehicles.

These two seemingly contradictory bits of evidence strongly suggest that there was indeed some sort of underlying weakness in the Firestone tires that caused them to succumb to tread separation at a somewhat greater rate than other tires of the same general class, but that this propensity was significantly greater when the tires were installed on Ford Explorers. The reason for this seems to be almost certainly Ford's decision to lower the recommended inflation pressure to 26 p.s.i. from a more typical 35 p.s.i. and its refusal to upgrade to a more expensive grade of tire that could better handle the additional strain associated with use at that lower pressure.[38]

The fact that the tires made by Goodyear seem to have held up somewhat better than those made by Firestone to this harsh use suggests that Firestone made a less durable tire than Goodyear. Whether or not the Firestone tires were defective in and of themselves is a difficult question, in part because our ordinary understanding of the concept of a "defect" is not well suited to situations in which we are dealing with differences between very small failure rates. Every product could be improved in some respects, and no product can be expected to be completely perfect. In practice, determining whether a product is defective often amounts to determining whether the product exhibits failures above what is considered a normal or acceptable rate.[39] The failure rates of Firestone tires on Ford Explorers were certainly abnormally high. But the fact that these elevated failure rates were strongly correlated with the Ford Explorer suggests that the "defect" was not an inherent property of the tires, but rather a complex situation created by the interaction of some underlying weakness or defect in the tires with the lower inflation pressures recommended for Ford Explorers.

Whether or not we decide that the underlying weaknesses that caused the Firestone tires to fail when subjected to the harsh conditions that Ford's engineers had mandated constitute a true defect may be, in the end, a question with no answer. What seems clear, however, is that a major contributing factor in the increased failure rate for Firestone tires on the Ford Explorer was Ford's decision to do what every educated member of the driving public knows is generally a very bad idea—to let some air out of the tires. Ford does not appear to have taken any extra steps to ensure against the possibility that flaws in the tires that might never have created an unsafe situation at inflation pressures closer to the middle of the safe range might well appear at pressures that push the limits (or at even lower pressures that would

predictably result from the typical American driver's unfortunate tendency to fail to keep a close watch on tire pressure). Indeed, there is considerable evidence to suggest that Ford looked the other way at evidence that suggested early on that the Firestone tires might not be up to the harsher task of running constantly at 26 rather than 35 p.s.i. In so doing, Ford violated a moral duty to select and use components—or quasi-components, if you will—that are and will remain safe when integrated into the composite product that they put into the hands of the consumer.

VII. CONCLUSION

We have argued that the suggestion that Ford is a mere retailer for tires is untenable. While tires fall into an intermediate category between a clear case of a separate product and a clear case of a component, the Firestone tires were sufficiently integrated into the design of the Explorer that Ford must assume a degree of responsibility for them that is greater than that of a mere retailer. They are, if not a true component, at least a quasi-component of the Ford Explorer. We have argued that the moral duty to produce safe products implies a moral duty on the part of assemblers to choose non-defective components (and this includes quasi-components) and to use them in ways that will not render them dangerous or defective. We have suggested that even if there was an underlying defect in the Firestone tires, Ford is still at least partly to blame because of its decision to use the tires in a way that it knew would tend to exacerbate any underlying and so far undetected defects. In the end, the evidence strongly suggests that an important contributing factor in the Firestone tires' elevated failure rate was Ford's decision to lower the pressure to which they would be inflated. In making this decision, Ford treated the tires as an integral part of the complex system that they were designing, changing their characteristics in order to effect a desired change elsewhere in the system. Tragically, their attempt to fix a problem with one aspect of the system seems to have contributed to the premature failure of another part of that system. It is ironic that Ford has been so successful in avoiding blame for the resulting tragedy by maintaining that the tires in question are a completely distinct product.

NOTES

Earlier drafts of this paper were read at the 11th annual meeting of the *Association for Practical and Professional Ethics* in Cincinnati, Ohio on March 3, 2002, and to an audience at Central Michigan University in the spring of 2001. The authors wish to thank the discussants there for providing a number of comments and criticisms that were helpful in further developing the arguments presented in this paper. Much of the paper was written while Dan Palmer was a Post-Doctoral Fellow at Central Michigan University's Center for Applied, Professional and Practical Ethics at Central Michigan University, and the authors would like to express their gratitude for the support provided by the Center and by CMU.

1. As fate would have it, Firestone had also presided over the largest recall of tires in U.S. history when it called back 14.5 million Firestone 500 tires in 1978.
2. "Firestone Tires Recalled," *CNNfn*, August 9, 2000. Http://cnnfn.cnn.com/2000/08/09/news/fireston e_recall.
3. Ibid.
4. Sara Nathan, "Tires Linked to 29 More Deaths," *USA Today*, December 7, 2000, p. 3B. A comprehensive chronology of the Ford/Firestone tire crisis, including references to the relevant NHTSA figures, court cases, and internal company memos, can be found at the *Public Citizen* web site, http://www.citizen.org/index.cfm.
5. Information concerning Ford's knowledge of these stability concerns can be found in James Healey and Sara Nathan. "Further Scrutiny Puts Ford in the Hot Seat, *USA Today*, September 21, 2000. http://www.usatoday.com/money/consumer/autos/mauto 850htm. "Report Ford Passed Up Improvement,"

Yahoo! News, October 18, 2000. http:// dailynews. yahoo.com/h/ap/20001018/bs/ford_explorers_1 .html, and *Public Citizen*, op. cit.
6. John Greenwald, "Tired of Each Other," *Time*, June 4, 2001, pp. 51–56.
7. See Keith Bradsher, "Documents on Design of Explorer Reveal a Series of Compromises," *New York Times*, December 7, 2000, pp. A1 and C6, Greenwald, op. cit., and *Public Citizen*, op. cit.
8. For a history of the lawsuits related to the Ford/Firestone Tire Crisis, see *Public Citizen*, op. cit.
9. Thomas Fogarty, "Can Courts' Cloak of Secrecy Be Deadly? Judicial Orders Protecting Companies Kept Tire Case Quiet," *USA Today*, October 16, 2000, p. 1–2B.
10. See, for instance, Matthew Stannard, "Ford, Firestone Knew Tires Were Bad, Suit Alleges," *San Francisco Chronicle*, August 30, 2000. http:www.sfgate. com/cgi-bin/article.cgi?file=/chronicle/archive/2000/08/30/MN19328.DTL, as well as the summery of the various internal documents related to this case that can be found at the Public Citizen web site noted above.
11. James Healey, "Firestone Leaves an Indelible Mark," *USA Today*, December 26, 2000, p. 2B.
12. Karen Miller, "Memo: Ford Had Wrong Tires in Mideast," *Yahoo! Business News*, October 19, 2000. http://dailynews.yahoo.com/h/ap/20001016/bs/ti re_deaths_middle_east_1.html, and Alfonso Chardy, "Venezuela Inquiry: Firestone, Ford Hid Tire Flaws," *The Miami Herald*, October 8, 2000. http://www.herald.com/content/today/news/national/digdocs/019021.htm.
13. Lawrence Ulrich, *Detroit Free Press*, September 25, 2000. http://www.freep.com/money/business/tire25_20000925.html.
14. Jennifer Bott, "The Big Blowout: Maneuvering by Bridgestone/Firestone, Ford May Have Made a Bad Situation Worse," *Auto.com*, October 5, 2000 and John Greenwald, op. cit.
15. "Firestone Letter to Belo & KHOU Executives," February 10, 2000. http://www.khou.com/news/stories/1290.html.
16. Janet Fix, "Conflict Preceded Firestone Recall," *Auto.com*, September 26, 2000. http://www.auto.com/autonews/tire26_20000926.htm.
17. Earle Eldridge and Thomas Fogarty, "Firestone Puts 'Best Theory' Forward," *USA Today*, September 13, 2000. http://www.usatoday.com/money/consumer/autos/mauto836.htm.
18. Jennifer Bott, op. cit.
19. For convenience, we will often simply say "Firestone tires" to refer to these models of tires which were installed on the Ford Explorers. Similarly, we sometimes will use "Firestone" to refer to Bridgestone/Firestone.

20. Early common law required retailers to bear full legal liability to consumers for any defective products. In cases where the retailer was a middleman for products created by a separate manufacturer, consumers could not sue the manufacturer directly. The reason for this was a doctrine known as "privity of contract." Essentially this doctrine conceptualized product liability as an aspect of a retail contract. Since a consumer had no such contract with a manufacturer unless she bought directly from it, she could only sue the retailer if the product was defective. Obviously this was exactly backwards relative to common sense moral intuition. This counter-intuitiveness, together with some utilitarian public policy arguments, led courts gradually to tear down the so-called "privity barrier" and allow consumers to sue the ultimate manufacturer of a product, no matter how many middlepersons were in the way. For more on the history of product liability law, and especially the judicial reasoning behind its evolution, see David Owen, M. Stuart Madden, and Mary Davis, *Madden & Owen on Products Liability,* 3rd edition (St. Paul, MN: WestGroup, 2000), volume 2, and Jerry J. Phillips, *Products Liability in a Nutshell,* 5th edition (St. Paul, MN: WestGroup, 1998).

21. For a comprehensive discussion of the legal issues, see Madden and Owen, op. cit., volume 2, pp. 335–60.

22. Madden and Owen, pp. 335 and 351.

23. Second Restatement of Torts, Section 400, comment d.

24. Richard D. Cunningham, "Apportionment Between Partmakers and Assemblers in Strict Liability," *The University of Chicago Law Review,* 49 (1982) pp. 544–63.

25. Of course there are further questions one might ask about whether Firestone could have produced a defective product and been blameless. Here moral intuitions and legal practices may part company. Intuitively, it seems at least prima facie unreasonable to blame a company for something that it could not have avoided; thus, if it were the case that there was no way for Firestone to detect or prevent the defects in its tires, then some people might want to hold Firestone *morally* blameless. (Holding an agent blameworthy for something that was, ex hypothesi, impossible for it to avoid may seem to violate the Kantian doctrine that ought implies can.) However, the law of product liability assigns strict liability to producers, so that a producer is liable for defects in its products regardless of whether it would have been possible to avoid or detect them, and regardless of how much care the producer exercised in its design and production process. The rationale for the legal doctrine of strict liability is partly utilitarian: as a matter of public policy, the doctrine provides maximum incentive to producers to go beyond ordinary standards of care. However,

there is also a fairness rationale as well: even though it may have been, ex hypothesi, impossible to prevent or detect, it is still fair to hold the producer liable for it, since the main alternative is to allow the consumer to bear the full brunt of the damage without compensation. In this paper we will focus mainly on cases in which the producer could have detected the defect; all of our hypothetical examples will be of this sort, and we will assume that Firestone and/or Ford could have detected or prevented whatever defects caused tragedies under discussion here. (This assumption is a reasonable one since, as we noted in section I, some tests done by Ford and Firestone did in fact suggest a problem with the tires.) By keeping to cases in which the producer could have done something to detect or prevent the defect in its product, we will keep the moral judgments pretty much in line with the legal judgments. Thus we will avoid the tough but interesting question of whether the legal doctrine of strict product liability is morally justified.

26. The reasons that we will suggest for thinking that Firestone tires are a component of the Ford Explorer rather than a separate product suggest a more general theory of what we might call "product metaphysics." However, we will not go on to develop such a theory in full in this paper. While the considerations we will offer here are, we think, sufficient to refute Ford's suggestion that the tires are a separate product and thus "not Ford's responsibility," on their own they do not provide necessary conditions for something's being a part of another product.

27. Unless, of course, they are the same company. For the purposes of this paper, we are imagining that one company, say Joe's Flashlight Factory, has agreed to have its product bundled with batteries produced by a separate company, say Betty's Battery Works.

28. Compare this, for instance, to the specialized batteries that are used in some electronic devices, such as cellular phones, laptop computers, etc. These seem to be much more integrated into the respective devices, and consequently we are more likely to regard them as components of larger products than as products in their own right.

29. Compare the disposable flashlights popular several years ago: these had non-replaceable batteries which, for all the consumer might care, could be in any novel size or configuration. A battery of this kind is integrated into the flashlight in a way that the replaceable battery is not.

30. Lawrence Ulrich, op. cit.

31. News Archive, *Automotive Fleet,* January 3, 2001. http://www.fleet-central.com/af/passnews_c.cfm?rank=761.

32. The law of products liability has reached a fairly clear consensus about cases in which a non-defective component is rendered defective and/or dangerous

by the assembler. In a number of important decisions, courts have held that if an assembler's own actions create a dangerous or defective situation from a component that was non-defective as supplied by the supplier, then the supplier is not at fault. In *City of Franklin V. Badger Ford Truck Sales* (58 Wis. 2d 641, 207 N.W. 2d 866 [Wisconsin Supreme Court, 1973], the court found that if a defect exists in the component part at the time that it is supplied to the assembler, then the component part maker is liable, but if the component part is "subject to further processing or substantial change, or where the . . . injury is not directly applicable to defective construction of the component part" then the component part maker is not liable. This assessment is echoed in *Lee v. Butcher Boy* (169 Cal. App. 3d. 215 [California, 1985]), in which a plaintiff whose hand was injured in a meat grinder sued the manufacturer of the motor. The suit was denied on the ground that the motor itself was not defective, but rather the defect arose because of how the motor was incorporated into the meal grinder itself. The court wrote that "We have found no case in which a component part manufacturer who had no role in designing the finished product and who supplied a non-defective component part, was held liable for the defective design of the finished product." These cases are nicely summarized and commented upon in David Owen, John Montgomery, and W. Page Keeton, *Products Liability and Safety: Case Materials*, Third Edition (Westbury, N.Y.: Foundation Press, 1996), pp. 755–63.

33. For the most part, we will not try to answer the important but difficult questions about the nature and stringency of this implied duty. For our present purposes, we will simply draw the weakest and thus least controversial conclusion from the example, namely that a company which is "assembling" a product from other components and raw materials has a duty to choose components that are safe for the uses it proposes to make of them. No doubt there is also a utilitarian/public policy case to be made for imposing a legal (if not moral) duty of strict liability here as well, for such a duty would give the assembler additional incentive to be careful. Since the component maker is also under a legal duty of strict liability, the consumer would be doubly protected by having two separate businesses doing everything possible to guard against defects. For an interesting discussion of the pros and cons of various rules for locating the legal liability for defective component parts, see Richard D. Cunningham, op, cit. Be that as it may, our conclusions will rest only on what we think is the uncontroversial claim that an assembler can be morally culpable for using a defective component part supplied by another company if it knew or should have known of a significant danger that the components were defective.

34. Notice that bad design decisions can also cause a component that was not defective as supplied to become defective. If a bad design places too much stress on a particular component, then that component may in fact fail, and it may do so in some, but not in all, of the products. In such a case, the defect might well appear to be the fault of the component maker. After all, if the component maker had supplied a more durable component, it might well not have failed. Yet the component may be perfectly fine when used in any number of other designs.

35. This claim does not necessarily imply that BBW would be at fault if it had only used the rope to carry, say 200 or 300 pounds, and it still failed. That question seems more controversial. A case could certainly be made either way: on the one hand, holding assemblers strictly liable for defects in component parts, while perhaps offending against the "ought implies can" principle, might be sound public policy. For it would give assemblers maximum incentive to ensure that the components used are safe and free from defects. On the other hand, holding assemblers strictly liable for defects in component parts of which it has no reason at all to be suspicious may seem to be both unfair and inefficient, for it might well require each assembler to set up its own testing program for every component or raw material that is being used. (Of course for ropes, such testing may present no major difficulties, but certainly some components are sufficiently sophisticated that requiring an assembler to do its own testing on them would probably constitute an unreasonable burden.)

36. See Ralph Vartabedian, "Getting a Grip on Tire Ratings is No Easy Task," *latimes.com*, September 20, 2000. http://www.latimes.com/cgi-bin/print.cgi.

37. See James Grimaldi and Frank Swoboda, "Ford Offers Tire Data Comparison," *The Washington Post*, September 18, 2000, p. A10.

38. It is also important to keep in mind the strong probability that the poor stability characteristics of the Ford Explorer made rollover far more likely once a tread-separation blow out had occurred. Although this paper focuses mainly on the issue of responsibility for the tread separation in the first place, it is important to note that in a better designed vehicle, a tire blow-out does not result in a vehicle rollover at anything like the alarming rate experienced by the Ford Explorer. Thus, once we determine how to apportion moral and legal blame for the tire blow-outs, there will remain the important issue of apportioning moral and legal blame for the resulting tragic accidents.

39. Recall that the vast majority of the Firestone tires in question never failed or gave rise to any problems for drivers. Indeed, by one estimate, less than 1 per 100,000 of the Firestone tires under consideration failed: see Ulrich, op. cit.

Case Study

A. H. Robins: The Dalkon Shield

Al Gini
T. Sullivan

On August 21, 1985, A. H. Robins of Richmond, Virginia—the seventeenth largest pharmaceutical house in America and corporately rated as number 392 in the Fortune 500—filed for reorganization under chapter 11 of the 1978 Federal Bankruptcy Code. On the surface, Robins seemed to be a thriving company. Its popular products, including Robitussin cough syrup, Chap Stick lip balm, and Sergeant's flea and tick collars for cats and dogs, generated record sales in 1985 of $706 million with a net income in excess of $75 million. Robins' petition for protection under Chapter 11 stems directly from the "blitz of litigation" over a product it has not produced since 1974, the Dalkon Shield intrauterine birth control device. At the time it filed for bankruptcy Robins had been deluged with more than 12,000 personal injury lawsuits charging that the Dalkon Shield was responsible for countless serious illnesses and at least 20 deaths among the women who used it.

In many ways this bankruptcy petition mimes and mirrors (Johns-) Manville's unprecedented request for reorganization in 1982. Manville, the nation's, if not the world's, largest producer of asbestos, claimed that it was succumbing to a "blitz of toxic torts" and therefore could not carry on with business as usual. In August 1982 Manville was facing 16,500 suits on behalf of people who claimed to have contracted cancer and other diseases caused by asbestos and the asbestos-related products that the company produced.

Like Manville, A. H. Robins is defending and explaining its actions by claiming that it simply cannot go on and fulfill its immediate and potential obligations to its stockholders, customers, employees, and litigants (claimants) unless it takes dramatic financial action. In filing for Chapter 11 Robins has won at least temporary respite from its legal woes. Although the company will continue operating during the reorganization, all suits now pending are frozen and no new suits can be filed. While the company develops a plan to handle its liabilities, it is up to the bankruptcy courts to deal with all present claims as well as to establish guidelines for the handling of any future claims.[1] Whatever the final results, the Dalkon Shield case may well turn out to be the worst product liability nightmare that a U.S. drugmaker or major corporation has ever suffered.[2] The A. H. Robins company is essentially a family owned and operated organization. The original company was founded by Albert Hartley Robins, a registered pharmacist, in 1866 in Richmond, Virginia. His grandson, E. Claiborne Robins, built and directed the company into a multinational conglomerate which was able to obtain Fortune 500 status by the middle of the twentieth century. While E. Claiborne Robins remains Chairman of the Board, E. Claiborne Junior is now the firm's president and CEO. Both the family and the company are much liked and respected in their home state. Generations of employees have repeatedly claimed that E. Claiborne Senior was at his worst a "benevolent despot" and at his best a kind and gentle man sincerely interested in quality control as well as his employees' well being. By all reports E. Claiborne Junior seems to be following in his father's footsteps. Moreover, the family's kindness has not been limited to its employees. In 1969 E. Claiborne Senior personally donated over $50 million to the University of Richmond. Since then the Robins family has given at least $50 million more to the university, and additional millions to other universities and to diverse other causes. In December 1983 *Town and Country* magazine listed Claiborne Senior among the top five of "The Most Generous Americans."

Both the family and the company take pride in having "always gone by the book" and always giving their customers a good product at a fair price. In its 120 years of operation the company had done business without having a single product-liability lawsuit filed against it. Critics now claim that Robins has been involved in a directly ordered, prolonged institutional cover-up of the short- and long-term effects of the use of the Dalkon Shield. Moreover, many critics, claim that, more than just stonewalling the possible side effects of the Shield, Robins is guilty of marketing a product they knew to be relatively untested, undependable, and therefore potentially dangerous. Robins is accused of having deceived doctors, lied to women, perjured itself to federal judges, and falsified documentation to the FDA. According to Morton Mintz, Robins' most outspoken critic, thousands, probably tens of thousands, of women who trusted the doctors who trusted A. H. Robins paid a ghastly price for the use of the Dalkon Shield: chronic pelvic infections, impairment or loss of childbearing capacity, children with multiple birth defects, unwanted abortions, recurring health problems, and chronic pain.

IUDs are among the most ancient forms of contraception, known for more than two thousand years. Exactly how an IUD prevents conception is not known. It may interfere with the fertilization of the eggs, but most experts believe that when inserted into the uterus it prevents pregnancy by making it difficult for a fertilized egg to attach itself to the wall of the uterus. Over the centuries the materials used in the fabrication of IUDs include ebony, glass, gold, ivory, pewter, wood, wool, diamond-studded platinum, copper, and plastic.[3] The Dalkon Shield was developed by Dr. Hugh J. Davis, a former professor of obstetrics and gynecology at the Johns Hopkins University, and Irwin Lerner, an electrical engineer. In 1970 they sold their rights to the Shield to Robins, who agreed to pay royalties on future sales and $750,000 in cash. Between 1971 and 1974 Robins sold 4.5 million Dalkon Shields around the world, including 2.85 million in the United States.

By the late 1960s large numbers of women had become concerned about the safety of the Pill. These women formed an ever-growing potential market for an alternative means of birth control. Many of these women switched to "barrier" methods of birth control, particularly the diaphragm, which, when used with spermicidal creams or jellies, can be highly effective, though inconvenient. Others turned to IUDs, which, although convenient, previously had been considered unsafe—causing pelvic infections, irregular bleeding, uterine cramps, and accidental expulsion. Robins leapt at an opportunity to develop a new market with their product. The company's task was to convince physicians that the Shield was as effective as oral contraceptives in preventing pregnancies and that it was safer, better designed, and afforded greater resistance to inadvertent expulsion from the uterus than other IUDs.[4]

In January 1971 Robins began to sell the Dalkon Shield, promoting it as the "modern, superior," "second generation" and—most importantly—"safe" intrauterine device for birth control. The Shield itself is a nickelsized plastic device that literally looks like a badge or a shield with spikes around the edges and a thread-sized "nylon tail string," which allowed both the wearer and the physician a means to guarantee that the device had not been expelled. The Shield was relatively inexpensive. The device itself sold for between $3.00 and $4.50 (its production costs were an incredibly low figure of $.25 a Shield). The only other cost associated with the Shield was the doctor's office fee for insertion and a recommended yearly pelvic examination. Dr. Hugh Davis claimed that the Dalkon Shield was the safest and most effective IUD because it is "the only IUD which is truly anatomically engineered for optimum uterine placement, fit, tolerance, and retention."[5] Davis was able to persuade a large number of physicians of the effectiveness of the Shield in an article he published in the "Current Investigation" section of the *American Journal of Obstetrics and Gynecology* in February 1970. The article described a study conducted at the Johns Hopkins Family Planning Clinic involving 640 women who had worn the Shield for one year. His analysis was based on 3,549 women-months of experience. Davis cited five pregnancies, ten expulsions, nine removals for medical reasons, and three removals for personal reasons. His startling results: tolerance rate (non-expulsion), 96 percent; pregnancy rate, 1.1 percent. The A. H. Robins Company reprinted no fewer than 199,000 copies of the Davis article for distribution to physicians.[6]

While various executives strongly recommended that other studies be commissioned to validate Davis's results, in January 1971 Robins began to market and sell the Shield on the basis of Davis's limited analysis. Robins' decision to produce and sell the Shield based on Davis's statistics may not coincide with the highest standards of scientific research, but it did not violate any FDA statutes and was therefore perfectly legal. At the time Robins produced the Shield, FDA had no regulatory policies in force regarding IUDs of any kind. While FDA had the authority to regulate the production, testing, and sales of all new prescriptions, it could only *recommend* testing on new medical devices. It could not monitor, investigate, or police a device unless charges of lack of effectiveness, injury, or abuse were formally leveled against the device or the producer.

In December 1970 Robins commissioned a major long-term study to reinforce Davis's results. The study concentrated on ten clinics, seven in the United States and one each in Canada, Nova Scotia, and British Columbia. Between December 1970 and December 1974 (six months after Robins suspended domestic sales) 2,391 women were fitted with the Shield. The first results came out in November 1972, and only about half of the women enrolled in the study. The statistics showed a sixteen month pregnancy rate of 1.6 percent. The Robins home office was more than pleased and immediately communicated this information to its sales staff. Thirteen months later, with all the women now participating in the program, less happy figures began to show up. The pregnancy rate after six months was 2.1 percent; after twelve months, 3.2 percent; after eighteen months, 3.5 percent; and after twenty-three months, 4.1 percent. In a final report published as a confidential internal document in August 1975 the final figures and results were even more devastating. The pregnancy rate after six months was 2.6 percent; after twelve months, 4.2 percent; after eighteen months, 4.9 percent; and after twenty-four months 5.7 percent. Two of the scientists involved in this project submitted a minority report claiming that the Shield was even less effective than these already damaging figures indicated. They claimed that the pregnancy rate during the first year was much higher; after six months, 3.3 percent; and after twelve months, 5.5 percent. This twelve-month pregnancy rate is exactly five times *higher than* the rate Robins advertised and promoted—1.1 percent—to catapult the Shield to leadership in the IUD business.[7] This minority report was never disclosed to the medical community by Robins. Nor did Robins communicate these results to its own sales force. It did report some of these findings to FDA in July 1974, but only after the company had suspended domestic sales earlier that June.

Soon after the Shield entered the marketplace, independent research results began to appear in both national and foreign journals of medicine. In 1970 and 1971 Dr. Mary O. Gabrielson, working out of clinics in San Francisco and Oakland, did an eighteen-month study on 937 women with results that Robins would not want to advertise. The rate of medical removals was 26.4 percent; the pregnancy rate, 5.1 percent. In 1973 the *British Medical Journal* published a study showing a 4.7 percent pregnancy rate in Shield users.[8] Again because there was no law requiring disclosure of this new research information, Robins did not rush to inform the general public, the medical community, or the FDA.

At the same time that the Robins Company was receiving research results pointing to poor statistical effectiveness of the Shield, they also began to receive more and more "single physician experience" reports warning and complaining about some of the medical consequences from using the Shield. These physician's reports plus the statistics generated from controlled clinical reports began to portray the Shield as neither effective nor safe.

The primary cause of concern for Shield users proved to be a much higher incidence of uterine/pelvic bacterial infections. PID (pelvic inflammatory disease) is a highly virulent and very painful, difficult to cure, life threatening infection, which more often than not impairs or destroys a woman's ability to bear children. Of those women who conceived with the Shield in place (approximately 110,000 in the United States), an estimated 60 percent of them miscarried after suffering severe bacterial infections (PID). In 1974 FDA reported that over 245 women in their fourth to sixth month of pregnancy suffered the relatively rare bacterially-induced miscarriage called septic spontaneous abortions. For fifteen women, these septic abortions were fatal.[9] Moreover, hundreds of women throughout the world who had conceived while wearing the Shield gave birth prematurely to children with grave congenital defects, including blindness, cerebral palsy, and mental retardation.[10]

Scientists now believe that the systemic cause for these virulent forms of bacterial infection is the nylon tail of the Shield itself. The Dalkon Shield tail string runs between the vagina, where bacteria are always present, and the uterus, which is germ free. It then passes through the cervix, where cervical mucus is the body's natural defense against bacterial invasion of the uterus. Robins claimed that cervical mucus would stop all germs from entering and infecting the uterus. To the naked eye, the Dalkon Shield tail string is an impervious monofilament, meaning that bacteria on it could not get into it. Actually, however, it is a cylindrical sheath encasing 200 to 450 round monofilaments separated by spaces. While the string was knotted at both ends, neither end was actually sealed. Therefore, any bacteria that got into the spaces between the filaments would be insulated from the body's natural antibacterial action while being drawn into the uterus by "wicking," a phenomenon similar to that by which a string draws the melting wax of a candle to the flame. Scientists believe that the longer the Shield and its string/tail is in place, the greater the chances for its deterioration and infiltration, thereby inducing infection in the uterus. Scientists now also contend that the "syndrome of spontaneous septic abortions" that occurred to women who had the Shield in place in the early second trimester of their pregnancy was caused by the tail string. That is, radical and sudden infection occurred with the uterus expanded to the point where it tended to pull the tail string into itself thereby bringing on instant, often lethal, contamination.[11]

In the summer of 1983 the Centers for Disease Control in Atlanta and the FDA recommended that all women still using the Shield should contact their physicians and have it immediately removed. The Agencies found that women using the Shield had a fivefold increase in risk for contracting PID as compared to women using other types of IUDs. No change in contraceptive practice was recommended for women using any other type of IUD.[12] In April 1985 two studies funded by the National Institute of Health announced yet another dire warning. These studies showed that childless IUD wearers who have had PID run a higher risk of infertility if their devices were Shields than if they were other makes.[13]

Throughout all of this, A. H. Robins officials appeared to be unaware of, or at best indifferent to, the issues, facts, and effects of their product. The company assumed the position of complete denial of any intentional wrongdoing or any malicious intent to evade full public disclosure of pertinent medical information about the safety and effectiveness of the Shield. On numerous separate occasions both in public forums and under oath, E. Claiborne Robins, Senior, has claimed near ignorance of Robins' sixteen-year involvement with the Dalkon Shield. At a series of depositions taken in 1984 Robins Senior swore that he was unable to recall ever having discussed the Shield with his son, the company's chief executive officer and president. When asked, "You certainly knew, when you started marketing this device, that PID was a life-threatening disease, did you not?" Robins testified: "I don't know that, I never thought of it as life-threatening." Did he know it could destroy fertility? "Maybe I should, but I don't

know that. I have heard that, but I am not sure where." Carl Lunsford, senior vice-president for research and development, swore he could recall no "expression of concern" by any company official about PID, and he didn't remember having "personally wondered" about the toll it was taking. He had not tried to find out how many users had died. He had not "personally reviewed" *any* studies on the Shield's safety or effectiveness. When asked if he had "any curiosity" regarding the millions of dollars the company had been paying out in punitive damages to settle lawsuits, his answer was, "No."[14] The case of William Forrest, vice-president and general counsel of A. H. Robins, further strains belief. He has been described by E. Claiborne Junior as one of the company's "two most instrumental" persons in the Dalkon Shield situation. He was in effect in charge of all Shield matters and related legal issues for over a decade. In a trial proceeding, Forrest testified that his wife had worn a Shield until it was surgically removed. She had also had a hysterectomy. Although IUD removals and hysterectomies were frequently connected and simultaneous events for many infected Shield wearers, Forrest steadfastly denied any connection in his wife's case and gave vague and widely differing dates for the two events. He and his wife, he explained, did not discuss such matters in detail. Indeed, Forrest gave a series of confusing accounts of his wife's hysterectomy and its possible relationship to the Shield she had worn.

Q: Did her doctor advise her that her hysterectomy was in any way related to the Dalkon Shield?

A: Not that I know of, no, sir.

Q: Did you ever ask her that?

A: I don't recall. I may have asked her that, I don't recall the doctor telling her that. . . .

Q: . . . Are you telling the ladies and gentlemen of the jury that you and your wife have never had a discussion concerning whether or not the Dalkon Shield played a part in her hysterectomy?

A: Well, certainly, as I indicated to you, we have very general discussions. Now, if I asked her whether that played a part, I don't recall specifically if I did. If I did, to my knowledge, there was no indication that it did.[15]

The company's response to all claims of faulty product design and limited testing procedures has been counter assertions or counter claims regarding the faulty or improper use of the product by the user or the physician. The company has steadfastly maintained that there were no special dangers inherent in the device. In a report to FDA they stated: "Robins believes that serious scientific questions exist about whether the Dalkon Shield poses a significantly different risk of infection than other IUDs." Their continuous theme has been that doctors, not the device, have caused any infections associated with the Shield. The company was committed to the notion that pregnancy and removal rates could be kept extremely low by proper placement of the Shield. They also contended that user abuse played a part in the Shield's supposed malfunctioning. They defined user abuse as poor personal hygiene habits, sexual promiscuity or excessive sexual activity, or physical tampering with the device itself.

According to three different independent investigative reports,[16] the company's public face of calm denial and counterargument masked an internal conspiring to conceal information from the public, the court system, and the FDA. These reports (books) claim documented evidence of the multilevel cover-up. They claim that Robins quashed all documentation debating and contesting Dr. Hugh Davis's celebrated pregnancy rate of only 1.1

percent, and that Robins knew of the real significance and traumatic effect of the wicking process of the tail string but did nothing about it. Not only did the company know that the nylon cord used on the tail could degenerate and cause infection, but as early as the summer of 1972 the company was warned in writing by one of its chief consultants, Dr. Thad Earl, that pregnant women should have the Shield immediately removed to avoid "abortion and septic infection." These reports also contend that on at least three separate occasions executives and officials of Robins lost or destroyed company files and records specifically requested by the Federal Appellate Courts and the FDA.

By May 1974 Robins could no longer avoid the evidence presented to it by FDA implicating the Shield in numerous cases of spontaneous septic abortions and in the death of at least four women as a result. These findings were disclosed in a letter sent by the company to 120,000 doctors. In June 1974 Robins suspended the U.S. distribution and sale of the Shield. In January 1975 Robins called back and completely removed the Shield from the market. The company termed the action a "market withdrawal," not a recall, because it was undertaken voluntarily and not at the direct order of FDA. In September 1980 Robins again wrote the medical community suggesting as a purely precautionary measure that doctors remove the Shield from their patients. In October 1984 Robins initiated a $4 million television, newspaper, and magazine advertising campaign warning and recommending that all women still wearing the device have it removed at Robins's expense. In April 1985 Robins publicly set aside $615 million to settle legal claims from women who had used the Shield. This reserve is the largest provision of its kind to date in a product liability case. In May 1985 a jury in Wichita, Kansas, awarded nearly $9 million to a woman who had charged that the use of the Shield caused her to undergo a hysterectomy. The award was the largest ever made in the history of litigation involving the Shield. Officials of the Robins Company felt that adverse decisions of this magnitude could mean that their $615 million fund would prove to be inadequate. On August 21, 1985, Robins filed for Chapter 11 protection, citing litigation relating to the Shield as the main cause for its actions. Company spokesmen said that it hoped that the Federal Bankruptcy Court in Richmond would set up a payment schedule that would enable it to survive while insuring that victims "would be treated fairly." E. Claiborne Robins, Junior, called it "essential that we move to protect the company's economic viability against those who would destroy it for the benefit of a few."[17] The intriguing financial irony in all of this is that when Robins filed for Chapter 11 it had already spent, at a conservative estimate, $500 million in settlements, litigation losses, and legal fees for a product it had only manufactured for three years and from which it had only realized $500,000 in real profits![18]

In all candor it must be remembered that Robins's actions are not without danger. To the extent that Robins is using Chapter 11 as a shelter against the rush of product-liability litigation, the company is nevertheless taking a gamble. Robins must now operate under the eye of a federal bankruptcy judge, and as Lawrence King, Professor of Law at NYU, has said in regard to the Manville case, "Once you file, there is always a risk of liquidation."[19] For example, as part of their reorganization arrangement with the court, Robins agreed to a class action procedure in which they would begin a 91 nation advertisement campaign to announce to all former users their right to file a claim for compensation for any health problems that may have been caused by the Shield. All potential claimants are given a case number and sent a questionnaire to determine if they qualify for a financial settlement. As of June 1986 more than 300,000 claims have been filed against Robins![20] Numbers such as these may completely overwhelm the bankruptcy court's ability to reorganize and reestablish the company on a sound financial basis.

Given all of this data, perhaps there is only one thing we can say with certainty in regard to Robins's production of the Dalkon Shield: "In the pharmaceutical world, products that fail can cripple companies as well as people."[21]

AN UPDATE

Since filing for Chapter 11 in 1985 A. H. Robins has received at least three serious takeover bids. Two of these bids were made by the Rorer Group of Philadelphia and Sanoli the Paris-based pharmaceutical and cosmetics house. Both were rejected primarily because of their inability or unwillingness to guarantee the $2.475 billion escrow fund that the court has mandated be established for the payment of all possible liability and injury claims now pending against Robins.[22] On July 26, 1988, however, Judge Robert R. Merhige approved a plan for the acquisition of Robins by American Home Products of New York. Under this plan, American Home would pay Robins' shareholders about $700 million in American Home stock and provide for most of the Dalkon Shield trust fund with Aetna Life and Casualty Co. contributing $425 million. The judge decreed that since 94 percent of the Shield claimants and 99 percent of the Robins' stockholders approved of the plan, the reorganization, pending appeal, would become final on August 25, 1988.[23]

Yet even in an era of corporate raiders and mergers, why would so many major organizations want to take over a company bogged down in bankruptcy proceedings?

The answer lies in such mundane but popular items as Robitussin and Dimetapp cold medicines, Chap Stick lip balm and Sergeant's flea-and-tick collars. These are among the products that make Robins one of the most profitable bankrupt companies in history. In the first three quarters of 1987, Robins earned $60 million on sales of $621 million, compared with profits of $55 million on revenues of $579 million during the same period of 1986.[24]

Nevertheless, as Guerry Thorton Jr., a lawyer for the Dalkon Shield Victims Association, has pointed out, "the plans confirmation was a phenomenal success story. It has set a precedent by not allowing Robins to escape liability by filling for bankruptcy."[25]

NOTES

1. Al Gini, "Manville: The Ethics of Economic Efficiency?" *Journal of Business Ethics*, 3 (1984), p. 66.
2. *Time*, September 2, 1985, p. 32.
3. Morton Mintz, *At Any Cost* (New York: Pantheon Books, 1985), p. 25.
4. Ibid., p. 29.
5. Ibid., p. 82.
6. Ibid., pp. 29–31.
7. Ibid., pp. 86–88.
8. Ibid., pp. 81, 82.
9. *FDA Consumer*, May 1981, p. 32.
10. Morton Mintz, "At Any Cost," *The Progressive*, November 1985, p. 21.
11. *At Any Cost*, pp. 131–48 and 149–72.
12. *FDA Consumer*, July–August 1983, p. 2.
13. *Wall Street Journal*, April 11, 1985, p. 1.
14. Mintz, "At Any Cost," *The Progressive*, p. 24.
15. Mintz, *At Any Cost*, p. 111.
16. Mintz, *At Any Cost* (New York: Pantheon Books, 1985). Sheldon Engelmayer and Robert Wagman, *Lord's Justice* (New York: Anchor Press/Doubleday, 1985). Susan Perry and Jim Dawson, *Nightmare: Women and the Dalkon Shield* (New York: Macmillan Publishing, 1985).
17. *New York Times*, August 22, 1985, pp. 1, 6.
18. *Time*, November 26, 1984, p. 86.
19. Gini, "Manville: The Ethics of Economic Efficiency?" p. 68.
20. *Wall Street Journal*, June 26, 1986, p. 10.
21. *U.S. News and World Report*, September 2, 1985, p. 12.
22. *Time*, January 11, 1988, p. 59.
23. *New York Times—National Edition*, July 27, 1988, p. 32.
24. *Time*, January 11, 1988, p. 59.
25. *New York Times—National Edition*, July 27, 1988, p. 32.

Chapter Seven

•

Multinationals

W E LIVE IN amazing times. We can go to our local market and buy products from all over the world. Widespread international and transnational commerce is helping to transform our global village into a global marketplace. "Sales territories" are now seen as more important than national boundaries. Corporate boards as more powerful than all but a handful of national governments. Moreover, it is becoming increasingly difficult to discern the "nationality" of the products we buy. Our car may have been designed in the United States and assembled in Mexico, from parts fabricated in Japan, Korea, the United States, and Singapore. It is now commonplace for finished products made in one country to be routinely sold around the world. We can even log onto the Internet and buy things from some of the remoter parts of the world directly, without even leaving the comfort of our own home. We've come a long way from the era when we purchased only locally produced goods, with an occasional smattering of merchandise traded to or from neighboring villages.

As we increasingly ponder the international nature of our buying habits, as well as our investments, I don't believe we devote nearly as much attention to questions regarding what it is like to live and work in other parts of the world. As consumers and investors, we are often self-absorbed and prone to consider our business transactions solely from the perspective of getting the best deal for the money—either in goods and services, or in a high return on investment. Moreover, I do not think that we reflect sufficiently on how companies from other parts of the globe can and should act when setting up shop on foreign soil.

Television and the Internet allow us to see that the world is populated by a variety of different cultures and societies, and that, to put it in the simplest terms, "things are different over there." These differences raise an additional ethical complication beyond the already difficult considerations regarding how business ought to be transacted. How should a business act on foreign soil, in light of these differences? Are these differences simply differences, or do they determine what constitutes right or wrong? Business practices within and among different cultures or societies can either mesh, remain neutral with respect to each other, or clash. In the latter case, how shall we decide on the proper ethical course of action? Can competing views concerning ethical standards be equally valid? And how can and should cultural differences affect business conduct and business ethics?

In addition, it is abundantly clear that not all nations' economies are equally strong, vigorous, or thriving. Besides differing cultural mores and accepted practices, we must consider the economic disparities that exist between nations participating in the global marketplace. How then should the stronger deal with the weaker, particularly in business activity? What should ethics say regarding consumers from a more affluent society enjoying lower prices directly resulting from having their goods produced by workers abroad, particularly when those workers toil in conditions that would not be tolerated within their own society? In other words, for example, should we condone sweatshops simply because they give us access to goods at lower prices? The question is simple to state but difficult to answers; "How do we go about creating a new global business ethics model to meet the needs of our new global marketplace?"

We begin our discussion with the "Ethical Wealth of Nations," which considers matters of international business ethics from the "social contract" perspective, examining how national boundaries are not a barrier to ethical concerns. "AIDS and Life-Saving Medicines: Responsibilities" examines the role that pharmaceutical companies should play in helping underdeveloped countries face critical medical crises. "Chrysler and Gao Feng: Corporate Responsibility for Religious and Political Freedom in China" considers the behavior of American automakers operating in China and asks us to consider how differing standards can be accommodated in an ethically sensitive manner. "The Great Non-Debate over International Sweatshops" asks us to consider whether sweatshops actually produce any benefits for their host countries, thereby complicating the moral analysis of what appears to be an exploitive labor practice. We conclude with "Shell Oil in Nigeria" which deals with oil, national rights, and international corporate needs and desires; and, "Levi Strauss and China" which deals with labor practices in China.

Essay

The Ethical Wealth of Nations

Thomas Donaldson

Not all nations are created equal. Michael Porter and others argue that some nations manifest a competitive advantage deriving from key elements of their economic structure. Some nations are thus disposed by structure to possess what Porter calls a "competitive advantage of nations" (Porter, 1990).

Extending the concept, Fukuyama has argued that cultural phenomenon, including a "propensity for spontaneous sociability" or, more simply, trust, can mark the difference between efficient and inefficient economic processes (Fukuyama, 1995). If so, then not only traditional forms of capital but "social capital" must be counted when determining the wealth of nations. It follows too, that if some nations are taller and richer than others, and have become so not by dint of hard work or natural resources, but by a form of social capital, then we should attempt to identify the key elements of such social capital. Certainly, the popular analyses of many current events suggest that ethical attributes or their absence have impacted economic events. Crony capitalism and the lack of transparency have been implicated in the Asian melt down of 1997–1998, and the failure of markets in the former Soviet Union has been linked to widespread bribery and corruption.

In this paper I want to examine the prospect of an ethical advantage of nations, and in particular, of a set of advantages that extend far beyond the simple dimension of trust so often discussed. I wish to consider, further, how such a range of ethical features would be structured, and what the implications of those features would be. In exploring the possible meaning of the "ethical wealth of nations" my task in this paper is to consider a proposition analogous to sociologist Robert Putnam's that certain inherent cultural tendencies make a society more likely to succeed with democratic institutions (Putnam et al., 1994).[1]

What ethical factors, then, might promote high levels of national economic performance? Can we make sense of such factors and, in turn, interpret their implications for national and corporate policy? Before beginning, a caveat should be made. The theses of social capital theorists qualify as empirical claims that must eventually find empirical confirmation. Fuzzyheaded speculation has sometimes passed for rationality in the discussion of social capital, and the plausibility of a claim must be remembered to be only one of many steps in securing its empirical truth (and perhaps not even a necessary step). Robert Solow (1995) may be right, for example, when he criticizes Fukuyama's thesis for its lack of rigor.[2] For this reason I wish to limit my aims in this paper. I shall attempt not to demonstrate the truth of any particular claim, but only show how those claims exhibit particular logical structures and to draw implications from those structures. In this vein, I will do two things.

First, I want to construct a typography of current claims, evidence, and rationale made for the existence of an ethical economic advantage. Such claims may be divided into four categories. Each claim has the following generic form: a more prosperous economy can be driven by that economy's possessing a certain ethical characteristic. The claims vary in terms of the characteristic asserted to drive higher prosperity. The four most popular characteristics are:

1. Fairer distribution of goods
2. Better government
3. More ingrained social cooperation
4. Inculcation of economic "duties" by citizens

It is noteworthy that all factors are primarily ethical in character, rather than economic.

Second, after having developed these four categories, I want to establish three further points:

1. Many purported ethical success factors can be interpreted as a means of circumventing market imperfections—but some cannot.

    In other words, the claims for economic advantage extend beyond the traditional logic of Pareto Optimality. In short, morality may create an economic advantage for nations in ways broader than the notion of an idealized market.
2. The success criteria for plausible success factors require that the values associated with those success factors possess the status of intrinsic value. In other words, people must ascribe independent value to the ethical factor, irrespective of its economic contribution.
3. If such claims for national ethical success factors are true, then nations should attend to the issue of moral education.

FAIRER DISTRIBUTION OF GOODS

One ethical factor claimed to influence economic success is the fairer distribution of goods. Put more technically, increased distributional equity or fairness enhances economic efficiency and productivity. An extreme example of distributional inequity occurs in countries where a handful of rich families control all of a country's capital resources. Broadly speaking distributional inequity occurs whenever a grossly unfair distribution in society exists of what Rawls and others have called society's "primary goods" (Rawls, 1971) such as wealth or health care. Such distributional inequity is said to dampen incentive and misallocate scarce resources. Some data appear to support the hypothesis, notably, data indicating than many of the world's most successful economies have less extreme gaps between their rich and poor than do the most successful ones. . . .

BETTER GOVERNMENT

Economic success has also sometimes been said to be enhanced by the existence of better government. Most claims are made on behalf of democracy as not only the "more ethical" form of government, but also the all-around "better" form of government, and an important part of being all-around better is economic efficiency. The economic argument for democracy is clearly not new. Lipset's now-famous argument that greater economic growth increases the likelihood that stable democratic forms of politics will emerge suggests a compatibility between democracy and economic growth (Lipset, 1980) Later 31, no. 1 (May 2001) theorists and statesmen have asserted that open and democratic political systems constitute catalysts for economic success. As early as the 1960s Milton Friedman argued that economic freedom stands in need of political freedom (Friedman, 1962).

How, he asks, can we be assured of labor mobility, access to resources, availability of knowledge, and opportunities for entrepreneurship when political freedom is absent? If, as in the Soviet Union of the 1930s, all members of society must work, and, indeed, must work at jobs formed and allocated by the central government, then how can the economic freedom necessary to fuel innovation and incentive exist? In light of the widely held assumption that the type of government most compatible with political freedom is democracy, democracy thus has often been viewed as a positive factor in economic success.

More recently, James Wolfensohn, president, the World Bank, has remarked that,

> We must recognize this link between good economic performance and open governance. Irrespective of political systems, public decisions must be brought right out into the sunshine of public scrutiny. Not simply to please the markets, but to build the broad social consensus without which even the best conceived economic strategies will ultimately fail (1998, p. 34, back cover).

In turn, the importance of having a democratic v. non-democratic government is heightened if one believes that a democracy is better able to reflect the true needs of consumers, and to embody the market's value of consumer sovereignty. This importance of a market-compatible government is heightened further if one agrees with Amartya Sen that the governments typically must make up for private sector shortcomings in dealing with familiar problems discussed in the literature, such as public goods and situations of strong externalities (Sen et al., 1990).

INGRAINED SOCIAL COOPERATION

A nation's embodiment of underlying cooperative tendencies may help it prosper because those tendencies can avoid forms of self-destructive economic interaction such as prisoner dilemmas. Robert Frank, an economist who writes frequently about game theoretic issues explains why moral motives are important in commerce. In "Can Socially Responsible Firms Survive in a Competitive Environment?" Frank discusses ways in which economic activity is more efficient when guided, at least in part, by principles and values (Frank, 1996). These ways depend heavily on the increased ability of market actors to solve what Frank calls "commitment" problems, i.e., problems that create failures and inefficiencies unless parties are able to behave responsibly to one another. A disposition to take ethics seriously can solve commitment problems with employees, with customers, and with other firms. For example, piece rates are efficient tools for managing production but not when firms are perceived to be untrustworthy. If workers do not believe the firm has committed itself to a given production rate schedule, and that it will simply raise rates when workers produce more, then they are more likely to maintain artificially low production rates. Or to take another example, employees will be reluctant to invest time and energy into developing company specific skills, i.e., skills that have negligible value on the open market, unless they believe the company is committed to rewarding them fairly. Shirking and opportunism, career lock-in, rising wage profiles, confidentiality requirements, quality assurance issues, subcontractor hold-up problems, and customer support issues are all ones that Frank argues can be solved more efficiently through socially responsible behavior . . . .

INCULCATION OF ECONOMIC DUTIES BY CITIZENS

The efficient functioning of any economic system, whether it be seventh century Japanese Confucianism, free market capitalism, or Communism, requires its participants to embrace certain system-specific duties. To be sure, some economic systems are inherently more efficient than others. Free market capitalism is undoubtedly more efficient and fair than Soviet style communism. Nonetheless we ought not to lose sight of the fact that any economic system, including Soviet style communism, will be more or less efficient depending on whether its participants accept or fail to accept key duties that support that system's essential transactions. Still further, it is worth noting that the economic duties necessary for the efficient functioning of an economy vary significantly depending on the kind of system in place. The obligations a Wall Street banker may owe to the system (such as engaging in free and fair competition) are different from that owed by an economic magistrate in the Nara period of Feudal Japan. By identifying what those duties are, one arrives at a much clearer picture of what business ethics entails.

Thomas Dunfee and I have described the generic duty that any participant of a legitimate economic system should take seriously: the "structural hypernorm of necessary social efficiency" or (shortened) the "efficiency hypernorm," At its broadest, the efficiency hypernorm requires observance of duties generated by the array of institutions and organizations that taken together provide the basic fabric of a given political economy. This fundamental moral precept addresses those institutions and coexistent duties designed to enable people to achieve the basic or "necessary" social goods of economic welfare and social justice (Donaldson and Dunfee, 1999).

Because of the widespread adoption of market structures around the globe, and because of a shared intuition among most theorists that markets require a certain amount of moral cooperation, many writers have concluded that failing to taking market-related duties seriously negatively affects economic performance. Here is a selective list of economic duties important for a market system:

1. Respect for intellectual property. One common claim for the impact of good ethics on economic performance is tied to the social promotion of economic incentives. To the extent that people fail to respect intellectual property, and to the extent they engage in intellectual property violations such as software piracy, the incentive to create new and better forms of intellectual property is said to diminish.[3] Why should intellectual property be protected? It should be protected because and to the extent that it enhances aggregative economic welfare. (To be sure, notions of intellectual property may vary somewhat depending upon culture. As Alford notes, stealing a book has been called an "elegant offense" by the Chinese (Alford, 1995).) But there is widespread agreement that without some protection of intellectual property, incentives to invest time and other resources in developing new property diminished. It is also well known that legal mechanisms are notoriously inept at policing many forms of intellectual property theft, as for instance with software piracy. Data show that countries with similar geographic and economic systems (such as the nations of Europe) often have strikingly variable software piracy rates. This suggests that not only regulation and government control are important in securing respect for intellectual property, but also social mores (Donaldson, 1996).

2. Engaging in fair competition and avoiding monopolies. To the extent that a John D. Rockefeller or a William Gates is able by virtue of monopoly power to demand artificially inflated prices, consumers are harmed. John Locke, the English philosopher renowned for his seminal defense of private property articulated the "no-monopoly requirement" of fairness convincingly. No one, he notes, may take the only water hole in the desert and charge what he will (Locke, 1948). A natural right to property, when properly understood, prohibits such an action.

3. Avoiding nepotism and "crony capitalism." Examples of the pernicious impact of nepotism and behavior nicknamed "crony capitalism" are not difficult to find. Indonesia's political and economic demise in 1998 brought striking abuses of nepotism and cronyism to light. The Suharto family's nepotistic economic arrangements were targeted by critics as a lynchpin of the country's economic troubles. Industries and foreign company relations (including both Chinese conglomerates and many large Western corporations) were blatantly divided among Suharto family members: Suharto daughter Tutut, son Sigit, daughter Titiek, and son Tommy were allocated sweeping spheres of influence. Tommy, in particular, was placed in charge of an infamous national auto production scheme that utilized Korean auto production facilities while protecting sales of the car in Indonesia through government tariffs. To the extent capital is allocated in the economy on the basis of nepotism, not the underlying value of the investment, economic efficiency suffers.

4. Not abusing government relationships. At one extreme, Boddewyn and Brewer (Boddewyn and Brewer, 1994) have argued that managers should consider the host company government on all fours with any other competitive factor. From this perspective the government has no special status over and above any other factor of production. Government is viewed simply as one player in the competitive game that international firms should try to win. The government, hence, can be "gained" to the advantage of the foreign corporation in the process of one company's exploiting its chain of economic value-adding activities in cross-border activity (Boddewyn and Brewer, 1994, p. 126). For his part, Boddewyn has even argued that when companies seek competitive advantages, bribery, smuggling, and buying absolute market monopolies (as discussed in the duty to avoid monopolies above) are not necessarily ruled out (Boddewyn, 1986).

Yet the role of government in maintaining market freedom is obvious. If and when government relationships are abused, the government's role in protecting and sustaining the market is compromised. For example, when taxes are not collected, courts cannot function, and the protection owed properly in a free market is destroyed.

5. Providing accurate information to the market (including transparency of relevant information). The importance of accurate information in fueling efficient economic activity is well substantiated. Rational choice demands accurate information. When companies fail to provide investors with accurate information, investors make worse decisions and any market, in turn, becomes less efficient. Indeed, another of the three "principal objectives" asserted at the end of 1998 by the head of the World Bank, James Wolfensohn, in the wake of the financial turmoil at Asia was "Improving the quality and transparency of key government institutions, including addressing issues of corruption and accountability" (Wolfensohn, 1998).

6. Avoiding bribery. Bribery distorts markets by allocating resources away from higher quality and lower prices towards the self-interest of agents. The company manager who pockets a bribe and buys goods for his company from a bribing supplier violates not only his duty to his company (by pocketing the money himself), but a duty he owes to the integrity of the market economy. Having taken the bribe he purchases a product or service that only through accident would constitute the best buy for his company. Such a misallocation, repeated hundreds of thousands of times, damages national economic efficiency. . . .

The view sometimes circulated in rich nations that emerging economies tolerate widespread bribery is slowly being exposed as false. As Heimann notes, "There is no country in the world where bribery is either legally or morally acceptable. That bribes have to be paid secretly everywhere, and that officials receiving bribes have to resign in disgrace if the bribe is disclosed, makes clear that bribery violates the moral standards of the South and the East, just as it does in the West" (Heimann, 1994) (footnote #73 quoted in Nichols, 1997).

Respecting Environmental Integrity

One of the more important so-called "public goods" is a livable environment. Most economists agree that the public goods inherent in the environment will not be efficiently achieved through the mere interplay of self-interested behavior. Even Milton Friedman speaks of the "neighborhood effects" problem and the need in turn to address the problem through more than market forces (Friedman, 1962). Even if one believes as Friedman may have—that the only solution to protecting the environment lies in legally imposed sanctions rather than ethical responsibility, it follows that market participants have a duty to support reasonable legal sanctions in order to insure environmental public goods.

Duties to Honor Contracts, Promises, and Other Commitments

If businesspeople regularly broke contracts, promises, and other commitments, the law would be powerless to insure remedies. In a sense, business law is like the policeman who is able to control a community, but only on the assumption that criminal activity is the exception, not the rule. Were people never independently motivated to engage in law abiding, non-criminal behavior, then the policeman would be overwhelmed. Similarly, the law of torts would be powerless to control a world of business in which firms and individuals had no independent respect for handshakes and contracts.

These, then, are the major items on the list of contemporary claims about how ethical factors may promote national economic advantage, or the "ethical wealth of nations." The fairer the distribution of goods, the better the government, the more ingrained the social cooperation, and the better inculcated are economic "duties" by citizens, the higher national efficiency and productivity will be—or so the assertions would have us believe. Leaving aside the critical question of the truth of these claims, what threads, if any, link the items in this long list of claims? Moreover, what, if anything, follows if the claims on the list turn out to be true?

It is tempting to suppose that what unites the items on the list is simply the concept of market imperfections. By the concept of "market imperfections." I mean a deviation from the perfect functioning of the ideal market as defined through the notion of Pareto Optimality. Pareto Optimality refers to a market in which all voluntary transactions have been consummated, in other words, a market where no one can be made better off without someone being made worse off. This interpretation is especially tempting for those economists who relegate ethics entirely to the study of economic externalities and other Pareto sub-optimal outcomes. Of course, not all nations subscribe fully to market capitalism. Nonetheless, most nations today do make some sort of systemic commitment to a market system—although the form of that commitment can vary enormously. For better or worse, Communism, Confucianism, and even radical socialism, are unpopular forms of government today.

Yet while many of the purported success factors on the list are a function of market imperfections, some, notably, are not. To be sure, key ethical assumptions flow from neoclassical economic theory. For example, Julienne Nelson has shown that because the assumptions of a perfectly competitive market are not met, certain duties follow (Nelson, 1994). A perfectly competitive market assumes, for example, that:

1. We all have the same information.
2. We all behave competitively in both spot and futures markets (i.e., neither producers nor consumers expect to influence the prices of goods and serves offered for sale).
3. We do not use technologies that cause externalities or that exhibit increasing returns to scale at relevant levels of production.

Failure to meet these conditions occurs every day in business. It follows that such imperfections impose certain duties to "maintain the system" upon market participants (duties which often are conveniently handed by citizens to government institutions such as courts and bureaucracies). To deny these conditions flatly would be to undermine the health of the free market system (Nelson, 1994). These duties have been interpreted differently by theorists, but most concur they involve obligations surrounding information disclosure and fair competition. For example Nelson asserts that an informed seller sometimes has obligations to notify a buyer of hidden product defects, and that sellers have a duty to "promote accurate and informative advertising."

Hence, many of the ethical success factors in the list above fall under the banner of the remedies for market imperfections. For example, each of the items on the list of "economic duties" that citizens should inculcate implicitly refers to market imperfections. In other words, respect for intellectual property, engaging in fair competition, not abusing government relationships, providing accurate information to the market, avoiding bribery, duties to honor contracts, promises, and other commitments, and avoiding bribery all reflect norms that would be rendered unnecessary were a Pareto Optimal state to exist. Were the market to function at a perfect level of competitiveness, then no need would exist for participants to adopt duties of the kind listed under the economic duties category above. [4]

But the same cannot be said for the other kinds of factors listed above. Consider, for example, the call for the fair distribution of goods throughout society. If one form of social capital is the fair distribution of goods throughout society, there is no reason to suppose that a perfect market will achieve such fairness. Pareto Optimality, for example, is compatible with wildly disparate levels of wealth. As has sometimes been noted, it is compatible with one person owning the entirety of an island, and the others relegated to the status of impoverished servants. (it might be the case that nobody could be made better off through a voluntary transaction without making the owner of the island worse off.) This is not to condemn the mechanism of the market, for markets deliver enormous social benefits. It is only to say that markets cannot do everything: distributive justice has never been claimed, even by extreme market proponents, to be an automatic consequence of pure market activity.

Nor does the concept of "better government" automatically flow from the fact of a perfectly competitive market. It may be, as suggested before, that democratic governments are "better" for market economies. But this proposition is logically distinct from the proposition that a perfect market, exhibiting a Pareto Optimal state, will automatically generate a "better" and hence democratic form of government. It may, or it may not.

Finally, the notion of ingrained social cooperation is not a necessary logical implication of a perfectly competitive market. Indeed the very notion of a prisoner's dilemma, which highlights the importance of cooperation as a social phenomenon, is one that presupposes that in the absence of confidence in a cooperative tendency of others, the dominant option from the standpoint of self-interest is defection. The market, as economists are quick to note, assumes self interest and presumes no preexisting level of cooperation among economic actors.

And so morality creates an economic advantage for nations in ways broader than the notion of an idealized market. Correcting market imperfections stands as an important economic function for morality, but does not constitute a universal link.

One characteristic, however, does link all of the success criteria listed above. In order to function successfully the values referenced above must have in the minds of market participants some "intrinsic worth." By "intrinsic worth" is meant value attributed by an individual to something, where that value is not tied to the value of something else. The term references an individual's attribution of independent value to something, a value that is separate from that thing's instrumental usefulness, or which in other words, lies apart from its usefulness in attaining some additional object that satisfies the individual's self interest. Whatever one seeks for the sake of something else by definition has instrumental value and lacks intrinsic value. One example of something with instrumental value (and hence no intrinsic value) is money; most people seek it not for the sake of money itself but for its capacity to secure goods, services, and

human happiness. For most people, then, money lacks "intrinsic value.". . .

We ought not to be surprised by the role played by intrinsic value in economic activity. In daily life we prefer doing business with people who show independent concern for values. Think of integrity. If we believe that our lawyer or banker is constantly lying in wait, looking for the moment he can abandon integrity, and that he is routinely seeking the hidden moment when acting unscrupulously will fatten his advantage and decrease ours, then we suppose it is time to hire a new lawyer or banker. Most of us prefer doing business with a lawyer or banker who places some intrinsic value on integrity.

So, too, the values that serve national economies require the status of intrinsic value from the standpoint of individual firms and persons. The values referenced in the list above demand some level of independent commitment on the part of citizens. In some instances the requirement is practical, in others, a matter of logic. If economic activity is to be enhanced through a fairer distribution of goods, better government, ingrained social cooperation, and the adoption of economic duties, then it is hard to imagine such conditions being met by citizens simply pursuing maximal self-interest and treating such goods as having merely instrumental worth. The problem lies in the logical probability that in many specific instances a self-interested calculation will indicate that abandoning the value at issue will lead to maximal satisfaction of self-interest.

Consider, for example, the value of democratic government and the act of voting. Voting, as many have noted, is a fundamentally irrational act from the standpoint of self-interest. I may realize that a society in which large numbers of citizens vote is critically important for the general satisfaction of my own self-interest. I may thus interpret the act of voting as having important instrumental value. Further, my instrumental interpretation of voting may be enhanced if I also believe that a democratic government is, all other things being equal, more effective in generating a healthy economy (as suggested in the analysis above). But the calculation undertaken from the standpoint of my own self-interest relative to any particular act of voting invariably reaches a negative recommendation. My loss of time and mental energy in undertaking the act of voting will consistently overwhelm the nearly nonexistent projected benefits from the tiny possibility that my vote will actually make a difference.

This is true for the other values argued to be important for economic success. Practically speaking, concern for a fair distribution of primary goods, commitment to cooperation, respect for intellectual property, attention to fair competition, avoidance of nepotism, respect for government relationships, integrity in providing information to the market, the rejection of bribery, respect for the environment, and belief in the importance of honoring contracts, promises, and other commitments, all must hold at least partial intrinsic worth for individual market participants for their successful realization. Without an individual's independent commitment to such values, they easily fall prey to rational, self-interested calculations.

Of course we have not in this paper set out to prove that the ethical factors listed in the early part of this article are in fact important for national economic success. Next, however, for the purpose of argument, let us presume they have been shown to be important in this way. Given, as we have seen, that such values must possess a component of intrinsic worth, implications follow for what nations should do. In particular, nations should attend to the issue of ethical education.

First, the ethical education that a nation undertakes must be of a kind that generates the commitment to the intrinsic worth of values. It will not do to educate economic participants merely in the niceties of enlightened self-interest. It will not do simply to instruct the young in the importance of "appearing ethical" in order to be financially successful. It will not even do to educate prospective business managers by merely explaining how successful economies rest upon the bedrock of moral principles. The task, rather, is to educate people, children and managers alike, in a way so that they are capable of ascribing independent (i.e., intrinsic) value to concepts such as integrity, democracy, the environment, and distributive fairness. Nor does it seem likely that such education will occur spontaneously. The right form of values-based education occurring without special effort seems especially unlikely in economies that must adjust themselves to modern markets from a past steeped in more familial, communal economic patterns. Evidence suggests that individual values bend only slightly in the presence of a new economic ideology.

Hence, a more complete "value bending" will probably require some form of educational initiative. Not all education around economic values needs to be of a traditional form, for example, schooling, or government communication. Some education may be multinational and organized through NGOs. The NGO "Transparency International," for example, has worked with nation states and to develop anticorruption education initiatives. Transparency International has worked in cooperation with General Electric Corporation in Italy and Canada. And, it has cooperated with a broad cross section of groups in Uganda and Tanzania. With corporate help, Transparency International also recently formed a national chapter in Russia.

None of the foregoing would make sense were it true that nation states should all adopt one, single, monolithic blueprint of ethics. But while evidence accumulates that some fundamental ethical principles are transnational in character, it also suggests strongly that nations and cultures possess at least some "moral free space" in which to shape their own religious, cultural, and historic identities (Donaldson and Dunfee, 1999). Hence, within this range of moral free space lie the important questions about ethics and economic efficiency.

Gibbon in his book *The Decline and Fall of the Roman Empire* asks why so many religions were allowed to flourish in ancient Rome. He answers his own question by commenting that the elite in Rome thought that all religions were equally false; the common people thought they were all equally true; and the bureaucrats thought they were all equally useful (Gibbon, 1993). Gibbon's clever comment underscores an important truth. With religion, ideology, and ethics we must sometimes ask more than the question "Is it true?" Ethical precepts are the kinds of thing that must stand on their own, and must entail intrinsic value. But they are also the kinds of thing about which we must ask "What do they make possible?" If, as it seems increasingly likely, successful economies rely at least in part on the collective morality of their participants, then we must ask the follow-up questions of what and how. What kinds of values are important? And how are such values inculcated?

These questions have pressing practical importance. Amartya Sen has referred recently to the economic corruption in Italy and the "grabbing culture" in Russia. In doing so he shows how the presence or absence of particular features of business ethics can influence the operation of all economies (Sen, 1997, p. 1). Clearly, in Italy it makes sense to ask how economic corruption impacts the economy, and in Russia how the presence of a "grabbing culture" may hinder economic performance. And because it makes sense to ask in any country what values enable healthy economic performance, and how those values are created, this paper has sought answers. The answers are that the values necessary to drive successful economies must maintain an element of intrinsic worth, and must be inculcated, at least partially, through a process of education.

NOTES

The research for this article was undertaken with a generous grant from The Carol and Lawrence Zicklin Center for Business Ethics Research at the Wharton School of the University of Pennsylvania. An earlier draft of this article is scheduled to appear in the *Journal of Business Ethics* sometime in 2000.

1. Indeed, it was Putnam who more than anyone popularized the term "social capital" despite the fact that his work was primarily aimed at the conditions for democracy rather than economic success.
2. Discussing Fukuyama's account in *Trust* (Fukuyama, 1995), Solow writes, "The trouble with this sort of thinking is that it is vague and often, in any concrete sense, uninformative. How would you ever know if the thesis is true or false?" (Solow, 1995). Solow's interpretation seems accurate. For "social capital" and especially "ethical capital" to attain the degree of acceptance among economists that Gary Becker and Theodore W Schultz have brought to "human capital" (including the idea that investment in education can be a national asset), we would no doubt need some means of measuring the phenomenon, of saying that there is "more" and "less" of it in certain places and times, and perhaps even an understanding of how it can diminish, i.e., "depreciates."
3. Morality sometimes influences intellectual property in a direct way. As Mullan notes, the European Patent Office, through its Guidelines for Examination, tests whether it is probable that the general public would regard the invention as so abhorrent that the protection of its patent would be inconceivable (Mullan, 1993).
4. Granted, one item in this list seems difficult to fit under the "market imperfections" label, namely, avoiding nepotism and crony capitalism. Yet even favoring a friend over a more attractive price might be construed as a step down from purely competitive behavior, and hence a form of market imperfection.

REFERENCES

1998, *Development and Human Rights: The Role of the World Bank* (Internal Working Group Report) (The World Bank, Washington, DC).

Alford, W. P.: 1995, *To Steal a Book Is an Elegant Offense: Intellectual Property Law in Chinese Civilization* (Stanford University Press, Stanford, CA).

Bobrowsky, D.: 1999, *Outsourcing Rights: Multinational Codes of Conduct and the Social Construction of Transaction Costs* (Department of Politics, New York University, New York), p. 16.

Boddewyn, J. J.: 1986, *International Political Strategy: A Fourth "Generic" Strategy* (Annual Meeting of the American Academy of Management, and the Annual Meeting of the International Academy of Business).

Boddewyn, J. J. and T. L. Brewer: 1994, "International-Business Political Behavior: New Theoretical Directions," *The Academy of Management Review* 19(1), 119–143.

Chakraborty, S. K.: 1997, "Business Ethics in India," *Journal of Business Ethics* 16(14), 1529–1538.

Donaldson, T.: 1996, "Values in Tension: Ethics Away from Home," *Harvard Business Review* 74(5), 48–56.

Donaldson, T. and T. Dunfee: 1999, *Ties that Bind: A Social Contracts Approach to Business Ethics* (Harvard University Business School Press).

Frank, R. H.: 1987, "If Homo Economicus Could Choose His Own Utility Function, Would He Want One with a Conscience?" *American Economic Review* 77(4), 593–604.

Frank, R. H.: 1996, "Can Socially Responsible Firms Survive in a Competitive Environment?" in D. M. Messick and A. E. Tenbrunsel (eds.), *Codes of Conduct: Behavioral Research into Business: Ethics* (Russell Sage Foundation, New York), pp. 86–103.

Friedman, M.: 1962, *Capitalism and Freedom* (University of Chicago Press, Chicago).

Fukuyama, F.: 1995, *Trust: The Social Virtues and the Creation of Prosperity* (The Free Press, New York).

Gauthier, D. P.: 1986, *Morals by Agreement* (Clarendon Press, Oxford).

Gibbon, E.: 1993, *The Decline and Fall of the Roman Empire* (Distributed by Random House, New York, Knopf).

Heimann, F. E.: 1994, "Should Foreign Bribery Be a Crime?" *Transparency International* 2.

Lipset, S. M.: 1980, *Political Man* (Johns Hopkins University Press, Baltimore).

Contracting (Free Press, New York).

Locke, J.: 1948, *The Second Treatise of Civil Government and a Letter Concerning Toleration* (Basil Blackwell, Oxford).

Mullan, K.: 1993, "Shock, Horror, Scandal! Is Your IP Wholesome Enough?" *Managing Intellectual Property* 32, 33–38.

Nelson, J.: 1994, "Business Ethics in a Competitive Market," *Journal of Business Ethics* 13(9), 663–667.

Nichols, P. M.: 1997, "Outlawing Transnational Bribery Through the World Trade Organization," *Law and Policy in International Business* 28(2), 305–386.

Porter, M. E.: 1990, *The Competitive Advantage of Nations* (Free Press, New York).

Putnam, R. D. and R. Leonardi et al.: 1994, *Making Democracy Work: Civic Traditions in Modern Italy* (Princeton University Press).

Quinn, D. P and T. M. Jones: 1995, "An Agent Morality View of Business Policy," *Academy of Management Review* 20(1), 22–42.

Ralston, D. A. and D. H. Holt et al.: 1995, "The Impact of Culture and Ideology on Managerial Work Values: A Study of the United States, Russia, Japan, and China," *Academy of Management Journal* (Best Papers Proceedings 1995), 187–191.

Ralston, D. A. and D. H. Holt et al.: 1997, "The Impact of National Culture and Economic ideology on Managerial Work Values: A Study of the United States, Russia, Japan, and China," *Journal of International Business Studies* (First Quarter), 177–207.

Rawls, J.: 1971, *A Theory of Justice* (Harvard University Press, Cambridge).

Sen, A.: 1997, "Economics, Business Principles and Moral Sentiments," *Business Ethics Quarterly* 7 (3), 5–15.

Sen, A. and N. Stern et al.: 1990, "Development Strategies: The Roles of the State and the Private Sector," *World Bank Research Observer*. 421–435.

Solow, R. M.: 1995, "But Verify: Review of *Trust: The Social Virtues and the Creation of Prosperity*" by Francis Fukuyama, *The New Republic*.

Williamson, O. E.: 1985, *The Economic Institutions of Capitalism: Firms, Markets, Relational.*

Wolfensohn, J.: 1998, "Asia: The Long View," *Financial Times*. London: 10.

Case Study

AIDS and Life-Saving Medicines: Responsibilities

Oliver F. Williams

THE EXECUTIVE'S DILEMMA

Moses Mpunthe stared at his company's absenteeism figures for the past six months and pondered the tough decision ahead. Should he provide antiretroviral drugs for his workers? Like many businesses in South Africa, his firm had experienced increasing numbers of employees with full-blown AIDS and many workers between 20 and 40 years old were dying. What is the right thing to do?

BLACK EMPOWERMENT AND THE NEW SOUTH AFRICA

Less than 5 years ago, Mpunthe bought three old, underutilized gold mines from some of the industry giants and found a way to make them profitable. Talented and well educated, Mpunthe was able to borrow the money to start the business because the major South African financial institutions were trying to overcome their apartheid past by making significant concessions in loan policies to talented blacks; it was their version of affirmative action. Although whites are only 12% of the population, they control 98% of the market capitalization of the Johannesburg Stock Exchange (JSE). With the overcoming of statutory apartheid in 1994, the new challenge is to overcome economic apartheid. (See Appendix A.) Yet Mpunthe knew that the coin of the realm here was ultimately business competence; more than one third of the black-controlled companies listed on the JSE in 1998 had failed by 2002 due to poor management.

With about 5,000 employees, Mpunthe's company is small by industry standards but it is doing well. Recently listed on the Johannesburg Stock Exchange, the firm has a small number of highly trained and experienced managers but the great majority of the workers are low-skilled. With an unemployment rate of at least 20% in South Africa and higher in neighboring countries, replacing workers is not a problem. Unemployed South Africans are desperate for any job. Yet beyond the economies of the situation, Mpunthe worried about the moral equation. While there is still no cure for AIDS, antiretrovirals allow most victims of the disease to live relatively normal lives, prolonging their working life by at least 10 years.

ANTIRETROVIRALS FOR THE VERY FEW

Mpunthe had been closely following the business response to AIDS in South Africa. A small number of large companies, for example, Anglo Gold, De Beers, Heineken, Coca-Cola, Ford, Daimler Chrysler and Anglo American, recently decided to provide antiretrovirals to their workers and to some family members. Providing the medicines and the medical care that must accompany them for safe and effective use, however, is no small expense. Unlike many medicines, antiretrovirals can only be taken under close supervision of a doctor or paramedical to ensure proper dosage and to avoid mutations of the virus. The finance firm, Old Mutual, offered free drugs and care to infected workers and, after voluntary testing, found that 5 percent of its employees (600 workers) had the disease. Chief executive, Roddy Sparks commented: "We're always closely watching our bottom line, but we have made this decision on a corporate conscience basis." Mining companies estimate that their infected workers range more in the area of twenty-five percent. Anglo American, a mining company with 134,000 employees and the largest employer in southern Africa, has an infection rate of 23 percent and budgets $3–5 million a year for antiretroviral medicines. Anglo negotiated a good price for the drugs from three major pharmaceutical firms: GlaxoSmithKline, Merck and Boehringer Ingelhein. If Mpunthe could get the same price for the medicines and if his firm's infection rate were in the range of the industry average, the total cost of coverage would be a big financial hit but it would not be impossible. Most companies in

South Africa had decided not to provide anti-retrovirals and he wondered if he should. The 2002 UNAIDS report indicates that of the 29.4 million people with HIV in Sub-Saharan Africa, only about 300,000 are receiving life-saving medicines.

A PUBLIC-PRIVATE PARTNERSHIP?

Mpunthe found much helpful data on the Internet. In 2002, estimates were the one in nine of South Africans, about 4.7 million people, were infected with HIV. A study by the Actuarial Society of South Africa (ASSA 2000) projects that in the next 10 years, 5 to 6 million people would die of AIDS and that without changes in sexual behavior 45% of adults would likely be infected. Heterosexual activity is the chief mode of transmission and the great majority of those infected are black. Because of poor public health services, there is a high prevalence of sexually transmitted diseases and this exacerbates the spread of HIV. Poverty and its attendant problems worsened the situation. Also low condom usage, high levels of migrant labor and low levels of circumcision all are contributing factors. Measures taken by the South African government under President Thabo Mbeki were puzzling to Mpunthe. On the one hand, there was a *National HIV/AIDS Strategic Plan for South Africa* (2000–2005), which outlined an action plan that seemed to be most appropriate for the pandemic. Yet the constant haggling by government officials about whether antiretrovirals were an effective and appropriate remedy for South Africa confused many. It was unclear that any significant behavioral change was taking place although one bright spot was that HIV infection levels for pregnant women under 20 fell from 21% in 1998 to 15.4% in 2001. HIV prevalence levels for women from 20 to 29 years old continued to rise, however.

In spite of this, the government had yet to provide any antiretrovirals in the public health clinics or hospitals. Given that most all infected were poor, the only hope of medications was from the public sector. There has been great hope that government policy might change when in April 2002, the new initiative The Global Fund to Fight HIV/AIDS, Tuberculosis and Malaria (GFAT) awarded South Africa some $160 million to fight HIV/AIDS over the next 5 years. (See Appendix B.) The government continues to claim lack of sufficient funds, personnel and infrastructure. Although there was clearly some truth to this claim, neighboring countries, such as Botswana, had teamed up with the Merck Pharmaceutical Company and the Bill and Melinda Gates Foundation in a partnership that would deliver free antiretrovirals, education, counseling, and new laboratories. The company and the foundation are providing $100 million for the project over 5 years for Botswana.

THE COMPANY RESPONSE

Mpunthe had canvassed the Internet for the best resources to inform his decision and discovered the most helpful web site to be that of the NGO the *Global Business Coalition on HIV/AIDS.* Headed by Richard Holbrooke, former U.S. Ambassador to the UN, the group includes over one hundred of the major multinational companies and has as it key goal the dramatic increase of business sector involvement in the HIV issue. The *Global Business Coalition* offers some Principles for Action for companies (see Appendix C). The action principles include: Risk assessment; non-discriminatory policy; prevention and awareness program; voluntary counseling and testing; and care, support and treatment. On the question of treatment, the Principles say this: "Where possible, companies should implement antiretroviral treatment programs for infected employees and their families, taking advantage of the major reductions in the prices of these drugs." Mpunthe wondered what he should do.

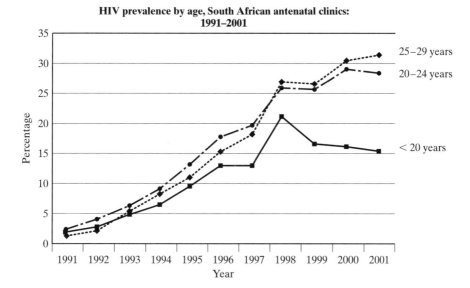

HIV prevalence by age, South African antenatal clinics:
1991–2001

Source: Summary Report, National HIV and Syphilis Sero-Prevalence Survey of Women Attending Public Antenatal Clinics in South Africa, 2001, Department of Health, South Africa, 2002.

Although, up to this point, AIDS had not actually cost the company since workers were so available and easily trained for the low-skilled jobs; the future was not so clear. Morale was becoming a problem with so many deaths, and the absentee rate was high not only for sickness but also for attending funerals. Recent studies had indicated the epidemic could cost the country as much as 17% in GDP growth by 2010. (See the profile of South Africa, Appendix A.) Moses Mpunthe also knew that the 2002 King Report on Corporate Governance for South Africa had made disclosure of HIV/AIDS risks a matter of good corporate governance. The Johannesburg Stock Exchange was about to require listed companies to report on how the disease could have an impact on bottom-line earnings and what it was doing about it. Not only increased social spending, but labor and training costs and new employee benefits were to be discussed in the shareholder report. Reflecting on all the information, Moses knew there must be a creative response to his dilemma; he just had not figured it out yet.

REFERENCES

Web Sites

ANC Today: www.anc.org.za/ancdoes/anctoday.

Ford Motor Company: www.ford.com.

Global Business Council on HIV/AIDS: www.businessfightsaids.org.

JSE Securities Exchange South Africa: www.jse.co.za.

Notre Dame Center for Ethics and Religious Values in Business (with links to other centers and institutes): www.nd.edu/ethics.

South African King Committee on Corporate Governance: www.iodsa.co.za.

South African Newspapers: www.ecola.com/news/press/of/za.

UNAIDS/WHO (Published *Global Summary of the HIV/AIDS Epidemic, December 2002*): www.unaids.org.

The United Nations Global Compact: www.unglobalcompact.org.

U.S. Department of State: www.state.gov/r.

Articles/Books

Acharya, K. "Coming Together For a Cause," *Business Line*, September 2, 2002.

Aita, J. "HIV/AIDS Epidemic Continues to Spread Worldwide," *UNAIDS Release*, November 26, 2002.

BBC News Online, "Old Mutual Offers Staff Anti-AIDS Drugs," September 12, 2002.

Bisseker, C. "It's Worse Than You Thought—Unless Behavior Changes," *Financial Mail*, June 15, 2001.

Bisseker, C. "Botswana and Uganda Lead the Way in the Battle," *Financial Mail*, June 15, 2001.

Bridge, S. "Aids Risk May Become an Accounting Item," *Business Report*, July 4, 2000.

Cauvin, H. E. "Mining Company to Offer HIV Drugs to Employees," *The New York Times*, August 7, 2002.

Deloitte and Touche Human Capital Corporation, "Evaluation of Workplace Responses to HIV/AIDS in South Africa," May 2002. Available on the web: www.redribbon.co.za.

Economist, "AIDS and South African Business: Strategic Caring," October 5, 2002.

Lamont, J. "UN Looks to Business for Help in Fight Against AIDS," *Financial Times*, August 30, 2002.

Lamont, J. "Anglo American Set to Be the First Group to Offer Staff Free AIDS Drugs," *Financial Times*, September 13, 2002.

Mail and Guardian online. "AIDS 'bringing social collapse,' " November 27, 2002.

New York Times-Editorial. "AIDS as a Threat to Global Stability," October 4, 2002.

Schoofs, M. "Holbrooke Enlists Multinational Firms to Battle AIDS," *The Wall Street Journal*, November 30, 2001.

"South African Business Coalition on HIV and AIDS: A South African Business Response to the HIV and AIDS Epidemic," South African Business Coalition on HIV/AIDS. Available on the web: www.redribbon.co.za.

Sternbert, S. "Former Diplomat Holbrooke Takes on Global AIDS," *USA Today*, June 11, 2002.

van der Vilet, V. "AIDS: Losing 'The New Struggle'?" *Daedalus*, Winter 2001, pp. 151–184.

Whiteside, A., and Sunter, C. *AIDS: The Challenge for South Africa*. Cape Town: Human and Rousseau, 2000.

APPENDIX A

Profile of South Africa

Excerpts from U.S. Department of State Bureau of African Affairs, April 2002

(For the full text of this profile, see *http://www.state.gov/r/pa/ei/bgn/2898.htm*).

OFFICIAL NAME

Republic of South Africa

GEOGRAPHY

Area: 1.2 million sq. km. (470,462 sq. mi.).

Cities: *Capitals*—Administrative, Pretoria; Legislative, Cape Town; Judicial, Bioemfontein. *Other cities*—Johannesburg, Durban, Port Elizabeth. Terrain: Plateau, savanna, desert, mountains, coastal plains. Climate: Moderate; similar to southern California.

PEOPLE

Nationality: *Noun and adjective*—South African(s).
Annual growth rate (2000): 1.5%.
Population (2001, 44.6 million): *Composition*—black 77.8%; white 10.2%; colored 8.7%; Asian (Indian) 2.5%; other 0.8.5%.

Languages: Afrikaans, English, Ndebele, Pedi, Sotho, Swazi, Tsonga, Tswana, Venda, Xhosa, Zulu (all official languages).

Religions: Predominantly Christian; traditional African, Hindu, Muslim, Jewish.

Education: *Years compulsory*—7–15 years of age for all children. The South African Schools Act, Act 84 of 1996, passed by Parliament in 1996, aims to achieve greater educational opportunities for black children, mandating a single syllabus and, more equitable funding for schools.

Health (official): *Infant mortality rate* (1998)—45.4 per live births. Estimates from international organizations range from 50 to 60 per live births. *Life expectancy*—54 yrs. Women; 52 yrs. Men.

GOVERNMENT

Type: *Executive*—president; bicameral Parliament.

Independence: The Union of South Africa was created on May 31, 1910; became sovereign state within British Empire in 1934; became a Republic on May 31, 1961; left the Commonwealth in October 1968.

Constitution: Nonracial, democratic constitution came into effect April 27, 1994; rejoined the Commonwealth in May 1994.

In 1991, the Group Areas Act, Land Acts, and the Population Registration Act—the last of the so-called "pillars of apartheid"—were abolished. A long series of negotiations ensued, resulting in a new constitution promulgated into law in December 1993. The country's first nonracial elections were held on April 26–29, 1994, resulting in the installation of Nelson Mandela as president on May 10, 1994.

Nelson Mandela stepped down as president of the ANC at the party's national congress in December 1997, when Thabo Mbeki assumed the mantle of leadership. Mbeki won the presidency of South Africa after national elections in 1999, when the ANC won just shy of a two-thirds majority in parliament. President Mbeki shifted the focus of government from reconciliation to transformation, particularly on the economic front. With political transformation and the foundation of a strong democratic system in place after two free and fair national elections, the ANC recognized the need to begin to focus on bringing economic power to the black majority in South Africa, as well as political power. In this, progress has come somewhat more slowly.

ECONOMY

GDP (2000): $126 billion. (2001 GDP—at market prices—R975, 196 million)
    GDP growth rate (2001): 2.0%.
    GDP per capita (2000): $2,900.
    Unemployment (2000): 23.3%.
    Natural resources: Almost all essential commodities, except petroleum products and

bauxite. Only country in the world that manufactures fuel from coal.

Industry: Types—minerals, mining, motor vehicles and parts, machinery, textiles, chemicals, fertilizer, information technology, electronics, other manufacturing, and agroprocessing.

Trade (2000): *Exports*—$31.5 billion (2001 merchandise exports R232.4 billion; 2001 gold exports R29.4 billion): gold, other minerals and metals, agricultural products, motor vehicles and parts. *Major markets*—U.K., U.S., Germany, Italy, Japan, East Asia, Sub-Saharan Africa. *Imports*—$27.3 billion (2001 merchandise imports R219.9 billion): machinery, transport equipment, chemicals, petroleum products, textiles, and scientific instruments. *Major suppliers*—Germany, U.S., Japan, U.K., Italy.

GDP composition (2000): *Agriculture and mining* (primary sector)—9.7%; *industry* (secondary sector)—24.4%; *services* (tertiary sector)—65.9%. World's largest producer of platinum, gold, and chromium; also significant coal production.

CHALLENGES AHEAD

The post-apartheid Government of South Africa has made remarkable progress in consolidating the nation's peaceful transition to democracy. Programs to improve the delivery of essential social services to the majority of the population are underway. Access to better opportunities in education and business is becoming more widespread. Nevertheless, transforming South Africa's society to remove the legacy of apartheid will be a long-term process requiring the sustained commitment of the leaders and people of the nation's disparate groups.

Although South Africa's economy is in many areas highly developed, the exclusionary nature of apartheid and distortions caused in part by the country's international isolation until the 1990s have left major weaknesses. The economy is now in a process of transition as the government seeks to address the inequities of apartheid, stimulate growth, and create jobs. Business, meanwhile, is becoming more integrated into the international system, and foreign investment has increased dramatically over the past several years. Still, the economic disparities between population groups are expected to persist for many years, remaining an area of priority attention for the government.

HIV/AIDS

South Africa is one of the countries most affected by HIV with 5–6 million HIV infected individuals. Nearly 20% of the 15–49 year old population is infected and in parts of the country up to 40% of women of child-bearing age are infected. Overall, 12–13% of the population is infected and by 2005 this rate could reach 15%. About 2,300 new infections occur each day or over 850,000 annually. Approximately 40% of adult deaths and 25% of all deaths in 2000 were due to AIDS. Without effective prevention and treatment 5–7 million cumulative AIDS deaths are anticipated by 2010 (with 1.5 million deaths in 2010 alone), and there will be over 1 million sick with AIDS. Recent studies predict the epidemic could cost South Africa as much as 17% in GDP growth by 2010. The extraction industries, education, and health are among the sectors that will be severely affected. Over the last decade, national government leadership has not effectively addressed the epidemic although a good HIV prevention strategy was initiated. In April 2002 a revitalization of the HIV/AIDS program was announced by the Cabinet with substantial funding increases anticipated in 2003–04.

APPENDIX B

The Global Business Council on HIV/AIDS

WHY IS HIV/AIDS MY BUSINESS?

The HIV/AIDS epidemic is one of the greatest social challenges of our generation, and the greatest public health crisis in over 600 years. In the most affected countries, notably in Sub-Saharan Africa, the epidemic is destabilizing markets and societies, and threatening economic development and security. HIV/AIDS especially affects workforces, both skilled and unskilled, and imposes enormous costs on businesses through declining productivity, increasing labor costs and loss of skilled and experienced workers.

Like other epidemics throughout history, HIV/AIDS spreads rapidly. However, unlike other epidemics, it can be years before a person infected with the virus starts showing symptoms, making it hard to evaluate the scale of the problem. Furthermore, about 95% of those who are HIV positive in the world do not know it. This is a major obstacle to implementing effective HIV/AIDS prevention and care responses. Business, therefore, must act early and decisively to protect themselves and to assist in dealing with this crisis.

WHAT SHOULD I DO?

While there are a variety of responses business can make. The Global Business Council on HIV/AIDS firmly believes that the greatest immediate responsibility—and opportunity—for individual companies is to protect their workforces and their families against the spread of this epidemic and to assist employees infected with HIV in remaining healthy and able to contribute to the business for as long as possible.

Businesses have begun to establish workplace policies and programs to combat HIV/AIDS. In addition, international agencies and non-governmental organizations have produced guidelines for employers. Recognizing that policies and programs need to be tailored to an individual company's size, location and type of business, the Council has identified the key elements of any effective program.

- **Risk Assessment**—Each company needs to evaluate the scale of the problem on its own workforce, reviewing what existing barriers may hinder effective action.
- **Non-Discriminatory Policy**—Company-wide policies should be developed to ensure employee confidentiality.
- **Prevention and Awareness Program**—Businesses should initiate HIV education for all employees explaining in simple, easily understood language, how HIV is—and is not—transmitted. The leadership and commitment of senior management is critical to the success of these programs. Programs typically include the treatment of sexually transmitted diseases, distribution of condoms to staff, and collaboration with local AIDS organizations to devise information materials and to provide counseling and support for staff.
- **Voluntary Counseling and Testing**—Businesses can offer confidential testing and counseling in on-site clinics or in partnership with other local health services. It is vital that confidentiality about test results is guaranteed, although generalized anonymous information about HIV rates in the workforce can assist future planning.
- **Care, Support and Treatment**—Employers can help their employees living with HIV/AIDS continue to contribute to the business for as long as possible through a range of care and support services through company clinics or in partnership with other healthcare providers. This should also include treatment of opportunistic infections, such as TB. Where possible, companies should implement antiretroviral treatment programs for infected employees and their families, taking advantage of the major reductions in the prices of these drugs.

The Global Business Council on HIV/AIDS has produced further information on setting up HIV workplace policies and programs. For more information contact Ben Plumley, the Executive Director at the Council. The Global Business Council on HIV and AIDS c/o Viacom 1515 Broadway, 45th floor, New York, NY 10036. TEL + 1 \ 212 846 5893. FAX + 1 \ 212 846 1939. WEB www.businessfightsaids.org.

APPENDIX C

U.S. Department of State Fact Sheet—September 3, 2000

(For an update, see http://www.state.gov/r/pa/prs/ps/2002/13227htm).

HIV/AIDS IN SUB-SAHARAN AFRICA

Background

- 28.5 million living with HIV AIDS at end-2001
- 2.2 million deaths in 2001
- 3.5 million new infections in 2001
- 12 countries have infection rates of 10 percent or more among 15–49 year olds
- 11 million AIDS orphans in 2001; UNAIDS predicts 20 million by 2010

Seventy-five percent of those living with HIV/AIDS are in Sub-Saharan Africa. The pandemic is changing the demographic structure of Africa and wiping out life expectancy gains. In many African countries, life expectancy is dropping from more than 60 years to around 45 years. In Botswana, it has dropped to 39; without AIDS, it is estimated to have been 72 years.

The estimates of the impact of HIV/AIDS on economic growth rates vary but the trend is clear. A World Bank researcher estimated that the average 0.4% per capita income growth rates Africa achieved in 1990–1997 would have been 1.1% per year without HIV/AIDS. In countries with prevalence rates around 20%, the effect is more dire; GDP growth rates will be about 2.6% less than they would have been without the epidemic.

While the long-term effect of the pandemic is not known, studies to date paint a grim picture. According to the World Bank, "Labor productivity is likely to drop, the benefits of education will be lost, and resources that would have been used for investments will be used for health care, orphan care, and funerals. Savings rates will decline, and the loss of human capital will affect production and the quality of life for years to come." By 2005, South Africa, for example, is projected to lose 11% of its workforce to AIDS; Zimbabwe nearly 20%.

This crushing HIV burden comes on top of Africa's significant share of global health problems generally. For example, 80 percent of the world's tuberculosis cases occur in Africa and respiratory infections, parasitic diseases, diarrheal diseases, and malaria remain major killers of children and adults across the continent.

U.S. INTERESTS

The U.S. has recognized that HIV is not only a threat to the health and economic well-being of Africans but a national security issue as well. As HIV/AIDS strains the economic, social and security fabric of Africa, it affects U.S. policy interests across the board. HIV undermines hard-fought development gains and can destroy communities and destabilize regions. It is also disproportionately affecting African militaries, with prevalence rates in some armed services possibly reaching 50%. The severe ripple effects of HIV/AIDS, if not contained, pose a clear threat to U.S. interests in a peaceful, prosperous and stable Africa.

Early intervention is important. As prevalence rates grow, per capita costs of addressing the epidemic also grow, thereby making a strong case for early intervention. When HIV rates are below 5%, the cost of programs is about $3 per capita. Once the rates hit 15%, the cost becomes $10–$12 per capita (this does not include antiretroviral treatment).

The U.S. focuses its programs on prevention, care and support through multifaceted programs that include preventing new infections, reducing risky behavior, social marketing of condoms, preventing mother-to-child transmission, voluntary counseling and testing, treating other sexually transmitted diseases, and programs to address the needs of AIDS orphans and communities caring for them. The U.S. is also supporting programs to strengthen vaccine research and testing and overall health system capacities. USAID and HHS (CDC) administer the bulk of USG resources but DoD and DoL have targeted programs to address HIV/AIDS in the military and workplace, respectively.

The issue of treatment, especially access to antiretroviral drugs at affordable prices has been at the forefront of the AIDS debate domestically and internationally. With encouragement from the U.S., a number of pharmaceutical companies have responded by agreeing to make their antiretroviral drugs available in developing countries at greatly reduced cost. While cost is an important issue and even reduced costs pose a challenge for very poor African countries, delivery/monitoring challenges associated with poor health care infrastructure are as important a consideration as cost. WTO Doha Ministerial Declaration on TRIPS and Public Health clarified the flexibility the TRIPS agreement offers in addressing health care emergencies, while retaining the integrity of the agreement and recognizing that TRIPS, and the incentives it offers for innovation and research, is part of the solution to health care crises. At their recent summit in Kananaskis, G-8 leaders reiterated their commitment to continue to promote the availability of an adequate supply of life-saving medicines in an affordable and medically effective manner.

CURRENT INITIATIVES

The USG is the single largest donor to international AIDS efforts. The FY '02 budget for the USG's international HIV/AIDS programs is about $800 million including $200 million of our $500 million pledge to the Global Fund. In FY '03, the request is about $1.1 billion. Just over half of U.S. support for bilateral HIV/AIDS programs goes to Africa. The U.S. bilateral program to date has focused about 70% of its resources on prevention efforts.

In June, President Bush announced a major new initiative to accelerate and expand U.S. efforts to fight mother and child HIV infection. The $500 million initiative will target 12 countries in Sub-Saharan Africa and the Caribbean. Within five years, the goal is to treat one million women and reduce mother-to-child transmission by 40 percent. The initiative includes elements to improve the health care delivery systems by pairing U.S. hospitals with African clinics, facilitating the implementation of prevention, care and treatment programs, and providing AIDS drugs where appropriate. Kenya, South Africa, and Uganda and Nigeria are slated to receive support in FY 2002; Nigeria will be added in FY 2004.

The U.S. is also the major contributor to the Global Fund to Fight AIDS, Tuberculosis, and Malaria. The U.S. has pledged $500 million to the Fund, which announced its first round of grants in April. The Board approved grants worth $378 million over two years for 40 programs in 31 countries. Another 18 proposals worth $238 million were put on a fast track for approval once some modifications are made to meet Fund criteria. About half of the value of the approved grants are for countries in Sub-Saharan Africa. The Fund has issued its second call for proposals and will announce additional grants in January 2003.

Case Study

Chrysler and Gao Feng: Corporate Responsibility for Religious and Political Freedom in China

Michael A. Santoro

INTRODUCTION

For multinational corporations, doing business in China presents many complex ethical issues. The Gao Feng incident exemplifies the challenging decisions that confront corporate executives trying to run a business in a country run by a totalitarian government that violates the human rights of its own citizens.

THE GAO FENG INCIDENT

In May 1994, Gao Feng, a devout Christian, was arrested in Beijing for planning a private worship service and candlelight vigil to commemorate the fifth anniversary of the Tiananmen Square massacre. Gao was a 26-year employee of Beijing Jeep, Chrysler's joint venture with the Chinese government. Gao was accused of violating Chinese laws against the practice of religion outside of a state-authorized venue.

Technically, Gao appears to have violated Chinese law. Article 36 of the Chinese Constitution nominally provides for freedom of religious belief. However, the government restricts religious practice to government-sanctioned organizations in order to control the growth and scope of activity of religious groups. State Council Regulation 145, signed into law by then Premier Li Peng in January 1994, requires all places of worship to register with government religious affairs bureaus and come under the supervision of official "patriotic" religious organizations. There are almost 85,000 approved venues for religious activities in China. Many religious groups, however, have been reluctant to comply with the regulation either out of principled opposition to state control of religion or due to fear of adverse consequences if they reveal, as the regulations require, the names and addresses of church leaders.

The Universal Declaration of Human Rights, endorsed by a resolution of the United Nations General Assembly in 1948, contains the following relevant provisions:

> **Article 18.** Everyone has the right to freedom of thought, conscience and religion; this right includes freedom to change his religion or belief, and freedom, either alone or in community with others and in public or private, to manifest his religion or belief in teaching, practice, worship and observance.
>
> **Article 19.** Everyone has the right to freedom of opinion and expression; this right includes freedom to hold opinions without interference and to seek, receive and impart information and ideas through any media and regardless of frontiers.
>
> **Article 20.** (1) Everyone has the right to freedom of peaceful assembly and association. (2) No one may be compelled to belong to an association.

According to press reports, Gao remained under administrative detention for five weeks. He was never formally charged. In early July, Gao returned to work at Beijing Jeep and told his supervisor that the Chinese Public Safety Bureau had imprisoned him for over a month. Chrysler asked Gao to produce proof of his detention. The Chinese police gave Gao a note that said that he had been detained for three days and then released without trial.

Beijing Jeep's general manager was faced with a tough decision. The Chinese joint venture partner was pressuring Chrysler to fire Gao Feng. If he does not fire him, millions of dollars of Chrysler's invested capital in China would be put at risk. If, however, Chrysler fires Gao Feng, the company would become complicit in the violation of his right to religious freedom and political expression.

The commercial interests at stake for Chrysler cannot be ignored. One of the keys to success in the Chinese markets is good relations with the Communist Party which keeps rigid control over the economy. Multinational corporations spend years cultivating good *guanxi* or connections in China. They are thus extremely vulnerable to retaliation. Even powerful corporations such as Motorola, Hewlett-Packard and General Motors are well aware that they could jeopardize billions of dollars of investments if they take a position on human rights that angers the Chinese government. At the time of the Gao Feng incident, for example, Chrysler was very aware that failure to accede to the government's request could result in losing a valuable minivan contract to its German competitor Daimler-Benz. (United States–based Chrysler subsequently merged its worldwide businesses with the Germany-based Daimler-Benz.) As a consequence, the basic instinct of most foreign businesspeople in China is to stay as far away from the subject of human rights as possible. However, when a situation like the Gao Feng incident arises, corporate executives must make a decision and take action. Avoidance is simply not an option.

THE DECISION

Put yourself in the position of Chysler's general manager. How would you handle the situation? Would you fire Gao Feng? Would you refuse to fire him? Is there some other course of action you would consider?

Would it be a sign of "cultural imperialism" if Chrysler refused to fire Gao Feng? After all, didn't Gao Feng violate Chinese law on the practice of religion? Does it matter that the enforcement of the law would appear to be in violation of the Universal Declaration of Human Rights?

How much should you factor in the financial consequences of your decision? What if your refusal to fire Gao Feng cost Chrysler millions of dollars in potential profits? Is there some way of handling the situation that would minimize the potential financial consequences?

When asked how he would handle the Gao Feng scenario, one executive with many years of business experience in China replied as follows: "The first thing I would do is to tell my secretary to hold my calls and then I would close my door to think. Because this would be a very serious situation, which, if not handled properly, could have serious repercussions for my company. I would take this very seriously."

OUTCOME

Chrysler, presumably reasoning that Gao Feng had no documented reason for failing to report to work for the bulk of the time he was missing, fired him for poor attendance. Gao Feng's case became widely publicized when the advocacy group Human Rights Watch took up his cause. Due to the personal intervention of Chrysler's chairman, Robert J. Eaton, Gao was eventually reinstated, but his case dramatically illustrates the moral and financial pitfalls of operating in a country where there are serious and pervasive human rights abuses.

Gao's freedom was, however, short-lived once the publicity surrounding his case subsided. A few months after his reinstatement at Chrysler, Gao was rearrested and without benefit of a legal proceeding sent to a reeducation through labor camp. Gao Feng was again released in 1998 following the highly publicized visit of a interdenominational group of clergy appointed by President Clinton to investigate religious freedom in China.

Essay

The Great Non-Debate over International Sweatshops

Ian Maitland

In recent years, there has been a dramatic growth in the contracting out of production by companies in the industrialized countries to suppliers in developing countries. This globalization of production has led to an emerging international division of labor in footwear and apparel in which companies like Nike and Reebok concentrate on product design and marketing but rely on a network of contractors in Indonesia, China, Central America, etc., to build shoes or sew shirts according to exact specifications and deliver a high quality good according to precise delivery schedules. As Nike's vice president for Asia has put it, "We don't know the first thing about manufacturing. We are marketers and designers."

The contracting arrangements have drawn intense fire from critics—usually labor and human rights activists. These "critics" (as I will refer to them) have charged that the companies are (by proxy) exploiting workers in the plants (which I will call "international sweatshops") of their suppliers. Specifically the companies stand accused of chasing cheap labor around the globe, failing to pay their workers living wages, using child labor, turning a blind eye to abuses of human rights, being complicit with repressive regimes in denying workers the right to join unions and failing to enforce minimum labor standards in the workplace, and so on.

The campaign against international sweatshops has largely unfolded on television and, to a lesser extent, in the print media. What seems like no more than a handful of critics has mounted an aggressive, media-savvy campaign which has put the publicity-shy retail giants on the defensive. The critics have orchestrated a series of sensational "disclosures" on prime time television exposing the terrible pay and working conditions in factories making jeans for Levi's or sneakers for Nike or Pocahontas shirts for Disney. One of the principal scourges of the companies has been Charles Kernaghan who runs the National Labor Coalition (NLC), a labor human rights group involving 25 unions. It was Kernaghan who, in 1996, broke the news before a Congressional committee that Kathie Lee Gifford's clothing line was being made by 13- and 14-year-olds working 20-hour days in factories in Honduras. Kernaghan also arranged for teenage workers from sweatshops in Central America to testify before Congressional committees about abusive labor practices. At one of these hearings, one of the workers held up a Liz Claiborne cotton sweater identical to ones she had sewn since she was a 13-year-old working 12 hours days. According to a news report, "[t]his image, accusations of oppressive conditions at the factory and the Claiborne logo played well on that evening's network news." The result has been a circus-like atmosphere—as in Roman circus where Christians were thrown to lions.

Kernaghan has shrewdly targeted the companies' carefully cultivated public images. He has explained: "Their image is everything. They live and die by their image. That gives you a certain power over them." As a result, he says, "these companies are sitting ducks. They have no leg to stand on. That's why it's possible for a tiny group like us to take on a giant like Wal-Mart. You can't defend paying someone 31 cents an hour in Honduras. . . ."[1] Apparently most of the companies agree with Kernaghan. Not a single company has tried to mount a serious defense of its contracting practices. They have judged that they cannot win a war of soundbites with the critics. Instead of making a fight of it, the companies have sued for peace in order to protect their principal asset—their image.

Major U.S. retailers have responded by adopting codes of conduct on human and labor rights in their international operations. Levi-Strauss, Nike, Sears, JCPenney, Wal-Mart, Home Depot, and Philips Van-Heusen now have such codes. As Lance Compa notes, such codes are the result of a blend of humanitarian and pragmatic impulses: "Often the altruistic motive coincides with "bottom line" considerations related to

From Ian Maitland, "The great non-debate over international sweatshops," *British Academy of Management Annual Conference Proceedings*, September, pp. 240–265, 1997. Reprinted with permission.

brand name, company image, and other intangibles that make for core value to the firm."[2] Peter Jacobi, President of Global Sourcing for Levi-Strauss has advised: "If your company owns a popular brand, protect this priceless asset at all costs. Highly visible companies have any number of reasons to conduct their business not just responsibly but also in ways that cannot be portrayed as unfair, illegal, or unethical. This sets an extremely high standard since it must be applied to both company-owned businesses and contractors. . . ."[3] And according to another Levi-Strauss spokesman. "In many respects, we're protecting our single largest asset: our brand image and corporate reputation."[4] Nike recently published the results of a generally favorable review of its international operations conducted by former American U.N. Ambassador Andrew Young.

Recently a truce of sorts between the critics and the companies was announced on the White House lawn with President Clinton and Kathie Lee Gifford in attendance. A presidential task force, including representatives of labor unions, human rights groups and apparel companies like L.L. Bean and Nike, has come up with a set of voluntary standards which, it hopes, will be embraced by the entire industry. Companies that comply with the code will be entitled to use a "No Sweat" label.

OBJECTIVE OF THIS PAPER

In this confrontation between the companies and their critics, neither side seems to have judged it to be in its interest to seriously engage the issue at the heart of this controversy, namely: What are appropriate wages and labor standards in international sweatshops? As we have seen, the companies have treated the charges about sweatshops as a public relations problem to be managed so

as to minimize harm to their public images. The critics have apparently judged that the best way to keep public indignation at boiling point is to oversimplify the issue and treat it as a morality play featuring heartless exploiters and victimized third world workers. The result has been a great non-debate over international sweatshops. Paradoxically, if peace breaks out between the two sides, the chances that the debate will be seriously joined may recede still further. Indeed, there exists a real risk (I will argue) that any such truce may be a collusive one that will come at the expense of the very third world workers it is supposed to help.

This paper takes up the issue of what are appropriate wages and labor standards in international sweatshops. Critics charge that the present arrangements are exploitative. I proceed by examining the specific charges of exploitation from the standpoints of both (a) their factual and (b) their ethical sufficiency. However, in the absence of any well-established consensus among business ethicists (or other thoughtful observers). I simultaneously use the investigation of sweatshops as a setting for trying to adjudicate between competing views about what those standards should be. My examination will pay particular attention to (but will not be limited to) labor conditions at the plants of Nike's suppliers in Indonesia. I have not personally visited any international sweatshops, and so my conclusions are based entirely on secondary analysis of the voluminous published record on the topic.

WHAT ARE ETHICALLY APPROPRIATE LABOR STANDARDS IN INTERNATIONAL SWEATSHOPS?

What are ethically acceptable or appropriate levels of wages and labor standards in international sweatshops? The following three possibilities just about run the gamut of standards or principles that have been seriously proposed to regulate such policies.

1. *Home-country standards:* It might be argued (and in rare cases has been) that international corporations have an ethical duty to pay the same wages and provide the same labor standards regardless of where they operate. However, the view that home-country standards should apply in host-countries is rejected by most business ethicists and (officially at least) by the critics of international sweatshops. Thus Thomas Donaldson argues that "[b]y arbitrarily establishing U.S. wage levels as the benchmark for fairness one eliminates the role of the international market in establishing salary levels, and this in turn eliminates the incentive U.S. corporations have to hire foreign workers."[5] Richard DeGeorge makes much the same argument. If there were a rule that said that "that American MNCs [multinational corporations] that wish to be ethical must pay the same wages abroad as they do at home, . . . [then] MNCs would have little incentive to move their manufacturing abroad; and if they did move abroad they would disrupt the local labor market with artificially high wages that bore no relation to the local standard or cost of living."[6]

2. *"Living wage" standard:* It has been proposed that an international corporation should, at a minimum, pay a "living wage." Thus DeGeorge says that corporations should pay a living wage "even when this is not paid by local firms."[7] However, it is hard to pin down what this means operationally. According to DeGeorge, a living wage should "allow the worker to live in dignity as a human being." In order to respect the human rights of its workers, he says, a corporation must pay "at least subsistence wages and as much above that as workers and their dependents need to live with reasonable dignity, given the general state of development of the society."[8] As we shall see, the living wage standard has become a rallying cry of the critics of international sweatshops. Apparently, DeGeorge believes that it is preferable for a corporation to provide no job at all than to offer one that pays less than a living wage. . . .

3. *Classical liberal standard:* Finally, there is what I will call the classical liberal standard. According to this standard a practice (wage or labor practice) is ethically acceptable if it is freely chosen by informed workers. For example, in a recent report the World Bank invoked this standard in connection with workplace safety. It said: "The appropriate level is therefore that at which the costs are commensurate with the value that informed workers place on improved working conditions and reduced risk."[9] Most business ethicists reject this standard on the grounds that there is some sort of market failure or the "background conditions" are lacking for markets to work effectively. Thus for Donaldson full (or near-full) employment is a prerequisite if workers are to make sound choices regarding workplace safety: "The average level of unemployment in the developing countries today exceeds 40 percent, a figure that has frustrated the application of neoclassical economic principles to the international economy on a score of issues. With full employment, and all other things being equal, market forces will encourage workers to make trade-offs between job opportunities using safety as a variable. But with massive unemployment, market forces in developing countries drive the unemployed to the jobs they are lucky enough to land, regardless of the safety."[10] Apparently there are other forces, like Islamic fundamentalism and the global debt "bomb," that rule out reliance on market solutions, but Donaldson does not explain their relevance.[11] DeGeorge, too, believes that the necessary conditions are lacking for market forces to operate benignly. Without what he calls "background institutions" to protect the workers and the resources of the developing country (e.g., enforceable minimum wages) and/or greater equality of bargaining power exploitation is the most likely result.[12] "If American MNCs pay workers very low wages . . . they clearly have the opportunity to make significant profits."[13] DeGeorge goes on to make the interesting observation that "competition has developed among multinationals themselves, so that the profit margin has been driven down" and developing countries "can play one company against another."[14] But apparently that is not enough to rehabilitate market forces in his eyes.

THE CASE AGAINST INTERNATIONAL SWEATSHOPS

To many of their critics, international sweatshops exemplify the way in which the greater openness of the world economy is hurting workers. . . . Globalization means a transition from (more or less) regulated domestic economies to an unregulated world economy. The superior mobility of capital, and the essentially fixed, immobile nature of world labor, means a fundamental shift in bargaining power in favor of large international corporations. Their global reach permits them to shift production almost costlessly from one location to another. As a consequence, instead of being able to exercise some degree of control over companies operating within their borders, governments are now locked in a bidding war with one another to attract and retain the business of large multinational companies.

The critics allege that international companies are using the threat of withdrawal or withholding of investment to pressure governments and workers to grant concessions. "Today [multinational companies] choose between workers in developing countries that compete against each other to depress wages to attract foreign investment." The result is a race for the bottom—a "destructive downward bidding spiral of the labor conditions and wages of workers throughout the world. . . ."[15] . . . Thus, critics charge that in Indonesia wages are deliberately held below the poverty level or subsistence in order to make the country a desirable location. The results of this competitive dismantling of worker protections, living standards and worker rights are predictable: deteriorating work conditions, declining real incomes for workers, and a widening gap between rich and poor in developing countries. I turn next to the specific charges made by the critics of international sweatshops.

Unconscionable Wages

Critics charge that the companies, by their proxies, are paying "starvation wages" and "slave wages." They are far from clear about what wage level they consider to be appropriate. But they generally demand that companies pay a "living wage." Kernaghan has said that workers should be paid enough to support their families and they should get a "living wage" and "be treated like human beings."[16] . . . According to Tim Smith, wage levels should be "fair, decent or a living wage for an employee and his or her family." He has said that wages in the maquiladoras of Mexico averaged $35 to $55 a week (in or near 1993) which he calls a "shockingly substandard wage," apparently on the grounds that it "clearly does not allow an employee to feed and care for a family adequately."[17] In 1992, Nike came in for harsh criticism when a magazine published the pay stub of a worker at one of its Indonesian suppliers. It showed that the worker was paid at the rage of $1.03 per day which was reportedly less than the Indonesian government's figure for "minimum physical need."[18]

Immiserization Thesis

Former Labor Secretary Robert Reich has proposed as a test of the fairness of development policies that "Low-wage workers should become better off, not worse off, as trade and investment boost national income." He has written that "[i]f a country pursues policies that . . . limit to a narrow elite the benefits of trade, the promise of open commerce is perverted and drained of its rationale."[19] A key claim of the activists is that companies actually impoverish or immiserize developing country workers. They experience an absolute decline in living standards. This thesis follows from the claim that the bidding war among developing countries is depressing wages. . . .

Widening Gap Between Rich and Poor

A related charge is that international sweat-shops are contributing to the increasing gap between rich and poor. Not only are the poor being absolutely impoverished, but trade is generating greater inequality within developing countries. Another test that Reich has proposed to establish the fairness of international trade is that "the gap between rich and poor should tend to narrow with development, not widen."[20] Critics charge that international sweatshops flunk that test. They say that the increasing GNPs of some developing countries simply mask a widening gap between rich and poor. "Across the world, both local and foreign elites are getting richer from the exploitation of the most vulnerable."[21] And, "The major adverse consequence of quickening global economic integration has been widening income disparity within almost all nations. . . ."[22] There appears to be a tacit alliance between the elites of both first and third worlds to exploit the most vulnerable, to regiment and control and conscript them so that they can create the material conditions for the elites' extravagant lifestyles.

Collusion with Repressive Regimes

Critics charge that, in their zeal to make their countries safe for foreign investment. Third World regimes, notably China and Indonesia, have stepped up their repression. Not only have these countries failed to enforce even the minimal labor rules on the books, but they have also used their military and police to break strikes and repress independent unions. They have stifled political dissent, both to retain their hold on political power and to avoid any instability that might scare off foreign investors. Consequently, critics charge, companies like Nike are profiting from political repression. "As unions spread in [Korea and Taiwan], Nike shifted its suppliers primarily to Indonesia, China and Thailand, where they could depend on governments to suppress independent union-organizing efforts."[23]

EVALUATION OF THE CHARGES AGAINST INTERNATIONAL SWEATSHOPS

The critics' charges are undoubtedly accurate on a number of points: (1) There is no doubt that international companies are chasing cheap labor. (2) The wages paid by the international sweatshops are—by American standards—shockingly low. (3) Some developing country governments have tightly controlled or repressed organized labor in order to prevent it from disturbing the flow of foreign investment. Thus, in Indonesia, independent unions have been suppressed. (4) It is not unusual in developing countries for minimum wage levels to be lower than the official poverty level. (5) Developing country governments have winked at violations of minimum wage laws and labor rules. However, most jobs are in the informal sector and so largely outside the scope of government supervision. (6) Some suppliers have employed children or have subcontracted work to other producers who have done so. (7) Some developing country governments deny their people basic political rights. China is the obvious example; Indonesia's record is pretty horrible but had shown steady improvement until the last two years. But on many of the other counts, the critics' charges appear to be seriously inaccurate. And, even where the charges are accurate, it is not selfevident that the practices in question are improper or unethical, as we see next.

Wages and Conditions

Even the critics of international sweatshops do not dispute that the wages they pay are generally higher than—or at least equal to—comparable wages in the labor markets where they operate. According to the International Labor Organization (ILO), multinational companies often apply standards relating to wages, benefits, conditions of work, and occupational safety and health, which both exceed statutory requirements and those practiced by local firms."[24] The ILO also says that wages and working conditions in so-called Export Processing Zones (EPZs) are often equal to or higher than jobs outside. The World Bank says that the poorest workers in developing countries work in the informal sector where they often earn less than half what a formal sector employee earns. Moreover, "informal and rural workers often must work under more hazardous and insecure conditions than their formal sector counterparts.[25]

The same appears to hold true for the international sweatshops. In 1996, young women working in the plant of a Nike supplier in Serang, Indonesia were earning the Indonesian legal minimum wage of 5,200 rupiahs or about $2.28 each day. As a report in the *Washington Post* pointed out, just earning the minimum wage put these workers among higher-paid Indonesians: "In Indonesia, less than half the working population earns the minimum wage, since about half of all adults here are in farming, and the typical farmer would make only about 2,000 rupiahs each day."[26] The workers in the Serang plant reported that they save about three-quarters of their pay. A 17-year-old woman said: "I came here one year ago from central Java. I'm making more money than my father makes." This woman also said that she sent about 75 percent of her earnings back to her family on the farm.[27] Also in 1996, a Nike spokeswoman estimated that an entry-level factory worker in the plant of a Nike supplier made five times what a farmer makes.[28] Nike's chairman. Phil Knight, likes to teasingly remind critics

that the average worker in one of Nike's Chinese factories is paid more than a professor at Beijing University.[29] There is also plentiful anecdotal evidence from non-Nike sources. A worker at the Taiwanese-owned King Star Garment Assembly plant in Honduras told a reporter that he was earning seven times what he earned in the countryside.[30] In Bangladesh, the country's fledgling garment industry was paying women who had never worked before between $40 and $55 a month in 1991. That compared with a national per capita income of about $200 and the approximately $1 a day earned by many of these women's husbands as day laborers or rickshaw drivers.[31]

The same news reports also shed some light on the working conditions in sweatshops. According to the *Washington Post*, in 1994 the Indonesian office of the international accounting firm Ernst and Young surveyed Nike workers concerning worker pay, safety conditions and attitudes toward the job. The auditors pulled workers off the assembly line at random and asked them questions that the workers answered anonymously. The survey of 25 workers at Nike's Serang plant found that 23 thought the hours and overtime worked were fair, and two thought the overtime hours too high. None of the workers reported that they had been discriminated against. Thirteen said the working environment was the key reason they worked at the Serang plant while eight cited salary and benefits.[32] The *Post* report also noted that the Serang plant closes for about ten days each year for Muslim holidays. It quoted Nike officials and the plant's Taiwanese owners as saying that 94 percent of the workers had returned to the plant following the most recent break. . . .

There is also the mute testimony of the lines of job applicants outside the sweatshops in Guatemala and Honduras. According to Lucy Martinez-Mont, in Guatemala the sweatshops are conspicuous for the long lines of young people waiting to be interviewed for a job.[33] Outside the gates of the industrial park in Honduras that Rohter visited "anxious onlookers are always waiting, hoping for a chance at least to fill out a job application [for employment at one of the apparel plants]."[34]

The critics of sweatshops acknowledge that workers have voluntarily taken their jobs, consider themselves lucky to have them, and want to keep them. . . . But they go on to discount the workers' views as the product of confusion or ignorance, and/or they just argue that the workers' views are beside the point. Thus, while "it is undoubtedly true" that Nike has given jobs to thousands of people who wouldn't be working otherwise, they say that "neatly skirts the fundamental human-rights issue raised by these production arrangements that are now spreading all across the world."[35] Similarly the NLC's Kernaghan says that "[w]hether workers think they are better off in the assembly plants than elsewhere is not the real issue."[36] Kernaghan, and Jeff Ballinger of the AFL-CIO, concede that the workers desperately need these jobs. But "[t]hey say they're not asking that U.S. companies stop operating in these countries. They're asking that workers be paid a living wage and treated like human beings."[37] Apparently these workers are victims of what Marx called false consciousness, or else they would grasp that they are being exploited. According to Barnet and Cavanagh, "For many workers . . . exploitation is not a concept easily comprehended because the alternative prospects for earning a living are so bleak."[38]

Immiserization and Inequality

The critics' claim that the countries that host international sweatshops are marked by growing poverty and inequality is flatly contradicted by the record. In fact, many of those countries have experienced sharp increases in living standards—for all strata of society. In trying to attract investment in simple manufacturing, Malaysia and Indonesia and, now, Vietnam and China, are retracing the industrialization path already successfully taken by East Asian countries like Taiwan, Korea, Singapore and Hong Kong. These four countries got their start by producing labor-intensive manufactured goods (often electrical and electronic components, shoes, and garments) for export markets. Over time they graduated to the export of higher value-added items that are skill-intensive and require a relatively developed industrial base.[39]

As is well known, these East Asian countries achieved growth rates exceeding eight percent for a quarter century. . . . The workers in these economies were not impoverished by growth. The benefits of growth were widely diffused: These economies achieved essentially full employment in the 1960s. Real wages rose by as much as a factor of four. Absolute poverty fell. And income inequality remained at low to moderate levels. It is true that in the initial stages the rapid growth generated only moderate increases in wages. But once essentially full employment was reached, and what economists call the Fei-Ranis turning point was reached, the increased demand for labor resulted in the bidding up of wages as firms competed for a scarce labor supply.

Interestingly, given its historic mission as a watchdog for international labor standards, the ILO has embraced this development model. It recently noted that the most successful developing economies, in terms of output and employment growth, have been "those who best exploited emerging opportunities in the global economy."[40] An "export-oriented policy is vital in countries that are starting on the industrialization path and have large surpluses of cheap labour." Countries which have succeeded in attracting foreign direct investment (FDI) have experienced rapid growth in manufacturing output and exports. The successful attraction of foreign investment in plant and equipment "can be a powerful spur to rapid industrialization and employment creation." "At low levels of industrialization, FDI in garments and shoes and some types of consumer electronics can be very useful for creating employment and opening the economy to international markets; there may be some entrepreneurial skills created in simple activities like garments (as has happened in Bangladesh). Moreover, in some cases, such as Malaysia, the investors may strike deeper roots and invest in more capital-intensive technologies as wages rise."

According to the World Bank, the rapidly growing Asian economies (including Indonesia) "have also been unusually successful at sharing the fruits of their growth."[41] In fact, while inequality in the West has been growing, it has been shrinking in the Asian economies. They are the only economies in the world to have experienced high growth *and* declining inequality, and they also show shrinking gender gaps in education. . . .

Profiting from Repression?

What about the charge that international sweatshops are profiting from repression? It is undeniable that there is repression in many of the countries where sweatshops are located. But economic development appears to be relaxing that repression rather than strengthening its grip. The companies are supposed to benefit from government policies (e.g., repression of unions) that hold down labor costs. However, as we have seen, the wages paid by the international sweatshops already match or exceed the prevailing local wages. Not only that, but incomes in the East Asian economies, and in Indonesia, have risen rapidly. . . .

The critics, however, are right in saying that the Indonesian government has opposed independent unions in the sweatshops

out of fear they would lead to higher wages and labor unrest. But the government's fear clearly is that unions might drive wages in the modern industrial sector *above* market-clearing levels—or, more exactly, further above market. It is ironic that critics like Barnet and Cavanagh would use the Marxian term "reserve army of the unemployed." According to Marx, capitalists deliberately maintain high levels of unemployment in order to control the working class. But the Indonesian government's policies (e.g., suppression of unions, resistance to a higher minimum wage and lax enforcement of labor rules) have been directed at achieving exactly the opposite result. The government appears to have calculated that high unemployment is a greater threat to its hold on power. I think we can safely take at face value its claims that its policies are genuinely intended to help the economy create jobs to absorb the massive numbers of unemployed and underemployed.[42]

LABOR STANDARDS IN INTERNATIONAL SWEATSHOPS: PAINFUL TRADE-OFFS

Who but the Grinch could grudge paying a few additional pennies to some of the world's poorest workers? There is no doubt that the rhetorical force of the critics' case against international sweatshops rests on this apparently self-evident proposition. However, higher wages and improved labor standards are not free. After all, the critics themselves attack companies for chasing cheap labor. It follows that, if labor in developing countries is made more expensive (say, as the result of pressure by the critics), then those countries will receive less foreign investment, and fewer jobs will be created there. Imposing higher wages may deprive these countries of the one comparative advantage they enjoy, namely low-cost labor.

We have seen that workers in most "international sweatshops" are already relatively well paid. Workers in the urban, formal sectors of developing countries commonly earn more than twice what informal and rural workers get. Simply earning the minimum wage put the young women making Nike shoes in Serang in the top half of the income distribution in Indonesia. Accordingly, the critics are in effect calling for a *widening* of the economic disparity that already greatly favors sweatshop workers.

By itself that may or may not be ethically objectionable. But these higher wages come at the expense of the incomes and the job opportunities of much poorer workers. As economists explain, higher wages in the formal sector reduce employment there and (by increasing the supply of labor) depress incomes in the informal sector. The case against requiring above-market wages for international sweatshop workers is essentially the same as the case against other measures that artificially raise labor costs, like the minimum wage. In Jagdish Bhagwati's words: "Requiring a minimum wage in an overpopulated, developing country, as is done in a developed country, may actually be morally wicked. A minimum wage might help the unionized, industrial proletariat, while limiting the ability to save and invest rapidly which is necessary to draw more of the unemployed and nonunionized rural poor into gainful employment and income."[43] The World Bank makes the same point: "Minimum wages may help the most poverty-stricken workers in industrial countries, but they clearly do not in developing nations. . . . The workers whom minimum wage legislation tries to protect—urban formal workers—already earn much more than the less favored majority. . . . And inasmuch as minimum wage and other regulations discourage formal employment by increasing wage and nonwage costs, they hurt the poor who aspire to formal employment."[44]

The story is no different when it comes to labor standards other than wages. If standards are set too high they will hurt investment and employment. The World Bank report points out that "[r]educing hazards in the workplace is costly, and typically the greater the reduction the more it costs. Moreover, the costs of compliance often fall largely on employees through lower wages or reduced employment. As a result, setting standards too high can actually lower workers' welfare. . . ."[45] Perversely, if the higher standards advocated by critics retard the growth of formal sector jobs, then that will trap more informal and rural workers in jobs which are far more hazardous and insecure than those of their formal sector counterparts.

The critics consistently advocate policies that will benefit better-off workers at the expense of worse-off ones. If it were within their power, it appears that they would reinvent the labor markets of much of Latin America. Alejandro Portes' description seems to be on the mark: "In Mexico, Brazil, Peru, and other Third World countries, [unlike East Asia], there are powerful independent unions representing the protected sector of the working class. Although there rhetoric is populist and even radical, the fact is that they tend to represent the better-paid and more stable fraction of the working class. Alongside, there toils a vast, unprotected proletariat, employed by informal enterprises and linked, in ways hidden from public view, with modern sector firms." . . .

Of course, it might be objected that trading off workers' rights for more jobs is unethical. But, so far as I can determine, the critics have not made this argument. Although they sometimes implicitly accept the existence of the trade-off (we saw that they attack Nike for chasing cheap labor), their public statements are silent on the lost or forgone jobs from higher wages and better labor standards. At other times, they imply or claim that improvements in workers' wages and conditions are essentially free. . . .

In summary, the result of the ostensibly humanitarian changes urged by critics are likely to be (1) reduced employment in the formal or modern sector of the economy, (2) lower incomes in the informal sector, (3) less investment and so slower economic growth, (4) reduced exports, (5) greater inequality and poverty.

CONCLUSION: THE CASE FOR NOT EXCEEDING MARKET STANDARDS

It is part of the job description of business ethicists to exhort companies to treat their workers better (otherwise what purpose do they serve?). So it will have come as no surprise that both the business ethicists whose views I summarized at the beginning of this paper—Thomas Donaldson and Richard De-George—objected to letting the market alone determine wages and labor standards in multinational companies. Both of them proposed criteria for setting wages that might occasionally "improve" on the outcomes of the market.

Their reasons for rejecting market determination of wages were similar. They both cited conditions that allegedly prevent international markets from generating ethically acceptable results. Donaldson argued that neoclassical economic principles are not applicable to international business because of high unemployment rates in developing countries. And DeGeorge argued that, in an unregulated international market, the gross inequality of bargaining power between workers and companies would lead to exploitation.

But this paper has shown that attempts to improve on market outcomes may have unforeseen tragic consequences. We saw how raising the wages of workers in international sweatshops might wind up penalizing the most vulnerable workers (those in the informal sectors of developing countries) by depressing their wages and reducing their job opportunities in the formal sector. Donaldson

and DeGeorge cited high unemployment and unequal bargaining power as conditions that made it necessary to bypass or override the market determination of wages. However, in both cases, bypassing the market in order to prevent exploitation may aggravate these conditions. As we have seen, above-market wages paid to sweatshop workers may discourage further investment and so perpetuate high unemployment. In turn, the higher unemployment may weaken the bargaining power of workers vis-à-vis employers. Thus such market imperfections seem to call for more reliance on market forces rather than less. Likewise, the experience of the newly industrialized East Asian economies suggests that the best cure for the ills of sweatshops is more sweatshops. But most of the well-intentioned policies that improve on market outcomes are likely to have the opposite effect.

Where does this leave the international manager? If the preceding analysis is correct, then it follows that it is ethically acceptable to pay market wage rates in developing countries (and to provide employment conditions appropriate for the level of development). That holds true even if the wages pay less than so-called living wages or subsistence or even (conceivably) the local minimum wage. The appropriate test is not whether the wage reaches some predetermined standard but whether it is freely accepted by (reasonably) informed workers. The workers themselves are in the best position to judge whether the wages offered are superior to their next-best alternatives. (The same logic applies *mutatis mutandis* to workplace labor standards).

Indeed, not only is it ethically acceptable for a company to pay market wages, but it may be ethically unacceptable for it to pay wages that exceed market levels. That will be the case if the company's above-market wages set precedents for other international companies which raise labor costs to the point of discouraging foreign investment. Furthermore, companies may have a social responsibility to transcend their own narrow preoccupation with protecting their brand image and to publicly defend a system which has greatly improved the lot of millions of workers in developing countries.

NOTES

1. Steven Greenhouse, "A Crusader Makes Celebrities Tremble." *New York Times* (June 18, 1996), p. B4.
2. Lance A. Compa and Tashia Hinchliffe Darricarrere, "Enforcement Through Corporate Codes of Conduct," in Compa and Stephen F. Diamond, *Human Rights, Labor Rights, and International Trade* (Philadelphia: University of Pennsylvania Press, 1996), p. 193.
3. Peter Jacobi in Martha Nichols, "Third-World Families at Work: Child Labor or Child Care." *Harvard Business Review* (Jan–Feb., 1993).
4. David Sampson in Robin G. Givhan, "A Stain on Fashion: The Garment Industry Profits from Cheap Labor." *Washington Post* (September 12, 1995), p. B1.
5. Thomas Donaldson, *Ethics of International Business* (New York: Oxford University Press, 1989), p. 98.
6. Richard DeGeorge, *Competing with Integrity in International Business* (New York: Oxford University Press, 1993), p. 79.
7. Ibid., pp. 356–7.
8. Ibid., p. 78.
9. World Bank, *World Development Report 1995, "Workers in an Integrating World Economy"* (Oxford University Press, 1995), p. 77.
10. Donaldson, *Ethics of International Business*, p. 115.
11. Ibid., p. 150.
12. DeGeorge, *Competing with Integrity*, p. 48.
13. Ibid., p. 358.
14. Ibid.
15. Terry Collingsworth, J. William Goold, and Pharis J. Harvey, "Time for a Global New Deal," *Foreign Affairs* (Jan–Feb., 1994), p. 8.
16. William B. Falk, "Dirty Little Secrets," *Newsday* (June 16, 1996).
17. Tim Smith, "The Power of Business for Human Rights." *Business & Society Review* (January 1994), p. 36.
18. Jeffrey Ballinger, "The New Free Trade Heel." *Harper's Magazine* (August, 1992), pp. 46–7. "As in many developing countries, Indonesia's minimum wage, . . ., is less than poverty level." Nina Baker, "The Hidden Hands of Nike," *Oregonian* (August 9, 1992).
19. Robert B. Reich, "Escape from the Global Sweatshop; Capitalism's Stake in Uniting the Workers of the World." *Washington Post* (May 22, 1994). Reich's test is intended to apply in developing countries "where democratic institutions are weak or absent."
20. Ibid.
21. Kenneth P. Hutchinson, "Third World Growth." *Harvard Business Review* (Nov–Dec., 1994).
22. Robin Broad and John Cavanaugh, "Don't Neglect the Impoverished South." *Foreign Affairs* (December 22, 1995).
23. John Cavanagh and Robin Broad, "Global Reach; Workers Fight the Multinationals." *The Nation*, (March 18, 1996), p. 21. See also Bob Herbert, "Nike's Bad Neighborhood." *New York Times* (June 14, 1996).
24. International Labor Organization, *World Employment 1995* (Geneva: ILO, 1995), p. 73.
25. World Bank, *Workers in an Integrating World Economy*, p. 5.
26. Keith B. Richburg, and Anne Swardson, "U.S. Industry Overseas: Sweatshop or Job Source?: Indonesians Praise Work at Nike Factory." *Washington Post* (July 28, 1996).
27. Richburg and Swardson, "Sweatshop or Job Source?" The 17 year-old was interviewed in the presence of managers. For other reports that workers remit home large parts of their earnings sea Seth Mydans. "Tangerang Journal; For Indonesian Workers at Nike Plant: Just Do It." *New York Times* (August 9, 1996), and Nina Baker, "The Hidden Hands of Nike."
28. Donna Gibbs, Nike spokeswoman on ABC's *World News Tonight*, June 6, 1996.
29. Mark Clifford, "Trading in Social Issues: Labor Policy and International Trade Regulation," *World Press Review* (June 1994), p. 36.
30. Larry Rohter, "To U.S. Critics, a Sweatshop; for Hondurans, a Better Life." *New York Times* (July 18, 1996).
31. Marcus Brauchli, "Garment Industry Booms in Bangladesh." *Wall Street Journal* (August 6, 1991).
32. Richburg and Swardson, "Sweatshop or Job Source?"
33. Lucy Martinez-Mont, "Sweatshops Are Better Than No Shops." *Wall Street Journal* (June 25, 1996).
34. Rohter, "To U.S. Critics a Sweatshop."
35. Barnet and Cavanagh, *Global Dreams*, p. 326.
36. Rohter, "To U.S. Critics a Sweatshop."
37. William B. Falk, "Dirty Little Secrets." *Newsday* (June 16, 1996).
38. Barnet and Cavanagh, "Just Undo It: Nike's Exploited Workers." *New York Times* (February 13, 1994).
39. Sarosh Kuruvilla, "Linkages Between Industrialization Strategies and Industrial Relations/Human Resources Policies: Singapore, Malaysia, The Philippines, and India." *Industrial & Labor Relations Review* (July, 1996), p. 637.

40. The ILO's Constitution (of 1919) mentions that: ". . . the failure of any nation to adopt humane conditions of labour is an obstacle in the way of other nations which desire to improve the conditions in their own countries." ILO, *World Employment 1995*, p. 74.

41. World Bank, *The East Asian Miracle* (New York: Oxford University Press, 1993), p. 2.

42. Gideon Rachman, "Wealth in Its Grasp, a Survey of Indonesia." *Economist* (April 17, 1993), pp. 14–15.

43. Jagdish Bhagwati and Robert F. Hudec, eds. *Fair Trade and Harmonization* (Cambridge: MIT Press, 1996), vol. 1, p. 2.

44. World Bank, *Workers in an Integrating World Economy*, p. 75.

45. Ibid., p. 77. As I have noted, the report proposes that the "appropriate level is therefore that at which the costs are commensurate with the value that informed workers place on improved working conditions and reduced risk. . . ." (p. 77).

Case Study

Shell Oil in Nigeria

John Boatright

On November 2, 1995, the Nigerian writer and activist Ken Saro-Wiwa was found guilty of ordering the murder of several Ogoni chiefs who were suspected of collaborating with the military government of Nigeria.[1] The Nigerian junta, headed at the time by General Sani Abacha, was criticized worldwide for bringing trumped-up charges against Saro-Wiwa and fourteen co-defendants in order to suppress a resistance movement that had criticized the operations of Shell Oil Company in the oil-rich Ogoniland region of Nigeria. A specially created tribunal, widely regarded as a kangaroo court, sentenced Saro-Wiwa and six others to death by hanging (eight of the accused were acquitted). Many world leaders and human rights organizations called upon Shell Oil Company to persuade the Nigerian government not to execute Ken Saro-Wiwa, but Shell executives were reluctant to intervene. According to one company official, "It is not for a commercial organization like Shell to interfere in the legal processes of a sovereign state such as Nigeria." Another executive said, "Our responsibility is very clear. We pay taxes and [abide by] regulation. We don't run the government." However, critics charged that Shell had been actively involved all along in the military suppression of the Ogoni people. A *New York Times* editorial described Shell's position as "untenable." "If the company is determined to stay in Nigeria, it must use its considerable influence there to restrain the government."

Royal Dutch/Shell is the world's largest oil company, earning profits of $6.2 billion in 1994 on $94.9 billion in revenues. With headquarters in both London and The Hague, Netherlands, and with operations in more than one hundred countries, this joint Anglo-Dutch enterprise is truly a transnational corporation. When oil was discovered in the Niger River delta in 1956, Royal Dutch/Shell was the first major company to begin production. Today, Nigeria pumps approximately two million barrels of crude oil, which provides about $10 billion a year for the military government or more than 80 percent of total government revenues. Almost half of this amount is produced by Shell Nigeria, in which the Nigerian government has a 55 percent stake and Royal Dutch/Shell a 30 percent stake (the remaining 15 percent is owned by a French and an Italian company). The Nigerian government mainly sits back and rakes in the profits; for its efforts in Nigeria, Royal Dutch/Shell receives about $312 million in profits each year. Nigeria is, arguably, the most corrupt country in the world and, for the vast majority of its people, one of the poorest. Most Nigerians live on less that $300 a year, while the country's elite maintain lavish lifestyles. A military government that came to power in 1993 annulled that year's election for president, abolished the major democratic institutions, closed many newspapers, and silenced all opposition. The country's infrastructure continued to deteriorate because funds for public works are siphoned off by government officials and their benchmen into guarded villas, fleets of luxury cars, and foreign bank accounts. General Abacha was rumored to have stashed more than a billion dollars abroad.

Shell's operations are centered in Ogoniland, a four-hundred-square-mile area at the mouth of the Niger River, where approximately one-half million Ogoni live in crowded, squalid conditions among some of the world's worst pollution. Although much of the pollution is due to overpopulation, oil spills and atmospheric discharges foul the environment. The most serious oil-related harm is due to flaring, which is the burning of the natural gas that results from oil production. Flares from tall vents create an eerie orange glow in the sky and emit greenhouse gases along with heat, soot, and noise. Very little of the wealth that comes from the ground in Ogoniland reaches the local population. Between 1958 and 1994, an estimated $30 billion worth of oil was extracted from the area. Under the formula for sharing revenue with the states, the federal government was obligated to return only 1.5 percent to Ogoniland (the percentage was increased to 3 percent in 1992), but much of these revenues is diverted by corruption. Shell Nigeria also returned some profits to the region, contributing $20 million in 1995 for schools, hospitals, and other services. However, some of this money was also used to build roads to oil installations, and a World Bank study concluded that the impact of the oil company's investment on the quality of life in Ogoniland was "minimal."

Ken Saro-Wiwa was a successful Ogoni businessman turned writer and television producer, who developed an interest in political activism in his late forties. He was instrumental in drafting an Ogoni Bill of Rights that demanded a "fair proportion" of oil revenues and greater environmental protection, and he helped form the Movement for the Survival of the Ogoni People (MOSOP). Saro-Wiwa traveled widely in the United States and Europe to build support for the new organization, and for his efforts he was nominated for the Nobel Peace Prize. Although MOSOP sought change from the federal government (and, to dramatize its cause, issued a symbolic demand for $10 billion in compensation from Shell), the organization opposed the use of violence and the idea of secession from Nigeria. Despite the calls for nonviolence, gangs of armed youths staged raids on oil installations, looting and vandalizing the facilities and attacking workers. In January 1993, Shell Nigeria abruptly ceased production in Ogoniland and evacuated its employees from the region. Amid growing civil unrest and military crackdowns, the leadership of MOSOP split. Ken Saro-Wiwa rejected a strategy of cooperating with the federal government to reduce violence in return for concessions. In particular, he called for a boycott of elections scheduled for June

1993, while some other leaders urged participation. On May 21, 1993, several hundred young men attacked a house where a group of dissident Ogoni chiefs (known as the "vultures") was meeting and killed most of them before the police could intervene. Although Saro-Wiwa was far away from the scene of the killings—he had been prevented from attending a MOSOP rally and had returned home—he was arrested the next day and imprisoned for eight months before his trial.

After the first attacks on Shell installations in Ogoniland, the company accepted the protection of the Nigerian police and provided some support for their services. Shell admits that the company provided firearms to the police, but human rights organizations charge the Shell-owned vehicles were used to transport police and soldiers and Shell officials participated in the planning of security operations. In an effort to induce Shell to resume operations in Ogoniland, General Abacha formed a special Internal Security Task Force to suppress opposition to the company's operations in the area. In a memo dated May 12, 1994, the commander of the task force proposed "wasting" operations to undermine the support for MOSOP and advised the government to seek "prompt regular inputs" from the oil companies. Shell denied making any payments for this purpose.

In May and June of 1994, the task force attacked at least thirty towns and villages, assaulting and killing the inhabitants and looting and destroying homes, fields, and livestock. By the time of Ken Saro-Wiwa's trial, Shell had not returned to Ogoniland, but its operations elsewhere in Nigeria were conducted with round-the-clock military protection. Critics generally accept Shell's arguments that withdrawing from Nigeria would harm the Nigerian people, but a *New York Times* editorial concluded that "Shell can no longer pretend that the political life of Nigeria is none of its business." To the argument that the company is merely a guest in the country, the editorial responds, "Shell, surely, has never hesitated to use its influence on matters of Nigerian tax policy, environmental rules, labor laws and trade policies."

POSTSCRIPT: Eights days after being sentenced to death, Ken Saro-Wiwa was hanged along with eight others. The United States, Canada, South Africa, and many European countries withdrew their ambassadors in protest, and a consumer boycott was organized by several human rights and environmental organizations. A Shell statement expressed "deep regret" over the executions. Although the company admitted that its top official had appealed privately to General Abacha for clemency on "humanitarian grounds," a spokesperson said, "We can't issue a bold statement about human rights because . . . it could be considered treasonous by the regime and employees could come under attack. It would only inflame the issues." Within a week of Ken Saro-Wiwa's death, Shell announced plans for a $4 billion liquefied natural gas plant in a partnership with the Nigerian government.

NOTES

1. This case is based on "Shell Oil in Nigeria," by Anne T. Lawrence, in *Case Research Journal*, 17 (Fall–Winter 1997), 1–21; Joshua Hammer, "Nigeria Crude," *Harper's Magazine*, June 1996, 58–68; Paul Lewis, "Rights Groups Say Shell Oil Shares Blame," *New York Times*, 11 November 1995, sec. 1, p. 6; "Shell Game in Nigeria," *New York Times*, 3 December 1995, sec. 4, p. 14; Andy Rowell, "Shell Shocked: Did the Shell Petroleum Company Silence Nigerian Environmentalist Ken Saro-Wiwa?" *The Village Voice*, 21 November 1995, 21; Andy Rowell, "Sleeping with the Enemy: Worldwide Protests Can't Stop Shell Snuggling up to Nigeria's Military," *The Village Voice*, 23 January 1996, 23; Paul Beckett, "Shell Boldly Defends Its Role in Nigeria," *Wall Street Journal*, 27 November 1995, A9.

Case Study

Levi Strauss & Co. and China

Edwin M. Epstein
Timothy Perkins
Colleen O'Connell
Carin Orosco
Mark Rickey
Matthew Scoble

Senior project team of students in the Financial Services
Honors Program, School of Economics and Business
Administration, St. Mary's College of California: under supervision
of Dean Edwin M. Epstein

PART A

The market that is the People's Republic of China consists of more than 1 billion consumers and offers low production costs, but its human rights violations have long been condemned by international bodies. In 1993, Levi Strauss & Co. (LS & Co.) faced one of its more difficult decisions in a long corporate history. Would it continue to conduct business in this enormously promising market or honor its relatively high ethical standards and withdraw?

Levi Strauss: History and Ethical Stance

Founded in the United States in 1873, LS&Co. enjoyed consistent domestic growth for generations and began overseas operations during the 1940s. The company became the world's largest clothing manufacturer in 1977 and achieved $2 billion in sales by the end of the decade. Having offered stock to the public during the 1970s to raise needed capital, management decided fourteen years later to reprivatize in a $2 billion leveraged buyout, the largest such transaction to date. Management's reasons included its heightened ability to "focus attention on long-term interests (and) . . . to ensure that the company continues to respect and implement its important values and traditions."[1] By 1993, LS&Co. produced merchandise in 24 countries and sold in 60.

LS&Co. has been a leader among U.S.-based corporations in recognizing the importance of business ethics and community relationships. Two 1987 documents developed by management summarize the unique values operating at LS&Co. The Mission Statement . . . affirms the importance of ethics and social responsibility, while the Aspirations Statement . . . lists the values intended to guide both individual and corporate decisions.

CEO Robert Haas frequently explains the importance of the Aspirations Statement as a way employees can realize the company Mission Statement and otherwise address factors that did not receive adequate consideration in the past. Efforts to take the values seriously have led to specific changes in human resources policies and practices. For instance, LS&Co. extends liberal domestic partner benefits, offers flexible-work programs, and has established child-care voucher programs. A series of classes for senior managers focuses on the Aspirations Statement. The company has also earned a reputation as an industry leader in facing controversial social issues. It was one of the first companies to establish programs to support AIDS victims.

In 1990, the company closed a Dockers' plant in San Antonio, Texas, transferring production to private contractors in Latin America where wages were more competitive. LS&Co. provided a generous severance package for the laid-off workers that included 90-day notice of the plant closing and extended medical insurance benefits. LS&Co. also contributed $100,000 to local support agencies and $340,000 to the city for extra services to the laid-off workers.[2] Despite these efforts, the company received serious criticism for relocating the plant.

Ethical Standards for International Business

In early 1992, LS&Co. established a set of global sourcing guidelines to help ensure that its worldwide contractors' standards mesh with the company values. A group of 10 employees from different areas of the company spent nine months developing the guidelines. The group used an ethical decision-making model that ranked and prioritized all stakeholders to help design the guidelines. The model examines the consequences of each action and suggests a decision based on a balance between ethics and profits.

The ensuing guidelines, "Business Partner Terms of Engagement" . . . cover environmental requirements, ethical standards, worker health and safety, legal requirements, employment practices, and community betterment. Contractors must: provide safe and healthy work conditions, pay employees no less than prevailing local wages, allow LS&Co. inspectors to visit unannounced, limit foreign laborers' work weeks to a maximum of 60 hours, and preclude the use of child and prison labor.[3]

In addition, the company established "Guidelines for Country Selection" . . . These guidelines cover issues beyond the control of one particular business partner. Challenges such as brand image worker health and safety, human rights, legal requirements, and political or social stability are considered on a national basis. The company will not source in countries failing to meet these guidelines.

The question would soon be raised: Does China meet these guidelines?

Human Rights and Labor Practices in China

China is ranked among the world's gravest violators of human rights, although Chinese officials do not regard their actions as such. The U.S. State Department says that China's human rights record falls "far short of internationally accepted norms."[4] Two more-egregious violations include arbitrary arrest and detention (with torture that sometimes results in death). Despite laws prohibiting arbitrary arrest and providing limits on detention, a commonly referenced clause states that family notification and timely charging are not required if such actions would "hinder the investigation."[5] Judicial verdicts are believed by many observers to be predetermined.

Chinese prison conditions are deplorable, and a long-standing practice holds that all prisoners, including political, must work. Chinese officials say that the fruits of prison-labor are used primarily within the prison system or for domestic sale.

Personal privacy is severely limited in China. Telephone conversations are monitored, mail is often opened and examined, and people and premises are frequently subjected to search without the necessary warrants. China has also engaged in forced family planning, with monitoring of a woman's pregnancy occurring at her place of employment.[6] Official rights to free speech and assembly are extremely restricted, as the world witnessed during the Tiananmen Square massacre in 1989.

Regarding labor conditions, China's leaders have refused to ratify the 10 guidelines prohibiting use of forced labor for commercial purposes established by the International Labor Organization Convention. Although China has regulations prohibiting the employment of children who have not completed nine compulsory years of education, child labor is widespread, especially in rural areas. Surveys show a recent increase in the dropout rate among southern Chinese lower-secondary schools, presumably because the booming local economy lures 12 to 16-year-olds away. At the time of LS&Co.'s deliberations regarding China, no minimum wage existed and safety conditions were found to be "very poor."

LS&Co. in China

This combination of government practices and labor conditions increased pressure within LS&Co. to rethink its decision to operate in China. In 1992, operations in the country generated some 10 percent of the company's total Asian contracting and 2 percent of worldwide contracting. Its Chinese operations produced approximately one million pants and shirts in 1993 and operated directly or indirectly through some 30 Chinese contractors. Over one half the goods produced in China were shipped to Hong Kong to be refined for sale in other countries.

These contracts were estimated to be worth $40 million.

LS&Co. is only one of thousands of foreign firms operating in China. The other companies, especially prominent *Fortune 500* companies with factories or manufacturing contracts in China, are cognizant of the human rights and labor conditions. Most of these companies lobbied President Clinton to renew China's Most Favored Nation (MFN) trading status, arguing that the continuing presence of U.S. companies would have a positive influence on reform. According to this viewpoint, investments made by companies such as LS&Co. could transform working conditions and thereby accelerate movement toward the social, economic, and political standards favored by the United States and other western countries.

Should Levi Strauss Stay or Leave?

In assessing the objectionable conditions in China, LS&Co. management felt it could not improve the situation because the violations were well beyond what could be remedied strictly through company communication and cooperation with contractors. At issue were practices that had to be addressed on a larger, national scale.

Leaving the country would expose LS&Co. to the high opportunity cost of foregoing business in a large emerging market. Some managers and employees felt the company would be supporting a repressive regime if it remained in China, while others argued that LS&Co. is a profit-making business enterprise, not a human rights agency. This latter group saw as positive management's acknowledged responsibility to society, but it felt the company also needed to consider its responsibilities to shareholders and employees. Some employees argued that staying in China would enable LS&Co. to improve conditions for Chinese citizens. But other stakeholders countered that remaining in China would violate the company's own guidelines about where it would and would not conduct business.

Important issues that complicated the decision include: the possibility that China might not accept LS&Co. back if the company left until conditions improved. If the company ceased production in China, it might be difficult for it to sell product there due to high tariffs imposed on imported apparel. But, some voices argued, continuing to manufacture in China would have a damaging impact on Levi's reputation, possibly putting at risk its valuable brand image.

PART B

To address the many issues regarding LS&Co's continued operations in China, the company organized a China Policy Group (CPG). Composed of 12 employees who together devoted approximately 2,000 hours to reviewing the China situation, the CPG consulted human rights activists, scholars, and executives in its attempt to fully address the critical issues.

The group examined all the issues highlighted in Part A and found itself divided on the question. In March 1993, the CPG delivered a report to LS&Co.'s Executive Management Committee. On April 27, after a half-day of deliberation, this most-senior management group remained undecided over what to do.

Robert Haas Acts

Confronted by the indecision of the Executive Management Committee, LS&Co.'s CEO and Chairman, Robert Haas, ended the stalemate by recommending the company forgo direct investment in China and end existing contracts over a period of three years due to "pervasive violations of basic human rights."[7] He maintained that the company had more to gain by remaining true to its ideals than by continuing to produce in China.

Reactions to the Decision

LS&Co. did not publicly announce its decision, but the news hit the airwaves with a speed and volume that surprised all involved. John Onoda, LS&Co.'s vice president of corporate communications, explained: "We never intended to get in the spotlight. . . . It was leaked and got out in 20 minutes."

Many people were highly skeptical of the company's stated intentions. Some asserted it was only a public relations ploy engineered to make the company look good. "I don't see broad support of it," claimed Richard Brecher, director of business services at the U.S.-China Business Council. "[It] would be regarded much more seriously if Levi's had made a direct investment in China."

In one respect, Brecher is right. The company did not directly invest in China; it produced its merchandise through Chinese contractors. In fact, on the sales side, LS&Co. jeans continue to sell in China through Jardine Marketing Services. Moving production contracts to other countries in Asia raised costs between four and ten percent, depending on which location was chosen. LS&Co. recognized this cost and considers it the price it must pay to uphold its integrity and protect its corporate and brand images.

Vice President Bob Dunn explained, "There's the matter of protecting our brand identity. Increasingly, consumers are sensitive to goods being made under conditions that are not consistent with U.S. values and fairness."[8] Linda Butler, director of corporate communications for LS&Co., iterated this sentiment when she affirmed that it was "better for us to honor our company's values."[9] Some even believe that the decision may ultimately prove profitable to the company. As one person claimed, "In many ways, it strengthens the brand. . . . This is a brand that thinks for itself, and these are values which people who buy the brand want for themselves. They're a badge product for youth who want to say 'I'm different.' "[10]

Impact in China

China's leadership showed no interest in the company's decision. One Chinese foreign ministry official was quoted, "At present there are tens of thousands of foreign companies investing in China. If one or two want to withdraw, please do."[11] Coincidentally, the LS&Co. decision-making process occurred as the United States considered extending China's MFN status. U.S. Trade Representative Mickey Kantor voiced his support for LS&Co. by stating, "As far as what Levi Strauss has done, we can only applaud it; we encourage American companies to be the leader in protecting worker rights and worker safety and human rights wherever they operate."[12]

More recently President Clinton renewed China's MFN trading status without requiring steps to improve human rights.[13] Clinton explained, "I believe the question . . . is not whether we continue to support human rights in China, but how we can best support human rights in China and advance our other very

significant issues and interests. I believe we can do it by engaging the Chinese."[14]

The position of the Clinton administration is that the United States should continue trading with China and hope that economic involvement will contribute to improvement in the conditions of Chinese citizens. As one might surmise from the case, LS&Co. takes a different position.

NOTES

1. *San Francisco Chronicle*, July 16, 1985, p. 51.
2. *The 100 Best Companies to Work for in America*, p. 502.
3. *Across the Board*, May 1994, p. 12.
4. *Far Eastern Economic Review*, April 14, 1994, p. 60.
5. *U.S. News & World Report*, August 2, 1993. p. 49.
6. Levi Strauss & Co. executive John Onoda, interview, February 1, 1995.
7. The CPG defined "pervasive human rights violations" as meaning when "the greater majority of the population are denied virtually all human rights. Most human rights violations are severe. Government has taken few or no actions to improve human rights climate and positive change is unlikely or, at best, uncertain."
8. *Wall Street Journal*, May 5, 1994, p. A18.
9. *Far Eastern Economic Review*, April 14, 1994, p. 60.
10. *Wall Street Journal*, May 5, 1994, p. A18.
11. *Far Eastern Economic Review*, April 14, 1994, p. 60.
12. *The New Republic*, June 14, 1993, p. 8.
13. *U.S. Department of State Dispatch*, May 30, 1994, p. 345.
14. *Across the Board*, May 1994, p. 12.

Chapter Eight

———————•———————

Privacy, Ethics, and Technology

Technology has had a profound effect in the business arena, and not just in the areas of command and control. Technology's effect also encompasses the moral arena, creating new moral problems as well as accelerating the impact of existing ethical issues' impact on all participants in the economy. Technology allows us to do things we couldn't do before as well as things we could do before—only now more quickly, efficiently, and accurately. However, it's not enough simply to discuss whether we *can* do a particular thing; we must also consider whether we *ought* to do that thing or not.

Information flow is at the forefront of technology's use in business, enabling business to create, store, merge, analyze, and recombine data in ways never before possible. What was once merely a cash box is now a sophisticated data terminal/cash register that, at the same time, provides a receipt for the customer, deletes the items from inventory, prints targeted coupons, flags items for reorder, credits a particular salesperson's commission check, and allows management to know what's being sold, when, by whom, and to whom. Businesses now know what *you've* bought—information many businesses are willing to pay to get. Particular businesses can then sell or share this information with their partners, as well as with data services. While this sharing is obviously beneficial to business, whose success thrives on information, it also can add up to the famous dictum from George Orwell's 1984: "Big Brother is watching!"

Information abounds in the market and, once placed in an electronic format, can no longer be sequestered and protected from prying eyes, both legitimate and unwelcome. That information can now be archived, manipulated, and stolen. With the invention of planes, trains, and automobiles came the observation that the world was becoming a smaller place. Technology, particularly television, telephones, and the Internet, has made the world an even smaller place. Nowadays news travels fast, and not always the news we want to travel, nor to whom. While the protection of privileged information is a *business* problem, the alleged invasion of privacy is a moral problem. Who owns information? Who should have access to that information?

The cases and essays in this chapter seek to begin the process of sorting out some of these new issues. "Technology and Ethics: Privacy in the Workplace" examines privacy in the workplace from both legal and ethical perspectives. "Virtual Morality: A New Workplace Quandary" is a short essay considering some specifics regarding employees' use of computers in the workplace, including e-mail and non-business use of computers. "Rippers, Portal Users, and Profilers: Three Web-Based Issues for Business Ethicists" continues with the ethical issues surrounding Napster-like downloading of music from the Internet, portals, and the collection of consumer marketing data via Internet log-ins. Excerpts from "Cyberethics" give us short but specific cases regarding employee e-mails, spam, and cookies. Also included in this section in a case on corporate confidentiality and communications: "E-mail Policy at Johnson & Dresser."

Essay

Technology and Ethics: Privacy in the Workplace

Laura P. Hartman

Privacy in the workplace is one of the more troubling personal and professional issues of our time. But privacy cannot be adequately addressed without considering a basic foundation of "ethics." We cannot reach a meaningful normative conclusion about workplace privacy rights and obligations without a fundamental and common understanding of the ethical basis of justice and a thorough understanding of the individual and organizational concerns and motivations.

In this article I discuss the status of privacy in the workplace from a technological as well as a legal perspective. What was once considered an inalienable right has now been reassessed as our society and the business world have grown ever more complex. Traditional ethical analysis offers some guidance on how to evaluate the balance between a worker's right to privacy and an employer's need for information with which to manage the workplace. But guidance is not the same as resolution; as concerns workplace privacy

rights, there are many more questions than answers.

I then address the vexing issues of privacy, drawing on ethical theory to advance a means by which to identify the appropriate ethical balance for workplace privacy. My focus is on employee privacy in particular, because this is a critical area where technological advancement is spurred by our desire for information and the ease of its collection. We must ensure that our ethical analysis remains current with the possibilities created by innovations.

ETHICS AS "PERCEPTION"

Individual views of appropriate bases for assessing the ethical nature of acts and consequences vary widely. For me, the concept of perception is critical for ethical assessment, since perception plays such a paramount role in framing issues. Our ethical decisions are influenced by our own perception of ourselves, by others' perception of our actions, and by our perception of "universal laws." Our final choices are determined by the perception that has the greatest impact or weight at the time.

For example, perhaps you have a certain hat that you love to wear; and it is simply the ugliest hat in the world. But it keeps you warm, and you're just going to wear it. You do not care what anyone thinks. You do not care if people stare at you walking down the block. All you care about is that you are comfortable. *Your* perception is all that matters. This same circumstance might exist for you in connection with an ethical dilemma. Sometimes you believe so strongly in what *you* think that, even if the entire universe believes what you are doing is wrong, you will go ahead and do it because you believe it is right. You are following your own values. It is your particular perception that defines what is ethical.

Now contrast the influence of personal perception to the origin of the second potential influence on our actions: what concerns us may be whether *society* perceives what we are doing is right. Society can be defined as one's mother, colleagues, other family members, even the larger American or global society.

Ethicists often call this the *New York Times* or CNN test. Perhaps now we should call it the *Web* test. When reaching a resolution to an ethical dilemma, you might test how you will feel if you saw what you did today all over the Internet tomorrow. The question becomes, would you feel all right if everyone else (in your circle or society) knew about what you did? In fact, you might believe that what you did is absolutely right, but the world (or your mother) does not understand it, misunderstands it, or misperceives it. You can probably imagine scenarios where you know what you are doing is right, but everyone is going to get the wrong impression so you simply choose not to do it. What matters to you in this decision

is what other people think. There are certainly situations where all of us might be subject to that type of influence.

The third scenario is where one's determination of whether something is ethical is based on one's interpretation of some universal rule or rules (such as a religious guidance or the direction of universally held principles). For some people, the question they ask themselves is, What would Buddha or Jesus or some other universalist do in this circumstance? It is the "perception" of that religion, spiritual leader, or other "omniscient" being that is critical to your decision. In the end, you believe that the rule is the word of God, or another being or force, and that is what is going to influence your decision, whether or not society or you independently agree with it.

So your determination of that which is ethical in any one circumstance truly depends on whose opinion is important to you. I will give one example of the importance of perception in decision-making. When I first took my three and a half year old daughter on an airplane, about a year and a half ago. I was concerned about her comfort level since I am no fan of airline takeoffs or landings. I was trying to prepare Emma for the takeoff, so I said, "Emma, the plane is going to run, run, run and then jump in the air, and it's going to jump just like you do, but it's going to stay in the air, and it's going to be okay."

As we take off from the ground, of course, Emma looks out the window and starts getting upset. But she is all upset about something to do with the *ground*, and I couldn't figure out what she meant until I realized that she perceived that *the ground was falling away* rather than the plane flying in the air. She could not see that we were in an airplane that was lifting up into the air. She saw that the ground was falling away; and it never would have occurred to me that she would perceive it that way. Yet that is what upset her to such a great extent.

Now maybe if I had considered how she might perceive the takeoff. I might have addressed it differently. Do you ever go to sleep at night thinking that something you did was just fine, but wake up the next morning with everyone angry at you? Or you hand in a memo to some manager, thinking it is perfectly clear; but she or he hands it back to you later saying. "I don't know what the heck you're talking about here, you've got to be more clear"? You thought you were so clear. In that regard it may be very helpful to engage in a bit of analysis to try to view things from the perspective of each of those individuals who might be impacted by your decision. I discuss the importance of this type of analysis further.

I do not believe that our ethics are fundamentally different; but often we care about different perspectives. Certain perspectives seem more valid, depending on the circumstances. Addressed this way, it is clear that businesses, in particular, generally care about what their primary stakeholders consider to be ethical because they are perceived to have the greatest impact on the business.

THE IMPACT OF ETHICS AS PERCEPTION IN BUSINESS DECISION-MAKING

There are a number of factors that influence businesses to care about how they are perceived by society. The law persuades us to be ethical using deterrents or punishments. The Federal Sentencing Guidelines prescribe hundreds of millions of dollars in fines or jail time for violations. Businesses are also influenced by pragmatic reasons. The Ethics Resource Center in Washington, D.C., found that firms with written codes of conduct are a better investment than those that do not have written codes. When firms engage in strong decentralization efforts, perhaps ethics is the only thing that creates a consistent link within the firm.

Society is also persuasive in its forms of chastisement or praise (consider the *New York Times* test, mentioned earlier). Consider, as well, the Johnson & Johnson case in connection with the tainted Tylenol containers. That situation arose decades ago; yet I still discuss it in my classes as a laudable way to respond to a situation. Wouldn't you like to believe that decades from now people in your firm will say, "oh, you should always do that the way ___ [input your name] did it in 2000"? Or would you rather that people decades from now say, "do it any way, but never do it the way that ___ did it back in 2000," such as the individual at Ford who recommended that they *not* recall the Ford Pinto?

There are also additional incentives for firms to engage in ethical behavior. First, unethical behavior imposes terrible costs. Nestle continues to feel the backlash resulting from an insensitive marketing campaign for infant formula in developing economies that cost many children their lives. This happened over twenty years ago; yet I still discuss that case, as well. Texaco has paid out almost $200 million for their failure to pay attention to diversity. Mercury Finance, Genentech, Bausch & Lomb, Microsoft: each of these firms has seen financial turmoil arise from ethical violations that were not originally anticipated.

OUR HABITUAL BUSINESS DECISION-MAKING PROCESS

Business decision-making is not all that different from decision-making by reasonably rational individuals. (Of course neither businesses nor people are completely rational.) So now that we have a more clear understanding of ethics and the impact of perception, as well as an awareness of the incentives toward ethical behavior, how do you *do* it? Usually, we make decisions *considering limited alternatives*. I may say to you, what do you do, choice a or choice b? You consider the options, feeling the pressure. You think, "oh my gosh, a or b, a or b . . . I'll take choice a!" But another option exists, does it not? One might say, "wait a minute, I need to think about this. There are other choices that you did not offer me—choices c, d, e, f." But usually, we consider only the limited alternatives.

We use *simplified decision rules*. You must make the choice to terminate someone. You choose to follow a rule of thumb such as firing the last one hired. "I'm sorry, there's nothing I can do." Rules of thumb relieve the decision-maker of the accountability for that decision. It feels better to say, "there is nothing I can do" than to explain that you have all the discretion in the world, but are still firing the person.

Finally, we usually select alternatives that merely *satisfy minimum criteria*. I believe this normal habit is one of the most detrimental of our habitual decision-making practices. If all of us need to reach a compromise on something, we would naturally find a solution on which we all could agree, and then stop. It is often difficult to believe there is a better answer than the first possible solution over which there is no dispute. But, instead, it is seldom that one continues to seek alternative, *better* solutions at this point. Does anyone ever say, "Wait, that might not be the best; let's keep trying"? It does not happen very often. You can imagine that one might miss out on the *best possible* decision instead of the *earliest or easiest* possible decision. This process is how we *usually* make decisions.

THE ETHICAL PROCESS OF DECISION-MAKING

What follows is a discussion of the *ethical* process of decision-making. It may appear to be awfully complicated. But let me tell you this: it becomes habitual, so habitual that it becomes *uncomfortable* when you are in circumstances where you cannot conduct an ethical decision-making process.

If you have ever learned how to drive a stick shift car, you will understand the following metaphor. Consider the first time you sat in a stick shift car. You had eighty-five thousand, three hundred and thirteen things to remember. Stick shift driving is pretty complicated. You have to remember when to pop the clutch, when to put in the clutch, when to put the brake or the gas on, what to do with this hand over here, what gear you are in, and so on. You begin to drive and the car dies often, you stall, and you deal with it, and then you learn. However, once you become proficient at stick shift driving, you do not really think about when you have to put in the clutch anymore. I drive a stick shift car and I do not think about putting in the clutch. I do not think about which gear I should be in. I just drive. And, in fact, when I drive an automatic car, my left foot keeps going down to try to push the clutch in! I am uncomfortable driving an automatic car these days.

So, compare these circumstances to the ethical decision-making process. It will be difficult or challenging or burdensome in the beginning; but later it will evolve into a habitual process—a process that, if you do not have the ability to follow it in certain circumstances, you are still pushing that left foot in. You are trying to do it. It is uncomfortable that you cannot.

The ethical decision-making process is as follows:

1. **Issue(s):** Identify the dilemma.
2. **Facts:** Obtain all of the unbiased facts.
3. **Alternatives:** Identify the choices that you have (look not only to a and b, but also to y and z!).
4. **Stakeholders:** Identify those who have an interest. What are their motivations? How much power does each hold over you or your firm?

5. **Impact:** Identify the impact of each alternative on each stakeholder and the stakeholders' resulting impacts on you or your firm.
6. **Additional assistance/theoretical guidance:** Do theories uncover any hidden implications? Do they support one alternative over another?
7. **Action:** Decide how to respond and act.
8. **Monitor:** Monitor outcomes and make adjustments where necessary.

There are a few other questions that business practitioners usually ask themselves that might offer a bit of guidance or direction.

1. How'd I get here in this dilemma in the first place?
2. Is my action legal? Where's the legal line?
3. Am I being fair and honest (is it "just")?
4. Am I acting in line with my personal integrity? The firm's core values? The character traits I endeavor to exhibit?
5. Am I being only self-serving or am I considering others?
6. Will it stand the test of time?
7. Is this a model of "right" behavior?
8. How will I feel afterwards? (Am I proud?)
9. Will someone get the wrong idea?
10. Is my loyalty in the "right" place?
11. Is this something a *leader* should do?
12. *How do I never get here again? What should I have done a while ago to avoid getting to this horrible place?*

The important factor in ethical decision-making is not necessarily arriving at a correct or right decision, but is instead to be conscious of the impact of the decision on one's self and others. It is practically impossible not to be affected by this consciousness in one's decision-making if one follows the process set forth above. The end result is a world of more conscious, considerate decisions rather than those based on rapid-fire, gut-based instincts.

Ethical Decision-Making with Regard to Employee Privacy. Applying this ethical decision-making process to the complicated challenge of employee privacy, one must first identify the issue and understand the dilemma. Then one must obtain all of the facts, identify the variety of alternatives available to both employees and employers, and identify all of the stakeholders. The next step is to attempt to understand the impact of the different alternatives in terms of workplace monitoring, surveillance, and so forth. Perhaps ethical theories will provide some insight. The issue of whether a fundamental "right" exists in personal autonomy or, conversely, managing the workplace may be illuminated by ethical theories. Finally, one needs to make a recommendation and monitor the outcomes. In the course of my research in this area, I am at the point of making a recommendation. I do not yet have evidence monitoring the outcomes.

ETHICS IN INFORMATION TECHNOLOGY AND WORKPLACE PRIVACY

Ethical Issues Unique to Information Technology

It appears to me that in ethics the difficulties are mainly due to the attempt to answer questions without first discovering precisely what question it is which you desire to answer.

—*George Edward Moore*

Information technology provides us with a host of ethical challenges. New technology imposes new implications for the balance of power in the workplace. We now have in-home offices, allowing for greater invasions. Moreover, the line between personal and professional lives has become blurred as workers conduct personal business in the office and professional business at home. The office usually provides faster, cheaper, and easier access to the Internet, while some work must be done at home in order to be completed according to our modern, technologically enhanced pace.

Faculty members, for instance, do not go home and become people other than faculty members. We often conduct work at home such as grading, class preparation, and so on. Similarly, our profession affords us a great deal of autonomy in terms of how we spend our days. We do not punch a clock nor hand in a time sheet. All of my students have my home number. My professional and personal lives are awfully blurred. (Sometimes, I wish they were not so blurred!)

Technology allows employers to ask more of each employee because we are now capable of greater production; we have greater abilities due to technology. We do not seem to know any longer when our work day is over. I used to be a lawyer and the understanding in that profession was, if you can work more hours, you do. This is because you will then be viewed as the preferred colleague. You will be the one who is going to get the plum assignments because you work so darned hard.

Other issues are raised by enhanced technology. For instance, should the technological ability to find something out make it relevant? With new employment testing technology, you can find out all sorts of personal information. Through genetic testing, hair follicle testing, drug testing, and so on, your employer can find out anything it wants to know about you. Should the employer find out the information simply because it can?

In addition, new technology allows for a more faceless communication.[1] If you have to fire someone, it is significantly easier to fire that person by e-mail than to walk into her or his office. In the latter case, you see the individual, desperate, perhaps disappointed, frustrated with the fact that you've worked them so hard and now you are terminating them. It is a lot easier to be nasty when you do not have to look your stakeholders in the face.

Finally, there is research that shows that the excessive exertion of power and authority may lead to what the researchers call a "semi-

schizoid response," including insecurity, "disruption of biographical continuity," feelings of being overwhelmed and powerless, and doubts about worthiness. The implication is that if someone questions you too much or takes away too much of your power, the ultimate cost may be your emotional security. Somewhat prophetically, Lawrence Lessig wrote in his bestseller *Code*, "We have been as welcoming and joyous about the net (and other technologies) as the earthlings were of the aliens in *Independence Day*. But at some point, we too will come to see a potential threat . . . and its extraordinary power for control."

Ethical Issues in the Privacy Arena

Specifically in connection with privacy, ethical issues arise with gathering information, assessing its accuracy, correcting it, and disclosure, as well as the substance of the information itself. Simply knowing that someone knows personal information about you can feel invasive or violating. For that amorphous reason, privacy is a slightly difficult concept to define. Ethan Catch says it is "the ability to control what others can come to know about you." Why do we care that someone knows our personal information? We can imagine items of personal data that we simply do not want others knowing, whether or not they would actually do something with that information. We do not like people knowing things about us; it comes down to one's ability to be autonomous in controlling one's personal information.

Do you, personally, care about the information others know about you? Would you care if your boss knew of all of your off-work activities? Consider Milton Hershey. Milton Hershey would tour Hershey, Pennsylvania, making note of workers' lawns that were not kept up, or homes that were not maintained. He would even hire private detectives to find out who was throwing trash in Hershey Park. Another business owner, Henry Ford, used to condition wages on workers' good behavior outside the factory. He had a hundred and fifty inspectors in his "sociological department" to keep tabs on workers' hygiene habits and housekeeping. Imagine!

Only recently did OSHA retract a statement that the occupational safety and health standards apply equally to workplaces and personal homes, when you work as a telecommuter. Can you imagine if you had to maintain the same standards of safety in your home that your employer must maintain at the traditional workplace?

Status of New Technology with Regard to Workplace Privacy

A multitude of basic and inexpensive computer monitoring products allow managers to track Web use, to observe downloaded files, to filter sites, to restrict employee access to certain sites, and to know how much time employees spend on various sites. Products include WebSense, Net Access Manager, WebTrack, and Internet Watchdog.

One particular firm. SpyShop.com, claims to service one-third of the *Fortune* 500 firms. This firm sells items such as a truth-telling device that links to a telephone. One can interview a job candidate on the phone and the device identifies those who lie. Another firm, Omnitracks, sells a satellite that fastens to the top or inside of a truck. The product allows trucking firms to locate trucks at all times. If a driver veers off the highway to get flowers for her or his partner on Valentine's Day, the firm will know what happened.

SpyZone.com sells an executive investigator kit that includes the truth phone and a pocket recording pen. Other outlets sell pinhole lens camera pens and microphones that fit in your pocket. The motto of one firm is "In God we trust. All others we monitor." That

firm offers a beeper buster, a computer program that monitors calls placed to beepers within a certain vicinity. A computer screen shows the manager all of the numbers so that he or she can determine whether the employee is being distracted during working hours.

Competing Interests

The predominant question I have sought to answer by my recent research is whether a balance is possible between the employer's interest in managing the workplace and the employees' privacy interest. Do employees even have a right to privacy? If one believes the answer is "no," then the entire issue becomes moot. If the employee does have some, even limited, right to privacy, one must seek to find a balance of interest. I will return to the consideration of "rights" as we apply ethical theories. First, it is helpful to identify the proposed rights in dispute.

The employer has a right to manage the workplace. In more specificity, employers want to manage the workplace so they can place workers in the appropriate positions. They want to ensure compliance with affirmative action and administer workplace benefits. They want to ensure effective or productive performance. They need to know what their workers are doing in their workplace. The employer's perspective is as follows: "I am paying them to be there working. If they are not working. I should know that and either pay them less, or hire different workers." It seems like a relatively understandable concern.

Employees, on the other hand, want to be treated as free, equal, capable, and rational individuals who have the ability to make their own decisions about the way their lives will unfold. They are interested in their own personal development and valued performance (the lack of privacy may prevent "flow"); conducting *some* personal business at the office; being free from monitoring for performance reasons (wary of increased stress/pressure from monitoring): being free from monitoring for privacy reasons; and in being able to review and to correct misinformation in data collected.

Consider the issue of personal work conducted at the office. I get to work some days at 7:00 A.M. and I do not leave until 7:00 P.M. on some days. Last I heard, many doctors' offices are not open before or after 7:00 in the morning or night. So when is one supposed to call and make an appointment, much less ever go to an appointment, if one is punching the clock with those hours? The employer has to understand that workers must be able to call the doctor and make an appointment. Workers need to be able to conduct *involuntary* personal matters at the office. Now, they might not need to e-mail their mother or chat on the phone with friends. Should workers still have the right to conduct that *voluntary* personal business, as well? Perhaps the resolution lies in the precise definition of voluntary or involuntary business.

THE LAW, NEW TECHNOLOGY, AND WORKPLACE PRIVACY

As dictated by the ethical decision-making process, one must obtain all the unbiased facts before responding to an ethical dilemma. Where new technology impacts the dilemma, the "facts" may be all the more difficult to ascertain since we are not yet completely equipped to obtain the necessary information. For example, some scholars contend that nearly everyone who has a computer (estimated to be about 80% of the people in the workforce in the United States) is subject to some form of information collection, no matter how much we protect ourselves.[2] Another source reports that more than 30 million workers were subject to workplace monitoring last year, up from only 8 million

in 1991.[3] We are not yet at a point where we can even determine whether this information is realistic.

We are relatively certain about the ways in which information is collected. As of 1999, two-thirds of mid- to large-sized firms conduct some form of monitoring, whether computer-based monitoring, video monitoring, monitoring of personal investments, or maybe simply monitoring key card access to the building or parking garage (up from 30% in 1993).[4] Our style of working, even of communicating, has created greater possibilities for monitoring. In connection with e-mail, for instance, over 90 million American workers now send over 2.8 billion e-mail messages per day, an average of 190 e-mails per day per worker.[5] We might not be too concerned about some forms of monitoring, while others might feel it to be particularly invasive.

Federal Legislation

Over 100 bills on privacy protection have been introduced in Congress, but as of this writing only one on the collection of personal information from kids on the Internet has been approved. Also, the White House is only supporting privacy protections related to medical information privacy because they believe that this type of uncertainty will dissolve as firms and employees become more comfortable with the medium.

Constitutional Protections

The Fourth Amendment to the U.S. Constitution protects the "right of the people to be secure in their persons, houses, papers, and effects, against unreasonable searches and seizures." This protection implies a reasonable expectation of privacy against intrusions *by the State, only.* As this provision of the Constitution does not apply to actions by private sector employers, their employees must rely instead on state-by-state laws and the common law made and accepted in the courts. Similar limitation exists in connection with the First Amendment's protection of personal autonomy and the Fifth Amendment's protection against self-incrimination—each of these only protects the individual from invasions by the State. Currently there is proposed employment-related privacy legislation in several states that would apply to private sector employers, but those states fall in the distinct minority.

What the courts will generally consider in cases involving both the Fourth Amendment and common law privacy protections is (a) whether the employer has a legitimate business interest in obtaining the information and (b) whether the employee has a reasonable expectation of privacy. Several examples of common law actions by the courts are illustrative of the courts' attempts at creating this balance, but perhaps more significant are the settlements reached by firms concerned about the *prospect* of a judge's decision.

Case Law

In one case, two McDonalds restaurant employees used voicemail to transmit love messages during an affair. They believed that these messages were private since the firm told them that only *they* had the access codes. The franchise owner monitored the voicemail messages and later played messages for the wife of one of the workers. The lovers sued for invasion of privacy. They settled for several million dollars, so we do not yet have any judge's decision in a situation like this.

In another case that never made it to the courts, the Minnesota Attorney General sued several banks for revealing personal information about clients to marketers in exchange for more than $4 million in fees. One bank eventually agreed to pay attorney fees plus $2.5 million to Habitat for Humanity.

As of this writing the law has not yet settled in connection with monitoring or the privacy of obtained information, hence the settlements. However, monitoring does seem justified by several cases where e-mail was later used as evidence to encourage a settlement. Within the past several years several large firms, including R. R. Donnelly, Morgan Stanley, and Citicorp, have found that cases often hinged on e-mail transmissions that people originally thought were deleted. In one case this included an e-mail containing 165 racial, ethnic, and sexual jokes sent to the entire firm. In another, the e-mail included sexual jokes about why beer is better than women. Had the firms enforced stringent policies about the use of e-mail and monitored to enforce these policies, perhaps these e-mails would never have been sent.

The *New York Times* also had some problems. They fired 24 employees at a Virginia payroll processing center for sending "inappropriate and offensive e-mail in violation of corporate policy." The public sector is not immune from similar challenges: The U.S. Navy reported that it had disciplined over 500 employees at a supply depot for sending sexually explicit e-mail. It happens all the time, and it's continuing to happen. You would think that people would actually learn.

In cases where the courts have been able to address the issue, it seemed at first that notice of monitoring might emerge as the critical factor. Perhaps persuaded by early case law, of the 67% of mid- to large-sized firms that monitor, 84% notify their employees of this activity. Notice might range from a one-line comment in the middle of an employee manual that someone receives on the first day of work to a dialogue box reminding you that e-mail may be monitored that pops up each time you hit the "send" button to transmit an e-mail.

In an early case addressing this topic, the court in *K-mart v. Trotti* held that the search of an employee's company-owned locker was not appropriate where the workers were told to use their own personal lock. The basis for the decision was that the employees were left with the legitimate, reasonable expectation of privacy because they used their own locks. On the other hand, an employer's search of employee lunch buckets was held reasonable by another court only two years earlier.[6]

In a later 1990 case, *Shoars v. Epson*, Epson won a suit filed by an employee who complained about e-mail monitoring.[7] In that case, the court distinguished the practice of *intercepting* an e-mail transmission from *storing and reading* e-mail transmissions once they had been sent, holding that the latter was acceptable. In a 1992 action, Northern Telecom settled a claim brought by employees who were allegedly secretly monitored over a 13-year period. In this case, Telecom agreed to pay $50,000 to individual plaintiffs and $125,000 for attorneys' fees.[8]

Similarly, an employee-plaintiff in a 1995 federal action won a case against his employer where the employer had monitored the worker's telephone for a period of 24 hours in order to determine whether the worker was planning a robbery. The court held that the company had gone too far and had insufficient evidence to support its claims.[9]

One might therefore conclude that, if an employer adequately notifies workers that it will conduct monitoring, it has effectively destroyed any reasonable expectation of privacy on the part of the workers. It would now be *unreasonable* to expect privacy since one is told not to expect it. However, in a case where the alternative extreme was true, where a firm notified workers that it would *not* monitor, the court did not follow congruent logic. It did not find a reasonable expectation of privacy based on a firm's pledge not to read e-mail.

In this case, *Smyth vs. Pillsbury*, Smyth sued the firm after a manager read his e-mail. At the time, Pillsbury had a policy saying that it would not read e-mail. One might presume that this policy should have created this reasonable expectation of privacy. But, instead, this was the first federal decision to hold that a private sector, at-will employee has no right of privacy in the contents of e-mail sent over the employer's e-mail system. The court held, "We do not find a reasonable expectation of privacy in the contents of e-mail communications voluntarily made by an employee to his supervisor over the company e-mail system, notwithstanding any assurances that such communications would not be intercepted by management."

THE LIMITATIONS OF THE LEGAL SYSTEM: A CALL FOR ETHICS

The law offers little, if any, guidance in this area in connection with workplace monitoring, and technology as a whole. In fact, "the development of our moral systems has not been able to keep pace with technological and medical developments, leaving us prey individually and societally to a host of dangers."[10] And does this not represent our current situation in terms of technological advances? It never occurred to most workers that some of this information was available or that they could be monitored in various ways. When it does not occur to them, they do not adequately protect themselves against it. Failure to completely understand the new technology may prevent people from completely understanding their exposure or potential vulnerability.

In his State of the Union address in January 2000, Clinton said, "Technology has to be carefully directed to assure that its reach does not compromise societal values. We have to safeguard our citizens' privacy."[11] The primary ethical issue for analysis is therefore whether the employee's fundamental right to privacy outweighs the employer's right to administer the workplace according to its desires. If not, is there a way to satisfy both parties? As law does not yet provide the answers, we turn to ethics for guidance.

The strongest, most persuasive, and most consistent guidance in this area is based in a theory called Integrative Social Contracts Theory (ISCT), promulgated by Tom Donaldson and Tom Dunfee, both faculty in Wharton's ethics program. ISCT seeks to differentiate between those values that are fundamental across culture and theory ("hypernorms"[12]) and those values that are culturally specific, determined within moral "free space," and that are not hypernorms. In identifying values as hypernorms, Donaldson and Dunfee propose that one look to the convergence of religious, cultural, and philosophical beliefs around certain core principles.[13] Included as examples of hypernorms are the freedom of speech, the right to personal freedom, the right to physical movement, and informed consent.[14] In fact, individual privacy is at the core of many of these basic, minimal rights and is, arguably, a necessary prerequisite to many of them.[15]

Specifically, ISCT seeks evidence of the widespread recognition of ethical principles that support a hypernorm conclusion, such as:

1. Widespread consensus that the principle is universal;
2. Component of well-known industry standards;
3. Supported by prominent nongovernmental organizations such as the International Labour Organization or Transparency International;
4. Supported by regional government organizations such as the European Union, the OECD, or the Organization of American States;
5. Consistently referred to as a global ethical standard by international media;
6. Known to be consistent with precepts of major religions;
7. Supported by global business organizations such as the International Chamber of Commerce or the Caux Roundtable;

8. Known to be consistent with precepts of major philosophies;
9. Generally supported by a relevant international community of professionals, e.g., accountants or environmental engineers;
10. Known to be consistent with findings concerning universal human values;
11. Supported by the laws of many different countries.[16]

With regard to privacy, a key finding of a recent survey of the status of privacy in fifty countries around the world included the following conclusion:

> Privacy is a fundamental human right recognized in all major international treaties and agreements on human rights. Nearly every country in the world recognizes privacy as a fundamental human right in their constitution, either explicitly or implicitly. Most recently drafted constitutions include specific rights to access and control one's personal information.[17]

Accordingly, it would appear that the value of privacy to civilized society is as great as the value of the various hypernorms to civilized existence. Ultimately, the failure to protect privacy may lead to an inability to protect personal freedom and autonomy.[18]

The application of ISCT, however, has limitations. ISCT does not quantify critical *boundaries* for rights. If employees have a right to privacy based on a hypernorm, how far does it extend and what should happen in a conflict? Does not the employer have certain hypernorm-based rights that might be infringed by the protection of the employees' privacy right? To quantify the boundaries of the universal rights, one must therefore look beyond ISCT to a more fairness-based methodology.

Ethicist John Rawls' theory of distributive economic justice provides fairness-based guidance for quantifying the boundary levels of fundamental rights. Distributive justice is a teleological approach to ethical decision-making that defines *ethical* acts as those that lead to an *equitable* distribution of goods and services. To determine a fair method for distributing goods and services. Rawls suggests that one consider how we would distribute goods and services if we were under a "veil of ignorance" that prevented us from knowing our status in society (i.e., our intelligence, wealth, or appearance). He asks that we consider what rules we would impose on this society if we had no idea whether we would be princes or paupers. Without knowing what role we might play in our society, would we devise a system of constant employee monitoring or complete privacy in all professional and personal endeavors? Rawls contends that those engaged in the exercise would build a cooperative system that was sensitive to the interests of all stakeholders. The reason Rawls believes that such a standard would emerge is that the members of the exercise do not know whether they would be among the employer population or employee population. Actions consistent with a system devised under a veil of ignorance are deemed ethical because of the inherent fairness of the system.

Rawls' theory of distributive justice does not provide guidance for identifying the categories of fundamental rights. What Rawls does provide is a method for establishing distribution rules that avoid market transgressions of the boundaries of ethical actions.

Conjoining ISCT and Rawlsian methods enables one to identify basic human rights and boundaries, and provides for a reasonable balance between economic and ethical consequences of privacy protection for both employees and employers. ISCT establishes the underlying, or foundational hypernorms within a society, whereas distributive justice offers guidance on the extent of those hypernorms and the means by which to implement them.

Scholars are not in complete agreement as to whether a right to privacy is a hypernorm, though most would agree that some form of personal autonomy must be protected. As mentioned above, evidence of a hypernorm such as freedom from slavery unequivocally supports this conclusion—personal autonomy serves as a cornerstone of this protection. On the other hand, the *quantification* of one's right to privacy, in particular workplace privacy, is better identified using a Rawlsian analysis. A proposal for such a fairness-based balance follows.

The implementation of an Ethical Resolution. Assuming for the purposes of this argument that privacy is a hypernorm, but one that may be limited by the employer's congruent right to managerial autonomy, how should the matter be resolved? I suggest a fairness-based decision based on two values: integrity and accountability.

Integrity, meaning consistency in values, would require that the decision-maker define her or his values, as well as create a prioritization of those values. This effort is often accomplished by a firm's mission statement or statement of values. Then, when faced with a dilemma or conflict between two or more of these values, the decision-maker will have internal as well as external guidance regarding the direction her or his decision should take. Second, no matter which direction is taken, the decision-maker must be accountable to anyone who is impacted by this decision. That would require a consideration of the impact of alternatives on each stakeholder, a balancing of that impact with the personal values addressed in the first step, and actions that represent the accountability to the stakeholders impacted by the decision.

Applying this process to a firm's response to monitoring and its impact on employee privacy, the firm may obtain guidance from its mission statement or alternative statement of values. Does monitoring satisfy or further the mission or values of the firm? Assuming monitoring satisfies or furthers the values of the firm (since a negative relationship here would end the discussion and resolve the dilemma), the employer must impose monitoring in a manner that is accountable to those affected by the decision to monitor.

To be accountable to the impacted employees, the employer must respect their privacy rights and their right to make informed decisions about their actions. Accordingly, this model would require that the employer should give adequate notice of the intent to monitor, including the form of monitoring, its frequency, and the purpose of the monitoring. In addition, in order to balance the employer's interests with those of the workforce, the employer should offer a means by which the employee can control the monitoring in order to create personal boundaries. In other words, if the employer is randomly monitoring telephone calls, there should be a notification device such as a beep whenever monitoring is taking place or the employee should have the ability to block any monitoring during personal calls. This latter option would address an oft-cited challenge to notification: if employees have notice of monitoring, there is no possibility of random performance checks. However, if employees can merely block personal calls, they remain unaware of which *business-related* calls are being monitored.

If it feels wrong, it probably is. Ethicist Gary Marks suggests that we look to a number of questions about monitoring, and he proposes that if you answer "yes" to these questions, your monitoring is more likely to be unethical.

- Does the *collection* of the data involve physical or psychological harm?
- Does the technique cross a personal boundary without permission?
- Could the collection produce invalid results?
- Are you being more intrusive than necessary?
- Is the data subject prohibited from appealing or changing the information recorded?
- Are there negative effects on those beyond the data subject?

- Is the link between the information collected and the goal sought unclear?
- Is the data being used in such a way as to cause a disadvantage to the subject?

As a manager, you are not without additional guidance on these issues. Kevin Conlon. District Counsel for the Communication Workers of America, suggests additional guidelines that may be considered in formulating an accountable process for employee monitoring:

- There should be no monitoring in highly private areas, such as restrooms.
- Monitoring should be limited to the workplace.
- Employees should have full access to any information gathered through monitoring.
- Continuous monitoring should be banned.
- All forms of *secret* monitoring should be banned.
- Advance notice should be given.
- Only information relevant to the job should be collected.
- Monitoring should result in the attainment of some business interest.[19]

Moreover, in its bargaining demands for last year, the Union of the United Auto Workers demanded concessions with regard to monitoring, including:

- Monitoring only under mutual prior agreement.
- No secret monitoring—advance notice required of how, when, and for what purpose employees will be monitored.
- Employees should have access to information gathered through monitoring.
- Strict limitations regarding disclosure of information gained through monitoring.
- Prohibition of discrimination by employers based on off-work activities.

RESOLUTION?

I am emphatic in much of what I have presented here because I passionately believe that there is a balance possible between workers and employers—not simply in the privacy/monitoring debate, but in many of the ethical challenges presented by new technological advances. Ultimately, employees and employers share a common vision with regard to the purpose of work and of the market in general. When the personal interests of both sides are considered, viable alternatives emerge.

Extreme opinions exist. An employer may believe that employees should simply quit if they don't want to be monitored, while certain employees may believe that they should have the ultimate control over their personal communications and other information. Two extremes. Yet, there is an absolute middle. One can absolutely respect the interest of the employee while also protecting the interest of the employer. A monitoring program that is developed according to and guided by the mission of the firm, then implemented in a manner that is accountable to the employees, follows the integrity/accountability approach I explored earlier.

From the employees' perspective, this type of resolution would respect their personal autonomy by providing for personal space, by giving notice of where that space ends, by giving them access to and the right to change or correct the information gathered, and by providing for monitoring that is directed toward the personal development of the employee and not merely to catch wrongdoers.

From the employer's perspective, this balance offers a way to effectively but ethically supervise the work done by their employees. It protects the misuse of resources, while also allowing them to better evaluate their workers and to encourage their workers to be more effective. I contend that any program that fails to satisfy these basic elements has the potential not only for ethical lapses, but also for serious economic problems.

Former vice president and presidential candidate Al Gore, who of course is an appropriate person to quote since he "invented" the Internet, claims that "new technology must not reopen the oldest threats to our basic rights: liberty and privacy. But government should not simply block or regulate all that electronic progress. If we are to move at full speed ahead into the information age, government must do more to protect your rights—in a way that empowers you more, not less. We need an electronic bill of rights for this electronic age."

CONCLUDING THOUGHTS

Before I conclude, I ask that you consider the following questions not only with regard to information technology and the impact that technology has on your particular workplace, but also with regard to the ethical issues that arise in other areas of your work. Consider what you might be willing to quit over. What would be so damaging, so intrusive, so much of a violation of your personal space that you would simply quit right then and there? What could be so bad?

Second, and perhaps it seems extreme in this particular circumstance, what would you be willing to give your life for? You may not believe right now that information technology is going to present life-and-death ethical dilemmas, and yet when we consider the ultimate usage of some of that technology, it really does have a life-and-death impact. If you knew that it would have a fatal, negative impact, would you quit if your firm or client failed to ameliorate it? Monitoring probably does not fall within this range, but you can imagine situations where technology does allow such an extreme unethical and certainly illegal act.

The reason why I want to conclude with this query is because this is really the purpose of this article. The world is a better place because you have thought about these questions now, rather than when you are first faced with these challenges in the workplace.

Have you ever had a situation where you act impulsively in the face of some dilemma, and you realize hours later that, if you'd only thought about it, there were other alternatives or there were other ways to look at it? It did not occur to you at the time. The best solution is to consider these situations now, in advance, so that your gut tells you more information when you need to know it. In speaking of inventor Charles Lindbergh, it is said that, "of all the man's accomplishments, and they were very impressive, the most significant is that he spent most of his life considering and weighing the values by which you should live."

If I ask you what your personal mission statement was so that you could actually implement the integrity and then accountability steps, would you know what it would be right now? Could you recite to me what you think are your critical values? Maybe not, but now is the time to think about them and not when those values are ultimately challenged.

Stanley Milgram conducted an experiment in the 1960s. In that experiment he called in two people. We'll take Megan and Jim. Megan and Jim come into my laboratory at Yale University, and I am wearing a white lab coat. I give to Jim fifty cards that have printed on them fifty pairs of symbols, i.e., a square and a heart, a diamond and a star, etc. Jim has a few minutes to memorize these. "Okay, Megan," the laboratory technician explains, "you are going to come into another room and test Jim. You're going to read off one of these symbols and, if he gets it correct, you'll continue. If he doesn't, you'll shock him with this electric shock machine, and then continue higher and higher voltages each time. It's just a little uncomfortable." Megan says that she understands.

Minutes later, the experiment begins. Jim remembers a few pairs in the beginning, but on the fourth card, he makes a mistake. He gets shocked and Jim says, "ah, that really hurt!" Megan says, "well, sorry." They keep going. They continue through a few more and Jim's saying. "wait a minute. This really hurts. Let me out of here! Let me out of here!" Later we hear, "I have a heart condition! Please let me out of here. This is horrible! I can't bear this any longer!" Megan's asking the experimenter, "what should I do?" The technician responds, "the experiment requires that you continue. You're being paid to participate in the experiment. There is no permanent tissue damage."

Continuing, Megan gets to number forty-eight, and she hears no sound from Jim's chamber. She looks to the technician who informs her that "no response is the same as a negative response." So she swallows, takes a deep breath and she zaps him. Forty-nine, no response. Fifty, no response. She stands up, gets out of the chair and says, "go, go, see if he's okay!"

And, of course, Jim is okay. He's reading from a script. He's not hooked up to a machine. He's part of the experiment. What is being tested is whether Megan will do what she has been told to do by an authority figure in a business or medical environment, against what she believes to be this person's best interest. One can now understand how this might be relevant to ethics and business ethics in particular.

Would you do something you knew was wrong because your boss tells you to do it? Oftentimes people say, "well if I didn't, I'd be fired." Well, so is it worth being fired? Should you do it or not do it? You still have a choice. You have a choice in everything.

In my lecture (the basis for this article) I asked my listeners the following question: "How many of you sitting here this afternoon believe that you might actually continue the whole experiment and go through number fifty?" Probably very few, and certainly significantly fewer than the more than 60% that completed the experiment for Milgram.

Now, the essential question: What is the difference between my listeners and those tested?

Are my listeners unique? Well actually yes, because they have read a discussion about ethics and have had the opportunity to consider the issues for a moment. It creates a bit of skepticism. Moreover, they have had the opportunity to observe the ethical dilemma and to have a slightly more objective opinion as to what they might do.

I believe that if you went into a psychological experiment tomorrow in real life, you would still challenge that experiment early in its process. Why? Because you have actually thought about what you might do in that circumstance. You have thought about the power or lack of power that this lab person would have over you. I am hoping that, as we consider ethics more and more on a regular basis, when ethical dilemmas come up, perhaps you will already have considered your response or at least your values with regard to the dilemma.

Simply by virtue of considering a dilemma beforehand, considering how you would act or what is important to you, you are going to make a different decision. The process cannot help but modify how you act. And so that's why I appreciate you caring about and reading about this subject.

NOTES

1. For additional insight in this area (and perhaps foresight, given the original date of publication), see William S. Brown, "Ontological Security, Existential Anxiety and Workplace Privacy," *Journal of Business Ethics* 23: 1 (2000), 61; citing in addition R. D. Laing, *The Divided Self* (New York: Penguin Books, 1965).

2. "More US firms checking email, says AMA," http://www.amanet.org/research/specials/monit.htm.

3. Julie Cook, "Big Brother Goes to Work," *Office Systems* (Aug. 1999), 43–45; John Macintyre, "Figuratively Speaking," *Across the Board* (Jan. 1999), 17.

4. Ibid.

5. Ibid.

6. *Simpson v. Commonwealth of Pa., Unemployment Compensation Bd. of Review.* 450 A.2d 305 (Pa. Comm. St. 1982). *cert. den'd.* 464 U.S. 822.

7. No. SCW112749 Cal. Sup. Ct., L.A. Cty., 1989, *appeal den'd.* Sup. Ct. Ca., 994 Cal. LEXIS 3670 (6/29/94); James McNair, "When You Use Email at Work, Your Boss May Be Looking In." *Telecom Digest.* http://icg.stwing.upenn.edu/cis500/reading.062.htm. reprinted from *The Miami Herald.*

8. Bureau of National Affairs. "Northern Telecom Settles with CWA on Monitoring." *Individual Employment Rights* (Mar. 10, 1992), 1.

9. Winn Schwartau. "Who Controls Network Usage Anyway?" *Network World* (May 22, 1995), 71.

10. John Haas, "Thinking Ethically About Technology," http://www.nd.edu/~rbarger/haas.ethic.

11. http//www.whitehouse.gov/WH/SOTU00/sotu-text.html (Jan. 27, 2000).

12. Thomas Donaldson and Thomas Dunfee. "Toward a Unified Conception of Business Ethics: Integrative Social Contracts Theory," *Academy of Management Review* 19 (1994), 252, 264 (hereinafter "Donaldson and Dunfee") (defining hypernorms as those principles that would limit moral free space, analogizing hypernorms to "hypergoods," "goods sufficiently fundamental as to serve as a source of evaluation and criticism of community generated norms [within moral free space]." Ibid.).

13. Donaldson and Dunfee, 252, 265.

14. Ibid.

15. Donaldson and Dunfee suggest that one look to international rights documents and statements of human rights for evidence of or support for certain hypernorms (Donaldson and Dunfee, 265–267). Evidence of privacy and data protection as a hypernorm may be found in the Organization for Economic Co-operation and Development's "Recommendation of the Council Concerning Guidelines Governing the Protection of Privacy and Transborder Flows of Personal Data" [O.E.C.D. Doc. C(80) 58 final (Oct. 1, 1980), *reprinted in* 20 I.L.M. 422 (1981)], the Council of Europe's "Council of Europe, Convention for the Protection of Individuals with Regard to Automatic Processing of Personal Data" [Jan. 28, 1981, EUR. T.S. No. 108, *reprinted in* 20 I.L.M. 317 (1981)], or the Commission of the European Community's Council Directive on the Protection of Individuals with Regard to the Processing of Personal Data and on the Free Movement of Such Data [COM(92)422 final 1992], European Commission Press Release IP/95/822 (7/25/95). "Council Definitively Adopts Directive on Protection of Personal Data." In support of the claim that privacy is either a hypernorm or a prerequisite to fundamental human rights, Charles Fried (*An Anatomy of Values* [n.p., 1970]. 142) contends that privacy is necessary to other values such as love and trust.

16. Thomas Donaldson and Thomas Dunfee. *Ties That Bind* (Boston: Harvard University Press, 1999), 60.

17. Global Internet Liberty Campaign. "Privacy and Human Rights: An International Survey of Privacy Laws and Practice," http://www.gile.org/privacy/survey/exec-summary.html (1998).
18. For a discussion on identifying Donaldson's and Dunfee's Integrative Social Contracts Theory-relevant ethical attitudes and the establishment of hypernorms, see Donaldson and Dunfee, 274–275, 276–277.
19. Kevin Conlon. "Privacy in the Workplace," *Labor Law Journal* (Aug. 1997), 444, 447. See also Organization for Economic Cooperation and Development (OECD). "Guidelines on the Protection of Privacy and Transborder Flows of Personal Data," available from the OECD at 202/785-6323.

Essay

Virtual Morality: A New Workplace Quandary

Michael J. McCarthy

Where do you draw the line.com? The explosion of the Internet into the workplace has empowered millions of employees, in a matter of keystrokes, to quietly commandeer company property for personal use. And ethical questions are mushrooming well beyond the propriety of workers frittering away a morning shopping online or secretly viewing pornographic Web sites.

Cautionary tales are piling up—from United Parcel Service of America Inc., which caught one employee using a UPS computer to run a personal business, to Lockheed Martin Corp., where a single e-mail heralding a religious holiday that was sent to 60,000 employees disabled company networks for more than six hours. The flood of e-mail traffic cost Lockheed Martin hundreds of thousands of dollars in lost productivity, and the employee lost his job.

Every day, companies face unexpected twists in the world of virtual morality. With the surge in day trading, is it OK for employees to log on to make a quick stock deal? How about sending out e-mails from work supporting a politician? Or using office computers to hunt for a new job? And if any of this is permissible occasionally, just when does it cross into excess?

This is a new spin on the old nuisance of employees making personal phone calls at work, but with greatly magnified possibilities. For one thing, the Web can be extremely seductive, lulling users to click screen after screen for hours at a time. Productivity can indeed suffer when dozens or hundreds of workers succumb to the temptation. What's more, unlike phone calls, electronic messages are often retrievable months or years later, and can be used as evidence in litigation against companies or individual employees.

In addition, though many workers don't realize it, when they surf the Web from work they are literally dragging their company's name along with them. Most Web sites can, and often do, trace the Internet hookups their visitors are using and identify the companies behind them. That leaves a serious potential for embarrassment if employees are visiting any number of places, from job-search sites to racist chat rooms. Caught off guard by the geometric growth of such issues, many companies have lost all hope of handling matters case by case. Some are using sophisticated software that monitors when, how and why workers are

---

From *Wall Street Journal*, October 21, 1999, pp. 81–84. Reprinted with permission of Dow Jones Inc.

using the Internet. Others are taking first stabs at setting boundaries.

Boeing Co., for one, seems to accept the inevitable with a policy specifically allowing employees to use faxes, e-mail and the Internet for personal reasons. But the aerospace and aircraft company also sets guidelines. Use has to be of "reasonable duration and frequency" and can't cause "embarrassment to the company." And chain letters, obscenity and political and religious solicitation are strictly barred.

Other companies are more permissive, but make it abundantly clear that employees can't expect privacy. Saying it recognizes that employees may occasionally need to use the Web or e-mail for personal reasons, Columbia/HCA Healthcare Corp. issues this warning in its "electronic communication" policy: "It is sometimes necessary for authorized personnel to access and monitor their contents." And, it adds, "in some situations, the company may be required to publicly disclose e-mail messages, even those marked private."

Attorneys have been advising companies to write such policies and alert employees that online activities will be monitored and that they can be disciplined. Such warnings make it difficult for employees to win any suit asserting that they expected their communications to be private—already an uphill claim given that the equipment belongs to the company in the first place.

Some 27% of large U.S. firms have begun checking employee e-mail, a huge jump from 15% in 1997, the American Management Association recently found. Some routinely do this to search for obscene language or images. Passed along employee to employee, those could constitute grounds for a sexual-harassment suit.

But the practice has generated controversy, particularly when workers are not forewarned. Earlier this month, California Gov. Gray Davis vetoed a measure that would have barred employers from secretly monitoring e-mail and computer files. Under the bill, companies would be allowed to do so only after they established monitoring policies and notified employees of them. Asserting that employers have a legitimate need to monitor company property, Gov. Davis said, "Every employee also understands that expense reports submitted for reimbursement are subject to employer verification as to their legitimacy and accuracy."

But even if a manager is within legal rights to peek at employee e-mail, does that make any kind of digital fishing expedition ethical? What's an employer to do, for example, if such a search of an employee's e-mail reveals that he has an undisclosed drug problem or is looking for another job?

To balance employee rights and a company's legal interests, some privacy advocates say, employers should check e-mail only after a worker is suspected of misconduct. "Just because companies own bathrooms doesn't mean they have the right to install cameras and monitor whatever goes on in there," says Marc Rotenberg, executive director of the Electronic Privacy Information Center, an advocacy group in Washington.

Against the tide, some companies and government agencies are trying to cling to "zero tolerance" policies, prohibiting any personal use of company equipment. One is Ameritech Corp., whose business code of conduct specifically states that computers and other company equipment "are to be used only to provide service to customers and for other business purposes," says a spokeswoman for the telecommunications company. The "policy ensures our employees are focused on serving customers," she adds. Reminders about the policy are sent periodically.

BellSouth was a similar hard-liner until the summer of 1998, when it caved. "We got a lot of questions from people saying they were afraid to give someone their company e-mail address for things like weekend soccer clubs," says Jerry Guthrie, the company's ethics officer.

"We work long hours—we wanted to offer it as a benefit to employees."

Before BellSouth employees can log on to their computers, however, they now must click "OK" to a message warning them against misuse of e-mail and the Internet, and alerting them that their actions can be monitored. Since the company changed the policy to allow for personal use, its security department has conducted more than 60 investigations of abuse. Some employees were suspended or fired for violations including accessing pornographic sites and spending too much time on nonbusiness Web pages, including sports sites.

BellSouth, like many other companies, uses filtering technology to block certain sites, but even that is a chore. Since each division currently filters different sites, the company is in the process of standardizing which sites will be blocked company-wide. "Some [other] companies block sports and financial sites," says Mr. Guthrie, though BellSouth doesn't intend to. But, he says, BellSouth will probably block access to "sex sites, hate sites and gambling sites."

In May, Zona Research Inc., an Internet market researcher in Redwood City, Calif., found that fully one-third of companies screen out any sites not on an approved list. In its survey of more than 300 companies. Zona also found that 20% of companies filter sites based on the user's job and another 13% based on the time of day.

But companies trying to construct such dams are discovering leaks all the time. Gambling, adult and other controversial sites are sanitizing or disguising their address names to operate under the radar of firms monitoring and blocking Internet content. One site remained undetected to cyber-smut police until it made headlines recently. Not to be confused with 1600 Pennsylvania Avenue, www.whitehouse.com offers X-rated content.

Essay

Rippers, Portal Users, and Profilers: Three Web-Based Issues for Business Ethicists

Martin Calkins

Recent controversies surrounding Napster—the popular Internet music file transference provider—illustrate the challenges by Internet users to our conventions about intellectual property. Although interesting, the Napster debate is just the beginning of what promises to be a string of like disputes about the extent of ownership of digitized material. Although we seem to be resolving some of the legal aspects of the Napster case, we have not begun to tackle the case's moral aspects nor have we attempted to address the broader ethical issues involving file transference via the Internet. These, we will see, are ripe areas for exploration by business ethicists.

In addition, the Internet has spawned all sorts of gateways to the Internet. These so-called portals cull, order, and display selected information. At first glance, portals appear to be innocuous but, as we will see, on further inspection they can be seen to influence and limit our moral worldview. Portals, then, bear watching and examination by business ethicists.

Finally, the information gathering practices of companies such as DoubleClick and Toysmart illustrate the problems attendant to use of the Internet to collect data on web browsers. Such data gathering—whether accomplished through tracking software or the application of search bots—challenges our notion of personal privacy as well as our conventional understanding of our commercial relationships. This web-related issue, like the others, is of growing concern for today's business ethicists.

With these issues in mind, this article will show how particular Internet technologies are influencing our moral standards. It then will suggest that business ethicists become more interested and involved in these issues and show how ethicists might begin to address the concerns of those caught up in today's fast-growing Internet-based world.

ISSUE 1: WEB-BASED FILE SHARING

In 1999, Napster.com, a music file transference database provider that allows users to freely evade copyright restrictions, set off a storm of controversy about the rightful distribution of digitized information in the form of music. For those unfamiliar with it. Napster allows users who have "ripped" music from CDs to mp3 file format to upload and transfer sound files to multiple unknown recipients.[1] Napster became a target for music industry lawyers recently because of the reach of its Internet-based distribution network and because Napster relied on easily identifiable Internet conduits, databases, and controlling interests. The series of closely watched trials that took place recently resulted in changes to Napster's day-to-day operations. At the same time, the public's fixation on the trial tended to obscure the fact that a number of Napster-like companies such as MP3.com (another music provider) and Scour.com (a provider of file-swapping programs for music, movies, photos, and other materials) either settled with the music industry or ceased their file exchange operations altogether.[2]

Furthermore, the Napster trials revealed the conflicted nature of the recording industry as a whole. While certain the music industry's corporate lawyers were going after Napster on copyright violation grounds, other corporate representatives—sometimes those within the same companies—were working for the defense of similar file web-based companies. Sony Music Entertainment Inc., for example, was a plaintiff in the lawsuit against Napster, claiming that Napster aided in the theft of copyrighted works by letting people trade music for free. At the same time, however, Sony Corporation is a member of the Consumer Electronics Association that, along with the Digital Future Coalition, opposed the July 2000 court ruling against Napster on the grounds that it could expand copyright law in unprecedented ways to the detriment of new technologies.[3]

Despite these and other conflicts, the legal case involving Napster is slowly being resolved. Even so, the issue of the dissemination of digitized files via the Internet has not gone away. Today more than ever, people are strongly committed to access to copyrighted material via the Internet. As *Wall Street Journal* reporter Lee Gomes recently quipped, "Napster, Schmapster. It's replaceable."[4]

Today, many open-source software (OSS) aficionados who previously supported Napster now disapprove of Napster's shift in policies after the recent court rulings.[5] Abandoning Napster, they turned instead to Song Spy, iMesh, WinMX, AngryCoffee, Gnutella, Freenet, and a host of other web-based file transfer networks that lack detectable central databases.[6] They use Freenet, for example, a network that uses a key system that effectively hides the identity of the user and does not rely on stored information at fixed locations nor subject information to any kind of centralized control.[7] Unlike Napster users, Freenet users are difficult, if not impossible to monitor. They can trade files in chat rooms on the Internet Relay Chat (IRC) network or through underground transient web sites. Their dispersal of material is so complete that even the programs' authors admit they cannot control the programs' use. As Ian Clarke, Freenet's primary creator, recently stated. "I've got no direct control over how people use [Freenet] . . . If someone put a gun to my head and said 'shut this down,' I would be unable to do so."[8]

In the long run, it seems likely that the mainstream media industries' attempts to stop or slow the growth of Internet-based challengers such as Napster will fall.[9] As the *New York Times* reporter Amy Harmon recently noted, people are increasingly digging in to maintain their access to free-ware.[10] The commentary in the "Talkback" section of *ZDNet News* supports her assertion.[11] As one reader recently quipped.

> Lawmakers are irrelevant. If I buy it, it's mine. As long as I'm not making money with it. I will do with it what I please. If my friends want to see it—I'll make the decision. If my friends want to hear it—I'll make the decision. If my friends want to borrow it—I'll make the decision. It's mine—I'll decide. They can write whatever law they want. It's mine. Government cannot rule without consent of the governed. MILLIONS of people are using Napster. The governed have spoken.[12]

In response to Napster's decision to become a pay site, one user commented. "I will *not* pay for use of Napster as it is. . . . Why should I?"[13]

Along with growing public resistance to control of web-based information sharing, it is not clear how long U.S. courts will be willing to support copyright holders as they do now. Free-ware providers are already beginning to proliferate globally in regions having legal systems less stringent than those of the United States or Europe and this is likely to cause greater strain on the current U.S. position regarding intellectual property. In addition, U.S. businesses outside the entertainment industry are beginning to regard constraints on file-sharing as restrictive of open markets.[14] Increasingly, as Lawrence Lessig points out, today's commonly held belief that copyrights are not protected enough is giving way to the understanding of the copyright as being not so much a copy-right as a copy-duty, that is, "the duty of owners of protected property to make that property accessible."[15] Indeed, the notion that we should appeal first and foremost to the courts to resolve issues such as these may be modified in the information age, for even when they are amended, laws tend to be either too general to apply to particular complex situations or too narrow to apply appropriately beyond a narrow range of cases. The Napster case seems to bear this out.

The attention given to Napster's legal proceedings has somewhat obscured the fact that Internet-based file-swapping involves a number of moral issues—the place of individual choice in society, our conception of stealing, whether code is something to be shared freely or a commodity, the justice of certain power relationships, and so forth. Interestingly, however, business ethicists have been rather slow to pick up on these ethical concerns. Instead, journalists have pursued them. One of the best treatments to date, for example, is Charles C. Mann's in-depth analysis of Napster in *The Atlantic Monthly*.[16] Similarly, newspaper reporters such as Harmon (*NY Times*) and Gomes (*Wall Street Journal*) are noteworthy for their coverage of the ethics of Napster, OSS, and web-based file-swapping. Gomes's recent interviews of Larry Wall (developer of the Perl language) and Linus Torvalds (creator of

Linux and one of the leaders in the open source software movement) about piracy via the Internet are particularly significant:

Wall:

Open source should be about giving away things voluntarily.

When you force someone to give you something, it's no longer giving, it's stealing. Persons of leisurely moral growth often confuse giving with taking.[17]

Torvalds:

Of course you should be able to sue over copyrights. The one good lawsuit in the whole Napster case is the one by Metallica: a suit by the actual authors. While it's probably motivated mostly by money. I can still at least hope that there is a strong feeling of morals there, too.[18]

While journalists are to be commended for introducing the ethical aspects of Napster and Internet-based file-swapping, they cannot be expected to investigate the ethics of the issue in depth. This is the domain of business ethicists and it is time for us to get to work. Currently, we have a rare opportunity to help Internet users, mainstream copyright holders, and others move beyond certain exclusively self-interest positions to work toward a deeper understanding of this complex moral problem. At present, it seems we have at least two competing views on digital file-sharing via the Internet. These are summarized in Table 8.1.

With these perspectives in mind, we might begin to deal with the ethics of Internet-based file-swapping by entertaining the following questions:

Questions to Ponder

- Is there a difference between downloading music from the web and taking music off the shelf of a music store?
- What moral dispositions are developed by repeatedly downloading others' work?
- Do music downloading feeding frenzies correlate with other forms of consumerism?
- Can (or do) on-line companies capitalize on these dispositions?
- If we accept unlimited file swapping of others' work, would we also allow others unlimited access to our files?
- Who controls (and to what extent) web-based information?
- Do OSS proponents have legitimate claims?
- Should digital information be controlled by its authors, distributors, governmental agencies, or the public?
- What other cases correlate to Internet file-sharing?
- What would such a casulstry look like?

TABLE 8.1   Web-based File Sharing and Property Rights

Perspective	Description	Examples	
Digital files are property	On-line sharing • a violation of property rights	Recording Industry of America	
No constraints on on-line file sharing	On-line sharing • should not be regulated by government or recording industry	Napster iMesh Song Spy WinMX	Gnutella Newtella FreeNet AngryCoffee

ISSUE 2: INTERNET PORTALS

A second area of potential concern for business ethicists is the use of Portals—web pages that serve as gateways to the Internet. Portals' general purpose is to cull, order, and disseminate information. Typically, they contain links to a variety of sites and are associated with a search engine or web directory. They can be broken down into three types, "broad door," "welcome, customer!," and "daily me." See Table 2.

The first sort of portal, my so-called broad door portal, is a site entrance through which everyone passes in the same way. This portal, typified by sites such as Yahoo.com and Go.com, routes all users through a single entry page.[19] There, one encounters a customizable database and simply keys in a word or phrase to locate, identify, and edit material on the Internet. The broad portal format is potentially lucrative because those who maintain it can offer advertising space to e-tailers.[20] Moreover, page providers can use pages to route visitors to shopping sites of their own or their sponsors. Not surprisingly then, "broad door" portals tend to have lots of ads for recommended e-tailers. Accordingly, Yahoo! currently promotes FTD.com, Nordstrom, and macys.com, and makes statements such as, "Yahoo! prefers Visa."[21]

The second sort of portal, the "welcome, customer!" portal, provides visitors with a list of suggestions immediately after arriving at the site. Epitomized by Amazon.com, the "welcome, customer!" portal uses cookies to identify the visitor, then suggests products or sites based on the visitor's prior purchases.[22] Each time a visitor arrives at a site with cookies turned on, the cookie is read and a list of hyperlinks or advertisements for products and services tailored to the intended customer's prior inquiries is brought forward. For example, if a woman happened to buy a Japanese cookbook for her daughter through Amazon.com, each time the woman returns to Amazon.com, she will get a list of books related to Japanese cooking, Japan, or cooking without requesting such information. In this way, Amazon.com, hopes to tap the woman's interests to spur new sales. The problem, of course, is that profiling based on past purchases may not reflect the woman's real interests at all. The woman purchased the Japanese cookbook for her daughter in this case and may not care at all for Japanese food. Regardless, each time she returns to Amazon.com, she will receive information about Japanese cuisine. Even so, "welcome, customer!" portals are useful to e-tailers and visitors to sites because they streamline the

TABLE 8.2 Portals

Portal Type	Description	Examples	
Broad door	Single entrance to a customizable database	Go Yahoo! AOL	Excite Lycos Dogpile
Welcome, customer!	Cookies • target past preferences • used to suggest new products or services	Amazon.com A.T. Cross Co.	
Daily me	User selects narrow preferences • Information is updated on each access to the site	AvantGo	

visitor's search, making it likely that the visitor will remain at a web site and (ultimately) make a purchase.

The third sort of portal, the "daily me" portal, is customizable by users. Not unlike the StartUp folder in the Microsoft Windows Start Menu, the "daily me" portal allows the visitor (again, with cookies turned on) to select certain areas of interest from a menu. Each time the individual returns to the site with cookies turned on and enters a password, information based on the preselected menu is provided. Some merchants, such as A. T. Cross, demand that cookies be turned on to access the web site (usually "cookies on" is optional). At sites that rely on this sort of profiling, ads targeted to user past preferences will be included on accessed pages.

The advantage of the "daily me" format is that visitor interests can be more narrowly defined and page information can more accurately reflect the true interests of the visitor. AvantGo.com. for example, uses this technology successfully.[23] Its so-called channels—user-stated preferences for handheld organizers such as the Palm Pilot and Handspring Visor—allow users to upload up-to-date information from a variety of commercial and noncommercial sites. These are appealing because they save time—a complete set of highly specific information can be uploaded in a single synchronization. The process is fast, reliable, and thorough. From the e-tailer's perspective, the arrangement is appealing because it provides an accurate picture of the consumer's preferences. E-tailers can use the data they gather from users to target potential customers more effectively.

Though seemingly a positive sum game, the use of portals is not without its drawbacks. Chief among these is the fact that the narrowing of interests just described constrains the flow of information to the user. Although the information provided reflects the user's stated preferences, the user is effectively shielded from other information that may be discomforting. Exclusive use of portals might easily facilitate user blindness to wrongdoing or injustices in the world.

Since portals cull, order, and disseminate web-based data for the user, they rely on a taxonomy of user preferences that is essentially value-laden and moral in nature. This taxonomy needs to be examined by ethicists. Thus, business ethicists would do well to entertain the following questions:

Questions to Ponder

- What values and moral principles ground the taxonomies of Internet portal users?
- What set of truth-bearing cases—what sort of casuistry—might inform the discussion of portal use?
- How are people's dispositions to world affairs influenced by repeated access to the narrowly defined informational preferences of Internet portals?
- How do e-tailers use the data they gather from users' access to Internet portals?

ISSUE 3: WEB-BASED PROFILING

The use of Internet portals invites a consideration of the wider issue of the invasion of personal privacy via the Internet. As we saw, portals regulate the distribution of information provided to users. Site maintainers or e-tailers may use the information they gather from user selections to suggest products and services to them.

To facilitate the effectiveness of such target marketing, software designers have developed site trackers to collect and collate visitor information, often without the visitor's knowledge. These so-called profilers—collectors of sets of data about the web surfing and buying habits of individuals—can track site visitors and determine how and how often someone accesses a web page.

eXTReMe Tracking is an example of such a tracker.[24] It is free and available for download by anyone. Once the eXTReMe Tracking icon is installed on a web page, the site monitor can look for visitors per time period (day, week, hour of the day, month, etc.), domain, country of origin, and browser type, search engine, and keywords used to locate the site. eXTReMe Tracking is not a covert technology because the eXTReMe Tracking icon must be displayed on the page for the software to work properly. Even so, it illustrates how any user can monitor the hits on his or her web page and develop a profile of his or her visitors.

Second, profilers can also use computer programs called "search bots" (short for robots) to search out new information. Search bots effectively ferret out Internet user information and then forward unsolicited email to the user, respond to user newsgroup messages, update the user profile with new information about the user, and so forth. Unlike trackers, search bots operate without the target person's knowledge or approval. Consequently, they are more intrusive and morally questionable than trackers.

One company that recently raised public concern about its tracking and profiling practices on the web was DoubleClick.com, a global Internet advertising company that specializes in ads for the Internet. In 2000, DoubleClick claimed to have worked with 4,400 advertisers to deliver over 30 billion ads every month. It came under fire, however, for allegedly providing advertisers with personal information of web browsers without the users' approval. It then adopted a privacy policy that assured readers it did not collect any personally identifiable information.[25] Even so, it admitted that it collects "non-personally identifiable information" that it uses for targeting ads and measuring ad effectiveness on behalf of their advertisers and web publishers who specifically request it.[26]

DoubleClick became a concern for privacy advocates when it combined with Abacus, the nation's largest proprietary database of consumer, retail, business-to-business, publishing, and online transactions used for target-marketing purposes.[27] The new DoubleClick-Abacus alliance intended to use statistical modeling of online behavioral and intent data to target their customers' Internet ads to the most responsive anonymous online prospects.[28] While they offered clear privacy statements, they established an "opt-out" policy regarding data gathering—in other words, people had to choose NOT to have DoubleClick/Abacus collect data on them.[29] This did not sit well with many and last year DoubleClick was forced to modify its plan to combine web-tracking data with offline databases.

In addition to the intrusiveness of on-line retailers, we have seen the potential for harm caused by e-tailers' indiscretion. Toysmart.com, for example, recently created a furor when it announced a plan to sell its customer database to the highest bidder when it decided to shut down its operations. Fortunately, as Thomas Weber of the *Wall Street Journal* reported. "Walt Disney Co., a Toysmart investor, offered to purchase and then destroy the data after the Federal Trade Commission moved to block Toysmart's plan."[30]

Not surprisingly, these and other privacy violations have spurred public concern. Consequently, groups such as the Privacy Rights Clearinghouse—a nonprofit consumer information and advocacy program established in 1992 that won a number of awards recently for its work on behalf of identity theft victims—have become increasingly prominent.[31] So, too, have discussion groups such as the Privacy Forum of Vortex Technology, a moderated e-mail digest for the discussion and analysis of issues related to on-line privacy.[32]

In addition, users have begun to adopt protective technologies to offset e-tailers' intrusiveness. One such technology by AdSubtract.com blocks ads, cookies, pop-up windows, animations, music, and other annoyances from the user's computer.[33] This software—distributed freely—also tallies the number of ads and cookies it disallows and enables the user to select against the dissemination of certain information. Most tellingly, AdSubtract has a special filter that targets and disables information transference to DoubleClick.

Another product that limits on-line data collection is that provided by Anonymizer.com whose mission, bolstered by reference to the United Nations' Universal Declaration of Human Rights, is to "ensure that an individual's right to privacy is not compromised by going on-line.[34] To promote its services, Anonymizer freely distributes a trial version that allows visitors to surf the web anonymously.

In short, these and other services and products attempt to return control of information gathering via the Internet to the user. While this is commendable, it is doubtful they will be entirely effective against e-tailer intrusiveness given the profits associated with information gathering.

Perhaps the most disturbing aspect of Internet-based tracking and profiling is what it portends for the future—specifically in regard to privacy and the emerging field of nanotechnology.

Popularized by K. Eric Drexler, undeveloped at present but looming on the horizon, nanotechnology (also called molecular technology) involves precision technology at the level of atoms and molecules.[35] It conceives of technology beyond microcircuits (where parts are measured in micrometers or millionths of a meter)—at the level of nanometers, or one thousand times smaller than a micrometer. It holds particular promise for medicine as computers are envisioned to be miniaturized such that they can be inserted into the body to relay information to receivers located outside the body. Doctors will then be able to monitor a patient's health without invasive procedures and, perhaps, without the patient even being present in the room.

Fitness enthusiasts also might appreciate the benefits of nanotechnology as computers might be injected into the bloodstream to monitor the individual's lipids, heart rate, blood flow, temperature and so forth, while exercising. This information might be transmitted to an external monitoring and storage device (e.g., a Palm organizer or a personal computer) and then used to construct an effective workout program, diet, or health regimen. Since data would be gathered by wireless

TABLE 8.3 Web-based Tracking

	Reasons	*Examples*
For	User profiling	eXTReMe
	Market research	DoubleClick
	Transaction ease	Toysmart
Against	Privacy violation	Anonymizer
	ID theft	AdSubtract
		Privacy Rights Clearinghouse
		Vortex Technologies

means, a fitness center's receivers might also collect the data. The fitness center might then offer inducements (discounted memberships and such) to users to allow it to sell the data to health and fitness related e-tailers. This information could, of course, eventually find its way to certain health care providers, insurance companies, or employer—with disastrous consequences.

As the above scenario suggests, our increasing reliance on web-based technologies challenges our notions of privacy and personal control. Clearly, the development of web-based technologies bears watching and ongoing commentary by business ethicists, for it holds potential harms and presses the boundaries of our moral norms. We would do well then to entertain questions such as the following:

Questions to Ponder

- What sort of casuistry might guide our deliberations about information gathering, confidentiality, and so forth?
- Should we limit personal electronic information gathering?
- If we would not prohibit it altogether, what limits would we impose on information gathering?
- How do we keep the guardians honest, that is, how do we know that companies such as AdSubtract are not duping us?
- How (or should) we establish a "need to know" basis for dissemination of personal information?
- What is business' place in this discussion?
- What role does fear play in our concerns about on-line privacy?
- What bridges are business ethicists forging with bioethicists and medical ethicists as business and medical issues increasingly overlap?

CONCLUSION

Recently, Jacob Schlesinger observed that e-commerce has helped to complicate our understanding of what is right and wrong

about information distribution by "sowing confusion over such long-settled matters as the way information is owned and shared."[36]

I think he is right.

As this article has shown, issues such as web-based information sharing, profiling, and tracking challenge many of our assumptions and norms. In each instance, we have seen the need for the involvement of business ethicists. The issues laid out here and those forecast for the future suggest that business ethicists have a rare opportunity to help users, e-tailers, and others advance in an understanding of the moral aspects of a web-based world that is confused, confusing, and sorely in need of direction.

NOTES

1. "Ripping" a song involves the use of a software program to digitally copy the song from a CD into a different format such as MP3, WAV, AIFC, or some other. ComputerUser.com Inc., *High-Tech Dictionary*, 2000. (accessed 19 Feb. 2001) http://www.computeruser.com/resources/dictionary/dictionary.html.

2. Don Clark, Anna Wilde Mathews, and Martin Peers, "Key Change: Napster Ruling Shifts Balance of Web Power Back to Music Industry," *Wall Street Journal,* 28 July 2000, A1.

3. Lisa M. Bowman, "Napster Case Makes Strange Bedfellows," *ZDNet News* 14 (Sept. 2000), (accessed 19 Feb. 2001) http://www.zdnet.com/zdnn/stories/news/0,4586,2627767,00.html.

4. Lee Gomes, "Napster Ruling May Be Just the Overture—The Free-Music Movement Is Morphing in Directions More Difficult to Control." *Wall Street Journal,* 28 July 2000, B1.

5. Open source software (OSS) is computer software in which the program source code is shared freely with developers and users. Proponents hold that OSS developers can customize programs and that these innovations can be shared within the programming community in such a way that everyone learns from each other. It is the basis of a number of hardware platforms and software languages. Linux is one popular example. Ibid. (accessed).

6. This is true for movie file transference as well. A Gnutella-like program called DivX;—a hacked version of the Microsoft MPEG-4 standard video-compression

system that enables users to store high-quality digital movies in 10% to 20% of a film's original space—is now available. With this program, users can download full-length movies in an hour or two using high-speed DSL or cable-modem connections. Film executives fear its distribution because it threatens to do to movies what the MP3 music compression system did to music CD sales. Lee Gomes, "E-Business: Now, the 'Napsterization' of Movies," *Wall Street Journal*, 19 July 2000, B1; and "Software Developers Race to Create New Movie-Download Format," *Wall Street Journal*, 14 Sept. 2000, B1.

7. Free Network Project. *Freenet Frequently Asked Questions*. Accessed 19 Feb. 2001, http://freenet.sourceforge.net/index.php?page=faq#sec1.1.

8. Amy Harmon, "Fans of Swapping Music on Internet Not Deterred by Court Order." *New York Times*, 28 July 2000, A1.

9. Jess Bravin, "Napster Ruling May Be Just the Overture—In Court. Old Media Beats Technology—For Now." *Wall Street Journal*, 28 July 2000, B1.

10. Harmon, "Fans of Swapping Music."

11. Bowman, "Napster Case."

12. NicX, *Talkback Central*, ZDNet News. (accessed 19 Feb. 2001). http:// www.zdnet.com/tlkbck/comment/22/0.7056.97352-564205.00.html.

13. Matthew Rothenberg, *TalkBack Central: Will Subscriptions Stifle Napster?* ZDNet News, 29 Jan. 2001. (accessed 19 Feb. 2001). http://www.zdnet.com/zdnn/stories/comment/0,5859.2679911.00.html.

14. As Mark Lemley summarizes, "the more complex you make the rules, the more difficult it is for markets to work." Quoted in Jacob M. Schlesinger. "The Outlook—The Web: Friend or Foe of Capitalism?" *Wall Street Journal*, 24 July 2000, A1.

15. Lawrence Lessig, *Code and Other Laws of Cyberspace* (New York: Basic Books, 1999), 127.

16. Charles C. Mann, "The Heavenly Jukebox," *The Atlantic Monthly*, Sept. 2000, 39–59.

17. Lee Gomes, "E-Business: Linux Gurus, Followers Differ on Napster Use," *Wall Street Journal*, 22 May 2000, B1.

18. Ibid.

19. Yahoo!, reputed to stand for, "Yet Another Hierarchical Officious Oracle," provides an interesting history of web-based databases. See Yahoo! Inc., *Yahoo!—Company History* (accessed 19 Feb. 2001) http://docs.yahoo.com/info/misc/history.html.

20. "E-tailing" refers to the buying and selling of goods and services over the Internet. E-tailers include e-commerce companies, Internet retailers, or virtual storefronts, e.g., Amazon.com, ETRADE, eBay, Buy.com, and so forth. E-tailers generate revenue from on-line sales and advertising partnerships and can manage complex distribution networks. Joint Venture: Silicon Valley Network, *Joint Venture's Internet Cluster Analysis* (San Jose, CA: Joint Venture: Silicon Valley Network, Inc., 1999), 18.

21. Much of the section on portals here was inspired by Judith V. Boettcher's (Executive Director, Corporation for Research and Educational Networking) talk at an informal panel discussion at the Syllabus 2000 Conference in Santa Clara, CA on 25 July 2000.

22. A cookie is a set of data that a web site server gives to a browser the first time the user visits the site. It updates the cookie with each return visit. A remote server saves the information the cookie contains about the user and the user's browser does the same, as a text file stored in the Netscape or Explorer system folder. Most, but not all, browsers support cookies. ComputerUser.com Inc. *High-Tech Dictionary*, 2000. (accessed 19 Feb. 2001) http://www.computeruser.com/resources/dictionary/dictionary.html.

23. AvantGo, Inc., *AvantGo Home Page*, 2000. (accessed 25 Feb. 2001). http://avantgo.com/frontdoor/.

24. eXTReMe digital, *eXTReMe Tracking Home Page*, 2000, (accessed 25 Feb. 2001). http://www.extreme-dm.com/tracking/.

25. DoubleClick Inc., *DoubleClick Privacy Statement*, 19 Feb. 2001. (accessed 19 Feb. 2001). http://www.doubleclick.net/us/corporate/privacy/default.asp?asp_object_1=&.

26. Ibid.

27. Abacus, *Home Page*, 2000. (accessed 19 Feb. 2001).

28. Abacus, *Corporate Profile*, 2001. (accessed 19 Feb. 2001). http://www.abacus-direct.com/corporate_profile.htm.

29. Ibid.

30. Thomas E. Weber, "Network Solutions Sells Marketers Its Web Database," *Wall Street Journal*, 15 Feb. 2001, B1.

31. Privacy Rights Clearinghouse, *About the PRC*, 15 Jan. 2001. (accessed 19 Feb. 2001). http://www.privacyrights.org/fs/services.htm.

32. Vortex Technology. *The Privacy Forum*, 2001. (accessed 19 Feb. 2001). http://www.vortex.com/privacy.

33. InterMute, Inc., *AdSubtract Home Page*, (accessed 19 Feb. 2001). http://www.adsubtract.com/index.html.

34. Anonymizer.com. *Home Page*, 2000 (accessed 19 Feb. 2001). http://www.anonymizer.com/corporate/index.shtml.

35. K. Eric Drexler. *Engines of Creation: The Coming Era of Nanotechnology* (New York: Doubleday, 1987).

36. Schlesinger. "The Outlook—The Web."

Case Study

Cyberethics: Seven Short Cases

Richard A. Spinello
Herman T. Tavani

CASE STUDY I

The Librarian's Dilemma (Hypothetical)

Assume that you have just taken over as the head librarian of a library system in a medium-size city in the United States. You discover that the main library building in the heavily populated downtown area has six Macintosh computers, but they are used only sporadically by this library's many patrons. The computers lack any interesting software and do not have Internet connectivity. As one of your first orders of business, you decide to purchase some popular software packages and to provide Internet access through Netscape's Navigator browser. The computer room soon becomes a big success. The computers are in constant use, and the most popular activity is Web surfing. You are pleased with this decision because this is an excellent way for those in the community who cannot afford computer systems to gain access to the Internet.

Soon, however, some problems begin to emerge. On one occasion, some young teenagers (probably about twelve or thirteen years old) are seen downloading graphic sexual material. A shocked staff member tells you that these young boys were looking at sadistic obscene images when they were asked to leave the library. About ten days later, an older man was noticed looking at child pornography for several hours. Every few weeks, there are similar incidents.

Your associate librarian and several other staff members recommend that you purchase and immediately install some type of filtering software. Other librarians remind you that this violates the ALA's code of responsibility. You re-read that code and are struck by the following sentence: "The selection and development of library resources should not be diluted because of minors having the same access to library resources as adult users." They urge you to resist the temptation to filter, an activity they equate with censorship. One staff member argues that filtering is equivalent to purchasing an encyclopedia and cutting out articles that do not meet certain standards. Another librarian points out that the library does not put pornographic material in its collection, so why should it allow access to such material on the Internet?

As word spreads about this problem, there is also incipient public pressure from community leaders to do something about these computers. Even the mayor has weighed in—she too is uncomfortable with unfettered access. What should you do?

Questions

1. Is filtering of pornographic Web sites an acquisition decision or does it represent an attempt to censor the library's collection?
2. Do libraries have any legal and/or moral duty to protect children from indecent and obscene material?
3. What course of action would you take? Defend your position.

CASE STUDY II

Spam or Free Speech at Intel?

Mr. Kenneth Hamidi is a disgruntled, former employee of Intel who has problems with the way Intel treats its workers. Hamidi is the founder and spokesperson of an organization known as FACE, a group of current and former Intel employees, many of whom claim that they have been mistreated by Intel. Hamidi was dismissed from Intel for reasons that have not been made public, but he claims to be a victim of discrimination.

Shortly after his dismissal in the fall of 1996, Hamidi began e-mailing Intel employees, informing them of Intel's unfair labor practices. He alleges that the company is guilty of widespread age and disability discrimination, but Intel firmly denies this allegation. According to Intel, Hamidi sent about 30,000 e-mail messages complaining about Intel's employment policies between 1996 and 1998. One message, for example, accused Intel of grossly underestimating the size of an impending layoff.

Intel's position was that Hamidi's bulk e-mail was the equivalent of spam, congesting its e-mail network and distracting its employees. Intel's lawyers have contended that these unsolicited mailings were intrusive and costly for the corporation. Moreover, the unwanted messages are analogous to trespass on Intel's property: just as a trespasser forces his or her way onto someone's else's property so these messages were being forced upon Intel and its employees.

In summary, their basic argument is that Hamidi does not have a right to express his personal views on Intel's proprietary e-mail system. They also point out that Hamidi has many other forums to express his opinions, such as the FACE Web site.

In November 1998, a California Superior Court judge agreed with these arguments and issued an injunction prohibiting Hamidi from sending any more bulk e-mail to Intel's employees.

Defenders of Hamidi's actions argue that the injunction is an unfair overreaction and that his free speech rights are being violated. They claim that this bulk e-mail should not be categorized as spam because it took the form of noncommercial speech, which deserves full First Amendment protection. Hamidi's speech involves ideas; it is not an attempt to sell goods or services over the Internet. Hamidi, therefore, has a First Amendment right to disseminate his e-mail messages to Intel's employees, even if the company is inconvenienced in the process.

Questions

1. Does Hamidi's speech deserve First Amendment protection? Should he be allowed to send these messages without court interference?
2. What do you make of Intel's argument that its censoring of Hamidi's bulk e-mail amounts to protecting its private property?
3. Should there be new laws to clarify this issue? How might those laws be crafted?

CASE STUDY III

The www.nga Domain Name Dispute (Hypothetical)

The National Gun Association (NGA) of America is a powerful lobbying organization established more than fifty years ago to protect the public's constitutional right to own firearms. The organization has millions of members concentrated in the western and southern regions of the country. It has a strong presence in Washington, D.C., where it advocates against efforts to restrict the right to own a gun. The NGA's vocal support of that right has spawned opposition groups, which believe that the NGA helps contribute to a climate of violence through its encouragement of gun ownership.

The NGA has a Web site, www.nga.org, where it disseminates information about the right to bear arms and other issues related to gun ownership and gun control. The site also informs members about impending legislation and advises them how to register their opinions with elected officials. The Web site is popular with members and averages more than 25,000 hits a day.

One of the more radical groups opposing the NGA, called Pacifists for Gun Control (PGC), has set up a nonprofit organization that distributes literature and organizes its own lobbying efforts. It has created a Web site for which it was able to secure the domain name www.nga-assassins.org. The PGC has admitted that one purpose in using this accusatory domain name is to intercept users looking for www.nga.org through its meta tags. Its home page has the following message.

> Don't be fooled by the NGA. Look here to see the damage that guns can really do!

The PGC's Web site is filled with material on the perils of gun ownership and the virtues of gun controls, particularly for automatic weapons and handguns. There are also links to other sites that discuss the excesses and the tendentious views of the NGA. Through the contents of this Web page, the PGC seeks to convert gun owners and others sympathetic to the NGA's objectives to its ideological views regarding violence and firearms.

The NGA has filed a lawsuit to block this Web site on the grounds that the domain name is deceptive and misleading. It also alleges that its trademark, "NGA," has been violated and diluted. The PGC contends that it is merely exercising its free speech rights. It is using this derivative domain name to help propagate its political ideas about gun ownership. It also points out that NGA members who are temporarily diverted to this site can easily move on to the real NGA Web site, so no harm is done. A court in the NGA's home state of Texas has taken up the matter and will soon issue a preliminary ruling.

Questions

1. Is this a free speech issue? Does the PGC have any right to use the domain name www.nga.assassins.org?
2. If you were litigating this case on behalf of the National Gun Association, which arguments would you use to support their position?
3. Can the PGC's unorthodox actions be morally justified in any way?

CASE STUDY IV

Framing as Property Theft?

In May 1998, a significant property dispute arose between *The Journal Gazette*, a major daily newspaper published in Fort Wayne, Indiana, and a Web site called www.Ft-Wayne.com. This Web site was created as a public service to provide announcements about community activities and local social events in Fort Wayne and its environs.

The newspaper alleged that when the Web site linked to its newspaper articles, the article would appear within a "frame," that is, surrounded by Ft-Wayne.com's own ads and banners along with its site address. *The Journal Gazette* filed suit against the Web site, claiming that its property was being systematically "looted" by this practice. The lawsuit cited federal trademark and copyright infringement as the basis for its claim. *The Journal Gazette* also alleged that Ft.Wayne.com was acting as a free rider by exhibiting the *Journal*'s articles surrounded by its own advertisements.

The Ft-Wayne.com Web site did stop framing the newspaper's articles after the lawsuit was filed but insisted that it did not violate any laws or do anything wrong. Defenders of the Web site observed that they were guilty only of providing more readers for *The Journal Gazette*. One of the Web site's creators also defended the practice "as a means to keep viewers from roaming away form the Ft-Wayne.com site.[1]

Questions

1. Comment on the merits of this lawsuit. Should there be unambiguous laws that prohibit framing? Does it make any difference that this was a community service site?
2. Defenders of framing use the analogy that this practice is similar to a newsstand running advertising banners over the area where it sells its newspapers. Does this analogy make any sense to you?

CASE STUDY V

Using Cookies at greatcareers.com (Hypothetical)

You have just opened a new Web site called *www.greatcareers.com*. The purpose of this Web site is to be a clearing house of information for people looking for jobs, especially in the Boston and New York areas. Users can sign up for this site free of charge to look through the extensive job listings, which are displayed weekly. The major sections of the Web page are divided according to different fields of work and different professions.

Your projected source of revenues is primarily from the ads that display on each page. One advertising agency that supplies you with some of your advertisers requests to be provided with some "cookie" information of your subscribers. They intend to use the "cookie"

information, which includes the user's search criteria, to generate a more personalized stream of ads for each user. Thus, individuals searching for teaching jobs would see different ads than someone looking for a nursing job. Such customized ads have the potential to generate more revenue.

This seems like a reasonable proposition, but you wonder whether it is legitimate to use cookie technology in this way. If so, should your users be informed about this practice? Should they be given an opportunity to "opt-out?"

Questions

1. Discuss the pros and cons of this proposal. What would you choose to do?
2. Is the principle of informed consent applicable here?

CASE STUDY VI

AOL and On-Line Privacy

Steve Case and other executives at America Online (AOL) were not prepared for the firestorm of controversy that greeted their latest press release. In that release, AOL verified that it was planning to sell the home phone numbers of their 8.5 million customers to selected telemarketers. Many AOL customers and even some government leaders called or e-mailed the company to register their dissatisfaction. In the wake of this strident protest, AOL needed to make some quick decisions.

Before their acknowledgment of this plan, AOL had signed deals with two marketing organizations: CUC International, a vendor of discount shopping services, and TelSave Holdings, Inc., a discount phone service. Apparently, AOL planned to give these two companies the phone numbers of their customers so that they could follow up with targeted telemarketing calls.

This was the second time in less than six months that AOL, America's largest on-line service provider, found itself besieged with customer complaints. In January of 1997, AOL began offering a flat monthly fee of $19.95 in exchange for unlimited Internet access. However, the company failed to upgrade its network capacity to accommodate peak traffic. As a result, AOL could not handle the added volume generated by this promotion and it was forced to provide rebates to many irate subscribers. The company was just recovering from the ill-effects of this public relations debacle, and in the view of many outsiders, it could ill-afford another publicity setback.

As AOL executives read over some the more vehement complaints of their subscribes, they reflected upon their options. They could forge ahead with their plans or perhaps use their own employees to make the marketing phone calls on behalf of CUC International and TelSave. AOL had assembled a proficient telemarketing group within its organization to peddle goods such as the AOL Visa card to its customer base. Under this plan, their role would simply be expanded.

As the controversy intensified, AOL managers faced some difficult questions. Should it stick with its plans to disseminate the phone numbers of its on-line subscribes and hope that the negative attention would soon dissipate? Also, how should it deal with those subscribers who did not want to receive these calls?

Questions

1. Recommend a specific course of action for AOL. Which philosophical or ethical principle underlies your position?
2. Should these phone numbers be off limits for AOL under any circumstances? Is the company violating their subscribers' privacy by making these calls?

CASE STUDY VII

The Case of the Pretty Good Privacy Encryption Program

In June 1991, Philip Zimmerman completed a complex and elaborate encryption program, which he called *Pretty Good Privacy*, or PGP. The program is based on public key cryptography (RSA) and allows ordinary users to encrypt their messages so that they cannot be deciphered by unauthorized individuals, including law enforcement authorities. To the dismay of government officials, the program was made available free of charge to the general public. Zimmerman handed PGP over to an unidentified "friend" in the summer of 1991. That individual subsequently placed the program on a bulletin board system on the Internet for anyone to access, with no fees to pay, registration forms to fill out, or questions to answer.

Since Zimmerman has distributed this user-friendly program, it has become the most widely used encryption program in cyberspace. Zimmerman himself never shipped the product to other countries (in violation of U.S. export laws), but there is no doubt that others have taken this free program and made it available to users all over the globe. According to Zimmerman, PGP was dispersed through cyberspace "like thousands of dandelion seeds blowing in the wind."

Although Zimmerman is admired by many civil libertarians and those who oppose U.S. export controls on encryption products, he does not enjoy the same status with law enforcement officials. They have contended for years that PGP interferes with their efforts to apprehend criminals and stop crime. The problem is that PGP makes it possible for terrorists or criminals to encrypt their communications, thereby making them off limits for surveillance.

According to the government's perspective, PGP has undermined U.S. export controls of encryption software and efforts to prevent uncrackable encryption programs from falling into the wrong hands. Several years ago, California police reported that PGP encryption prevented them from reading the electronic diary of a pedophile, which would have helped them crack an expanding ring of child pornographers.

Zimmerman has been investigated by the FBI and by a federal grand jury, but he has never been convicted of any wrongdoing. He has explained and justified his actions in many forums. In an essay written when PGP was just completed, he cites the need for privacy protection for all citizens as his primary motivation for writing this program:

> If privacy is outlawed, only outlaws will have privacy. Intelligence agencies have access to good cryptographic technology. So do the big arms and drug traffickers. So do defense contractors, oil companies, and other corporate giants. But ordinary people and grassroots political organizations mostly have not had access to affordable "military grade" public-key cryptographic technology. Until now.
>
> PGP empowers people to take their privacy into their own hands. There's a growing social need for it. That's why I wrote it.[2]

Questions

1. From a moral standpoint, do you agree with Zimmerman's decision to release PGP so freely on the Internet?
2. Are U.S. legal restrictions on programs such as PGP sound and warranted?

NOTES

1. Kaplan, C. Lawsuit may determine whether framing is thieving. *Cyber Law Journal.* Available at http://www.nytimes.com/library/tech/98/05/cyberlaw.
2. Zimmerman, P. 1996. How PGP works/why do you need PGP? In Ludlow, P. (Ed.), *High noon on the electronic frontier.* Cambridge, MA: MIT Press, p. 184.

Case Study

E-Mail Policy at Johnson & Dresser

Richard A. Spinello

Jason Perry left the executive office suite of Johnson & Dresser shortly after 3:30 p.m. and returned to his own office on the floor below. He had made a rare visit to the company's Chief Operating Officer (COO) in order to discuss the company's questionable e-mail policies. The meeting had gone reasonably well and Perry was wondering about his next steps. As he checked over his notes and waited for his next appointment he reviewed the events leading up to this meeting.

Perry had joined Johnson & Dresser, a moderate sized retail brokerage firm, about seven years ago. He was hired as a senior systems analyst but within two years he was promoted to the position of Information Systems (IS) Director. He was relatively well known in the industry and aspired to work for one of the major brokerage houses on Wall Street.

A year or two after Perry's promotion he oversaw the purchase and installation of an advanced electronic mail system that would be used throughout the company. Although many were slow to make the transition to an on-line communication system, within a short time almost the entire organization became dependent on e-mail.

The new product had been introduced at several training sessions where electronic mail was frequently compared to regular postal mail and where the confidentiality of one's communications was certainly intimated. Users were not told that all of the company's e-mail messages were archived and available for future inspection at any time. Moreover, users were strongly encouraged to use e-mail for communicating with their fellow employees. The firm clearly saw this form of electronic communication as preferable to the use of phone calls or quick office visits.

Perry did not expect that Johnson & Dresser would make much use of the archived messages, but when an insider trading scandal broke at the firm it was decided to check the e-mail of several brokers who had been implicated. All of the brokers involved resigned quietly and nothing further came of the matter. The brokerage house had a strong reputation on Wall Street for integrity, and always acted quickly when there were problems of this nature. The company was keenly aware of the importance of an unimpeachable reputation in order to maintain its current clients and attract new business.

In the aftermath of this potential scandal senior managers at the firm decided to routinely inspect employee e-mail. This was to make sure that no one else was involved in the insider trading scandal and to ferret out any other compliance problems or suspicious behavior. As a result some managers regularly asked for a compilation of e-mail messages before an employee's annual review. In the vast majority of cases they found nothing incriminating or damaging in these messages and the individuals never knew that anyone had been checking their electronic mail messages.

But there were some exceptions to this. One incident that bothered Perry a great deal involved a young analyst named Lisa Curry. She was a 10-year veteran at the company responsible for following the utility industry. She worked closely with brokers, providing reports and advice on various utility stocks. Like others at Johnson & Dresser, she was a little wary at first of using the e-mail system. Soon, however, she came to heavily rely on electronic mail for a large portion of her communications with her fellow employees. Indeed over time she felt much less inhibited when she composed e-mail messages. Thus, although she was usually pretty diffident around the company, she found herself engaging in some intense e-mail discussions with one of the few women brokers at the firm, Margaret Leonard. She often sent Leonard messages that complained about sexist corporate policies or messages that conveyed the latest company gossip. None of these messages were especially incendiary or provocative but they were fairly critical of Johnson & Dresser. Also, on occasion she criticized her boss for his lack of sensitivity on certain issues; she was perturbed, for example, at his condescending attitude toward some of the other women analysts.

Curry never dreamed that anyone would ever see these messages. Leonard assured her that she promptly erased the messages right after she read them. Curry let her know that she did the same with Leonard's messages. Both of them assumed that when they hit the delete key the messages would be permanently erased from the system. When Curry was due for her annual review her manager decided to check her e-mail communications and found the messages which she sent to Leonard. He was furious that she was so critical of Johnson & Dresser and also chastised her for wasting so much time sending "trivial, gossipy" e-mail messages. He told her that she did not seem to be a real team player and that maybe she should look around for a company that had a philosophy closer to her own. The end result was that despite her excellent track record as an analyst Curry received a small salary increment and a mixed performance review.

Curry was completely shocked by this. She could not believe that her messages were not considered completely confidential. She expected such confidentiality especially since she was not told anything to the contrary indeed, in her view she had been led to believe by the IS department that her privacy would be protected.

Among those she called in the company to complain about her treatment was Perry. She told him that his department's training sessions had duped people into believing that their e-mail messages would be confidential. She also pointed out that users should be told that messages would be archived and might be available for future scrutiny. Finally she stressed that she would be loath to continue using e-mail if everything she wrote would one day be scrutinized by her manager and "God knows who else at this paranoid company!"

Perry was sympathetic. He had received a few other complaints, and was beginning to question the company's fairness. He told Curry that he would look into the matter and try to craft a more open and responsible policy. He could make no promises since he knew that others in the company would need to be involved in any such policy emendations. Perry felt sorry for what happened to Curry, and he did not want to see other employees get blindsided in the same way that she did.

Consequently, Perry decided to ask for a meeting with the Chief Operating Officer in order to broach the issue of a revised e-mail policy that would better protect the privacy of Johnson & Dresser employees. During this session Perry argued that the company should probably at least take steps to inform employees that their messages were being stored and might be intercepted. However, while the COO did not disagree, he was worried about the ramifications of announcing to everyone that e-mail was being monitored. For one thing users might be less inclined to use e-mail, and the productivity gains realized by adopting this technology would be lost.

When asked about the legal implications of all this, Perry noted that according to current law the company was well within its rights to read an employee's e-mail. He wondered, however, if the company was living up to its high moral ideals by inspecting these messages. Isn't it a violation of confidentiality to read someone's postal letters? Why should electronic mail be any different? Should the company be proactive and declare electronic mail off limits except under unusual circumstances? Should it even continue to collect and store the large volume of e-mail messages generated by its many employees?

The COO was ambivalent about these suggestions, and he pointed out to Perry how the policy of archiving and inspecting e-mail helped the firm to uncover the insider trading scandal and take swift action. Maybe it needed to compromise employee privacy sometimes in order to protect the company against such abuses in the future. The more sources it could tap, the better it could discover problems and ensure that everyone at Johnson & Dresser was complying with the regulations of the Securities and Exchange Commission (SEC).

As the meeting came to a conclusion Perry was told to propose and defend a tenable and responsible e-mail policy that could be presented to the Executive Committee. He now began to think about what that policy should be. Clearly, there were many complex issues to untangle and key decisions to make.

Chapter Nine

———————•———————

Leadership

I N THIS LAST section we return the primary questions of this text: Why is it so hard for businesses to do the right thing? Why is it so hard to be ethical? I am convinced that without committed ethical leadership, ethical standards will not be established, maintained, and retained in the life of any organization. Ethical ideas, standards, and values can and may originate anywhere within the structure of an organization, but without the backing, encouragement, and financial support of leadership, the best of intentions and ideas more often than not will wither on the vine.

The ethics of all forms of leadership—whether they be good or bad, positive or negative—affects the ethos of the workplace and thereby helps to form the ethical choices and decisions of the workers in the workplace. Leaders help to set the tone, develop the vision, and shape the behavior of all those involved in organizational life. The critical point to understand here is—like it or not—that business and politics serve as the metronome for our society. And the meter and behavior established by leaders set the patterns and establish the model for workers' behavior as individuals and as a group. Although the term "business ethics" and "moral leadership" are technically distinguishable, in fact, they are inseparable components in the life of every organization.

The fundamental principle that underlies my thesis regarding leadership and ethical conduct is age-old. In his *Nichomachean Ethics*, Aristotle suggested that one cannot learn morality simply by reading a treatise on virtue. The spirit of morality, said Aristotle, is awakened in the individual only through the behavior and conduct of a moral person. In claiming that workers/followers derive their models for ethical conduct from the behavior of leaders, I am in no way denying that workers/followers share responsibility for the overall conduct and culture of an organization. My argument does not exonerate workers; rather, it tries to explain the process involved. The actions of leaders both communicates the ethics of our institutions and establishes the standards and expectations leaders want and often demand from their fellow workers and followers. Although it would be naïve to assert that employees simply and unreflectively absorb the manners and mores of the workplace, it would be equally naïve to suggest that they are unaffected by the modeling and standards of their respective places of employment. Work is how we spend our lives, and the lessons we learn there, good or bad, play a part in the development of our moral perspective and how we formulate and adjudicate ethical choices. Many business ethicists believe that without the active intervention of effective moral leadership, we are doomed to forever wage a rear-guard action. Students of organizational development are never really surprised when poorly managed, badly led business wind up doing unethical things.

This last section offers cases and essays that both positively and negatively support the thesis that for good or ill, leadership directly influences the conduct and character of organizational life. The first two essays, "Leadership: An Overview" and "The Call of Leaders," offer a working definition of and theoretical perspective on the roles, rights, and responsibilities of leaders and the function of leadership. "Ethics: Take It from the Top" and "Moral Mazes: Bureaucracy and Managerial Work" wind up arguing for the same thesis: Leaders influence and sometimes dictate the standards, values, and behavior of organizations—but with radically different outcomes. "Ways Women Lead" offers some interesting and provocative insights into the differences between men and women in leadership roles.

The story of Aaron Feurstein and Maulden Mills, "Not a Fool, Not a Saint" is a case that celebrates the difficulties, discipline, integrity, and commitment it takes to do the right thing. On the other side of the equation are two cases involving Enron ("Visionary's Dream Led to Risky Business") and Tyco ("Former Tyco Executives Are Charged") and what happens when leadership decides on a code of conduct.

Essay

Leadership: An Overview

Al Gini

INTRODUCTION

In 1948, Chester Barnard, noted management scholar, wrote that research in "leadership has been the subject of an extraordinary amount of dogmatically stated nonsense."[1] In 1978, the dean of modern leadership studies, James MacGregor Burns, put it slightly more charitably when he wrote: "Leadership is one of the . . . least understood phenomena on earth."[2]

The sting and the irony of this criticism is even more painful when you consider that no other topic in the behavioral sciences has been more studied and more written about than leadership.[3] Ralph Stogdill and Bernard Bass, in their separate and combined works, itemized and analyzed some 4,725 studies of leadership prior to 1981; and a recent study claims that, not counting magazine and newspaper articles, there were 132 books published on leadership during the 1980s alone.[4]

The problem then is not a lack of research, but rather a lack of agreement on fundamentals. As one wag has put it: "Next to economic theory never has so much been written on the same topic—resulting in so little agreement on the most elemental propositions in the field."

© 1997 Kluwer Academic Publishers. *Journal of Business Ethics* 16: 323–330, 1997. Reprinted with permission.

Joseph C. Rost in his important book *Leadership for the Twenty-First Century*, claims that the problem is rock-bottom basic. The field of leadership studies lacks definitional clarity and consensus regarding its two most primary terms leadership and leader(s).

Rost claims that most leadership scholarship has been a mishmash of mythology, mistakes, and misunderstanding.[5] Of the 587 books, chapters and articles (written between 1900 and 1989) Rost researched in preparation for his text, only 221 of them gave a definition of leadership. The other 366 offered no definition, either, he claims, because they assumed knowledge on everyone's part or because they feared that an explicit definition would be proven wrong. Moreover, said Rost, of the 190 definitions offered, most did not distinguish leadership from the numerous other social processes which human beings use to coordinate, direct, control, and govern others. And worse still, all of them, after analysis, can be reduced to the equation: "Good Leadership is equal to Good Management." (What Rost refers to as the fallacy of the "Industrial Paradigm of Leadership.") Rost contends that, for any discipline to be on solid ground and to pursue its topic in a focused manner, it must at least be able to define itself clearly.[6]

Unfortunately, even with this admonition, the problem which remains is that leadership is still conventionally defined, by scholars and laymen alike, either by the social role of leadership or by what leaders do.

According to John Gardner, leadership should never be confused with status, power, position, rank, or title.

> Even in large corporations and government agencies, the top-ranking person may simply be bureaucrat number one. We have all occasionally encountered top persons who couldn't lead a squad of seven-year-olds to the ice cream counter.[7]

Jill Graham has correctly pointed out: "Appropriate labels for the person giving orders, monitoring compliance, and administering performance-contingency rewards and punishment include 'supervisor' and 'manager', but *not* 'leader'."[8]

Just as leadership is not equivalent to office-holding, prestige, authority, or decision making,[9] a true and complete definition of leadership cannot be drawn simply from the personality traits and behaviors of particular leaders. Such an attempt may produce an informative biographical account of the leader in question, but may not result in any real insights into the art of leadership.

So the question remains, what is leadership and how can it be defined? I believe that leadership is a delicate combination of the *process*, the techniques of leadership, the *person*, the specific talents and traits of a/the leader, and the general requirements of the *job* itself. I am convinced that although the concept of leadership can and must be distinguishable and definable separately from our understanding of what and who leaders are, the phenomenon of leadership can only be known and measured in the particular instantiation of a leader doing a job. In other words, while the terms "leadership" and "leader" are not synonymous, the reality of leadership cannot be separated from the person as leader and the job of leadership. . . .

THE PROCESS

Leadership is a power and value laden relationship between leaders and followers/constituents who intend real change(s) that reflect their mutual, purpose(s) and goal(s).[10]

Given this definition there are a number of essential elements that must be present if leadership exists or is occurring.

Power

All forms of leadership must make use of power. However, power need not be coercive, dictatorial, or punitive to be affective. Power can also be used in a non-coercive manner to orchestrate, mobilize, direct, and guide members of an institution or organization in the pursuit of a goal or series of objectives.

The term power comes from the Latin *posse*: to do, to be able, to change, to effect. In general power is about control, the ability to produce intended effects or results. To have power is to possess the capacity to control or direct change. . . .[11]

The central issue of power in leadership is not will it used; but, rather, will it be used wisely and well? In the best of all possible worlds scenario, those who seek power should seek it out of a sense of stewardship and not for the purposes of personal aggrandizement and career advancement. The ideal model of this can be found in *The Republic* where Socrates' guardians see their office as a social responsibility, a trust, a duty and not as a symbol of their personal identity, prestige and lofty status.

Of course, the juggling act of wielding power ultimately lies in the ability to balance and integrate the natural conflict which exists between standard definitions, utopian ideals, historic necessity and the peculiar quirks and needs of the individual personalities who aspire to power.

Value Laden

I believe that Tom Peters and Bob Waterman were correct when they stated: "The real role of leadership is to manage the values of an organization."[12] All leadership is value laden. All leadership, whether good or bad, is moral leadership.

To put it more accurately, all leadership is ideologically driven or motivated by a certain philosophical perspective which may or may not prove to be moral in a more colloquial or normative sense. The point is, all leadership claims a particular point of view or philosophical package of ideas it wishes to advocate and advance. All forms of leadership try to establish the guidelines, set the tone, and control the manners and morals of the constituency of which they are a part.

Although we regularly hold up for praise the moral leadership of Lincoln, Churchill, Gandhi, and Mother Teresa; like it or not Hitler, Stalin, Hussein, and David Koresh must also be considered moral leaders of a sort!

Leaders and Followers/Constituents

One of the most common errors in leadership literature is the equation of leadership with the ability of a leader to lead.[13] Leadership, however, does not exclusively reside in the leader. Rather it is a dynamic relationship between leaders and followers alike. Leadership is always plural; it always occurs within the context of others.

E. P. Hollander has argued that while the leader is the central and often the most vital part of the leadership phenomenon, followers are important and necessary factors in the equation.

> Without responsive followers there is no leadership . . . (Leadership) involves someone who exerts influence, and those who are influenced . . . The real "power" of a leader lies in his or her ability to influence followers . . . Leadership is a process of influence which involves an ongoing transaction between a leader and followers.[14]

In fact, I believe the argument can be advanced—in partial response to the "be-whiskered question"[15] are leaders born or made?—that leaders, good or bad, great or small arise out of the needs and opportunities of a specific time and place. I believe that great leaders require great causes, great issues, and most importantly, a hungry and willing constituency. If this were not true, at least in part, would any of us have ever heard of Lech Walesa, Martin Luther King, Jr., or Nelson Mandela? "Leaders and followers,"

Burns wrote, "are engaged in a common enterprise; they are dependent on each other, their fortunes rise and fall together."[16]

Leaders and Followers Intend Real Change(s)

All forms of leadership are essentially about transformation.[17] Leadership is not about maintaining the status quo; it is about initiating change in an organization. Simply sustaining the status quo is equivalent to institutional stigmatism. "The leadership process," said Burns, "must be defined . . . as carrying through from decision-making stages to the point of concrete changes in people's lives, attitudes, behaviors (and) institutions . . ."[18] While the process of leadership always involves a certain number of transactional exchanges—that is, short-term changes and the trading of benefits to meet immediate and appropriate wants and needs—transformational change means the pursuit of new concrete, substantive, and not incidental changes.

Of course, while the ultimate test of practical leadership is the realization of actual change that meets people's enduring the long term needs, the real issue in the process is the Kantian one of intent.[19] Transformation is about leaders and followers *intending* real changes to happen and pursuing them actively. As John Gardner has pointed out, consequences are never a reliable assessment of leadership.[20] The quality and worth of leadership cannot be measured solely in terms of achievements. Ultimately and ethically, commitment and concerted effort are as important as outcome.

Mutual Purposes and Goals

If leadership is an active and ongoing relationship between leaders and followers, then the central requirement of the leadership process is for leaders to evoke consensus in their constituencies, and conversely, for followers to inform and influence their leadership.

"Leadership mobilizes, naked power coerces," said Burns.[21] Leadership must "engage" its followers, not merely direct them. Leaders must serve as models and mentors, not martinets. Leaders must be effective teachers and through education and the policy of empowerment make their followers "collaborators"[22] and reciprocally co-responsible in the pursuit of a common enterprise. In the end, says Abraham Zaleznik, "Leadership is based on a compact that binds those who lead with those who follow into the same moral, intellectual and emotional commitment."[23]

However, as both Burns and Rost warn us, the nature of this "compact" is inherently unequal because the influence patterns existing between leaders and followers are unequal. Responsive and responsible leadership requires, as a minimum, that democratic mechanisms be put in place which recognize the right of followers to have adequate knowledge of alternative leadership styles, goals and programs, as well as the capacity to choose between them. In leadership, writ large, mutually agreed upon purposes help people achieve consensus, assume responsibility, work for the common good and build community.[24]

THE PERSON

Given my definition of leadership and the thesis that the process of leadership cannot be separated from the person as leader, I now want to examine those traits and talents that are required of an individual if he or she is going to adequately fulfill the role of leader.

Character

In *Character: America's Search for Leadership*, Gail Sheehy argues, as did Aristotle, that character is the most crucial and most illusive element of leadership. The root of the word "character" comes from the Greek word for engraving. As applied to human beings, it refers the enduring marks, engravings, or etched-in factors in our personality which include our inborn talents as well as the learned and acquired traits imposed upon us by life and experience. These engravings define us, set us apart, and motivate our behavior.

In regard to leadership, says Sheehy, character is both fundamental and prophetic. The "issues (of leadership) are today and will change in time. Character is what was yesterday and will be tomorrow."[25] For Sheehy, character establishes both our day-to-day demeanor and our destiny. Therefore it is not only useful but essential to examine the character of those who desire to lead us. As a journalist and long time observer of the political scene, Sheehy contends that the Watergate affair of the early 1970s serves as a perfect example of the links between character and leadership. As Richard Nixon demonstrated so well: "The Presidency is not the place to work out one's personal pathology . . ."[26]

Leaders rule us, run things, wield power. Therefore, says Sheehy, we must be careful about who we chose to lead. Because who we chose, is what we shall be. If character is destiny, the destiny our leaders reap will be our own.

Charisma

While the exact role, definition, and function of a charismatic leader is the center of much controversy in the literature of leadership, I want to make a much more modest claim for the necessity of charisma in the person of the leader.

I am convinced that leadership is as much an emotional relationship between leaders and followers as it is a jural or legalistic one.[27] Whether through personality, performance, presentation, image, mind, or message, effective leaders must win-over, at a very basic human level, those they lead.

By charisma I do not mean spiritual aura, celebrity status, hypnotic powers, or even rhetorical eloquence. I mean, as a minimum, that leaders must possess enough self esteem to be seen, heard, and understood in order to engender confidence and cooperation from their constituency. Warren Bennis in his book, *On Becoming a Leader*, offered a definition of a leader which he did not specifically refer to as charismatic, but one, I think, that nicely sums up the definition I am suggesting

> [Leaders are] People who are able to express themselves fully. They know who they are, what their strengths and weaknesses are, and how to fully deploy their strengths and compensate for their weaknesses. They also know what they want, why they want it, and how to communicate what they want to others in order to gain their cooperation and support.[28]

Political Ambition

Although I have argued against those that covet power for purposes of personal aggrandizement or career advancement, there must be those who seek and want power. Without ambition we are caught in the Socratic conundrum of having to force leadership on otherwise reluctant individuals by dint of mythology, prescribed duty, and the force of law.

Ambition is not necessarily bad or pathological, and political ambition need not simply be the quest for power to the exclusion of other motives. Citing the works of Abraham Maslow, Burns contends that ambition, fueled by a strong sense of self esteem, is the most potent and beneficial motivator for those who seek power. According to Maslow, people who possess self esteem (self-actualization) have a clearer sense of self and others, egoism and objectivity, individual and communal rights, basic and growth needs and are not threatened by ambiguity, conflict and consensus. Self actualizers, Maslow believes, are not motivated by unfulfilled ego needs. They do not need "recognition" or to "make a mark." Rather they seek to "make a difference," by contributing to the collective whole."[29] They seek to contribute in the way that John Adams sought to contribute.

> I must study politics and war, that my sons may have liberty to study mathematics and philosophy. My sons ought to study mathematics and philosophy, geography, natural history and naval architecture, in order to give their children the right to study painting, poetry, music, architecture, statuary, tapestry and porcelain.[30]

Know-How

Perhaps the most important contribution of Joseph Rost's *Leadership for the Twenty-First Century* is his thesis that leadership should not be studied solely from the perspective of a single discipline such as business leadership, educational leadership, or political leadership. Leadership studies, he claims, requires a multidisciplinary and interdisciplinary approach to fully understand and practice leadership.[31]

While I want to agree with this overall thesis, I also want to uphold the principle that leadership as practiced in a particular profession is different from leadership as practiced in other professions. In other words, while the general techniques of leadership and the qualities of the leader remain the same, the specific task requirements of leadership vary with the "business" at hand.

Leadership in different areas requires different technical expertise. To use Warren Bennis' term, leaders must possess "business literacy." That is, leaders must have knowledge of and be experts at what they are doing. They must have horizontal and vertical knowledge of how the "business" works and a full understanding of what is required to do the task well.[32]

THE JOBS OF LEADERSHIP

Lifting a page from John Gardner, I want to turn to a short list of the jobs of leadership and the leader. While individuals differ strikingly in how well they perform these various jobs, how they perform them will determine, to a large extent, how their leadership skills will be evaluated.[33]

Vision

The first and central job of leadership is that effective leaders must create and communicate a clear vision of what they stand for, what they want to achieve and what they expect from their followers. . . .

However, even though vision is central to leadership, the visions offered need not always be Nobel Prize winning accomplishments or involve Herculean efforts. For success to be possible, visions must be doable, attainable. Any task or vision—no matter how vital or important—when too large, will, more often than not, prove too overwhelming to accomplish or even attempt. At the very least, the visions of leadership must offer direction as well as hope.

Managing

Leadership and management are not the same thing. One can be a leader without being a manager. Conversely, one can manage without leading. Nevertheless, logistically these two jobs often overlap.

Abraham Zaleznick offers a reasonably neutral definition and distinction between the two terms.

> The crucial difference between managers and leaders is in their respective commitments. A manager is concerned with *how* decisions get made and *how* communications flow; a leader is concerned with *what* decisions get made and *what* he or she communicates.[34]

This definition implies that leaders are involved in strategy, and that managers are more concerned with the operational side of a given enterprise. But what this definition does not imply is the all-too-common fallacy of associating the people practicing leadership with the "good guys in white hats"; and the people practicing management as the "bad guys in black hats" who are mediocre, bungling, bureaucrats, unqualified, and unsuited to lead.[35] Nor does this definition imply that management is an important but insufficient process in the operation of organizations; whereas leadership is necessary and needed at all times.

Management and leadership are two distinct and necessary ingredients in the life of every organization. Leadership is not just good management, but good management is part of the overall job description of every leader. To turn around a quote from H. Ross Perot: "In successful organizations, both its people and its inventories are well led and well managed."[36] Moreover, given our definition of leadership as a dynamic relationship between leaders and followers, at times— leaders must manage managers, and managers must manage by leading.

Stakeholdership

Through their conduct and policy, leaders, within the context of any job, must try to make their fellow constituents aware that they are all stakeholders in a conjoint activity that cannot succeed without their involvement and commitment. Successful leadership believes in and communicates some version of the now famous Hewlett Packard motto: "The achievements of an organization are the results of the combined efforts of each individual."

At the operational or "shop-floor" level, at least three overlapping policies must be operative in order to translate the concept of stakeholdership from theory to fact. *Participation*: Leaders must actively participate in the life of an organization. But it is not enough to just walk through the shop, say hello, and be seen. Participation means asking questions, getting involved, spending time, and trouble shooting.[37] *Trust*: Trusting one's constituents means living out the belief that people will respond well when treated like adults. Certainly, some individuals will abuse that trust, but the hope is that most will thrive, grow, and prove more productive because of it. *Risk taking*: Successful leaders must clearly communicate that creativity and innovation are prized commodities. Therefore, autonomy and experimentation are encouraged, and, conversely, failure is tolerated and not viewed negatively. The message here should be a clear one: "Only those with confidence and ability sometimes fail. The mediocre and those who are insecure in what they are doing never dare to risk either success or failure."

Responsibility

"Leadership", said Burns, "is grounded in conscious choice among real alternates. Hence, leadership assumes competition and conflict, and brute power denies it."[38] Leaders, of whatever particular profession, do not shun conflict; they confront it, exploit it and ultimately take responsibility for the choices and decisions they are able to hammer out of it.[39]

Leaders must assume full responsibility for their choices and commitments, successes and failures. If and when they promise certain kinds of change and cannot bring about that change, they must be willing to stand down.

The final job of leadership is knowing when to go.

CONCLUSION

Leadership is never tidy. "Any attempt to describe a social process as complex as leadership inevitably makes it seem more orderly than it is."[40] Few examples neatly fit into the definitional molds we have fashioned. Nevertheless, I want to conclude my remarks with an example which, perhaps, brings together the three issues of this paper "the *Process*, the *Person*, and the *Job*."

In a recent book, *The Mask of Command*, the British war historian John Keegan argues that Alexander the Great was one of the most, if not the most, effective generals in history. Keegan's contention is based on the fact that Alexander both made the plans for battle and then literally led his troops into battle.

Keegan maintains that Alexander's men followed him, had confidence in him as well as in themselves, because Alexander shared their life and all of their risks. In many ways, said Keegan, Alexander's army was a collection of individuals who shared the same ideals and goals. They knew that their literal survival—not just financial success and career advancement—was totally dependent on the commitment and energy of their fellow worker-warriors.

For Keegan, Alexander was an heroic leader because he inspired achievement and took the risks. Alexander did not simply command or demand obedience from his men. Rather, he convinced them of his vision and lived it out with them.

Not so surprisingly, said Keegan, when, because of his many wounds. Alexander was no longer able to participate in battle and lead by example, he lost control of his army and they voted to stop their conquests, turn back, and go home.[41]

To reiterate the words of Abraham Zaleznick: "Leadership is based on a compact that binds those that lead with those who follow into the same moral, intellectual and emotional commitment."[42]

NOTES

1. C. I. Bernard: 1948, *Organizations and Management* (Harvard University Press, Cambridge), p. 80.

2. James MacGregor Burns: 1979, *Leadership* (Harper Torchbooks, New York), p. 2.

3. W. B. Bennis: 1959, "Leadership Theory and Administrative Behavior: The Problem With Authority." *Administrative Science Quarterly* 4, 259–301.

4. J. C. Rost: 1993, *Leadership for the Twenty-First Century* (Praeger, Westport, L/CT), p. 69.

5. Rost, p. 149.

6. Rost, pp. 94, 136, 179.

7. J. W. Gardner: 1990, *On Leadership* (The Free Press, New York), p. 2.

8. J. W. Graham: 1988, "Transformational Leadership: Fostering Follower Autonomy, Not Automatic Followership." In J. G. Hunt, B. R. Baliga, H. P. Crachler and C. A. Schriescheim (eds.), *Emerging Leadership Vistas* (Lexington Books, Lexington, MA), p. 74.

9. P. Selznick: 1957, *Leadership in Administration* (Row, Peterson, Evanston, IL). p. 24.

10. Rost, p. 102.

11. A. A. Berle: 1969, *Power* (Harcourt, Brace and World, Inc., New York), p. 37.

12. T. Peters, B. Waterman: 1982, *In Search of Excellence* (Harper and Row, New York), p. 245.

13. Rost, p. 43.

14. E. P. Hollander: 1978, *Leadership Dynamics* (The Free Press, New York), pp. 4, 5, 6, 12.

15. Gardner, p. 6.

16. Burns, p. 426.

17. Rost, p. 123.

18. Burns, p. 414.

19. Burns, p. 461.

20. Gardner, p. 8.

21. Burns, p. 439.

22. B. Nanus: 1989, *The Leader's Edge* (Contemporary Books, Chicago), pp. 51, 52.

23. A. Zaleznik: 1990, "The Leadership Gap," *Academy of Management Executive* 4(1), 12.

24. Rost, p. 124.

25. G. Sheehy: 1990, *Character: America's Search for Leadership* (Bantam Books, New York), p. 311.

26. Sheehy, p. 66.

27. W. H. Kracke: 1978, *Force and Persuasion: Leadership in an Amazonian Society* (University of Chicago Press, Chicago), p. 34.

28. W. G. Bennis: 1989, *On Becoming a Leader* (Addison-Wesley, Reading, MA), p. 89.

29. Burns, pp. 116, 117.

30. Burns, p. 31.

31. Rost, pp. 1, 2.

32. W. G. Bennis: Sept. 7, 1992, *NPR—Marketplace* (USC Radio).

33. Gardner, p. 11.

34. Zaleznik, p. 14.

35. Rost, pp. 140, 141.

36. Rost, p. 141. (H. Ross Perot, "People cannot be managed, Inventories can be managed, but people must be led").

37. John McDonald: 1989, *Global Quality* (Mercury Books, John Piggott Lowdon).

38. Burns, p. 36.

39. Burns, p. 39.

40. Gardner, p. 22.

41. J. Keegan: 1987, *The Mask of Command* (Viking Press, New York).

42. Zaleznick, p. 12.

Essay

The Call of Leaders

Gary Wills

I had just turned seventeen, did not know Los Angeles, had never even driven in a big city. I had certainly never backed a swivel trailer up to a loading dock. But my father gave me a map, marked a warehouse's location, and told me to deliver a refrigerator there. I would have to get someone to help me unload it when I arrived. It was very clever of him. I knew what he was doing. But I complied anyway.

I had a chip on my shoulder, since my father had left my mother to marry a (much younger) Hollywood model. While I was in California for a high school contest, he asked me to work at his nascent business for the rest of the summer. But for that offer, I would not have stayed—I needed a job in any event. He knew that the way to recruit a resisting son-employee was to give me independence—not only in things like deliveries, but in sales and purchasing of household equipment. If I failed, that might break down my resistance. If I didn't, pride in the work might renew a bond that had been broken. Paradoxically, by giving me independence he got me to do his will. That is the way leadership works, reciprocally engaging two wills, one leading (often in disguised ways), the other following (often while resisting). Leadership is always a struggle, often a feud.

Why, after all, should one person do another person's will? The answer that used to be given is simple: the leader is a superior person, to whom inferiors should submit. But modern democracies are as little sympathetic to this scheme as I was to the authority of my father. Patriarchal society, it is true, was rooted in a radical inequality between leaders and followers. Even ancient Athens, the first western democracy, submitted to "the best man," according to Thucydides:

> [Pericles], a man clearly above corruption, was enabled, by the respect others had for him and his own wise policy, to hold the multitude in a voluntary restraint. He led them, not they him; and since he did not win his power on compromising terms, he could say not only what pleased others but what displeased them, relying on their respect.[1]

Some still subscribe to that notion of leadership. How often have we heard that we lack great leaders now, the clearly virtuous kind, men like George Washington and Abraham Lincoln? The implication is that we could become great again with a great man to guide us. We would not mind submitting to anyone *that* good. (Of others we continue to be wary.)

I shall be arguing in this book that the Periclean type of leadership occurs rarely in history, if at all. Scholars have questioned Thucydides' description of Pericles' position—Athenians seemed quicker than most to *ostracize* leaders who thought themselves above the people.[2] Why *should* people immolate their own needs and desires to the vision of some superior being? That has happened in some theocratic societies—but then people were obeying *God* in his representative; and it was their own belief in God's will that constrained them.

In a democracy, supposedly, the leader does not pronounce God's will to the people but carries out what is decided *by* the people. Some might object that the leader is, in that case, mainly a follower—he or she does what the community says when it "speaks" through elections, through polls, through constituent pressure. Such leaders are not, like the Pericles of Thucydides, able to displease their followers. They compromise their principles. They are bribed, if not with money, then with acceptance, or office, or ego satisfaction.

We seem stuck, then, between two unacceptable alternatives—the leader who dictates to others, or the one who truckles to them. If leaders *dictate*, by what authority do they take away people's right to direct their own lives? If, on the contrary, they truckle, who needs or respects such weathervanes?

Most of the how-to manuals on leadership assume one or other of these models—or, inconsistently, both. The superior-person model says the leader must become *worthy* of being followed—more disciplined than others, more committed, better organized. This sends aspiring leaders to the mirror, to strike firm-jawed poses, to cultivate self-confidence and a refusal to hedge.

Or the leader is taught to be ingratiating. This is the salesmanship or Dale Carnegie approach—how to win friends and influence people. It treats followers as customers who "buy" the leader's views after these have been consumer-tested and tailored to maximum acceptance.

The *followers* are, in this literature, a hazy and not very estimable lot—people to be dominated or served, mesmerized or flattered. We have thousands of books on leadership, none on followership. I have heard college presidents tell their students that schools are meant to train leaders. I have never heard anyone profess to train followers. The ideal seems to be a world in which everyone is a leader—but who would be left for them to be leading?

Talk about the nobility of leaders, the need for them, our reliance on them, raises the clear suspicion that followers are *not* so noble, not needed—that there is something demeaning about being a follower. In that view, leaders only rise by sinking others to subordinate roles. Leaders have a vision. Followers respond to it. Leaders organize a plan. Followers get sorted out to fit the plan. Leaders have willpower. Followers let that will replace their own.

We have long lists of the leader's requisites—he or she needs determination, focus, a clear goal, a sense of priorities, and so on. We easily forget the first and all-encompassing need. The leader most needs followers. When those are lacking, the best ideas, the strongest will, the most wonderful smile have no effect. When Shakespeare's Welsh seer, Owen Glendower, boasts that "I can call spirits from the vasty deep," Hotspur deflates him with the commonsense answer: "Why, so can I, or so can anyone. But will they come when you do call them?"[3] It is not the noblest call that gets answered, but the *answerable* call.

Abraham Lincoln did not have the highest vision of human equality in his day. Many abolitionists went farther than he did in recognizing the moral claims of slaves to instant freedom and something approaching a recognition of their human dignity. Lincoln had limited political goals, and he was willing to compromise even those. He knew that no one could be elected in or from Illinois if he espoused full equality for blacks—so he unequivocally renounced that position:

> I am not, nor ever have been, in favor of bringing about, in any way, the social and political equality of the white and black races . . . I am not, nor ever have been, in favor of making voters or jurors of negroes, nor of qualifying them to hold office, nor of intermarrying with white people; and I will say, in addition to this, that there is a physical difference between the white and black races which I believe will forever forbid the two races living together on terms of political and social equality. And inasmuch as they cannot so live, while they do remain together, there must be the position of superior and inferior; and I, as much as any other man, am in favor of having the superior position assigned to the white race.[4]

But for that pledge, Lincoln had no hope of winning office. The followers were setting the terms of acceptance for their leader. He could not issue calls they were unprepared to hear. (He *could* do it, of course—as Owen Glendower can shout summonses down into the deep. But it would be a waste of time.)

This Lincoln has disappointed people who think followers should submit to a leader's superior vision, those who want the leader to be active, the followers passive. Lincoln's career shows response from both sides of the process. His leadership was a matter of *mutually* determinative activity, on the part of the leader *and* the followers. Followers "have a say" in what they are being led to. A leader who neglects that fact soon finds himself without followers. To sound a certain trumpet does not mean just trumpeting one's own certitudes. It means sounding a specific call to specific people capable of response.

Does this remove or reduce the heroic note from Lincoln's leadership—as if he were only *allowed* to lead, by followers who could withhold their response? Well, what is the alternative—people who cannot refuse to follow? If that were the case, the leader would be marshaling automatons, not voluntary respondents.

It is odd that resentment should be felt toward the demands of followers when the limiting power of *circumstance* is so readily accepted. Even the most ardent hero worshipers of Winston Churchill admit that he needed an occasion for the exercise of his skills. But for World War II, we would never have known what he could do in the way of rallying English spirit. Yet the followers are even more intimate in their cooperation with the leader than are external circumstances. The leader can have the skill for his or her role, the occasion for its use, and still lack followers who will respond to the person or the moment.

So much for the idea that a leader's skills can be applied to all occasions, that they can be taught outside a historical context, learned as a "secret" of control in every situation. A leader whose qualities do not match those of potential followers is simply irrelevant. The world is not playing his or her game. My favorite example of this is the leadership of Syrian holy men in the fifth century of the Common Era.[5] Those men, who made policy for whole communities, were revered for their self-ravaging austerity. The man who had starved himself most spectacularly was thought the best equipped to advise pious consultants. So delegations went to consult Simeon the "Stylite" (Pillar Man), perched in his midair hermitage. Leadership was entirely conditioned by the attitudes of contemporary followership. Who would now write a manual called *The Leadership Secrets of Simeon Stylites*, telling people to starve and whip and torture themselves into command positions?

Closer to our time, Thomas Jefferson thought the French Revolution had been less successful than the American one, not because the French lacked leaders but because they lacked discerning followers. A corrupt people is not responsive to virtuous leadership. The French spirit had been sapped, he claimed, by superstition (Catholicism) and despotism (monarchy). Napoleon, to retain the people's allegiance, had to revert to both, calling on the pope to crown him emperor.[6]

It may seem that the Lincoln example has moved us too far from the Periclean "best man" toward the Dale Carnegie accommodator. If the leader is just an expediter of what other people want, a "resource" for their use, the people are not being led but serviced.

But Lincoln had no clear expression of popular will to implement. He had to *elicit* the program he wanted to serve, and that always involves *affecting* the views one is consulting. Even pollsters, seeking to understand what is on the minds of people, affect the outcome by their mode of questioning. In Lincoln's constituency were some abolitionists, many defenders of slavery, many more who wanted to avoid facing the issue of slavery. Unlike the abolitionists, who were leaders of a small elite putting pressure on the government from outside, Lincoln had to forge a combination of voters who would join him in at least minimal disapproval of slavery. He had to convince some people that it was in their own interest not to let the problem fester—he told them they could not *afford* to take Stephen Douglas's "hands-off" attitude.

Many voters resisted Lincoln—as I did my father in the summer of 1951. Lincoln deferred to some of their prejudices—left them independent in that sense—in order to win agreement on a policy of (at least) some hope for ultimate manumission. He argued in terms of his listeners' own commitment. They celebrated the Declaration of Independence, with its claim that all men are created equal. How could they stay true to their political identity, based on the Declaration, if they did not at some level oppose slavery? By keeping this option open for gradual approximation, Lincoln was able to move at a later period for more direct action on the problem. In that sense, he temporized not to evade the problem but to

prevent its evasion. G. K. Chesterton perfectly captured the delicacy of his operation:

> He loved to repeat that slavery was intolerable while he tolerated it, and to prove that something ought to be done while it was impossible to do it. . . . But, for all that, this inconsistency beat the politicians at their own game, and this abstracted logic proved most practical after all. For, when the chance did come to do something, there was no doubt about the thing to be done. The thunderbolt felt from the clear heights of heaven.[7]

In order to know just how far he could go at any moment, Lincoln had to understand the mix of motives in his fellow citizens, the counterbalancing intensities with which the different positions were held, and in what directions they were changing, moment by moment. This is the time-consuming aspect of leadership. It explains why great thinkers and artists are rarely the leaders of others (as opposed to influences on them). The scientist absorbed in the solution of his problems does not have the energy or patience to understand the needs of a number of other people who might be marshaled to deal with the problem. That is something the popularizer of the great man's thought usually does. More important, the pure scientist does not *tailor* his view of, say, the atom to whatever audience he hopes to influence, as Lincoln trimmed and hedged on slavery in order to make people take small steps in the direction of facing the problem.

My father was a natural leader who acted in small arenas. Even as a child, I thought it childish of him to want to get his way all the time. I did not notice then that he got his way by entering into the minds of others and finding something there that would respond to his attentions—as, on a vastly different scale, Lincoln found a grudging acceptance of the Declaration's pledge on which to build his strategy of emancipation. My father's tactics were different with me, with my sister, with the golfing friends I observed him with while caddying. There is something selfless in the very selfishness of leaders—they must see things as the followers see them in order to recruit those followers.

If the followers get marshaled toward action by a leader, the leader need not be loved or admired (though that can help). I had no great admiration for my father when I found myself responding to his initiatives. Conversely, one can admire or love people who are not, by virtue of that love, leaders.

Imagine a meeting called to consider a course of action—let us say, to mount a protest against an employer whose hiring and promotion practices discriminate against women. A speaker rises who is stunningly eloquent. Listener A knows and admires the speaker, would go anywhere to hear her speak, hopes to emulate her eloquence in his own way; but he does not care about the issue, and the speech does not bring him any closer to caring. Listener B, on the contrary, has never met the speaker, does not particularly like her, is disposed to resent the employer but had no hope of finding allies to resist him, and is now heartened to act in conjunction with others responding to the speaker. Who is the follower here? If, as seems certain, it is Listener B, then admiration, imitation, and affection are not necessary to followership. Agreement on a *goal* is necessary.

So far I have been discussing just two things—leaders and followers. That is better at least, than treatments dealing with only one thing—leaders. But the discussion cannot get far without a third thing—the goal. This is not something *added on* to the other two. It is the reason for the other two's existence. It is also the equalizer between leader and followers. The followers do not submit to the person of the leader. They *join* him or her in pursuit of the goal. My father and I were working together for the success of his new business. Of course, he had separate motives for wanting me there, and I had motives for

not wanting to be there. We could not share *those* motives, unique to our own situation. It was the thing we *could* share that created the possibility of leadership.

It is time for a definition: the leader is one who mobilizes others toward a goal shared by leader and followers. In that brief definition, all three elements are present, and indispensable. Most literature on leadership is unitarian. But life is trinitarian. One-legged and two-legged chairs do not, of themselves, stand. A third leg is needed. Leaders, followers, and goals make up the three equally necessary supports for leadership.

The goal must be *shared,* no matter how many other motives are present that are not shared. Go back to the meeting that called for a protest at employer discrimination. The speaker may have had many ancillary motives for speaking—to show off her rhetorical style, to impress a sexual partner in the audience, to launch a larger political career. Her listeners surely would have many motives—some to improve their prospects with the employer, or their regard among fellow workers. But the followers *become* followers only insofar as they agree with the speaker on a plan of action against the employer.

This plan is cast in terms of justice, though it is easy to think this is only a rationale for the mix of various motives, some shared, some not. Each is in this to get something different. David Hume, the eighteenth-century philosopher, said people obey others for their *own* advantage, and this writhing of various wormlike urges for advantage is far from the picture of idealistic leaders and docile followers.

Yet Hume, perceptive as he was, knew that people follow most reliably when they are convinced that what they are doing is right. He knew the *utility* of that belief.[8] If, at the meeting to discuss discrimination, only those who would benefit directly by the protest were to join the speaker, that would limit the followership from the outset. And that small number would always be fraying away. The boss could buy off dissent by special favors to a few of the activists, or threats to the weak-hearted. Once one person got what *she* wanted, there would be no future motive for supporting her sisters. Private advantage shifts constantly, and is a poor basis for public action. That is why Lincoln based his policy on the *moral* claim of the Declaration of Independence. Some thought he did not go far enough, others that he went too far; but the moral ground of the Declaration was both broad and narrow enough to accommodate many positions while remaining fixed itself.

Lincoln had to persuade voters. He could not force them. Where coercion exists, to the extent of its existence, leadership becomes unnecessary or impossible. Loose uses of the word "lead" can mislead. We talk of a policeman leading his prisoner to jail. But the captor is not a leader in our sense—he is a captor. Though he is mobilizing another toward a goal, it is not a goal they share in their intentions. The prisoner's goal is to get as far away from the prison as possible.

A slave master buying labor can "lead" slaves to his plantation, but that does not make him their leader. He is their owner. If I had worked for my father only because I needed the money and could get it nowhere else, I would not have been a follower, just an employee. Coercion is not leadership, any more than is mesmerism. Followers cannot be automatons. The totalitarian jailer who drugs a prisoner into confession of a crime has not *led* him to some shared view of reality.[9]

James MacGregor Burns's well-known definition of leadership, though it tries to cover all bases, is inadequate precisely because it leaves out this note of a goal *shared* by leader and followers:

> Leadership over other human beings is exercised when persons with certain motives and purposes mobilize, in competition or conflict with others, institutional, political, psychological, and other resources so as to arouse, engage, and satisfy the motives of followers.[10]

Any person who *affects* others is a leader, by this definition. Hitler's enormities, let us say, arouse hatred in me, mobilize me, and that hatred is satisfying to me—am I, then, a follower of Hitler? Not when the goals of our action are so different. My aim is to destroy Hitler. That is not his aim. Hitler's followers shared, at some level, his goals—vindication of German complaints about the Versailles treaty, the restoration of discipline in society, the glorification of the German nation (and, to varying degrees, the German race) at the expense of others.

Burns's definition would cover all kinds of influence on others—a musician's arousing of pleasure in the audience, a celebrity's gratification of curiosity. A person does not become a "follower" of Bach by being aroused and satisfied. A reader of the *National Enquirer* "follows" reports on Cher or Michael Jackson, but is not a follower of them toward some shared goal. A thinker may be influenced by the philosophy of Ludwig Wittgenstein, but their wills were never consciously engaged in cooperative movement toward a goal. A fan of Madonna is not like a soldier in Joan of Arc's army. Influence is not, of itself, leadership. The weather influences us. So do earthquakes, or background music in public places.

The leader does not just vaguely affect others. He or she takes others toward the object of their joint quest. That object defines the *kind* of leadership at issue. Different types of leaders should be distinguished more by their goals than by the personality of the leader (the most common practice). The crisis of mere subsistence on a life raft calls for one type of leader. Democratic stability for another. Revolutionary activity for still a third. The compromise and flexibility of Lincoln were appropriate for his kind of leadership. But in his own time other leaders had to be quite different in their methods. General Grant could not sound out his military "constituents." William Lloyd Garrison could not temporize on principle when leading the abolitionists. Harriet Tubman, organizing raids to rescue slaves in the South, could not lead by discussion-group methods.

It is one of the major disservices of the "superman" school of leadership that it suggests a leader can command *all* situations with the same basic gifts. Businessmen study the leadership style of General Patton. People assume that Napoleon would make a good CEO—which is like assuming that he would make a good Simeon Stylites. General Grant proved that a great military commander is not necessarily, by reason of his marital success, a good political leader in an electoral democracy—as Lyndon Johnson proved that a superb Senate leader can make a poor president.

Since leadership must differ from situation to situation, it will not be treated in the book as a single thing. I have considered sixteen different *kinds* of leadership—and, of course, there are subdivisions within those. Those chosen are not the "greatest" leaders, but the ones who seemed to exemplify the distinctive type. Skills overlap from type to type, without obscuring the fact that the military leader's goal is quite different from the social reformer's. A Napoleon's leadership resembles only very distantly an Eleanor Roosevelt's. It is the goal that, in the first place, sets the type. The tactics will be affected, also, by the followers available.

It is easier to see the type when the exemplar is large in scale. Yet not every military leader can be (or should be) a Napoleon, not every politician an FDR, not every intellectual leader a Socrates. What is said about the outsize figure can be applied, *mutatis mutandis*, to leaders in a smaller sphere. The military adjutant has something to ponder in the career of Napoleon, or the precinct worker in Roosevelt's techniques. Templates from the past can be laid over living leaders around us.

I try further to define each person I study by considering an *antitype* to him or her, one who exemplifies the same characteristics by contrast. Roger Smith shows how Perot succeeded by the way he (Smith) failed. The marketing leadership Perot had is made clearer by considering its lack in Smith. For both types and the antitypes I do not offer brief biographies. Only the aspects of their careers that exemplify the stated kind of leadership (or its lack) will be emphasized. Thus Napoleon's military career is considered apart from his legislative and imperial politics.

Most important, I hope that readers will keep in mind the different types of *followers* appropriate to historically conditioned goals. Not many of us will be leaders; and even those who are leaders must also be followers much of the time. This is the crucial role. Followers judge leaders. Only if the leaders pass that test do they have any impact. The potential followers, if their judgment is poor, have judged themselves. If the leader takes his or her followers to the goal, to great achievements, it is because the followers were capable of that kind of response. Jefferson said the American people responded to revolution in a way that led to a free republic, while the French responded to their revolution in a way that led to an imperial dictatorship. The followers were as much to blame for the latter development as was Napoleon. In the same way, the German people were jointly responsible for Hitler's atrocities. He was powerless to act without followers.

Show me your leader, and you have bared your soul. You respond only to one who has set certain goals. You are responsible for that activity, for motion toward those goals. If leadership is mysterious and often scary, so is followership. That is why some would prefer not to follow at all. At the dawn of the ancient

Greek achievement, Hesiod had already identified the problem with people who will neither lead nor follow:

> The best is he who calls men to the best.
>
> And those who heed the call are likewise blessed.
>
> But worthless who call not, heed not, but rest.[11]

Some people lament a current lack of leaders, implying that they would become wonderful followers if only some leader worthy of them came along. But perhaps they have not been looking very hard. Others think that if the president is not a leader to their liking, the whole national scene is empty. But, throughout our history, the great leaders have not been only or mainly in the White House. Except in time of war or other crisis, a democratic leader is usually a reconciler of voting blocs rather than a leader of embattled causes. Resisted change has been accomplished by abolitionists, suffragists, labor organizers, civil rights defenders, antiwar activists.

In our own day, vast changes have been taking place, with strong leaders on both sides of each issue. Dr. King led the integration struggle, and George Wallace opposed it, with great skill. No social change has been more vast than that of women's place in society. Leaders on one side, like Gloria Steinem and Faye Wattleton, have been met and resisted by a Phyllis Schlafly or a Beverly LaHaye. The environmental movement, the consumer movement, the gay rights movement have had devoted leaders, and devoted opposition. Randall Terry and his followers have been inventive and determined in their opposition to abortion. A Ralph Nader on the left faces a leader on the right like William F. Buckley. We do not lack leaders. Various trumpets are always being sounded. Take your pick. We lack sufficient followers. That is always the real problem with leadership. Calls are always going down into the vasty deep; but what spirits will respond?

Essay

Ethics: Take It from the Top

Maynard M. Dolecheck
Carolyn C. Dolecheck

"History teaches us that no free society or free economy can long survive without an ethical base. It is only through a shared moral foundation—a set of binding rules for fair conduct—that free associations, be they social, diplomatic, or commercial, can flourish and endure. Far from being a luxury, a sound business ethic is essential to preservation of free enterprise."[1]

Few in the business community would disagree with the foregoing statement by William Simon, businessman and former U.S. Secretary of the Treasury. However, the problem of unethical business practices needs to be periodically reviewed, interpreted, and analyzed. Therefore, this article discusses unethical business practices and suggests steps business executives might take to reduce or alleviate such practices.

SCALE OF ETHICAL/UNETHICAL PRACTICES

Ethical/unethical business practices can be viewed on a scale from Highly Ethical to Highly Unethical as shown in Exhibit 1. Practices to the left of Point A on the scale represent unethical actions, while practices to the left of Point B represent not only unethical but illegal actions. A gray area exists as to whether a practice is ethical or unethical, since different individuals may locate Point A differently on the scale. Most individuals, however, agree that Point A is to the right of Point B. In other words, business practices occur which are unethical but not illegal. Such agreement was confirmed by the authors' 1986 study of business persons employed in the southern United States; 89% of those responding thought that business ethics is more than operating a business organization in such a way as to stay within the law.[2]

This example of a business practice that would fall into the gray area of ethical/unethical was reported in the 6 January 1988 *Wall Street Journal*: The Best Western Hotel in Winter Park, Florida, charges guests daytime long-distance rates 24 hours a day without informing the guests; the hotel then pockets the difference between what the telephone company charges and what the guest pays. When the general manager was asked about the practice, his reply was, "There's nothing in the Florida law that requires us to (inform the guests), so we don't."[3]

In this case the manager apparently believes that Points A and B coincide on the ethical/unethical scale and therefore the practice is ethical. One could even argue that use of the telephone is no different from the hotel's buying soft drinks for $0.25 and selling them to its guests for $2.00. Therefore, the practice in question is ethical. However, most people would argue that the practice is unethical because the hotel does not inform the guests that it is charging daytime rates at all times; guests probably assume they are paying night rates for nighttime calls and thus they are being misled.

SERIOUS PROBLEM OF UNETHICAL PRACTICES

Conceding that some business practices fall into a gray area of ethical/unethical, the apparent frequency of unethical practices indicates a serious and continuing problem facing American business organizations. Reporters and commentators have publicly exposed business wrongdoing with seemingly ever-greater frequency. During the 1970s, the media focused on illegal activities involving political contributions; discrimination due to age, sex, and race; lack of concern for workers' and the public's health and safety; mishandling of pension funds; and bribing of foreign officials. During the 1980s, the media has concentrated on flagrant abuses of financial information, overcharging the government for military supplies,

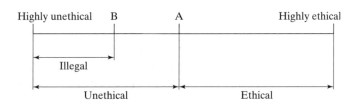

Exhibit 1:   Scale of ethical/unethical practices

and mislabeling of products. *Time* magazine recently stated, "While common street crime costs the United States an estimated $4 billion/year in losses, white-collar lawbreaking drains at least $40 billion—and probably much more—from corporations and government."[4] A study by Amitai Etzioni, professor of sociology at George Washington University, concluded that during the past ten years about two-thirds of America's 500 largest corporations have been involved in some form of illegal behavior.[5]

Managers themselves acknowledge the problem exists. A *Wall Street Journal* article on 8 September 1987 noted that one-fourth of 671 managers surveyed by a research firm believed ethics can impede a successful career and that better than one-half of all executives they know would bend the rules to get ahead.[6]

Furthermore, the general public believes that fraud, lying, and shoddy practices are typical of American business. A New York Times/CBS News Poll conducted in June 1985 revealed that 55% of the American public believe that most corporate executives are dishonest; 59% think that white-collar crime occurs very often.[7]

Most of the wrongdoing just noted is not only unethical but illegal. Illegal behavior compared to unethical, but legal, behavior is easier to document (measure) because it stems from litigation and is usually more sensational. If illegal behavior occurs as frequently as reports indicate, unethical practices that may not be illegal also occur frequently.

CHANGING ENVIRONMENT CONTRIBUTES

The frequency of unethical business practices appears to have several basic causes, but many seem to stem from changing environmental conditions. Examples are changing regulations, widespread mergers and acquisitions, rapid computerization, and increased international trade. Changing environmental conditions can result in the breaking down of established corporate cultures, widening the previously noted gray area of ethical/unethical practices, creating areas where appropriate controls are nonexistent and fostering extreme pressures to achieve organizational goals—all of which can lead to unethical behavior.

An example of changing regulations is the lessening of government intervention in business. The United States has a long history of establishing laws, regulations, and agencies for the protection of consumers, investors, employees, and the public. The current U.S. government administration and, to a lesser extent the previous two administrations, have curtailed and even dismantled many regulatory agencies. Examples are the trucking, airline, and banking industries. Deregulation may have resulted in managers feeling compelled or pressured to cut corners to compete with rivals, as the airline industry appears to have done. If media reports are true, some airlines have acted unethically, if not illegally, in an effort to compete with other airlines particularly in areas of flight delays, and the maze of ticket prices and restrictions that tend to confuse and mislead the public.

The decline in American business's ability to compete internationally with foreign firms has added impetus to the pressures that managers perceive in order to regain lost markets. Such pressures can result in unethical actions, such as paying bribes to foreign governments.

Large business organizations, particularly those formed by mergers and acquisitions, typically decentralize by establishing profit centers as a means of control. Such profit centers can easily lead to pressures for managers to act unethically to achieve organizational goals (primarily profits). Research has shown that managers at the lower levels in an organization feel greater pressure to do this than do managers higher up.[8]

The ethical problems that business organizations are facing are analogous to ethical problems the U.S. government is currently encountering. Examples are government officials abusing Civil Service rules, misspending government money, conspiring to end enforcement actions against a client represented by a relative, participating in conflicts of interest, and using government personnel for private business. The House Subcommittee on Civil Service has compiled an index that lists 225 top administration personnel or nominees who have been the subject of allegations of ethical infractions. Whitney North Seymour who prosecuted and convicted former White House aide Michael Deaver recently stated, "Unless the attitudes of government leaders change, there is little that prosecutors can do except put a thumb in the dike."[9]

ALLEVIATING THE ETHICS PROBLEM

Realistically, unethical practices in business can never be totally eliminated—it is an imperfect world. As in government, the legal system—even with more laws and regulations—is not the answer nor is an attempt to slow environmental change. However, with appropriate management attitudes and actions, businesses can alleviate or control the problem.

Business organizations should strive to employ only individuals with integrity. Too often companies are careless about checking prospective employees' statements concerning education, military service, and accomplishments in previous jobs. Regardless of a business organization's efforts to employ only individuals with impeccable integrity, it is not always possible to perform thorough background checks.

All is not lost, however. While clichés such as "ethics is learned at home" or "once a thief—always a thief" may be partially true, attitudes of unethical individuals can be changed or at the very least held in check by an ethical business organization.

Attitudes toward ethics involve a complex set of values derived from experiences and emotions that are learned at home, church, and school as well as the many varied influences of other formal and informal groups to which one belongs. Business organizations also have a great influence on the attitudes and values systems of individuals; this is particularly true since employees spend a minimum of eight hours a day at work. In fact, those in some quarters propose that a business organization can have a conscience.[10]

To achieve a corporate conscience requires that management focus on three areas: (1) commit to the goal of ethical conduct and serve as a role model; (2) strive toward openness; and (3) establish and implement rules, policies, and procedures to achieve the goal.

Commit to Ethical Goals and Serve as a Role Model: It is mandatory that an organization as a whole—from top to bottom—make a commitment to ethical behavior; however, the commitment has to originate from the top. One study of business executives of manufacturing firms located in the Southeast found that in a listing of eight factors that could influence ethical standards, the factor selected most frequently (32.6%) was "Top management emphasis on ethical action."[11] Traditionally, mission statements of a business refer to market niches in terms of goods and services. To incorporate the relative importance of values within the organization, the mission statement should also embrace ethical behavior. Top management must then continually stress that ethical behavior is demanded and that company loyalty will not be accepted as an excuse for unethical acts. Such a philosophy must be reiterated at every level and each manager held responsible for seeing that ethical behavior occurs at all lower levels.

What management says is important, but management action is even more important. Management serves as an ethical role model; through its capacity to set highly visible personal examples of sound ethical behavior, it establishes the tone for the entire organization. Serving as an ethical role model also requires sound employee relations, such as dealing with employees in a fair and just manner, never attempting to use subordinates in such a way as to profit from their efforts without considering their welfare, and representing subordinates' points of view at higher management levels. Sound employee relations result in a climate of trust and confidence within the organization. Without such a climate, total commitment to ethical behavior cannot be attained.

The daily contact between supervisor and subordinate provides the best opportunity for integrating the top management commitment to ethical activity into everyday conduct and decision making throughout all levels of an organization. Research has shown that an individual's immediate supervisor plays a very important role in ethical/unethical behavior. In the authors' 1986 study, U.S. business personnel in the South were asked to rank by relative importance six factors contributing to unethical behavior. Behavior of superiors was ranked first, with behavior of one's peers and personal financial need ranked a distant second and third.[12] Other studies have consistently indicated that behavior of superiors ranks first as a contributor to unethical behavior.[13] Also, in the authors' 1986 study, when asked who of eight possible individuals they consulted when faced with an ethical dilemma on the job, 42% of those responding indicated that they consulted their boss.[14] The percentage would probably have been even higher if more employees believed their bosses were ethical.

A personal example may illustrate the importance of supervisors' leading by example:

Early in his career one of us worked as a management trainee for a large alcoholic beverage distillery. Shortly after he began work, it was learned that an error had been made in the selection of barrels of aged whiskey. Only whiskey aged in oak barrels for at least six years was to be bottled, since the label on the bottles indicated that it had been aged six years. But in this particular batch, about 4% of the whiskey had been aged less than six years by only one to four months. The whiskey had already been bottled but not shipped to the wholesaler when the error was detected. Retrieving all the cases and emptying each bottle by hand (the whiskey itself could have been reused in a blend) would have been very time-consuming and costly. It was the author's judgment as well as that of three other management trainees that nothing should be done since (1) only 4% of the whiskey was aged less than six years, (2) the average age of the whiskey was considerably in excess of six years, (3) research had shown that individuals cannot detect any taste difference after five years of aging in a barrel, and (4) no one except a few people within the department knew that the error had occurred.

The production foreman, however, without a second thought, ordered all bottles from the batch dumped. The gist of the foreman's comment was, "When the company states 'aged six years in an oak barrel,' that's what it means." The point was well made, and it had a profound effect on all four management trainees. Furthermore, over time it became apparent that ethical behavior consistently permeated all levels of the organization.

The performance review between supervisor and subordinate is an opportune time to emphasize the importance of discussing an ethical situation with someone—preferably the superior. Counseling with others about ethical situations in the workplace can provide perspective, understanding, and comfort. Sanford McDonnell, chairman of McDonnell

Douglas Corporation, recently stated, "When you talk things out, you get a better feel for the company's value system."[15] Recently, a partner in an accounting firm knowingly approved another firm's false financial statements and is now facing a prison sentence. He stated in retrospect, "If I had sought counsel from someone that I had respect for, if I had even talked to my wife . . ."[16]

During a performance review, goals to be met by a subordinate are usually agreed on. Realistic goals must be set. If goals are too high, the temptation is to cut corners to achieve them. Certainly, setting a goal that requires effort to achieve is sound management practice, but the effort should be reasonable or the subordinate may feel the goal can be attained only through unethical practices. Supervisors must demand that ethical practices be maintained even at the expense of not achieving profit goals. During such contacts it is also important to attempt to identify situations (sometimes referred to as forward control) that may arise in pursuit of goals where ethical or legal problems are likely to occur.

Strive for Openness: Openness is essential to the establishment of mutual confidence and trust within an organization; therefore, openness must be an integral part of management's commitment to ethical conduct. Business organizations tend to be very secretive both internally and externally. Secretiveness too often enables managers to avoid responsibility for their decisions. Any decision not open for scrutiny is too often unethical. Even ethical actions and decisions that are not open for all to see or are only partially known by others in an organization (often through the grapevine) are often perceived as unethical because not all facts and circumstances are known. False perceptions may be as detrimental to an organization as reality. Furthermore, openness allows employees to feel comfortable when speaking out and discussing ethical questions and problems. Openness encourages employees to talk freely about an organization's policies and procedures, thus reducing the gray area on the ethical/unethical scale. Optimum decisions in terms of ethics are made only after discussion and debate within an organization.

An argument can be made against openness in certain situations. For instance, performance evaluations should be strictly between a supervisor and the subordinate. However, most arguments against openness are specious and usually benefit only those who wish to maintain secrecy at the expense of the organization.

Openness is also the best way to reduce outsiders' suspicions of an organization's motives and actions. Sir Adrian Cadbury, chairman of Cadbury Schweppes, recently stated, "Disclosure is not a panacea for improving the relations between business and society, but the willingness to operate an open system is the foundation of those relations."[17] The recent disclosure that Chrysler cars with disconnected speedometer cables were driven by company employees and then sold as new (a practice which most would describe as unethical) was diffused by openness concerning the incident. Chrysler President Lee Iaccoca publicly admitted the practice, offered compensation to buyers of such cars, and promised such a practice would not occur again.

Openness also involves top management's acknowledgment that it is accountable for unethical behavior occurring at lower levels. Too often, one hears a manager saying, "But I didn't know such an activity was going on"; or, "It's impossible for me to know everything going on below me." Such statements may be partially true, but too often they are only an excuse. Marshall Clinard, professor emeritus at the University of Wisconsin, found in his survey of retired middle managers that 72% believed that upper management knew about improper conduct either while it was going on or soon after.[18] Furthermore, a truly open organization with appropriate controls reduces the likelihood that managers really do not know what is going on at lower levels.

Establish Rules, Policies, and Procedures: Appropriate rules, policies, and procedures must be established to reinforce and augment management's commitment toward achievement of the ethical goal—

1. A code of ethics should be established. In recent years, most large business organizations have devised codes. The Center for Business Ethics at Bentley College found that of 279 large companies surveyed, 208 had written codes.[19] While most large firms have an ethics code, many, if not most, smaller firms have not taken the time or effort to establish one. Even firms with ethics codes have too often devised them for the wrong reason—an erroneous belief that having a code absolves top managers from responsibility if wrongdoing occurs at lower levels.

   A meaningful ethics code should be both general and specific. The code should contain general statements outlining management's total commitment to ethical behavior; these statements serve as a guide to behavior and decision making within the total organization. A code should also contain specific "do" and "don't" statements that are enforceable. An example of a specific statement would be "All facts necessary for an informed purchase of a product or service must be provided to a potential customer." Such a statement would have been clearly violated in the earlier example of the hotel that did not inform guests they were being charged daytime telephone rates for night calls. Even supposedly specific statements can be open to interpretation, and codes should indicate that when a question of interpretation is involved, it must be referred to a higher level in the organization. Ethics codes must be continually updated. As environmental changes occur, revisions and additions to the code may be needed. For instance, rapid computerization or a merger may require updating an organization's ethics code.

2. Policies and procedures for reporting ethical problems must be established. The traditional upward communication channel flowing from subordinate through superior is not always appropriate. As previously noted, an individual's supervisor may be part of the problem. An organization must designate individuals to whom information can be communicated. The Bentley College study of 279 top U.S. companies found that only 17 had an ombudsman or a telephone hot line for employees to use when they wished to bypass normal channels.[20]

   The establishment of a hot line is an effective upward communication channel. A hot line also serves notice that the organization encourages individuals to report what they believe is unethical behavior within the organization, sometimes referred to as whistle-blowing. The fate of whistle-blowers in some organizations—demotion or even termination—has been frequently publicized in the media. Thus, it is management's responsibility to convince employees of the following:

   - Whistle-blowing is encouraged.
   - Confidentiality will be maintained.
   - Appropriate action will be taken when wrongdoing is reported.

   Management's total commitment to ethical behavior can overcome most employees' fears concerning use of an ombudsman. However, establishing an ombudsman who is an outsider (for example a retired executive) can aid in overcoming fears of confidentiality and reprisals. At the very least, the ombudsman should be a manager near the top of the organization.

3. Policies and procedures must be devised to communicate downward to employees. Methods for communicating downward are many and include bulletin boards, policy manuals, company newsletters, and meetings. Too often a company sends out a memo to all employees citing the organization's commitment to ethical behavior, and the subject is never mentioned again. As previously noted, each supervisor is the key to downward communication and is responsible for the following:

   - Reemphasizing the ethical commitment of the organization.
   - Explaining policies and procedures such as the hot line.
   - Reiterating that performance will be measured first in terms of ethical standards and second in terms of profitability.

Training sessions are often useful in communicating downward and to some extent upward. Training sessions should include employees from all levels in order to promote common understanding of management's commitment to ethical behavior as well as to discuss the policies and procedures for implementing the commitment. It is doubtful that such sessions can teach ethics per se, but they should accomplish the following:

- Sensitize employees as to the importance of ethical conduct.
- Alert employees to possible ethical situations.
- Help individuals think more clearly about relevant issues and discuss concerns and doubts.
- Reduce the gray area on the ethical/unethical scale.

4. A formal enforcement system is necessary to put teeth into rules. Regardless of an organization's positive commitment to ethical behavior, it is imprudent to rely solely on good intentions. Human behavior still necessitates deterrents. People must be afraid to break the rules because they know they are likely to be punished. A formal auditing system should be devised to detect unethical behavior and a judicial board (ethics committee) empowered to judge internal violations and to guarantee due process to those accused of wrongdoing. Membership on a judicial board depends on many factors, such as size of the organization, number of levels within the organization, and so forth, but the members must be individuals whose impeccable integrity is generally recognized throughout the organization.

When unethical behavior is found, prompt action (commensurate with the misdeed) must be taken. Management should publicize the misconduct and the punishment should be administered for all to see—the element of openness. Too often, a manager's first reaction is to avoid an embarrassing situation which to some extent derives from the feeling that "I'm at least partially responsible." However, little or no action sends a clear message to other employees about what top management really thinks is or is not important. If an infraction is deemed very serious, frequently the action is to allow the guilty individual to resign, and the whole affair is handled as quietly as possible. Companies have even been known to give a good recommendation for the individual who was asked to resign. Such actions do not serve as a deterrent to unethical behavior.

One must remember, however, that while an enforcement system is necessary, an organization has to be careful to address issues of ethics in a positive manner. Instituting a police-state atmosphere only intimidates and alienates employees and results in a loss of confidence in and loyalty to the organization.

In the final analysis, top management must set the ethical tone and send a clear and pragmatic message to all employees that ethical conduct is demanded regardless of other organizational goals. To ensure compliance, such a mandate must be supplemented by appropriate rules, policies, and procedures. The key, however, is for an organization to never let up on its vigilance to achieve ethical practices. Only then can an organization have a conscience.

NOTES

1. William E. Simon, "A Challenge to Free Enterprise," in *The Ethical Basis of Economic Freedom*, Ivan Hill, ed. (Chapel Hill, North Carolina: American Viewpoint, 1976), 405–06.

2. Maynard M. Dolecheck, James Caldwell, and Carolyn C. Dolecheck, "Ethical Perceptions and Attitudes of Business Personnel," *American Business Review* (January 1988): 47–54.

3. Jonathan Dahl, "Tracking Travel," *Wall Street Journal* 6 January 1988, 17.

4. Stephen Koepp, "Having It All, Then Throwing It All Away," *Time*, 25 May 1987, 23.

5. Saul W. Gellerman, "Why Good Managers Make Bad Ethical Choices," *Harvard Business Review* (July/August 1986): 85.

6. "Ethics Are Nice, but They Can Be a Handicap Some Executives Declare," *Wall Street Journal*, 8 September 1987, 1.

7. *Hong Kong Business Today* reporting the New York Times/CBS News poll, September 1985, 42.

8. Barry Z. Posner and Warren H. Schmidt, "Values and the American Manager: An Update," *California Management Review* (Spring 1984): 210–11.

9. "Ethical Problems Plague Reagan's Administration," *News-Star-World*, 20 December 1987, 11A.

10. Kenneth Goodpaster and John Mathews, "Can a Corporation Have a Conscience?" *Harvard Business Review* (January/February 1982): 132–41.

11. S. J. Vitell and T. A. Festervand, "Business Ethics Conflicts, Practices and Beliefs of Industrial Executives," *Journal of Business Ethics* (May 1987): 116.

12. Dolecheck, Caldwell, and Dolecheck, "Ethical Perceptions."

13. Ibid.

14. Ibid.

15. Alan J. Otten, "Ethics on the Job: Companies Alert Employees to Potential Dilemmas," *Wall Street Journal*, 1 July 1986, 17.

16. Martha Brannigan, "Auditor's Downfall Shows a Man Caught in Trap of His Own Making," *Wall Street Journal*, 4 March 1987, 31.

17. Sir Adam Cadbury, "Ethical Managers Make Their Own Rules," *Harvard Business Review*, (September/October 1987): 69.

18. Stan Crock, "How to Take a Bite Out of Corporate Crime," *Business Week*, 15 July 1985, 122.

19. Otten, "Ethics on the Job."

20. Ibid.

Essay

Ways Women Lead

Judy B. Rosener

The command-and-control leadership style associated with men is not the only way to succeed.

Women managers who have broken the glass ceiling in medium-sized, nontraditional organizations have proven that effective leaders don't come from one mold. They have demonstrated that using the command-and-control style of managing others, a style generally associated with men in large traditional organizations, is not the only way to succeed.

The first female executives, because they were breaking new ground, adhered to many of the "rules of conduct" that spelled success for men. Now a second wave of women is making its way into top management, not by adopting the style and habits that have proved successful for men but by drawing on the skills and attitudes they developed from their shared experience as women. These second-generation managerial women are drawing on what is unique to their socialization as women and creating a different path to the top. They are seeking and finding opportunities in fast-changing and growing organizations to show that they can achieve results—in a different way. They are succeeding because of—not in spite of—certain characteristics generally considered to be "feminine" and inappropriate in leaders.

The women's success shows that a nontraditional leadership style is well suited to the conditions of some work environments and can increase an organization's chances of surviving in an uncertain world. It supports the belief that there is strength in a diversity of leadership styles.

In a recent survey sponsored by the International Women's Forum, I found a number of unexpected similarities between men and women leaders along with some important differences. Among these similarities are characteristics related to money and children.

I found that the men and women respondents earned the same amount of money (and the household income of the women is twice that of the men). This finding is contrary to most studies, which find a considerable wage gap between men and women even at the executive level. I also found that just as many men as women experience work-family conflict (although when there are children at home, the women experience slightly more conflict than men).

But the similarities end when men and women describe their leadership performance and how they usually influence those with whom they work. The men are more likely than the women to describe themselves in ways that characterize what some management experts call "transactional" leadership. That is, they view job performance as a series of transactions with subordinates, which includes exchanging rewards for services rendered or punishment for inadequate performance. The men are also more likely to use power that comes from their organizational position and formal authority.

The women respondents, on the other hand, described themselves in ways that characterize "transformational" leadership—getting subordinates to transform their own self-interest into the interest of the group through concern for a broader goal. Moreover, they ascribe their power to personal characteristics like charisma, interpersonal skills, hard work, or personal contacts rather than to organizational stature.

Intrigued by these differences, I interviewed some of the women respondents who described themselves as transformational. These discussions gave me a better picture of how these women saw themselves as leaders and a greater understanding of the important ways in which their leadership style differs from the traditional command-and-control style. I call their leadership style "interactive leadership" because these women actively work to make their interactions with subordinates positive for everyone involved. More specifically, the women encourage participation, share power and information, enhance other people's self-worth, and get others excited about their work. All these things reflect their belief that allowing employees to contribute and to feel powerful and important is a win-win situation—good for the employees and the organization.

INTERACTIVE LEADERSHIP

From my discussions with the women interviewees, several patterns emerged. The women leaders made frequent reference to their efforts to encourage participation and share power and information—two things that are often associated with participative management. But their self-description went beyond the usual definitions of participation. Much of what they described were attempts to enhance other people's sense of self-worth and to energize followers. In general, these leaders believe that people perform best when they feel good about themselves and their work, and they try to create situations that contribute to that feeling.

Encourage participation. Inclusion is at the core of interactive leadership. In describing nearly every aspect of management, the women interviewees made reference to trying to make people feel part of the organization. They try to instill this group identity in a variety of ways, including encouraging others to have a say in almost every aspect of work, from setting performance goals to determining strategy. To facilitate inclusion, they create mechanisms that get people to participate and they use a conversational style that sends signals inviting people to get involved.

One example of the kinds of mechanisms that encourage participation is the "bridge club" that one interviewee, a group executive in charge of mergers and acquisitions at a large East Coast financial firm, created. The club is an informal gathering of people who have information she needs but over whom she has no direct control. The word bridge describes the effort to bring together these "members" from different functions. The word club captures the relaxed atmosphere.

Despite the fact that attendance at club meetings is voluntary and over and above the usual work demands, the interviewee said that those whose help she needs make the time to come. "They know their contributions are valued, and they appreciate the chance to exchange information across functional boundaries in an informal setting that's fun." She finds participation in the club more effective than memos.

Whether or not the women create special forums for people to interact, they try to make people feel included as a matter of course, often by trying to draw them into the conversation or soliciting their opinions. Frieda Caplan, founder and CEO of Frieda's Finest, a California-based marketer and distributor of unusual fruits and vegetables, described an approach she uses that is typical of the other women interviewed: "When I face a tough decision, I always ask my employees, 'What would you do if you were me?' This approach generates good feedback and introduces my employees to the complexity of management decisions."

Of course, saying that you include others doesn't mean others necessarily feel included. The women acknowledge the possibility that their efforts to draw people in may be seen as symbolic, so they try to avoid that perception by acting on the input they receive. They ask for suggestions before they reach their own conclusions, and they test—and sometimes change—particular decisions before they implement them. These women use participation to clarify their own views by thinking things through out loud

and to ensure that they haven't overlooked an important consideration.

The fact that many of the interviewees described their participatory style as coming "naturally" suggests that these leaders do not consciously adopt it for its business value. Yet they realize that encouraging participation has benefits. For one thing, making it easy for people to express their ideas helps ensure that decisions reflect as much information as possible. To some of the women, this point is just common sense. Susan S. Elliott, president and founder of Systems Service Enterprises, a St. Louis computer consulting company, expressed this view: "I can't come up with a plan and then ask those who manage the accounts to give me their reactions. They're the ones who really know the accounts. They have information I don't have. Without their input I'd be operating in an ivory tower."

Participation also increases support for decisions ultimately reached and reduces the risk that ideas will be undermined by unexpected opposition. Claire Rothman, general manager of the Great Western Forum, a large sports and entertainment arena in Los Angeles, spoke about the value of open disagreement: "When I know ahead of time that someone disagrees with a decision, I can work especially closely with that person to try to get his or her support."

Getting people involved also reduces the risk associated with having only one person handle a client, project, or investment. For Patricia M. Cloherty, senior vice president and general partner of Alan Patricof Associates, a New York venture capital firm, including people in decision making and planning gives investments longevity. If something happens to one person, others will be familiar enough with the situation to "adopt" the investment. That way, there are no orphans in the portfolio, and a knowledgeable second opinion is always available.

Like most who are familiar with participatory management, these women are aware that being inclusive also has its disadvantages. Soliciting ideas and information from others takes time, often requires giving up some control, opens the door to criticism, and exposes personal and turf conflicts. In addition, asking for ideas and information can be interpreted as not having answers.

Further, it cannot be assumed that everyone wants to participate. Some people prefer being told what to do. When Mary Jane Rynd was a partner in a Big Eight accounting firm in Arizona (she recently left to start her own company—Rynd, Carneal & Associates), she encountered such a person: "We hired this person from an out-of-state CPA firm because he was experienced and smart—and because it's always fun to hire someone away from another firm. But he was just too cynical to participate. He was suspicious of everybody. I tried everything to get him involved—including him in discussions and giving him pep talks about how we all work together. Nothing worked. He just didn't want to participate."

Like all those who responded to the survey, these women are comfortable using a variety of styles. So when participation doesn't work, they act unilaterally. "I prefer participation," said Elliott, "but there are situations where time is short and I have to take the bull by the horns."

Share power and information. Soliciting input from other people suggests a flow of information from employees to the "boss." But part of making people feel included is knowing that open communication flows in two directions. These women say they willingly share power and information rather than guard it and they make apparent their reasoning behind decisions. While many leaders see information as power and power as a limited commodity to be coveted, the interviewees seem to be comfortable letting power and information change hands. As Adrienne Hall,

vice chairman of Eisaman, Johns & Laws, a large West Coast advertising firm, said: "I know territories shift, so I'm not preoccupied with turf."

One example of power and information sharing is the open strategy sessions held by Debi Coleman, vice president of information systems and technology at Apple Computer. Rather than closeting a small group of key executives in her office to develop a strategy based her own agenda, she holds a series of meetings over several days and allows a larger group to develop and help choose alternatives.

The interviewees believe that sharing power and information accomplishes several things. It creates loyalty by signaling to coworkers and subordinates that they are trusted and their ideas respected. It also sets an example for other people and therefore can enhance the general communication flow. And it increases the odds that leaders will hear about problems before they explode. Sharing power and information also gives employees and coworkers the wherewithal to reach conclusions, solve problems, and see the justification for decisions.

On a more pragmatic level, many employees have come to expect their bosses to be open and frank. They no longer accept being dictated to but want to be treated as individuals with minds of their own. As Elliott said, "I work with lots of people who are bright and intelligent, so I have to deal with them at an intellectual level. They're very logical, and they want to know the reasons for things. They'll buy in only if it makes sense."

In some cases, sharing information means simply being candid about work-related issues. In early 1990, when Elliott hired as employees many of the people she had been using as independent contractors, she knew the transition would be difficult for everyone. The number of employees nearly doubled overnight, and the nature of working relationships changed. "I warned everyone that we were in for some rough times and reminded them that we would be experiencing them together. I admitted that it would also be hard for me, and I made it clear that I wanted them to feel free to talk to me. I was completely candid and encouraged them to be honest with me. I lost some employees who didn't like the new relationships, but I'm convinced that being open helped me understand my employees better, and it gave them a feeling of support."

Like encouraging participation, sharing power and information has its risks. It allows for the possibility that people will reject, criticize, or otherwise challenge what the leader has to say or, more broadly, her authority. Also, employees get frustrated when leaders listen to—but ultimately reject—their ideas. Because information is a source of power, leaders who share it can be seen as naïve or needing to be liked. The interviewees have experienced some of these downsides but find the positives overwhelming.

Enhance the self-worth of others. One of the byproducts of sharing information and encouraging participation is that employees feel important. During the interviews, the women leaders discussed other ways they build a feeling of self-worth in coworkers and subordinates. They talked about giving others credit and praise and sending small signals of recognition. Most important, they expressed how they refrain from asserting their own superiority, which asserts the inferiority of others. All those I interviewed expressed clear aversion to behavior that sets them apart from others in the company-reserved parking places, separate dining facilities, pulling rank.

Examples of sharing and giving credit to others abound. Caplan, who has been the subject of scores of media reports hailing her innovation of labeling vegetables so consumers know what they are and how to cook them, originally got the idea from a farmer. She said that whenever someone raises the subject, she credits the farmer and downplays her role. Rothman is among the many note-writers; when someone does something out of the ordinary, she writes them a personal note to tell them she noticed. Like many of the women I interviewed, she said she also makes a point acknowledging good work by talking about it in front of others.

Bolstering coworkers and subordinates is especially important in businesses and jobs that tend to be hard on a person's ego. Investment banking is one example because of the long hours, high pressures, intense competition, and inevitability that some deals will fail. One interviewee in investment banking hosts dinners for her division, gives out gag gifts as party favors, pass out M&Ms at meetings, and throws parties "to celebrate ourselves." These things, she said, balance the anxiety that permeates the environment.

Rynd compensates for the negativity inherent in preparing tax returns: "In my business we have something called a query sheet, where the person who reviews the tax return writes down everything that needs to be corrected. Criticism is built into the system. But at the end of every review. I always include a positive comment—your work paper technique looked good, I appreciate the fact that you got this done on time, or something like that. It seems trivial, but it's one way to remind people that I recognize their good work and not just their shortcomings."

Energize others. The women leaders spoke of their enthusiasm for work and how they spread their enthusiasm around to make work a challenge that is exhilarating and fun. The women leaders talked about it in those terms and claimed to use their enthusiasm to get others excited. As Rothman said, "There is rarely a person I can't motivate."

Enthusiasm was a dominant theme throughout the interviews. In computer consulting: "Because this business is on the forefront of technology, I'm sort of evangelistic about it, and I want other people to be as excited as I am." In venture capital: "You have to have a head of steam." In executive search: "Getting people excited is an important way to influence those you have no control over." Or in managing sports arenas: "My enthusiasm gets others excited. I infuse them with energy and make them see that even boring jobs contribute to the fun of working in a celebrity business."

Enthusiasm can sometimes be misunderstood. In conservative professions like investment banking, such an upbeat leadership style can be interpreted as cheerleading and can undermine credibility. In many cases, the women said they won and preserved their credibility by achieving results that could be measured easily. One of the women acknowledged that her colleagues don't understand or like her leadership style and have called it cheerleading. "But," she added, "in this business you get credibility from what you produce, and they love the profits I generate." While energy and enthusiasm can inspire some, it doesn't work for everyone. Even Rothman conceded, "Not everyone has a flame that can be lit."

PATHS OF LEAST RESISTANCE

Many of the women I interviewed said the behaviors and beliefs that underlie their leadership style come naturally to them. I attribute this to two things: their socialization and the career paths they have chosen. Although socialization patterns and career paths are changing, the average age of the men and women who responded to the survey is 51—old enough to have had experiences that differed because of gender.

Until the 1960s, men and women received different signals about what was expected of them. To summarize a subject that many experts have explored in depth, women have been expected to be wives, mothers, community volunteers, teachers, and nurses. In all these roles, they are supposed to be cooperative, supportive, understanding, gentle, and to provide service to others. They are to derive satisfaction and a sense of self-esteem from helping others, including their spouses. While men have had to appear to be competitive, strong, tough, decisive, and in control, women have been allowed to be cooperative, emotional, supportive, and vulnerable. This may explain why women today are more likely than men to be interactive leaders.

Men and women have also had different career opportunities. Women were not expected to have careers, or at least not the same kinds of careers as men, so they either pursued different jobs or were simply denied opportunities men had. Women's career tracks have usually not included long series of organizational positions with formal authority and control of resources. Many women had their first work experiences outside the home as volunteers. While some of the challenges they faced as managers in volunteer organizations are the same as those in any business, in many ways, leading volunteers is different because of the absence of concrete rewards like pay and promotion.

As women entered the business world, they tended to find themselves in positions consistent with the roles they played at home: in staff positions rather than in line positions, supporting the work of others, and in functions like communications or human resources where they had relatively small budgets and few people reporting directly to them.

The fact that most women have lacked formal authority over others and control over resources means that by default they have had to find other ways to accomplish their work. As it turns out, the behaviors that were natural and/or socially acceptable for them have been highly successful in at least some managerial settings.

What came easily to women turned out to be a survival tactic. Although leaders often begin their careers doing what comes naturally and what fits within the constraints of the job, they also develop their skills and styles over time. The women's use of interactive leadership has its roots in socialization, and the women interviewees firmly believe that it benefits their organizations. Through the course of their careers, they have gained conviction that their style is effective. In fact, for some, it was their own success that caused them to formulate their philosophies about what motivates people, how to make good decisions, and what it takes to maximize business performance.

They now have formal authority and control over vast resources, but still they see sharing power and information as an asset rather than a liability. They believe that although pay and promotion are necessary tools of management, what people really want is to feel that they are contributing to a higher purpose and that they have the opportunity as individuals to learn and grow. The women believe that employees and peers perform better when they feel they are part of an organization and can share in its success. Allowing them to get involved and to work to their potential is a way of maximizing their contributions and using human resources most efficiently.

ANOTHER KIND OF DIVERSITY

The IWF survey shows that a nontraditional leadership style can be effective in organizations that accept it. This lesson comes especially hard to those who think of the corporate world as a game of survival of the fittest, where the fittest is always the strongest, toughest, most decisive, and powerful. Such a workplace seems to favor leaders who control people by controlling resources, and by controlling people, gain control of more resources. Asking for information and sharing decision-making power can be seen as serious disadvantages, but what is a disadvantage under one set of circumstances is an advantage under another. The "best" leadership style depends on the organizational context.

Only one of the women interviewees is in a traditional, large-scale company. More typically, the women's organizations are medium-sized and tend to have experienced fast growth and fast change. They demand performance and/or have a high proportion of professional workers. These organizations seem to create opportunities for women and are hospitable to those who use a nontraditional management style.

The degree of growth or change in an organization is an important factor in creating opportunities for women. When change is rampant, everything is up for grabs, and crises are frequent. Crises are generally not desirable, but they do create opportunities for people to prove themselves. Many of the women interviewees said they got their first break because their organizations were in turmoil.

Fast-changing environments also play havoc with tradition. Coming up through the ranks and being part of an established network is no longer important. What is important is how you perform. Also, managers in such environments are open to new solutions, new structures, and new ways of leading.

The fact that many of the women respondents are in organizations that have clear performance standards suggests that they have gained credibility and legitimacy by achieving results. In investment banking, venture capital, accounting, and executive placement, for instance, individual performance is easy to measure.

A high proportion of young professional workers—increasingly typical of organizations—is also a factor in some women's success. Young, educated professionals impose special requirements on their organizations. They demand to participate and contribute. In some cases, they have knowledge or talents their bosses don't have. If they are good performers, they have many employment options. It is easy to imagine that these professionals will respond to leaders who are inclusive and open, who enhance the self-worth of others, and who create a fun work environment. Interactive leaders are likely to win the cooperation needed to achieve their goals.

Interactive leadership has proved to be effective, perhaps even advantageous, in organizations in which the women I interviewed have succeeded. As the work force increasingly demands participation and the economic environment increasingly requires rapid change, interactive leadership may emerge as the management style of choice for many organizations. For interactive leadership to take root more broadly, however, organizations must be willing to question the notion that the traditional command-and-control leadership style that has brought success in earlier decades is the only way to get results. This may be hard in some organizations, especially those with long histories of male-oriented, command-and-control leadership. Changing these organizations will not be easy. The fact that women are more likely than men to be interactive leaders raises the risk that these companies will perceive inter-

active leadership as "feminine" and automatically resist it.

Linking interactive leadership directly to being female is a mistake. We know that women are capable of making their way through corporations by adhering to the traditional corporate model and that they can wield power in ways similar to men. Indeed, some women may prefer that style. We also know from the survey findings that some men use the transformational leadership style.

Large, establishing organizations should expand their definition of effective leadership. If they were to do that, several things might happen, including the disappearance of the glass ceiling and the creation of a wider path for all sorts of executives—men and women—to attain positions of leadership. Widening the path will free potential leaders to lead in ways that play to their individual strengths. Then the newly recognized interactive leadership style can be valued and rewarded as highly as the command-and-control style has been for decades. By valuing a diversity of leadership styles, organizations will find the strength and flexibility to survive in a highly competitive, increasingly diverse economic environment.

Essay

Moral Mazes: Bureaucracy and Managerial Work

Robert Jackall

Corporate leaders often tell their charges that hard work will lead to success. Indeed, this theory of reward being commensurate with effort has been an enduring belief in our society, one central to our self-image as a people

where the "main chance" is available to anyone of ability who has the gumption and the persistence to seize it. Hard work, it is also frequently asserted, builds character. This notion carries less conviction because businessmen, and our society as a whole, have little patience with those who make a habit of finishing out of the money. In the end, it is success that matters, that legitimate striving, and that makes work worthwhile.

What if, however, men and women in the big corporation no longer see success as necessarily connected to hard work? What becomes of the social morality of the corporation—I mean the everyday rules in use that people play by—when there is thought to be no "objective" standard of excellence to explain how and why winners are separated from also-rans, how and why some people succeed and others fail?

This is the puzzle that confronted me while doing a great many extensive interviews with managers and executives in several large corporations, particularly in a large chemical company and a large textile firm. I went into these corporations to study how bureaucracy—the prevailing organizational form of our society and economy—shapes moral consciousness. I came to see that managers' rules for success are at the heart of what may be called the bureaucratic ethic.

This article suggests no changes and offers no programs for reform. It is, rather, simply an interpretive sociological analysis of the moral dimensions of managers' work. Some readers may find the essay sharp-edged, others familiar. For both groups, it is important to note at the outset that my materials are managers' own descriptions of their experiences.[1] In listening to managers, I have had the decided advantages of being unencumbered with business reponsibilities and also of being free from the taken-for-granted views and vocabularies of the business world. As it happens, my own research in a variety of other settings suggests that managers' experiences are by no means unique; indeed they have a deep resonance with those of other occupational groups.

WHAT HAPPENED TO THE PROTESTANT ETHIC?

To grasp managers' experiences and the more general implications they contain, one must see them against the background of the great historical transformations, both social and cultural, that produced managers as an occupational group. Since the concern here is with the moral significance of work in business, it is important to begin with an understanding of the original Protestant Ethic, the world view of the rising bourgeois class that spear-headed the emergence of capitalism.

The Protestant Ethic was a set of beliefs that counseled "secular asceticism"—the methodical, rational subjection of human impulse and desire to God's will through "restless, continuous, systematic work in a worldly calling."[2] This ethic of ceaseless work and ceaseless renunciation of the fruits of one's toil provided both the economic and the moral foundations for modern capitalism.

On one hand, secular asceticism was a ready-made prescription for building economic capital; on the other, it became for the upward-moving bourgeois class—self-made industrialists, farmers, and enterprising artisans—the ideology that justified their attention to this world, their accumulation of wealth, and indeed the social inequities that inevitably followed such accumulation. This bourgeois ethic, with its imperatives for self-reliance, hard work, frugality, and rational planning, and its clear definition of success and failure, came to dominate a whole historical epoch in the West.

But the ethic came under assault from two directions. First, the very accumulation of wealth that the old Protestant Ethic made possible gradually stripped away the religious basis of the ethic, especially among the rising middle class that benefited from it. There were, of course, periodic reassertions of the religious context of the ethic, as in the case of

John D. Rockefeller and his turn toward Baptism. But on the whole, by the late 1800s the religious roots of the ethic survived principally among the independent farmers and proprietors of small businesses in rural areas and towns across America.

In the mainstream of an emerging urban America, the ethic had become secularized into the "work ethic," "rugged individualism," and especially the "success ethic." By the beginning of this century, among most of the economically successful, frugality had become an aberration, conspicuous consumption the norm. And with the shaping of the mass consumer society later in this century, the sanctification of consumption became widespread, indeed crucial to the maintenance of the economic order.

Affluence and the emergence of the consumer society were responsible, however, for the demise of only aspects of the old ethic—namely, the imperatives for saving and investment. The core of the ethic, even in its later, secularized form—self-reliance, unremitting devotion to work, and a morality that postulated just rewards for work well done—was undermined by the complete transformation of the organizational form of work itself. The hallmarks of the emerging modern production and distribution systems were administrative hierarchies, standardized work procedures, regularized time-tables, uniform policies, and centralized control—in a word, the bureaucratization of the economy.

This bureaucratization was heralded at first by a very small class of salaried managers, who were later joined by legions of clerks and still later by technicians and professionals of every stripe. In this century, the process spilled over from the private to the public sector and government bureaucracies came to rival those of industry. This great transformation produced the decline of the old middle class of entrepreneurs, free professionals, independent farmers, and small independent businessmen—the traditional carriers of the old Protestant Ethic—and the ascendance of a new middle class of salaried employees whose chief common characteristic was and is their dependence on the big organization.

Any understanding of what happened to the original Protestant Ethic and to the old morality and social character it embodied—and therefore any understanding of the moral significance of work today—is inextricably tied to an analysis of bureaucracy. More specifically, it is, in my view, tied to an analysis of the work and occupational cultures of managerial groups within bureaucracies. Managers are the quintessential bureaucratic work group; they not only fashion bureaucratic rules, but they are also bound by them. Typically, they are not just *in* the organization; they are *of* the organization. As such, managers represent the prototype of the white-collar salaried employee. By analyzing the kind of ethic bureaucracy produces in managers, one can begin to understand how bureaucracy shapes morality in our society as a whole.

PYRAMIDAL POLITICS

American businesses typically both centralize and decentralize authority. Power is concentrated at the top in the person of the chief executive officer and is simultaneously decentralized; that is, responsibility for decisions and profits is pushed as far down the organizational line as possible. For example, the chemical company that I studied—and its structure is typical of other organizations I examined—is one of several operating companies of a large and growing conglomerate. Like the other operating companies, the chemical concern has its own president, executive vice presidents, vice presidents, other executive officers, business area managers, entire staff divisions, and operating plants.

Each company is, in effect, a self-sufficient organization, though they are all coordinated by the corporation, and each president reports directly to the corporate CEO.

Now, the key interlocking mechanism of this structure is its reporting system. Each manager gathers up the profit targets or other objectives of his or her subordinates, and with these formulates his commitments to his boss; this boss takes these commitments, and those of his subordinates, and in turn makes a commitment to *his* boss. (Note: henceforth only "he" or "his" will be used to allow for easier reading.) At the top of the line, the president of each company makes his commitment to the CEO of the corporation, based on the stated objectives given to him by his vice presidents. There is always pressure from the top to set higher goals.

This management-by-objectives system, as it is usually called, creates a chain of commitments from the CEO down to the lowliest product manager. In practice, it also shapes a patrimonial authority arrangement which is crucial to defining both the immediate experiences and the long-run career chances of individual managers. In this world, a subordinate owes fealty principally to his immediate boss. A subordinate must not overcommit his boss; he must keep the boss from making mistakes, particularly public ones; he must not circumvent the boss. On a social level, even though an easy, breezy informality is the prevalent style of American business, the subordinate must extend to the boss a certain ritual deference: for instance, he must follow the boss's lead in conversation, must not speak out of turn at meetings, and must laugh at the boss's jokes while not making jokes of his own.

In short, the subordinate must not exhibit any behavior which symbolizes parity. In return, he can hope to be elevated when and if the boss is elevated, although other important criteria also intervene here. He can also expect protection for mistakes made up to a point. However, that point is never exactly defined and always depends on the complicated politics of each situation.

Who Gets Credit?

It is characteristic of this authority system that details are pushed down and credit is pushed up. Superiors do not like to give detailed instructions to subordinates. The official reason for this is to maximize subordinates' autonomy; the underlying reason seems to be to get rid of tedious details and to protect the privilege of authority to declare that a mistake has been made.

It is not at all uncommon for very bald and extremely general edicts to emerge from on high. For example, "Sell the plant in St. Louis. Let me know when you've struck a deal." This pushing down of details has important consequences:

1. Because they are unfamiliar with entangling details, corporate higher echelons tend to expect highly successful results without complications. This is central to top executives' well-known aversion to bad news and to the resulting tendency to "kill the messenger" who bears that news.
2. The pushing down of detail creates great pressure on middle managers not only to transmit good news but to protect their corporations, their bosses, and themselves in the process. They become the "point men" of a given strategy and the potential "fall guys" when things go wrong.

Credit flows up in this structure and usually is appropriated by the highest ranking officer involved in a decision. This person redistributes credit as he chooses, bound essentially by a sensitivity to public perceptions of his fairness. At the middle level, credit for a particular success is always a type of refracted social honor; one cannot claim credit even if it is earned. Credit has to be given, and acceptance of the gift implicitly involves a reaffirmation and strengthening of fealty. A superior may share some credit with subordinates in order to deepen fealty relationships and induce greater future efforts on his behalf. Of course, a different system is involved in the allocation of blame, a point I shall discuss later.

Fealty to the "King"

Because of the interlocking character of the commitment system, a CEO carries enormous influence in his corporation. If, for a moment, one thinks of the presidents of individual operating companies as barons, then the CEO of the parent company is the king. His word is law; even the CEO's wishes and whims are taken as commands by close subordinates on the corporate staff, who zealously turn them into policies and directives.

A typical example occurred in the textile company last year when the CEO, new at the time, expressed mild concern about the rising operating costs of the company's fleet of rented cars. The following day, a stringent system for monitoring mileage replaced the previous casual practice.

Great efforts are made to please the CEO. For example, when the CEO of the large conglomerate that includes the chemical company visits a plant, the most important order of business for local management is a fresh paint job, even when, as in several cases last year the cost of paint alone exceeds $100,000. I am told that similar anecdotes from other organizations have been in circulation since 1910; this suggests a certain historical continuity of behavior toward top bosses.

The second order of business for the plant management is to produce a complete book describing the plant and its operations, replete with photographs and illustrations, for presentation to the CEO; such a book costs about $10,000 for the single copy. By any standards of budgetary stringency, such expenditures are irrational. But by the social standards of the corporation, they make perfect sense. It is far more important to please the king today than to worry about the future economic state of one's fief, since if one does not please the king, there may not be a fief to worry about or indeed any vassals to do the worrying.

By the same token, all of this leads to an intense interest in everything the CEO does and says. In both the chemical and the textile companies, the most common topic of conversation among managers up and down the line is speculation about their respective CEOs' plans, intentions, strategies, actions, styles, and public images.

Such speculation is more than idle gossip. Because he stands at the apex of the corporation's bureaucratic and patrimonial structures and locks the intricate system of commitments between bosses and subordinates into place, it is the CEO who ultimately decides whether those commitments have been satisfactorily met. Moreover, the CEO and his trusted associates determine the fate of whole business areas of a corporation.

Shake-Ups & Contingency

One must appreciate the simultaneously monocratic and patrimonial character of business bureaucracies in order to grasp what we might call their contingency. One has only to read the *Wall Street Journal* or the *New York Times* to realize that, despite their carefully constructed "eternal" public image, corporations are quite unstable organizations. Mergers, buy-outs, divestitures, and especially "organizational restructuring" are commonplace aspects of business life. I shall discuss only organizational shake-ups here.

Usually, shake-ups occur because of the appointment of a new CEO and/or division president, or because of some failure that is adjudged to demand retribution; sometimes these occurrences work together. The first action of most new CEOs is some form of organizational change. On the one hand, this prevents the inheritance of blame for past mistakes; on the other, it projects an image of bareknuckled aggressiveness much appreciated on Wall Street. Perhaps most important, a shake-up rearranges the fealty structure of the corporation, placing in power those barons whose style and public image mesh closely with that of the new CEO.

A shake-up has reverberations throughout an organization. Shortly after the new CEO of the conglomerate was named, he reorganized the whole business and selected new presidents to head each of the five newly formed companies of the corporation. He mandated that the presidents carry out a thorough reorganization of their separate companies complete with extensive "census reduction"—that is, firing as many people as possible.

The new president of the chemical company, one of these five, had risen from a small but important specialty chemicals division in the former company. Upon promotion to president, he reached back into his former division, indeed back to his own past work in a particular product line, and systematically elevated many of his former colleagues, friends, and allies. Powerful managers in other divisions, particularly in a rival process chemicals division, were: (1) forced to take big demotions in the new power structure; (2) put on "special assignment"—the corporate euphemism for Siberia (the saying is: "No one ever comes back from special assignment"): (3) fired; or (4) given "early retirement," a graceful way of doing the same thing.

Up and down the chemical company, former associates of the president now hold virtually every important position. Managers in the company view all of this as an inevitable fact of life. In their view, the whole reorganization could easily have gone in a completely different direction had another CEO been named or had the one selected picked a different president for the chemical company, or had the president come from a different work group in the old organization. Similarly, there is the abiding feeling that another

significant change in top management could trigger yet another sweeping reorganization.

Fealty is the mortar of the corporate hierarchy, but the removal of one well-placed stone loosens the mortar throughout the pyramid and can cause things to fall apart. And no one is ever quite sure, until after the fact, just how the pyramid will be put back together.

SUCCESS & FAILURE

It is within this complicated and ambiguous authority structure, always subject to upheaval, that success and failure are meted out to those in the middle and upper middle managerial ranks. Managers rarely spoke to me of objective criteria for achieving success because once certain crucial points in one's career are passed, success and failure seem to have little to do with one's accomplishments. Rather, success is socially defined and distributed. Corporations do demand, of course, a basic competence and sometimes specified training and experience; hiring patterns usually ensure these. A weeding-out process takes place, however, among the lower ranks of managers during the first several years of their experience. By the time a manager reaches a certain numbered grade in the ordered hierarchy—in the chemical company this is Grade 13 out of 25, defining the top 8 1/2% of management in the company—managerial competence as such is taken for granted and assumed not to differ greatly from one manager to the next. The focus then switches to social factors, which are determined by authority and political alignments—the fealty structure—and by the ethos and style of the corporation.

Moving to the Top

In the chemical and textile companies as well as the other concerns I studied, five criteria seem to control a person's ability to rise in middle and upper middle management. In ascending order they are:

1. *Appearance and dress.* This criterion is so familiar that I shall mention it only briefly. Managers have to look the part, and it is sufficient to say that corporations are filled with attractive, well-groomed, and conventionally well-dressed men and women.

2. *Self-control.* Managers stress the need to exercise iron self-control and to have the ability to mask all emotion and intention behind bland, smiling, and agreeable public faces. They believe it is a fatal weakness to lose control of oneself, in any way, in a public forum. Similarly, to betray valuable secret knowledge (for instance, a confidential reorganization plan) or intentions through some relaxation of self-control—for example, an indiscreet comment or a lack of adroitness in turning aside a query—can not only jeopardize a manager's immediate position but can undermine others' trust in him.

3. *Perception as a team player.* While being a team player has many meanings, one of the most important is to appear to be interchangeable with other managers near one's level. Corporations discourage narrow specialization more strongly as one goes higher. They also discourage the expression of moral or political qualms. One might object, for example, to working with chemicals used in nuclear power, and most corporations today would honor that objection. The public statement of such objections, however, would end any realistic aspirations for higher posts because one's usefulness to the organization depends on versatility. As one manager in the chemical company commented: "Well, we'd go along with his request but we'd always wonder about the guy. And in the back of our minds, we'd be thinking that he'll soon object to working in the soda ash division because he doesn't like glass."

Another important meaning of team play is putting in long hours at the office. This requires a certain amount of sheer physical energy, even though a great deal of this time is spent not in actual work but in social rituals—like reading and discussing newspaper articles, taking coffee breaks, or having informal conversations. These rituals, readily observable in every corporation that I studied, forge the social bonds that make real managerial work—that is, group work of various sorts—possible. One must participate in the rituals to be considered effective in the work.

4. *Style.* Managers emphasize the importance of "being fast on your feet"; always being well organized; giving slick presentations complete with color slides; giving the appearance of knowledge even in its absence; and possessing a subtle, almost indefinable sophistication, marked especially by an urbane, witty, graceful, engaging, and friendly demeanor.

I want to pause for a moment to note that some observers have interpreted such conformity, team playing, affability, and urbanity as evidence of the decline of the individualism of the old Protestant Ethic.[3] To the extent that commentators take the public images that managers project at face value, I think they miss the main point. Managers up and down the corporate ladder adopt the public faces that they wear quite consciously; they are, in fact, the masks behind which the real struggles and moral issues of the corporation can be found.

Karl Mannheim's conception of self-rationalization or self-streamlining is useful in understanding what is one of the central social psychological processes of organizational life.[4] In a world where appearances—in the broadest sense—mean everything, the wise and ambitious person learns to cultivate assiduously the proper, prescribed modes of appearing. He dispassionately takes stock of himself, treating himself as an object. He analyzes his strengths and weaknesses, and decides what he needs to change in order to survive and flourish in his organization. And then he systematically undertakes a program to reconstruct his image. Self-rationalization curiously parallels the methodical subjection of self to God's will that the old Protestant Ethic counseled; the difference, of course, is that one acquires not moral virtues but a masterful ability to manipulate personae.

5. *Patron power.* To advance, a manager must have a patron, also called a mentor, a sponsor, a rabbi, or a godfather. Without a powerful patron in the higher echelons of management, one's prospects are poor in most corporations. The patron might be the manager's immediate boss or someone several levels higher in the chain of command. In either case the manager is still bound by the immediate, formal authority and fealty patterns of his position; the new—although more ambiguous—fealty relationships with the patron are added.

A patron provides his "client" with opportunities to get visibility, to showcase his abilities, to make connections with those of high status.

A patron cues his client to crucial political developments in the corporation, helps arrange lateral moves if the client's upward progress is thwarted by a particular job or a particular boss, applauds his presentations or suggestions at meetings, and promotes the client during an organizational shake-up. One must, of course, be lucky in one's patron. If the patron gets caught in a political crossfire, the arrows are likely to find his clients as well.

Social Definitions of Performance

Surely, one might argue, there must be more to success in the corporation than style, personality, team play, chameleonic adaptability, and fortunate connections. What about the bottom line—profits, performance?

Unquestionably, "hitting your numbers"—that is, meeting the profit commitments already discussed—is important, but only within the social context I have described. There are several rules here. First, no one in a line position—that is, with responsibility for profit and loss—who regularly "misses his numbers" will survive, let alone rise. Second, a person who always hits his numbers but who lacks some or all of the required social skills will not rise. Third, a person who sometimes misses his numbers but who has all the desirable social traits will rise.

Performance is thus always subject to a myriad of interpretations. Profits matter, but it is much more important in the long run to be perceived as "promotable" by belonging to central political networks. Patrons protect those already selected as rising stars from the negative judgments of others; and only the foolhardy point out even egregious errors of those in power or those destined for it.

Failure is also socially defined. The most damaging failure is, as one middle manager in the chemical company puts it, "when your boss or someone who has the power to determine your fate says: 'You failed.'" Such a godlike

pronouncement means, of course, out-and-out personal ruin; one must, at any cost, arrange matters to prevent such an occurrence.

As it happens, things rarely come to such a dramatic point even in the midst of an organizational crisis. The same judgment may be made but it is usually called "nonpromotability." The difference is that those who are publicly labeled as failures normally have no choice but to leave the organization; those adjudged nonpromotable can remain, provided they are willing to accept being shelved or, more colorfully, "mushroomed"—that is, kept in a dark place, fed manure, and left to do nothing but grow fat. Usually, seniors do not tell juniors they are nonpromotable (though the verdict may be common knowledge among senior peer groups). Rather, subordinates are expected to get the message after they have been repeatedly overlooked for promotions. In fact, middle managers interpret staying in the same job for more than two or three years as evidence of a negative judgment. This leads to a mobility panic at the middle levels which, in turn, has crucial consequences for pinpointing responsibility in the organization.

Capriciousness of Success

Finally, managers think that there is a tremendous amount of plain luck involved in advancement. It is striking how often managers who pride themselves on being hardheaded rationalists explain their own career patterns and those of others in terms of luck. Various uncertainties shape this perception. One is the sense of organizational contingency. One change at the top can create profound upheaval throughout the entire corporate structure, producing startling reversals of fortune, good or bad, depending on one's connections. Another is the uncertainty of the markets that often makes managerial planning simply elaborate guesswork, causing real economic outcome to depend on factors totally beyond organizational and personal control.

It is interesting to note in this context that a line manager's credibility suffers just as much from missing his numbers on the up side (that is, achieving profits higher than predicted) as from missing them on the down side. Both outcomes undercut the ideology of managerial planning and control, perhaps the only bulwark managers have against market irrationality.

Even managers in staff positions, often quite removed from the market, face uncertainty. Occupational safety specialists, for instance, know that the bad publicity from one serious accident in the workplace can jeopardize years of work and scores of safety awards. As one high-ranking executive in the chemical company says, "In the corporate world, 1,000 'Attaboys!' are wiped away by one 'Oh, shit!' "

Because of such uncertainties, managers in all the companies I studied speak continually of the great importance of being in the right place at the right time and of the catastrope of being in the wrong place at the wrong time. My interview materials are filled with stories of people who were transferred immediately before a big shake-up and, as a result, found themselves riding the crest of a wave to power; of people in a promising business area who were terminated because top management suddenly decided that the area no longer fit the corporate image desired; of others caught in an unpredictable and fatal political battle among their patrons; of a product manager whose plant accidentally produced an odd color batch of chemicals, who sold them as a premium version of the old product, and who is now thought to be a marketing genius.

The point is that managers have a sharply defined sense of the *capriciousness* of organizational life. Luck seems as good an explanation as any of why, after a certain point, some people succeed and others fail. The upshot is that many managers decide that they can do little to influence external events in their favor. One can, however, shamelessly streamline oneself, learn to wear all the right masks, and get to know all the right people. And then sit tight and wait for things to happen.

"GUT DECISIONS"

Authority and advancement patterns come together in the decision-making process. The core of the managerial mystique is decision-making prowess, and the real test of such prowess is what managers call "gut decisions," that is, important decisions involving big money, public exposure, or significant effect on the organization. At all but the highest levels of the chemical and textile companies, the rules for making gut decisions are, in the words of one upper middle manager: "(1) Avoid making any decisions if at all possible; and (2) if a decision has to be made, involve as many people as you can so that, if things go south, you're able to point in as many directions as possible."

Consider the case of a large coking plant of the chemical company. Coke making requires a gigantic battery to cook the coke slowly and evenly for long periods; the battery is the most important piece of capital equipment in a coking plant. In 1975, the plant's battery showed signs of weakening and certain managers at corporate headquarters had to decide whether to invest $6 million to restore the battery to top form. Clearly, because of the amount of money involved, this was a gut decision.

No decision was made. The CEO had sent the word out to defer all unnecessary capital expenditures to give the corporation cash reserves for other investments. So the managers allocated small amounts of money to patch the battery up until 1979, when it collapsed entirely. This brought the company into a breach of contract with a steel producer and into violation of various Environmental Protection Agency pollution regulations. The total bill, including lawsuits and now federally mandated repairs to the battery, exceeded $10 million. I have heard figures as high as $150 million, but because of "creative accounting," no one is sure of the exact amount.

This simple but very typical example gets to the heart of how decision making is intertwined with a company's authority structure and advancement patterns. As the chemical company managers see it, the decisions facing them in 1975 and 1979 were crucially different. Had they acted decisively in 1975—in hindsight, the only rational course—they would have salvaged the battery and saved their corporation millions of dollars in the long run.

In the short run, however, since even seemingly rational decisions are subject to widely varying interpretations, particularly decisions which run counter to a CEO's stated objectives, they would have been taking a serious risk in restoring the battery. What is more, their political networks might have unraveled, leaving them vulnerable to attack. They chose short-term safety over long-term gain because they felt they were judged, both by higher authority and by their peers, on their short-term performances. Managers feel that if they do not survive the short run, the long run hardly matters. Even correct decisions can shorten promising careers.

By contrast, in 1979 the decision was simple and posed little risk. The corporation had to meet its legal obligations; also it had to either repair the battery the way the EPA demanded or shut down the plant and lose several hundred million dollars. Since there were no real choices, everyone could agree on a course of action because everyone could appeal to inevitability. Diffusion of responsibility, in this case by procrastinating until total crisis, is intrinsic to organizational life because the real issue in most gut decisions is: Who is going to get blamed if things go wrong?

"Blame Time"

There is no more feared hour in the corporate world than "blame time." Blame is quite different from responsibility. There is a cartoon of Richard Nixon declaring: "I accept all of the responsibility, but none of the blame." To blame someone is to injure him verbally in public; in large organizations, where one's image is crucial, this poses the most serious sort of threat. For managers, blame—like failure—has nothing to do with the merits of a case; it is a matter of social definition. As a general rule, it is those who are or who become politically vulnerable or expendable who get "set up" and become blamable. The most feared situation of all is to end up inadvertently in the wrong place at the wrong time and get blamed.

Yet this is exactly what often happens in a structure that systematically diffuses responsibility. It is because managers fear blame time that they diffuse responsibility; however, such diffusion inevitably means that someone, somewhere is going to become a scapegoat when things go wrong. Big corporations encourage this process by their complete lack of any tracking system. Whoever is currently in charge of an area is responsible—that is, potentially blamable—for whatever goes wrong in the area, even if he has inherited others' mistakes. An example from the chemical company illustrates this process.

When the CEO of the large conglomerate took office, he wanted to rid his capital accounts of all serious financial drags. The corporation had been operating a storage depot for natural gas which it bought, stored, and then resold. Some years before the energy crisis, the company had entered into a long-term contract to supply gas to a buyer—call him Jones. At the time, this was a sound deal because it provided a steady market for a stably priced commodity.

When gas prices soared, the corporation was still bound to deliver gas to Jones at 20¢ per unit instead of the going market price of $2. The CEO ordered one of his subordinates to get rid of this albatross as expeditiously as possible. This was done by selling the operation to another party—call him Brown—with the agreement that Brown would continue to meet the contractual obligations to Jones. In return for Brown's assumption of these costly contracts, the corporation agreed to buy gas from Brown at grossly inflated prices to meet some of its own energy needs.

In effect, the CEO transferred the drag on his capital accounts to the company's operating expenses. This enabled him to project an aggressive, asset-reducing image to Wall Street. Several levels down the ladder, however, a new vice president for a particular business found himself saddled with exorbitant operating costs when, during a reorganization, those plants purchasing gas from Brown at inflated prices came under his purview. The high costs helped to undercut the vice president's division earnings and thus to erode his position in the hierarchy. The origin of the situation did not matter. All that counted was that the vice president's division was steadily losing big money. In the end, he resigned to "pursue new opportunities."

One might ask why top management does not institute codes or systems for tracking responsibility. This example provides the clue. An explicit system of accountability for subordinates would probably have to apply to top executives as well and would restrict their freedom. Bureaucracy expands the freedom of those on top by giving them the power to restrict the freedom of those beneath.

On the Fast Track

Managers see what happened to the vice president as completely capricious, but completely understandable. They take for granted the absence of any tracking of responsibility. If anything, they blame the vice president for not recognizing soon enough the dangers of the situation into which he was being drawn and for not preparing a defense—even perhaps finding a substitute scapegoat. At the same time, they realize that this sort of thing could easily happen to them. They see few defenses against being caught in the wrong place at the wrong time except constant wariness, the diffusion of responsibility, and perhaps being shrewd enough to declare the ineptitude of one's predecessor on first taking a job.

What about avoiding the consequences of their own errors? Here they enjoy more control. They can "outrun" their mistakes so that when blame time arrives, the burden will fall on someone else. The ideal situation, of course, is to be in a position to fire one's successors for one's own previous mistakes.

Some managers, in fact, argue that outrunning mistakes is the real key to managerial success. One way to do this is by manipulating the numbers. Both the chemical and the textile companies place a great premium on a division's or a subsidiary's return on assets. A good way for business managers to increase their ROA is to reduce their assets while maintaining sales. Usually they will do everything they can to hold down expenditures in order to decrease the asset base, particularly at the end of the fiscal year. The most common way of doing this is by deferring capital expenditures, from maintenance to innovative investments, as long as possible. Done for a short time, this is called "starving" a plant; done over a longer period, it is called "milking" a plant.

Some managers become very adept at milking businesses and showing a consistent record of high returns. They move from one job to another in a company, always upward, rarely staying more than two years in any post. They may leave behind them deteriorating plants and unsafe working conditions, but they know that if they move quickly enough, the blame will fall on others. In this sense, bureaucracies may be thought of as vast systems of organized irresponsibility.

FLEXIBLITY & DEXTERITY WITH SYMBOLS

The intense competition among managers takes place not only behind the agreeable public faces I have described but within an extraordinarily indirect and ambiguous linguistic framework. Except at blame time, managers do not publicly criticize or disagree with one another or with company policy. The sanction against such criticism or disagreement is so strong that it constitutes, in managers' view, a suppression of professional debate. The sanction seems to be rooted principally in their acute sense of organizational contingency; the person one criticizes or argues with today could be one's boss tomorrow.

This leads to the use of an elaborate linguistic code marked by emotional neutrality, especially in group settings. The code communicates the meaning one might wish to convey to other managers, but since it is devoid of any significant emotional sentiment, it can be reinterpreted should social relationships or attitudes change. Here, for example, are some typical phrases describing performance appraisals followed by their probable intended meanings:

Stock Phrase	Probable Intended Meaning
Exceptionally well qualified	Has commited no major blunders to date
Tactful in dealing with superiors	Knows when to keep his mouth shut
Quick thinking	Offers plausible excuses for errors
Meticulous attention to detail	A nitpicker
Slightly below average	Stupid
Unusually loyal	Wanted by no one else

For the most part, such neutered language is not used with the intent to deceive; rather, its purpose is to communicate certain meanings within specific contexts with the implicit understanding that, should the context change, a new, more appropriate meaning can be attached to the language already used. In effect, the corporation is a setting where people are not held to their word because it is generally understood that their word is always provisional.

The higher one gets in the corporate world, the more this seems to be the case; in fact, advancement beyond the upper middle level depends greatly on one's ability to manipulate a variety of symbols without becoming tied to or identified with any of them. For example, an amazing variety of organizational improvement programs marks practically every corporation. I am referring here to the myriad ideas generated by corporate staff, business consultants, academics, and a host of others to improve corporate structure; sharpen decision making; raise morale; create a more humanistic workplace; adopt Theory X, Theory Y, or, more recently, Theory Z of management; and so on. These programs become important when they are pushed from the top.

The watchword in the large conglomerate at the moment is productivity and, since this is a pet project of the CEO himself, it is said that no one goes into his presence without wearing a blue *Productivity!* button and talking about "quality circles" and "feedback sessions." The president of another company pushes a series of managerial seminars that endlessly repeats the basic functions of management: (1) planning, (2) organizing, (3) motivating, and (4) controlling. Aspiring young managers attend these sessions and with a seemingly dutiful eagerness learn to repeat the formulas under the watchful eyes of senior officials.

Privately, managers characterize such programs as the "CEO's incantations over the assembled multitude," as "elaborate rituals with no practical effect," or as "waving a magic wand to make things wonderful again." Publicly, of course, managers on the way up adopt the programs with great enthusiasm, participate in or run them very effectively, and then quietly drop them when the time is right.

Playing the Game

Such flexibility, as it is called, can be confusing even to those in the inner circles. I was told the following by a highly placed staff member whose work requires him to interact daily with the top figures of his company:

"I get faked out all the time and I'm part of the system. I come from a very different culture. Where I come from, if you give someone your *word*, no one ever questions it. It's the old hard-work-will-lead-to-success ideology. Small community, Protestant, agrarian, small business, merchant-type values. I'm disadvantaged in a system like this."

He goes on to characterize the system more fully and what it takes to succeed within it:

"It's the ability to play this system that determines whether you will rise. . . . And part of the adeptness [required] is determined by how much it bothers people. One thing you have to be able to do is to play the game, but you can't be disturbed by the game. What's the game? It's bringing troops home from Vietnam and declaring peace with honor. It's saying one thing and meaning another.

"It's characterizing the reality of a situation with *any* description that is necessary to make that situation more palatable to some group that matters. It means that you have to come up with a culturally accepted verbalization to explain why you are *not* doing what you are doing. . . . [Or] you say that we had to do what we did because it was inevitable; or because the guys at the [regulatory] agencies were dumb; [you] say we won when we really lost; [you] say we saved money when we squandered it; [you] say something's safe when it's potentially or actually dangerous. . . . Everyone knows that it's bullshit, but it's *accepted*. This is the game."

In addition, then, to the other characteristics that I have described, it seems that a prerequisite for big success in the corporation is a certain adeptness at inconsistency. This premium on inconsistency is particularly evident in the many areas of public controversy that face top-ranking managers. Two things come together to produce this situation. The first is managers' sense of beleaguerment from a wide array of adversaries who, it is thought, want to disrupt or impede management's attempts to further the economic interests of their companies. In every company that I studied, managers see themselves and their traditional prerogatives as being under siege, and they respond with a set of caricatures of their perceived principal adversaries.

For example, government regulators are brash, young, unkempt hippies in blue jeans who know nothing about the business for which they make rules; environmental activists—the bird and bunny people—are soft-headed idealists who want everybody to live in tents, burn candles, ride horses, and eat berries; workers' compensation lawyers are out-and-out crooks who prey on corporations to appropriate exorbitant fees from unwary clients; labor activists are radical troublemakers who want to disrupt harmonious industrial communities; and the news media consist of rabble-rousers who propagate sensational antibusiness stories to sell papers or advertising time on shows like *60 Minutes.*

Second, within this context of perceived harassment, managers must address a multiplicity of audiences, some of whom are considered adversaries. These audiences are the internal corporate hierarchy with its intricate and shifting power and status cliques, key regulators, key local and federal legislators, special publics that vary according to the issues, and the public at large, whose goodwill and favorable opinion are considered essential for a company's free operation.

Managerial adeptness at inconsistency becomes evident in the widely discrepant perspectives, reasons for action, and presentations of fact that explain, excuse, or justify corporate behavior to these diverse audiences.

Adeptness at Inconsistency

The cotton dust issue in the textile industry provides a fine illustration of what I mean. Prolonged exposure to cotton dust produces in many textile workers a chronic and eventually disabling pulmonary disease called byssinosis or, colloquially, brown lung. In the early 1970s, the Occupational Safety and Health Administration proposed a ruling to cut workers' exposure to cotton dust sharply by requiring textile companies to invest large amounts of money in cleaning up their plants. The industry fought the regulation fiercely but a final OSHA ruling was made in 1978 requiring full compliance by 1984.

The industry took the case to court. Despite an attempt by Reagan appointees in OSHA to have the case removed from judicial consideration and remanded to the agency they controlled for further cost/benefit analysis, the Supreme Court ruled in 1981 that the 1978 OSHA ruling was fully within the agency's mandate, namely, to protect workers' health and safety as the primary benefit exceeding all cost considerations.

During these proceedings, the textile company was engaged on a variety of fronts and was pursuing a number of actions. For instance, it intensively lobbied regulators and legislators and it prepared court materials for the industry's defense, arguing that the proposed standard would crush the industry and that the problem, if it existed, should be met by increasing workers' use of respirators.

The company also aimed a public relations barrage at special-interest groups as well as at the general public. It argued that there is probably no such thing as byssinosis; workers suffering from pulmonary problems are all heavy smokers and the real culprit is the government-subsidized tobacco industry. How can cotton cause brown lung when cotton is white? Further, if there is a problem, only some workers are afflicted, and therefore the solution is more careful screening of the work force to detect susceptible people and prevent them from ever reaching the workplace. Finally, the company claimed that if the regulation were imposed, most of the textile industry would move overseas where regulations are less harsh.[5]

In the meantime, the company was actually addressing the problem but in a characteristically indirect way. It invested $20 million in a few plants where it knew such an investment would make money; this investment automated the early stages of handling cotton, traditionally a very slow procedure, and greatly increased productivity. The investment had the side benefit of reducing cotton dust levels to the new standard in precisely those areas of the work process where the dust problem is greatest. Publicly, of course, the company claims that the money was spent entirely to eliminate dust, evidence of its corporate good citizenship. (Privately, executives admit that, without the productive return, they would not have spent the money and they have not done so in several other plants.)

Indeed, the productive return is the only rationale that carries weight within the corporate hierarchy. Executives also admit, somewhat ruefully and only when their office doors are closed, that OSHA's regulation on cotton dust has been the main factor in forcing technological innovation in a centuries-old and somewhat stagnant industry.

Such adeptness at inconsistency, without moral uneasiness, is essential for executive success. It means being able to say, as a very high-ranking official of the textile company said to me without batting an eye, that the industry has never caused the slightest problem in any worker's breathing capacity. It means, in the chemical company, propagating an elaborate hazard/benefit calculus for appraisal of dangerous chemicals while internally conceptualizing "hazards" as business risks. It means publicly extolling the carefulness of testing procedures on toxic chemicals while privately ridiculing animal tests as inapplicable to humans.

It means lobbying intensively in the present to shape government regulations to one's immediate advantage and, ten years later, in the event of a catastrophe, arguing that the company acted strictly in accordance with the standards of the time. It means claiming that the real problem of our society is its unwillingness to take risks, while in the thickets of one's bureaucracy avoiding risks at every turn; it means as well making every effort to socialize the risks of industrial activity while privatizing the benefits.

THE BUREAUCRATIC ETHIC

The bureaucratic ethic contrasts sharply with the original Protestant Ethic. The Protestant Ethic was the ideology of a self-confident and independent propertied social class. It was an ideology that extolled the virtues of accumulating wealth in a society organized around property and that accepted the stewardship responsibilities entailed by property. It was an ideology where a person's word was his bond and where the integrity of the handshake was

seen as crucial to the maintenance of good business relationships. Perhaps most important, it was connected to a predictable economy of salvation—that is, hard work will lead to success, which is a sign of one's election by God—a notion also containing its own theodicy to explain the misery of those who do not make it in this world.

Bureaucracy, however, breaks apart substance from appearances, action from responsibility, and language from meaning. Most important, it breaks apart the older connection between the meaning of work and salvation. In the bureaucratic world, one's success, one's sign of election, no longer depends on one's own efforts and on an inscrutable God but on the capriciousness of one's superiors and the market; and one achieves economic salvation to the extent that one pleases and submits to one's employer and meets the exigencies of an impersonal market.

In this way, because moral choices are inextricably tied to personal fates, bureaucracy erodes internal and even external standards of morality, not only in matters of individual success and failure but also in all the issues that managers face in their daily work. Bureaucracy makes its own internal rules and social context the principal moral gauges for action. Men and women in bureaucracies turn to each other for moral cues for behavior and come to fashion specific situational moralities for specific significant people in their worlds.

As it happens, the guidance they receive from each other is profoundly ambiguous because what matters in the bureaucratic world is not what a person is but how closely his many personae mesh with the organizational ideal; not his willingness to stand by his actions but his agility in avoiding blame; not what he believes or says but how well he has mastered the ideologies that serve his corporation; not what he stands for but whom he stands with in the labyrinths of his organization.

In short, bureaucracy structures for managers an intricate series of moral mazes. Even the inviting paths out of the puzzle often turn out to be invitations to jeopardy.

NOTES

I presented an earlier version of this paper in the Faculty Lecture Series at Williams College on March 18, 1982. The intensive field work done during 1980 and 1981 was made possible by a Fellowship for Independent Research from the National Endowment for the Humanities and by a Junior Faculty Leave and small research grant from Williams College.

1. There is a long sociological tradition of work on managers and I am, of course, indebted to that literature. I am particularly indebted to the work, both joint and separate, of Joseph Bensman and Arthur J. Vidich, two of the keenest observers of the new middle class. See especially their *The New American Society: The Revolution of the Middle Class* (Chicago: Quadrangle Books, 1971).

2. See Max Weber, *The Protestant Ethic and the Spirit of Capitalism*, translated by Talcott Parsons (New York: Charles Scribner's Sons, 1958), p. 172.

3. See William H. Whyte, *The Organization Man* (New York: Simon & Schuster, 1956), and David Riesman, in collaboration with Reuel Denney and Nathan Glazer, *The Lonely Crowd: A Study of the Changing American Character* (New Haven: Yale University Press, 1950).

4. Karl Mannheim, *Man and Society in an Age of Reconstruction* [London: Paul (Kegan), Trench, Trubner Ltd. 1940), p. 55.

5. On February 9, 1982, the Occupational Safety and Health Administration issued a notice that it was once again reviewing its 1978 standard on cotton dust for "cost-effectiveness." See *Federal Register*, vol. 47, p. 5906. As of this writing (May 1983), this review has still not been officially completed.

Essay

Not a Fool, Not a Saint

Thomas Teal

Malden Mills owner Aaron Feuerstein was both ridiculed and canonized when he kept his 1,000 employees on the payroll after a fire burned down his factory last Christmas. But now he's proving that treating workers well is just plain good business.

At a European trade show in Brussels during the first week of September, Malden Mills of Lawrence. Massachusetts, introduced a broad new line of high-end upholstery fabrics. Buyers snapped up the sleek material, derived from the company's hugely successful line of Polartec and Polarfleece apparel knits. A victory, certainly. And one more step in an uphill comeback by a factory that suffered one of the biggest industrial fires in New England history less than a year ago, a factory whose owner achieved heroic stature by keeping more than 1,000 jobless employees at full pay for several months after the blaze.

Yet Aaron Feuerstein, owner, president, and CEO of Malden Mills, has good reason to feel unappreciated. It's true that his work force adores him, that almost every newspaper, TV station, and business magazine in the U.S. has sung his praises, that Bill Clinton invited him to Washington for the State of the Union address, and that columnists, unions, and religious leaders all across the country have declared him a saint. But much of this celebrity is based on the misleading premise that this 70-year-old acted selflessly, against his own best interests, which is another way of saying that he acted the way a saint might act: irrationally.

In fact, it seems pretty clear that some people call Feuerstein a saint because they don't quite have the courage to call him a fool. They don't think he should be rebuilding his mill, at least not in Lawrence. They think he should have pocketed the insurance proceeds, closed the business, and walked away. Or else they think he should have grabbed the chance to move the company to some state or country with lower labor costs.

Some commentators have even accused him of risking the very survival of his business with a lot of grandstanding magnanimity that served no purpose but self-advertisement. There's a suggestion that real businessmen are tougher than Feuerstein, that responsible owners never pay any employee a dime more than they have to, and that no factory owner could possibly have done what Feuerstein has done unless he'd been touched by God or is just touched, period. These people, for instance, argue that Feuerstein certainly could have skipped the grand gesture of paying out some $15 million in wages and benefits to already overpaid workers when they no longer had a place to work. One business school professor has suggested pointedly that not everyone should look to him as a model.

Most of this carping is nonsense. But in a way, so is much of the praise. Why in the world should it be a sign of divinely inspired nuttiness to treat a work force as if it was an asset, to cultivate the loyalty of employees who hold the key to recovery and success, to take risks for the sake of a large future income stream, even to seek positive publicity? These are the things Aaron Feuerstein has done, and most people stand in amazement as if they were witnessing a miracle or a traffic accident.

I was one of them until I discovered that Feuerstein is at heart a hard-nosed businessman. He has some minor eccentricities—a weakness for little bursts of Shakespeare, a tendency to wander off into far corners of the room as he thinks and talks—and his Old Testament intensity and biblical pronouncements can be slightly intimidating, despite his

warmth. The two hours I spent with him, however, convinced me that he is as tough-minded as he is righteous, a man entirely up to the job of running a factory for profit.

Take downsizing. Would anyone have guessed that Feuerstein was a devotee? At one point, as he was warming to an attack on the unconscionable Al Dunlap (the man who dismantled Scott Paper and fired a third of its work force). I interrupted to suggest that maybe Scott Paper was overstaffed and Feuerstein surprised me: "If one-third of the people in that company were wastefully employed, then Dunlap did the right thing." And then the new patron saint of working Americans surprised me some more. "Legitimate downsizing as the result of technological advances or as a result of good industrial engineering? Absolutely. I'm in favor of it. And we do it here all day long. . . . We try to do it in such a way as to minimize human suffering, but the downsizing must be done." Under the benevolent, angular exterior lurks a businessman—a businessman who understands labor. The trick, he told me, is to keep growing fast enough to give new jobs to the people technology displaces, to weed out unnecessary jobs "without crushing the spirit of the work force." If all you're after is cutting costs, if you "just have a scheme to cut people—that sort of thing is resented by labor, and you're never forgiven." Feuerstein has a union shop, has long invested heavily in technology that eliminates jobs, and has never had a strike—not exactly the hallmarks of a fool.

Or take the insurance question. Feuerstein could certainly have closed the factory, sold the business, pocketed the proceeds, and spent the rest of his days in a hammock. But men in their 70s who still come to work every day for the sheer exhilaration of the job don't turn to hammocks in a crisis. His decision to rebuild seems to have been spontaneous and immediate, made more or less by the light of the flames and without much thought to the insurance proceeds. And still it was a rational decision Factories are insured for their replacement cost and if you don't replace them you may have to settle for the depreciated value of the lost building and machinery, in this case a lot of modern machinery and several antediluvian buildings. You can solve this equation without the higher math. An insurance payoff is likely to be much larger when it's taken as a contribution toward a state-of-the-art manufacturing facility, partly because it has the potential to produce income for your family for two or three generations to come. Last year's pre-fire, pretax profit was $20 million on sales of $400 million. Twenty million times two or three generations comes to an awful lot of money.

Or take self-advertisement. Feuerstein has not been shy with the media. Malden Mills has been featured everywhere from *People* to *Dateline* to the Land's End catalogue, and it's all been free. What's more, if the insurance settlement should wind up in court—not wildly improbable—will it hurt Feuerstein's chances of winning that half the people in the country worship the ground he walks on? Do insurance companies care about their reputations? You bet.

As for the idea that he might relocate the company somewhere with lower wages. Feuerstein moved the company to Lawrence (from Malden, just outside Boston) in 1956, at a time when New England textile mills thought local labor too expensive and were streaming south like carpetbaggers. A great many of those companies failed anyway, despite the lower wages they spent so much money to find, and Feuerstein is sure he knows why: They gave too much attention to costs and not enough to quality. He responds with contempt to suggestions that Malden Mills should move offshore (Labor in the South is no longer such a bargain.)

"Why would I go to Thailand to bring the cost lower when I might run the risk of losing the advantage I've got, which is superior

quality?" In any case, he goes on, lower wages are a temporary advantage. Quality lasts. At least it can last if you focus hard on expertise and the freedom to innovate. But to do that, you have to focus hard on employees. When Feuerstein came to Lawrence, he wasn't looking for cheap labor but for skilled labor—capable, experienced textile designers, engineers, and workers who could give him the edge he needed to compete more effectively.

It's here he has shown his real genius. Any idiot with a strong enough stomach can make quick money, sometimes a lot of it, by slashing costs and milking customers, employees, or a company's reputation. But clearly that's not the way to make a lot of money for a long time. The way to do that is to create so much value that your customers wouldn't dream of looking for another supplier. Indeed, the idea is to build a value creation system of superior products, service, teamwork, productivity, and cooperation with the buyer. Reduced to its essence, that means superior technology and superior employees. Reduced still further, as Aaron Feuerstein can tell you, it means superior employees. The correlation between loyal customers and loyal employees is no coincidence.

For Malden Mills, the first test and the breakthrough came in the early 1980s with the total collapse of the market for what was then a company mainstay—artificial furs. It was the R&D and production employees who saved the company over the next few years, using their superior expertise in synthetic fibers, napping, and finishing to create a series of lightweight, thermal, resilient, woollike fabrics under the brand names Polarfleece and Polartec. They look good, feel good, wick well, don't pill, and hold up to repeated washing. Moreover, they're all engineered to order. The retailer wants, say, a fabric for cyclists that's windproof and light but also soft, absorbent, and quick-drying. Malden's ability to satisfy such orders has made Polartec a favorite of upscale retailers like

Land's End, L. L. Bean, Patagonia, the North Face, Eddie Bauer, and a dozen more.

Best of all, these customers are loyal. Customer retention at Malden Mills runs roughly 95%, which is world class. Employee retention runs above 95%, which is prodigious but can hardly come as a surprise to anyone familiar with Feuerstein's approach to personnel. As for productivity, from 1982 to 1995, revenues in constant dollars more than tripled while the work force barely doubled. Compare that with an overall productivity increase for the U.S. of a little better than 1% per year. Thanks to its employees, Malden Mills has risen from at least one five-alarm crisis in the past. No wonder Aaron Feuerstein loves those employees enough to risk $15 million to keep them available and motivated and to help him rise from the literal ashes of last year's catastrophe. This isn't the work of a saint or a fool, it's the considered and historically successful policy of a genial manufacturing genius who might serve as a model for every man and woman in business.

Essay

Visionary's Dream Led To Risky Business

Peter Behr
April Witt

For Vince Kaminski, the in-house risk-management genius, the fall of Enron Corp. began one day in June 1999. His boss told him that Enron president Jeffrey K. Skilling had an urgent task for Kaminski's team of financial analysis.

A few minutes later, Skilling surprised Kaminski by marching into his office to explain. Enron's investment in a risky Internet start-up called Rhythms NetConnections had jumped $300 million in value. Because of a securities restriction, Enton could not sell the stock immediately. But the company could and did count the paper gain as profit. Now Skilling had a way to hold on to that windfall if the tech boom collapsed and the stock dropped.

Much later, Kaminski would come to see Skilling's command as a turning point, a moment in which the course of modern American business was fundamentally altered. At the time Kaminski found Skilling's idea merely incoherent, the task patently absurd.

When Kaminski took the idea to his team—world-class mathematicians who used arcane statistical models to analyze risk—the room exploded in laughter.

The plan was to create a private partnership in the Cayman Islands that would protect—or hedge—the Rhythms investment, locking in the gain. Ordinarily, Wall Street firms would provide such insurance, for a fee. But Rhythms was such a risky stock that no company would have touched the deal for a reasonable price. And Enron needed Rhythms: The gain would amount to 30 percent of its profit for the year.

The whole thing was really just an accounting trick. The arrangement would pay Enron to cover any losses if the tech stock dropped. But Skilling proposed to bankroll the partnership with Enron stock. In essence, Enron was insuring itself. The risk was huge, Kaminski immediately realized.

If the stocks of Enron and the tech company fell precipitously at the same time, the hedge would fail and Enron would be left with heavy losses.

The deal was "so stupid that only Andrew Fastow could have come up with it," Kaminski would later say.

In fact, Fastow, Enron's chief financial officer, had come up with the maneuver, with Skilling and others. In an obvious conflict of interest, Fastow would run the partnership, sign up banks and others as investors, and invest in it himself. He stood to make millions quickly, in fees and profits, even if Enron lost money on the deal. He would call it LJM, after his wife and two children.

Stupid or not, Enron did it and kept doing more like it, making riskier and riskier bets. Enron's top executives, who fancied themselves the best of the brightest, the most sophisticated connoisseurs of business risk, finally took on more than they could handle.

Fastow's plan and Skilling's directive would sow seeds of destruction for the nation's largest energy-trading company, setting in motion one of the greatest business scandals in U.S. history.

On Oct. 16, 2001, Enron was forced to disclose $1 billion in losses, more than half from LJM deals gone bad. Thus began a chain of events that would drive Enron's stock price into the dirt and force the company into bankruptcy proceedings, wiping out thousands of jobs and tens of billions of dollars in savings.

Enron was the first of the recent business scandals that have devastated investor faith, contributed to a multitrillion-dollar market downturn and made corporate reform a political imperative.

The Washington Post examined Enron's epic collapse, focusing on the final five months, drawing on dozens of interviews with former Enron executives and employees and thousands of pages of Enron documents, records from an internal investigation, and sworn testimony from court cases and congressional hearings.

The company's story provides a powerful parable. Policymakers, investors, and executives must grapple with its lessons today; business students and historians will study them for decades.

Enron was a fundamentally self-destructive institution, a house of cards where human error and a culture of ambition, secrecy, and greed made collapse inevitable.

While Skilling has previously attributed Enron's demise to innocent misfortune—a "classic run on the bank"—the Houston firm was a victim of its own making, a virtual company with vastly overstated profits.

Skilling and Enron founder and chairman Kenneth L. Lay said they believe Enron remained profitable until its sudden collapse late year. Skilling and Fastow declined to be interviewed for this article. Skilling has testified that he was unaware of any improper accounting or falsified financial statements. A spokeswoman for Lay said in a statement yesterday that Lay believes Enron's profits "were not inflated in any way."

Lay, who had turned day-to-day control over to Skilling in the late 1990s, was obliged as chairman of a company with 25,000 employees in 30 countries to "rely on talented people whose trustworthiness he had no reason to doubt," according to his spokeswoman, Kelly Kimberly.

Skilling, Lay's personally chosen successor as chief executive, was directly involved in the overstatement of profit, according to interviews and investigators' reports. He sponsored and approved accounting and tax gimmicks with private partnerships and funds that contributed billions in improper or questionable earnings. Those deals helped elevate Enron's stock price during the market's boom in the 1990s. Enron executives and directors sold $1 billion worth of shares in the three years before the company collapsed.

Enron hailed 2000 as a breakout year with $101 billion in revenue, more than double that of the year before, putting it at No. 7 on the list of largest U.S. corporations. Skilling, Lay and 17 other officers and directors signed the 2000 financial statements, declaring them to be a true picture on which investors could rely.

The numbers were shams and the portrait was a fake, the record shows.

In 2001, Enron spent money faster than it was coming in. Most of its huge revenue gains came from power sales on its highly touted Internet energy-trading site. But revenue was padded in various ways. Traders swapped power with each other, internal memos state. Billions in loans were counted as cash from operations. And Enron's accounting inflated revenue from long-term contracts, former executives say.

Enron's profits were a mirage.

The company claimed that it earned $979 million in 2000. But $630 million of that came from improper accounting involving LJM and other partnerships, investigators for the company's board concluded. Another $296 million in "profit" came from hidden tax-cutting transactions, not normal business operations.

Take away the accounting tricks and the company was making little profit, if any.

Enron used the bewildering complexity of its finances to hide its true nature. Some people had nagging suspicious. But like the cowed townspeople in the children's story, few questioned the emperor's new clothes.

"It's so complicated everybody is afraid to raise their hands and say, 'I don't understand it,'" Louis B. Gagliardi, an analyst with John S. Herold Inc. in Norwalk, Conn., said last year.

Enron's arc toward scandal and bankruptcy exposed the failure of watchdogs at every level. Its board defaulted on its oversight duties. Outside accountants ceded their independence and violated their profession's rules. Outside

lawyers approved misleading deals and failed to vigorously pursue a crucial allegation of accounting misdeeds. Wall Street analysts led a cheering section while their firms collected enormous banking fees from the company. Regulators were overwhelmed by Enron's complexity. The media were blinded by its image of success.

Nobody looked inside the company and saw what wasn't there.

After Skilling gave Kaminski the assignment involving the LJM partnership in June 1999, the researcher and a member of his team worked through the weekend to check and recheck their analysis. On Monday morning, Kaminski was confident that it was a bad, even dangerous, deal for Enron. He told his immediate boss, Chief Risk Officer Richard Buy, that the Rhythms NetConnections–LJM partnerships venture should not go forward.

Kaminski described the deal as "heads the partnership wins, tails Enron loses."

Enron could not make the deal without the approval of its outside accounting firm, Arthur Andersen LLP. But accountants there had the same reaction as Kaminski. Andersen partner Benjamin Neuhausen e-mailed his colleague David B. Duncan, head of Andersen's Enron audit team, to complain about Fastow's proposed role in LJM.

"Setting aside the accounting, idea of a venture entity managed by CFO is terrible from a business point of view. Conflicts galore. Why would any director in his or her right mind ever approve such a scheme?"

Duncan responded: "I really couldn't agree more."

But Duncan did not try to oppose the deal. In his e-mail to Neuhausen, Duncan wrote that Andersen would go along if Lay and Enron's 18-member board of directors approved the arrangement.

In a one-hour teleconference on June 28, 1999, that included five other items of business, the board approved the LJM proposal presented by Lay, Skilling and Fastow. It also gave Fastow permission to work simultaneously for LJM and Enron, despite the conflict of interest.

"I couldn't stop it," Buy told Kaminski. Kaminski wondered how hard he had tried.

Paraphrasing Winston Churchill's rebuke of Neville Chamberlain's appeasement of Hitler, Kaminski told a colleague that Buy had chosen shame over confrontation. The confrontation would come, Kaminski predicted.

Several days later, Kaminski was sitting in his office when the phone rang, according to one executive's account. It was Skilling, saying Kaminski was being transferred out of Buy's risk-management division because he was acting like a cop, trying to kill deals. People did not like it.

To understand Enron's fate, it helps to start with its beginnings.

In June 1984, when Ken Lay became chairman and chief operating officer of Enron's precursor, Houston Natural Gas, the firm's finances were a lot simpler. It was just a pipeline company. Lay quickly doubled its size by acquiring a Florida pipeline company.

But Lay's dreams were bigger still. Pipelines were profitable, and Lay wanted to create the largest pipeline system in the nation. The next year, Lay's firm merged with InterNorth Inc. Together, they owned about 40,000 miles of pipeline.

The company changed its name to Enron in 1986. It was just the beginning. Lay, its patriarchal visionary, was determined to create one of the biggest, most successful companies in the world.

With an ideological fervor for deregulation and a knack for winning influential friends, Lay campaigned for changes in federal energy rules that would allow natural gas to be sold on open markets like wheat or pork bellies. In doing so, he helped create an industry and made Enron a corporate political powerhouse.

In 1990, Lay hired the 36-year-old Skilling, a brilliant Harvard MBA who was a longtime Enron consultant, to pioneer the company's energy-trading operations. Skilling created the "gas bank," making Enron the first company to buy large volumes of gas from producers and resell it to industrial customers on long-term contracts. That stabilized the U.S. gas market, expanded gas production nationwide and fueled the phenomenal growth that Enron reported during the decade.

The synthesis of Lay and Skilling proved potent, putting Enron at a confluence of major political and financial currents. The deregulation of energy markets, spurred by the Reagan administration, created great opportunities. And Skilling's foray into energy trading came just as financial institutions were unleashing exotic investment tools—a flow of money looking for opportunities.

A guru-like pitchman with a disdain for traditional business practices. Skilling was perfectly placed to ride the new wave. He gave the impression that pipelines were hopelessly boring. As he rose at Enron, he retooled the company in his own image: smart and arrogant, confident and flashy. He assembled a fast-moving band of self-described pioneers who embraced risky new ideas as the route to profits.

"We like risk because you make money by taking risks." Skilling said in an interview with University of Virginia business school professors two years ago. "The key is to take on risk that you manage better than your competitors."

Skilling was proud of pushing boundaries. He persuaded federal regulators to let Enron use "mark-to-market" accounting, an approved mechanism used by brokerages for securities trading. Skilling applied it throughout Enron's operations, from the Rhythms Net-Connections transaction to its commodities trading. It allowed Enron to calculate revenue from long-term contracts and count much of it as immediate profit, although the money would not come in for years, if ever. For example, the company booked a $65 million profit in 1999 based on its projection of natural-gas sales from a South American pipeline project. The pipeline had yet to be built.

In a bold stroke, Enron moved its gas and electricity trading on-line. Going far beyond energy, Skilling's young MBAs created unheard-of commodities markets—even offering weather derivatives, contracts that gave businesses financial protection against the costs of heat waves or blizzards.

"We made the gas market in the United States what it is today," said Robert Hermann, Enron's former chief tax counsel. "We decided we could do the same thing with electricity, and we were well on our way to doing it. Then we thought we could do it with anything. We had people who thought they could sell hairballs if they could find the buyers."

Wall Street and the business press were dazzled. For six years running, *Fortune* magazine ranked Enron as the most innovative company in the nation. At an exclusive conference of intellectuals and political leaders at Davos, Switzerland, in 2000, Lay declared Enron the prototype of the "new economy" corporation. Lay described Enron executives as guerrillas fashioning bullets out of ideas.

"Somewhere out there is a bullet with your company's name on it, a competitor . . . that will render your strategy obsolete," Lay said. "You've got to shoot first."

As the nation's tech sector boomed in the late 1990s, Skilling said the transformed energy firm, with its on-line trading arm, deserved the sky-high stock price of a dot-com company. The market bought it. From 1998 to 2000, Enron's stock tripled in value.

"We're the world's coolest company," Skilling told the University of Virginia professors.

Lay even considered the idea of draping a giant pair of sunglasses around Enron's headquarters tower in Houston, Skilling joked.

"It was an intoxicating atmosphere," said Jeff S. Blumenthal, an Enron tax lawyer. "If you loved business and loved being challenged and working with unique, novel situations . . . it was the most wonderful place."

It wasn't just the ideas. The place was giddy with money. Enron paid employees $750 million in cash bonuses in 2000, an amount approaching the company's reported profit that year.

The princes of Enron were its dealmakers or "developers," in-house entrepreneurs who launched businesses and structured deals so they could immediately claim huge profits for the company—and bonuses for themselves—while saving the problems for later.

From the company's earliest days, those princes flew around the world, overpaying for power plants in India, Poland and Spain, a water plant in Britain, a pipeline in Brazil, and thousands of miles of Internet cable. Enron accumulated 50 energy plants in 15 countries. Virtually none of them were profitable.

Lou L. Pai, a Skilling favorite, set up an Enron division that sold electricity to businesses. Pai received numerous stock options as compensation. He sold $270 million worth of Enron stock in the 16 months before he left the company last year.

"The culture at Enron is all about 'me first, I want to get paid,' " Hermann said "I used to tell people if they don't know why people are acting a certain way, go look up their compensation deal and then you'll know. There were always people wanting to do deals that didn't make sense in order to get a bonus."

Porsches replaced pickup trucks in the company parking lot as even secretaries became paper millionaires. There were mansions in Houston's posh River Oaks neighborhood, vacation homes in Aspen. Everybody went along for the company's wild ride.

In June 1999, when Kaminski opposed the Rhythms deal that Skilling and Fastow were promoting, his boss's wry response was telling.

"Next time Fastow is going to run a racket, I want to be part of it," Kaminski recalled his boss, Buy, saying.

To much of the world, Jeff Skilling looked like a genius. Between January and May 2000, the stock price had risen nearly 80 percent, to $77 a share. Enron insiders—Lay and Skilling among them—had cashed out more than $475 million worth of stock. Everybody was getting rich.

But Enron had created only an illusion of ever-expanding revenue and profits.

The company still needed increasing amounts of cash for its profligate new ventures and expanding energy-trading operations. Its grab bag of pipelines and plants could not produce enough money to drive the growth that Lay and Skilling demanded.

As Fastow explained in a *CFO* magazine article, Enron could not keep borrowing in traditional ways without scaring lenders away and damaging its credit rating. Enron's investment-grade credit was just high enough to ensure that it could get the cash it needed to settle its energy contracts when they came due.

So Enron turned itself into a factory for financial deals that would pump up profit, protect its credit rating, and drive up its stock price.

In the 1990s, banks and law firms began aggressively peddling "structured finance," complex deals in which companies set up separate affiliates or partnerships to help generate tax deductions or move assets and debts off the books. With Skilling's ascension to the presidency in 1997. Enron became increasingly dependent upon such deals to hit its financial targets.

"Skilling's participation in the LJMs and the other vehicles was probably the most important part of his job," said John Ballentine, a former president of an Enron pipeline subsidiary and a corporate vice president.

The company teamed up with the brightest minds in banking, accounting and law to create scores of secretive deals with exotic code names such as Braveheart, Backbone, Rawhide, Raptor, and Yosemite.

Enron used the deals for various purposes. The LJM partnerships hedged risky stock investments such as Rhythms. An affiliate named Whitewing took billions of dollars of debt off the company's books. In some cases, Enron "sold" money-losing foreign assets to the partnerships, added the proceeds to its quarterly financial statement and then bought the assets back in the next reporting period.

To entice banks and others to invest in the deals. Enron privately pledged millions of shares of its stock to guarantee against any losses. It was a risky gambit, exposing the company to losses if the price of its shares dropped and it could not cover its obligations.

It worked well for the short term, when Enron needed a quick boost for its quarterly earnings. But as Enron's trading expanded, its other businesses underperformed. Its debt and cash needs kept growing, so the company needed to make more and bigger "structured transactions" to keep the game going—pledging increasing amounts of stock. Enron's strategy began to resemble what members of Congress would later call a high-tech Ponzi scheme.

In May 2000, Alberto Gude, an Enron vice president, went to see Lay just before Gude retired. He had known Lay since 1977 and wanted to warn him about the "selfishness" and "arrogance" of the team that had transformed the company. Lay said through his spokeswoman that he does not recall this specific conversation.

"I really believe you are in trouble," Gude recalled telling Lay. "Jeff Skilling and his team are not the same kind of people we are used to managing Enron."

According to Gude, Lay responded, "They are okay guys."

One of Skilling's "okay guys" was Andrew S. Fastow, then 38, Enron's chief financial officer since 1998. Skilling hired him from a Chicago bank where he specialized in numbingly complex deals to raise money for clients.

As the top finance man at Enron, Fastow was responsible for Enron's overall financial stability.

He was known as an intimidating and single-minded self-promoter. He liked to say that capitalism was about survival of the fittest. He flogged his team so furiously to close deals that they often made business calls in the middle of the night. Executives who attended meetings with Fastow recall him freely putting down older colleagues or anybody he perceived as weak.

As unpopular as he was, Fastow was untouchable. Skilling was positively enamored of him. "Fastow was Skilling's favorite," Enron lawyer Jordan Mintz said later.

But even Skilling later conceded to investigators that Fastow could be a "prickly guy that would tell you everything wrong about others and everything right about himself."

Fastow was also something of a mystery. He rarely attended the quarterly briefings Enron staged for financial analysts, making him the butt of a Wall Street wisecrack: "Name Enron's CFO."

He spent much of his time as managing partner of the LJM partnerships. Although he later said he spent only three hours a week on the partnerships, colleagues complained that he was constantly working on his own deals. He jetted to New York, California, Florida and the Caribbean, hunting investors.

For Enron, Fastow's effort was time well spent. LJM1 had been a huge success.

The Rhythms stock was worth nearly $60 a share when the second quarter of 1999 ended, giving Enron a paper profit of about $300 million. That windfall exceeded Enron's net income for the quarter. By the end of the year, Rhythms stock had dropped to about $30 a share—but thanks to the hedge with LJM1, Enron avoided reporting any losses on the decline.

It was easy to see the deal as an act of financial wizardry.

So Skilling supported Fastow's drive to create a much bigger private equity fund, LJM2, capitalized with more than $300 million from outside investors—more than 20 times the size of LJM1. This time, the board required Fastow's colleague, Chief Accounting Officer Richard A. Causey, to monitor what Fastow was doing.

But nobody reined in Fastow.

In raising money for LJM2, he was both ruthless and charming, colleagues said.

Fastow strong-armed Enron's major Wall Street banking partners, threatening to take away Enron's banking business if they did not put money into his fund, former Enron treasurer Jeffrey McMahon said later.

The banks put up a "huge outcry," but many ultimately invested, including J.P. Morgan Chase & Co., Citigroup Inc., and Merrill Lynch & Co.

"The banks complained they were being told that investing in LJM2 was a quid pro quo for future Enron business," McMahon later told investigators.

Fastow used the soft touch with people like Joe Marsh. A wealthy Floridian, Marsh had been approached in 2000 by his Merrill Lynch stock adviser about investing $1 million in LJM2 Fastow's partnership would do deals with Enron, promising gaudy annual returns of 20 percent or more.

At first, Marsh was skeptical, "It sure sounded like a conflict of interest," he said. So his broker arranged for Marsh to do a conference call with other investors and Fastow.

Fastow was knowledgeable, at ease, and persuasive, Marsh said. "He said he was putting in $5 million of his own. His wife was mad at him for doing it, but he really believed in it," Marsh said. Enron's lawyers and accountants, the board, Merrill Lynch, everyone had approved it. "It got flying colors." Marsh was convinced. He put in $1.6 million.

Fastow had married into a wealthy Houston family. He wanted wealth of his own, colleagues said.

At Enron, Fastow made about $2.4 million in salary, bonus and incentives. But he had long chafed at the huge bonuses that division chiefs were getting from big power plant and pipeline deals. He wanted a similarly lucrative payday for himself. He got one from LJM1 in the spring of 2000, when Enron and the partnership ended the Rhythms transaction.

Three London bankers who have been accused in criminal fraud complaints of joining with Fastow to cheat their bank in the Rhythms deal had a pithy take on what motivated him. "We should be able to appeal to his greed," one of the bankers e-mailed another in February 2000.

Fastow's dealings with the British bankers were not revealed until much later. Fastow's secret profit from LJM1 and the Rhythms deal was staggering a $1 million investment turned into a $22 million profit in less than a year.

For a while, LJM2 looked like a great deal for everyone.

From 2000 on, the LJM deals provided most of Enron's profits, though they remained invisible to outside investors.

At the end of each financial quarter, whenever Enron needed to sell a pipeline or Internet cable, or execute a helpful commodities trade, it would turn to Fastow for almost instant results.

Even inside Enron, the exact details were a closely held secret. People gossiped that Fastow was getting rich, but nobody asked how rich.

Enron's board, which twice waived the company's code of ethics to allow Fastow's dual roles, could have asked, but it did not until too late. Board members later said they were misled by Enron executives. The board set up an elaborate system for monitoring Fastow, with three committees assigned to the task. But board members put little energy into it, repeatedly failing to ask pointed questions, a

Senate subcommittee later concluded. As Enron's chief financial officer, Fastow was supposed to be the company's financial watchdog, even in the LJM transactions. But Fastow personally profited if LJM bested Enron in negotiations. Some Enron colleagues say Fastow bullied subordinates to win an advantage for LJM. He pressured one, William Brown, to close a deal on terms unfair to Enron, Brown later told investigators.

As more colleagues came to believe that Fastow was enriching himself and a few close to him, the deals became a source of envy and suspicion.

In early 2000, McMahon complained to Skilling about Fastow's conflict of interest, McMahon later told investigators. Soon afterward Fastow confronted McMahon.

Fastow told McMahon that he "should have known everything said to Skilling would get back to him," McMahon recalled.

A week later, Skilling encouraged McMahon to take a job in another part of the company. Skilling replaced him with Ben F. Glisan, one of Fastow's closest aides.

The message flashed throughout Enron: Don't mess with Fastow.

When Mintz, a lawyer who worked under Fastow, later complained to Buy about the conflict, Mintz said Buy warned him not to "stick his neck out."

Enron had publicly identified Fastow as LJM's general manager in its proxy statements in 2000 and 2001. But in its quarterly and annual financial statements field with the Securities and Exchange Commission, Enron had not named him. It merely referred in footnotes to "a senior officer of Enron," a vague description that troubled some Enron executives and left some investors in the dark.

But the word was getting out.

By spring 2001, Fastow's identify—and his LJM role—attracted attention from a few Wall Street analysts, financial speculators, and journalists.

In May, a column on TheStreet.com cited a very critical analysis of Enron's finances by a private research firm, Off Wall Street, that alerts subscribers to high-priced stocks that are primed to fall. The analysis concluded that Enron's stock was worth only half of its $59 price.

"It probably should come as no surprise that Enron management appears to have resorted to a variety of transactions that are of questionable quality and sustainability to manage and to boost its earnings," the analysis said.

In the center of the TheStreet.com's column was Fastow's name as the head of one of the questionable Enron partnerships that "consistently bugs analysts."

Others questioned why so many top Enron executives were leaving—after cashing in stock. In June, *U.S. News & World Report* quoted skeptics asking whether Enron's financial reports masked an underachieving company. After starting 2001 in the $80 range, the stock had drifted downward. By July it was below $50.

Once investors and journalists started asking about LJM, Skilling "got concerned," Mintz and one of Enron's outside lawyers. Ronald T. Astin, later told investigators.

Some Enron lawyers had been saying all year that they wanted Fastow out of LJM. They were worried that the company would have to provide more details about Fastow's partnership to comply with SEC disclosure rules.

Mintz had written an internal memo stating there was "no possible legal argument" for not disclosing how much Fastow had profited personally from the LJM partnerships in the company's next proxy statement.

Enron was expecting a routine SEC review in the coming months, making it more urgent to get Fastow out of LJM.

But he was reluctant to walk away from the partnership. He tried at first to reduce his role, but the Andersen accountants said that Enron would have to disclose the relationship anyway.

Skilling sat down with Fastow and gave him a choice, Skilling later told investigators. He could be Enron's chief financial officer or run LJM, but he could not keep doing both.

Fastow wanted to think about it.

Ultimately, Fastow had what Mintz later described as a "melodramatic moment" and resolved to sell his interest to one of his closest associates, Michael J. Kopper, who left the company in order to take over LJM. Mintz did not know the terms.

Several Enron lawyers met to discuss whether Enron should know. A lawyer for Enron's main outside firm, Vinson & Elkins LLP, advised that Enron didn't have any obligation to know. So Enron didn't ask.

That summer, accounting professor Bala G. Dharan pointed out some opaque financial transactions in Enron's published financial statements to a class at Rice University in Houston. He flashed the cryptic reference to the "senior officer" on the screen. He wondered aloud about the executive's identity.

After class, a student—an Enron employee—approached. "Everybody knows that, Professor Dharan. It's Andy Fastow."

On July 12, 2001, in one of those routine rites of business, Skilling fielded questions from Wall Street analysts about the company's second-quarter financial results. Skilling batted away the analysts' mild queries. Enron had "outstanding" results, he said, a 40 percent increase in profit.

Finally, Skilling was asked an obscure sounding question by Carol Coale, a securities analyst with Prudential Securities Inc. in Houston and a growing skeptic.

What about Enron's transactions with your "MLT affiliate" she asked, groping for the correct name, LJM.

Skilling mentioned there were "a couple of real minor things" with LJM, before dismissing the question: "There are no new transactions in LJM."

"He's lying to me," Coale thought. She, too, had been piecing together the sketchy clues from Enron's financial statements. She suspected that Enron was using LJM to hide big losses.

But she did not press him. People who dealt with Skilling knew not to do that. And despite her misgivings, Coale did not feel that she had enough information to advise investors to sell their Enron stock. By the end of July 2001, Lay and Skilling were on the road again, telling analysts that Enron had never been stronger.

The response was nearly unanimous: "Buy, buy, buy."

The full story of LJM remained hidden.

UPDATE

In August, Michael Kopper, a former assistant to Enron CFO Andrew Fastow, pled guilty to charges of wire fraud and money laundering, admitting that he, Fastow, and others used off-balance-sheet partnerships to misappropriate millions of dollars. Kopper agreed to pay $12 million in restitution, and still faces the possibility of up to 15 years in jail. In early October, Fastow was charged with securities fraud, wire fraud, mail fraud, and conspiracy in connection with the secret partnerships he set up and ran at Enron. Fastow faces up to 140 years in prison if convicted on all counts. At the time this book went to press, he had not yet entered a plea in the case. The SEC, meanwhile, filed civil charges against Fastow, seeking to bar him from ever acting as an officer or director of a public company again, and to have him give up all his "ill gotten gains." As for Enron the company, it remains in business, operating under bankruptcy protection. A recent government report on the California energy crisis of 2000–2001 found evidence that Enron deceived regulators and manipulated prices in order to boost profits, and recommended further investigation into "possible misconduct" charges.

Essay

Former Tyco Executives are Charged

Mark Maremont
Jerry Markon

New York prosecutors charged Tyco International Ltd.'s former chief executive, L. Dennis Kozlowski, and its former chief financial officer, Mark H. Swartz, with stealing more than $170 million from the company, and accused them of running a "criminal enterprise" aimed at defrauding investors.

Manhattan District Attorney Robert M. Morgenthau charged the two executives with numerous counts of grand larceny, enterprise corruption and falsifying business records. Mr. Morgenthau also charged Messrs. Kozlowski and Swartz with illegally obtaining a total of more than $400 million by selling Tyco shares while concealing information from investors about executive compensation and loans. They could each face a maximum of 30 years in jail.

Mark A. Belnick, the company's former general counsel, was separately charged with six counts of falsifying business records, and faces as many as four years in prison.

The indictment, and a related civil complaint filed by the Securities and Exchange Commission, allege that Mr. Kozlowski siphoned money from the company for personal uses, including to buy yachts and fine art, to build a mansion for himself in Florida, and to buy a $5 million estate on the Massachusetts island of Nantucket. Mr. Swartz similarly used company funds improperly to buy a yacht and invest in real estate, among other things, the SEC said. A front-page article by *The Wall Street Journal* last month detailed a pattern of unauthorized use of Tyco funds by Mr. Kozlowski dating back to 1997.

The Manhattan district attorney obtained a restraining order from a state judge, unsealed Thursday, temporarily freezing $600 million in assets owned by Messrs. Kozlowski and Swartz. A hearing will be held on that proceeding on September 24.

The indictment represents a marked escalation in the Tyco scandal that began in June with the indictment of Mr. Kozlowski on charges of conspiring to evade $1 million in sales tax on art purchases. Mr. Kozlowski resigned from Tyco the day before that indictment, and Mr. Belnick was fired in June. Mr. Swartz left the company in August.

Mr. Kozlowski "looted the company by granting himself and others excessive compensation, including bonuses, without regard for restrictions put on compensation by the board of directors," prosecutors said. At a news conference, Mr. Morgenthau said it was unfortunate the defendants weren't caught sooner, but expressed confidence that the severity of the charges would deter others. "I hope that a number of corporate officers aren't going to sleep well tonight," he said.

All three defendants pleaded not guilty in State Supreme Court in Manhattan. "These charges are exactly that—they're accusations, and they are unproven," Mr. Kozlowski's lawyer, Stephen Kaufman, said. "When they are aired in their entirely, they will prove to be unfounded." Charles Stillman, a lawyer for Mr. Swartz, said his client "is going to answer these charges, and I tell you he is going to be acquitted at the end of the day." An attorney for Mr. Belnick, Robert Katzberg, declined to comment after the hearing. The three men were released, but were ordered to post bonds by Thursday. Mr. Kozlowski is required to post $100 million, Mr. Swartz $50 million, and Mr. Belnick $1 million.

Although some Tyco shareholders were glad that charges were confined to former executives, others said the apparent extent of the chicanery raised new questions about the reliability of Tyco's accounting under Messrs. Kozlowski and Swartz. "In all my years of following companies, when executives are stealing money they're also cooking the books," said Mare Cohodes of Rocker Partners LLC, a hedge fund that is shorting Tyco's stock, or betting on its decline. Mr. Kozlowski served as CEO from 1992 until he resigned in June.

Tyco, which has been seeking to distance itself from Mr. Kozlowski, on Thursday filed a civil lawsuit against him seeking to recover more than $100 million it claims he misappropriated. The company also announced the nomination of five new directors to its 11-person board, and said its board had voted not to support the re-election of any of the nine Kozlowski-era directors at its annual meeting in March. Tyco, which is registered in Bermuda, is an industrial conglomerate with roughly $35 billion in annual revenue.

In a sign of a boardroom rift, three Tyco directors dissented from the 8-3 board vote and said they have hired an attorney to explore whether the wholesale replacement of the board is in accord with proper corporate-governance procedures. The three—Wendy Lane, Stephen Foss, and Richard Bodman—believe directors did nothing wrong, and were duped by Mr. Kozlowski and other executives.

"It looks like the directors were asleep, but we were not," said Ms. Lane, adding that she knows of no board—including Enron Corp.'s—that has been totally replaced. She argues that it isn't good for such a complex company as Tyco for the entire board and top management learn to be replaced within a few months.

A person close to the directors who voted for the majority plan called that argument "ridiculous," and pointed out that Mr. Foss was head of Tyco's compensation committee, while Mr. Bodman was a member of its audit committee. "Look what happened to the company while they were in charge," this person said.

Tyco said it doesn't believe at this point that any material adjustments to its prior financial statements will be required. Still, a Tyco spokesman said that to reassure shareholders, newly appointed CEO Edward Breen recently ordered an in depth review of the company's past accounting practices, which is scheduled to be finished in "late fall."

The complaints by New York prosecutors and the SEC focus on compensation and loans granted to Messrs. Kozlowski and Swartz without board approval. From 1997 to 2002, the SEC said Mr. Kozlowski improperly borrowed $242 million from a Tyco program intended to help executives pay taxes on restricted-stock grants. Instead of using the funds for that purpose, Mr. Kozlowski spent the money on yachts, fine art, estate jewelry, and luxury apartments. Mr. Swartz similarly used $72 million in loans from the program for personal investments and business ventures, the SEC said.

Messrs. Kozlowski and Swartz also borrowed a total of $78 million from Tyco for real-estate "relocation" loans that weren't in accord with Tyco policies, the SEC said. Mr. Kozlowski used the money to build a mansion in Florida and to buy a $5 million estate in Nantucket for himself, and to buy a $7 million New York apartment for his first wife, whom

he since has divorced. Mr. Swartz used some of the funds to buy a yacht and invest in real estate, the SEC said.

Rather than repay all of these borrowings, the Tyco executives allegedly found various ways to get Tyco to forgive huge sums, without board approval or disclosure to shareholders. In 1999, for example, the two executives simply wiped clean $25 million in loans to Mr. Kozlowski and $12.5 million in loans to Mr. Swartz, the SEC claimed. The SEC also alleges that Tyco purchased one of Mr. Kozlowski's New Hampshire houses for $4.5 million, or three times its market value, without disclosure to shareholders.

The SEC also charged that Messrs. Kozlowski and Swartz covered up some of their unauthorized compensation by directing subordinates at Tyco "to bury" the amounts in unrelated accounts, in one case by offsetting them against gains from the sale of a unit. In addition, New York prosecutors said Mr. Kozlowski had the company's internal auditors report to the board through himself, and "ensured they would not audit" a Tyco unit through which the loans and other payments were made.

Tyco's civil suit against Mr. Kozlowski also details an array of questionable conduct. Mr. Kozlowski, the company alleges, spent $700,000 of company funds for a personal investment in a movie, titled *Endurance*, and billed Tyco for $1.1 million for personal expenses including jewelry, clothing, wine, and flowers.

The company also says the former chief executive spent $43 million of its money on charitable donations made in Mr. Kozlowski's name or to benefit him. One donation, of $1.3 million, went to a Nantucket conservation group to purchase land adjacent to Mr. Kozlowski's property to prevent development.

David Dreman of Dreman Value Management, which owns seven million Tyco shares, said of Mr. Kozlowski and other executives: "I'm a little dazed about how much money they siphoned off." But Mr. Dreman praised

Tyco for taking steps to rid the company of directors lied to Mr. Kozlowski and to try to recover money they believe he was improperly paid. "It seems to me to be almost a clean sweep," Mr. Dreman said.

UPDATE

Just days after prosecutors indicted the former Tyco executives, the company released a report showing just how adept Dennis Kozlowski and his cronies had been at lining their own pockets at shareholders' expense. Among the items for which Kozlowski had the company pick up the tab were a $6,000 shower curtain, a $2,200 wastebasket, and a $17,100 traveling toilette box. In 2000, Kozlowski had Tyco give out $96 million in unapproved bonuses to select employees, with Kozlowski and former CFO Mark Swartz allegedly taking home $50 million. Kozlowski also had Tyco shell out $1 million to pay for his wife's birthday party in Sardinia. At press time, Kozlowski and Swartz were out on bail awaiting trial.